VALUES IN GLOBAL ADMINISTRATIVE LAW

Global Administrative Law has recently emerged as one of the most important contemporary fields in public law scholarship. Concerned with developing fuller understandings of patterns in global governance, it represents one of the most insightful ways of viewing the multifarious forms of public power that now exist beyond the State. Focusing in particular on the search for accountability and legitimacy, it carries with it testing questions about democracy in post-Westphalian society; the meaning of ideas of 'publicness' and 'public good'; and the global relevance of values that include due process, equality and fundamental rights. These, and other issues, are key to critiquing the form of governance that now envelops the globe.

The present collection of essays brings together some of the leading public law scholars who are working in the field of global administrative law. Based on papers presented at a workshop held at Sciences-Po in Paris, it addresses past and future challenges related to global governance. Each of the contributions picks up on the more general theme of the values that do or should inform global administrative law, and the book in this way provides a novel and thought-provoking commentary on this most engaging area of debate.

Values in Global Administrative Law will be of interest not just to public lawyers, but also to social and political scientists working on globalisation and/or international relations. It will also be an invaluable resource for undergraduate and postgraduate courses that touch partly or exclusively on the challenges of global governance.

Values in Global Administrative Law

Edited by

Gordon Anthony

Jean-Bernard Auby

John Morison

and

Tom Zwart

·HART·
PUBLISHING

OXFORD AND PORTLAND, OREGON
2011

Published in the United Kingdom by Hart Publishing Ltd
16C Worcester Place, Oxford, OX1 2JW
Telephone: +44 (0)1865 517530
Fax: +44 (0)1865 510710
E-mail: mail@hartpub.co.uk
Website: http://www.hartpub.co.uk

Published in North America (US and Canada) by
Hart Publishing
c/o International Specialized Book Services
920 NE 58th Avenue, Suite 300
Portland, OR 97213–3786
USA
Tel: +1 503 287 3093 or toll-free: (1) 800 944 6190
Fax: +1 503 280 8832
E-mail: orders@isbs.com
Website: http://www.isbs.com

British Library Cataloguing in Publication Data

Data Available

ISBN: 978-1-84946-009-5

Typeset by Columns Design XML Ltd, Reading
Printed and bound in Great Britain by
CPI Antony Rowe Ltd, Chippenham, Wiltshire

Preface

This collection of essays is the result of a workshop on 'Values in Global Administrative Law' that was held in Sciences-Po, Paris, in late 2008. The decision to organise the workshop was motivated by two factors. The first was a desire to allow leading public law scholars from Europe, the US, and Latin America to contribute to increasingly important debates about the role that law might play in legitimating global governance. Within those debates global administrative law has emerged as one of the most prominent schools of thought, and the workshop was intended to facilitate critical and complementary perspectives on the values that should inform that body of law. The chapters presented here thus offer a range of views on issues that include the viability of global administrative law, its relationship to values found in constitutional law and European law, and the limits to the use of national administrative law constructs in an era of post-State decision-making.

The second factor was a wish to mark the contribution that Professors Spyridon Flogaitis and Gérard Timsit have made to European Public Law and, by extension, Global Public Law. Both professors have added greatly to debates about law beyond the State through their activities as scholars and through their work as founding members of (what is now) the European Public Law Organisation in Greece. Most of the participants at the workshop are members of the affiliated European Group of Public Law, and they each wanted to use the workshop to acknowledge the institutional and personal links that have been created through Spyros and Gérard's endeavours. We would very much hope that they will enjoy reading and critiquing the chapters that have been written for them.

As editors of the essays we would, of course, wish to thank each of the contributors for agreeing to participate in the collection and for being so faithful to deadlines and protocols. We would also like to thank a number of people and organisations who facilitated the Paris workshop and the production of the book. Christine Briatte at Sciences Po provided us with the most wonderful logistical support in the run-up to the workshop and it is no exaggeration to say that it could not have been held without her. It is also true that the workshop could not have been held without generous financial support from a number of sources and we would thank the British Academy; the Law School at Queen's University Belfast; the Research Master at Utrecht School of Law; and the Chaire Mutations de l'Action Publique et Du Droit Public at Sciences Po. Lastly, at Hart Publishing we would thank Richard for all his interest in the project and Rachel Turner for her patience and professionalism as the chapters were assembled and edited.

Gordon Anthony, Jean-Bernard Auby, John Morison, Tom Zwart

Table of Contents

List of Contributors

Gordon Anthony is a Reader in Law at Queen's University Belfast. His books include: *UK Public Law and European Law: The Dynamics of Legal Integration* (Hart Publishing, Oxford, 2002); and (with Peter Leyland) *Textbook on Administrative Law* (OUP, 6th ed, 2008).

Jean-Bernard Auby is Professor of Law and Director of the Chaire Mutations de l'Action Publique et Du Droit Public, Insitut d'Études Politiques (Sciences-Po), Paris. His books include: *La globalisation, le droit et l'État* (Paris, Montchrestien, 2nd ed, 2010); and (with Mark Freedland, eds), *The Public Law/Private Law Divide: Une entente assez cordiale?* (Hart Publishing, Oxford, 2006).

Stefano Battini, is Professor of Administrative Law at the University of Tuscia (Viterbo) and member of Irpa (Istituto di ricerche sulla pubblica amministrazione). He has authored many texts in the area of global administrative law including *Amministrazioni senza Stato. Profili di diritto amminstrativo internazionale* (Milan, Giuffrè, 2003).

Sabino Cassese is Professor of Theory and History of the State at the 'Scuola Normale Superiore' of Pisa, and currently a judge of the Constitutional Court of Italy. One of the first scholars to write on global administrative law, his books include S Cassese, *Lo Spazio Giuidico Globale* (Laterza, Bari, 2003); and S Cassese, *La Crisi dello Stato* (Laterza, Bari, 2001), *Il diritto globale* (Einaudi, Torino, 2009), and *When Legal Orders Collide* (Global Law Press, Editorial Derecho Global, Sevilla, 2010).

Sérvulo Correia, Emeritus Professor at the Faculty of Law, Universidade de Lisboa. A leading academic and practising lawyer in Portugal, his books include *Direito do Contencioso Administrativo* (Lex Publishing, Lisbon, 2005).

Paul Craig is Professor of English Law at the University of Oxford. His recent publications include *EU Administrative Law* (Oxford University Press, 2006) and *The Lisbon Treaty: Law, Politics, and Treaty Reform* (Oxford University Press, 2010).

Jacqueline Dutheil de la Rochère Professeur à l'Université Paris II, and formerly Présidente de l'Université Panthéon-Assas (Paris-II). A leading commentator on EU law, her publications include, with Jean-Bernard Auby (eds), *Droit Administratif Européen* (Bruylant, Brussels, 2007).

George Gerapetritis is Assistant Professor of Constitutional Law at the University of Athens. His books include *Proportionality in Administrative Law* (Ant N Sakkoulas ed, Athens, 1997, in English); *Reasoning of Administrative Acts* (Ant N Sakkoulas ed, Athens, 1998, in Greek); and *Equality and Affirmative Action* (Ant N Sakkoulas ed, Athens, 2007, in Greek).

Agustin Gordillo, Emeritus Professor, University of Buenos Aires. Judge of the Administrative Tribunal, Organization of American States, Washington, DC (2002–2007); Judge of the Administrative Tribunal, International Monetary Fund, Washington, DC, since 1994; Judge of the Administrative Tribunal, International Labor Organization, Geneva, since 2004; Judge of the Administrative Tribunal, United Nations, since 2008. Author of many leading texts, including a comprehensive 4 volume *Treatise of Administrative Law* (9th ed, 2006) and *The Future of Latin America: Can the EU Help?* (2003).

Flora Goudappel is Associate Professor in the Faculty of Law, Erasmus University Rotterdam, and previously was a legal advisor to the Ministry of Justice in the Netherlands. She has published widely in leading Dutch journals and in foreign publications including the *European Review of Public Law*, and the *Tulane Forum of European and Civil Law*. Her most recent book is *The Effects of EU Citizenship* (Asser 2010).

Carol Harlow QC, FBA is Emerita Professor of Law at the London School of Economics and Political Science and author of many books on public law, including *State Liability: Tort Law and Beyond* (Oxford University Press, 2004) and *Accountability in the European Union* (Oxford University Press, 2002). With Professor Richard Rawlings, she has also published *Law and Administration* (Cambridge University Press, 3rd ed, 2009).

Tim Koopmans is a Former judge at the European Court of Justice and Advocate General at the Hoge Raad, Den Haag. He is the author of numerous articles on the nature and origins of European public law, and is the author of *Courts and Political Institutions: A Comparative View* (Cambridge University Press, 2003).

John Morison FRIA is Professor of Jurisprudence at Queen's University Belfast. His books include: *Reshaping Public Power: Northern Ireland and the British Constitutional Crisis* (Sweet and Maxwell, London, 1995); and (with K McEvoy and G Anthony, eds), *Judges, Transition and Human Rights: Essays in Memory of Stephen Livingstone* (OUP, 2007).

Luis Ortega Alvarez, Professor Catedrático de Derecho Administrativo, Facultad de Ciencias Jurídicas y Sociales, Toledo, Spain is a leading expert in Spanish Administrative law in a European context. He has authored, co-authored and edited many books, including *Spanish Administrative Law under European Influence* (Europa Law Publishing, 2010).

Eberhard Schmidt-Aßmann is Professor of Law in the Institute of German and European Law, Rupert-Karls Universitat Heidelberg. He is the author of many leading texts on German and European administrative law, including *Grundrechtspositionen und Legitimationsfragen im öffentlichen Gesundheitswesen* (De Gruyter, Berlin 2001) and *Das Allgemeine Verwaltungsrecht als Ordnungsidee* (Springer, Berlin, Heidelberg, 2004).

Peter L Strauss is Betts Professor of Law at Columbia Law School. His many publications include *Administrative Justice in the United States*, (2d ed. Carolina Academic Press 2002) and *Legal Methods: Understanding and Using Cases and Statutes* (Foundation Press, 2nd ed, 2008). In 2008 he was Fernand Braudel Senior Fellow, European University Institute, Florence, Italy.

Ton van den Brink is Associate Professor in European Union law at the Europa Institute of Utrecht University. His research focuses on topics of European constitutional law and national dimensions of the European integration process and he has published extensively in this area. His books include *Regelgeving in Nederland ter implementatie van EU-recht* (2004). In 2008, he led a research project on the implementation of EU law commissioned by the Dutch Ministry for Justice.

Tom Zwart is Professor of Human Rights Law at the University of Utrecht. His books include: *The Admissibility of Human Rights Petitions: The Case Law of the European Commission of Human Rights and the Human Rights Committee* (Martinus Nijhoff, 1994).

Table of Cases

Ordered alphabetically by jurisdiction, except for certain national jurisdictions (France, Germany, Greece and Italy) which are ordered chronologically by court.

European Union

CFI/General Court

ECJ/Court of Justice

International

ECtHR

National

Belgium

Canada

France

Germany

Greece

India

Italy

Table of Legislation and Related Instruments

Bilateral

European Union

International

National

1

Values in Global Administrative Law: Introduction to the Collection

GORDON ANTHONY, JEAN-BERNARD AUBY, JOHN MORISON, AND TOM ZWART

INTRODUCTION

THIS IS A collection of essays about an emerging and contested field of legal scholarship—global administrative law—and its search for grounding values in the processes of governance beyond the State. The aim of the collection is to further debates about what global administrative law is, what it is not, and how it might contribute to the broader quest for legitimacy in an era of global governance.[1] That era has been characterised by a shift away from State-centric conceptions of power towards one in which international and supranational institutions, as well as informal networks and private actors, exert an increasing influence on policy preferences and outcomes.[2] However, while this has long generated a body of literature on the attendant problems of globalisation,[3] it is only more recently that contributions have sought to provide new legal frameworks for understanding global decision-making. In doing so, the literature on global administrative law has suggested that much of global governance is administrative in form and that its corresponding decision-making processes can

[1] M Zürn, 'Global Governance and Legitimacy Problems' (2004) *Government & Opposition* 260.

[2] See A Hurrell, *On Global Order: Power, Values, and the Constitution of International Society* (Oxford, Oxford University Press, 2007) ch 4.

[3] The literature on globalisation is voluminous and includes: A Giddens, *Runaway World: How Globalization is Reshaping Our Lives* (London, Profile, 2002); U Beck, *What is Globalization?* (Polity, 2000); J-A Scholte, *Globalization: A Critical Introduction* (London, Macmillan, 2000); D Held et al, *Global Transformations* (Stanford University Press, 1999); JH Mittelman (ed), *Globalization: Critical Reflections* (Boulder, Colorado, Lynne Rienner, 1996); and D Held, *Democracy and the Global Order: From the Modern State to Cosmopolitan Governance* (Cambridge, Polity Press, 1995). For more critical perspectives see, eg, Z Bauman, *Globalisation: The Human Consequences* (Cambridge, Polity Press, 1998) and H Henderson, *Beyond Globalization: Shaping a Sustainable Global Economy* (Connecticut, Kumarian Press, 1999).

be analysed with reference to requirements that include accountability, transparency, rationality, and legality.[4] The global administrative law thesis is, in that sense, about using familiar administrative law constructs in the admittedly less familiar setting of extra-State decision-making.

It is in looking for the wider values that can and should underpin requirements of accountability and so on that the idea of global administrative law becomes contested.[5] Values, for these purposes, may be viewed as the shared moral understandings that shape the political life of a community and which take form, in administrative law, as justiciable legal principles.[6] Scholarship here has historically linked such principles to national constitutional orders founded on values of democracy, equality, and political participation that correspond to a greater or lesser extent with conceptions of 'sovereignty' and 'State'.[7] Of course, in Europe, elements of that modelling have long been thrown into doubt by the emergence of an ever-more elaborate body of EU administrative law, but even then questions about post-national law have remained and projected difficulties for any more large-scale global law project.[8] For instance, what is, or can be, the meaning of democracy in the post-Westphalian order, and what can that enquiry reveal about the nature of accountability in a global polity?[9] What, too, of constitutionalism and the consolidation of values within formal documents that delineate authority amongst institutions and provide mechanisms for controlling exercises of public power? Is it important to base a body of global administrative law upon pre-established constitutional norms and, if so, should those norms be regarded

[4] eg, B Kingsbury, N Krisch, R Stewart & J Weiner, 'Global Governance as Administration—National and Transnational Approaches to Global Administrative Law' (2005) 68 *Law and Contemporary Problems* 1, 5.

[5] See too C Harlow, 'Global Administrative Law: The Quest for Principles and Values' (2006) 17 *European Journal of International Law* 187.

[6] A Barak, *The Judge in a Democracy* (New Jersey, Princeton University Press, 2006) at 57. Compare Bozeman's approach: '"Public values" are those providing normative consensus about (a) the rights, benefits, and prerogatives to which citizens should (and should not) be entitled; (b) the obligations of citizens to society, the state, and one another, and (c) the principles on which governments and policies should be based": see B Bozeman, *Public Values and Public Interest* (Washington, Georgetown University Press, 2007) at 13.

[7] See generally K Dyson, *The State Tradition in Western Europe* (Oxford, Oxford University Press, 1980). On the implications for administrative law see JWF Allison, *A Continental Distinction in the Common Law: A Historical and Comparative Perspective on English Public Law* (Oxford, Oxford University Press, 2000); and on the global debate see J McLean, 'Divergent Legal Conceptions of the State: Implications for Global Administrative Law' (2005) 68 *Law and Contemporary Problems* 167.

[8] G della Cananea, 'Beyond the State: The Europeanization and Globalization of Procedural Administrative Law' (2003) 9 *European Public Law* 565. And on the EU's body of law see J-B Auby and J Dutheil de la Rochère (eds), *Droit Administratif Européen* (Brussels, Bruylant, 2007); P Craig, *EU Administrative Law* (Oxford, Oxford University Press, 2006); and J Schwarze, *European Administrative Law*, 2nd edn (London, Sweet & Maxwell, 2006).

[9] See P Cerny, 'Globalization and the End of Democracy' (1999) 36 *European Journal of Political Research* 1. But compare A Moravcsik, 'Is there a "Democratic Deficit" in World Politics? A Framework for Analysis' (2004) *Government & Opposition* 336; G de Búrca, 'Developing Democracy Beyond the State' (2008) 46 *Colombia Journal of Transnational Law* 221; and T Fleiner and LR Basta Fleiner, *Constitutional Democracy in a Multicultural and Globalised World* (Berlin, Springer-Verlag, 2009).

as fixed or fluid? And what of the role of human rights in global governance, particularly when some have suggested that they encapsulate 'values for a godless age'?[10]

In this chapter we address such questions when introducing the themes that run through the essays in the collection. As will become apparent, we prefer not to make a bright line distinction between global administrative law and debates about constitutionalism; and neither do we think that global administrative law can properly be analysed as something that is distinct from EU administrative law. Such distinctions have informed some of the extant literature, which regards global administrative law as a more modest project than global constitutionalism and as something that has analytical force only in respect of decision-makers with a global reach.[11] Doubting the sustainability of such distinctions, we suggest that many of the values that underlie global administrative law are unavoidably constitutional in nature and that recognising them as such provides a fuller framework for understanding the normative and empirical dimensions to global governance. We also suggest that EU law should be regarded as an integral part of the global administrative law regime precisely because globalisation entails decision-making processes that are overlapping rather than mutually exclusive and in which regional standards exist as important elements of the broader global dynamic.[12]

DELIMITING 'GLOBAL ADMINISTRATIVE LAW'

The starting point for debate about global administrative law is Benedict Kingsbury, Nico Krisch and Richard Stewart's seminal paper, *The Emergence of Global Administrative Law*.[13] Complemented by the work of scholars who include Professor Sabino Cassese,[14] their paper proposes a schema for research that is

[10] The term is borrowed from Francesca Klug: see *Values for a Godless Age: The History of the Human Rights Act and its Political and Legal Consequences* (London, Penguin, 2000).

[11] On the administrative law/constitutionalism distinction see N Krisch, 'Global Administrative Law and the Constitutional Ambition', *LSE Legal Studies Working Paper No 10/2009*, available through www.lse.ac.uk/collections/law/wps/; and for an approach which gives only limited attention to the significance of the EU experience see A von Bogdandy, P Dann, and M Goldmann, 'Developing the Publicness of Public International Law: Towards a Legal Framework for Global Governance Activities' (2008) 9 *German Law Journal* 1375.

[12] On such arguments see generally Scholte, n 3 above; and J-B Auby, *La globalisation, le droit et l'État* (Paris, Montchrestien, 2003).

[13] (2005) 68 *Law and Contemporary Problems* 15. But for earlier forays see, among others, della Cananea, n 8 above; A Aman Jr, 'The Limits of Globalization and the Future of Administrative Law: From Government to Governance' (2001) 8 *Indiana Journal of Global Legal Studies* 379; and C Harlow, 'European Administrative Law and the Global Challenge' in P Craig and G de Búrca (eds), *The Evolution of EU Law* (Oxford, Oxford University Press, 1999) at 261.

[14] See, among others, S Cassese, B Carroti, L Casini, M Macchia, E MacDonald and M Savino (eds), *Global Administrative Law: Cases, Materials, Issues*, 2nd edn (New York, Institute for International Law and Justice, 2008), available at www.iilj.org/GAL/; S Cassese, 'Global Standards for National Administrative Procedure' (2005) 68 *Law and Contemporary Problems* 109; S Cassese,

based upon two key observations about governance in a post-State constellation.[15] The first concerns the fact that global governance is driven by five categories of actors that exist in a 'global administrative space' and which engage, to a greater or lesser extent, in decision-making processes that can have implications for States, individuals, corporations, and non-governmental organisations (NGOs). Of these actors, some are formal international organisations such as the United Nations or World Health Organisation (WHO) (category one) or treaty based systems for distributed administration like the World Trade Organisation (WTO) (category two), and global administration here has historically been analysable with reference to norms of international law. However, the remaining categories are said to reveal the fuller complexities of global administration as the actors in them exist outside international law orthodoxy and blur the lines that divide public from private. Category three thus consists of transnational networks of administrative and governmental actors who are engaged in agenda setting and related activities; category four includes private or hybrid bodies that perform delegated regulatory functions with a global reach (for instance, the Commission on Food Safety Standards); and category five consists of private, self-regulating bodies in the realms of, most notably, sport (the paradigm example is the International Olympic Committee).

The second observation, which positions the central thrust of their paper, is that such actors are often insufficiently accountable. Of course, in general terms, this is merely one way of restating familiar criticisms of globalisation and, in particular, the argument that the post-Westphalian order challenges core understandings of democracy and related ideas of control.[16] However, in offering a fuller explanation for that problem, Kingsbury, Krisch and Stewart suggest that the lack of accountability is caused by the fact that the various global actors fall between a number of conceptual stools. This is because they exist at one remove from national legal disciplines where conceptions of accountability are at their most advanced; because international law does not have equivalent conceptions to constrain power above the level of the State; and because many of the actors involved are, in any event, private or semi-public and thereby ill-suited to public law analysis. There is, in the result, an 'accountability deficit' that informs the much wider problem of legitimacy in global governance.

'Administrative Law with the State? The Challenge of Global Regulation' (2005) 37 *New York University Journal of International Law and Politics* 663; S Cassese, 'The Globalization of Law' (2005) 37 *New York University Journal of International Law and Politics* 973; S Cassese, *Lo Spazio Giuridico Globale* (Bari, Laterza, 2003); and S Cassese, *La Crisi dello Stato* (Bari, Laterza, 2001).

[15] And for related commentary see the various contributions to the special issue of (2009) *Acta Juridica*; S Chesterman, 'Globalization Rules: Accountability, Power, and the Prospects for Global Administrative Law' (2008) 14 *Global Governance* 39; the various contributions to the special issues of (2006) 17(1) *European Journal of International Law*, (2005) 68(3–4) *Law and Contemporary Problems*, and (2005) 37(4) *New York University Journal of International Law and Politics*; and S Battini, *Amminstrazioni senza Stato. Profili di dirrito amminstrativo internazionale* (Milan, Giuffrè, 2003).

[16] Cerny, n 9 above.

It is with this in mind that Kingsbury, Krisch and Stewart posit the development of a body of global administrative law. In doing so, their paper does not state in final terms that such a body of law already exists but rather that it may exist and that, with fuller enquiry, it might give global processes increased legitimacy by tying them to requirements of, among others, legality. Their approach is therefore one that seeks to identify global administrative bodies and to ascertain, in the first instance, whether the decision-making processes of such bodies already adhere to fair hearing and transparency guarantees (for instance through the giving of reasons), as well as rights to appeal.[17] Indeed, it is here that their work is complemented by that of Sabino Cassese who has written about procedural developments of the kind heralded by the celebrated *Shrimp-Turtle* decision of the WTO Appellate Body.[18] But beyond identifying existing instances of accountability and control, Kingsbury, Krisch and Stewart's project also seeks to make proposals about how to increase accountability in those areas where it is less apparent or even absent. As they put it:

> Understanding global governance as administration allows us to recast many standard concerns about the legitimacy of the international institutions in a more specific and focused way . . . This inquiry usefully highlights the extent to which mechanisms of procedural participation and review, taken for granted in domestic administrative action, are lacking on a global level. At the same time it invites development of institutional procedures, principles, and remedies with objectives short of building a full-fledged (and at present illusory) global democracy. ... In our approach, global administrative law effectively covers all the rules and procedures that help ensure the accountability of global administration, and it focuses in particular on administrative structures, on transparency, on participatory elements in the administrative procedure, on principles of reasoned decision-making, and on mechanisms of review.[19]

Literature written in the light of the launch paper has addressed a wide range of issues that include institution specific case studies[20] and more abstract analyses of global administrative law's status as 'law'.[21] However, of most interest here are the contributions that have considered the question whether there is a nexus between global administrative law and post-national constitutionalism.[22] As indicated

[17] And for wider and related perspectives see P Nanz and J Steffek, 'Global Governance, Participation and the Public Sphere' (2004) *Government & Opposition* 314.

[18] WTO Appellate Body, United States—Import Prohibition of Certain Shrimp and Shrimp Products, WT/DS58/AB/R, Doc No 98–3899 (12 Oct 1998), discussed in Cassese, 'Global Standards' n 14 above.

[19] N 13 above, at 27–28.

[20] eg, RB Stewart and MR Sanchez Badin, 'The World Trade Organisation and Global Administrative Law' *IILJ Working Paper 2009/7*, available at: www.iilj.org/publications/documents/2009–7.StewartRatton-Sanchez.pdf.

[21] See D Dyzenhaus, 'The Concept of (Global) Administrative Law' (2009) *Acta Juridica* 3; and B Kingsbury, 'The Concept of "Law" in Global Administrative Law' (2009) 20 *European Journal of International Law* 23.

[22] On post-national constitutionalism see, eg, D Chalmers, 'Post-nationalism and the Quest for Constitutional Substitutes' (2000) 27 *Journal of Law and Society* 178.

above, we consider that global administrative law should be situated within a constitutional framework, albeit that begs the difficult question of 'which constitutionalism' should be chosen.[23] Others, in contrast, are less convinced that it is possible to develop a working constitutionalism for global governance largely because of the difficulties in overcoming the historic link between ideas of democracy, territory, and political community.[24] In some of the literature, global administrative law is thus 'separated-off' from constitutional law and given a free-standing analytical worth.

The question of constitutionalism

The principal proponent of separation is Nico Krisch.[25] Building upon his earlier contribution to the launch paper, Krisch has argued that global administrative law should be the foremost line of enquiry as it offers a more 'modest' means to understand and address problems of legitimacy in post-State decision-making. For Krisch, this follows from global administrative law's emphasis on accountability as this allows debate to focus upon discrete areas of decision-making without having to engage with the 'holistic' ambition of constitutionalism. In developing the argument, Krisch takes the example of 'foundational constitutionalism' that predominates in systems in which a constitution 'found(s) and comprehensively organis(es) the public power existing in a polity'.[26] Although he accepts that there is a normative appeal to arguments about having just such a constitution at the global level, he cautions that creating that constitution would entail 'a comprehensive reconstruction (that) would not only require massive institutional change but also a transformation of the societal basis on which the global order rests'.[27] For the present, Krisch thus prefers to disentangle global administrative law from global constitutionalism and to seek to understand global governance with first reference to mechanisms for accountability. As he explains, this may allow 'us to sharpen our focus and begin to answer crucial questions of global governance without leaping to grand designs borrowed from dissimilar contexts and likely at odds with the fluid and diverse character of the postnational polity'.[28]

The central difficulty with Krisch's thesis—which he himself concedes—is that it is not always possible or easy to distinguish between constitutional and administrative law matters in practice. This then invites the inverse reasoning that we prefer, viz that administrative law requirements of accountability and so

[23] On some of the definitional issues see P Craig, 'Constitutions, Constitutionalism, and the European Union' (2001) 7 *European Law Journal* 125.

[24] Although for the beginnings of a revised approach to democracy see de Búrca, n 9 above.

[25] N 11 above.

[26] ibid, at 8.

[27] ibid, at 10.

[28] ibid, at 22.

on can only ever properly be understood against a backdrop of constitutional values (an obvious example would be due process guarantees, which have long corresponded with anterior constitutional rights of access to justice even in settings where there is no written constitution).[29] In related accounts on the question of 'which constitution' is feasible in the global context, there appear to be two main—and competing—approaches. The first of these holds that public international law can provide constitutional norms for global governance whether in the form of a single (foundational) document that is complemented by general principles of law and *jus cogens*[30] or through a more reflexive approach to the interaction of national and international legal standards.[31] This, in turn, presupposes unifying and evolutionary qualities to public international law,[32] and those who argue in its favour note that a departure from international law's emphasis on common purposes would threaten the ideal of global order.[33] Of course, arguments of this kind resonate with the cosmopolitan thrust of earlier international law scholarship in which the shared bonds of humanity were taken to lend themselves to the ideal of government beyond the divisions represented by States.[34] However, such arguments are now also understood to by-pass well-worn critiques about power imbalances within the international community,[35] and they are faced, too, with criticisms of the normative and empirical limitations to the unity thesis. These start with the fact that there has been a 'fragmentation' of international law in recent years,[36] and end with Krisch's point that it would simply not be possible to agree upon a foundational constitution for the globe. Indeed, while it has previously been suggested that the UN Charter already provides such a constitution,[37] the pace of fragmentation has overtaken those claims and pointed to the need for a level of political agreement that has so far eluded even the smaller scale formalist ambition of the EU.[38]

[29] eg, the UK: see *R (Anufrijeva) v Secretary of State for the Home Department* [2004] 1 AC 604 at [26], Lord Steyn.

[30] B Fassbender, 'The UN Charter as Constitution of the International Community' (1998) 36 *Colombia Journal of Transnational Law* 529.

[31] eg M Kumm, 'Constitutional Law Encounters International Law: Terms of Engagement' in S Choudhry (ed), *The Migration of Constitutional Ideas* (Cambridge, Cambridge University Press, 2007) at 256. And for related perspectives see R St J Macdonald and DM Johnston (eds), *Towards World Constitutionalism: Issues in the Legal Ordering of the World Community* (Boston, M Nijhoff Publishers, 2005).

[32] On which see generally GZ Capaldo, *The Pillars of Global Law* (Aldershot, Ashgate, 2008).

[33] For a survey of the arguments see G de Búrca, 'The European Court of Justice, and the International Legal Order' (2009) 51 *Harvard International Law Journal* 1.

[34] See, eg, H Lauterpacht, *The Function of Law in the International Community* (Oxford, Clarendon Press, 1933).

[35] For one such perspective see D Vagts, 'Hegemonic International Law' (2001) 95 *American Journal of International Law* 843.

[36] See M Koskenniemi and P Leino, 'Fragmentation of International Law: Post-Modern Anxieties' (2002) 15 *Leiden Journal of International Law* 553.

[37] Fassbender, n 30 above.

[38] A Hurrelmann, 'European Democracy, the "Permissive Consensus" and the Collapse of the EU Constitution' (2007) 13 *European Law Journal* 343. On the pace of fragmentation see K Ziegler,

Public international law, in consequence, is left mainly with arguments about more reflexive approaches to the interface between national and international norms, and even then there are concerns about the tendency to over-emphasise State-centric visions of law in a post-State constellation.[39]

The competing argument—which we prefer—is that post-national constitutionalism can best be conceived of in terms of 'constitutional pluralism'. This approach holds, at its most basic, that there are a range of overlapping constitutional orders in globalising post-State society and that these are to be regarded as interdependent rather than mutually exclusive.[40] These multiple sites of constitutionalism can, moreover, either be established or emerging, and they are taken to interact with one another on a basis of heterarchy and accommodation.[41] Within this modelling, individual orders may have foundational constitutions of their own (for instance at the State level), although the essence of constitutional pluralism lies elsewhere. This is because it does not deny that different constitutional sites will have their own internal points of legitimation, but rather that those points of legitimation should be understood as partly conditioned by their overlap with other sites and the points of legitimation that define those. The idea of heterarchy likewise posits an equality of orders in which no single order's norms enjoy a hierarchical status and in which the interaction of norms can, for instance, allow decision-making in one system to prompt realignment in another. Constitutional pluralism, in this way, thus envisages a 'dialogue' between systems that are linked together by global processes that allow them to act as 'checks and balances' on one another.[42] To put the point differently, the emphasis is less on the pursuit of an elusive foundational constitution for the globe and more on the

'Strengthening the Rule of Law, but Fragmenting International Law: The *Kadi* Decision of the ECJ from the Perspective of Human Rights' (2009) 2 *Human Rights Law Review* 288. And on the resulting challenge for international law scholarship see M Koskenniemi, 'The Fate of Public International Law: Between Technique and Politics' (2007) 70 *Modern Law Review* 1.

[39] N Walker, 'The Idea of Constitutional Pluralism' (2002) 65 *Modern Law Review* 317, 322.

[40] See, eg, M Avbelj and J Komárek (eds), *Four Visions of Constitutional Pluralism*, EUI Working Papers, Law, 2008/21, available at www.cadmus.iue.it/dspace/bitstream/1814/9372/1/LAW_2008_21.pdf; G Anthony, 'Clustered Convergence? European Fundamental Rights Standards in Irish and UK Public Law' (2004) *Public Law* 282; MP Maduro, 'Contrapunctual Law: Europe's Constitutional Pluralism in Action' in N Walker (eds), *Sovereignty in Transition* (Oxford, Hart Publishing, 2003) at 501; MP Maduro, 'Europe and the constitution: What if this is as good as it gets?' in JHH Weiler and M Wind (eds), *European Constitutionalism Beyond the State* (Cambridge, Cambridge University Press, 2003) at 74; and Walker, n 39 above. See too, eg, P Berman, 'Global Legal Pluralism' (2007) 80 *Southern California Review* 1155.

[41] And see, by analogy, N Krisch, 'The Case for Pluralism in Postnational Law', *LSE Legal Studies Working Paper No 12/2009*, available at www.eprints.lse.ac.uk/24561/ and his 'The Pluralism of Global Administrative Law' (2006) 17 *European Journal of International Law* 247. Although note that, given his other work (eg, n 11 above), Krisch prefers not to use the term 'constitutional pluralism' as that 'would conceal, rather than bring into relief, the theoretical and practical differences that exist between constitutionalist, unity-oriented, and pluralist, heterarchical conceptions' ('Case for Pluralism' at 2).

[42] See further G Anthony, 'EU Law's Fundamental Rights Regime and Post-national Constitutionalism: *Kadi's* Global Setting' in P Birkinshaw and M Varney (eds), *The European Union Legal Order After Lisbon* (Dordrecht, Kluwer, 2010) at 179.

potential that is offered by a multifarious 'power limiting constitutionalism' that is focused upon the 'rule of law', 'rights' and 'review'.[43]

There are two points that we would emphasise at this stage. The first is that constitutional pluralism's focus on an equality of orders provides an anchor for global administrative law that should allow it to avoid, at least potentially, the allegations of Western hegemony that inform much of the literature on globalisation.[44] For instance, one of the main concerns about the original global administrative law thesis is that it can reduce to a search for a universal set of administrative law principles that may not be sensitive to the different contexts within which the principles exist.[45] We would endorse that view and, in doing so, would argue that the law of Kingsbury, Krisch and Stewart's 'global administrative space' can best be understood as a body of law that interacts with the administrative law of a wide range of intersecting national and regional spaces. This, to our minds, is in the very nature of an interdependent global polity, and it places the law of the global administrative space in a heterarchical relationship with other bodies of law that have been formed in different constitutional settings. There are, in that sense, many sites of global administrative law, which can exist above, beneath and beside the different versions found at State level.

The second point sounds directly on the question of values. Put shortly, the understanding that global administrative law engages a multiplicity of constitutional sites allows it to draw inspiration from the related social, cultural and political mores that define those sites. Of course, in a negative sense, this could be said (potentially) to legitimate otherwise repugnant value systems, as constitutional pluralism's emphasis on heterarchy would suggest equal recognition even for those orders that deny the legitimacy of other systems.[46] But that, by itself, is to take one extreme example by way of rejecting a more generally valid proposal for conceptualising global governance, and it also overlooks the extent to which there is a complementarity of values between the intersecting systems. The obvious instance here is fundamental rights, where there is a growing global consensus on their importance. Although that consensus can become strained around questions such as 'types of rights' and 'cultural relativity',[47] the growth of national, regional, and global rights instruments has embedded 'basic values that set down standards or boundaries which no agent, whether a representative of a global body, state or civil association, should be able to violate'.[48] Given this—and

[43] This is the distinction made by Krisch, n 11 above. But note that he does not suggest that 'power limiting constitutionalism' is necessarily viable in the global context.

[44] DB Goldman, *Globalisation and the Western Legal Tradition: Recurring Patterns of Law and Authority* (Cambridge, Cambridge University Press, 2007).

[45] Harlow n 5 above, at 207.

[46] On conflicts of norms see A Wiener and U Puetter, 'The Quality of Norms is What Actors Make of It' (2009) 5 *Journal of International Law and International Relations* 1.

[47] See generally J-M Coicaud et al (eds), *The Globalization of Human Rights* (Tokyo, United Nations University Press, 2003).

[48] D Held, 'Restructuring Global Governance: Cosmopolitanism, Democracy and the Global Order' (2009) 37 *Millenium* 535, 537.

given, too, the link between fundamental rights and ideas of deliberative democracy[49]—there is much to suggest a growing commonality of values that have originated in a variety of sources but which are now interdependent as a result of the linkages associated with globalisation. Cast in those terms, constitutional pluralism provides not a vision of polarity in global governance but one of mutuality and complementarity.

EU law and the 'global administrative space'

We can illustrate the above points with reference to EU law, which lends historical and contemporary dimensions to the debate. The historical dimension is essentially concerned with the evolution of the EU's constitutional order and the body of administrative law that exists within it. Although that process of evolution has stopped short of political agreement on a foundational constitution for the EU,[50] it is axiomatic that there is a supranational constitutionalism at work and that it interacts with, and has drawn inspiration from, national constitutional values.[51] Within that experience, it equally is axiomatic that the interaction of orders has not always been problem free[52] and it is against that background that much of the initial literature on constitutional pluralism has been written.[53] However, with that literature moving towards a position of orthodoxy—at least in European studies—it is clear that the EU provides one instance of how different orders can co-exist with, and learn from, one another. It is, in the result, possible to speak of European values such as 'democracy', 'rights' and the 'rule of law' informing EU administrative law and as thereby feeding into, and influencing, developments in the administrative law traditions of the Member States.[54] Indeed, there is even an element of historical return here as the very fact that the European values were first borrowed from national traditions means that they are, in effect, re-entering their traditional sites in a modified and modernised form.

[49] D Feldman, 'Constitutionalism, Deliberative Democracy, and Human Rights' in J Morison, K McEvoy and G Anthony (eds), *Judges, Transition and Human Rights: Essays in Memory of Stephen Livingstone* (Oxford, Oxford University Press, 2007) at 443.

[50] See Hurrelman, n 38 above.

[51] Art 2 TEU.

[52] The seminal instance of disaccord remains that associated with the decision-making of the German Federal Constitutional Court. See, as regards the Lisbon Treaty, D Doukas, 'The Verdict of the German Federal Constitutional Court on the Lisbon Treaty: Not Guilty but Don't Do it Again!' (2009) 34 *European Law Review* 866.

[53] N 40 above.

[54] On the relationship between the national and European orders see generally Auby and Dutheil de la Rochère, n 8 above and, e.g, L Ortega, L Arroyo and Carmen Plaza (eds), *Spanish Administrative Law Under European Influence* (Groningen, Europa Law Publishing, 2010) and J-B Auby (ed), *L'influence du droit européen sur les catégories du droit public* (Paris, Dalloz, 2010). And on indirect influences see further ML Fernandez Esteban, 'National Judges and Community Law: The Paradox of Two Paradigms of Law' (1997) 4 *Maastricht Journal of European and Comparative Law* 143.

The contemporary dimension then sounds on the EU's role as one actor among many in global governance. At its height, that role is direct in the sense that the EU has a legal personality that allows it to participate as a member of global decision-making organisations such as the WTO.[55] But it is also apparent that the EU can play an indirect role in global decision-making, viz where a decision that is internal to the EU's constitutional order has implications for orders that exist outside Europe's territorial boundaries. Jan-Arte Scholte terms such decisional effects as 'supraterritorial',[56] and the outstanding example of such effects is the European Court of Justice (ECJ) decision in *Kadi v EU Council*.[57] The case—which is already regarded as seminal[58]—saw the ECJ use EU law's fundamental rights standards to review the legality of EC Regulations that had implemented UN Security Council Resolutions that listed and imposed sanctions upon individuals suspected of involvement in international terrorism.[59] In doing so, the ECJ emphasised how the EU's internal constitutional order could protect the due process and property rights of individuals and that this was neither influenced by nor had implications for international law. While this effectively meant that the ECJ rejected arguments about the primacy of the UN Charter[60]—the decision has for that reason been criticised[61]—it added significant weight to arguments about the need to change the procedures whereby names were added to UN sanctions lists.[62] In a global polity of overlapping orders, *Kadi* thereby served, albeit indirectly, to check and balance UN decision-making that had violated long-established fundamental rights standards.

[55] Prior to the Lisbon Treaty it was, of course, the EC that had legal personality and membership of the WTO. But see now Art 47 TEU.

[56] N 3 above, ch 2.

[57] Joined Cases C 402/05P and C-415/05P, *Kadi & Al Barakaat International Foundation v Council and Commission* [2008] 3 CMLR 41.

[58] For commentary see, among others, de Búrca, n 33 above; Ziegler, n 38 above; G della Cananea, 'Global Security and Due Process of Law between the United Nations and the European Union: *Yassin Abdullah Kadi & Al Barakaat International Foundation v Council*' (2009) 15 *Colombia Journal of European Law* 511; T Tridimas and JA Gutierrez-Fons, 'EU Law, International Law and Economic Sanctions Against Terrorism: The Judiciary in Distress' (2009) 32 *Fordham International Law Journal* 660; D Halberstram and E Stein, 'The United Nations, the European Union and the King of Sweden: economic sanctions and individual rights in a plural world order' (2009) 46 *Common Market Law Review* 13; and G Harpaz, 'Judicial review by the European Court of Justice of UN "smart sanctions" against terror in the *Kadi* dispute' (2009) 14 *European Foreign Affairs Review* 65.

[59] Principally Council Regulation (EC) 881/2002, OJ L 139/9.

[60] Art 103 of which reads: 'In the event of a conflict between the obligations of the Members of the United Nations under the present Charter and their obligations under any other international agreement, their obligations under the present Charter shall prevail'.

[61] de Búrca, n 33 above.

[62] For earlier criticisms of the listing process see B Fassbender, *Targeted Sanctions and Due Process: The responsibility of the UN Security Council to ensure that fair and clear procedures are made available to individuals and entities targeted with sanctions under Chapter VII of the UN Charter*, Study Commissioned by the UN Office of Legal Affairs 2006, available at www.un.org/law/counsel/Fassbender_study.pdf. And on the current procedures see UNSC Resolution 1822 (2008).

It is important not to overstate the significance that one judgment may hold for broader patterns in global governance.[63] However, given our above comments about the nature of global administrative law and its relationship with constitutional values we would contend that *Kadi* provides a strong example of how 'the constitutional' informs 'the administrative' in decision-making within and beyond State structures. We would also suggest that the judgment speaks to constitutional pluralism's capacity to provide a heightened degree of legitimacy in global governance or, in the words of the original global administrative law thesis, to ensure accountability in extra-State decision-making. Although this perhaps posits a paradox whereby an order with well-known internal legitimacy problems is able to legitimate external governance processes,[64] there is still much within the judgment that complements wider arguments about how Europe may act as a buffer against the worst excesses of globalisation.[65] Those arguments hold, at their highest, that the EU's internal processes can perform an important stabilising function in global law and politics and that this has far-reaching implications for emergent models of democracy in a post-national context.[66] Seen from that perspective, *Kadi* reveals global administrative law as a complex system of mutually reinforcing bodies of law with no apex or singular reference point.

THE ESSAYS IN THE COLLECTION

What, then, of the essays in this collection? Certainly, each contribution touches directly or indirectly upon the above themes, albeit that the individual authors may not agree fully with the manner in which we have weaved those themes together. This much was apparent at a workshop held at Sciences Po in Paris in late 2008 at which the essays were first discussed in the light of the literature on global administrative law. The workshop, which had the added purpose of marking the contribution to European public law of Professors Spyridon Flogaitis and Gérard Timsit,[67] made clear that approaches to global administrative law are as varied as they are contested and we are aware that our preferences for 'constitutionalism' and 'pluralism' may not be shared by all. Nevertheless, the chapters in the book still cluster around the core theme of the challenge of post-State governance and the need to replace old public law orthodoxies with

[63] Albeit that it has been followed in other cases, eg, Case T-318/01, *Omar Mohammed Othman v Council and Commission*, 11 June 2009.

[64] On which see E Odvar and JE Fossum, 'Europe in Search of Legitimacy: Strategies of Legitimation Assessed' (2004) 25 *International Political Science Review* 435.

[65] J Habermas, *The Divided West* (Cambridge, Polity Press, 2006).

[66] ibid. See too J Habermas, *The Postnational Constellation: Political Essays* (Cambridge, Polity Press, 2001).

[67] The founding members and guiding lights of the European Group of Public Law, Athens, Greece: see www.eplo.eu/. Most of the contributors are members of the Group.

new. The chapters, in that way, complement one another and bring much to extant debates about global administrative law and its search for values and principles.

The nature of governance in the modern polity provides the focal point for chapters by Sabino Cassese, Stefano Battini, Paul Craig, Eberhard Schmidt-Aßmann and Peter Strauss. Cassese's chapter, 'A Global Due Process of Law?',[68] notes the exponential growth of regulatory regimes beyond the level of State and considers the scope for procedural participation in their corresponding decision-making processes. He observes that 'the global legal order is full of rules prescribing participatory rights' but that 'participation is far from being a global principle because the global law is made up of many different, separate and self-contained regimes'. The overall thrust of his chapter is therefore of the need to regard the issue of participation as multifaceted and something to be resolved through the interaction of various decision-making fora. Battini's chapter, 'Globalisation and Extraterritorial Regulation: An Unexceptional Exception',[69] builds upon the idea of overlapping orders and norms when assessing the significance of increased extraterritorial effect for regulatory measures. For Battini this is an unavoidable consequence of globalisation and he chronicles how such effect is now commonplace in the realms of economics, information technology, and the environment. Craig's chapter, 'Shared Administration and Networks: Global and EU Perspectives',[70] likewise examines the dynamics of transnational governance, this time with reference to policy networks of the kind that occupy Kingsbury, Krisch and Stewart's 'global administrative space'. Drawing upon the experience of networks that operate primarily in the EU context, Craig notes that they can be important vehicles for the delivery of policy but that their workings must always be tied to a quest for legitimacy and accountability. The importance of that quest is also emphasised in Schmidt-Aßmann's chapter on 'Principles of an International Order of Information',[71] which addresses the challenge of regulating the flow of personal information within the processes of global administration. While the chapter begins with some cautionary comments about the global administrative law venture, it goes on to suggest that existing international treaties, conventions and related human rights standards already point to data protection and freedom of information as pillars of an international order of information. Strauss' chapter—'Possible Controls Over the Bending of Regulatory Science'[72] —examines information from a different perspective, viz that of access to the scientific data that is used by decision-makers with regulatory responsibilities. Focusing largely on the US experience, he chronicles instances where transparency has been lacking and where reform may be needed. He

[68] At 17–54.
[69] At 55–74.
[70] At 75–110.
[71] At 111–18.
[72] At 119–66.

concludes by drawing the point more widely when saying that 'these are not simply American issues. One may be certain the issues of science-bending and the possible contributions to its control of transparency are present in *every* administrative law system'.[73]

The issue of accountability that is noted by Craig and Schmidt-Aßmann is central to the chapters by Carol Harlow and Tom Zwart. Harlow, one of the foremost commentators on the topic, uses her chapter, 'Accountability as a Value for Global Governance and Global Administrative Law'[74] to highlight how accountability is an essentially Western concept associated with the liberal democratic State. She next traces its evolution above the level of the State and notes that it has attained the status of a key value in many of the institutions of global governance. While Harlow does not regard this as problematic in and of itself, she does query whether the value is truly global and she leaves us with questions about Western values and hegemony in post-State law and governance. Zwart's chapter then takes the fact of a lack of accountability in many global processes when asking 'Would International Courts be Able to Fill the Accountability Gap at the Global Level?'.[75] Using procedural developments within the Appellate Body of the WTO as an example he answers this question in the affirmative while at the same time noting the sectoral role played by that court and others at the international level. Given the corresponding—and inevitable—lack of judicial control in some areas, Zwart posits the development of a Global Administrative Court to which global organs could subscribe.

Debates about accountability raise difficult questions about the nature of the 'publics' to which decision-makers must account, and the chapters by John Morison and Gordon Anthony, Jean-Bernard Auby, and Luis Ortega address some of those questions. In 'The Place of Public Interest'[76] Morison and Anthony consider the possible meanings of 'public interest' in global administrative law, particularly given the key role that the term has historically played in national administrative law traditions and in human rights law. Their argument is that the absence of a single polity at the global level creates formidable difficulties for normative ideas of public interest, and they conclude that the term has fullest relevance when nested within pluralist readings of post-State governance. Auby's chapter on 'Public Goods and Global Administrative Law'[77] in turn considers the relationship between globalisation, public goods theory (legal and economic) and the project initiated by Kingsbury, Krisch, and Stewart. His conclusion is that their global administrative law thesis enjoys much analytical force in relation to global decision-making about public goods but that the next step should be to

[73] At 150.

[74] At 167–86. Her other works include *Accountability in the European Union* (Oxford, Oxford University Press, 2002) and, with R Rawlings, 'Promoting Accountability in Multi-level Governance: A Network Approach' (2007) 13 *European Law Journal* 542.

[75] At 187–207.

[76] At 209–32.

[77] At 233–43.

link such decisions to ideas of citizenship, democracy and constitutionalism beyond the State. On this point, Luis Ortega's chapter, 'Global Citizenship and Global Legitimacy' provides valuable insights into questions of identity in a global polity with a decreasing emphasis on State-based models of nationality.[78]

Fundamental rights—which are central to our arguments, above, about the interface between constitutional law and administrative law—are discussed in chapters by George Gerapetritis, Jacqueline Dutheil de la Rochère, Sérvulo Correia, and Agustin Gordillo. Gerapetritis' chapter, 'Affirmative Action: A New Challenge for Equality',[79] provides an in-depth analysis of affirmative action measures in a range national settings as well as at the level of the EU, and suggests that substantive equality may now be emerging as quasi fourth generation right. Dutheil de la Rochère uses her chapter, 'Fundamental Rights in the Global and European Law Order',[80] to consider the normative place of rights within the multi-level system of law that characterises the modern day polity. Noting that assumptions about the universality of rights were essentially about the applicability of European standards, she chronicles how rights discourses have changed and how there are, in reality, a number of complementary rights regimes that exist at the national, European, and global levels. That element of complementarity is explored in depth in Sérvulo Correia's chapter, 'Administrative Due or Fair Process: Different Paths in the Evolutionary Formation of a Global Principle and a Global Right'.[81] Focusing on the different methodologies of the common law and Romano-Germanic traditions, he traces how due/fair process has emerged as a shared global norm that played such a vital role in the *Kadi* judgment of the ECJ. Gordillo's chapter[82] on 'Access to Justice, Legal Certainty, and Economic Rationality' likewise addresses issues of due/fair process, albeit that he cautions that fairness and so on can be meaningful only to the extent that legal orders prioritise anterior values such as the rule of law.

The remaining chapters look more closely at the specific lessons that EU law holds for the global enterprise. Flora Goudappel and Ton van den Brink's chapter on 'Processes of Transnationalization of Administrative Values: Administrative Regulation and Transparency in the EU'[83] focuses upon the interplay of legal standards within the framework of the EU. Their approach assesses the nature and limits of legal convergence, and their chapter reveals much about how legal principles are formed and disseminated in settings that juxtapose national and supranational orders. Tim Koopmans, a former judge at the ECJ, offers an historical perspective on the construction of EU administrative law in 'Globalisation of Administrative Law—the European Experience'.[84] His is a contribution

[78] At 245–55.
[79] At 257–90.
[80] At 291–305.
[81] At 307–55.
[82] At 357–66.
[83] At 367–86.
[84] At 387–400.

based upon experiences at the coalface of EU law, and he considers how far the European experience of integration might be replicated at the global level. He concludes that further international integration is almost inevitable and that, as with the European experience, administrative lawyers must continue to embrace the challenges and opportunities that such integration will present. This is a fitting conclusion, indeed, for a book that seeks to add to those efforts that have been made to date.

2

A Global Due Process of Law?

SABINO CASSESE*

THE IMMATURITY OF INTERNATIONAL LAW?

ADMINISTRATION IS BECOMING increasingly international. Regulatory regimes are being shifted from domestic authorities to global agencies. International organisations now enjoy regulatory, adjudicatory and dispute resolution powers. Their number is increasing (there were 123 international governmental organisations in 1951; 154 in 1960; 242 in 1971; 1,039 in 1981; there are now approximately 8,000).[1] They are growing both in terms of personnel and finances (the number of employees went from 65,000 in the year 1970 to 100–120,000 in 1981;[2] across the entire UN system, there were 52,107 officers in 1997 and 75,282 in 2007; the budget of the UN system was $6.4 billion in 2007, rising from around $5 billion in 1997).[3] Their influence is on the rise.

If a global administration is now well-established, is it also now subject to those special rules—the right to a hearing, the duty to give reasons, judicial

* An extended version of this paper was first presented at the 'I Ciclo de Conferencias em comemoraçao dos 10 años da FDUP' as 'A global due process of law' (University of Oporto, Law Department, 27 April 2006) and subsequently at the Hauser Colloquium on 'Globalization and its discontents' (New York University School of Law, 13 September 2006). The author wishes to express his gratitude to Stefano Battini, Francesca Bignami, Eleonora Cavalieri, Elisa D'Alterio, Maurizia De Bellis, Euan MacDonald, Bernardo Giorgio Mattarella, Elisabetta Morlino, Richard B Stewart and in particular Lorenzo Casini for their helpful comments on an earlier draft.

[1] For these data, see S Cassese, 'Relations between International Organizations and National Administrations' in International Institute of Administrative Sciences, XIXth International Congress of Administrative Sciences, *Proceeding* (Deventer, Kluwer, 1985) at 165; and B Kingsbury and L Casini, 'Global Administrative Law Dimensions of International Organizations Law' in L Boisson de Chazournes, L Casini, and B Kingsbury (eds), Symposium on 'Global Administrative Law in the Operations of International Organizations' (2009) 6(2) *International Organizations Law Review* 319, 326, fn 23. More generally, in 2006, there were 61,345 international governmental organisations (IGOs) and non-governmental organisations (NGOs); in 1981, there were 14,752; in 1960, 1,422; and in 1951, 955 (see *Yearbook of International Organizations* 2008, published by UIA).

[2] S Cassese, *Relations*, n 1 above, at 165.

[3] UN, Personnel Statistics (data as at 31 December 2007) and budgetary and financial situations of organizations of the United Nations system—UN website.

review—that we call administrative law? Or, at this early stage, is the global administration still ruled by secrecy, informality and arbitrariness?

Hans Kelsen, writing in 1934, argued that 'international law is a "primitive" system, in that it lacks organs for creating and applying legal norms, and so has to rely on the members of the international legal community to create norms and on individual states to enforce them'.[4]

Kelsen's diagnosis has been echoed by three recent authors. The first has remarked upon the 'continuing immaturity of international law in the failure of international organizations to provide the controls of the rule of law which are the mark of a mature legal order'.[5] The second has observed that an international organisation '.... operates .... in something of a legal vacuum, within what is literally a lawless environment'.[6] The third has noted that globalisation is the most dramatic assertion of the superiority of technocratic government, in

[4] H Kelsen, *Introduction to the Problems of Legal Theory* (Oxford, Clarendon Press, 1992), ch 9 (translation of the *Reine Rechtslehre*, 1934), as summarised by D Dyzenhaus, 'Emerging from self-incurred immaturity', paper presented at the New York University Law School, Globalization and its Discontents Colloquium, Spring 2004. Kelsen wrote: 'International law is still a primitive legal system, however, just at the beginning of a development that the state legal system has already completed. It is still marked by wide-ranging decentralization—at least in the field of general international law, and thus as it affects the entire international legal community. There are still no organs, whose respective functions reflect a division of labour, for creating and applying legal norms. The formation of general norms proceeds by way of custom or treaty, which is to say, by way of the members of the legal community themselves, and not by way of a special legislative organ. And the application of general norms to the concrete case proceeds in the same way. The state that considers its interests violated is to decide for itself whether there exists the material fact of an unlawful act for which another state is responsible. And if this other state denies the claimed unlawful act, then, for want of an objective authority to settle the dispute in a legally regulated procedure, the state whose law has been violated is itself authorized to respond to the violator with a coercive act of general international law, that is, with reprisal or war. This self-help technique, which also served as the point of departure for the development of the state legal system, emphasizes the principles of collective and absolute liability over the principles of individual liability and liability for fault. The consequence of an unlawful act is not directed against the human being who, functioning as an organ of the individual state, intentionally or negligently brought about the material fact of the unlawful act. Rather, the consequence is directed against others, who took no part in the unlawful act and were unable to prevent it. Reprisals and war do not strike the state organs whose acts or forbearences, imputed to the state, count as violations of international law; reprisals and war strike either the mass of human beings making up "the people", or they strike a particular state organ, the army—in so far as it is possible, in modern warfare, to separate the army from the people at all.': see *Introduction to the problems of legal theory* at 108 ff. See also H Kelsen, 'The Essence of International Law' in KW Deutsch and S Hoffmann (eds), *The Relevance of International Law* (Cambridge, Mass, Schenkman, 1968) at 87 ('International Law as a Primitive Legal Order').

[5] D Dyzenhaus, n 4 above, at 2.

[6] RA Gorman, 'The Development of International Employment Law: my Experience on International Administrative Tribunals at the World Bank and the Asian Development Bank' in (2004) 25 *Comp Labor Law and Pol'y Journal* 633, 638. See also A Fischer-Lescano and G Teubner, 'Regime Collisions: the Vain Search for Legal Unity in the Fragmentation of Global Law' (2004) 5 *Michigan Journal of International Law* 999; International Law Commission, *Conclusions of the work of the Study Group on the Fragmentation of International Law: Difficulties arising from the Diversification and Expansion of International Law* (United Nations, 2006); E Benvenisti and GW Downs, 'The Empire's New Clothes: Political Economy and the Fragmentation of International Law' (2007) 60 *Stanford Law Review* 595; IH Scheltema, *Fragmentation of International Law: Framing the Debate*, SSRN Working Paper, 20 February 2010.

contrast with the American 'enormous new apparatus of administrative law designed to maximize both the participation of interest groups in the bureaucratic policy-making process and the obligation of bureaucracies to make public every bit of their fact gathering, analysis, and public choice processes and to prove publicly their every claim of expertise'. 'Transnational or global governance .... raises .... serious problems for administrative law. Under this form of governance, decision-making processes are relatively new and tend to be elitist and opaque, with few participants and no agreed upon protocol. .... Lack of defined participatory mechanisms lead to street demonstrations that demand additional places at the table, but there are as yet few seating plans or even table manners.'[7]

An opposite point of view is that the regulatory dimension of international law has produced the emergence of global governance, and that among the hallmarks of the global governance there is 'international proceduralization and international insistence on domestic proceduralization'.[8]

In this chapter I shall not examine the entire problem of the development of the rule of law at the global level.[9] Instead, I shall focus only on one side of this problem: are mechanisms of procedural participation, which are taken for granted in domestic administrations, lacking in the global legal order? Do 'notice and comment' rights in rule-making procedures and the 'right to a hearing' in adjudicatory proceedings exist in the global arena?

The reason for this choice is that 'fair decision-making procedures have been very successful in gaining deference to decisions and to rules, authorities and institutions more generally'.[10] A fair procedure plays an important role in

[7] The two quotations are from two articles by M Shapiro, 'The Globalization of Law' (1993) 1 *Indiana Journal of Global Legal Studies* 45–47 and 'Administrative Law Unbounded' (2001) 8 *Indiana Journal of Global Legal Studies* 369, 374–75.

[8] JHH Weiler and I Motoc, 'Taking Democracy Seriously: The Normative Challenges to the International Legal System' in S Griller (ed), *International Economic Governance and Non-Economic Concerns-New Challenges for the International Legal Order* (Wien, Springer, 2003) at 68–69. See also A von Bogdandy, P Dann, M Goldmann, 'Developing the Publicness of Public International Law; Towards a Legal Framework for Global Governance Activities' in A von Bogdandy, R Wolfrum, J von Bernstorff, P Dann and M Goldmann (eds), *The Exercise of Public Authority by International Institutions. Advancing International Law* (Heidelberg, Springer, 2010) at 3 ff; E Benvenisti and GW Downs, 'Court Cooperation, Executive Accountability and Global Governance' (2009) 41 *New York University Journal of International Law and Politics* 931; AD Mitchell and J Farnik, 'Global Administrative Law: Can It Bring Global Governance to Account?' (2009) 37 *Federal Law Review* 237; CA Whytock, 'Domestic Courts and Global Governance' (2010) 84 *Tulane Law Review* (forthcoming).

[9] See S Chesterman, 'An International Rule of Law?' (2008) 56 *American Journal of Comparative Law* 331; J Waldron, 'The Rule of International Law' (2006) 30 *Harvard Journal of Law and Public Policy* 15; D Dyzenhaus, 'The Rule of (Administrative) Law in International Law' (2005) 68 *Law and Contemporary Problems* 127, and E Denninger, 'Lo Stato di diritto o "rule of law": che cosa è oggi?' in A Jellamo and F Riccobono, *In ricordo di Vittorio Frosini* (Milano, Giuffrè, 2004) p 74, where he raises the question of whether the rule of law ends with the end of the sovereignty of the nation State.

[10] TR Tyler, 'Social Justice: Outcome and Procedure' (2000) 35 *International Journal of Psychology* 124. See also K Murphy, 'Regulating More Effectively: The Relationship between Procedural Justice, Legitimacy, and Tax Non-compliance' (2005) 32 *Journal of Law and Society* 562 ff; N Luhmann,

building social consensus. Both process control and voice can encourage people's cooperation with authorities and lead to legitimacy. Recognising participatory rights in the global legal order may, therefore, increase international organisations' legitimacy.

This analysis will be divided into two parts. In section 2, I shall present a taxonomy of participatory rights and procedural rules. In section 3, I shall measure the degree of maturity of participation in the global administrative arena and compare global to domestic proceduralism. In particular, the analysis will show that the development of global administrative principles (such as due process, fair hearings, consultation or duty to give reasons) does not stem only from judicial decisions, but also—if not mostly—from legislation or regulation adopted by international institutions: global administrative law is not only judge-made law, but also legislative regulation.[11] Furthermore, these global norms, which are embodied in treaties, conventions, declarations, recommendations, guidelines, codes, or standards, can affect States and national administrations, private entities and individuals, or both.[12]

THE MAZE OF GLOBAL PARTICIPATORY RIGHTS

> In domestic settings, the right of affected individuals to have their views and relevant information considered before a decision is taken is one of the classical elements of administrative law. Versions of such a principle are increasingly applied in global administrative governance.[13]

In domestic legal orders, participatory rights have a simple structure. For example, if an authority has to take decisions that affect large populations, the law may require that the interested parties be consulted and due consideration be

Legitimation durch Verfahren, 2nd edn (Frankfurt, Suhrkamp, 1983); Italian translation *Procedimenti giuridici e legittimazione sociale* (Milano, Giuffré, 1995). According to Luhmann, procedure is a means for neutralising disappointment. An opposite point of view is that of LH Tribe, 'The Puzzling Persistence of Process-Based Constitutional Theories' (1980) 89 *Yale Law Journal* 1063: 'the constitutional theme of perfecting the processes of governmental decision is radically indeterminate and fundamentally incomplete'.

[11] From a different perspective, the legal nature of these norms has been analysed in-depth by B Kingsbury in 'The Concept of "Law" in Global Administrative Law' (2009) 20 *European Journal of International Law* 23. See also M Goldmann, 'Inside Relative Normativity: From Sources to Standard Instruments for the Exercise of International Public Authority' (2008) 9 *German Law Journal* 1865; and S Cassese, 'Is There a Global Administrative Law?' in A von Bogdandy et al (eds), n 8 above, at 772 ff.

[12] As B Kingsbury and L Casini, n 1 above at 358, have observed: 'many practical and normative activities of IOs, and of the other actors in complex governance regimes, must be managed not simply by formal norms and rules of jurisdiction or hierarchical or interpretive solutions to overlaps, but by a dynamic process of regulation in which global administrative law can play a useful part. … Regulatory approaches emphasize process, directions of change, gradual improvement rather than instant results, and dynamic rather than simply static analysis'.

[13] B Kingsbury, N Krisch, and RB Stewart, 'The Emergence of Global Administrative Law' (2005) 68 *Law and Contemporary Problems* 15, 37.

given to their opinions. Or, if an authority has to apply sanctions to private individuals, the law may provide that the affected parties be heard and due consideration be given to their views in reaching a decision (and possibly that reasons be given with the decision).

In the global legal order, things are more complex. In the global regulatory process, participation can be granted to national authorities or to private individuals. Domestic authorities may make comments in global procedures or in the domestic procedures of another State. Private individuals may be heard both by their domestic authorities and by foreign national authorities. The right to a hearing may be granted both vertically (for example, to a national government in conflict with an international organisation) and horizontally (for example, to a domestic authority in conflict with a domestic authority of another State). National governments appear before and within international organisations both as a unit and as a disaggregated set of bodies. Relations are usually triadic (the private party, the national government, the global institution), not dyadic. We are thus witnessing the growing complexity of participation in the global arena. The following provides some examples of the main types of participatory rights.

Participation granted to private parties vis-à-vis domestic authorities

First, global rules may provide for the participation of private parties in national decision-making. For example, the Rio Declaration on environment and development (3–4 June 1992) has established, as Principle 10, that

> [e]nvironmental issues are best handled with participation of all concerned citizens, at the relevant level. At the national level, each individual shall have appropriate access to information concerning the environment that is held by public authorities .... and the opportunity to participate in decision-making process.

Subsequently, the 1998 Aarhus Convention on access to information, public participation in decision-making and access to justice in environmental matters[14] establishes the principle of 'public participation' (Article 1.1). Furthering this principle, Article 6 provides that 'the public concerned shall be informed, either by public notice or individually as appropriate, early in an environmental decision-making'. The procedure must provide 'opportunities for the public to participate', a public hearing with comments or questions, sufficient time for informing the public, early public participation, when all options are open and effective public participation can take place. In reaching the decision due account is to be taken of the outcome of the public participation. The public authority

[14] G Handl, 'International "Lawmaking" by Conferences of the Parties and Other Politically Mandated Bodies' in R Wolfrum and V Röben (eds), *Developments of International Law in Treaty Making* (Berlin, Springer, 2005) at 135 ff. See also K Raustiala, 'The "Participatory Revolution" in International Environmental Law' (1997) 21 *Harvard Environmental Law Review* 537 ff.

has to 'make accessible to the public the text of the decision along with the reasons and considerations on which the decision is based'.[15]

A second example is the Code of Conduct for Responsible Fisheries, a voluntary agreement that serves as an 'instrument of reference to help States to establish or improve legal and institutional framework required for the exercise of responsible fisheries'.[16] According to Article 6.13 and 6.16, States,

> in accordance with appropriate procedures, should facilitate consultation and the effective participation of industry, fishworkers, environmental and other interested organizations in decision making with respect to the development of laws and policies related to fisheries management, development, international lending and aid . . . [States] 'should ensure that fishers and fishfarmers are involved in the policy formulation and implementation process'.[17]

A third example is the Cartagena Protocol on Biosafety to the 2000 Montreal Convention on Biological Diversity.[18] Article 23, on public awareness and participation, provides that '[t]he Parties shall: (a) Promote and facilitate public awareness, education and participation' and 'in accordance with their respective laws and regulations, consult the public in the decision-making process regarding living modified organisms and shall make the results of such decisions available to the public'.

[15] Art 7 recognises the right for the public to participate during the preparation of plans and programmes and of policies relating to the environment, while Art 8 establishes the right to 'effective public participation at an appropriate stage, and while options are still open, during the preparation by public authorities of executive regulations and other generally applicable legally binding rules that may have a significant effect on the environment'. To this end, 'draft rules should be published or otherwise made publicly available and the public should be given the opportunity to comment, directly or through representative consultative bodies. The result of the public participation shall be taken into account as far as possible'.

[16] Art 2. The Code has been followed by the International Plan of Action to Prevent, Deter, and Eliminate Illegal, Unreported and Unregulated Fishing (IPOA-IUU), another voluntary instrument. This provides that States encourage 'full participation of stakeholders in combating IUU fishing, including industry, fishing communities, and non-governmental organizations' (Art 9.1; see also Arts 25 and 83). See J Friedrich, 'Legal Challenge of Nonbinding Instruments: The Case of the FAO Code of Conduct for Responsible Fisheries' (2008) 9 *German Law Journal* 1539.

[17] Art 7.1.2 provides that 'within areas under national jurisdiction, States should seek to identify relevant domestic parties having a legitimate interest in the use and management of fisheries resources and establish arrangements for consulting them to gain their collaboration in achieving responsible fisheries'. According to Art 7.1.6, '[r]epresentatives from relevant organizations, both governmental and non-governmental, concerned with fisheries should be afforded the opportunity to take part in meetings of subregional and regional fisheries management organizations and arrangements' and 'should be given timely access to the records and reports of such meetings, subject to the procedural rules on access to them'. Finally, according to Art 11.3.2, 'States, in accordance with their national laws, should facilitate appropriate consultation with and participation of industry as well as environmental and consumer groups in the development and implementation of laws and regulations related to trade in fish and fishery products'.

[18] M Böckenförde, *Grüne Gentechnik und Welthandel* (Berlin, Springer, 2004).

A fourth example is that of World Trade Organization (WTO) Guidelines for arrangements on relations with non-governmental organisations (NGOs) (decision adopted by the General Council on 18 July 1996).[19] These point to 'the special character of the WTO'. As it is not possible for NGOs to be directly involved in the work of the WTO or its meetings, '[c]loser consultation and cooperation with NGOs can .... be met constructively through appropriate processes at the national level where lies primary responsibility for taking into account the different elements of public interest which are brought to bear on trade policy-making'.

A fifth example is the 1994 Agreement on Implementation of Article VI of the General Agreement on Tariffs and Trade (GATT). Article 6.1 provides that '[a]ll interested parties in an anti-dumping investigation shall be given notice of the information which the authorities require and ample opportunity to present in writing all evidence which they consider relevant in respect of the investigation in question'. Article 6.1.2 provides that 'evidence presented in writing by one interested party shall be made available promptly to other interested parties participating in the investigation'. Article 6.1.3 states: '[a]s soon as an investigation has been initiated, the authorities shall provide the full text of the written application received ... to the known exporters and to the authorities of the exporting Member and shall make it available, upon request, to other interested parties involved'. Article 6.2 continues by saying: '[t]hroughout the anti-dumping investigation all interested parties shall have a full opportunity for the defence of their interests'.[20]

[19] E Benvenisti, 'Public Choice and Global Administrative Law: Who's Afraid of Executive Discretion?', Draft 11 February 2004, Paper presented at the New York University Law School Globalization and its Discontents Colloquium, Spring 2004.

[20] And then '[T]o this end, the authorities shall, on request, provide opportunities for all interested parties to meet those parties with adverse interests, so that opposing views may be presented and rebuttal arguments offered .... Interested parties shall also have the right, on justification, to present other information orally'. Art 6.3 states that '[o]ral information provided under paragraph 2 shall be taken into account by the authorities only in so far as it is subsequently reproduced in writing and made available to other interested parties, as provided for in subparagraph 1.2' and Art 6.4 specifies that '[t]he authorities shall whenever practicable provide timely opportunities for all interested parties to see all information that is relevant to the presentation of their cases'. The following provisions regulate control of the accuracy of the information supplied by the interested parties and investigations carried out in order to verify the information provided or to obtain further details. Finally, according to Art 6.9, '[t]he authorities shall, before a final determination is made, inform all interested parties of the essential facts under consideration which form the basis for the decision whether to apply definitive measures. Such disclosure should take place in sufficient time for the parties to defend their interests', and Art 6.11 states that '[f]or the purposes of this Agreement, "interested parties" shall include: (i) an exporter or foreign producer or the importer of a product subject to investigation, or a trade or business association a majority of the members of which are producers, exporters or importers of such product; (ii) the government of the exporting Member; and (iii) a producer of the like product in the importing Member or a trade and business association a majority of the members of which produce the like product in the territory of the importing Member. This list shall not preclude Members from allowing domestic or foreign parties other than those mentioned above to be included as interested parties'.

Sixthly, the World Bank Guidelines for Joint Staff Assessment of a Poverty Reduction Strategy require that the programme called Heavily Indebted Poor Countries Initiative (HIPC), started in 1996, be based on participation. Civil society groups, women's groups, ethnic minorities, policy research institutes and academics, private sector trade unions, and representatives of different regions of the country must be involved in the design of the strategy at the national level in order to obtain concessional lending and debt relief.

Finally, the North American Agreement on Labor Cooperation (NAALC), which entered into force in 1994 and established the Commission for Labor Cooperation, provides (Article 5, paragraph 1) that:

> Each Party shall ensure that its administrative … proceedings for the enforcement of its labor law are fair, equitable and transparent and, to this end, each party shall provide that: a. such proceedings comply with due process of law; b. any hearings in such proceedings are open to the public …; c. the parties to such proceedings are entitled to support or defend their respective positions and to present information or evidence; and d. such proceedings are not unnecessarily complicated and do not entail unreasonable charges or time limits or unwarranted delays.[21]

This provision goes on to require that national governments provide reasoned decisions, based on information or evidence in respect of which the parties were offered the opportunity to be heard, and judicial review by independent and impartial tribunals.

Though global norms do not structure the procedure, in some instances a global supervisory board is established, which oversees the compliance of national authorities with global rules and develops them through a case by case process. Even where the applicable global norms are substantive, and procedure is not addressed, supervisory bodies have created procedural rights to ensure that the substantive rights are respected.

Global rules may guarantee participation in national decision-making processes, under the control of global regulators. This is a variant of the first type, as global rules impose on States the obligation to guarantee participation, but require that an international institution supervise and control the participation that is granted at the national level.

The WTO Agreement on Safeguards, Article 3.1, provides that:

> a member may apply a safeguard measure only following an investigation by the competent authorities of that member pursuant to procedures previously established and made public in consonance with article X of GATT 1994. This investigation shall include reasonable public notice to all interested parties and public hearings or other

[21] The Agreement has established 'a process whereby citizens, groups, or governments can raise questions of labor law enforcement in all three member countries. The Commission, through a network of National Administrative Offices in each country, coordinates the submission process, which can, in some cases, directly result in initiation of the government-to-government dispute settlement mechanism' (US General Accounting Office, *NAFTA–US Experience With Environment, Labor, and Investment Dispute Settlement Cases*, GAO-01–933, July 2001, 4.

> appropriate means in which importers, exporters and other interested parties could present evidence and their views, including the opportunity to respond to the presentations of other parties and to submit their views, inter alia, as to whether or not the application of a safeguard measure would be in the public interest. The competent authorities shall publish a report setting forth their findings and reasoned conclusions reached on all pertinent issues of fact and law.

In addition, Article 13 has established a Committee on Safeguards for the oversight of the agreement's implementation. This Committee has 'to find, upon request of an affected Member, whether or not the procedural requirements of this Agreement have been complied with in connection with a safeguard measure, and report its findings to the Council for Trade in Goods'. According to Article 12 of the same Agreement, a Member has the obligation to notify the Committee upon initiating an investigation, before taking a provisional safeguard measure and upon taking a decision, and provide the Committee with all pertinent information.

In this case, participation is granted by global rules to private parties before national authorities. Private parties may be nationals of the State in which participation takes place, or nationals of another State. Participation is intended to provide the parties with the possibility of defending their interests.[22]

Finally, global procedural norms have been extended to non-governmental regulatory bodies.

A first example is provided by the Programme for the Endorsement of Forest Certification (PEFC) Rules for Standard Setting. Article 3.4 regulates the participatory process for the standard setting process for forest certification in the following manner:

> 3.4.1 [t]he process of development of certification criteria shall be initiated by national forest owners' organisations or national forestry sector organisations having the support of the major forest owners' organisations in that country. All relevant interested parties will be invited to participate in this process. Their views will be documented and

[22] Also extremely interesting are cases in which the global law does not explicitly impose the principle of fairness on national governments, but where this principle is nevertheless recognised by a global court. Art 73.2 of the United Nations Convention on the Law of the Sea provides that 'arrested vessels and their crews shall be promptly released upon the posting of reasonable bond or other security'. The International Tribunal of the Law of the Sea (ITLOS), in the *Juno trader* case, on 18 December 2004 decided that '[t]he obligation of prompt release of vessels and crews includes elementary considerations of humanity and due process of law. The requirement that the bond or other financial security must be reasonable indicates that a concern for fairness is one of the purposes of this provision' (para 77). In a separate opinion Judge Treves wrote: 'the essential fact seems to me to be that between the time of arrest of the ship and the time of the application to the Tribunal … all domestic procedures held in the case … inaudita altera parte'. In fact, 'confiscation [had been] obtained in violation of due process' and 'fines [had been] imposed without procedural guarantees'. See also ITLOS, The 'Hoshinmaru' Case (*Japan v Russian Federation*), Case n 14, and ITLOS, The 'Tomimaru' Case (*Japan v Russian Federation*), Case n 15.

> considered in an open and transparent way. A Forum (e.g., committee, council, working group) shall be created to which interested parties are invited to participate in the process ...[23].
>
> 3.4.2 The start of the standard setting process shall be communicated to the public. Information on the development process shall be distributed and discussed and final draft standards shall be available to all interested parties, e.g. by posting it on the Internet.
>
> 3.4.3 The final draft standards are sent out for formal national consultation process. Consultation shall ensure that the views of interested parties are discussed. The Forum shall give general information on the changes made as the result of a consultation process.[24]

A second example is that of the International Organization of Securities Commission's (IOSCO) Objectives and Principles of Securities Regulation.[25] Article 6.5, on *Clear and consistent regulatory processes* provides that:

> in exercising its powers and discharging its functions, the regulator should adopt processes which are: ... transparent to the public; fair and equitable. In the formulation of policy, the regulator should: have a process for consultation with the public including those who may be affected by the policy; publicly disclose its policies in important operational areas; observe standards of procedural fairness; ... Many regulators have authority to publish reports on the outcome of investigations or inquiries, particularly where publication would provide useful guidance to market participants and their advisers. Any publication of a report must be consistent with the rights of an individual to a fair hearing ...[26]

A third example is that of the World Anti-Doping Agency (WADA) Code (World Anti-Doping Code). This sets forth rules and principles that are to be followed by

[23] Art 3.5.1 continues by saying: '[t]he invited parties should represent the different aspects of sustainable forest management and include, e.g. forest owners, forest industry, environmental and social non-governmental organisations, trade unions, retailers and other relevant organisations at national or sub-national level. Participation in the Forum shall be organised according to its respective consensus–building procedures which should provide for balanced representation of interest categories such as producers, buyers, consumers, etc. The interested parties' participation and views will be documented and considered in an open and transparent way. Formal approval of standards shall be based on evidence of consensus. The Forum shall define its own written procedures based on the consensus principle which governs the methods used for standards development. Copies of the procedures shall be made available to interested parties upon request. Such written procedures shall contain an appeal mechanism for the impartial handling of any substantive and procedural complaints'.

[24] A similar rule is established by Article 4 which sets standards for chain of custody certification. See E Meidinger, 'The Administrative Law of Global Private-Public Regulation: The Case of Forestry' (2006) 17 *European Journal of International Law*. See also C Segall, 'The Forestry Crisis as a Crisis of the Rule of Law' (2006) 58 *Stanford Law Review* 1539 ff, and M Howlett and J Rayner, 'Globalization and Governance Capacity: Explaining Divergence in National Forest Programs as Instances of "Next-Generation" Regulation in Canada and Europe' (2006) 19 *Governance* 251 ff.

[25] D Zaring, 'Informal Procedure, Hard and Soft, in International Administration' (2005) 5 *Chicago Journal of International Law* 547.

[26] IOSCO, Objectives and Principles of Securities Regulation, May 2003, available at www.iosco.org/library/pubdocs/pdf/IOSCOPD154.pdf.

all anti-doping organisations, understood as all organisations responsible for adopting, implementing or enforcing anti-doping rules within their authority (the International Olympic Committee, the International Paralympic Committee, international federations, major event organisations, and national anti-doping organisations).[27] In terms of participation, the Code requires that all anti-doping organisations provide a fair hearing process for any person who is alleged to have committed an anti-doping rule violation. This process must respect principles such as a timely hearing, a fair and impartial hearing panel, and the right of each party to present evidence, including the right to call and question witnesses.[28]

As mentioned above, these global rules are enacted by private global organisations, like the PEFC, or by semi-public global organisations, like IOSCO and WADA (which bring together domestic public authorities). These rules are imposed from above upon the relevant national authorities or organisations; they operate vertically or diagonally, granting the right to be heard (to nationals and to foreigners). The right to participate has the purpose of ensuring consultation or guaranteeing the right to a fair hearing.[29]

Participatory rights of private parties before domestic authorities are quite varied. They are provided by global law in informal procedures introduced in order to ensure the involvement of civil society in the preparation of policies (as in the cases of WTO Guidelines on relations with NGOs and of the World Bank Guidelines for the assessments of poverty reduction strategies); in rule-making procedures (as in the case of the Code of Conduct for Responsible Fisheries or in the case of the securities regulation); in procedures leading to administrative measures, like environmental impact assessments, transfer, handling or use of

[27] Note that, in this case, global procedural norms include international bodies as well. See P David, *A Guide to the World Anti-Doping Code. A Fight for the Spirit of Sport* (Cambridge, Cambridge University Press, 2008).

[28] See the World Anti-Doping Code, Art 8.1, which also includes the right to be represented by counsel at the person's own expense; the right to be informed in a fair and timely manner of the asserted anti-doping rule violation; the right to respond to the asserted anti-doping rule violation and resulting consequences; the person's right to an interpreter at the hearing, with the hearing panel to determine the identity, and responsibility for the cost, of the interpreter; and a timely, written, reasoned decision, specifically including an explanation of the reason(s) for any period of ineligibility. See L Casini, 'Hybrid Public-Private Bodies: The World Anti-Doping Agency (WADA)' in Symposium on 'Global Administrative Law in the Operations of International Organizations' (2009) 6:2 *International Organizations Law Review* 421, especially 433 ff. An overview of problems that emerged before the adoption of the World Anti-Doping Code, such as the lack of procedural guarantees for athletes, is in MS Straubel, 'Doping Due Process: A Critique of the Doping Control Process in International Sport' (2002) 106 *Dickinson Law Review* 523, specifically at 544 on the clash between US and civil law notion of due process, and 557–58 on procedural rules.

[29] One type of participatory right is granted to private parties before national agencies which act in the global arena. This type has two peculiarities: the participatory rights in question are not provided for by global rules, but by national law; and private parties participate in national proceedings, but these proceedings serve global decision-making processes. A significant example of this comes can be found in § 2578 of the United States Code, which provides for Notice of United States participation in international standard-setting activities.

living modified organisms, trade safeguard measures, forest certification, disqualification for doping and labour law enforcement in North America; and in dispute settlement proceedings (for example, anti-dumping investigations).

In these cases, participation is required by global rules, some voluntary, some binding. It is, therefore, imposed from above on the national legal orders. These global rules create a vertical opening, in the sense that they establish the duty of domestic authorities to hear private parties, whether they be individuals or groups. They strengthen national rules providing for participation in the domestic realm. But they also go beyond domestic rules, which generally grant participatory rights only to nationals, while global rules require domestic authorities to hear foreign parties as well.

In terms of their structure, the participatory rights examined here are incredibly diverse.

Provision for participation has been made before public authorities, semipublic bodies, and even private bodies as in the cases of forest certification, securities regulation and anti-doping measures. Only in the last case is an impartial hearing body required.

The relevant procedures are not normally designed in full detail, as participation is granted by global rules before national authorities, and global actors neither want nor need to interfere overly with domestic authorities' jurisdiction; the same can be said for the identification of the private parties who can participate, for the provisions on access to records, for the kind of participation envisaged (to make comments or to attend meetings) and for the obligation to take in due consideration the comments made by the parties.

Participation is variously granted to affected parties, concerned citizens or interested organisations. In some cases, as for fisheries, parties are more precisely defined as those having a legitimate interest in the use and management of fisheries resources. In other cases, notably the WTO anti-dumping and safeguard measures, foreign parties can participate and parties can respond to observations made by other parties.

In order to make participation possible in practice, some global rules guarantee access to the information, or the right to be informed, or the duty of the authorities to give notice or to disclose policies, as in the cases of environmental assessment, fisheries regulation, WTO anti-dumping and safeguard measures, forest certification, securities regulation and anti-doping disqualification.

The times for and methods of participation are also defined. Environmental proceedings must, for example, guarantee early public participation and antidoping hearings are required to be timely. Participation can be oral or written, through hearings or meetings, with or without counsel (see the cases of fisheries regulation, WTO anti-dumping and safeguard measures, forest certification, securities regulation and anti-doping measures).

The obligation of the authorities to take into account the points of view collected during consultation proceedings is established only in the cases of environmental matters, NGO consultation and in the proceedings for labour law enforcement in North America; the requirement of a reasoned decision is provided only in the cases of environment, WTO safeguard measures, anti-doping disqualification and North American labour law enforcement procedures; and the obligation to make the decision available or accessible to the public is established only in the cases of environment, living modified organisms procedures and North American labour law enforcement.

Moving from the structure to the function of participation, four main types can be observed. There are cases where participation has the purpose of involving civil society in the (public or private) decision-making process (for example, in environmental matters and in proceedings to regulate securities); cases where participation has the purpose of encouraging cooperation between governmental and intergovernmental action (as in the case of responsible fisheries); cases where participation is intended to gain the trust of people (as in the case of living modified organisms); and cases where participation plays the same role as the right of defence in a judicial process (as in the case of WTO anti-dumping and safeguard measures, anti-doping disqualification, and North American labour law enforcement).

Why do global organisations take measures to provide for participation in domestic matters, before national agencies? Three main reasons can be distinguished.

One reason is a need to harmonise not only goods, services and tariffs, but also procedures. This leads the rules and practices followed in many countries to be codified at the global level. The scope of these rules thus becomes wider, because they are imposed upon multiple national governments. This is the case of participation in environmental matters, in the proceedings for forest certification, in securities regulatory processes and in anti-doping procedures.

The obligation of national governments to hear private parties is established at the global level in another set of cases in order to promote the collaboration of domestic private parties in implementing global policies, because national agencies act in accordance with such policies. This is the case of the Code of Conduct for Responsible Fisheries, the Cartagena Protocol on Biosafety, the WTO Guidelines for arrangements in relations with NGOs, and the HIPC Programme of the World Bank.[30]

Thirdly, participation is provided at the global level because it involves foreign actors, who would not otherwise have a right to a hearing under domestic law. In the cases of anti-dumping investigation, safeguard measures, the UNCLOS, as interpreted in the well-known *Juno Trader* decision of the International Tribunal of the Law of the Sea, global law was needed to impose on States the obligation to provide a hearing to a party who did not enjoy that right under domestic law.

[30] Notice that, according to the WTO document mentioned above, the WTO is both a Treaty establishing rights and obligations and a forum for negotiations.

In these cases, either participation is granted by national norms to nationals but not to foreigners (and therefore global norms widen their scope), or participation is not granted at all by national rules (and global norms make it available to everybody, but foreign actors have a special interest in making use of it).

Participation granted to national governments vis-à-vis global organisations

A second type of participation is that granted to national governments in global decision-making processes. Like the previous type of participation discussed above, this too is vertically oriented.

The first example is that of the International Convention for the Regulation of Whaling.[31] This convention includes a schedule, which is an integral part of the convention. The schedule can be amended. Article V.3 provides that amendments 'shall be notified by the Commission to each of the Contracting Governments'. If any government presents to the Commission objection to any amendment, the amendment 'shall not become effective with respect to any of the Governments and any other Government may present an objection to the amendment'. The amendment becomes effective with respect to all governments that have not presented an objection.[32]

A second example is that of the 1987 Montreal Protocol on Substances that Deplete the Ozone Layer as adjusted and amended by Meetings of the Parties.[33] Article 2(9)(b) provides that proposals for adjustments and reductions of production or consumption of the controlled substances 'shall be communicated to the Parties by the Secretariat at least six months before the meeting of the Parties at which they are proposed for adoption'.[34]

[31] G Handl, n 14 above, at 133 ff.

[32] Art V.3 provides that '[e]ach of such amendments shall become effective with respect to the Contracting Governments ninety days following notification of the amendment by the Commission to each of the Contracting Governments, except that (a) if any Government presents to the Commission objection to any amendment prior to the expiration of this ninety-day period, the amendment shall not become effective with respect to any of the Governments for an additional ninety days; (b) thereupon, any other Contracting Government may present objection to the amendment at any time prior to the expiration of the additional ninety-day period, or before the expiration of thirty days from the date of receipt of the last objection received during such additional ninety-day period, which ever date shall be later; and (c) thereafter, the amendment shall become effective with respect to all Contracting Governments which have not presented objection but shall not become effective with respect to any Government which has so objected until such date as the objection is withdrawn. The Commission shall notify each Contracting Government immediately upon receipt of each objection and withdrawal and each Contracting Government shall acknowledge receipt of all notifications of amendments, objections, and withdrawals'.

[33] G Ulfstein, 'Reweaving the Fabric of International Law? Patterns of Consent in Environmental Framework Agreements' in Wolfrum and Röben (eds), n 14 above, at 147 ff.

[34] Art 9.2, lett c), continues by saying: '[i]n taking such decisions, the Parties shall make every effort to reach agreement by consensus. If all efforts at consensus have been exhausted, and no agreement reached, such decisions shall, as a last resort, be adopted by a two-thirds majority vote of

A third example is that of the Procedures for the Elaboration of Codex Alimentarius Standards and Related Texts. Part I on the 'Uniform procedure for the elaboration of codex standards and related texts' provides two consultations with Members of the Commission (ie Member Nations and Associate Members of the Food and Agriculture Organization (FAO) and the World Health Organization (WHO)).[35] The first concerns the *proposed draft standard*. This is sent to Members of the Commission and interested international organisations for comment.[36] The proposed draft standard is submitted to the Commission or to the Executive Committee for adoption as a draft standard. They will give due consideration to any comments that may be submitted by any of their Members regarding the implications which the proposed draft standard or any provisions thereof may have for their economic interests. The *draft standard* is sent to all Members and interested international organisations for comment on all aspects, including possible implications of the draft standard for their economic interests.[37] It is then submitted to the Commission 'together with any written proposals received from Members and interested international organizations for amendments with a view to its adoption as a Codex standard....'. A similar two-step consultation procedure is followed, according to Part II, for the 'uniform accelerated procedure for the elaboration of codex standards and related texts'.

A fourth example is that of the Operational Guidelines for the Implementation of the World Heritage Convention established by the Intergovernmental Committee for the Protection of the World Cultural and Natural Heritage.[38] These guidelines provide for the participation of the State Parties in the process for the inscription of properties on the World Heritage List. For this purpose, Articles 149 and 150 provide that:

> [t]he Advisory Bodies are requested to forward to States Parties ... any final question or request for information that they may have after the examination of their evaluation. The concerned States Parties are invited to send ... a letter to the Chairperson, with copies to the Advisory Bodies, detailing the factual errors they might have identified in the evaluation of their nomination made by the Advisory Bodies.

the Parties present and voting representing a majority of the Parties operating under Paragraph 1 of Article 5 present and voting and a majority of the Parties not so operating present and voting'.

[35] See M Livermore, 'Authority and Legitimacy in Global Governance: Deliberation, Institutional Differentiation, and the Codex Alimentarius' (2006) 81 *New York University Law Review* 766.

[36] The comments received are sent by the Secretariat to the subsidiary body or other body concerned, which has the power to consider such comments and to amend the proposed draft standard.

[37] The comments received are sent by the Secretariat to the subsidiary body or other body concerned, which has the power to consider such comments and amend the draft standard.

[38] On this, see L Boisson de Chazournes, 'Treaty Law-Making and Non-Treaty Law-Making: The Evolving Structure of the International Legal Order' in Wolfrum and Röben (eds), n 14 above, at 473 ff; D Zacharias, 'The UNESCO Regime for the Protection of World Heritage as Prototype of an Autonomy-Gaining International Institution' (2008) 9 *German Law Journal* 1833; and L Casini (ed), *La globalizzazione dei beni culturali* (Bologna, Il Mulino, 2010).

The dialogue between global institutions and States continues in the following way, regulated by Articles 159 and 160:

> [n]ominations which the Committee decides to refer back to the State Party for additional information may be resubmitted to the following Committee session for examination. The additional information shall be submitted to the Secretariat .... The Secretariat will immediately transmit it to the relevant Advisory Bodies for evaluation. ... The Committee may decide to defer a nomination for more in-depth assessment or study, or a substantial revision by the State Party.... These nominations will then be revaluated by the relevant Advisory Bodies[39]

A fifth example is that of the International Labour Organization (ILO). Article 26 of the ILO Constitution provides that 'any of the Members shall have the right to file a complaint with the International Labour Office if it is not satisfied that any other Member is securing the effective observance of any Convention which both have ratified in accordance with the foregoing articles'. The Governing Body may communicate with the government in question. If no satisfactory statement in reply is forthcoming, the Governing Body may appoint a Commission of Inquiry to consider the complaint and to report thereon.[40] In such cases, the Members are required to place at the disposal of the Commission of Inquiry all information in their possession which bears upon the subject-matter of the complaint (Article 27). According to Article 28, '[w]hen the Commission of Inquiry has fully considered the complaint it shall prepare a report embodying its findings on all questions of fact relevant to determining the issue between the parties and containing such recommendations as it may think proper as to the steps which should be taken to meet the complaint and the time within which they should be taken'. Finally, Article 29 provides that '[t]he Director-General of the International Labour Office shall communicate the report of the Commission of Inquiry to the Governing Body and to each of the governments concerned in the complaint, and shall cause it to be published. 2. Each of these governments shall within three months inform the Director-General of the International Labour Office whether or not it accepts the recommendations contained in the report of the Commission; and if not, whether it proposes to refer the complaint to the

[39] Arts 183, 184 and 196 provide that corrective measures and the deletion of properties shall be made in consultation with the State Party concerned.

[40] Art 26 continues: '4. The Governing Body may adopt the same procedure either of its own motion or on receipt of a complaint from a delegate to the Conference. 5. When any matter arising out of article 25 or 26 is being considered by the Governing Body, the government in question shall, if not already represented thereon, be entitled to send a representative to take part in the proceedings of the Governing Body while the matter is under consideration. Adequate notice of the date on which the matter will be considered shall be given to the government in question'.

International Court of Justice'. The International Court of Justice may affirm, vary or reverse any of the findings or recommendations of the Commission of Inquiry.[41]

A sixth example is the Financial Action Task Force on money laundering (FATF). Paragraph 10 ('Review process') of the 'Annual Review of Non-Cooperative Countries or Territories', 12 October 2007 states that:

> [t]he jurisdictions to be reviewed were informed of the work to be carried out by the FATF. The reviews involved gathering the relevant information, including laws and regulations, as well as any mutual evaluation reports, related progress reports and self-assessment surveys, where these were available. This information was then analysed against the twenty-five criteria and a draft report was prepared and sent to the jurisdictions for comment. . . . These comments and the draft reports themselves were discussed between the FATF and the jurisdictions concerned during a series of face-to-face meetings. Subsequently, the draft reports were discussed and adopted by the FATF Plenaries.[42]

A seventh example is the North American Agreement for Labor Cooperation (NAALC). Articles 23–27 of this Treaty provide that, if a matter is not resolved between the national governments through 'cooperative consultations', an 'Evaluations Committee of Experts' is established. This Committee 'may invite written submissions from the Parties and the public'. It 'may consider, in preparing its report, any information provided by ... the [National Administrative Authority] of each Party, organizations institutions and persons with relevant expertise, and the public'. Finally, '[e]ach Party shall have a reasonable opportunity to review and comment on information that the Evaluation Committee of Experts receives and to make written submissions to the Evaluation Committee' (Article 24, paragraphs 4–6).

[41] See ACL Davies, 'Global Administrative Law at the International Labour Organization: the Problem of Softer Standards', Paper presented at the New York University Law School Colloquium on Global Administrative Law, April 2005, at 3 ff (also on the recourse to soft law as a means of withholding participation rights).

[42] Additional information on the procedure were provided by the previous 'Report on Non-Cooperative Countries and Territories', 14 February 2000: '[t]he FATF and its members can implement focussed efforts, country by country, to convince non-cooperative jurisdictions to improve legislation and domestic practices and to participate actively in international co-operation. These efforts could take the form of a dialogue, in conjunction with the relevant FATF-style regional body or appropriate international organisation/body, with the identified jurisdictions in order to check that their situation has been estimated correctly and to establish whether improvements are already being undertaken. The dialogue could be pursued by a letter from the FATF President to the concerned government explaining the purpose of the FATF's work in this area once the consolidated list of non-cooperative jurisdictions has been established. This dialogue should prompt them to amend their laws and change their practices. To do so, they could be helped through advice and technical co-operation by FATF, its members, a FATF-style regional body, or an appropriate international organisation/body to implement the necessary changes. Specific actions could also be taken by other multi-lateral fora (e.g., the G-7, the OECD, the Basle Committee, IOSCO and the International Financial Institutions) to seek the issuance of public statements or other appropriate action'.

Within terms of the examples of participatory rights in the private parties-national authorities examples above, these cases display both similarities and important differences.

Participation of national governments in global institutions is established by global rules, imposed from above; but in the case of the FATF there are no rules, only practice.

Participation is granted not only in treaty-making, but also in rule-making procedures (as in the case of amendments to the International Convention for the Regulation of Whaling Schedule and in the case of adjustment and reduction of production of substances that deplete the ozone), in standard setting proceedings (as in those of the Codex Alimentarius Commission), in policy-making procedures (as in those of the NAALC), in adjudication proceedings (as in the process for the inscription on the World Heritage List or in the review processes of the FATF) and in dispute settlement procedures (as for the evaluation of the complaints to the ILO).

Here the participating party is not a private individual or organisation, but the State (although the NAALC does also allow for 'submissions' from 'the public').

The proceedings are more loosely structured than in the previous case. This may be due to the fact that national governments are parties to the global institutions and can therefore control them from the inside.

There are two features common to these participatory rights. A notification or communication is provided; and objections or comments by States are envisaged. In the case of the NAALC, there can be cross-examination, as parties can review and comment on the information received by the Committee. Only in the cases of food standards and of labour complaints do global norms require that objections or comments are given due consideration.

Some of these procedures are complex. Participation is 'serial', as in the case of objections to amendments to the schedule to the International Convention for the Regulation of Whaling and of the nominations for the inscription of properties in the World Heritage List. Furthermore, participation can be doubled in a two-step consultation procedure, as in the case of the Codex Alimentarius Commission Standards.

Decision-making can fall under the jurisdiction of the executive body of the global organisation in question, or it may be conferred upon a separate body (as in the case of the Commission of Inquiry which reports to the Governing Body of the ILO on complaints by Members).

The imposition by global rules on domestic agencies of a right to participate is much less important than requiring global institutions to allow national governments to participate in the global decision-making process. The first type is well known in domestic legal orders, while the second has a precedent in the federal and regional States and in supra-national governments (like the European Union), where there are participation procedures for States in decision-making relating to federal or supra-national matters.

Lastly, I will address the question raised at the end of the previous section: why are avenues of participation established by global rules? For this second type of participation, three kinds of reasons can be identified.

Participation is required by global law because it is a part of the negotiation process that characterises the international arena. It provides another way to ensure cooperation among States in establishing rules or amending treaties. This is the case of the regulation of whaling and of the substances that deplete the ozone layer. States have participatory rights because they are political principals in international decision-making and are parties to a Treaty that is implemented by an international organisation.

Participation of national authorities at the global level is required in order to integrate domestic authorities into global decision-making processes and to promote the collaboration of national government agencies in reaching a global decision (as in the case of the process for the inscription of properties on the World Heritage List). This is not a separate level of government, but is made up of a global and a multinational component (as in the case of the Codex Alimentarius Commission standard setting process).

Finally, participation is granted at the global level in order to provide the right to a hearing to a government which has been the subject of a complaint filed by another government for not having observed a convention (as in the case of the ILO) or a 'review' of a global organisation (as in the case of countries that do not cooperate in the fight against money laundering).

The first rationale for participation does not really fall into the field that I am examining, because participation in this sense is a Treaty-amending power. States establish participatory rights as a way to guarantee to each other the power to amend agreements.

Participation granted to national governments (and to interested parties) vis-à-vis other national governments

In the global legal order participatory rights do not only operate vertically (private parties are heard by the State; States are heard by global organisations), but also horizontally (national governments are heard by other national governments; global institutions participate in the decision-making process of other global institutions). I shall now discuss the first of these two types of participatory rights.

The first example is the General Agreement on Trade in Services (GATS). Article VI.4 provides that in order to ensure that measures relating to qualification requirements and procedures, technical standards and licensing requirements do not constitute unnecessary barriers to trade in services, the Council for Trade in Services shall, through appropriate bodies it may establish, develop any necessary disciplines. Such disciplines shall aim to ensure that such requirements are, inter alia: (a) based on objective and transparent criteria, such as competence and the ability to supply the service; (b) not more burdensome than necessary to ensure the quality of the service; (c) in the case of licensing procedures, not in themselves a restriction on the supply of the service.

As an example of the implementation of such rule, consider the WTO 'Disciplines on domestic regulation for the accountancy sector'. These have a chapter on transparency that provides, for instance, that members 'shall make publicly available, including through the enquiry and contact points, the names and addresses of competent authorities' (ie governmental or non-governmental entities responsible for the licensing of professionals or firms, or accounting regulations); or that when introducing measures which significantly affect trade in accountancy services, 'Members shall endeavour to provide opportunity for comment, and give consideration to such comments, before adoption'.

A second example is that of the Agreement on the Application of Sanitary and Phytosanitary measures. Article 7, on transparency, establishes that '[m]embers shall notify changes in their sanitary or phytosanitary measures and shall provide information on their sanitary or phytosanitary measures in accordance with the provisions of Annex B'. Annex B, on 'Transparency of sanitary and phytosanitary regulations', regulates the notification procedures in the following manner:

> [w]henever an international standard, guideline or recommendation does not exist or the content of a proposed sanitary or phytosanitary regulation is not substantially the same as the content of an international standard, guideline or recommendation, and if the regulation may have a significant effect on trade of other Members, Members shall: (a) publish a notice at an early stage in such a manner as to enable interested Members to become acquainted with the proposal to introduce a particular regulation; (b) notify other Members, through the Secretariat, of the products to be covered by the regulation together with a brief indication of the objective and rationale of the proposed regulation. Such notifications shall take place at an early stage, when amendments can still be introduced and comments taken into account; (c) provide upon request to other Members copies of the proposed regulation and, whenever possible, identify the parts which in substance deviate from international standards, guidelines or recommendations; (d) without discrimination, allow reasonable time for other Members to make comments in writing, discuss these comments upon request, and take the comments and the results of the discussions into account.[43]

[43] Annex B continues in the following terms: '9. The Secretariat shall promptly circulate copies of the notification to all Members and interested international organizations and draw the attention of developing country Members to any notifications relating to products of particular interest to them. 10. Members shall designate a single central government authority as responsible for the implementation, on the national level, of the provisions concerning notification procedures according to paragraphs 5, 6, 7 and 8 of this Annex'. The WTO document on 'How to apply the transparency provisions of the SPS agreement', nn 72–74, explains how to deal with comments from others: '[a] prime purpose of notifying proposed regulations is to allow countries that might be affected by them to be consulted during the drafting process. Government authorities that have notified proposed regulations might receive comments on such regulations. Comments will either go to the notification authority or any other address specified in the final box of the notification form. … The notification authority should establish good working relationships with relevant agencies, and documented administrative procedures to ensure this happens. When other countries make comments on a

A third example is provided by the Agreement on Technical Barriers to Trade (TBT). Article 2.9 provides a regulation similar to that of Annex B to the SPS Agreement, discussed above.[44]

A fourth example is that of the Basel Convention on the Control of Transboundary Movements of Hazardous Wastes and their Disposal (adopted by the Conference of the Plenipotentiaries on 22 March 1989).[45] Article 6, on the transboundary movement of such waste between Parties, provides that the State of export 'shall notify, or shall require the generator or exporter to notify, in writing, through the channel of the competent authority of the State of export, the competent authority of the States concerned of any proposed transboundary movement of hazardous wastes or other wastes'. The State of import 'shall respond to the notifier in writing, consenting to the movement with or without conditions, denying permission for the movement, or requesting additional information'. A copy of the final response of the State of import 'shall be sent to the competent authorities of the States concerned which are Parties'. The State of export 'shall not allow the generator or exporter to commence the transboundary movement until it has received written confirmation that: (a) the notifier has received the written consent of the State of import; and (b) the notifier has received from the State of import confirmation of the existence of a contract between the exporter and the disposer specifying environmentally sound management of the wastes in question'. Each State of transit which is a Party 'shall

notified SPS measure, the country notifying has certain obligations to meet. The country receiving comments should, without further request: (i) acknowledge the receipt of such comments; (ii) explain within a reasonable period of time, and at the earliest possible date before the adoption of the measure, to any Member from which it has received comments, how it will take these comments into account and, where appropriate, provide additional relevant information on the proposed sanitary or phytosanitary regulations concerned; (iii) provide to any Member from which it has received comments, a copy of the corresponding sanitary or phytosanitary regulations as adopted or information that no corresponding sanitary or phytosanitary regulations will be adopted for the time being; (iv) where possible make available to other countries comments and questions it has received and answers it has provided, preferably through electronic facilities'.

[44] Art 2.9 provides that '[w]henever a relevant international standard does not exist or the technical content of a proposed technical regulation is not in accordance with the technical content of relevant international standards, and if the technical regulation may have a significant effect on trade of other Members, Members shall: 2.9.1 publish a notice in a publication at an early appropriate stage, in such a manner as to enable interested parties in other Members to become acquainted with it, that they propose to introduce a particular technical regulation; 2.9.2 notify other Members through the Secretariat of the products to be covered by the proposed technical regulation, together with a brief indication of its objective and rationale. Such notifications shall take place at an early appropriate stage, when amendments can still be introduced and comments taken into account; 2.9.3 upon request, provide to other Members particulars or copies of the proposed technical regulation and, whenever possible, identify the parts which in substance deviate from relevant international standards; 2.9.4 without discrimination, allow reasonable time for other Members to make comments in writing, discuss these comments upon request, and take these written comments and the results of these discussions into account'.

[45] G Handl, n 14 above, at 131 ff.

promptly acknowledge to the notifier receipt of the notification'. It may subsequently respond to the notifier in writing, within 60 days, consenting to the movement with or without conditions, denying permission for the movement, or requesting additional information.[46]

A fifth example is that of the Principles for Food Import and Export Inspection and Certification System of the Codex Alimentarius Commission. Articles 13, 14, 15 and 16, which deal with transparency, set out several requirements such as, for instance, that the principles and operations of food inspection and certification systems should be open to scrutiny by consumers, their representative organisations and other interested parties; or that importing countries should provide information on existing requirements and proposed changes to requirements should be published and an adequate time period permitted for comment.[47]

A sixth example is that of the Code of Conduct for Responsible Fisheries. Article 11.3.4 provides that '[w]hen a State introduces changes to its legal requirements affecting trade in fish and fishery products with other States, sufficient information and time should be given to allow the States and producers affected to introduce, as appropriate, the changes needed in their processes and procedures. In this connection, consultation with affected States on the time frame for implementation of the changes would be desirable. Due consideration should be given to requests from developing countries for temporary derogations from obligations'.

A seventh example is the Agreement on Implementation of Article VI of the General Agreement on Tariffs and Trade (GATT) 1994. Article 5.5 provides: 'after receipt of a properly documented application and before proceeding to initiate an investigation, the authorities shall notify the government of the exporting Member concerned'. The above-mentioned Article 6.1.3 states that, after an investigation has been initiated, the authorities 'shall provide the full text of the

[46] Art 6 continues as follows: '[[t]he State of export shall not allow the transboundary movement to commence until it has received the written consent of the State of transit. However, if at any time a Party decides not to require prior written consent, either generally or under specific conditions, for transit transboundary movements of hazardous wastes or other wastes, or modifies its requirements in this respect, it shall forthwith inform the other Parties of its decision pursuant to Article 13. In this latter case, if no response is received by the State of export within 60 days of the receipt of a given notification by the State of transit, the State of export may allow the export to proceed through the State of transit.'

[47] It also provides that the views of exporting countries should be taken into account in taking a final decision. A reasonable period should be allowed before a new requirement takes effect in order to permit exporting countries, and in particular developing countries, to make necessary changes to methods of production and control measures. Importing countries should make available to the exporting countries, upon request, timely advice as to the basis of the decision they have taken regarding the compliance of foods with their relevant requirements. Upon request by the competent authorities of the importing countries, the exporting countries should provide access to view and assess the actual working of their relevant inspection and certification systems.

written application to the known exporters and to the authorities of the exporting Member and shall make it available, upon request, to other interested parties involved'.[48]

The eighth example is from the WTO Agreement on Safeguards. Article 12.3 provides: '[a] Member proposing to apply or extend a safeguard measure shall provide adequate opportunity for prior consultations with those Members having a substantial interest as exporters of the product concerned, with a view to, inter alia, reviewing the information provided under paragraph 2, exchanging views on the measure and reaching an understanding on ways to achieve the objective set out in paragraph 1 of Article 8'.

The last example is from the General Agreement on Tariffs and Trade (GATT) 1994 itself.[49] Article XIX of that Agreement regulates emergency action on imports of particular products. Paragraph 2 provides that '[b]efore any contracting party shall take action pursuant to the provisions of paragraph 1 of this Article, it shall give notice in writing to the contracting parties as far in advance as may be practicable and shall afford the contracting parties and those contracting parties having a substantial interest as exporters of the product concerned an opportunity to consult with it in respect of the proposed action'.[50] The treaty provides for an agreement. If the agreement is not reached, the affected parties can suspend equivalent concessions.[51]

[48] Art 6.11 states: '[f]or the purposes of this Agreement, "interested parties" shall include: (i) an exporter or foreign producer or the importer of a product subject to investigation, or a trade or business association a majority of the members of which are producers, exporters or importers of such product; (ii) the government of the exporting Member; and (iii) a producer of the like product in the importing Member or a trade and business association a majority of the members of which produce the like product in the territory of the importing Member. This list shall not preclude Members from allowing domestic or foreign parties other than those mentioned above to be included as interested parties'.

[49] Art X.3a. of the 1994 GATT provides that '[e]ach Member shall administer in a uniform, impartial and reasonable manner all its laws, regulations and decisions and rulings ...' and requires that Members maintain or institute judicial, arbitral or administrative tribunals or procedures to ensure prompt review and correction of administrative action.

[50] On Art XIX, para 2 of GATT, see GATT Analytical Index, at 523–24.

[51] On the basis of this provision the Appellate Body of the WTO has decided that the certifications envisaged by s 609 of the United States Public Law 101–162 'consist principally of administrative ex parte inquiry or verification by staff of the Office of Marine Conservation in the Department of State with staff of the United States National Marine Fisheries Service. With respect to both types of certification, there is no formal opportunity for an applicant country to be heard, or to respond to any arguments that may be made against it, in the course of the certification process before a decision to grant or to deny certification is made. Moreover, no formal written, reasoned decision, whether of acceptance ore rejection, is rendered on applications for either type of certification, whether under Section 609(b)(2)(A) and (B) or under Section 609(b)(2) ... The certification processes followed by the United States thus appear to be singularly informal and casual, and to be conducted in a manner such that these processes could result in the negation of rights of Members. There appears to be no way that exporting Members can be certain whether the terms of Section 609, in particular, the 1996 Guidelines, are being applied in a fair and just manner by the appropriate governmental agencies of the United States. It appears to us that, effectively, exporting Members applying for certification whose applications are rejected are denied basic fairness and due process, and are discriminated against, vis-à-vis those Members which are granted certification. The provisions of Article X:3 of the

Horizontal linkages among States, established by global rules, are as dense as vertical linkages between States and global organisations. Global governance is not made up of global institutions alone. It also consists of multinational and transnational processes. These open national governments up to each other and increase the dialogue between nations.

Yet participatory rights that operate horizontally also have an additional vertical effect. Many examples make clear that compliance by national governments with participatory requirements is supervised by global authorities (eg, the Council for Trade in Services or the WTO Secretariat). Therefore, the structure is not purely horizontal as it involves both vertical and horizontal elements.

This kind of participation occurs in rule-making (eg. in the context of the GATS, SPS and TBT Agreements and responsible fisheries regulations), adjudicating (eg, in the contexts of transboundary movements of hazardous wastes, food inspection, WTO safeguard measures, and GATT emergency action) and quasi-judicial (eg, in the context of the Agreement on Implementation of Article VI of the GATT 1994) procedures.[52]

The obligation to grant participation rights falls upon national governments, and the parties that participate are also national governments. Only in a few cases, such as the TBT Agreement, the Codex Alimentarius Commission Export Inspection and Certification System, and the Agreement on the Implementation of Article VI of the GATT 1994, can private parties also participate. Participation

GATT 1994 bear upon this matter. In our view, Section 609 falls within the 'laws, regulations, judicial decisions and administrative rulings of general application' described in Article X:1. Inasmuch as there are due process requirements generally for measures that are otherwise imposed in compliance with WTO obligations, it is only reasonable that rigorous compliance with the fundamental requirements of due process should be required in the application and administration of a measure which purports to be an exception to the treaty obligations of the Member imposing the measure and which effectively results in a suspension pro hac vice of the treaty rights of other Members. It is also clear to us that Article X:3 of the GATT 1994 establishes certain minimum standards for transparency and procedural fairness in the administration of trade regulations which, in our view, are not met here. The non-transparent and ex parte nature of the internal governmental procedures applied by the competent officials in the Office of Marine Conservation, the Department of State, and the United States National Marine Fisheries Service throughout the certification processes under Section 609, as well as the fact that countries whose applications are denied do not receive formal notice of such denial, nor of the reasons of the denial, and the fact, too, that there is no formal legal procedure for review of, or appeal from, a denial of an application, are all contrary to the spirit, if not the letter, of Article X:3 of the GATT 1994', WTO Appellate Body, United States—Import Prohibition of Certain Shrimp and Shrimp Products (AB-1998–4) (WT/DS58/AB/R) 12 October 1998, nn 180–83. See also WTO Appellate Body, United States—Restrictions on Imports of Cotton and Man-made Fibre Underwear (AB-1996–3) (WT/DS24/AB/R) 10 February 1997, para IV; WTO Appellate Body, Thailand—Anti-Dumping Duties on Angles, Shapes and Sections of Iron or Non-Alloy Steel and H-Beams from Poland (AB-2000–12) (WT/DS122/AB/R) 12 March 2001, paras 98–112; WTO Appellate Body, European Communities—Anti-Dumping Duties on Imports of Cotton-Type Bed Linen from India Recourse to Article 21.5 of the DSU by India (AB-2003–1) (WT/DS141/AB/RW) 8 April 2003, paras 101–46. G della Cananea, 'Beyond the State: the Europeanization and Globalization of Procedural Administrative Law' (2003) 9 *European Public Law* 574.

[52] RB Stewart and M Ratton Sanchez Badin, 'The World Trade Organization and Global Administrative Law', IILJ Working Paper 2009–7.

rights are extended to private economic actors in a way that is similar to the first set of cases examined, where global norms impose on national governments the obligation to hear private parties. In these cases, domestic governments, as participants, play a double role, as they also protect the interests of private actors.

Global norms require that national governments provide information, or publish notices, or notify information, and some also introduce time requirements, as information must be given at an early stage or giving sufficient or adequate time (as is the case with the SPS and TBT Agreements and of food inspection and fisheries regulation).

Information is required in order to allow for comments (and the SPS and TBT Agreements establish that comments must be made in writing) from the States (or other interested parties).

Finally, four instruments (the GATS, the SPS and TBT Agreements, and the Codex) require that the addressee government give consideration or take into account the comments received.

When participation provided by global norms is placed under global control, the relations established are not purely horizontal, but triangular, involving both horizontal (between national governments) and vertical (between national governments and global institutions) links.

Why does global law oblige national governments to hear other national governments? First of all, it is in order to ensure an exchange of information and the reciprocal adaptation of national rules and conduct, as in the case of the Code of Conduct for Responsible Fisheries.

A second reason is in order to provide not only for an exchange of information, but also to encourage a process of self-harmonisation among States, as in the cases of the GATS, the SPS and TBT Agreements, and the Food Import and Export Inspection and Certification System.

The third reason is to promote multinational cooperation, as in the case of transboundary movements of hazardous wastes, anti-dumping procedures and safeguards measures.

Participation granted to global institutions before other global institutions

A second type of horizontal participatory rights are those granted to global institutions vis-à-vis other global institutions.

The first example is the United Nations Environment Programme (UNEP). Rule 10 of the Rules of Procedure of the UNEP Governing Council regulates agenda setting:

> [a]fter the Governing Council has considered the provisional agenda for the following session, the provisional agenda, incorporating any amendments made by the Governing Council, shall be communicated by the Executive Director to all States Members of the United Nations or members of the specialized agencies and of the International Atomic Energy Agency, the Chairmen of subsidiary organs of the Governing Council as

> appropriate, the President of the General Assembly when the Assembly is in session, the President of the Economic and Social Council, the appropriate United Nations bodies, the specialized agencies, the International Atomic Energy, the intergovernmental organizations referred to in rule 68 below and the international non-governmental organizations referred to in rule 69 below.

A second example is that of the already-mentioned Codex Alimentarius Commission's standard-setting procedure. The 'Uniform procedure for the elaboration of Codex standards and related texts' (Part 1 of the 'Procedures for the Elaboration of Codex Standards and Related Texts') provides that both the 'proposed draft standard' and the 'draft standards' are sent not only to members of the Commission, but also to 'interested international organizations'. These organisations may make comments on all aspects and the 'subsidiary body' of the Commission (see Rule IX of the 'Rules of procedure of the Codex Alimentarius Commission'), usually a Committee, 'has the power to consider such comments'.

Participation, in the above cases, is granted in agenda setting and in standard setting proceedings. Other interested global institutions are entitled to participate. The usual procedure—communication–comments–consideration—applies.

Why do global rules impose participation in these cases? Global law is made up of sectoral regimes. But these regimes are interconnected. A global institution may be member of the governing board of another global institution, or it may—as is the case here—enjoy the right to participate in certain decision-making processes of another global body. Global rules granting participatory rights to a global organisation vis-à-vis other global organisations establish lines of communication between global regulatory regimes.

This function is no different from the function of inter-agency consultation and participation procedures within national governments. It ties up authorities and ensures cooperation.

Participation granted to private parties before global institutions

I now turn to the most important part of the picture: participatory rights that private parties may exercise directly before global organisations. Participation of private parties in domestic procedures (1) is well known, as the relevant rights are usually established by domestic legislation. Participation of national governments in global institutions (2) is also a widespread phenomenon. Participation of national governments in foreign governments' decision-making (3) is also common, as bilateral or multilateral agreements open up national legal systems vis-à-vis foreign ones. The peculiarity of the first, in this case, lies in the fact that it is established by global rules. Therefore, the duty to hear is imposed on the State. The peculiarity of the second and the third forms of participation lies in the fact that State participation in global organisations does not, in this case, occur at a 'constitutional' level but rather at an 'administrative' level. It is not participation in the 'legislative' process, but participation in the 'administrative' process.

What is entirely new is the participation of national civil society in the global decision-making process. This undermines the traditional view of the State as the only global actor: participation in global decision-making is no longer the province of national governments alone.

Participation of national civil society within global institutions is the result of the growth of global regulation of private actors: the more international organisations establish standards for private actors, the more these actors need to participate in the global standard setting processes.[53]

The first example is informal consultation with the financial industry by the Basel Committee on Banking Supervision (BCBS), established by the Governors of the Central Banks of the leading Western countries (Belgium, Canada, France, Germany, Italy, Japan, Luxembourg, the Netherlands, Spain, Sweden, Switzerland, United Kingdom and United States) at the end of 1974.[54] Its membership has recently been broadened to include representatives from the G20 countries.[55] The 'Introduction' to the document on the 'Application of Basel II to Trading Activities and the Treatment of Double Default Effects' (July 2005) states:

> [i]n releasing the Revised Framework ..., the BCBS re-iterated its intention to maintain its active dialogue with the industry to ensure that the new framework keeps pace with, and can be applied to, ongoing developments in the financial services sector .... Given the interest of both banks and securities firms in the potential solutions to these particular issues, the BCBS has worked jointly with the International Organization of Securities Commissions (IOSCO) to consult with industry representatives and other supervisors on these matters. ... The BCBS released a first version of this proposal ... for consultation purposes. Thirty-seven comments have been provided by banks, investment firms, industry associations, supervisory authorities, and other interested institutions. ... The BCBS and IOSCO worked diligently, in close cooperation with representatives of the industry, to reflect their comments in the present paper.[56]

A second example is the WTO's 23 July 1996 'Guidelines for arrangements on relations with non-governmental organizations', which states that Members recognise the role NGOs can play in increasing the awareness of the public with respect to WTO activities, and agree in this regard to improve transparency and develop communication with NGOs. Therefore, to contribute to achieving

[53] See S Cassese, 'Global Standards for National Administrative Procedure' (2005) 68 *Law and Contemporary Problems* 109.

[54] D Zaring, n 25 above.

[55] Central bank governors and heads of supervision from Argentina, Indonesia, Saudi Arabia, South Africa and Turkey, together with Hong Kong and Singapore are now members of the Committee: see BCBS, *Basel Committee Broadens its Membership*, Press Release, 10 June 2009, www.bis.org/press/p090610.htm.

[56] See also MS Barr and GP Miller, 'Global Administrative Law: the View from Basel' (2006) 17 *European Journal of International Law* 17 ff.

greater transparency, Members will ensure more information about WTO activities is publicised, in particular by making available documents, and the Secretariat will make available on-line the material which is open to the public, including derestricted documents. The interaction between the WTO Secretariat and NGOs should be developed through various means such as, inter alia, the organisation on an ad hoc basis of symposia on specific WTO-related issues, the making of informal arrangements for receiving any information that NGOs wish to make available for consultation by interested delegations, and the continuation of the practice of responding to requests for general information and briefings about the WTO.

A third example is that of the Commission for Environmental Cooperation (CEC), established by the North American Agreement on Environmental Cooperation (NAAEC) (1993).[57] The Commission comprises a council, a Secretariat and a 'Joint Public Advisory Committee (JPAC)' (Article 8.2). This Committee has adopted 'Public Consultation Guidelines'. Consultations are meetings held by the JPAC in which members of the public are allowed to provide their input on any matter within the scope of the NAEEC Agreement, thus contributing to the decision-making process on such matters. The principles for consultation embodied in the guidelines are that any consultation should advance the purpose for which it has been convened and should be organised to provide the most effective use of time and the resources dedicated to it. As for the structure of consultation, the guidelines provide that consultation meetings will be structured along the following lines: 'advance notification; introduction and information; early break-up into work groups or roundtables; opportunity for each participant to make a presentation; and a closing session to allow open discussion between participants and JPAC members'.

A fourth example is the already mentioned North American Agreement for Labor Cooperation (NAALC) that—as noted—provides that 'the public' may make 'submissions' to the Evaluation Committees of Experts, and that these Committees 'may consider' such submissions (Article 24, paragraphs 4 and 5).

A fifth example is that of the 'Code of Conduct for Responsible Fisheries'. As already noted, this provides for consultation and effective participation by States. But it also requires consultation with and participation by global institutions.

[57] On this treaty, DL Markell, 'The North American Commission for Environmental Cooperation after Ten Years: Lessons about Institutional Structure and Public Participation in Governance'; JH Knox, 'Separated at Birth: The North American Agreement on Labor and the Environment'; K Raustiala, 'Police Patrols and Fire Alarms in the NAAEC'; C Wold, L Ritchie, D Scott, and M Clark, 'The Inadequacy of the Citizen Submission Process of Articles 14 and 15 of the North American Agreement on Environmental Cooperation' all in (2004) *Loyola of Los Angeles International and Comparative Law Review* 341 ff, 359 ff, 389 ff, 415 ff; T Yang, 'The Effectiveness of the Nafta Environmental Side Agreement's Citizen Submission Process: a Case Study of Metales y Derivados' (2005) 76 *University of Colorado Law Review* 443 ff; DL Markell, 'Governance of International Institutions: A Review of the North American Commission for Environmental Cooperation's Citizen Submission Process' (2005) 30 *North Carolina Journal of International Law and Commercial Regulation* 759 ff.

Article 1. 2 states that '[t]he Code is global in scope, and is directed toward members and non-members of FAO, fishing entities, subregional, regional and global organizations, whether governmental or non-governmental, and all persons concerned with the conservation of fishery resources and management and development of fisheries, such as fishers, those engaged in processing and marketing of fish and fishery products and other users of the aquatic environment in relation to fisheries'.

A sixth example comes from the Constitution of a global private organisation, the International Accounting Standards Committee Foundation (IASCF). This Constitution establishes that the IASB (International Accounting Standards Board), in the preparation and adoption of standards, shall '(b) publish an Exposure Draft on all projects and normally publish a discussion document for public comment on major projects; ... (f) establish procedures for reviewing comments made within a reasonable period on documents published for comment; ... (j) consider holding public hearings to discuss proposed standards, although there is no requirement to hold public hearings for every project; ... (l) give reasons if it does not follow any of the non-mandatory procedures set out in (b), (g), (i), (j) and (k)'.[58] According to these provisions, accounting standards are developed through an 'international due process' that involves accountants, financial analysts and other users of financial statements, the business community, stock exchanges, regulatory and legal authorities, academics and other interested individuals and organisations from around the world.[59]

A seventh example is that of Article 34 of the 1970 Patent Cooperation Treaty, which regulates the procedure before the International Preliminary Examining Authority: '(2)(a) The applicant shall have a right to communicate orally and in writing with the International Preliminary Examining Authority. (c) The applicant shall receive at least one written opinion from the International Preliminary Examining Authority .... (d) The applicant may respond to the written opinion'. Article 34 goes on to specify rules for the restriction of claims.

Another example comes from the International Labour Organization (ILO) Constitution: Article 24 provides that '[i]n the event of any representation being made to the International Labour Office by an industrial association of employers or of workers that any of the Members has failed to secure in any respect the effective observance within its jurisdiction of any Convention to which it is a party, the Governing Body may communicate this representation to the government against which it is made, and may invite that government to make such statement on the subject as it may think fit'. Article 25 then states: '[i]f no statement is received within a reasonable time from the government in question, or if the statement when received is not deemed to be satisfactory by the

[58] Art 37. The Constitution, first approved in 2001, has been periodically reviewed. This article refers to the text as amended in March 2010.

[59] See IASB's *Due Process Handbook*, 2008 at 31, n 18, and 112–14 on the 'comply or explain requirement' and 18–53 for the six stages of standard-setting.

Governing Body, the latter shall have the right to publish the representation and the statement, if any, made in reply to it'.

A ninth example is that of the Internet Corporation for Assigned Names and Numbers (ICANN) Bylaws.[60] Article III, section 6 of these Bylaws provides for a notice and comment procedure on policy actions. With respect to any policies that substantially affect third parties, ICANN shall 'provide public notice' and 'a reasonable opportunity for parties to comment on the adoption of the proposed policies, to see the comments of others, and to reply to those comments'. Where the policy action affects public policy concerns, the opinion of the Governmental Advisory Committee must be requested. Subsequently, ICANN shall provide 'reconsideration' by a 'Reconsideration Committee' and 'independent review' by an 'Independent Review Panel'.

Finally, the above-mentioned World Anti-Doping Code has established the right to a fair hearing before every anti-doping organisation. As a consequence, this right is guaranteed to the affected parties not only before national anti-doping organisations, but also before the International Olympic Committee, the International Paralympic Committee and the International Federations (see Introduction to the Code and Article 8).

Before concluding on this point, it is important to note that private parties' participation in global decision-making procedures may also be the result of State action. The Aarhus Convention on Access to Information, Public Participation in Decision-Making and Access to Justice in Environmental Matters (25 June 1998), Article 3.7, provides that '[e]ach Party shall promote the application of the principles of this Convention in international environmental decision-making processes and within the framework of international organizations in matters relating to the environment'.

The United States Code, title 19, Chapter 22, Subchapter I, Paragraph 3536: Increased transparency states: '[t]he Trade Representative shall seek the adoption by the Ministerial Conference and General Council of procedures that will ensure broader application of the principle of transparency and clarification of the costs and benefits of trade policy actions, through the observance of open and equitable procedures in trade matters by the Ministerial Conference and the General Council, and by the dispute settlement panels and the Appellate Body under the Dispute Settlement Understanding'.

These cases illustrate that private participation in global decision-making can occur both on a 'de facto' (as in the case of the Basel Committee) and 'de iure' (as in the remaining cases) basis, and it can do so in regulatory, adjudicatory and compliance procedures.[61]

[60] As amended 28 October 2010 (http://www.icann.org/en/general/bylaws.htm#III).

[61] A different set of cases involves the participation of global organisations' employees in global decision-making (C de Cooker (ed), *Accountability, Investigation and Due Process in International Organizations* (Leiden, Martinus Nijhoff, 2005) is in large part devoted to this issue). In these cases, we see the participation of private parties who do not represent civil society. Take, for instance, the

Participation in global decision-making processes provided for by global rules is—as noted above—the most important step towards introducing direct links between civil society and global institutions. This may explain why this type of participation is regulated in a somewhat vague and ambiguous manner.

This type of participation has the following peculiarities. It can exist with respect to policy formulation proceedings (as in the case of NGO before the WTO or ICANN or that of the NAALC), regulatory procedures (as in the BCBS and in the fisheries cases), standard-setting proceedings (as is the case of accounting standards), procedures aimed at enforcing global standards in domestic jurisdictions (as in the case of environmental standards in North America), in adjudication proceedings (as in the cases of the patents, labour standards and anti-doping). In the case of the CEC, consultation is required for policy formulation, preparation of programmes and also for specific projects and issues.

This type of participation is also granted within public and semi-public bodies, and within 'ad hoc' bodies. It is open to private parties (interested or affected persons, concerned industry, NGO representatives), but also to domestic agencies (as in the case of the BCBS, where other supervisors can participate) and to national governments (as in the case of 'representations' to the ILO, where national governments play the role of respondents).

Global norms provide for consultation, cooperation, participation and for ancillary obligations, like making available information or documents (as in the cases of the WTO and the CEC).

Participants may respond or make comments (as in the cases of the BCBS, accounting standards, patent examination, and environmental and labour standards in North America), have meetings or symposia (as in the case of WTO with NGOs, and in that of the CEC) or public hearings (as happens in the development of accounting standards).

National governments may provide comments or responses on reports prepared by the global authority in question following the 'submissions' of the

conditions of service applicable to the staff of the WTO Secretariat (decision adopted by the General Council on 16 October 1998), in particular Reg 12.2: ('[i]n disputes relating to their conditions of service, staff members have the right to due process, as set out in the Staff Rules'). But what if the right to a hearing is not provided for by the relevant global rules? This is illustrated by the *Skandera* case, decided by the World Bank Administrative Tribunal on 5 June 1981 (No 2). The Tribunal held (Nos 28 and 29) that a '[n]otice of termination should communicate to the affected staff member the true reasons for the Bank's decision. It is in the interest of the Bank that the employment of qualified employees not be terminated on the basis of inadequate facts or ill-founded justifications, and one way to assure this is to furnish the staff member at the time of termination with a specific and true assessment which will provide a fair opportunity to the individual to dispute, and possibly to seek rectification of the decision of the Bank. The prompt communication of reasons for termination will also facilitate the preparation and presentation of appeals and other remedies provided in the Bank's dispute-resolution procedure. By failing ... to inform Mr. Skandera accurately of the reasons for the termination of his appointment, the Bank impaired his ability to protect his interests. Although prompt and candid disclosure of reasons might well not have affected the Tribunal's decision regarding the propriety of the termination, Mr. Skandera was delayed by four months in dealing in an informed manner with the Bank's action'. On this case, see RA Gorman, n 6 above, at 439–40.

parties, as in the cases of labour and environmental standards in North America. In the cases of the BCBS and the IASB, a requirement to reflect on or review the comments received is provided, although only the latter also establishes an obligation to give reasons.[62]

Participation of private parties at the global level is granted for two main reasons.

The first is to provide consultation. The Basel Committee—as already noted—consulted the regulated industry 'to ensure that the new framework keeps pace with, and can be applied to, ongoing developments in the financial services sector'. The interaction between the WTO Secretariat and NGOs is encouraged in order to 'contribute to accuracy and richness of the public debate'. The JPAC provides to the CEC Secretariat 'relevant technical, scientific or other information' and contributes to decision-making through consultation. The same purpose is furthered by the consultation procedures of global organisations in the field of fisheries regulation, the IASB in its development of accounting standards, and the North American Commissions for Environmental Cooperation and for Labor Cooperation.

The second purpose for granting participation is to provide the right to a hearing: to, for example, an individual seeking a patent in the international preliminary examination; to a State accused for having failed to observe an ILO Convention; and to persons who are accused of having violated an anti-doping rule (or to a UN international civil servant).

A GLOBAL DUE PROCESS?

'[A]s supranational organizations take on more of an autonomous decision-making role and face more controversial issues, they tend to develop better governance structures'.[63] The more global institutions expand their role as regulators, the more global administrative law matures.

The development of a global law is still challenged by those authors who think the supra-State to be an 'acephalous world', the product of negotiated understanding. Therefore, 'we should be very cautious in representing what are essentially negotiated orders at regional and global level as legal orders while they remain significantly different from those at the level of the state'.[64] But this point of view associates law only with the State (in the words of the same author, 'some of these expansive moves to represent law as present beyond the state, even as

[62] In the case of ICANN, the opinion of the Governmental Advisory Committee must be requested. A triangular relationship between private party-global institution-national government is therefore established.

[63] DC Esty, 'Good Governance at the Supranational Scale: Globalizing Administrative Law' (2006) 115 *Yale Law Journal* 1490.

[64] S Roberts, 'After Government? On Representing Law Without the State' (2005) 68 *Modern Law Review* 23.

having nothing to do with governing, leave us with a diminishing sense of what law is'),[65] whereas it has long been observed that wherever one finds a society, one finds law.

This analysis has shown that participation in global law is multi-faceted, in terms of who is granted the right to participate, which level of government is obliged to grant participation, and which decision-making processes must be open to participation.

The parties entitled to participate are private individuals or groups, national governments and global organisations. Participation is granted at the national level, both before national and foreign governments, and at the global level. Procedures in which participation is granted are concerned with law-making, regulation, adjudication and dispute settlement.

Global norms require that both domestic administrations and global institutions comply with due process principles. In both cases governments and/or private parties are entitled to participatory rights: while the domestic–international divide is respected in the first case, it is transcended in the second.

Participatory rights granted at the global level show more complexity, when compared with the same rights in the domestic governments. In the WTO system, for instance, global rules imposing the duty to hear private parties on States are reinforced by rules also obliging them to hear foreign States. In many regulatory regimes, there is continuity between participation and negotiation, and the former can even act as a surrogate for the latter.

This also produces some ambiguity, as it is difficult to draw the line between the political rights of national governments as political principals in international negotiations and participation rights more closely analogous to those granted to private parties with regard to domestic administrative regulatory authorities.

Secondly, participatory rights in global law have a wider sphere of application than in domestic law: participatory rights are granted by private governance regimes that mirror administrative law principles.

Thirdly, participatory rights in the global legal order are multi-polar, while in domestic law they are often dyadic. In the global arena there are many more conflicting interests than in the domestic domain. As the rule of law requires giving these interests a say, there can be numerous parties involved in global administrative proceedings, representing both public and private interests, national and supranational interests.

The maturity of global administrative law

But how mature is global administrative law? Are its principles well developed or are they in a primitive stage of growth? Is global proceduralism, as a consequence, similar to domestic proceduralism? To what extent are participatory rights in the

[65] ibid, at 3.

global law different from domestic participatory rights? Do participatory rights in the global arena follow the same path as their domestic counterparts? Do these procedures embody administrative law principles as traditionally understood, or just good governance principles?

This analysis has shown that participation in the global administrative arena is not precisely defined; moreover, it is loosely structured and is not always enforceable before a judge.[66]

Participatory rights at the global level are regulated in a somewhat rudimentary fashion. While in the domestic legal order both notice and comment procedures (ie participation in rule-making processes) and hearing procedures (ie participation in adjudicatory procedures) are subject to detailed rules, providing detailed procedural obligations, in the global legal order, such procedures are only summarily regulated.

In the global legal system, participatory rights are more or less structured depending on the sector or area. Their regulation is most developed in areas like environmental protection, sports, trade and Internet governance, because of the particular complexity of global regulation and the need to level the playing field.

Another reason why participatory rights are less rudimentary in certain areas is because of the need to grant participation to foreign actors in domestic legal systems. The global legal system has both a vertical dimension (global institutions are superimposed on domestic institutions) and a horizontal one (domestic legal orders are obliged to open up to each other). In the latter dimension, it is crucial to give foreign actors a say vis-à-vis domestic authorities.

Moreover, while in the domestic legal order participation is just one element of a larger body of law, requiring transparency (in order to let participants know that there is an administrative decision in preparation), reasoned decision (in order that participants can see that their positions have been taken in account) and judicial review (in order to ensure that the administrative agency respects procedural requirements), in the global legal order transparency, reasoned decision and judicial review requirements are in some regulatory regimes unknown, and in others exist only at a rudimentary stage of development. Consequently, one can raise the question of whether participation alone, without transparency, a requirement to provide reasons for decisions and judicial review, can be understood as equivalent to the due process of law in the domestic legal order.

[66] More examples of participatory rights in UN Economic and Social Council, Economic Commission for Europe, 'Survey of selected access to information, public participation, and access to justice rules and practices in international forums', MP.PP/2002/18/Add.1 CEP/2002/13/Add. 1 12 September 2002 and B Morgan, 'Turning Off the Tap: Urban Water Service Delivery and the Social Construction of Global Administrative Law', (2006) 17 *European Journal of International Law* 226 ff. See also C Harlow, 'Global Administrative Law: The Quest for Principles and Values' (2006) 17 *European Journal of International Law* 207: 'a universal set of administrative law principles, difficult in any event to identify, is neither welcome nor particularly desirable: diversity and pluralism are greatly to be preferred'.

The boundaries between participation and consultation, participation and negotiation, and participation and cooperation are not clear. Participation is granted in order to establish links between civil society and national governments, between national governments and global institutions, between national governments and other national governments, between global institutions and other global organisations, and between civil society and global institutions. But these links are—with a few exceptions—established without introducing a precise balance of powers.

The rights of individual participants and the obligations of the authorities necessary to ensure participation are not well defined. Rights and obligations are more loosely defined in adjudication procedures, while they tend to be better structured in rule-making procedures, as a consequence of the central role of rule-making in the global arena. They are more detailed when dealing with the participation of national governments, less when dealing with private actors, as a consequence of the leading role still played by the States in the global legal order.

Global agencies—as already noted—are not always required to give reasons for their decisions: therefore, the addressees of global decisions can often participate in the decision-making process without being entitled to know on which grounds the decision has been taken.

In a very few cases, participation rights are enforceable before a judge, who can review administrative action and quash decisions taken without consulting or hearing private parties.

Therefore, global proceduralism is at an elementary stage of development and the rule of law is not fully implemented in the global legal order.

The other side of the coin is that global procedures, more frequently than domestic procedures, are required to be based on scientific evidence, on independent evaluation and on deliberative democracy. Being younger than their national equivalents and more removed from politics, they can easily be subject to such rules. Moreover, the interaction between global and domestic norms produces at least two consequences. First, when global norms are added to domestic ones, they undergo a process of reciprocal interpenetration and strengthening. Secondly, the more global norms on participation are imposed on domestic administration, the more global institutions are themselves obliged to comply with due process requirements.

In conclusion, the extent of global participatory rights may not be comparable to that attained by participation rights provided in national legal systems, but it is nevertheless possible to state that they are no longer at a primitive stage of development. It is possible to predict that they will progress further through judicial enforcement at the global level, as courts will come to play a threefold role, consisting in the enforcement of existing rules, their expansion into new areas, and in the development of additional general principles, not bound to individual regulatory regimes and of more general application.

How global is global administrative law?

The global legal order is full of rules prescribing participatory rights. But how global is global due process? In spite of the great number of rules providing for participation, participation is far from being a global principle, because the global law is made up of many different, separate and self-contained regimes: each regime has its own due process principles, and not all of these regimes grant participatory rights. Indeed, there is a lack of overall principles that are applied within all regulatory regimes, as a general form of their functioning.

In 2005, the European Union Court of First Instance (now known as the General Court) stated that 'it appears that no mandatory rule of public international law requires prior hearing for the persons concerned in circumstances such as those of this case, in which the Security Council, acting under Title VII of the Charter of the United States, decides, through its Sanctions Committee, that the funds of certain individuals or entities suspected of contributing to the funding of terrorism must be frozen'.[67] As a consequence, no violation of the rights of the affected parties was found, on the grounds that global law provides neither a general 'principle of defence' nor a specific right to be heard in relation to the UN Sanctions Committee's freezing of private funds. In 2008, however, the European Court of Justice reversed this decision, on the basis that 'measures incompatible with respect for human rights are not acceptable in the Community (paragraph 284), and 'the obligations imposed by an international agreement cannot have the effect of prejudicing the constitutional principles of the EC Treaty', including respect for human rights (paragraph 285).[68]

There are strong asymmetries among the many different participatory rights granted at the global level. Therefore, although the many rules examined above do have a cumulative effect, they do not establish a general principle of the global legal order.

Although the global legal order consists of the sum of many self-contained regulatory regimes, and participatory rights are not granted everywhere or in general terms, there are, on the other hand, two forces at work that push toward the generalisation of participatory rights.

[67] Judgment of the Court of First Instance (Second Chamber, Extended Composition), 21 September 2005, in Case T-306/01, para 307.

[68] Judgment of the European Court of Justice (Grand Chamber), 3 September 2008, in Cases C-402/05 P and C-415/05 P. See G De Búrca, 'The European Court of Justice and the International Legal Order after *Kadi*' (2009) *Harvard International Law Journal*; N Lavranos, 'The Impact of the *Kadi* Judgment on the International Obligations of the EC Member States and the EC' (2009) *Yearbook of European Law*; KS Ziegler, 'Strengthening the Rule of Law, But Fragmenting International Law: The *Kadi* Decision of the ECJ from the Perspective of Human Rights' (2009) 9 *Human Rights Law Review* 288.

Participation in the global arena is becoming a 'human right'[69] and thus a universal principle. There is a tension between the limited scope of each regulatory regime providing for participation and participation conceived as a human right, and therefore as becoming universally applicable.

There is a powerful spill-over effect from one arena to another:[70] principles designed for one regulatory regime pass into others, in part because of the strong connections among these regimes (for example, the connecting regimes of 'trade and').

Secondly, in the many different regulatory regimes that together constitute global governance, the right to participate in decision-making processes is granted only when prescribed by a specific rule. The right to a hearing and notice and comment procedures are not as well-established in the global legal order as they are in domestic law. The reason for this weakness is the insufficient development of the global judiciary, because only courts can make these principles generally applicable.

What is the purpose of participation in the global legal order?

The functions or justifications of participation in the global legal order are not easy to analyse. As the different participation rights are loosely defined and structured, it is difficult to classify their highly diverse functions. In addition, these functions differ depending on the institutional context and nature of the right in question. Finally, participation is frequently multi-purpose. It is, therefore, possible to mention only a prevailing few of the most important functions.

Participation has a legitimacy-building function. Global regulatory agencies are like self-contained machines; but, through participation, civil society can get closer to the workings of power.

[69] BS Chimni, 'Co-Option and Resistance: Two Faces of Global Administrative Law' (2005) 37 *New York University Journal of International Law and Politics* 799. See also RP Peerenboom, 'Human Rights and Rule of Law: What's the Relationship' UCLA School of Law, UCLA Public Law Series, 2005, Paper 5–21. One good example is Art 6 of the European Convention on Human Rights. This provides a right of defence in judicial procedures. The Strasburg Court is widening this provision, also submitting some national administrative procedures to the participation requirement. See N Mole and C Harby, *The right to a fair trial. A guide to the implementation of Article 6 of the European Convention on Human Rights* (Strasbourg, Council of Europe, 2001) p 10; P Craig, 'The Human Rights Act, Article 6 and Procedural Rights' (2003) 4 *Public law* 753; C Ovey and R White, *Jacobs and White: The European Convention on Human Rights* (Oxford, Oxford University Press, 2002) 139 ff.

[70] G Silverstein, 'Globalization and the rule of law: "A machine that runs of itself?"' (2003) 1 *International Journal of Constitutional Law* 428.

Global institutions, whether established by national governments or by other global organisations, need to link themselves to civil society, in order to get the information, the support, the consensus and the cooperation required to govern.[71]

National governments themselves must be afforded greater levels of participation. On one hand, when they delegate powers to global institutions, they cannot control these institutions through mechanisms of vertical accountability (for example, budgetary controls) alone, but also need to be able to influence individual decision-making processes. On the other hand, national government controls 'need to be supplemented by an increase in horizontal accountability, that is, by an increase in the influence of the addressees of global regulation. This can be carried out by making regulators more transparent and by forcing them to publicly justify rules'.[72]

This legitimising function makes participation desirable for proponents of cosmopolitan democracy: 'we will need to develop a concept of transnational democracy better equipped to take the legacy of traditional rule of law-virtues seriously'.[73]

Participation in the global law has a second function: ensuring State involvement in global governance, furthering compliance with global decisions and fostering a horizontal dialogue between States. Participation integrates domestic authorities into global decision-making processes and provides a forum for national and sub-national interests in order to guarantee them a degree of protection. It has, in this sense, a corporatist function, because it is a means for exchanging information and establishing networks, as in the 'interest representation model'.[74]

The third prevailing function of participation in the global legal order is one that is well known in the domestic legal orders—that of defence: the right to a hearing provides national governments or private actors with an opportunity to present their views and to protect their interests, prior to a decision being taken.

Finally, participation as organised discussion and negotiation (a hallmark of the international legal order) is expanding in a piecemeal fashion. Global law is

[71] See L Boisson de Chazournes, 'Concluding Remarks—Changing Roles of International Organizations: Global Administrative Law and the Interplay of Legitimacies' in Symposium on 'Global Administrative Law in the Operations of International Organizations', n 1 above, at 655 ff.

[72] D Kerwer, 'Rules that Many Use: Standards and Global Regulation' (2005) 18 *Governance* 621–22.

[73] WE Scheuerman, 'Cosmopolitan Democracy and the Rule of Law' (2002) 15 *Ratio Juris* 454. See also D Archibugi, 'Democrazia cosmopolitica: una prospettiva partecipante' in *Rivista italiana di scienza politica*, A. XXXV, n 2, August 2005, 261–88, esp at 279. On the relations between democracy and rule of law, in general, see J Habermas, 'Il nesso interno tra Stato di diritto e democrazia' in J Habermas, *L'inclusione dell'altro. Studi di teoria politica* (Milano, Feltrinelli, 1988) at 249–59 and JM Maravall and A Przeworski (eds), *Democracy and the Rule of Law* (Cambridge, Cambridge University Press, 2003).

[74] RB Stewart, 'The Reformation of American Administrative Law' (1975) 88 *Harvard Law Review* 1667, and 'US Administrative Law: A Model for Global Administrative Law?' (2005) 68 *Law and Contemporary Problems* 55 ff.

based on reciprocity. Therefore, no State can avoid affording due process to foreign States and nationals, if it wants to benefit from the same principle.

There is a link between function and structure. If the purpose of participation is to provide legitimacy or interest representation, the parties included in the procedure will be 'all interested parties' (as in the case of environmental protection). If the purpose is to provide a defence, the parties will be the affected persons alone (as in the case of anti-doping procedures).

Participation at the global and domestic levels

What if more participation is provided at the national level than at the global level? 'Allocation of regulatory power to the global level withholds participation rights from domestic stakeholders and poses therefore potential legitimacy problems'.[75] The growth of global regulation can 'marginalize opportunities for public participation'.[76]

To solve this problem, different strategies can be employed. The first is to develop participation rights at the global level. The second is to enable interested parties to participate in the national government decision-making processes necessary for participating in global organisations. The third is the participation of public interest organisations in the official delegations to the meetings of global bodies.[77] In the first case, umbrella organisations can be established in order to bring the concerns of their constituencies to the attention of global regulators.[78] An example of the second case is the US law that requires public participation in the formulation of US negotiating priorities in multilateral negotiations. Costs are the main limitations upon the third strategy.

In conclusion, legal globalisation cannot be reduced to a process of Americanisation.[79] Global legalism—or at least global participation—accomplishes many functions: requiring reluctant national governments to respect the right to be heard; giving national governments a voice in global

[75] D Livshiz, 'Updating American Administrative Law: WTO, International Standards, Domestic Implementation, and Public Participation', (2007) 24 *Wisconsin International Law Journal* 961 ff, argues that participation ought to be available both domestically and internationally. See also SS Shapiro, 'International Trade Agreements, Regulatory Protection, and Public Accountability' (2002) 54 *Administrative Law Review* 435, esp at 449, on the preclusion of effective citizen participation because of globalisation.

[76] D Livshiz, n 75 above, at 30.

[77] ibid, at 33.

[78] eg, the Trans Atlantic Consumer Dialogue (TACD) and the Trans Atlantic Business Dialogue (TABD): see D Livshiz, n 70 above, at 43 ff.

[79] According to M Shapiro, n 7 above, at 48, 'Americanization and globalization partially overlap' because the American constitutional experience serves as a world model. According to D Keleman and EC Sibbitt, 'The Globalization of American Law' (2004) 58 *International Organization* 103, the factors of the spreading of American law are economic liberalisation, political fragmentation, judicialisation and the influx of American law firms. See also M-C Ponthoreau, 'Trois interprétations de la globalisation juridique' in *Actualite Juridique: Droit Administratif*, 2006, no 1, 9 January 2006, at 20–25.

organisations; opening up communication between States and between global institutions, compelling them to listen, if not to cooperate; and, ultimately, giving civil society a voice vis-à-vis international organisations. The participation of civil society or interest groups in the executive decision-making process is the dominant but not exclusive feature of the American experience.[80]

THE VALUE OF PARTICIPATION IN THE GLOBAL LEGAL ORDER

The most important participatory rights imposed by global rules are those addressed to national governments and international institutions for the benefit of private parties. The conclusion shall therefore focus on the first and the last of the five categories outlined above.

Both of these categories of participatory rights present peculiarities. With regard to the first, State relationships with private parties are traditionally reserved to regulation by the State. With regard to the second, the establishment of direct links between the global-level and civil societies entails the consequence that global rules bypass those set by national governments. Both types of participatory rights challenge the State.

'As the locus of regulatory activity has increasingly shifted "upwards", the actors and procedural rules that facilitate effective and fair regulation domestically have followed'.[81] Globalisation has produced two peculiar results. First, it has established an additional level of government, which makes normative claims upon national governments. This gave rise to a strong need for the development of mechanisms aimed at making national governments accountable at the global level.

This new level of government, however, lacks the features commonly presented by popular democracy. It is therefore in need of a means of legitimation.

These two peculiar features of the global legal order help to illustrate why its incorporation of liberal democratic principles would be crucial.[82] The global legal order redefines the relationships between governments and citizens at both national and global levels, both to ensure compliance with global rules at the national level and to legitimise global decision-making processes.

Consider the duty to hear private parties. This duty is established by global rules and directed at national governments. Does the global legal order seek to enhance the efficiency or the accountability of national governments by subjecting them to such an obligation? Or does this duty promote national governments' compliance with global rules?

Global actors need not worry about the efficiency or the legitimacy of national institutions. These institutions do not generally need to prove their legitimacy, as

[80] According to Stewart, n 69 above. See the symposium on Stewart's article in *Issues in Legal Scholarship* (San Francisco, Berkeley Electronic Press, 2005).

[81] K Raustiala, 'The "Participatory Revolution"' n 14, at 585.

[82] JH Knox, 'Separated at Birth' n 57, at 361.

popular elections accord them a certain degree of support. And it would be paradoxical if global institutions, which rely on States for their own legitimacy, were to concern themselves with the degree of legitimacy of States by imposing a duty upon national governments to consult their citizens before, for example, taking environmental decisions.

The participation rights created by global rules, by contrast, benefit global actors, as private actors are 'possessors of significant compliance-relevant information'.[83] Empowering private actors vis-à-vis national governments makes them actors in a 'fire alarm' process.[84] Their participation triggers investigations performed by national authorities, which must review their own actions in the light of global standards.[85]

Private parties are instrumental in the implementation of global rules. These rules are addressed to national governments, which must implement them. However, it would be much too complicated for global institutions to create a compliance control mechanism from above for the purpose of checking compliance with global standards at a national level. It is significantly easier to resort to the cooperation of private parties.

Establishing such a duty, incumbent upon national governments, to consult as a means of keeping States' actions under control is a crafty device, as the global legal order takes advantage of private parties, 'using' them as if these were its own agents. But how effective can this device be? More than a control mechanism, private participation may signal the need for a check. Private parties themselves are not necessarily instrumental to the purposes of global rules. National agencies may disregard private submissions. Compliance in this framework is, therefore, incidental.

This control function is strengthened by requiring national governments to hear private parties that are not nationals of the forum State, and by establishing international organs to monitor participation at the national level (as operated by the WTO Agreement on Safeguards, Article 3).

The duty imposed, by global rules, upon national governments to hear private parties aims less at making domestic institutions more efficient or accountable to their population, than at compelling them to comply with global rules.

While participation at the national level serves mainly to induce national compliance with global rules, participation at the global level is more effective as a legitimation mechanism.[86]

[83] K Raustiala, 'Police patrols' n 57, at 405.

[84] MD McCubbins and T Schwartz, *Congressional Oversight Overlooked: Police Patrols versus Fire Alarm*, 28 *American Journal of Political Science* (1984) 165 ff.

[85] There are more effective procedures for reaching the same result. An example is the right to make submissions to a supranational body to have a domestic decision reviewed.

[86] In general on interest representation as a way of promoting legitimacy of administrative governance, please see E Magill, *Images of Representation*, Be Press Issues in Legal Scholarship, The Reformation of American Administrative Law, Article 5 (2005) 1ff.

At the global level, there is less need to control compliance. Those who create the rules and those who implement them do not belong to different legal orders. On the contrary, there is a strong need for legitimation.

An analysis of accountability in the global legal order must be premised upon an important consideration: the members of global bodies are not directly elected. Abandonment of the domestic analogy may, therefore, be necessary. The global legal order has created unique mechanisms for ensuring accountability, based mainly on the diffusion of information. This has been called 'a pluralistic accountability system for world politics'.[87]

In confronting the problem of legitimating global decision-making processes, it is crucial to establish the conditions under which a given procedure can be considered legitimate.

Drawing upon studies on procedural justice, it is possible to affirm that a parallel can be drawn between legislative legitimacy and procedural legitimacy. 'For the exercise of legislative power to be legitimate, the legislation must be the outcome of a process that satisfies norms of democratic participation'. Similarly, for proceedings to be legitimate, the affected parties must become the 'authors' (even if not the only authors) of the proceedings. Participation has an independent value that 'cannot be reduced to a function of the effect of participation on outcomes'.[88]

Four crucial questions arise here. Should decision-making processes – and thus participation – be located at the local, national or global level? To whom should participation extend, if legitimacy is to be conferred upon the proceedings? How wide should the scope of participation be, in order to legitimise the proceedings? Do legitimate global decision-making processes suffice to render global bodies legitimate?

An answer to these questions has yet to be found, but a few sub-questions can be suggested, which may serve to facilitate the work of those willing to venture into this minefield.

First, if the decision is shifted from the local and national levels to the global one, local and national participation becomes more difficult. However, local interest groups can take advantage of participative opportunities offered at the global level as means of decision-making and participation that remain beyond the reach of national authorities.[89] This has the effect of crowding out national agencies, which are no longer the final arbitrating authority over national interests.

[87] RO Keohane, *Accountability in World Politics* (2006) 29 *Scandinavian Political Studies*, 82.

[88] LB Solum, *Procedural Justice* (2005) University of San Diego School of Law, Law and Economics Research Paper Series, 12, in The Berkeley Electronic Press (bepress), at 276, 280 and 321.

[89] As occurred in the case of land protection, giving rise to national reactions, such as the proposal of the 'American Land Sovereignty Protection Act' (May 13, 1999). See J Rabkin, *The Yellowstone Affair: Environmental Protection, International Treaties and National Sovereignty*, Competitive Enterprise Institute, Environmental Studies Program, May 1997 (www.heartland.org/Article.cfm?artId=3966).

As for the second question, it is clear that if the affected parties are to be the co-authors of the decision, all such parties must be entitled to participate (or at least to waive their right to participation). But who can classify as an affected party? Those whom are bound by the final decision? Or those with a substantial interest in the final decision? And what is to be made of the situation in which such parties are simply an indeterminate entity or mass of entities?

Thirdly, it is clear that participation should occur on a timely basis and include, at least, notice of the proceedings and provision of the opportunity to be heard. However, there can be no discussion between competing interests unless the possibility for cross-examination is provided. The final decision remains inscrutable unless the proceeding authority is under a duty to provide reasons. There is no appeal unless some kind of judicial review is available.

As for the fourth and most difficult question, participation does not necessarily imply actual decision-making. Participants only enjoy the generic right to be heard: therefore, 'participation is a weak substitute for self-government'.[90] But consider the fact that what we call democracy at the national level is, in fact, an oligarchy: officials, that are elected periodically by the people, take decisions in their name; the People itself does not take decisions (except in the case of referenda), but only choose their representatives. This is the reason why national legal orders supplement simple electoral democracy with interest representation in domestic decision-making processes (deliberative democracy).

CONCLUSION

While national administrative laws date back two centuries, a general obligation incumbent upon administrative agencies to consult affected parties has developed at the domestic level only recently, and not without several difficulties. Such a general duty was established by legislators only in 1925 in Austria, in 1946 in the United States, in 1978 in Germany, and in 1990 in Italy; in France and in the United Kingdom, it has not yet been recognised by statute.

Why, at the global level, has an obligation to consult developed so rapidly and spread so widely? Is there an explanation for such a maze of participatory rights (vertical and horizontal on one hand; local, national and global on the other), that does not constrain data within received conceptual categories and distinctions?[91]

First, context is relevant. The global legal order consists of a mosaic of legal systems, presenting several different layers (local, national, regional, global) and a

[90] C Möllers, *Patterns of Legitimacy in Global Administrative Law: Trade-offs between due process and democratic accountability*, presented at the Second Global Administrative Law Seminar, Viterbo, 9–10 June 2006, p 3.

[91] L Nader, *Le forze vive del diritto. Un'introduzione all'antropologia giuridica* (Napoli, Edizioni Scientifiche Italiane, 2003) 62–63, 68.

plurality of sectorial regulatory regimes. Competition and overlapping do arise, but so do lack of communication and coordination. It is far from being an harmonious system of law.[92]

Secondly, the institutional setting is also significant. Such a setting is characterised by an atrophy of the legislative and judicial branches. At the global level, there is no participation through elections. The availability of a means of recourse to courts is limited. Instead, negotiation plays a dominant role.[93]

Thirdly, of relevance is the nature of institutional relations. These are not international relations, in which national governments – the States – play the part of the main actors. They are, instead, inter-administrative relations, in which national bureaucracies have a dominant role.

The context, the institutional setting and the nature of institutional relations are all wholly new and unknown to lawyers and political scientists alike. These figures are accustomed to dealing with unitary legal orders (or with a plurality of legal orders organised in some form of hierarchical structure), with institutional settings in which there are three equally developed branches (legislative, judicial and executive), which interact through relationships that are clearly defined by rules.

The nature of these three elements determines the modes of decision and solution of conflicts.[94] Consultation and participation are instrumental to establishing links between national legal orders, to enabling a dialogue among the local, national, regional and global levels of management, to giving rise to a surrogate of parliamentary and judicial procedures, and to preventing conflicts. Consultation and participation mimic – albeit in a very inefficient way – parliaments and courts.

[92] Again, compare with the legal systems studied by the anthropologists: ibid, 68, 85, 97.
[93] L Nader, ibid, at 21.
[94] L Nader, ibid, at 66.

3

Globalisation and Extraterritorial Regulation: An Unexceptional Exception

STEFANO BATTINI

INTRODUCTION

IN HIS FAMOUS dissenting opinion in the *Lotus* case,[1] Justice Loder linked the strictly territorial effect of national regulation to the principle of sovereignty and thus the mutual independence of States, which is a 'postulate' of international law. The 'fundamental consequence' of that postulate, according to Loder, 'is that no municipal law ... can apply or have binding effects outside the national territory'.

This cornerstone of classical international law[2] is mirrored in national public law principles, which traditionally regard the extraterritoriality of domestic regulation as an exception to the opposite rule.

In an influential 1895 work, the German scholar Otto Mayer wrote that 'notre Etat ne prétend que par exception à exercer son autorité dans la sphère du territoire étranger'.[3]

About 15 years later, in the United States (US), Justice Holmes was equally clear in expressing the same concept: 'the general and almost universal rule is that the character of an act as lawful or unlawful must be determined wholly by the law of the country where the act is done'.[4] This sentence is probably the most frequently quoted statement of the 'presumption against extraterritoriality', a

[1] Case of *SS Lotus (France v Turkey)*, Judgment No 9, 7 September 1927, PCIJ Reports 1928, Series A, No 10.

[2] See AL Parrish, *Reclaiming International Law from Extraterritoriality*—electronic copy available at: www.ssrn.com/abstract=1013740, at 26.

[3] O Mayer, *Deutsches Verwaltungsrecht* (Leipzig, 1895–96). The quotation given is from the French edition: O Mayer, *Le droit administratif allemand* (Paris, Giard-Briére Editeurs, 1906), § 62, (*Le droit administratif international*) at 354.

[4] *American Banana Co v United Fruit Co*, 213 US 347, 357 (1909).

long-standing canon of statutory interpretation according to which the 'legislation of Congress, *unless a contrary intent appears*, is meant to apply only within the territorial jurisdiction of the United States'.[5]

Thus, the principle of the mutual independence of States has traditionally permitted extraterritoriality only as an exception to the rule.

Today, however, the interdependence between States is making extraterritoriality increasingly unexceptional.

This chapter addresses the change. It argues, on the basis of an analysis of recent case law, that the increasing extraterritoriality of domestic regulation, either de jure or de facto, is an unavoidable effect of globalisation.

Globalisation is of course a multifaceted phenomenon, and a careful description of it must consider at least three dimensions. First of all, the economic dimension: a global market, in which most, if not all, countries participate, has been realised. Second, the information technology (IT) dimension: people can share and communicate a mass of data and information every day and in real time, irrespective of their geographical location, provided they have access to the Internet. Finally, the environmental dimension: sustainable development is a truly global common good, which can only be achieved by people from every country, and is likewise jeopardised by them.

The impact of each of these dimensions upon the territorial reach of domestic regulation is examined in the following sections. Section 2 addresses the relationship between market integration and extraterritorial antitrust regulation. Section 3 illustrates how the IT dimension of globalisation leads domestic authorities to regulate foreign Internet content. Section 4 examines transboundary pollution and the extraterritorial application of environmental regulation. Section 5 concludes by briefly highlighting the fundamental public law problem raised by extraterritoriality, which is democratic legitimacy: the national extraterritorial regulator is not accountable to foreign regulated subjects.

THE ECONOMIC DIMENSION: GLOBAL MARKETS AND EXTRATERRITORIAL ANTITRUST REGULATION

Hartford Fire is the leading US case on extraterritorial antitrust regulation.[6] The facts in *Hartford Fire* are also a perfect demonstration of the relationship between economic integration and the extraterritoriality of economic regulation.

Four major US primary insurers decided to promote an industry-wide change from 'occurrence-based' to 'claims-made' insurance policies.[7] Their efforts were

[5] *EEOC v Arabian American Oil Co* ('*Aramco*'), 499 US 244, 248 (1991).

[6] *Hartford Fire Insurance Co v California*, 509 US 764 (1993).

[7] The reasons for this are well-explained by KW Dam, *Extraterritoriality in an Age of Globalization: The Hartford Fire Case* (1993) *Supreme Court Review* 289, 297: 'the core of their concern was their liability to insureds under "occurrence-based" policies, which cover claims with regard to any occurrences during the period in which the policy was in force whenever the claim might later arise.

successful thanks to the assistance of British reinsurers, who agreed to reinsure American primary insurers only for claims-made policy forms. The Attorneys General for several states and many private plaintiffs brought antitrust suits against American and British insurance companies, including the British reinsurers, maintaining that their conduct amounted to an illegal conspiracy under the Sherman Antitrust Act.

National antitrust legislation normally aims at protecting domestic consumers from anti-competitive activities carried out on the national territory by producers or service providers. However, economic integration breaks down this spatial congruence between regulations and the regulated activities. In a global market, the anti-competitive activities of producers or service providers can affect consumers in every country in which their goods are sold or their services are provided. In the *Hartford Fire* case, the conduct of the British reinsurers had a direct, negative impact on US policy holders. In order to adequately protect them, US antitrust rules would have had to reach the British reinsurers as well. But how can US antitrust rules apply to British reinsurers doing business in London? Can national antitrust regulations apply *extraterritorially* to activities taking place entirely beyond national borders?

US courts have given different answers to this question over time. The general trend, however, has been away from strict territoriality and towards a broad extraterritoriality. A strict territoriality approach was first adopted by the Supreme Court in 1909. In *American Banana Co v United Fruit Co*, Justice Holmes firmly rejected the extraterritorial application of the Sherman Act, using the words quoted above. In 1945, however, Holmes' strict territorial approach was abandoned. In the *Alcoa* case,[8] the Court of Appeals for the Second Circuit, acting for the Supreme Court, announced the new 'effects test' approach. Under this rule, the Sherman Act would be deemed to apply to wholly foreign conduct if it was intended to, and did, have some *effects* within the US market. As Judge Learned Hand stated: 'any state may impose liabilities … for conduct outside its borders that has consequences within its borders which the state reprehends'. The effects test was modified about 30 years later by the consideration of 'international comity'. In the 1976 *Timberlane* decision, the Court of Appeals for the Ninth Circuit held that the effects test is 'by itself … incomplete, because it fails to consider other nations' interests'.[9] Consequently, the Court set forth a new

Policies written on occurrence forms therefore subjected the insurers to liability that could not be quantified or even known until years or even decades after the policy had expired. To deal with this problem, the insurers sought to eliminate the occurrence form not just from their own set of forms but for the industry as a whole. They sought to substitute an industry-wide "claims-made" form. Under the latter form the policy covered only claims made during the policy period. Since such a form for newly written policies would otherwise expose them to retroactive and unforeseeable liability with regard to prior occurrences, they included in the claims-made industry form a cut-off date before which no claims would be recognized'.

[8] *United States v Aluminium Co Of Am* ('*Alcoa*'), 148 R 2d 416, 444 (2d Cir 1945).

[9] *Timberlane Lumber Co v Bank of Am*, 549 F.2d 597, 611–12 (9th Cir 1976) (*Timberlane I*).

balancing test that involved taking a number of factors into account. This enabled US courts to limit their jurisdiction over foreign anti-competitive conduct having effects within the US when considerations of international comity suggested deferring to the foreign State, whose interests were stronger.[10] Finally, however, in the 1993 *Hartford Fire* decision, the Supreme Court refused the *Timberlane* balancing test. The Supreme Court held that US antitrust rules are applicable to the conduct of British reinsurers, because it is 'well established by now that the Sherman Act applies to foreign conduct that was meant to produce and did in fact produce some substantial effect in the United States'.[11] In such a case, according to Justice Souter, international comity considerations could prevent the exercise of US jurisdiction only when there was a 'true conflict' between US and foreign law. But a true conflict does not exist 'where a person subject to regulations by two states can comply with the laws of both'.[12] Therefore, since the British reinsurers did not argue that British law required them to act in violation of US law, there was no reason to decline jurisdiction. Ultimately, in *Hartford Fire* the US Supreme Court embraced a pure 'effects test', without any international comity limitation: that is, a broad extraterritorial approach.

A similar approach has come to prevail in Europe. The European Commission first affirmed the extraterritoriality principle in 1977, stating that the Commission 'can act against restrictions of competition whose effects are felt within the territory under its jurisdiction, even if the companies involved are locating and doing business outside the territory, and of foreign nationality, have no link with that territory, and are acting under an agreement governed by foreign law'.[13] This approach was later embraced in 1988 by the European Court of Justice in the

[10] The factors to be balanced are the following: 'the degree of conflict with foreign law or policy, the nationality or allegiance of the parties and the locations or principal places of business of corporations, the extent to which enforcement by either state can be expected to achieve compliance, the relative significance of effects on the United States as compared with those elsewhere, the extent to which there is explicit purpose to harm or affect American commerce, the foreseeability of such effect, and the relative importance to the violations charged of conduct within the United States as compared with conduct abroad' (*Timberlane I* 549 F2d 597, at 614). In 1987, the *Restatement (third) of the Foreign Relations Law of the United States* adopted a similar balancing test The factors to consider include: '(a) the link of the activity to the territory of the regulating state, i.e. the extent to which the activity takes place within the territory, or has a substantial, direct and foreseeable effect upon or in the territory; (b) the connections, such as nationality, residence, or economic activity, between the regulating state and the person principally responsible for the activity to be regulated, or between that state and those whom the regulation is designed to protect; (c) the character of the activity to be regulated, the importance of regulation to the regulating state, the extent to which other states regulate such activities, and the degree to which the desirability of such regulation is generally accepted; (d) the existence of justified expectations that might be protected or hurt by the regulation; (e) the importance of the regulation to the international political, legal or economic system; (f) the extent to which the regulation is consistent with the traditions of the international system; (g) the extent to which another state might have an interest in regulating the activity; and (h) the likelihood of conflict with regulation by another state' (§ 403).

[11] *Hartford Fire Insurance Co v California*, at 796.

[12] ibid, at 799.

[13] M Ivaldi and O Bertrand, *European Competition Policy in International Markets* (October 2006). Available at www.ssrn.com/abstract=951594, at 8–9.

Wood Pulp case.[14] The ECJ was asked to determine whether Article 81 of the EC Treaty should apply to US, Canadian, Swedish and Finnish producers conspiring to fix wood pulp prices in the EU. Defendants claimed that the EU lacked jurisdiction over them, since they were not incorporated in the EU. Furthermore, as one of the US defendants was involved in an export cartel legally authorised in the United States, they also claimed that application of the EU law would actually violate the international public law duty of non-interference. The ECJ rejected both claims, using arguments very similar to those used by the US Supreme Court in *Hartford Fire*. As to the defendants' first claim, the ECJ reasoned that EU laws were applicable because 'the producers *implemented* their pricing agreements within the common market': therefore, 'what matters is not the place where the agreement or the decision is taken but where it is implemented, i.e., where products are sold'.[15] The European 'implementation doctrine'—as observed by an official from the Antitrust Division of the US Department of Justice—'is very close to, if not indistinguishable from the American effects test'.[16] As for the defendants' second claim, the ECJ stated that the international duty of non-interference could be violated where the duties in one country are prohibited by the laws of another country. Such a 'true conflict'—as the US Supreme Court would have probably characterised it—did not arise in *Wood Pulp*, where the agreements prohibited by EU laws were not also a duty under the US laws regulating export cartels.

To sum up, both the United States and the EU do apply their respective antitrust laws extraterritorially to anti-competitive conduct taking place outside their borders, but producing effects, or being implemented, within them. This is a form of de jure extraterritoriality, in which foreign producers or service suppliers, in acting overseas, are the formal addressees of decisions adopted by national judicial or administrative authorities enforcing domestic rules.

The de jure extraterritorial application of antitrust rules has many drawbacks.

First of all, it produces international conflicts, as Justice Scalia observed in his dissenting opinion in *Hartford Fire*, predicting that the majority's broad extraterritorial approach 'will bring the Sherman Act and other laws into sharp and unnecessary conflict with the legitimate interests of other countries—particularly our closest trading partners'.[17] The extraterritorial reach of US antitrust laws has

[14] ECJ, Joined Cases 89,104, 114, 116, 117 and 125 to 129/85, *A Ahlström Osakeytiö and others v Commission*, ECR 1988, at 5193.

[15] Ivaldi and Bertrand, n 13 above, at 9.

[16] MT Batz, 'A Comparative Analysis of United States and European Union Jurisdiction in Extraterritorial Antitrust Law and The Need for International Standards' (2007) *Duquesne Buinesss Law Journal* 65, 82; D Geradin, M Reysen, and H David, *Extraterritoriality, Comity and Cooperation in EC Competition Law* (July 2008). Available at www.ssrn.com/abstract=1175003 (stating that 'whether one applies the implementation doctrine or the effects doctrine similar outcomes should normally be reached, although it is arguable that the latter doctrine is wider in scope').

[17] See *Hartford Fire Insurance Co v California* at 820.

in fact created international tensions, leading several foreign countries to introduce blocking statutes, aimed at 'shortening the long arm of American antitrust jurisdiction'.[18]

Secondly, extraterritoriality produces *over-regulation*. Producers and service providers doing business in global markets, and thus operating in many different countries, also have to comply with many different antitrust laws. That means, at a minimum, the multiplication of the costs of doing business, as firms must satisfy the regulatory agencies in each country. Moreover, given the differences between various national regulations, all of which must be respected, firms are subject to a complex legal regime consisting 'of a medley of the strictest elements of each national regime'.[19] For example, a proposed merger between two large firms doing business in both the United States and Europe (such as Boeing and McDonnell Douglas, or General Electric and Honeywell) could go forward only if both US and EU authorities permitted it. Consequently, the merger must satisfy the strictest regulator: as it has been observed, 'in matters of antitrust, the most prohibitory nation wins'.[20]

Thirdly, both international conflicts and over-regulation may be exacerbated by the risk of bias. National regulators could be tempted to apply stricter standards to foreign anti-competitive conduct than to the same conduct by domestic producers and service providers. They could be tempted to externalise the costs of a restrictive policy (which are borne by producers abroad), while internalising its benefits (which are enjoyed by consumers and competitors locally). For example, in both the *McDonnell Douglas/Boeing* and *GE/Honeywell* cases, European antitrust authorities were accused of prohibiting a merger,

[18] DA Sabalot, 'Shortening the Long Arm of American Antitrust Jurisdiction: Extraterritoriality and the Foreign Blocking Statutes' (1982) 28 *Loyola Law Review* 213. See also 'Reassessment of International Application of Antitrust Laws: Blocking Statutes, Balancing Tests, and Treble Damages' (1987) 50 *Law and Contemporary Problems* 197 (stating that 'these blocking statutes evidence foreign disdain for American antitrust laws, and are designed to create a disincentive for the extraterritorial reach of U.S. antitrust laws. There are two kinds of blocking statutes: First, there are discovery blocking statutes aimed at preventing compliance with foreign state requests or orders for documents or information. Second, there are judgment blocking provisions that declare unenforceable in whole or in part the decisions or orders of a foreign court purporting to affect foreign nationals').

[19] A Guzman, 'The Case for International Antitrust' (2004) 22 *Berkeley Journal of International Law* 355, 360 (giving an example of the phenomenon: 'Suppose … the activities of a firm are subject to the competition laws of country A and country B. Assume that country A has, relative to country B, a restrictive policy with respect to horizontal restraints of trade and a permissive policy with respect to vertical restraints. … Country B, however, believes that its regime, which is relatively permissive with respect to horizontal restraints but restrictive with respect to vertical restraints, is optimal. Firms subject to the jurisdiction of both states face a de facto regime that includes the strict horizontal restraint regulations of country A and the strict vertical restraint regulations of country B. This is a stricter policy than either country A or country B believes should exist. In short, firms doing business in both the United States and the EU face an international competition policy regime that is more burdensome than the regime of either the EU or United States and very likely more restrictive than what either jurisdiction would choose if it were a closed economy').

[20] E Fox, 'National Law, Global Markets and *Hartford:* Eyes Wide Shut' (2000–01) 68 *Antitrust Law Journal* 73, 80.

approved by US antitrust authorities, in order to protect European producers from American competition, even to the detriment of European consumers.

Given the drawbacks of extraterritoriality, we must nevertheless reflect upon the consequences of the opposite approach. In a globalised economy, the alternative to de jure extraterritoriality is not actually strict territoriality, but rather de facto extraterritoriality.

As Law and Economics scholars have explained, antitrust authorities in countries that do not apply their antitrust law extraterritorially tend to be more relaxed in their enforcement. As they are not able to regulate foreign firms importing goods into their country, they tend to adopt a policy which is optimal for a net exporting country. This policy, while taking into account all the costs borne by (domestic) producers affected by potentially strict antitrust regulation, does not fully consider all of the potential benefits to consumers, specifically ignoring the benefits to foreign consumers. The result is a less restrictive policy, thus a form of *under-regulation*, which could also be exacerbated by the risk of bias. National regulators could be tempted to apply a preferential treatment to domestic anti-competitive conduct which only (or mainly) produces negative effects abroad. Export cartels' explicit or implicit exemptions are the clearest example: antitrust authorities internalise the benefits of exemptions (which are enjoyed locally by domestic firms), while externalising the costs (which are borne abroad by foreign consumers and competitors).

Although this *under-regulation* is not formally extraterritorial, it can nevertheless have a broad de facto extraterritorial impact. The same effects test which is applied to foreign anti-competitive conduct could be extended to the foreign antitrust regulations allowing this conduct. If American policy holders have been affected by the British reinsurers' behavior, they have been also affected by the British regulatory regime for the reinsurance market, in which that behavior is perfectly legitimate. Either the stricter American antitrust rules apply extraterritorially to the conduct of British reinsurers de jure, or the more relaxed British rules extraterritorially impact American policy holders de facto.

To sum up, the interaction between global markets and national antitrust laws necessarily implies extraterritoriality in one form or another, as well as its respective drawbacks. Either firms face the burden of over-regulation due to the de jure extraterritorial application of foreign antitrust rules, or consumers are harmed by the de facto extraterritorial impact of foreign under-regulation. Both firms and consumers are thus increasingly exposed to foreign administrative regulation.

THE IT DIMENSION: REGULATING FOREIGN INTERNET CONTENT

Two recent cases clearly illustrate the relationship between the IT dimension of globalisation and the increasing extraterritoriality of national regulation. The *Yahoo* case is probably the most familiar one, and thus worth discussing from the outset.

In 2000, two human rights organisations (Ligue Internationale Contre le Racisme et l'Antisémitisme (LICRA), and Union des étudiantes juifs de France (UEJF) filed a lawsuit against Yahoo in the Tribunal de Grande Instance de Paris. Yahoo was accused of permitting French Internet users to access its United States-based auction site, in which Nazi artifacts were offered for sale by other users, in conflict with Article R-645–1 of the French Penal Code.

The French Court ruled that Yahoo, by failing to implement a filtering system to identify French users and prevent them from accessing the prohibited content, was violating French law. The Court then ordered Yahoo 'to take all necessary measures to dissuade and render impossible any access via Yahoo.com to the Nazi artifact auction site and to any other site or service that may be construed as constituting an apology for Nazism or a contesting of Nazi crimes'. Yahoo was ordered to comply within three months or face a penalty for each day of non-compliance.[21]

Although Yahoo partially complied with the order,[22] it claimed that it could not fully comply without banning all Nazi-related material from Yahoo.com, which would infringe upon its rights under the First Amendment of the US Constitution. Yahoo then filed a lawsuit in California, seeking a declaration that the French Court's order was unenforceable in the US. The US District Court ruled that the First Amendment precludes the enforcement within the US of a French order intended to regulate the content of speech over the Internet: 'although France has the sovereign right to regulate what speech is permissible in France, this Court may not enforce a foreign order that violates the protections of the U.S. Constitution by chilling protected speech that occurs simultaneously within our borders'.[23]

The Supreme Court of Canada recently faced similar issues, though in the different field of copyright regulation.

[21] Tribunal de Grande Instance de Paris, Ordonnance de référé, 22 May 2000, *UEJF et Licra c/ Yahoo! Inc. et Yahoo France*; Tribunal de Grande Instance de Paris, Ordonnance de référé, 11 August 2000, *Association 'Union des Etudiants Juifs de France', la 'Ligue contre le Racisme et l'Antisémitisme' / Yahoo ! Inc. et Yahoo France*; Tribunal de Grande Instance de Paris, Ordonnance de référé, 20 November 2000, *UEJF et Licra c/ Yahoo! Inc.* Available at www.juriscom.net/txt/jurisfr/cti/tgiparis20000522.htm#texte.

[22] Specifically changing its auction policy to prohibit individuals from auctioning 'any item that promotes, glorifies or is directly associated with groups or individuals known principally for hateful or violent positions or acts, such as Nazi or the Ku Klux Klan'.

[23] *Yahoo! Inc v La Ligue Contre Le Racisme et l'Antisémitisme*, 145 F Supp 2d 1168, 1179 (ND Cal 2001), at 19, available at www.juriscom.net/en/txt/jurisus/ic/dccalifornia20011107.htm.

In 1995, the Society of Authors, Composers and Music Publishers of Canada (SOCAN), a collective society which administers the music copyrights of Canadians and foreigners in Canada, applied to the Canadian Copyright Board for approval of a tariff for the communication of musical work over the Internet (called Tariff 22). SOCAN wanted to collect royalties from Internet service providers located in Canada because, by allowing Canadian Internet users to download music from foreign websites, they were infringing the copyright owner's exclusive right to communicate the work to the public. The Board decided to deal with legal and jurisdictional issues separately from the determination of the tariff. After a hearing in 1999, the Board held that: a) copyright liability does not attach to Internet service providers, as they only provide the means of telecommunication necessary for the content provider to communicate a work; therefore, the Internet service provider is not liable unless it exerts a significant level of control over the activities of those who post content; b) even where the Internet service provider does more than act simply as a conduit, no copyright liability is incurred in Canada unless the communication originates from a server located in Canada.[24]

The Board's decision was reviewed by the Federal Court of Appeals[25] and subsequently appealed to the Supreme Court of Canada.[26] While upholding the first part of the decision, the Supreme Court disagreed with the Board on the issue of jurisdiction. The Board's view, according to which Canadian copyright laws only apply to Internet communication originating from a host server located in Canada, was shared by the dissenting Justice LeBel, who considered it the only approach fully consistent with the territoriality principle. However, the majority of the Court considered this approach to be 'unduly formalistic': 'a content provider is not immune from copyright liability by virtue only of the fact that it employs a host server outside the country'. Speaking for the majority, Justice Binnie stated that the existence of a 'real and substantial connection' to Canada is sufficient to support the application of Canadian copyright laws to a transnational Internet communication. The location of the point of origin of the communication, that is the *situs* of the content provider, is certainly an important 'connecting factor'. But it is not the only one. The location of the end user is also relevant. Therefore, the Court concluded that 'Canada could exercise copyright jurisdiction in respect both of transmissions *originating* here, and transmissions originating abroad but *received* here'.[27]

[24] Decision of the Board dated October 27, 1999, SOCAN – Tariff 22 (Transmission of Musical Works to Subscribers Via a Telecommunications Service Not Covered Under Tariff Nos. 16 or 17) [Phase I: Legal Issues] (SOCAN 22 (1999)).

[25] *Society of Composers, Authors and Music Publishers of Canada v Canadian Assn. of Internet Providers* (CA), 2002 FCA 166.

[26] *Society of Composers, Authors and Music Publishers of Canada v Canadian Assn. of Internet Providers*, 2004 SCC 45

[27] ibid.

Both the French and the Canadian courts affirmed a State's right to regulate foreign Internet content. Both courts affirmed the extraterritorial application of national laws limiting the free circulation of information to foreign websites in order to protect the public morality or intellectual property rights inside their borders.

The same rationale underlies extraterritoriality, both in these cases as well as in *Hartford Fire* or *Wood Pulp*: as an Internet communication takes place in both the originating and the receiving countries, courts can apply the receiving country's regulations to actions taken in the originating country, following an 'effects test' approach. What makes the *Yahoo* case 'uniquely challenging'—as observed by the US District Court in declaring the French order to be unenforceable—'is that the Internet allows one to speak in more than one place at the same time'. Because of that, the French High Court could have applied French criminal laws to limit 'a speech by a U.S. resident within the U.S., on the basis that such speech can be accessed by Internet users in France'. French jurisdiction was asserted because 'the damage is suffered in France'. In other words, the French court adopted an effects test approach: 'jurisdiction is asserted where the courts believe that the web-site has had an effect within the jurisdiction'.[28] Similarly, in the *SOCAN* case, Justice Binnie held that 'an Internet communication that crosses one or more national boundaries *occurs* in more than one country, at a minimum the country of transmission and the country of reception'. Because of that, the Supreme Court of Canada could have extended the reach of Canadian copyright laws to communications of musical works originating outside Canada, on the grounds that Canadian Internet users can receive those communications. The communication originating abroad produces an effect in Canada, where the 'harm is suffered' (ie, the infringement of the exclusive right of the Canadian copyright's owner to communicate the musical works to the Canadian public).

The IT dimension of globalisation leads to extraterritoriality for largely the same reasons, and with similar consequences, as the economic dimension.

The reasons for extraterritoriality are that both global markets and the Internet contribute enormously to the widening effects of human conduct. The effects of anti-competitive conduct occurring 'here' can be felt 'everywhere', that is wherever the relevant goods can be sold. Likewise, the effects of posting data on a website located 'here' can be felt 'everywhere', that is wherever people can access the Internet.

[28] See 'The legal implications of the Yahoo! Inc. Nazi memorabilia dispute: an interview with Professor Michael Geist' in 'An international discussion of the implications of the Yahoo! Inc. Nazi memorabilia dispute', interviews organised by Lionel Thoumyre, Juriscom.net, January/March 2001 at www.juriscom.net/en/uni/doc/yahoo/geist.htm: 'I would instead argue that … courts are moving toward an effects based analysis whereby jurisdiction will be asserted where the court believes that the Web site has had an effect within the jurisdiction. That … approach can be found in this case as the French judge reached a determination that the "Yahoo.com" site, despite being passive from a French perspective, still had an effect within France and was thus subject to French jurisdiction'.

The widening consequences of human activities inevitably drives the exterritorial regulation, de jure or de facto, of them.

On the one hand, regulatory agencies and courts increasingly take an 'effects approach', according to which something 'occurs' wherever its effects are felt. Therefore, they claim jurisdiction over conduct that physically takes place abroad, subjecting it to national regulation.

As we have seen, this de jure extraterritoriality has many drawbacks, particularly over-regulation. If a communication occurs both 'here' (ie, in the originating country) and 'there' (in the receiving country)—as the French and the Canadian courts have held—it can be regulated both from 'here' and 'there'. And as Internet communications can be received 'everywhere', Internet activities must then 'comply with all law'. An amici curiae brief submitted by various American non-governmental organisations (NGOs) in support of Yahoo clearly illustrates the risk of over-regulation: 'If French law can be enforced here, Yahoo! could likewise be required to block access to information that "sabotages national unity" in China, undermines "religious harmony and public morals" in Singapore, offends "the social, cultural, political, media, economic, and religious values" of Saudi Arabia, fosters "Pro-Israeli speech" in Syria ... just to name a few examples'. Similarly, in the *SOCAN* case, the dissenting Justice LeBel warned against the 'effects approach', stating that it 'could result in a layering of royalty obligations between States'[29] and even Justice Binnie had to admit that his conclusion 'raises the spectre of imposition of copyright duties on a single telecommunication in both the State of transmission and the State of reception'.[30]

On the other hand, the alternative to this de jure over-regulation of Internet content is the de facto extraterritorial impact of under-regulation of Internet content.

If the more restrictive French regulation of speech does not apply to US residents communicating over Internet, then the United States' heightened protection of freedom of speech impacts French users, by undermining the balance between freedom of speech and public morals that French citizens consider to be appropriate. Therefore, either the French Code Penal applies de

[29] *Society of Composers, Authors and Music Publishers of Canada v Canadian Assn. of Internet Providers*, 2004 SCC 45, para 152: 'The real and substantial connection test proposed by Binnie J is inconsistent with the territoriality principle in that it may reach out and grasp content providers located in Bangalore who post content on a server in Hong Kong based only on the fact that the copyrighted work is retrieved by end users in Canada. Unlike a broadcaster, a content provider does not know in advance which territories will receive its transmissions. ... A danger with Binnie J's approach is that it could result in a layering of royalty obligations between States. This danger is particularly acute with the Internet: content posted on a server is usually accessible from anywhere on the globe'.

[30] ibid, para 78: 'This conclusion also raises the spectre of imposition of copyright duties on a single telecommunication in both the State of transmission and the State of reception, but as with other fields of overlapping liability (taxation for example), the answer lies in the making of international or bilateral agreements, not in national courts straining to find some jurisdictional infirmity in either State'.

jure extraterritorially in the US, or the First Amendment of the US Constitution has a de facto extraterritorial impact on France. Likewise, either Canadian copyright laws apply extraterritorially, for instance, to 'content providers located in Bangalore who post musical works on a server in Hong Kong', or the potentially poor enforcement of copyright laws in Bangalore or Hong-Kong de facto impacts copyright owners in Canada.

THE ENVIRONMENTAL DIMENSION: DEALING WITH TRANSBOUNDARY POLLUTION

Like global trade and Internet communications, pollution also 'respects no borders'.[31] Economic activities in one country increasingly have an impact upon the environment of other countries. The adoption of an effects-based approach to problems of transboundary pollution inevitably leads countries affected by foreign pollution to extend their domestic environmental rules extraterritorially to activities taking place outside their borders.

Pakootas v Teck Cominco (the *Trail Smelter* case), provides a good illustration.

For nearly a century, from 1895 to 1995, a smelter located in the Canadian city of Trail, approximately 10 miles north of the US border, discharged its 'slag', a by-product of the smelting process composed of such dangerous substances as arsenic, cadmium, mercury and zinc, into the Upper Columbia River. The Columbia River carried the slag across the border into the US, polluting the surrounding area, including Lake Roosevelt in Washington State, which is occupied by the Confederated Tribes of the Colville Reservation. Acting upon the Tribes' petition, the US Environmental Protection Agency (EPA) determined that the US portion of the Upper Columbia River had been contaminated primarily by the slag discharged from the Trail Smelter. In 2003, the EPA issued an Unilateral Administrative Order, pursuant to the Comprehensive Environmental Response, Compensation, and Liability Act (CERCLA): Teck Cominco, the Canadian corporation operating the Smelter, as a 'responsible party', was directed to undertake an investigation and feasibility study finalised to clean-up actions. Cominco refused to comply, arguing that US law did not apply to a Canadian corporation operating in Canada, after which two members of the Tribes (Pakootas and Michaels) filed a suit seeking to compel Cominco to comply with the EPA order. Cominco moved to dismiss the complaints, but the District Court of the Eastern District of Washington denied the motion to dismiss[32] and the Court of Appeals for the Ninth Circuit affirmed.[33]

[31] MJ Robinson-Dorn, 'The Trail Smelter, Is What's Past Prologue? EPA Blazes a New Trail for CERCLA' (2006) 14 *New York University Environmental Law Journal* 233, 235.

[32] *Pakootas v Teck Cominco Metals Ltd*, No CV-04–256-AAM, 2004.

[33] *Pakootas v Teck Cominco Metals, Ltd*, 452 F3d 1066, 1069 n2 (9th Cir 2006).

The reasoning of the District Court is very interesting, as it transplants the 'effects-doctrine' from market to non-market issues,[34] supporting the extraterritorial application of US environmental regulation. According to the Court, 'the well-established principle that the presumption [against extraterritoriality] is not applied where failure to extend the scope of the statute to a foreign setting will result in *adverse effects* within the United States, leads ... to conclude that extraterritorial application of CERCLA is appropriate in this case'.[35] Therefore, US environmental regulation, like its antitrust law, could apply to a foreign corporation operating exclusively in a foreign country in accordance with that country's laws, just because the *effects* of its actions were felt within the US.

This de jure extraterritoriality is highly controversial, for reasons that are well known and clearly articulated in the various amici curiae briefs submitted to the US Supreme Court in support of Cominco's petition for *certiorari*.

First of all, as Canada's government argued in its brief, extraterritoriality violated the principle of comity of nations, infringing 'Canada's strong interest in regulating its own corporate citizens' and thus constituted an 'unreasonable interference with the sovereign authority of other nations'.[36]

Moreover, extraterritoriality led to environmental over-regulation, affecting not only the Canadian, but also the American, business community, which in fact strongly rejected the 'effects doctrine' in environmental matters. The arguments put forward in the US Chamber of Commerce's brief are very illustrative and worth highlighting:

[34] Traditionally US courts have accepted the extraterritorial application of antitrust and securities law, but have generally not accepted the extraterritorial application of environmental law. On this topic, see J Turley, 'When in Rome: Multinational Misconduct and the Presumption against Extraterritoriality' (1989–90) 84 Northwestern University Law Review 598, particularly at 663–64 (stating that 'Antitrust and Securities violations are generally viewed from a transnational perspective. Since the market is viewed transnationally, market violations and prohibitions are given similar meaning. Conversely, courts continue to view environmental and labor conditions as local matters and thus interpret ambiguous statutes in this area as limited to domestic applications .... Yet, at a time when the world is developing inexorably toward a unified and interdependent system of economies and environments, American courts continue to adopt an archaic territorialist view of labor and environmental disputes that is more reflective of the early 1900s. In the meantime, the presumption against extraterritoriality stands as a judicially maintained barrier to worker and environmental protections, behind which American multinationals can essentially turn back the clock on corporate responsibility').

[35] The reasoning of the Court of Appeals was different, but came to substantially the same conclusions. The Court determined that holding Teck liable did not constitute an extraterritorial application of CERCLA, because the release or threatened release of hazardous substances from the site into the environment, the act that created liability under CERCLA, actually occurred within the US. To sum up: according to the district court, extraterritorial application of CERCLA was appropriate because the effects of the polluter's conduct, which took place abroad, were felt within the US; according to the Court of Appeals, as the conduct (release of hazardous substances) took place where its effects were felt, that is within the US, CERCLA was not applied extraterritorially.

[36] See US Supreme Court, *Teck Cominco Metals Ltd v Pakootas, On Petition For a Writ of Certiorari To The United States Court of Appeals For the Ninth Circuit*, Brief of the Government of Canada as Amicus Curiae in Support of Petitioner, No 061188, available at www.law.washington.edu/Directory/docs/Robinson-Dorn/TrailSmelter/.

> Canadian companies faced with the unexpected requirement to comply not only with their country's domestic regulation but also with … U.S. environmental statutes when acting solely on Canadian soil will have every incentive to pressure their government to respond. … Canada could very well … impos[e] corresponding liability on companies operating within U.S. territory whenever their operations produce pollution that later ends up in Canada. [As a result], the need to become familiar with foreign laws and regulations, and to conform domestic company activities to these requirements, would impose a significant informational and operational cost on all business in the border regions.

The US Chamber of Commerce also warned against the risk that embracing the 'effects doctrine' could lead to a 'potentially unbounded' extraterritorial application of environmental statutes, extending to air and water pollution emanating not only from Canada, but also from non-border regions, such as Asian countries:

> Given the sweeping nature of cross-border contamination, a limitless range of foreign companies operating solely on foreign soil could be captured by the … expansive interpretation of our domestic laws. Correspondingly … any foreign nation that can trace at least some of its environmental pollution to economic activity occurring in the United States [could] subject the alleged polluter to protracted litigation and potential liability in that country.[37]

The US Solicitor General, invited by the Supreme Court to express the position of the US, did not share these concerns, arguing that under the 'effects doctrine' extraterritoriality is only justified when it is 'reasonable'. It would be reasonable in cases similar to the 'traditional example', in which a person in State A shot a victim across the border in State B. And the *Trail Smelter* does look like such a case, 'because it was inevitable that the river would carry the pollution directly into the United States', and because the slag is 'directly attributable' to Cominco's actions. On the contrary, extraterritoriality would certainly be unreasonable in the unanalogous case in which 'distant sources … contribute to widespread and diffuse air pollution'.[38]

It would often be difficult to determine—according to the Solicitor General's opinion—whether an environmental 'effect' in one country environment is caused 'directly' and 'foreseeably' enough by a foreign action to justify extraterritoriality. Moving away from the traditional example, when does reasonable extraterritoriality become unreasonable?

[37] See US Supreme Court, *Teck Cominco Metals Ltd v Pakootas, On Petition For a Writ of Certiorari To The United States Court of Appeals For the Ninth Circuit*, Brief of the Chamber of Commerce of the United States of America's Amicus Curiae in Support of Petition for a Writ of Certiorari, at 13–15, No 061188, available at www.law.washington.edu/Directory/docs/Robinson-Dorn/TrailSmelter/.

[38] See US Supreme Court, *Teck Cominco Metals Ltd v Pakootas, On Petition For a Writ of Certiorari To The United States Court of Appeals For the Ninth Circuit*, Brief of the United States as Amicus Curiae, at 17–18, No 061188, available at www.law.washington.edu/Directory/docs/Robinson-Dorn/TrailSmelter/.

However, no matter where one locates the threshold, when de jure extraterritoriality ends, de facto extraterritoriality begins.

Either the stricter US environmental laws can apply extraterritorially to the smelting process taking place in Canada de jure, *or* the more lax Canadian environmental regulations (or the more lax Canadian enforcement of those regulations when pollution is exported outside Canada) can have a de facto extraterritorial impact upon the health of Tribes resident in US territory.

Similarly, *either* the higher US environmental standards can be applied extraterritorially de jure to economic activities taking place in Asia, or the lower Asian environmental standards can extraterritorially impact US citizens' welfare de facto, due to the long-range transport of atmospheric pollutants. Therefore, *either* the business community bears the costs of environmental *over-regulation* through de jure extraterritoriality, *or* citizens are exposed to harmful environmental effects of economic activities due to the de facto extraterritorial impact of foreign *under-regulation.*[39]

The more the world shares one market, one Internet and one environment, the more meaningless the choice between territoriality and extraterritoriality becomes. The real choice is increasingly between de jure and de facto extraterritoriality.

REGULATION WITHOUT REPRESENTATION: A NEW CHALLENGE FOR (A GLOBAL) ADMINISTRATIVE LAW

Globalisation makes extraterritoriality less exceptional. It is useful to go back to *Lotus*, in order to understand how this happens. To review the well-known facts in *Lotus*, in August 1926, a collision occurred on the high seas between a French vessel (*SS Lotus*) and a Turkish one. The Turkish vessel sank and eight persons died. Turkish authorities arrested the first officer of the French ship for involuntary manslaughter. Before the Permanent Court of International Justice, the French government argued that international law did not allow Turkey to undertake proceedings with regard to offences committed by a French national on board a French vessel (that is to say, on French territory). The Court rejected the argument, stating that:

> [no rule of] international law forbade Turkey to take into consideration the fact that the offence *produced its effects* on the Turkish vessel and consequently in a place assimilated to Turkish territory .... On the contrary, it is certain that the courts of many countries ... interpret criminal law in the sense that offences, the authors of which at the moment

[39] The 'global impact' of national *under-regulation*, that is to say of failure to enforce environmental regulation by domestic agencies, has been recognised recently by the US Supreme Court in *Massachusetts v Environmental Protection Agency* (127 S Ct 1438—2007). See A Long, 'Standing & Consensus: Globalism in *Massachusetts v EPA*' (2008) 23 *Journal of Environmental Law & Litigation* (stating that '*Massachusetts* supports a globalist view of environmental law by integrating global environmental concerns into cognizable challenges to domestic agency regulation').

> of commission are in the territory of another State, are nevertheless to be regarded as having been committed in the national territory, if one of the constituent elements of the offence, *and more especially its effects*, have taken place there. (Emphasis added.)

This passage of the *Lotus* judgment highlights an important aspect of the relationship between territory and (prescriptive) jurisdiction. The more the territory in which the regulated conduct takes place is decoupled from the territory in which it produces its effects, the more a conflict over jurisdiction is likely to arise. Both the State regulating the place of conduct and the possibly different State regulating the place of its effects can claim territorial jurisdiction. In other words, if something happens both here and there, it could be regulated both here and there.

In 1926, human conduct and its effects rarely occurred in places subject to the overlapping territorial jurisdiction of different States. A manslaughter occurred either in France or Turkey. It could have occurred in both countries only in such an exceptional situation as when the high seas had brought two otherwise removed territories together.

The main effect of globalisation however is precisely to make the world smaller, bringing different, distant territories into closer communication and thus significantly increasing the transnational nature of economic and social relationships.

Today, globalisation makes commonplace what the high seas in *Lotus* made possible only exceptionally.

The various, highly intertwined dimensions of globalisation have set off a kind of 'spatial revolution',[40] whereby actions carried out in one place often produce effects in many different and sometimes very distant places. Consequently, national legislatures and administrative agencies are increasingly challenged to regulate transnational phenomena. Either they regulate conduct which occurs outside their borders and produces effects inside, or they regulate conduct which occurs inside their borders and produces effects beyond. In both cases, as shown above, national regulation has either a de jure or a de facto extraterritorial reach.

The increasing extraterritorial reach of national regulation raises the fundamental public law problem of 'regulation without representation'. On the one hand, national authorities adopt rules and administrative decisions which have a direct or indirect external impact on foreign citizens and firms. On the other hand, national authorities do not receive any legitimacy from—and are in no way accountable to—the foreign citizens and firms which are affected by their rules and decisions.

[40] C Schmitt, *Land and Sea* (Simona Draghici (trans)) (Washington DC, Plutarch Press, 1997, original publication: 1954).

This 'external accountability gap' is the consequence of an imbalance caused by a far-reaching economic and social integration (an 'openness boom', according to the European Commissioner Peter Mandelson)[41] without a similar political and legal integration.

How to achieve a recalibration is beyond the scope of this chapter. It is worth observing, however, that two paths can be and in fact have been pursued.

The first one is the path of vertical integration. States can delegate their power to regulate, or at least their power to harmonise the substantive content of their domestic regulations, to common global institutions, which are indirectly representative of the citizens of all of their Member States.

Vertical integration stimulates the development of a large body of global administrative regulation, produced by formal international organisations, global networks of national administrative agencies and hybrid organisations composed of public and private transnational institutions.

Vertical integration, however, has also its own drawbacks.

First of all, there is the legitimacy issue. International organisations only *indirectly* represents the citizens of their Member States and, moreover, their 'global regulation' is not itself regulated by the administrative law of any country. When the power to regulate is transferred to international institutions, affected citizens risk losing their domestic administrative law guarantees, which become useless. That is why international organisations are slowly creating a 'Global Administrative Law' applicable to their own rules and decision, which is, however, still at its embryonic stage of development.

The second drawback refers to the efficacy issue. The decision-making process of international organisations is inevitably cumbersome, as it is often very difficult, in order to harmonise national regulations, to reach multilateral consensus on substantive rules, let alone resolve the problem of their uniform enforcement. The sectors previously analysed provide good examples in this respect. As for antitrust, the WTO negotiations for a competition agreement have failed. The US has, over time, raised important objections to the EU position in favour of an international antitrust code enforced by the WTO. According to the US, 'there is no consensus on substantive competition rules … [and] an international code, even if enacted, would necessarily reflect a lowest common denominator approach … [and] would be a rigid and static set of rules that could not be

[41] P Mandelson, *Europe's openness and the politics of globalisation*, The Alcuin Lecture, Cambridge, 8 February 2008, available at www.ec.europa.eu/commission_barroso/mandelson/speeches_articles/sppm191_en.htm: 'So, in 1990, two in ten people on this planet lived in societies that were significantly integrated into a global economy. Today about nine in ten do. These may not be politically open societies, but they are economically open enough to have allowed for membership of the WTO and with it the open global trading system. That is more than three billion people and probably one billion workers entering the global economy—pretty much creating the modern global economy—in less than two decades. This is the single most important change you need to grasp to understand the modern world. We are living in the wake of an openness boom'.

adapted to the rapidly changing circumstances of the global market'.[42] As for the regulation of Internet content, the Convention on Cybercrime, adopted by the Committee of Ministers of the Council of Europe on 2001,[43] does not include, among the 'content related offences', the distribution of racist propaganda through computer system. The Committee drafting the convention discussed this possibility, but, as clarified in the 'Explanatory Report', did not reach consensus on the criminalisation of such a conduct because 'some delegations expressed strong concern about including such a provision on freedom of expression grounds'.

Vertical integration, however, is not the only path to be pursued in order to address the issue of de jure and de facto extraterritoriality and to remedy to the problem of 'regulation without representation'. The second path is horizontal integration. States can in fact retain their power to regulate, provided they follow common rules which oblige them to consider the interests and views of the different territorial communities affected by their decisions.

Let us consider two examples, referring to antitrust and environmental regulation.

As for antitrust, both the Organisation for Economic Co-operation and Development (OECD) Recommendations[44] and bilateral agreements such as the EU/US agreement on the application of their competition laws[45] include '*comity*' provisions. According to these provisions, a country is required 'to give full and sympathetic consideration to other countries' important interests while it is making decisions concerning the enforcement of its own competition laws'.[46]

On the one hand, '*negative comity*' provisions require a country to consider how it may prevent its law enforcement actions from harming another country's important interests. Article II of the EU/US bilateral agreement states that 'each Party shall notify the other whenever its competition authorities become aware that their enforcement activities may affect important interests of the other Party', for example when the enforcement actions 'involve anticompetitive activities … carried out in significant part in the other Party's territory'. That is to say that de jure extraterritorial application of antitrust law requires a previous notification to the authorities of the country in which the anti-competitive

[42] Spencer Weber Walzer, 'An International Common Law of Antitrust' (1999) 34 *New England Law Review* 1, electronic copy available at: www.ssrn.com/abstract=984490, at 164.

[43] See Convention on Cybercrime, Budapest, 23 November 2001, available at www.conventions.coe.int/Treaty/en/Treaties/Html/185.htm.

[44] Particularly OECD, *Recommendation of the Council concerning Co-operation between Member Countries on Anticompetitive Practices affecting International Trade*, 27 July 1995 – C(95)130/FINAL.

[45] *Agreement between the Government of the United States and the Commission of the European Communities regarding the application of their competition laws*, OJ L 95, 27 April 1995 at 47–52. Approved by the decision of the Council and the Commission of 10 April 1995 (95/145/EC, ECSC); See also *Agreement between the European Communities and the Government of the United States of America on the application of positive comity principles in the enforcement of their competition laws*, OJ L 173, 18 June 1998, at 28–31.

[46] See OECD, *CLP Report on Positive Comity*, DAFFE/CLP(99)19, Dist 14 June 1999, para 18.

conduct takes place. Moreover, the OECD Recommendations link this notification requirement to the duty of taking into account the views expressed by the notified country.[47] In a situation such as *Hartford Fire*, therefore, '*negative comity*' would have required US antitrust authorities, before opening a proceeding against London reinsurers, to notify British authorities and take into account their comments. An international 'notice and comment' mechanism, or a global 'due process' principle, would have then limited the de jure extraterritorial application of domestic antitrust laws.

On the other hand, '*positive comity*' provisions require national antitrust authorities to take into account 'another country's request that it open a law enforcement proceeding in order to remedy conduct that is substantially and adversely affecting another country's interests'.[48] Positive comity is thus a kind of international guarantee against the de facto extraterritorial impact of foreign under-regulation or, to put it a better way, against the extraterritorial impact of poor or ineffective enforcement of foreign antitrust regulation.

A similar rationale underlies—as for environmental regulation—the North American Agreement on Environmental Cooperation, to which Canada and the US are Party. Article 22 of the Agreement, for example, states that 'any Party may request in writing consultations with any other Party regarding whether there has

[47] See OECD, *Recommendation of the Council concerning Co-operation between Member Countries on Anticompetitive Practices affecting International Trade*, n 44 above, art I.A.1: 'When a Member country undertakes under its competition laws an investigation or proceeding which may affect important interests of another Member country or countries, it should notify such Member country or countries, if possible in advance, and, in any event, at a time that would facilitate comments or consultations; such advance notification would enable the proceeding Member country, while retaining full freedom of ultimate decision, to take account of such views as the other Member country may wish to express and of such remedial action as the other Member country may find it feasible to take under its own laws, to deal with the anticompetitive practices'. See also art. I.B.4: 'a) A Member country which considers that an investigation or proceeding being conducted by another Member country under its competition laws may affect its important interests should transmit its views on the matter to or request consultation with the other Member country; b) Without prejudice to the continuation of its action under its competition law and to its full freedom of ultimate decision the Member country so addressed should give full and sympathetic consideration to the views expressed by the requesting country, and in particular to any suggestions as to alternative means of fulfilling the needs or objectives of the competition investigation or proceeding'.

[48] OECD, *CLP Report on Positive Comity*, n 46 above, para 18. See OECD, *Recommendation of the Council concerning Co-operation between Member Countries on Anticompetitive Practices affecting International Trade*, n 44 above, art. I.B.5: 'a) A Member country which considers that one or more enterprises situated in one or more other Member countries are or have been engaged in anticompetitive practices of whatever origin that are substantially and adversely affecting its interests, may request consultation with such other Member country or countries recognising that entering into such consultations is without prejudice to any action under its competition law and to the full freedom of ultimate decision of the Member countries concerned; b) Any Member country so addressed should give full and sympathetic consideration to such views and factual materials as may be provided by the requesting country and, in particular, to the nature of the anticompetitive practices in question, the enterprises involved and the alleged harmful effects on the interests of the requesting country'. More generally, see *Agreement between the European Communities and the Government of the United States of America on the application of positive comity principles in the enforcement of their competition laws*, n 45 above.

been a *persistent pattern of failure* by that other Party to effectively enforce its environmental law'. The de facto extraterritorial impact of the ineffective enforcement of domestic environmental laws is remedied, by these provisions, allowing foreign authorities (and sometimes foreign citizens)[49] to request such an enforcement and, in this way, to introduce their interests in the decision-making process of another country. On the basis of this rules, in a situation like the *Trail Smelter* case, US authorities, instead of applying extraterritorially US environmental laws to a Canadian company operating in Canada, could have requested consultation with Canadian environmental authorities concerning the failure to effectively enforce Canadian environmental laws on the Canadian company.

As these examples make clear, horizontal integration involves the application, to national regulation, of international rules with a typical administrative law content: notice and comment, due process, etc. A kind of Global Rule of Law is thus emerging, in order to remedy the fundamental problem of 'regulation without representation' in our new globalised world. A promising future awaits Administrative Law, beyond the State.

[49] Arts 14–15 of the Agreement foresee a 'Citizen Submissions on Enforcement Matters mechanism', which enables members of the public to trigger the process by submitting to the Commission for Environmental Cooperation (CEC) a claim alleging a failure to enforce its environmental laws effectively on the part of any of the partners. Following a review of the submission, the CEC may investigate the matter and publish a factual record of its findings, subject to approval by the CEC Council.

More generally, on the perspective of 'diagonal environmental rights', see JH Knox, 'Diagonal Environmental Rights' in M Gibney and S Skogly (eds), *Extraterritorial Obligations in Human Rights Law* (University of Pennsylvania Press, Forthcoming), available at www.ssrn.com/abstract=1134863 (stating that 'Although most environmental treaties set out horizontal rights and duties, many of their *benefits* run diagonally. Those most affected by extraterritorial environmental harm are neither residents nor nationals of the state with territorial jurisdiction over the source of the harm. One could argue that the foreign residents affected by such harm are the real parties in interest in any dispute arising under such treaties, and to that degree they have diagonal interests implicit in the treaties. If those interests were expressed as rights, then IEL would give rise to diagonal environmental rights. *Such a conversion could occur if the individuals had rights to enforce the treaties against the states party to them.* This would not require amending the treaties to set out new *substantive* rights on the part of the individuals, but rather allowing them to have access to procedures that promote compliance with existing horizontal obligations').

4

Shared Administration and Networks: Global and EU Perspectives

PAUL CRAIG*

INTRODUCTION

THERE IS AN extensive literature in political science concerning policy networks, with divergent interpretations given to this term.[1] This chapter does not take sides in this debate. The object of the present inquiry is more limited. It is to examine the way in which networks are used by the EU in policy delivery in the light of the literature concerning networks and the global order, and global administrative law.

The chapter begins by examining some of this prominent literature. It will become apparent that such networks can have advantages, but that they can also be problematic from a number of perspectives. In section 2, the focus shifts to networks concerned with policy delivery in the EU. The terrain is mapped, there is analysis of different types of networks and the reasons why they are chosen. It will be argued in section 3 that networks are properly regarded as one part of shared administration in the EU.

The discussion in section 4 considers the rationale for use of networks in relation to policy delivery, to be followed in section 5 by analysis of the particular features of these EU networks. Section 6 is concerned with issues of legitimacy and accountability posed by networks in the EU. The chapter concludes by considering the lessons that can be learned about networks on the global level from experience within the EU.

* Professor of English Law, St John's College, Oxford. I am grateful for comments on an earlier version of this chapter from a seminar held in Paris in 2008, and from Carol Harlow.

[1] For an excellent overview, T Börzel, 'What's So Special about Policy Networks? An Exploration of the Concept and Its Usefulness in Studying European Governance', *European Integration online Papers (EIoP)*, 1 (16), www.eiop.or.at/eiop/texte/1997–016a.htm; T Börzel, 'Organising Babylon. On the Different Conceptions of Policy Networks' (1998) 76 *Public Administration* 253.

NETWORKS AND THE GLOBAL ORDER

> Terrorists, arms dealers, money launderers, drug dealers, traffickers in women and children, and the modern pirates of intellectual property all operate through global networks. So, increasingly, do governments. Networks of government officials—police investigators, financial regulators, even judges and legislators—increasingly exchange information and coordinate activity to combat global crime and address common problems on a global scale. These government networks are a key feature of world order in the twenty-first century, but they are underappreciated, undersupported and underused to address the central problems of global governance.[2]

Thus Anne-Marie Slaughter begins her important work on the way in which networks have transformed the global political order. She explains how networks are a prevalent feature of the global order, ranging from the environment to security, from financial regulation to international trade and from policing to macro-economic policy. The networks are normally horizontal in nature, in the sense that the relevant players are commonly bankers, trade officials or environmental activists from different countries. Networks can however be vertical, existing between players at different levels within a supranational organisation. The networks may be free-standing, external to any international organisation, but they commonly also feature within such organisations.

Slaughter adopts a broad view of network, using it to capture 'all the different ways that individual government institutions are interacting with their counterparts either abroad or above them'.[3] She defines a network as a 'pattern of regular and purposive relations among like government units working across the borders that divide countries from one another and that demarcate the "domestic" from the "international" sphere'.[4]

Slaughter distinguishes three different types of network, while recognising that some networks may have more than one role. There are enforcement networks, designed to render enforcement more efficacious across international boundaries. There are information networks, aimed at the exchange of information between governmental agencies or the like, on matters as diverse as security, the environment, policing, health, and fundamental rights. The third category is the harmonisation network, designed to foster closer uniformity in regulatory standards.

The purpose of Slaughter's study is not merely descriptive. It is also explicitly normative. Thus she argues that networks can be a positive force for good within the global order. They can foster convergence on an issue, or help to ensure that divergence of view is informed by reasoned dialogue based on understanding of the other side's perspective. Networks can, secondly, improve compliance with international rules. A third benefit is that networks can increase international cooperation.

[2] A-M Slaughter, *A New World Order* (New Jersey, Princeton University Press, 2004) at 1.
[3] ibid, at 14.
[4] ibid.

Slaughter is nonetheless mindful of the problems with networks, which relate both to input and output. Thus decision-making may be dominated by experts and enthusiasts, by technology and passion, to the exclusion of a broader spectrum of views.[5] Networks may lack transparency, which exacerbates the preceding problem. Networks may also circumvent the normal rules of representative democracy, allowing policy to be developed without the imprimatur of the elected legislature.

Slaughter responds by proposing five principles to alleviate these concerns.[6] *Global deliberative equality* is designed to counter the elitism/exclusion that can attend networks. The process of global governance is seen as a collective deliberation about common problems and hence 'all affected individuals, or their representatives, are entitled to participate'.[7] All government networks should therefore adopt clear criteria for participation that will be fairly applied.[8] *Legitimate difference* entails the idea that difference of view 'reflects a desirable diversity of ideas about how to order an economy or society',[9] with willingness to reconsider how an issue is dealt with at home, and respect different choices made by other societies. Thus legitimate difference 'enshrines pluralism as a basis for, rather than a bar to regulatory cooperation, leaving open the possibility of further convergence between legal systems in the form of mutual recognition or even harmonization, but not requiring it'.[10] The third of Slaughter's principles is *positive comity*, which is a principle of affirmative cooperation between government agencies of different nations. It requires 'regulatory agencies to substitute consultation and active assistance for unilateral action and noninterference',[11] as exemplified by international cooperation in relation to antitrust. The penultimate principle is *checks and balances*, with Slaughter providing the example of the relationship between national courts and the Community courts in the EU, and the hope that 'government institutions of the same type in different systems national and international, and of different types can check each other both vertically and horizontally'.[12] *Subsidiarity* is the final principle: decisions should be taken as closely as possible to the citizen, with the consequence that most decisions should still be taken at national level, or even closer to the citizen if feasible.

[5] P Alston, 'The Myopia of Handmaidens: International Lawyers and Globalization' (1997) 8 *European Journal of International Law* 441; M Shapiro, 'Administrative Law Unbounded: Reflections on Government and Governance' (2001) 8 *Indiana Journal of Global Legal Studies* 369; M Shapiro, '"Deliberative", "Independent" Technocracy v. Democratic Politics: Will the Globe Echo the EU' (2005) 68 *Law and Contemporary Problems* 341.

[6] Slaughter, n 2 above, ch 6.

[7] ibid, at 246.

[8] ibid.

[9] ibid, at 248.

[10] ibid, at 249.

[11] ibid, at 250.

[12] ibid, at 254.

Concerns about global and transnational networks are also apparent in the literature on global administrative law. Thus Kingsbury, Krisch and Stewart stress that underlying the emergence of global administrative law is the 'vast increase in the reach and form of transgovernmental regulation and administration designed to address the consequences of global administration'.[13] They note that global administrative bodies include 'formal intergovernmental regulatory bodies, informal intergovernmental regulatory networks and coordination arrangements, national regulatory bodies operating with reference to an international intergovernmental regime, hybrid public-private regulatory bodies, and some regulatory bodies exercising transnational governance functions of particular public significance'.[14] Thus transnational networks and coordination arrangements are one type of global administration generating interest in global administrative law.[15] The challenge is to consider how far administrative law precepts concerning matters such as procedural participation, transparency, reasoned decision-making, and judicial review, including substantive rationality or proportionality scrutiny, can be applied in such contexts.[16]

NETWORKS AND THE EU: MAPPING THE TERRAIN

The concept of network will strike a chord with those familiar with the EU, since networks abound.[17] This section analyses some prominent types of EU network, their rationale and the principal institutional players responsible for their existence.[18]

Networks and Policymaking: Member State and Commission Initiatives

It will be seen that horizontal networks have a prominent role in the enforcement of EU law. Networks of national officials also play an important role in the

[13] B Kingsbury, N Krisch, R Stewart, 'The Emergence of Global Administrative Law' (2005) 68 *LCP* 15, at 16.

[14] ibid, at 17.

[15] ibid, at 21, 24, 25.

[16] ibid, at 37–41. See also S Shapiro, 'International Trade Agreements, Regulatory Protection and Public Accountability' (2002) 54 *Administrative Law Review* 415; A Aman, 'Globalization, Democracy and the Need for a New Administrative Law' (2003) 10 *Indiana Journal of Global Legal Studies* 125; R Stewart, 'Administrative Law in the Twenty-First Century' (2003) 78 *New York University Law Review* 437; R Stewart, 'US Administrative Law: A Model for Global Administrative Law?' (2005) 68 *LCP* 63; S Cassese, 'Global Standards for National Administrative Procedure' (2005) 68 *LCP* 109; A von Bogdandy and P Dann, 'International Composite Administration: Conceptualizing Multi-Level and Network Aspects in the Exercise of International Public Authority' (2008) 9(11) *German Law Journal* 2013.

[17] R Dehousse, 'Regulation by Networks in the European Community: the Role of European Agencies' (1997) 4 *Journal of European Public Policy* 246.

[18] For discussion of the way in which courts and Ombudsmen in the EU can be seen in terms of networks, see C Harlow and R Rawlings, 'Promoting Accountability in Multilevel Governance: A Network Approach' (2007) 13 *European Law Journal* 542.

development of EU policy. On some occasions it has been the Member States, acting through the Council, that have driven such developments, while on other occasions the Commission has been the driving force.

The best known example of national network influence on policy-making is of course Comitology.[19] The EEC, from its inception, had to delegate power to the Commission to make regulations, in order to cope expeditiously with changing market circumstances. Thus the Council, through a 'parent' regulation, authorised the Commission to enact more specific regulations within a particular area. The Council was not, however, willing to give the Commission carte blanche to legislate in this manner. It made the exercise of delegated legislative power subject to institutional constraints, in the form of committees on which Member State interests were represented. This was in part because there might be disagreements between the States as to the content of the more detailed norms, and in part because the Council was wary of the Commission's federalising tendencies, and hence was unwilling to delegate power without the formal representation of Member State interests. The rest as they say is history. The Comitology regime originated in agriculture and customs and rapidly spread to all other areas. Comitology committees became part of the institutional landscape, and rules have been enshrined in Decisions.[20] The Commission may be content with advisory committees to help with implementation of EU law, but it has never been happy with the formal powers wielded by management and regulatory committees, regarding them as a constraint on implementation which it regards as its own prerogative, and it has striven for changes that would either diminish or bypass their powers.

The Commission is however happy to use national networks in policy-making provided that it, the Commission, has a firm hand on the reins of power and provided also that the national networks do not have formal powers of their own. This is more especially so where the Commission decides that this is the best

[19] R Pedler and GF Schaefer (eds), *Shaping European Law and Policy: The Role of Committees and Comitology in the Political Process* (Maastricht, European Institute of Public Administration, 1996); D Rometsch and W Wessels (eds), *The European Union and Member States, Towards Institutional Fusion?* (Manchester, Manchester University Press, 1996); C Joerges, K-H Ladeur and E Vos (eds), *Integrating Scientific Expertise into Regulatory Decision-Making: National Traditions and European Innovations* (Baden Baden, Nomos, 1997); C Joerges and E Vos (eds), *EU Committees: Social Regulation, Law and Politics* (Oxford, Hart Publishing, 1999); *Third Report of the House of Lords' Select Committee on European Legislation: Delegation of Powers to the Commission: Reforming Comitology* (HL 23; 1999); E Vos, *Institutional Frameworks of Community Health and Safety Legislation: Committees, Agencies and Private Bodies* (Oxford, Hart Publishing, 1999); M Andenas and A Turk (eds), *Delegated Legislation and the Role of Committees in the EC* (The Hague, Kluwer Law International, 2000); C Bergstrom, *Comitology, Delegation of Powers in the European Union and the Committee System* (Oxford, Oxford University Press, 2005); P Craig, *EU Administrative Law* (Oxford, Oxford University Press, 2006), ch 4; P Strauss 'Rulemaking in the Ages of Globalization and Information: What America can Learn from Europe, and Vice-Versa', (2005–6) 12 *Columbia Journal of European Law* 645.

[20] Council Decision 87/373/EEC of 13 July 1987, Laying Down the Procedures for the Exercise of Implementing Powers Conferred on the Commission, OJ 1987 L197/33; Council Decision 99/468/EC of 28 June 1999, Laying Down the Procedures for the Exercise of Implementing Powers Conferred on the Commission, OJ 1999 L184/23.

method of imbuing agreed legislative initiatives with greater specificity. This can be exemplified by the Commission's use of national networks in policy-making in relation to customs.

Thus it is generally agreed that it is desirable to prevent fraud, and protect security at borders. Horizontal networks have been used to decide on more specific application of these general principles, as exemplified by the Customs 2013 programme,[21] which gives the national customs administrations of the EU, together with the European Commission, the opportunity to cooperate in areas of common and high interest. The programme runs from 1 January 2008 to 31 December 2013 and provides a legal and financial base for: reinforcing security within the EU and at the external border; strengthening the fight against fraud; and increasing the competitiveness of European business by speeding up customs procedures. The programme has a budget of €324 million.

The Customs 2013 cooperation programme is implemented on the basis of annual work programmes, through which the national customs administrations work together to protect the EU's financial interests from fraud, which requires, inter alia, cooperation between national agencies, and exchange of information and best practices, to ensure good quality control throughout the customs territory. The objective of trade facilitation also entails important responsibilities for national customs administrations, requiring them to cooperate to minimise the burdens on trade in relation to customs legislation and procedures, and to facilitate implementation of a paperless customs environment.

This is particularly important since although EU customs operate under a common legal framework and a common customs tariff, implementation depends on individual national administrations with differing national responsibilities which are called upon to act 'as if they were one' when applying EU customs law. It is therefore crucial for there to be equivalent operational capacity of customs administrations including IT architectures, working methods and common training provisions.

Centralised/Direct Administration: National Networks as an Organisational Choice

The Financial Regulation 2002 distinguishes between centralised and shared administration.[22] Much EU administration falls into the latter category: the Commission and national administrations are accorded formal rights, powers

[21] www.ec.europa.eu/taxation_customs/customs/index_en.htm.

[22] Council Regulation (EC, Euratom) 1605/2002 of 25 June 2002 on the Financial Regulation applicable to the General Budget of the European Communities, OJ 2002 OJ L248/1, Art 54(2)(c), as amended by Council Regulation (EC, Euratom) No 1995/2006 of 13 December 2006 amending Regulation (EC, Euratom) No 1605/2002 on the Financial Regulation applicable to the general budget of the European Communities, OJ 2006 L390/1.

and duties under the relevant EU legislation, which both must fulfil if the aims of the legislation are to be fulfilled. Networks feature prominently within shared administration, as will be seen.

They can also be used in the context of centralised administration. The Financial Regulation provides that such activities can be directly managed within the Commission; management tasks can be undertaken by executive agencies; implementation can be entrusted to an EU body or agency; some tasks can be delegated to networks of national agencies; and certain activities can be contracted-out.

We are concerned here with the network option. Centralised management of EU activities can be undertaken by, inter alia, 'national or international public-sector bodies or bodies governed by private law with a public-service mission providing adequate financial guarantees and complying with the conditions provided for in the implementing rules'.[23] Such bodies must be chosen in an objective and transparent manner, following a cost-effectiveness analysis, to match the Commission's implementation requirements.[24] Where EU policy is implemented in this way the Commission will conclude agreements with such bodies specifying their tasks, the performance conditions and reporting rules.[25] The Commission must inform the relevant national legislative authority annually and justify the use of such bodies.[26]

The Commission can therefore devolve executive responsibilities to a network of national bodies, which are either public or have a public service mission guaranteed by the State.[27] These bodies are collectively referred to as 'national agencies', which act as a partner in the implementation of EU policies, but the Commission retains overall responsibility for service delivery.[28] The intention is to devolve detailed implementation to national agencies, where there is no 'large measure of discretion'[29] on EU policy. The implementing tasks entrusted to such agencies will 'in no way alter any choices taken by the Commission involving political judgment'.[30] The Commission perceives a number of advantages in using such national 'agencies':[31] it facilitates proximity to the beneficiaries of the policy; it fosters complementarity, since there will often be national agencies with

[23] ibid, Art 54(2)(c).

[24] Commission Regulation (EC, Euratom) 2342/2002 of 23 December 2002, Laying Down Detailed Rules for the Implementation of Council Regulation 1605/2002, OJ 2002 L357/1, Art 39, as amended by Commission Regulation (EC, Euratom) No 478/2007 of 23 April 2007 amending Regulation (EC, Euratom) No 2342/2002 laying down detailed rules for the implementation of Council Regulation (EC, Euratom) No 1605/2002 on the Financial Regulation applicable to the general budget of the European Communities, OJ 2007 L111/13.

[25] ibid, Art 41.

[26] ibid, Art 39(4).

[27] Communication from the Commission, Management of Community Programmes by Networks of National Agencies, COM(2001) 648 final.

[28] ibid, at 3.1.

[29] Reg 1605/2002, n 22 above, Art 54(1).

[30] COM(2001) 648 final, n 27 above, at 5.2.

[31] ibid, at 4.1.

experience of a particular policy; and it facilitates flexibility, since such 'agencies' can adapt to local circumstance.

Shared Administration: Enforcement Networks and Formal EU Legislation

It is not fortuitous that the most formal networks exist where there is the strongest incentive for effective enforcement of EU law across national borders. The Commission will normally be in the driving seat and will press for measures that enhance the enforcement capacities of the relevant national agencies to render the regulatory regime more effective. The Commission has pressed for formal law to establish a network of national enforcement agencies and the resultant regulations set out their powers and duties in considerable detail. The national agencies are willing to surrender some enforcement autonomy on their own territory, since they gain reciprocal powers of cross-border enforcement in other Member States.

This is exemplified by the regimes in customs and agriculture, where problems of cross-border fraud have been especially prevalent.[32] The recitals to Regulation 515/97 state that combating fraud in the customs union and the common agricultural policy (CAP) calls for close cooperation between the relevant national authorities, and for close cooperation between them and the Commission. The scope of the investigative and enforcement powers becomes readily apparent from Regulation 515/97.

There are provisions dealing with 'assistance on request'. Thus an administrative authority in one Member State, the applicant authority, can request the relevant authority in another Member State, the requested authority, to transmit to it any information which may enable it to ensure compliance with the provisions of customs or agricultural legislation.[33] The applicant authority can also ask the requested authority for a special watch to be kept on persons, on storage facilities or on modes of transport where there are reasonable grounds for believing that there may be breaches of customs or agricultural legislation.[34] The requested authority has a duty to make available when asked by the applicant authority any information concerning operations detected or planned which constitute, or appear to constitute, breaches of customs or agricultural legislation,[35] and the requested authority can be obliged to conduct administrative

[32] Council Regulation (EC) 515/97 of 13 March 1997 on mutual assistance between the administrative authorities of the Member States and cooperation between the latter and the Commission to ensure the correct application of the law on customs and agricultural matters, OJ 1997 L82/1, replacing earlier provisions dating from 1981. The Regulation was promulgated under Art 308 EC, since the Commission felt that the Treaty articles dealing specifically with customs and agriculture did not empower the Community to establish the system covered by the Regulation.

[33] ibid, Art 4(1).

[34] ibid, Art 7.

[35] ibid, Art 8.

enquiries concerning operations which constitute, or appear to the applicant authority to constitute, breaches of customs or agricultural legislation.[36]

Regulation 515/97 also contains provisions dealing with 'spontaneous assistance'. Thus the competent national authorities are obliged to assist their counterparts in other Member States without prior request where they consider it useful for ensuring compliance with customs or agricultural legislation. Such assistance consists of communicating information, including information about their customs/CAP operations, and sharing relevant documentation.[37]

Regulation 515/97 makes provision not only for the horizontal dimension of network cooperation, but also for the vertical dimension concerning relations between the national authorities and the Commission. The national authorities are obliged to communicate to the Commission information concerning both the 'micro' dimension of customs/CAP enforcement, data concerning goods that have violated the customs regulations, and also the more 'macro' dimension, methods or practices used to breach customs or agricultural legislation, and any information on shortcomings in customs and agricultural legislation that have become apparent,[38] more especially where they might have general EU relevance, or ramifications for other Member States.[39]

Shared Administration: Enforcement Networks, Formal EU Legislation and Upgrading Network Powers

Horizontal networks are not static. The Commission will strengthen a network by upgrading it and granting it formal powers where these are necessary for effective cross-border implementation of EU law. The Commission is once again the principal institutional catalyst for change. It will keep a watchful eye on the way a particular network operates and will not hesitate to strengthen its powers where it feels that this is needed for efficacious enforcement of EU law. The relevant Member State agencies that form the network may lose some autonomy, since the changes will at the very least imbue existing de facto obligations with a de jure quality lacking hitherto, and will often impose new obligations. This loss of national agency autonomy is nonetheless counterbalanced by the increase in the national agency's power to pursue violations of EU law in another Member State.

An important example is the 2004 Regulation on cooperation between national authorities responsible for enforcement of consumer protection laws.[40]

[36] ibid, Art 9(1).
[37] ibid, Arts 14–15.
[38] ibid, Art 17.
[39] ibid, Art 18.
[40] Regulation (EC) 2006/2004 of the European Parliament and of the Council of 27 October 2004 on cooperation between national authorities responsible for the enforcement of consumer protection laws, OJ 2004 L364/1.

The Regulation was premised on the assumption that existing national enforcement arrangements were inadequate for trans-border infringements of consumer protection laws. While there was a network of national authorities, the Commission felt that it was necessary to formalise the network and to give such authorities common investigation and enforcement powers.

This is made clear in the recitals to the Regulation, which state that existing national enforcement arrangements for consumer protection laws are not adapted to the challenges of the internal market, the consequence being barriers to cooperation between public enforcement authorities. This enabled sellers to evade enforcement by relocating within the EU, led to distortion of competition for law-abiding sellers and undermined the confidence of consumers in taking up cross-border offers. It was therefore necessary to establish a network of public enforcement authorities with common investigation and enforcement powers.

The Regulation accords national authorities in the network extensive powers and duties. Each competent national authority must have the investigation and enforcement powers necessary for the application of the Regulation. These powers, which are to be exercised where there is reasonable suspicion of an intra-EU infringement, include, inter alia, the right: to access to documents related to the infringement; to require the supply by any person of relevant information related to the infringement; to carry out necessary on-site inspections; to request that the seller cease the infringement; to require the cessation of any infringement; and to require the losing defendant to make payments to the public purse or to any beneficiary designated in or under national legislation, in the event of failure to comply with the decision.[41]

The Regulation makes extensive provision for mutual assistance in relation to investigations, imposing obligations on the requested authority to provide information to the applicant authority and to carry out investigations on its behalf.[42] It also empowers the enforcement authorities of one Member State to furnish their counterparts in other Member States with such information where there has been no request.[43]

The Regulation also makes detailed provision for reciprocal enforcement between members of the network. Thus a requested authority is obliged when requested by an applicant authority to take all necessary enforcement measures to bring about the cessation of the infringement, exercising the powers set out above.[44] There are moreover provisions designed to ensure coordination of market surveillance and enforcement activities. It is for the national authorities to coordinate these activities, such that when they become aware that an infringement harms the interests of consumers in more than two Member States, they

[41] ibid, Art 4.
[42] ibid, Art 6.
[43] ibid, Art 7.
[44] ibid, Art 8.

must coordinate their enforcement actions.[45] In its first eight months of operations, the network considered approximately 100 cases, and dealt with 20 alerts concerning possible breaches to consumer laws.[46]

In addition to detailed rules concerning investigation and enforcement in particular cases, the Regulation also makes provision for cooperation between network members at a more 'macro' level, concerning matters such as consumer information and advice, support for consumer representatives, support for bodies responsible for the extra-judicial settlement of consumer disputes, and support for consumers' access to justice.

Shared Administration: Enforcement Networks, Re-thinking Administration and Extending Network Powers

The role played by networks can also change because of fundamental re-thinking of the way in which an area of law should be administered. EU competition law provides the classic example.

The traditional approach to enforcement of EU competition law was that agreements had, subject to certain exceptions, to be notified to the Commission, and the Commission had a monopoly over exemptions dealt with in Article 81(3) EC. Thus national courts and national competition authorities (NCAs) could apply Articles 81 and 82, which had direct effect, but could not grant an individual exemption under Article 81(3). This approach came under increasing strain, since the Commission did not have the resources to deal with all notified agreements, nor did it have the resources to adjudicate on anything but a handful of individual exemptions. The Commission therefore encouraged national courts to apply Articles 81 and 82. However, in the *White Paper on Modernization*[47] it proposed a thorough overhaul of the enforcement regime, abolishing notification and the Commission's monopoly over Article 81(3). National courts and NCAs would be empowered to apply Article 81 in its entirety and Article 82.

[45] ibid, Art 9.

[46] www.ec.europa.eu/consumers/enforcement/index_en.htm.

[47] White Paper on Modernization of the Rules Implementing Articles 85 and 86 of the EC Treaty, Commission Programme 99/27, 28 April 1999; R Wesseling, 'The Commission White Paper on Modernisation of EC Antitrust Law: Unspoken Consequences and Incomplete Treatment of Alternative Options' [1999] *European Competition Law Review* 420; C-D Ehlermann, 'The Modernization of EC Antitrust Policy: A Legal and Cultural Revolution' (2000) 37 *Common Market Law Review* 537; A Schaub, 'Modernisation of EC Competition Law: Reform of Regulation No 17' in B Hawk (ed), *Fordham Corporate Law Institute* (New York, Fordham University, 2000), ch 10; R Whish and B Sufrin, 'Community Competition Law: Notification and Exemption—Goodbye to All That' in D Hayton (ed), *Law's Future(s): British Legal Developments in the 21st Century* (Oxford, Hart Publishing, 2000), ch 8.

The new regime was implemented by Regulation 1/2003,[48] and had a significant impact on individual national enforcement authorities and networks between them. NCAs and national courts can apply the entirety of Articles 101 and 102 TFEU.[49] The Commission continues to have enforcement power under the new regime: it can act on a complaint or on its own initiative and find an infringement of Article 101 or Article 102.[50]

There are provisions facilitating cooperation between an NCA and the Commission,[51] and NCAs cannot make rulings in relation to Articles 101 and 102 that are contrary to a decision of the Commission on the same subject matter.[52] There are also provisions facilitating cooperation between NCAs in different Member States,[53] and a European Competition Network has been established for discussion and cooperation between NCAs.[54] Where two or more NCAs have received a complaint or are acting on their own initiative against the same agreement, etc, 'the fact that one authority is dealing with the case shall be sufficient grounds for the others to suspend proceedings before them or to reject the complaint'.[55] The Commission may also reject a complaint on the ground that an NCA is dealing with the matter. Where a case has already been dealt with by an NCA, or by the Commission, any other NCA may reject it.[56]

There are separate provisions dealing with cooperation with national courts.[57] National courts may, in cases concerned with Articles 101 and 102, ask the Commission for information in its possession, or for its opinion on questions concerning the application of Community competition rules.[58] Member States are obliged to send the Commission copies of judgments applying Article 101 or 102.[59] NCAs may submit written observations to national courts in cases concerning Articles 101 and 102, and may submit oral argument with the permission of the national court. The Commission may do likewise where the coherent application of Articles 101 and 102 so requires.[60] National courts cannot make rulings in relation to Articles 101 and 102 that are counter to a Commission

[48] Council Regulation (EC) 1/2003 of 16 December 2002 on the implementation of the rules on competition laid down in Arts 81 and 82 of the Treaty, OJ 2003 L1/1.
[49] Reg 1/2003, n 48 above, Arts 5 and 6.
[50] ibid, Art 7.
[51] ibid, Arts 11–12, 16.
[52] ibid, Art 16(2).
[53] Commission Notice on cooperation within the Network of Competition Authorities, OJ 2004 C101/43; Joint Statement of the Council and the Commission on the Functioning of the Network of Competition Authorities, available at www.ec.europa.eu/comm/competition/ecn/more_details.html.
[54] www.ec.europa.eu/comm/competition/ecn/more_details.html.
[55] Reg 1/2003, n 48 above, Art 13(1).
[56] ibid, Art 13(2).
[57] Commission Notice on the cooperation between the Commission and the courts of the EU Member States in the application of Arts 81 and 82 EC [2004] OJ C101/54.
[58] Reg 1/2003, n 48 above, Art 15(1).
[59] ibid, Art 15(2).
[60] ibid, Art 15(3).

decision on the same subject matter, and they must avoid giving decisions that would conflict with a decision contemplated by the Commission in proceedings which it has initiated.[61]

Shared Administration: Support Networks, EU Initiatives and EU Sponsorship

The preceding discussion provides a natural bridge to that which follows. We saw that network members responsible for enforcement also have obligations to cooperate on matters such as consumer information and advice. It is moreover clear that the EU, in particular the Commission, will support not just horizontal networks of national enforcement agencies, but also networks that support those that the EU legislation is intended to benefit. There are a number of such horizontal support networks, as is apparent from the following three examples.

The Commission was instrumental in establishing the European Consumer Centres Network (ECC-Net) which was created in order to have better informed and educated consumers and also to help them obtain redress for violation of their consumer rights in cross-border transactions. The ECC-Net is an EU-wide network designed to promote consumer confidence by advising citizens on their rights and providing easy access to redress, particularly where the consumer has made a cross-border purchase.[62] There is also the European Consumer Consultative Group (ECCG)[63] which is the main forum for consultation of consumer interests.

In the case of the European Judicial Network (EJN), EU support was forthcoming from the European Council and the Commission, and was then embodied in a formal EU Act. The catalyst was the Tampere European Council in 1999, in which the Heads of State wished the European Commission to take initiatives to improve access to justice in Europe, one of which was the establishment of a network of national authorities responsible for civil and commercial law. The Commission presented a proposal in 2000, which was adopted by the Council in May 2001.[64] The network consists of national judicial and administrative authorities. It meets several times each year to exchange information and experience and boost cooperation between the Member States as regards civil and commercial law. The main objective is to facilitate litigation where there is a transnational element, although it does not provide legal advice about a specific situation.[65]

[61] ibid, Art 16(1).

[62] www.ec.europa.eu/consumers/redress_cons/index_en.htm.

[63] Commission Decision 2003/709/EC of 9 October 2003 setting up a European Consumer Consultative Group, OJ 2003 L258/35.

[64] Council Decision 2001/470/EC of 28 May 2001 establishing a European Judicial Network in civil and commercial matters, OJ 2001 L174/25.

[65] www.ec.europa.eu/civiljustice/index_en.htm.

A third example of what I have termed a horizontal support network is SOLVIT, which has been operational since July 2002.[66] It is an on-line problem solving network in which Member States work together to solve without legal proceedings problems caused by the misapplication of internal market law by public authorities.[67] There is a SOLVIT centre in every Member State (as well as in Norway, Iceland and Liechtenstein). They are part of the national administration and are committed to providing solutions within 10 weeks. Using SOLVIT is free of charge. The Commission coordinates the network, provides the database facilities and, when needed, helps to expedite resolution of problems. The Commission also passes formal complaints it receives on to SOLVIT if there is a good chance that the problem can be solved without legal action. When a case is submitted to SOLVIT, the local SOLVIT Centre, known as the 'Home' SOLVIT Centre, checks the application to ensure that it concerns misapplication of internal market rules and that all necessary information has been made available. It then enters the case into an on-line database, and it is forwarded automatically to the SOLVIT Centre in the Member State where the problem has occurred, known as the 'Lead' SOLVIT Centre, which confirms within a week whether or not it will take the case. This depends on whether it considers that the case is well-founded and can be resolved pragmatically. The two SOLVIT Centres work together to resolve the problem and the Home SOLVIT Centre keeps the complainant informed of progress. SOLVIT therefore functions as an alternative dispute resolution mechanism, but if a problem is unresolved, or the complainant considers that the proposed solution is unacceptable, a formal legal action is still possible.

Shared Administration: Regulatory Networks, Standardisation and the Privatisation of Standard Setting

The role played by networks in the regulatory process of standard setting has been as important as the role played by Comitology networks in the policy-making process. The story here is well known and can be briefly related.

The revitalisation of the single market in the 1980s required not only reform in the legislative process, which was achieved through the Single European Act 1986, but also a new approach to harmonisation to facilitate the passage of these measures. Traditional harmonisation techniques were slow, and generated excessive uniformity.[68] The Commission recognised these shortcomings in its White

[66] Effective Problem Solving in the Internal Market (SOLVIT), COM(2001) 702 final.

[67] www.ec.europa.eu/solvit/.

[68] J Pelkmans, 'The New Approach to Technical Harmonization and Standardization' (1987) 25 *Journal of Common Market Studies* 249, 252–53; M Egan, *Constructing a European Market* (Oxford, Oxford University Press, 2001) at 78–81; N Burrows, 'Harmonisation of Technical Standards: Reculer Pour Mieux Sauter?' (1990) 54 *Modern LawReview* 597.

Paper,[69] and proposed a New Approach to Technical Harmonization and Standards.[70] There was to be mutual recognition through the *Cassis de Dijon* principle;[71] national rules which did not come within the mandatory requirements would be invalid. Legislative harmonisation was to be restricted to laying down health and safety standards; and there would be promotion of European standardisation.[72]

The principal bodies responsible for standardisation are the European Committee for Standardization (CEN),[73] the European Committee for Electrotechnical Standardization (CENELEC),[74] and the European Telecommunications Standards Institute (ETSI).[75] These bodies are private organisations, with CEN and CENELEC being non-profit technical organisations established under Belgian law in 1961 and 1973 respectively, and ETSI being a non-profit organisation set up under French law in 1986.

The detailed organisational structure varies as between the three bodies, but there are nonetheless common features. Thus, for example, in CEN there are 30 national members, which are the national standards organisations of the respective countries; they have voting rights in the General Assembly and Administrative Board of CEN and provide delegations to the Technical Board which defines the work programme. The precise status of the national standards organisations varies, but many are private enterprises.[76] It is the responsibility of the CEN National Members to implement European Standards as national standards, to distribute and sell them and to withdraw any conflicting national standards. There are seven associate members, which are European organisations, representing particular sectors of industry as well as consumers, environmentalists, workers, and small and medium-sized enterprises. They do not have voting rights in the CEN General Assembly, but can participate in policy discussion and sit on Technical Boards.

The essence of the standardisation process is as follows. A directive passed pursuant to the new approach to harmonisation will establish in general terms the health and safety requirements that the goods must meet. The setting of standards helps manufacturers prove conformity to these essential requirements.

[69] COM(85) 310, para 64.

[70] Bull EC 1–1985; www.newapproach.eu/.

[71] Case 120/78 *Rewe-Zentrale AG v Bundesmonopolverwaltung für Branntwein* [1979] ECR 649.

[72] Commission, Enhancing the Implementation of New Approach Directives, COM(2003) 240; Council Resolution of 7 May 1985 on a new approach to technical harmonization and standards, OJ 1985 C 136/1; Green Paper on the Development of European Standardisation: Action for Faster Technological Integration in Europe', COM(90) 456 final.

[73] www.cen.eu/cenorm/homepage.htm.

[74] www.cenelec.eu/Cenelec/Homepage.htm.

[75] www.etsi.org/WebSite/homepage.aspx.

[76] See, eg, in the UK, British Standards Institute, www.bsigroup.com/en/About-BSI/About-BSI-Group/BSI-History/; in Germany, Deutsches Institut fur Normung e. V. (DIN) www.din.de/cmd?level=tpl-home&contextid=din; in Italy, Ente Nazionale Italiano di Unificazione (UNI), www.cen.eu/cenorm/members/national+members/italy/index.asp; in Denmark, Dansk Standard, www.ds.dk/en-GB/Sider/default.aspx.

The relevant standardisation organ will formulate the technical standards, on the basis of which industry needs to manufacture products complying with the directives. These technical specifications are not binding as such and retain their character as voluntary European standards, but, the governments must assume that products manufactured in accordance with the European standards comply with the 'fundamental requirements' stipulated in the directive, thereby enhancing free market access. Thus, when a standard has been approved by the Commission and published in the Official Journal all Member States must accept goods which conform to it. If a Member State disputes whether the standard conforms to the directive's safety objectives, the burden of proof will be on the State to prove that this is so. While a manufacturer can still produce goods according to other standards, it has the burden of proof of showing that the goods meet the essential requirements in the directive. The Commission may request the standardisation organisations to develop standards in support of their policies by issuing formal 'mandates', but these bodies can also proceed without such a mandate.

The attractions of the new approach to harmonisation for the EU are considerable. Directives can be drafted more easily since they are less detailed. The manufacturers retain some choice as to whether to comply with the standards, but if they choose not to do so they have the burden of proving that their goods nonetheless comply with the essential health and safety requirements of the directive. The technical work of standard setting can be delegated to private bodies such as CEN, CENELEC and ETSI, which constitute networks of the national standardisation bodies and hence have technical expertise. Thus far approximately 30 such directives have been enacted based on the new approach or principles analogous thereto.[77] This may seem a small number, but each measure deals with a general product area, such as personal protective equipment, toys, construction products, explosives, medical devices and the like, and can therefore apply to hundreds or thousands of products that fall within the generic category.

There have been concerns as to the standardisation process, relating to matters such as the efficiency of the standardisation bodies, and the representation of consumer interests.[78] It is however clear from a political perspective that the EU

[77] www.ec.europa.eu/enterprise/newapproach/standardization/harmstds/reflist.html.

[78] B Farquhar, 'Consumer Representation in Standardisation' (1995) 3 *Consumer Law Journal* 56; K Armstrong and S Bulmer, *The Governance of the Single European Market* (Manchester, Manchester University Press, 1998) at 157–63; E Vos, *Institutional Frameworks of Community Health and Safety Regulation: Committees, Agencies and Private Bodies* (Oxford, Hart Publishing, 1999); C Joerges, H Schepel and E Vos, *The Law's Problems with the Involvement of Non-Governmental Actors in Europe's Legislation Processes: The Case of Standardisation,* EUI Working Paper 99/9; European Association for the Coordination of Consumer Representation, ANEC, *Consumer Participation in Standardisation* (ANEC, 2000); H Schepel, *The Constitution of Private Governance* (Oxford, Hart Publishing, 2005); The Broader Use of Standardization in Community Policy, COM(95) 412 final; General Guidelines for the Cooperation between CEN, CENELEC and ETSI and the European Commission and EFTA, OJ 2003 C91/04.

continues to regard standardisation as central to the attainment of the single market[79] and indeed for other policies.[80] There have been numerous initiatives designed to increase its effectiveness, including, inter alia:[81] expediting the standardisation process; improving the effective participation of all interested parties, which is recognised to be inadequate at EU level and within Member States;[82] addressing the financing of the standardisation bodies; and dealing with the relationship between EU and global standards.

Shared Administration: Regulatory Networks, Agency Creation and the Instrumental View of Networks

We have seen from the preceding discussion that the Commission is often supportive of national networks, nurturing them as the optimal way to enforce EU law. It should however also be acknowledged that the Commission's view of networks is 'instrumental' in two respects. Thus, on the one hand, if the agencies that constitute the network are perceived to have deficiencies then the Commission will not hesitate to intervene via formal legislation to strengthen them. On the other hand, if the network is not doing its job as identified by the Commission then it may be incorporated into an agency structure; the network may continue to exist, but it will be do so within a modified legal and political environment.

This is exemplified by developments in the energy sector. The regime for electricity is embodied in Directive 2003/54,[83] which replaced the earlier provision dating from 1996. The main aim of Directive 2003/54 is to complete the internal market in electricity and to expedite market liberalization. The Directive therefore establishes common rules for the generation, transmission, distribution and supply of electricity. It lays down rules for the functioning of the electricity

[79] www.ec.europa.eu/enterprise/standards_policy/index_en.htm.

[80] On the role of European standardisation in the framework of European policies and legislation, COM(2004) 674, at 4; www.ec.europa.eu/enterprise/standards_policy/role_of_standardisation/index.htm.

[81] COM(2004) 674, n 80 above; Towards an increased contribution from standardisation to innovation in Europe, COM(2008) 133; 2891st Competitiveness Council Meeting, 25 September 2008, available at www.ec.europa.eu/enterprise/standards_policy/standardisation_innovation/index.htm.

[82] COM(2004) 674, n 80 above, at 9; COM(2008) 133, n 81 above, at 8. The standardisation bodies are certainly keen to present themselves as fostering transparency and participation, www.cen.eu/cenorm/homepage.htm, but compare the views of ANEC, the body that represents consumer interests, www.anec.eu/anec.asp.

[83] Directive 2003/54/EC of the European Parliament and of the Council of 26 June 2003 concerning common rules for the internal market in electricity and repealing Directive 96/92, OJ 2003 L176/37. See also Directive 2005/89/EC of the European Parliament and of the Council of 18 January 2006 concerning measures to safeguard security of electricity supply and infrastructure investment, OJ 2005 L33/22. The analogous provision relating to gas is Directive 2003/55/EC of the European Parliament and of the Council of 26 June 2003 concerning common rules for the internal market in natural gas and repealing Directive 98/30, OJ 2003 L176/57.

sector, access to the market, the criteria and procedures for tenders, the granting of authorizations and the operation of the system. The market-orientation of the Directive is qualified by public service obligations to protect the customer.[84] National regulatory authorities have a central role in applying the Directive.

There were, however, real difficulties in breaking down barriers to trade between Member States and reforms introduced in 2007 were designed to remedy this problem. There were also institutional changes to reduce deficiencies in the national decision-making structure.[85] The powers of the national regulators have been strengthened, and a new agency created.

The rationale for the reforms relating to the national regulatory agencies is the variation between them across the Member States, with some being relatively weak, while others were strong. The Commission regarded strong regulators as necessary for a properly functioning internal market, and the reforms are directed towards ensuring that such authorities exist within the Member States, with the requisite financial independence to perform their tasks and increased powers overall.

The strengthening of national regulatory authorities is but one part of the 2007 reforms. The other is the creation of a new agency at EU level. There were, prior to the 2007 reforms, certain networks to foster discussion of cross-border issues, the Florence Forum for electricity[86] and the Madrid Forum for gas.[87] There was in addition an advisory group established in 2003, the European Regulators Group for Electricity and Gas (ERGEG),[88] composed of representatives of the national regulatory authorities. The ERGEG facilitates coordination and cooperation between the national regulatory authorities, and between them and the Commission.

The Commission was positive about the contributions of these self-regulatory networks, but it felt nonetheless that they had not produced common standards necessary to make 'cross-border trade and the development of first regional markets, and ultimately, a European energy market a reality'.[89] The Commission considered differing organisational options to cope with this problem. It rejected the idea that the matter should be done by the Commission itself, since it did not possess the requisite expertise. The Commission concluded that the tasks could be best undertaken by a separate entity, outside the Commission. This view was endorsed by the European Council and the European Parliament.

[84] Dir 2003/54, Art 3(9).

[85] Directive 2009/72/EC of the European Parliament and of the Council concerning common rules for the internal market in electricity, OJ 2009 L 211/55; Regulation (EC) 713/2009 of the European Parliament and of the Council of 13 July 2009 establishing an Agency for the Co-operation of Energy Regulators, OJ 2009 L211/1.

[86] www.ec.europa.eu/energy/electricity/florence/index_en.htm.

[87] www.ec.europa.eu/energy/gas/madrid/index_en.htm.

[88] www.ergeg.org/portal/page/portal/ERGEG_HOME/ERGEG.

[89] COM(2007) 530 final, at 9–10.

The Commission was careful to ensure that the new Agency for the Cooperation of Energy Regulators (ACER) fitted the established mould for EU agencies. The powers given to ACER therefore complement the tasks performed by national regulatory authorities. In more specific terms,[90] ACER provides a framework for national regulators to cooperate in order to improve the handling of cross-border situations, increase the exchange of information and the apportionment of competence where more than one Member State is involved. ACER is to exercise regulatory oversight of the cooperation between transmission system operators. The Agency will have responsibility for monitoring the activities of the European Network of Transmission System Operators for Electricity and of the European Network of Transmission System Operators for Gas. In relation to technical and market codes, the Agency will be empowered to ask transmission system operators to modify their drafts, or address issues in greater detail. ACER can recommend that the Commission make these codes legally binding where voluntary implementation by transmission system operators does not suffice. ACER is also to have individual decision-making powers in certain types of case, and a general advisory role, with the power to issue non-binding guidelines on good practice.

Shared Administration: Information Networks and Efficient Pooling of Knowledge

We have seen from Slaughter's analysis that information networks are common in the international arena. The EU provides many examples of this same phenomenon. Two examples from among many will suffice for present purposes.

The European Agency for Health and Safety at Work (EU-OSHA) provides a classic example of an agency with responsibility for information and coordination that works with and through a network of national agencies. In order to encourage improvements in the safety and health of workers the agency is charged with providing the EU, Member States, the social partners and those involved in the field with technical, scientific and economic information on workplace health and safety.[91] The information is intended to identify risks and good practices. The agency supplies the EU and Member States with such information as they require to implement effective policies to protect workers' health and safety, and provides such information to the Commission when it is preparing legislation.[92] In order to attain its goals EU-OSHA is instructed to set up a network comprising the main elements of national information networks,

[90] ibid, draft Arts 5–8.

[91] Council Regulation (EC) 2062/94 of 18 July 1994 establishing a European Agency for Safety and Health at Work, OJ 1994 L216/1, Arts 2, 3(1)(a)-(d), as amended by Council Regulation (EC) 1112/2005 of 24 June 2005, Amending Regulation 2062/94 establishing a European Agency for Safety and Health at Work, OJ 2005 L184/5.

[92] ibid, Art 3(1)(e).

including national social partners' organisations, national focal points and what are called future topic centres. Member States must inform the agency of their national health and safety information networks.[93]

The European Network and Information Agency (ENISA)[94] functions in a similar way. It was established because of the increased importance of communication networks and information systems, and to prevent them from being jeopardised by accident, attack and mistake. ENISA is therefore charged with provision of information concerning such risks and analysing ways of dealing with them, and assists the Commission with EU legislation. The enabling Regulation emphasises that ENISA should facilitate coordination between the EU and Member States on network security.[95] This is reflected in the organisational structure of ENISA, which works through two types of administrative network. There is a Permanent Stakeholders' Group (PSG) which is composed of national experts representing the relevant stakeholders, such as the Information and Communication Technologies industry, consumer groups and academic experts. The PSG advises the Executive Director as to ENISA's work programme.[96] The other network used by ENISA is the ad hoc working group, which gives advice on more technical and scientific issues. The framework for such working groups is in a decision of ENISA's management board.[97]

Shared Administration: Policy Formation, Policy Execution and the Open Method of Coordination

Networks are also a central feature of the Open Method of Coordination, OMC, which although it did not begin in 2000, was nonetheless given prominence by the Lisbon Summit in March 2000.[98] The EU was 'to become the most competitive and dynamic knowledge-based economy in the world, capable of sustainable economic growth with more and better jobs and greater social cohesion'.[99] The plan was in part economic, and in part social. There was to be education and training for those in the knowledge society, the development of an active employment policy, modernisation of social protection, and the promotion of social inclusion.

The implementation of this strategy was to be by 'improving the existing processes, introducing a new open method of coordination at all levels, coupled with a stronger guiding and coordinating role for the European Council to ensure

[93] ibid, Arts 3(1)(f), 4.

[94] Regulation (EC) 460/2004 of the European Parliament and of the Council of 10 March 2004, Establishing the European Network and Information Agency, OJ 2004 L77/1.

[95] ibid, Arts 2(1)–(3), 3.

[96] http://www.enisa.europa.eu/pages/01_02.htm; The PSG Vision for ENISA (2006), available at http://www.enisa.europa.eu/doc/pdf/news/psgvisionforenisafinaladoptedmay2006version.pdf

[97] http://www.enisa.europa.eu/doc/pdf/management_board/decisions/ad_hoc_wg.pdf

[98] Lisbon European Council, Presidency Conclusions, 23–24 March 2000.

[99] Ibid at para 5.

more coherent and strategic direction and effective monitoring of progress'.[100] The OMC was to be a decentralized process, with the Member States, regional and local government, the social partners and civil society actively involved.[101]

The general features of OMC were said to be:[102] fixing EU guidelines plus timetables for achieving the goals; establishing, where appropriate, quantitative and qualitative indicators and benchmarks against the best in the world to compare best practice; translating these European guidelines into national policies by setting targets and adopting measures; and periodic monitoring, evaluation and peer review organized as mutual learning processes.

The Lisbon approach was developed further at the Nice European Council in December 2000,[103] and was re-launched at the Brussels European Council in the March 2005 Summit.[104] Networks are integral to the OMC methodology. The emphasis on fostering deliberation, learning and discourse through exchange of best practice has generated formal and informal networks in the areas where the OMC technique has been applied.

SHARED ADMINISTRATION AND NETWORKS

There is an extensive literature on administrative interaction in the EU. It is generally agreed that much of this should be regarded in terms of shared administration, mixed administrative proceedings or composite administration, with little turning on the precise nomenclature adopted.[105] The discussion thus far has been agnostic about the utility of the label 'network' to evaluate forms of

[100] Ibid at para 7.
[101] ibid, at para 38.
[102] ibid. at para 37.
[103] Nice European Council, Presidency Conclusions, 7–9 December 2000.
[104] European Council, Presidency Conclusions, 22–23 March 2005.
[105] S Cassese, 'Il sistema amministrativo europeo e la sua evoluzione' (1991) *Rivista Trimestrale di Diritto Pubblico* 769; C Franchini, 'L'impatto dell'integrazione comunitaria sulle relazioni al vertice dell'amministrazione. Poteri governativi e poteri amministrativi' (1991) *Rivista Trimestrale di Diritto Pubblico* 775; E Schmidt-Aßmann, 'Verwaltungskooperation und Verwaltungskooperationsrecht in der Europäischen Gemeinschaft' (1996) *Europarecht* 270; S Cassese, 'La signoria comunitaria sul diritto amministrativo' (2002) *Rivista Italiana di Diritto Pubblico Comunitario* 291; E Chiti and C Franchini, *L'Integrazione Amministrativa Europea* (Bologna, Il Mulino, 2003); C Franchini, 'I principi applicabili ai procedimenti amministrativi europei' (2003) *Rivista Italiana di Diritto Pubblico Comunitario* 1037; S Cassese, 'Diritto amministrativo europeo e diritto amministrativo nazionale: signoria o integrazione?' (2004) *Rivista Italiana di Diritto Pubblico Comunitario* 1135; S Cassese, 'European Administrative Proceedings' (2004) 68 *LCP* 21; M Chiti, 'Forms of European Administrative Action' (2004) 68 *LCP* 37; G della Cananea, 'The European Union's Mixed Administrative Proceedings' (2004) 68 *LCP* 197; C Franchini, 'European Principles Governing National Administrative Proceedings' (2004) 68 *LCP* 183; E Chiti, 'Administrative Proceedings involving European Agencies' (2004) 68 *LCP* 219; P Craig, *EU Administrative Law* (Oxford, Oxford University Press, 2006), chs 1–7; S Cassese, 'Diritto amministrativo comunitario e diritti amministrativi nazionali', in M Chiti and G Greco (eds), *Tratatto di diritto amministrativo europeo* (Milano, Giuffrè, 2007), vol I at 1–13; H Hofmann and A Türk, 'The Development of Integrated Administration in the EU and its Consequences' (2007) 13 *ELJ* 253; E Schmidt-Aßmann, 'Introduction: European Composite Administration (*Verwaltungsverbund*) and the role of European administrative law' in O Jansen and B Schöndorf-Haubold (eds), *The*

administrative interaction in the EU. My view is that most such networks are best regarded as a sub-part of shared administration, as is apparent from the preceding discussion. This view is reinforced by the fact that the language of networks is embedded in the very nomenclature of certain EU organisations, and in EU primary law and official documentation, as well as being prominent in the secondary literature on political science.

It has been argued in the context of international administrative interaction that the concept of composite administration is a better lens through which to view forms of administrative interaction, and that it is preferable to both multi-level governance, which implies a top-down hierarchy, and network, which implies the absence of hierarchy.[106] This analysis relates to administrative interaction at the international level. It nonetheless warrants some comment when thinking about networks at the EU level.

There is however no a priori reason why the concept of multi-level governance necessarily insinuates a top-down hierarchy, or why the network concept connotes the absence of hierarchy. They may have such a connotation in literature concerning the disposition of power within Germany, but the concepts are not used predominantly in this way in the literature on international relations, or political science.[107] The concept of multi-level governance, whether at the international or EU level, is agnostic as to which players have the major input into policy development, and debate about the primary locus of this power for any particular policy area is often the subject of vibrant debate.[108] Nor is the literature on networks, whether at international or EU level, premised on an absence of hierarchy. The nature of power relations, de jure and de facto, within any particular network is a matter for analysis.[109]

Any disagreement on this issue is nonetheless more formal than substantive.[110] It is certainly true that mere invocation of the network concept tells one little

European Composite Administration (Mortsel, Belgium, Intersentia, 2008), ch 2; P Craig, 'Community Administration, History, Typology and Accountability' in M D'Alberti (ed), *Le nuove mete del diritto amministrativo* (Bologna, Il Mulino, 2010) 11–66.

[106] von Bogdandy and Dann, n 16 above, at 2018, 2034.

[107] It may be that the concepts have this connotation.

[108] See, eg, G Marks, L Hooghe and K Blank, 'European Integration from the 1980s: State-Centric v Multiple-Level Governance' (1996) 34 *Journal of Common Market Studies* 341; M Pollack, 'Regional Actors in Intergovernmental Play: The Making and Implementation of EC Structural Policy', in C Rhodes and S Mazey (eds), *The State of the European Community, Vol. 3: Building a European Polity* (London, Longman, 1995); T Risse-Kappen, 'Exploring the Nature of the Beast: International Relations Theory and Comparative Policy Analysis Meet the European Union' (1996) 34 *JCMS* 53; J Golub, 'State Power and Institutional Influence in European Integration: Lessons from the Packaging Waste Directive' (1996) 34 *JCMS* 313; J Caporaso, 'The European Union and Forms of State: Westphalian, Regulatory or Post-Modern' (1996) 34 *JCMS* 29; F Scharpf, 'The Problem Solving Capacity of Multi-Level Governance' (1997) 4 *Journal of European Public Policy* 520.

[109] See, eg, Slaughter, n 2 above; Kingsbury, Krisch and Stewart, n 13 above; M Pollack and G Shaffer (eds), *Transatlantic Governance in the Global Economy* (Boulder, Colorado, Rowman and Littlefield, 2001).

[110] The general analysis provided by von Bogdandy and Dann, n 16 above, is a valuable addition to the literature.

about the kind of network, the rationale for its establishment, and the disposition of power therein. These are matters for inquiry and analysis of the kind undertaken in the previous section. This is however equally true of concepts of shared administration, mixed administrative proceedings or composite administration. The reality is therefore that the same issues need to be considered whether through the language of network, or that of shared, mixed or composite administration. My own preference is, as stated above, to regard networks as a sub-part of the more general conception of shared or mixed administration.

NETWORKS AND THE EU: RATIONALE

Administrative Efficacy

An important rationale for EU networks is administrative efficacy. Many important parts of EU law are formally dependent upon shared administration, with the Commission and national authorities having complementary rights, powers and duties laid down by EU regulation and where both sides must fulfil their assigned role for the effective discharge of the relevant Treaty scheme. The efficacy of such regimes will depend upon close collaboration between national agencies, more especially where there is a significant cross-border dimension, and this is facilitated by a network.

Administrative efficacy and networks may also be pertinent where centralised administration prevails. The fact that the Commission is accorded centralised responsibility for a certain task does not mean that it will undertake the entirety in-house. It may use an executive agency, or decide that the optimal administrative strategy is a network of national agencies, which explains why the Financial Regulation makes provision for this option.[111]

Efficiency

A second rationale for the prevalence of networks is efficiency, which is closely related to the first, but nonetheless distinct. There are areas where the EU's competence is limited and where its actions will be confined to supporting or coordinating action taken by the Member States. There are other areas where even though the EU's competence is greater the tasks assigned to a particular branch of the administration, such as a an EU agency, are limited. Thus, as seen from the preceding analysis, many EU agencies perform what are primarily information gathering and coordination roles, to help both the Commission and the Member States.

[111] COM(2001) 648 final, n 27 above.

Networks are a prominent feature of such institutional regimes. Thus EU-OSHA will work through a network of national agencies to improve standards of health and safety at work, and it is common for there to be a network of national officials working with Community agencies to provide and coordinate information.

The sharing of information is clearly an efficient way to combat collective problems, whether those relate to security, health, racism or fundamental rights. It also enhances efficiency by facilitating the sharing of expertise in the salient area, enabling network members to draw on the experience of others as to ways of dealing with a specific problem, which is significant given the differential experience of national regulators, and the advent of new Member States.

Power

It would nonetheless be mistaken to assume that the rationale for networks is captured wholly by administrative efficacy or efficiency. We should recognise that power has also been an important factor for certain networks, the most prominent example being Comitology committees. Now to be sure it can be accepted that collaboration between the Commission and national experts may be helpful for the efficacious implementation of secondary norms produced by the Comitology process. It would however be blinkered to see this as constituting the entirety, or indeed, even the principal theme, of the Comitology story. If it were then the Member States might have rested content with advisory committees.

The rationale for management and regulatory committees was primarily because the Member States wished to influence the content of secondary norms in a way not provided for in the original Treaty. This was perfectly rational from the Member States' perspective, given that policy choices are not infrequently made or fine-tuned in such Comitology regulations. The fact that the committees' formal powers are used relatively rarely does not undermine their significance, since committee decision-making will take place in the shadow of these formal powers. This is so even if one subscribes to the view that Comitology decision-making is best regarded in terms of deliberative supranational governance. The bottom line is still that the creation, retention and extension of the Comitology regime have been markedly influenced by the disposition of power between the Member States in the Council, and the Commission.

Rational Delegation

There is an extensive literature on the rationale for delegating certain tasks to bodies outside the traditional bureaucracy:[112] it facilitates use of experts who are not part of the normal bureaucratic structure; it frees up the parent department to concentrate on strategic policy; it insulates resolution of technical regulatory issues from the vagaries of day-to-day political change and hence increases the credibility of the choices thus made.

There is moreover an emerging literature concerning the rationale for choosing a private agent as the delegate,[113] which is relevant for the delegation of standard setting to private networks in the EU. The primary reason is that the public body will often lack the requisite expertise, which would be costly to acquire, and even more costly to maintain. A further rationale for choosing a private agent is that it facilitates 'blame avoidance' and the 'shifting of responsibility' by the public authority, since delegation to a private agent creates a distance between it and the public authority. Thus the political benefits foregone by the public authority's not being able to claim direct credit for a successful standard will often be outweighed by the fact that it will avoid some of the blame if the relevant stakeholders are dissatisfied with the resultant standard.

Inclusion

A further rationale for networks is that they facilitate inclusion. Thus networks are viewed as one way of promoting inclusion in EU deliberation. This operates to varying degrees in the areas where the Open Method of Coordination applies. It is also a factor that explains what were termed Community support networks, the positive sponsorship for networks, such as those concerning consumer protection, which support EU policies.

Networks can foster such inclusion not only in instrumental terms, by enabling the relevant national players to participate with the expectation that the resultant EU norm will be better as a result, but also for non-instrumental reasons, by providing such players with some 'voice' in decision-making within the EU polity, irrespective of the precise causal relationship between their input and the resulting output.

[112] D Epstein and S O'Halloran, *Delegating Powers: A Transaction Cost Politics Approach to Policy Making under the Separation of Powers* (Cambridge, Cambridge University Press, 1999); M Thatcher and A Stone Sweet, 'Theory and Practice of Delegation to Non-Majoritarian Institutions' (2002) 25 *West European Politics* 1; M Pollack, *Engines of European Integration: Delegation, Agency and Agenda-Setting in the European Union* (London, Blackwell, 2003); W Mattli and T Büthe, 'Global Private Governance: Lessons from a National Model of Setting Standards in Accounting' (2005) 68 *LCP* 225.

[113] Mattli and Buthe, n 112 above, at 230–31.

NETWORKS AND THE EU: FEATURES

The identification of the rationales for networks in the EU is important; so too are the features of such networks.

'Institutional Orchestrator'

It is axiomatic that networks require creation. They do not spontaneously 'emerge' by magic or nature. Networks in the global order may nonetheless develop from a less structured form of meeting between the participants, as the result of the initiative of a particular state, from institutional needs within an international organisation or doubtless in a number of other ways.

There is however some contrast with the EU in this respect. This is because there will normally be an 'institutional orchestrator' within the EU, which will be the prime mover behind the establishment of a particular network, or even if the network existed hitherto the institutional orchestrator will have a considerable impact on its role. This is readily apparent from the preceding discussion.

The Commission has been the principal mover behind the establishment of many EU networks, especially the classic enforcement networks. It was the Commission that had first-hand experience of the difficulties of cross-border fraud and recognised the need for more formal collaboration between national agencies. The Commission's incentive for improvement was heightened because it was regularly criticised by the Court of Auditors when loss to EU funds was revealed.

The Commission's role as institutional orchestrator is also evident in other contexts. Thus the Commission has significant input into the creation of what was termed Community support networks. It has done much to orchestrate regulatory networks in the context of standardisation, determining the role played by the standardisation bodies. It was moreover the Commission that took the instrumental view of particular regulatory networks, not hesitating to enhance the network's powers by creating a new agency. The significance of the institutional orchestrator role played by the Commission is no surprise, given its role within decision-making and its overall responsibility for implementation of EU law.

It should not however be thought that it has a monopoly in this respect. The Council was the principal catalyst behind the creation of the networks that constitute Comitology. The European Council has also been of importance. The Lisbon strategy that developed the OMC originated in the European Council, and became an important topic for subsequent European Council meetings. The European Council and the Council have also taken a keen interest in some Community support networks, such as the EJN.

The fact that an institutional orchestrator will often exist does not imply that its power will be the same for all networks. That would be counter-intuitive given the heterogeneity that characterises this overall area. It does mean that the institutional orchestrator is able to: initiate changes in network relations where these are not working optimally, as exemplified by developments in the energy sphere; significantly alter the enforcement regime, with consequential implications for the powers of national networks, as in the case of competition; be proactive in the creation of support networks, as attested by the establishment of the EJN; and press for the formalisation of network powers in order to increase their efficacy, as exemplified by developments in consumer protection.

Formal and Informal

A second noteworthy feature of EU networks is that they vary considerably concerning their degree of formality.

At one end of the spectrum are networks formally established by regulation, with the members given formal legal powers to achieve the ends of the relevant enforcement or regulatory regime. The enforcement networks that exist in agriculture, customs and consumer protection exemplify this type of network regime.

At the other end of the spectrum are networks that may have no formal basis in EU law, where the establishment of the network and its powers are dependent on soft law. This typifies some, although by means all, of the networks which operate pursuant to the OMC.

There are moreover networks which fall somewhere along the preceding spectrum. Thus, for example, regulation may make provision for information networks within a particular area, while leaving much unsaid as to their more precise role. Or the existence and powers of the network may be recognised to some extent within formal law, while still leaving much of the network's practical operation to be supplemented by soft law, as with some other areas to which the OMC applies.

Public and Private

It is also clear that the members of the network may be public or private bodies, subject to constraints imposed by EU law, in particular through the 2002 Financial Regulation.

In many areas, the network members will be national public bodies. Thus the members of the enforcement networks which operate in relation to customs, agriculture, and consumer protection are national public authorities. This is also the case with many regulatory networks that apply EU law concerning utilities and telecommunications at national level. The paradigm once again is a national regulatory authority, which will be a public body in its own right.

In other areas, the network members will be private undertakings per se, or private undertakings with a public service mission. This captures, for example, the networks that administer the standardisation regime pursuant to the new approach to harmonisation. It also captures some of the support networks, such as ECC-Net, which have been sponsored by the Commission because they further the aims of important EU policies.

EU Courts

The EU courts may well be regarded as part of an enforcement network with national courts.[114] The very existence of an institutionalised system of adjudication is also of more general significance for the networks considered above, since it shapes the very way they operate. This is so for a variety of reasons, three of which are presented here.

Thus at the most basic level, the EU courts will adjudicate on formal legal networks to ensure that their powers are exercised in compliance with the precepts of judicial review. It should moreover be recognised that judicial review has a Janus-like quality. It can be used to ensure that network members remain within their assigned power. It also offers the ECJ and General Court the opportunity to interpret the relevant powers teleologically in order to effectuate the aims of the EU legislation.[115]

The EU courts will also play a role in deciding on the legitimacy and modus operandi of particular networks. Comitology would never have become the regime that it is today had the ECJ not rejected an early challenge to such committees.[116] The ECJ, while willing to consider the legality of the choice between management and regulatory committees, also boosted the Comitology regime by adopting a broad concept of implementation. Thus while the ECJ insisted that the primary norm should embody the 'essential elements' of the relevant matter, it interpreted this relatively loosely, thereby allowing a broad range of implementing measures to be adopted through regulations according to Comitology procedures from which the European Parliament (EP) was effectively excluded.[117]

The ECJ's judgments can moreover have a significant impact on the way in which networks operate, even if they are not given in the context of those networks. Thus the ECJ has held that the right to be heard does not apply to the making of legislative-type norms. They have therefore denied consultation rights unless they are expressly provided by a Treaty article, regulation, directive or

[114] Harlow and Rawlings, n 18 above.

[115] See, eg, Craig, n 19 above, at 277–79.

[116] Case 25/70, *Einfuhr- und Vorrasstelle für Getreide und Futermittel v Köster, Berodt & Co* [1970] ECR 1161. See also Case 23/75, *Rey Soda v Cassa Conguaglio Zucchero* [1975] ECR 1279; Case 5/77, *Carlo Tedeschi v Denkavit Commerciale Srl* [1977] ECR 1555.

[117] Case C-156/93, *European Parliament v Commission* [1995] ECR I-2019, at paras 18–22; Case C-417/93, *European Parliament v Council* [1995] ECR I-1185, at para 30.

decision governing the area.[118] This has important consequences for the operation of, for example, standardisation. There have been continuing problems about consumer groups, small and medium-sized enterprises and NGOs being able to contribute to the standardisation process, but they are precluded by the ECJ's jurisprudence from claiming that they ought to be accorded such consultation rights.

NETWORKS AND THE EU: LEGITIMACY AND ACCOUNTABILITY

It is important to reflect on legitimacy and accountability concerning network governance and administrative interaction in the EU. Limits of space preclude detailed treatment of these issues, since this could occupy a chapter in its own right. The objective is to convey the nature of the legitimacy and accountability issues applicable to the different kinds of networks.

Formal Networks and Formal Powers: Enhancing Legitimacy and Accountability

A paradox, which is more apparent than real, should be acknowledged at the outset: the most powerful networks, which include the classic enforcement networks, may be the most legitimate and accountable. The reason is not hard to discern. These networks were established by Community legislation, which specifies in detail the powers and duties of network members.

Thus judged in terms of input legitimacy, such networks fare well. The classic enforcement networks operating in customs, agriculture, consumer protection and competition were established by formal legislation enacted by the EP and the Council. Thus insofar as input legitimacy is determined by legislative assent in the manner specified by the particular legal system, these networks have it. They have received the imprimatur of the EU legislature.

These networks also fare relatively well in terms of accountability. The fact that the network regime is contained in a regulation normally renders it easier to understand the powers of network members, which are commonly specified in detail, hence promoting legal clarity, this being an important feature of the rule of law. The formal legal foundation for such networks also facilitates legal accountability and judicial review. It is clear in principle that acts of network members can be legally challenged for compliance with the Treaty, the enabling regulation, and general principles of EU law.

This does not of course mean that the regulations embodying such networks are immune from criticism. A commentator might feel that the powers given to network members are too extensive, or indeed that they do not go far enough. It might be argued that the powers are ineffective for the task at hand. This does not

[118] Case C-104/97 P, *Atlanta AG v Commission* [1999] ECR I-6983; Craig, n 19 above, ch 10.

however alter the preceding point, which is that formal regulations foster both input legitimacy and accountability.

Formal Networks and Formal Powers: Embedding Controversial Criteria

It should however also be acknowledged that the existence of formal networks with formal powers will not necessarily guarantee legitimacy or accountability. The reasons are instructive, as the Comitology example will make clear.

The Comitology regime enjoys input legitimacy, as judged by the criterion used above. Comitology committees will be established by an article in the enabling regulation that governs the particular area. Thus the common format is that where EU legislation regulates a new area it will make provision for a Comitology committee, which will oversee implementing regulations enacted by the Commission. This formal input legitimacy is further enhanced by the Comitology Decisions,[119] which contain the rules that govern advisory, management and regulatory committees, and provide indicia as to when each should be used.

The Comitology regime nonetheless remains controversial in terms of legitimacy. A legislative norm may well have input legitimacy in the formal sense that it is enacted in accord with the rules for the passage of that kind of legal norm, but it may embody and embed criteria that are open to criticism.

Thus the continuing debate concerning input legitimacy and Comitology is explicable in part because of the controversial nature of the criteria that govern committee deliberations in the Comitology Decisions of 1987 and 1999. The 1987 Decision[120] largely excluded the EP from any significant role in the passage of implementing regulations, since the technocrats on the committees were national appointees, and the EP had little say over the resulting measures. This was irksome to the EP, more especially after the creation of the co-decision procedure in the Maastricht Treaty, since it saw its victories from increased input into the making of primary EU norms being undermined by the fact that it had so little impact over implementing regulations. The 1990s was therefore a stormy decade, with numerous battles and skirmishes waged by the EP over this issue.[121] The 1999 Comitology Decision[122] improved the EP's input into implementing regulations, but it was still dissatisfied and pressed for further reforms that were finally forthcoming in 2006. The legal reality even now is that the EP is not an equal partner with the Council in relation to such measures.

The accountability of Comitology decision-making composed of networks of national technocrats working with the Commission has also been questioned.

[119] N 20 above.
[120] Decision 87/373, n 20 above.
[121] Bergstrom, n 19 above.
[122] Decision 99/468, n 20 above.

There have been longstanding concerns as to transparency. Many have questioned the role assigned to national technocrats in the framing of implementing regulations, contending that the issues are often as much political/social as they are technical, and that choices proffered by the technocrat incumbents may well conceal values that are implicit.[123] It remains unclear who is the agent and who is the master in these deliberations. The fact moreover that participation by interested parties in the shaping of Comitology norms is not fostered by the EU political or legal process, reduces the possibility of reinforcing legitimacy and accountability from the 'bottom', via consultation.[124]

Informal Networks, Hard Law and Soft Law: The Tension between Aspiration and Reality

There are, as seen above, networks that do not have a formal legal foundation, being the product of political choice from the EU political organs, and operating through soft law. The resultant issues concerning legitimacy and accountability may well vary between such networks, and their significance will be affected by the tasks that they undertake.

The concerns about legitimacy and accountability can nonetheless be exemplified in relation to the OMC. It should be noted at the outset that while OMC deliberations will normally take the form of recommendations rather than hard-edged legal norms, the picture of OMC as being purely soft law is nonetheless flawed. The governing instruments that frame the OMC will normally take the form of hard law. The framework for OMC in economic and employment policy is found in Treaty articles combined with EU legislation, and the same is true for the provisions on social exclusion, the difference being that the relevant Treaty article does not embody the OMC regime, this being set out in the form of a binding Decision.[125] The Treaty articles and legislation will often be couched in mandatory terms in relation to the procedure for coordination.[126]

The most pressing concern in relation to input legitimacy has been the marginalisation of the EP. It has been supportive of this mode of policy delivery, but has nonetheless voiced concerns about its use. Thus the Committee on Employment and Social Affairs stated that leaving aside employment, the areas

[123] Shapiro, n 5 above; C Harlow, *Accountability in the European Union* (Oxford, Oxford University Press, 2002) at 175; R Dehousse, 'Towards a Regulation of Transnational Governance? Citizen's Rights and the Reform of Comitology Procedures', in C Joerges and E Vos (eds), *EU Committees: Social Regulation, Law and Politics* (Oxford, Hart Publishing, 1999) at 111–14; J Weiler, 'Epilogue: "Comitology" as Revolution—Infranationalism, Constitutionalism and Democracy', in Joerges and Vos (eds), n 19 above, at 342–49.

[124] Craig, n 19 above.

[125] Decision 50/2002/EC of the European Parliament and of the Council of 7 December 2001 establishing a programme of Community action to encourage cooperation between Member States to combat social exclusion, OJ 2002 L10/1.

[126] See, eg, Arts 99 and 128 EC.

where the OMC was to be preferred to other executive instruments were not specified by the Treaty, by other regulatory provisions or by an interinstitutional agreement.[127] The choice of the OMC was 'taken on a case-by-case basis by the Council acting on a proposal from the Commission or on its own initiative'.[128] It felt that the EP was 'at risk of being marginalized or sidelined by these new political procedures'.[129] The Committee noted that the EP's role in OMC procedures was unspecified, with the exception of the EES, where it had a right to be consulted, but that its role in this area was severely constrained by time constraints.[130] It proposed that the OMC procedure should only be used in any policy area after the EP and the Council had given their approval. Similar concerns were voiced by the Committee on Economic and Monetary Affairs.[131]

There have also been concerns as to accountability. Limits of space preclude detailed treatment, but some issues can be touched on here. There has been disquiet as to transparency, which is clearly central to the OMC, both in itself and as a pre-condition for fostering participation, debate and the like. Doubts have been raised concerning transparency in relation to the employment and pensions OMC,[132] and more generally as to the transparency or opacity of the decision-making process itself.[133] It has been suggested that there should be an obligation that the OMC should be conducted as transparently as possible, so as to ensure the fullest participation of all relevant bodies.[134] Analogous concerns have been raised as to participation, which is once again central to the ideal of the OMC, connoting the idea that the process should be inclusive, not exclusive. Empirical evidence in the context of the European Employment Strategy has however found participation to be limited,[135] and the EP's Committee on Employment and Social Affairs voiced the opinion that 'as things stand, the open method of coordination is, in many cases, a process conducted between and on behalf of elites, the outcome of intergovernmental negotiation and bargain'.[136] There are also significant question marks as to the susceptibility of the OMC to judicial

[127] Committee on Employment and Social Affairs, Report on Analysis of the Open Coordination Procedure in the Field of Employment Social Affairs and Future Prospects, Rapporteur, Miet Smet, A5–0143/2003.

[128] ibid, Rec D.

[129] ibid, Rec G.

[130] ibid, Rec I.

[131] Committee on Economic and Monetary Affairs, On the Commission Communication on Streamlining the Annual Economic and Employment Policy Coordination Cycles, Rapporteur, Othmar Karas, A5–0400/2002, at 7, 10–11.

[132] C de la Porte and P Nanz, 'The OMC—A Deliberative-Democratic Mode of Governance? The Cases of Employment and Pensions' (2004) 11 *JEPP* 267, at 276–77.

[133] D Hodson and I Maher, 'The Open Method as a New Mode of Governance: The Case of Soft Economic Policy Co-ordination' (2001) 39 *JCMS* 719.

[134] G de Búrca and J Zeitlin, 'Constitutionalising the Open Method of Coordination: What Should the Convention Propose?' (2003) Centre for European Policy Studies Brief No 31.

[135] De la Porte and Nanz, n 132 above, at 278–79.

[136] Committee on Employment and Social Affairs, n 127 above, at 13.

review, and this is so notwithstanding the willingness of the EU courts to review EU norms in the form of guidelines and the like that are not formally binding.

Private Networks and Standardisation: Competing Visions

It should also be recognised that discussion of legitimacy and accountability may well be dependent upon prior assumptions as to how a particular area should be conceptualised. This may be contested by those who hold competing visions, with consequential implications for legitimacy and accountability. This can be exemplified by three contrasting views of private networks and standardisation.

We can begin with the Commission's 'official view'. The Commission emphasises its role in ensuring the efficiency, accountability and transparency of the standardisation process, which satisfies the needs of all stakeholders, while stressing that it does not determine the detailed content of the resulting standards. It accepts that governments do not have the requisite expertise to influence the content of standards, while stressing the governmental role in establishing the objectives and targets, leaving it to the standardisation bodies to decide on the content of the standards and the best way of meeting the governmental objectives.[137]

A second view regards the official regime as deficient in terms of legitimacy and accountability. It is argued that the regulatory regime is suspect since it entails delegation of power to private bodies, subject only to vague legislative standards, and hence violates the *Meroni* non-delegation doctrine,[138] a claim voiced most strongly by German authors.[139] The problem is then said to be compounded by: scant public control over the standardisation bodies; concerns over the lack of internal democracy therein;[140] and difficulties of rendering standards amenable to judicial review since they do not form an integral part of the directive. On this view the Commission's Green Paper from 1990,[141] while not perfect, was nonetheless a step in the right direction, since it proposed a Community institutional structure on the standardisation bodies to define the role of participants at national and EU level and allow for greater transparency

[137] DG Enterprise, Vademecum on European Standardisation, Standardisation and Governance (November 2003), available at www.ec.europa.eu/enterprise/standards_policy/vademecum/index.htm.

[138] Case 9/56, *Meroni & Co, Industrie Metallurgiche SpA v. High Authority* [1958] ECR 133; Craig, n 19 above, ch 5.

[139] See also Previdi, 'The Organization of Public and Private Responsibilities in European Risk Regulation: An Institutional Gap Between Them?', in C Joerges, K-H Ladeur and E Vos (eds), *Integrating Scientific Expertise into Regulatory Decision-Making-National Traditions and European Innovations* (Baden-Baden, Nomos, 1997) at 225.

[140] Joerges, Schepel and Vos, n 78 above, at 11.

[141] Commission Green Paper on the Development of Standardization: Action for Faster Technical Integration in Europe, COM(90) 456 final.

and participation of interested parties. The Green Paper was however defeated by an admixture of opposition from the standardisation bodies, and national governments.[142]

A third view is premised on different assumptions, with consequential implications for legitimacy and accountability. Proponents of this view reject what they regard as the unduly hierarchical and formalistic assumptions about legitimacy and accountability integral to the view adumbrated above. They maintain that while standardisation may be too important to be left entirely to the standardisation community, it is too complex a mixture of 'cognitive, normative and political aspects' to be taken over by administrators.[143] They do not contend that the existing regime is perfect, but argue that it is best conceived in terms of deliberative supranationalism.[144]

This is not the place to 'resolve' the debate between these contending views. Some comment is however warranted. The 'official view' is premised on the distinction between specification of essential objectives, to be determined by the EU legislature, and the delineation of standards to comply with those objectives. Subject to this, the Commission does not regard itself as setting the standards; in fact it goes out of its way to asseverate that it is not doing so.[145] The corollary is that although the 'new approach directives' allow Commission intervention in relation the standard set by CEN etc, this is not a power that the Commission uses often, so that emphasis is placed on process-based constraints on the standardisation bodies, rather than substantive control.

This is, from one perspective, predictable from the principal/agent literature. The Commission does not have the expertise to undertake standard setting, delegation to a private agent becomes rational, and the desire to 'avoid blame' is echoed in the Commission's forceful statement that it does not set the standards. The legitimacy of this conceptualisation is however crucially dependent on two variables.

There is the extent to which the EU legislature really does specify the essential objectives in the enabling directive. Such directives do contain a section or annex on such matters. But the devil is truly in the detail. A glance at 'new approach' directives indicates that the essential objectives are specified at some level of generality. Thus the essential requirements in the Construction Directive stipulate that construction must be carried out to prevent 'major deformations to an inadmissible degree', 'damage to an extent disproportionate to the original cause', 'the presence of dangerous particles or gases in the air' and the like.[146] The

[142] Joerges, Schepel and Vos, n 78 above, at 20–24.
[143] ibid, at 43.
[144] ibid, at 40–63; K-H Ladeur, 'Towards a Legal Concept of the Network in European Standard-Setting', in Joerges and Vos, n 19 above, ch 9.
[145] N 137 above.
[146] Council Directive 89/106/EEC of 21 December 1988 on the approximation of laws, regulations and administrative provisions of the Member States relating to construction products, OJ 1989 L40/12, Annex 1.

meaning of such phrases is necessarily open to a range of interpretations. The particular substantive meaning will be chosen by the standardisation body, and will embody a view as to what risks are deemed acceptable. Technical expertise may be a necessary component in this evaluation, but it is not sufficient, since the level of acceptable risk is not a purely technocratic inquiry. Nor is this conclusion altered if one views standardisation in deliberative supranational terms: even if one assumes that experts reach their decision in this manner, this does not alter the fact that they are making a choice concerning societal risk.

There is on the other hand the extent to which the standard-making procedures really are open to a wide constituency of stakeholders. Let us assume that the EU legislature could not realistically be more specific in stipulating the essential requirements. This nonetheless leaves considerable interpretative discretion to the standardisation bodies, and thereby increases the importance of transparency and procedural input from affected stakeholders. However in 2004 the Commission accepted that effective participation of interested parties did not yet exist at the EU standardisation level,[147] or within all Member States, and this was echoed in its latest Communication.[148] The difficulties of ensuring such access, and that certain players do not dominate the standard-setting process, should not therefore be underestimated.[149]

CONCLUSION

It is interesting to reflect by way of conclusion on the desiderata identified by Anne-Marie Slaughter for global networks in the light of EU experience with networks. Two points stand out in this respect.

First, there are clearly features of the EU that facilitate attainment of these desiderata. The enactment of hard law through an established legislative process enables deliberation as to the nature of the powers that should be afforded to network players, and greater transparency as to the result which is embodied in a formal EU norm. The EU courts are important to the system of checks and balances, and can impose administrative law constraints on network players. There are moreover features of EU law that allow legitimate difference to be taken into account, whether through differentiation, minimal harmonisation or by giving Member States choice of form and methods of implementation of a directive.

Second, there are however also aspects of the EU experience that give more pause for thought. EU legislation may well embody criteria for network inclusion that are controversial in terms of deliberative equality, as exemplified by Comitology and standardisation. More informal networks can lead to difficulties of

[147] COM(2004) 674, n 80 above, at 9.
[148] COM(2008) 133, n 81 above, at 8–9.
[149] Mattli and Büthe, n 112 above.

transparency and uncertainty as to the nature of the network's role in decision-making. The existence of an 'institutional orchestrator' may well have benefits, but it gives the holder of such power considerable influence in shaping EU networks. Moreover, while the EU courts can have a beneficial impact by imposing principles of administrative law on network players, judicial decisions can also reinforce questionable power hierarchies embodied in particular networks, either by, for example, legitimating such networks even though there may be shortcomings in terms of deliberative participation, or by refusing to accept that participation in rulemaking comes within general principles of EU law.

What is clear is that networks are an important feature of the administrative landscape in the EU. They are recognised in formal EU norms, and in much official EU documentation, as well as secondary literature. They are properly to be regarded as a sub-part of the shared administration/mixed proceedings/composite administration, which characterises much of the interaction between the EU and the Member States. The challenge is to ensure that such networks are legitimate and accountable within the overall scheme of EU governance.

5

Principles of an International Order of Information

EBERHARD SCHMIDT-AẞMANN

INTRODUCTION

OUR CENTRAL ISSUE—VALUES in global administrative law—is fascinating and precarious at the same time: it is *fascinating* since matters of values hit the core of any legal order (there is no law without values); and it is *precarious* since the notion of values is to a high degree undetermined and vague.

It is easy to reach a consensus on transparency, social equality or accountability as values of global administrative law. But it is far more difficult to define their exact meaning and in what way they are to be accentuated in a multi-level legal order or in global governance structures. I shall refer to this as the issue of definition of values.

The difficulty of defining values, well known in a national framework, is even more distinct in the global context: global administrative law cannot be established exclusively on values originating in the European and American legal cultures. Legal thinking of other cultures must be integrated as well. Highly-developed legal orders and progressive legal scholars may, of course, act as a driving force on the way to a global administrative law. Its concept as 'global' law will however be theoretically and practically mistaken if we do not make the effort to learn the values and legal thinking of other major, particularly Asian and South American, states which already play a role in global governance structures and will do so to an even greater extent in future. The challenge is to find comparable criteria according to which values are to be defined. This shall be referred to as the issue of sufficient diversity of cultural aspects.

In view of the large scope and indefinite nature of values, in this chapter I shall pursue a more precise approach: I shall not deal with values as such, but rather with 'principles', by which I understand values that have acquired a certain shape in their respective legal orders. Instead of analysing theoretical constructs I have preferred to gain insight by examining international treaties and conventions as well as recommendations by international organisations, including soft law. The material contained in these legal texts is to be analysed and put into a system. Of particular interest in this respect have proven to be multilateral treaties for they depict the legal practice of many States. With due caution, one can develop from the involved regulations *by means of an analogy* principles that can be applied in other legal contexts. This process is common to national administrative law. In the context of global administrative law this process is somewhat more complicated. Nonetheless, orientation on legal texts constitutes a sound basis since it leaves little space to purely theoretical speculation. Whilst the 'top down' and the 'bottom up' are the two most common approaches in global administrative law, I have chosen a third approach that is to be based as much as possible on positive law.

AN ORDER OF INFORMATION

In the following, I shall examine principles of an order of information. I have focused intentionally on the information issue.

– Traditionally, administrative law has aimed at reaching administrative decisions and their judicial control. We are used to deal with administrative decisions, legal remedies and the role of the courts.[1]
– In global administrative law a different approach will be required: international administrative relations and networks of global governance have been shaped by informality far stronger than national administrative law has (ever) been. Rather than by decisions of administrative bodies of a specific legal character this field is dominated by agreements, dissemination of information and concrete action of diverse actors. Apart from informality, a lack of judicial control has become apparent. There are some fields, eg WTO law, in which courts and court-like arbitration and litigation tribunals play an important role. However, such a dominant position as courts have taken in national and European administrative law has not been known to global administrative law so far and will not be in the near future either.

Hence, global administrative law is not decision-driven, nor court-oriented, but rather information-based. The major action modus of global governance has been collecting, processing and forwarding information. That means: it is necessary to examine which rules determine handling of information by the diverse actors.[2]

[1] E Schmidt-Aßmann, *Das Allgemeine Verwaltungsrecht als Ordnungsidee*, 2nd edn (Berlin, Springer 2004) at 277–375.

[2] E Schmidt-Aßmann, 'Die Herausforderung der Verwaltungsrechtswissenschaft durch die Internationalisierung der Verwaltungsbeziehungen' (2006) 45 *Der Staat* 315, 333; E Schmidt-Aßmann, 'The Internationalization of Administrative Relations as a Challenge for Administrative Law Scholarship' (2008) 9(11) *German Law Journal* 2061, 2074.

- How do the actors obtain information and to what extent are they authorised or obliged to pass this information to other actors?
- Who guarantees the quality of information obtained and who is authorised to revise it?
- Is the acquired information in general publicly available or does the non-disclosure principle apply?

These are elementary issues to be dealt with by global administrative law. It is to be analysed, first, whether there are common principles applicable to handling information and, second, which instruments and schemes for implementation of these principles are provided for by positive law. I shall discuss this using the examples of data protection (section 3) and free access to records (section 4)—the two pillars of an international order of information.

DATA PROTECTION

Rules on protection of personal data nowadays belong to the core stock of international public law.[3] They are meant to provide for standards applicable to transborder data exchange by national administrations. Such rules can be found mainly in bilateral and multilateral treaties, for example, in double taxation agreements and in agreements on cooperation in social security matters. Conventions and recommendations by international organisations are also important in this respect. Some early examples are the Convention for the Protection of Individuals with regard to Automatic Processing of Personal Data adopted by the Council of Europe in 1981[4] and the OECD Guidelines on the Protection of Privacy and Transborder Flows of Personal Data adopted in 1980.[5] Both documents lay down general principles of data protection and provide guidelines as to how these principles are to be abided by in the specific situation of transborder cooperation. Emphasis is laid on the human rights aspect and the requirement of transborder data flows which are as unhindered as possible. A modern and comprehensive regulation of the issue is the International Convention on Mutual Administrative Assistance in Customs Matters (so called Johannesburg-Convention),[6] although it has been signed by only a few States so far. In effect similar regulations have been established in a Memorandum of Understanding by

[3] Herbert Burkert, 'Internationale Grundlagen' in Alexander Roßnagel (ed), *Handbuch Datenschutzrecht* (Munich, Beck Juristischer Verlag, 2003) at 85–130.

[4] Convention for the Protection of Individuals with regard to Automatic Processing of Personal Data, 28 January 1981, EuropTS No 108.

[5] Recommendation of the Council Concerning Guidelines Governing the Protection of Privacy and Transborder Data Flows, OECD, 23 September 1980.

[6] International Convention on Mutual Administrative Assistance in Customs Matters, Arts 24–41, 27 June 2003.

national authorities cooperating in financial matters in the International Organisation of Security Commissions (IOSCO).[7]

A particularly interesting field is that of police law.[8] Police authorities very often deal with highly sensitive data. At the same time they are the most distinct representatives of national sovereignty. Rules on data protection can be found, for example, in bilateral police agreements, for example, in Articles 26 to 28 of the Swiss-German Police Agreement of 1999.[9] Multilateral regulations are contained in the Convention implementing the Schengen Agreement (Articles 126–130),[10] which is referred to in other agreements, for example, the German-French police agreement. Other complex regulations of data protection have been adopted in the Europol Convention (Articles 13–25).[11] Interpol has its own set of Rules adopted in 2003,[12] which, however, rank as soft law only.[13]

Data protection has been a major issue not only regarding administrative relations of European States or States of similarly liberal administrative traditions. Comparable regulations can be found also in treaties with States whose attitude to privacy and the rule of law has not been quite as pronounced in other respects. This can be exemplified by the readmission agreements between the EU and States like the Ukraine, Russia and China (in relation to Hong Kong)[14] or between Germany and the Syrian Arab Republic.[15] It is not essential whether such States apply data protection to purely national administrative procedures. As far as international intercourse is concerned they are in any case obliged to guarantee such protection and to accept the principles laid down in the treaties. Possibly, international law has a spill-over effect in the national legal

[7] Multilateral Memorandum of Understanding Concerning Consultation and Cooperation and the Exchange of Information, IOSCO, May 2002.

[8] B Schöndorf-Haubold, 'Internationale Sicherheitsverwaltung' in H-H Trute, T Groß, HC Röhl, C Möllers (eds), *Allgemeines Verwaltungsrecht—zur Tragfähigkeit eines Konzepts* (Tübingen, Mohr Siebeck Gmbh & Co. K, 2008) at 575–612.

[9] Vertrag zwischen der Bundesrepublik Deutschland und der Schweizerischen Eidgenossenschaft über die grenzüberschreitende polizeiliche und justitielle Zusammenarbeit [Agreement on cross-border cooperation in police and justice matters] 27 April 1999, Switz-FRG, Arts 26–28, 2001 BGBl. II 946, 955.

[10] Convention Implementing the Schengen Agreement of 14 June 1985 on the Gradual Abolition of Checks at Their Common Borders, 19 June 1990, Arts 126–130, 2000 OJ (L 239) 19, 50–52.

[11] Convention Based on Article K3 of the Treaty on European Union, on the Establishment of a European Police Office (Europol Convention), 27 November 1995, Arts 13–25, 1995 OJ (C 316), 2–32.

[12] Resolution AG-2003-RES-04, adopted by the General Assemby of Interpol, 2003, amended by Resolution AG-2005-RES-15, www.interpol.int/Public/ICPO/LegalMaterials/constitution/info/default.asp.

[13] B Schöndorf-Haubold, 'The Administration of Information in International Administrative Law—the Example of Interpol' (2008) 9(11) *German Law Journal* 1719, 1733.

[14] Agreement between the European Community and Ukraine on the Readmission of Persons, 18 June 2007, Art 13, 2007 OJ (L 332) 48; Agreement Between the European Community and the Russian Federation on Readmission, 25 May 2006, Art 17, 2006 OJ (L 129) 40; Agreement between the European Community and the Government of the Hong Kong Special Administrative Region of the People's Republic of China on the Readmission of Persons Residing without Authorisation, 24 January 2004, Art 15, 2004 OJ (L 17) 29.

[15] Agreement on Readmission, 14 July 2008, Syria-F.R.G, Art. 5, 2008 BGBl. II 811, 813.

orders of these States. But it would be better to remain realistic and note that sceptics will have their doubts regarding the implementation of data protection provisions in those countries. At least, the treaties mentioned above go some way to providing for special control schemes.

Western countries must be warned against arrogance. Even States of a liberal and democratic tradition can turn into problem cases in matters of data protection. I am talking here about the United States (US) and their 'War Against Terror'. It is true that data protection follows different concepts in Europe and the US. Nonetheless, what occurred during the negotiations on the Agreement on the processing and transfer of passenger name record 2006/2007 was more than a disparity of concepts. The negotiations exposed an elementary distrust of the Europeans towards handling data protection by the United States Department of Homeland Security (DHS). The Europeans gave their consent only upon an explanation by the DHS of its practice of handling data and giving respective guarantees.[16]

So, which principles do apply to transborder data flows? Two models can be identified:

(a) Under the harmonisation model, the participants, as a rule states, are obliged to adjust their respective legal orders to uniform substantive principles. Accordingly, Article 5 of the Council of Europe Convention reads as follows:

Personal data undergoing automative processing shall be:

- obtained and processed fairly and lawfully;
- stored for specified and legitimate purposes and not used in a way incompatible with those purposes;
- adequate, relevant and not excessive in relation to the purposes for which they are stored;
- accurate and, where necessary, kept up to date;
- preserved in a form which permits identification of the data subjects for no longer than is required for the purpose for which those data are stored.

Similarly, the OECD Recommendation of 1980 mentions and explains the following principles:

- Collection Limitation Principle: 'There should be limits to the collection of personal data and any such data should be obtained by lawful and fair means and, where appropriate, with the knowledge or consent of the data subject';
- Data Quality Principle: 'Personal data should be relevant to the purposes for which they are to be used, and, to the extent necessary for those purposes, should be accurate, complete and kept up-to-date';
- Purpose Specification Principle: 'The purposes for which personal data are

[16] Agreement on the Processing and Transfer of Passenger Name Record (PNR) Data by Air Carriers to the United States Department of Homeland Security (DHS) (2007 PNR Agreement), 23 July 2007, EU-US, 2007 OJ (L 204) 18.

collected should be specified not later then at the time of data collection and the subsequent use limited to the fulfilment of those purposes or such others as are not incompatible with those purposes and as are specified on each occasion of change of purpose';
- Use Limitation Principle: 'Personal data should not be disclosed, made available or otherwise used for purposes other than those specified in accordance with Paragraph 9 except: (a) with the consent of the data subject; or (b) by the authority of law';
- Security Safeguards Principle: 'Personal data should be protected by reasonable security safeguards against such risks as loss or unauthorised access, destruction, use, modification or disclosure of data';
- Openness Principle: 'There should be a general policy of openness about developments, practices and policies with respect to personal data. Means should be readily available of establishing the existence and nature or personal data, and the main purposes or their use, as well as the identity and usual residence of the data controller';
- Individual Participation Principle: 'An individual should have the right: (a) to obtain from a data controller, or otherwise, confirmation of whether or not the data controller has data relating to him; (b) to have communicated to him, data relating to him (i) within a reasonable time (ii) at a charge, if any, that is not excessive (iii) in a reasonable manner and (iv) in a form that is readily intelligible to him; (c) to be given reasons if a request made under subparagraphs (a) and (b) is denied, and to be able to challenge such denial; and (d) to challenge data relating to him and, if the challenge is successful, to have the data erased, rectified, completed or amended';
- Accountability Principle: 'A data controller should be accountable for complying with measures which give effect to the principles stated above'.

A comprehensive harmonisation of national law according to this model would establish a uniform protection standard and remove the problems of transborder data flow to the margins. However, such a far-reaching solution often is not possible.

(b) This is encountered by the second model that makes data flow dependent on the existence of an 'adequate level of protection'. Such regulation has been codified, for example, in the EC Directive on the protection of personal data with regard to transfer to third countries.[17] Reaching the required level of protection is subject to control by the transferring State; respective statements by the EC Commission are of general validity. What level of protection is adequate depends on the type of data, relevant legal practice and other factors. Often, the 'more sensitive' party will try to have further principles agreed on in order to reach a

[17] European Parliament and Council Directive 95/46/EC on the Protection of Individuals with Regard to the Processing of Personal Data and on the Free Movement of Such Data, Art 25, 24 October 1995, 1995 OJ (L 281) 31.

minimum harmonisation. This was the case, for example, in the negotiations preceding the above mentioned readmission agreements signed by the EU.

In general, there are a number of established principles applicable to protection of personal data in international legal relations. Among these, the purpose specification principle has acquired almost universal relevance. These principles can be denoted as constituents of global administrative law. They determine the practice of the cooperating parties in the framework for which they are intended. Moreover, the same contracting parties can resort to them when searching for solutions in comparable situations. Transferring these principles to administrative relations between other actors is, however, only possible if those actors are also obliged to obey by certain common rules such as privacy protection according to Article 8 ECHR[18] 'Data protection has indeed proven to be a global concept—even though with local variants', according to Burkert.[19]

FREEDOM OF INFORMATION

There is far less to be said about freedom of information. This second pillar of an order of information for international administrative law is still to be built. So far, the general access to information stored by administrations has been determined by the respective administrative tradition. In the 1980s, the Organisation for Economic Co-operation and Development (OECD) failed in its attempts to improve the access to documents maintained by administrations.[20] Nowadays, there has been stronger impetus to secure free access to data on an international level. Here, the EU has set the pace, for example, in the field of environmental law. Recently, international treaties such as the Aarhus Convention under ECOSOC have played a similar role.[21] Some international organisations have also increasingly promoted a policy of disclosure of information, for example, the World Bank and the UN-Development-Programme.[22] This process will go on. An informed public is regarded as an essential element of civil society. Here, the discourse will have to focus on the general issue of values first.

Specific transborder problems arise at points where different administrative cultures meet each other. Generally speaking, a national authority is not entitled to provide to the public information which it has obtained from an authority of a State whose legal order follows the non-disclosure principle.

[18] European Convention of Human Rights.

[19] Burkert, n 3 above.

[20] Burkert, n 3 above.

[21] Convention on Access to Information, Public Participation in Decision-Making and Access to Justice in Environmental Matters (Aarhus Convention), 25 June 1998.

[22] The World Bank, *The World Bank Policy on Disclosure of Information*, June 2002, www1.worldbank.org/operations/disclosure/documents/disclosurepolicy.pdf; United Nations Development Programme, *UNDP and Civil Society Organizations: A Practice Note on Engagement*, www.europeandcis.undp.org/files/uploads/Povertyr%20reduction/UNDP%20policies%201.pdf.

CONCLUSIONS

Having said this, I return to my opening statement: the issue of values in global administrative law is a fascinating, but precarious one. The matters examined in this chapter are also concerned with values. The principles of data protection are concrete derivations of human rights, in particular the right to privacy provided by Article 12 of the UN's Declaration of Human Rights and in Article 8 EHRC.[23] With respect to the general access to records I would name the principles of democracy and transparency as the essential values.

Since values are to a high degree indefinite, they are unfit for solving specific problems and cases of administrative law. They require specification through principles. As far as protection of personal data is concerned, this has now been achieved to a high degree not only on national but also on international level. It is essential to derive the principles from existing legal material. Legal material can be found not only on global level but first of all in bilateral treaties between states and in recommendations by organisations with a local scope of activity.

Talking about 'global administrative law', we disregard regional and local aspects. The denotation as 'global' is also somewhat misleading insofar as it does not express that, in spite of globalisation, nation states have remained the major actors in the governance structures. Therefore, the notion of international administrative law is more appropriate.[24] It comprises all levels of international administrative activities, including States as well as international organisations and their administrative tribunals.

The jurisdiction of all these taken together constitutes a rich source of developing principles of international administrative law. This was stated impressively by Spyros Flogaitis at the Conference of the European Group of Public Law in 2005:[25]

> The rules put forth by international administrative tribunals which contain all the wisdom of administrative law created in the various legal systems around the globe, must be studied fully and in depth in order to produce the rules and general principles of law as a feed back for the daily running of the administration of international organisations. Very important work has been done by international lawyers specializing in international organisations. It is about time for regular administrative lawyers to reorient their scientific forces in this direction.

[23] *Leander v Sweden*, 26 March 1987, § 48, ECHR A 116; *Rotaru v Romania*, 4 May 2000, § 43, 63 Rep 2000-V.

[24] Eberhard Schmidt-Aßmann, 'Die Herausforderung der Verwaltungsrechtswissenschaft durch die Internationalisierung der Verwaltungsbeziehungen' (2006) 45 *Der Staat* 315, 327; Eberhard Schmidt-Aßmann, 'The Internationalization of Administrative Relations as a Challenge for Administrative Law Scholarship' (2008) 9(11) *German Law Journal* 2061, 2067.

[25] S Flogaitis, 'Administrative Law of International Organizations—With Special Regard to the United Nations' (2006) 18 *European Review of Public Law* 271, 286.

6

Possible Controls over the Bending of Regulatory Science

PETER L STRAUSS*

INTRODUCTION

'BELLEROPHON TAMING PEGASUS', the monumental statue shadowing the formal entrance to Columbia Law School, states in metaphor the tension that motivates this piece. Nominally it reflects reason taming unreason, which is the role that law claims in society. One knowing a bit of its history sees more. Commissioned in the early 1960s, its earliest sketches reflected a proportion and a distance between man the master and the winged horse of unreason suggesting optimism that the outcome was secure. The golden bridle would do its work and reason would prevail. As the early 1960s became the late 1960s, Pegasus grew in the sketches, Bellerophon shrank, and ultimately the two merged. Now Pegasus was Bellerophon's own head; the bridle was around his own neck; the horse's expression of pain and rage was his own. And as Bellerophon could never completely tighten the noose around his own neck if he wished to live, one knew that the struggle could not be resolved. Reason and unreason continuously contend. What a metaphor for the project of law!

In particular, what a metaphor for the continuing tensions between objective ('scientific') and political inputs to regulatory decision-making. For science as for law, the ambition is for 'reason', for analysis as free as it can be of the influence of 'man'. Here's a strong statement of that position, that might be taken as scientists' equivalent of 'government of laws and not of men'.

> Science is, and can only be, descriptive and explanatory. Whether a scientific finding is judged to be accurate is dependent on the quality and rigor of the methods used and

* Betts Professor of Law, Columbia Law School, Columbia University, New York, NY. This chapter, first shown in draft to the conference on global administrative law in whose volume it appears, has gained much from colleagues at the European University Institute, the Universities of Sydney, Melbourne, Victoria, and Auckland and the Australian National University, where I was privileged to visit and present it, and also from able research assistant, Andrew Amend, Columbia 2008. Current through the fall of 2009, it remains very much a work in progress, during changing times.

> whether that finding is replicable. The scientific process is not democratic—no amount of desire for different results can establish them—and inconsistent findings create true controversy only when their methods are of comparable validity.[1]

Of course it is equally futile. For science as for law, 'man' *cannot* be eliminated. Judgements must be made in inevitable arenas of uncertainty—judgements that will be shaped by human predispositions and heuristics that need hardly correspond to the realities they seek to describe. And beyond these unavoidable human difficulties lie the incentives that in so many contexts twist human behaviours in ways that law seeks to control—greed for profit and lust for power central among them. The issue, then, is somehow giving the objective or perhaps one should just say the open side of scientific endeavour purchase—elevating judgement, suppressing simple will.

The American regulatory landscape has been littered with efforts to distort or suppress information relevant to the responsibilities of federal agencies responsible for protecting health, safety or the environment on the basis of sound science. While these efforts have a long historical pedigree—consider the industrial practices respecting such hazards as silicosis, tobacco and asbestos, or government behaviours in respect of nuclear weapons testing[2] or the Tuskeegee experiment[3]—recent times have seen them take particular prominence. Drug company failures to, for instance, alert regulators respecting hazards created by their products spread across the pages of two recent books describing a variety of means that have been used in the service of distorted outcomes: creation of research to produce intended outcomes; suppression of unwanted information; discrediting reliable research; interfering with the careers of those who produce unwanted information; and public relations campaigns.[4] 'The editors of our best international scientific and medical journals', one reports, 'are chagrined by their inability to weed out unreliable research emerging from a funding regime that is increasingly driven by the expectation of future economic gain.'[5] Within the science community, they suggest, organised insistence on recreating the conditions for honest inquiry will require such measures as mandatory disclosures of all financial interests (conflict of interest reporting) and the development of techniques for data-sharing that permit peer review while diminishing opportunities for harassment and other inappropriate behaviours—along with vigilant self-policing regimes. The situation, one might say, reflects only an ordinary

[1] JD Kraemer, LO Gostin, 'Science, Politics, and Values: The Politicization of Professional Practice Guidelines' (2009) 301(6) *Journal of the American Medical Association* 665–67 available at www.jama.ama-assn.org/cgi/content/full/301/6/665.

[2] www.hss.energy.gov/healthsafety/ohre/roadmap/experiments/index.html; www.historytogo.utah.gov/utah_chapters/utah_today/nucleartestingandthedownwinders.html.

[3] www.cdc.gov/tuskegee/timeline.htm.

[4] TO McGarity and WE Wagner, *Bending Science: How Special Interests Corrupt Public Health Research* (Cambridge MA, Harvard University Press, 2008); D Michaels, *Doubt is Their Product: How Industry's Assault on Science Threatens Your Health* (Oxford, Oxford University Press, 2008).

[5] McGarity and Wagner, n 4 above, at 229–30.

instance of a particular community's need to identify and suppress deviant behaviours that threaten its integrity and values. Theft and fraud, too, are social problems and we develop law and institutions to secure our sense of social honesty. But it is not, of course, simply an intra-community affair. The public consequences of distortion may be quite severe.

Similar alarms were widespread about the Bush administration's treatment of scientific issues. In what one journalist-reporter characterised as 'The Republican War on Science',[6] battles ranged over such disparate issues as global warming, day-after contraception, endangered species protection, environmental hazard regulation and politicised controls of advisory committee membership. Sixty-two prominent scientists issued a remarkable call for 'Restoring Scientific Integrity in Policy-Making' in February of 2004.[7] Thousands more signed it subsequently, and the signatories included 52 Nobel laureates, 63 National Medal of Science recipients, and 195 members of the National Academies.[8] A more recent journalist's account, 'Undermining Science: Suppression and Distortion in the Bush Administration',[9] suggested that little changed in its wake.

Politics certainly infected these alarms. The Union of Concerned Scientists, that catalysed both the petition and the more recent book, is not a neutral body. Conservative authors and columnists have persuasively pointed to similar episodes in Democrat administrations,[10] and the literature on science, policy and

[6] C Mooney, *The Republican War on Science* (New York, Basic Books, 2005).

[7] The text can be found on the website of the Union of Concerned Scientists, www.ucsusa.org/scientific_integrity/abuses_of_science/scientists-sign-on-statement.html.

[8] www.ucsusa.org/scientific_integrity/solutions/big_picture_solutions/prominent-statement-signatories.html.

[9] S Shulman, *Undermining Science: Suppression and Distortion in the Bush Administration* (Berkeley and Los Angeles, University of California Press, 2008).

[10] 'For the sake of argument, let's assume that the Bush administration has done all that UCS accuses it of doing. This problem is not particular to Republican administrations—the very linkage of government and science almost guarantees some chicanery. Let's recall the halcyon days of the Clinton administration. In 1993, Princeton University physicist William Happer was fired from the Department of Energy because he disagreed with Vice President Al Gore's views on stratospheric ozone depletion. In 1994, President Bill Clinton rejected the finding from the Embryo Research Panel of the National Institutes of Health which declared that the intentional creation of human embryos for genetic research was ethical. Clinton simply banned any federal funding for such research.

And in 1993, the EPA used a meta-analysis of a number of studies to find that second-hand smoke caused lung cancer in adult non-smokers and serious respiratory problems in children. That may well be, but the EPA had to put its thumb on the scales in order to get the result it wanted. The agency included just 11 out of 30 known studies on second-hand smoke in its meta-analysis, and even then found no increased risk to non-smokers at the 95 percent confidence level that had been the traditional agency standard. So the agency simply moved the confidence level from 95 percent to 90 percent in order to get the result it wanted.

At the time, I talked to a member of the EPA's scientific advisory board, an epidemiologist working at a leading east coast university who requested anonymity. He told me that he knew it was inadvisable to change the confidence level. He didn't oppose the change, though, because he was afraid he would be kicked off the board if he didn't go along. "I wanted to remain relevant to the policy process", he explained. He was also an EPA grant recipient.' Ronald Bailey, 'Why government isn't the best place to look for unbiased science', reasononline, www.reason.com/news/show/34774.html, (3 March 2004), visited 10 March 2009. And see the NY Times columns and posts to this point

politics is rich with suggestions that the economic importance and political salience of science and technology issues makes them inevitable.[11] As in the case of stem cell research, disputes may often really be about values (eg, the sanctity of human life, understood to begin at conception) rather than science as such, although what one author describes as 'stealth advocacy' may often invoke ostensible science in their support.[12]

One may add that a Republican administration encounters a civil service likely to be much less sympathetic to its preferences than a Democratic one.[13] Disregard for the work of the civil service could be seen as an understandable reaction to civil servants' resistance to legitimate political direction.

Still, it is striking that the two administrations prior to that of President Bush, one Republican and one Democratic, found about as many occasions to invoke the Endangered Species Act *each year* as the most recent Bush administration did through its whole term in office[14]—and when the latter did invoke it, that was largely under judicial compulsion. Nor had any prior presidency been so marked by the repeated, anguished phenomena of lifetime government scientists resigning jobs that they had not been permitted to serve in integrity, with repeated accounts of muffled reports of scientific views and findings.

President Obama made the issue of 'restoring scientific integrity' prominent in his successful political campaign, and an applauded theme of his inaugural address. On 9 March 2009, he issued a memorandum for the heads of executive departments and agencies purporting to address these issues. It appears in full in Appendix A to this chapter. It assigns to the Director of the Office of Science and Technology Policy, the White House office responsible for coordinating science matters in government, the task of developing recommendations that will produce merit-based (ie, not political) appointments, use of scientific methods (including peer review as appropriate) in developing information, heightened transparency, and improved protection for dissidents ('whistleblowers'). And scepticism whether this was a change in the service of science or of politics immediately followed.[15] What are the tools law can bring to improve the chance

by John Tierney in the New York Times, eg 'Politicizing Science', www.tierneylab.blogs.nytimes.com/2009/02/27/politicizing-science, visited 10 March 2009.

[11] R Pielke, Jr, *The Honest Broker—Making Sense of Science in Policy and Politics* (Cambridge, Cambridge University Press, 2007); DS Greenberg, *Science, Money and Politics* (Chicago, University of Chicago Press, 2001); S Jasanoff, *The Fifth Branch—Science Advisers as Policymakers* (Cambridge MA, Harvard University Press, 1990).

[12] Pielke, n 11 above.

[13] See n 28 below.

[14] See Shulman, n 9 above, at xii–xiii.

[15] S Stolberg, 'Obama Puts His Own Spin on Mix of Science with Politics', NY Times, 9 March 2009; J Tierney, 'Politics-Free Science?', www.tierneylab.blogs.nytimes.com/2009/03/09/politics-free-science, visited 10 March 2009. A later report was that:

> OSTP Director John Holdren met the 9 July deadline in the presidential memorandum for suggesting how executive agencies should improve their conduct on everything from vetting job

that sound judgement, 'reason', will prevail, and to diminish the influence of simple will, 'unreason'?

In asking this question, one must be aware of an important lacuna in the characterisation of science earlier quoted. If 'the scientific process is not democratic', it also will rarely be conclusive in those matters of greatest interest to regulators and politicians. No society committed to democracy can afford to ignore the frequently remarked variations between expert and public evaluations of risk. The observable differences in public willingness to accept risks of varying sorts, even when openly and reliably defined, will produce policy outcomes varying from those that straightforward comparison of objective risk levels would suggest. Motorcycle riders will notice no cognitive dissonance as they campaign vigorously against nuclear power. These are issues that might be addressed by education; but while certainly susceptible of political manipulation, they reflect preferences that cannot be discredited. One might distinguish here between political judgements that develop from democratic discussion processes, and political outcomes that are more directly the product of the exercise of simple, and usually covert, will. It is the latter that are the principal concern of this chapter.

SOME EXAMPLES OF WILL OVER JUDGEMENT

This section sketches four examples of settings in which it might be thought 'will' had prevailed over 'judgement', two drawn from American experience and two from abroad.

Treatment regimes for Lyme Disease

The quotation earlier set out was taken from an article in the Journal of the American Medical Association (JAMA) criticising a decision of the Attorney-General of Connecticut to prosecute the Infectious Diseases Society of America (IDSA) for state antitrust violations. In 2006, the IDSA issued updated clinical practice guidelines in 2006 for the diagnosis and treatment of Lyme disease, recommending against the use of longterm antibiotics to treat 'chronic Lyme disease (CLD)'. The IDSA is a private non-governmental organisation (NGO) that formulates recommendations about disease treatment regimens on the basis

applicants to protecting whistleblowers. But the details remain under seal until all relevant agencies have signed off on them.

www.blogs.sciencemag.org/scienceinsider/2009/09/lost-in-space-t.html, dated 1 September 2009 and visited 20 September 2009. In the interim his Office of Science and Technology Policy had conducted and reported numerous innovative programmes in e-government. See generally www.whitehouse.gov/open/, www.whitehouse.gov/open/blog/, and, in particular, www.mixedink.com/OpenGov/, where a government consultation on improving e-government was recently held.

of available studies. These recommendations are influential on physicians prescribing courses of treatment, and on insurance companies making determinations about coverage. CLD is a label that some use to describe a variety of non-specific symptoms persisting in some Lyme disease sufferers after evidence of bacterial infection has disappeared and for which, frequently, no evidence suggests the etiologic agent of Lyme disease is responsible. IDSA's study, for the authors of the JAMA article demonstrably the product of sound science, had led it to conclude that long-term treatment of these symptoms with antibiotics was ineffective, expensive, and posed the risks associated with long-term antibiotic use. For the International Lyme and Associated Diseases Society (ILADS), however, a CLD advocacy group supported by the manufacturer of the drug used for long-term treatment, and drawing on the work of a committee that included the president of a company that manufactures an alternative Lyme disease diagnostic test and multiple physicians whose practices are listed with the group's patient referral service, these results were anathema. ILADS immediately protested, asserting the superiority of its alternative guidelines; the JAMA article asserts that these guidelines were based on substandard review methods. Within days, the Connecticut Attorney-General launched an investigation, alleging IDSA had violated state antitrust law by excluding differing viewpoints from its guideline creation process and including members who had financial interests in, or ties to, Lyme disease diagnostic and treatment makers. IDSA had disclosed its panel members' potential conflicts of interest in its published guidelines, and the authors of the JAMA article assert that there was no evidence that any conflicts altered the guidelines' content. The committee that created the ILADS guidelines did not disclose the financial interests associated with its guideline document. To avoid exorbitant litigation costs, IDSA was forced to settle the claim and alter its guidelines.

Herceptin and Breast Cancer Treatment in New Zealand

Public subsidisation of medical treatment regimes in New Zealand depends importantly on the judgements reached by Pharmac, a governmental agency whose decisions are grounded in considerations of cost as well as effectiveness. Herceptin is a pharmaceutical that can be effective in treating certain forms of breast cancer, but which itself poses certain health risks if used for a long time, and is quite expensive; a full year's treatment might cost in the range of NZ $70,000 (depending on the patient's weight). From 2001, Pharmac had listed Herceptin as approved for extended use in the treatment of *metastatic* breast cancers. Subsequently, the question arose whether it should also be approved for treatment of women whose breast cancer had been detected at an earlier stage. In 2006, responding to advice from expert committees that called the drug's cost-effectiveness for these women into question, Pharmac decided not to schedule the drug for that use 'at this time'. To approve the use would have had implications for New Zealand's capacity to subsidise other treatment regimes for the full range of diseases. In 2007, responding to broad consultations and to a study suggesting that a nine-week course of treatment with the drug concurrent with chemotherapy showed a level of effectiveness comparable to that which might arise from a full year's treatment, it decided to list the nine-week course of treatment as approved for subsidisation, but did not reopen the one-year question. In April 2008, responding to review sought by breast cancer sufferers wishing the full year option, quite possibly with support from the drug's manufacturer, New Zealand's High Court found that Pharmac had failed to engage in the required level of consultation in reaching its first decision and, while approving the process attending the second decision, concluded that that process had not reopened the one-year question. It directed reconsideration of that question, after full consultation. Pharmac complied, and came to the same conclusion: the benefit of the one-year regimen was too uncertain in relation to its cost. Within the breast cancer community and to the drug's manufacturer, this was of course a highly disappointing outcome, although others understood it as preventing diversion of necessarily limited public funds from other, more promising uses to support health care generally. The matter became an issue in the national elections later that year, and one party promised as part of its campaign to assure full funding. It won, and promptly acted through the Ministry of Health—not Pharmac—to subsidise the full-year regimen.

A Wind Farm in Australia

The Australian Minister for Environment, a member of the Australian Senate, was required to approve the siting of a large wind-farm at Bald Hills, in southern Australia.[16] The siting was locally controversial for reasons grounded in aesthetics and concern over the noise it might produce. And an election was pending, in which a candidate of the minister's party (the minister was himself from a distant riding) had allied himself with the opposition to the farm. The minister refused to approve the application, citing the risk it posed to a critically endangered species of parrot. The parrot was indeed endangered, and wind farms pose unquestionable dangers to migratory birds. But, as has not been unknown in the United States,[17] ostensible concern for the parrot was a stalking horse for local residents unhappy about a projected intrusion on their amenities. When the reports and data on which the minister had relied became available, it proved that few, if any, of the endangered species had ever been seen in the vicinity of the projected wind farm; their population density, to the extent there was any, lay elsewhere, and the major threat to their survival was development and its

[16] This paragraph is based on J Prest, 'The Bald Hills wind farm debacle' in T Bonyhady and P Christoff, (eds), *Climate Law in Australia* (Sydney, Federation Press, 2007).

[17] *Scenic Hudson Preservation Conference v Federal Power Commission*, 354 F2d 608 (2d Cir 1965).

associated habitat changes. The data suggested that perhaps one parrot would fall to the wind farm every millennium; extinction from other causes was thought likely within 50 years. The availability of this data—and the passage of election day—resulted eventually in a settlement that permitted the wind farm's construction.

Setting the Secondary Level for Ozone in the United States

In the spring of 2008, the public became aware of disagreements between the Bush White House and the Environmental Protection Administration (EPA) about the level of ozone exposure appropriate for national ambient air quality standards to protect forest growth and other 'secondary' targets of protection from harm by air pollution.[18] ('Primary' standards are set for public health concerns.) Reflecting the differences they understood between the needs and vulnerabilities of human and forest lungs, the various scientific advisory committees and bureaucratic decision-makers within the EPA had settled on an ozone level marginally differing from the primary standard. It would have been somewhat more stringent than the primary level but also with a more forgiving measurement interval.

These standards are to be set following the public procedures of the Clean Air Act for rule-making, procedures building on but somewhat more stringent than those of the US Administrative Procedure Act (APA). (In many European countries, the development of similar measures would be described as subsidiary legislation or perhaps ministerial decrees; in the EU, as implementing measures.) Under these procedures as currently understood, the public receives notice of a proposed rule and access to the data and reports underlying it, and any person interested to do so is able to submit additional data and to comment on the proposal; the agency must then explain its decision in some detail and, as already indicated, its reasoning is subject to relatively close scrutiny on judicial review.

The EPA's Administrator, a politically responsible official comparable in dignity to a Cabinet Secretary and who by statute is given the authority to decide such matters, was prepared to accept and act on the advice he had received from his staff. Before he could do so, however, contemporary arrangements (established by the President for White House coordination and oversight of regulatory activity) required him to seek clearance from an office in the President's Office of Management and Budget, the Office of Information and Regulatory Affairs (OIRA). OIRA initially sought reconsideration of the matter, suggesting that the primary and secondary standards would most efficiently be identical—set at the somewhat more permissive level already determined for the primary standard. EPA staff generated a response detailing why, in their judgement, the best

[18] J Eilperin, 'Ozone Rules Weakened at Bush's Behest; EPA Scrambles To Justify Action', The Washington Post, 14 March 2008, at A1.

scientific evidence available about the differing vulnerabilities of humans and forests required differing standards under their statutory responsibilities. The EPA Administrator indicated to the White House, then, that he intended to stand by his staff's judgement. At this point he was directed—told President Bush had decided—that identical standards must be adopted. The Administrator acquiesced.

The resulting blizzard of newspaper stories and congressional inquiries suggested that something untoward had occurred. The relevant statute, placing the responsibility for this decision in the Administrator and not the President, both assumed and required that the decision would be made in accordance with the best available scientific information. Neither the President nor his agent OIRA has the resources or expertise to do good science on such an issue. Moreover, the relevant statute precludes using economic cost/benefit, as such, as a decisional consideration. (While this proposition might seem questionable as a policy matter, it had underlain the US Supreme Court's willingness just a few years earlier to accept the significant law-making authority the statute confers on the EPA's Administrator.[19] Permitting the EPA to make political trade-offs rather than base its actions on ostensibly objective judgements about best science would heighten concerns about the constitutionality of conferring this law-making authority on unelected officials.[20]) Suspicions were rife that the White House judgement about ozone was animated by raw political concerns for the well-being of favoured industries; or if not that, certainly by the factors of economic cost that the statutes had excluded from the Administrator's consideration. Congressional committees demanded, and the White House adamantly refused to provide, a variety of documentary evidence and testimony on the issue. The standard was issued in the form the White House had insisted upon, and in that form might be subject to judicial review.[21]

[19] *Whitman v American Trucking Ass'ns, Inc* 531 US 457, 475 (2001) ('While Congress need not provide any direction to the EPA regarding the manner in which it is to define "country grain elevators", which are to be exempt from [certain statutory requirements], it must provide substantial guidance on setting air standards that affect the entire national economy').

[20] *cf Boreali v Axelrod* 71 NY 2d 1 (1987) (New York's Public Health Council authorised to consider only public health factors in adopting a regulation controlling smoking in public places; it lacks the 'open-ended discretion' to construct 'a regulatory scheme laden with exceptions based solely upon economic and social concerns').

[21] On 16 September 2009, the EPA Administrator announced that she was reopening the standard, which presumably will moot any review petition that may have been filed. www.yosemite.epa.gov/opa/admpress.nsf/6424ac1caa800aab85257359003f5337/85f90b7711acb0c88525763300617d0d!OpenDocument, visited 20 September 2009.

In a similar Bush administration episode, OIRA delayed for years action on a proposed regulation to protect an endangered species, right whales, from collisions with large boats traveling at speeds that made evasion difficult; the regulation was eventually issued in the form the responsible agency had requested but only after more than a year later than the action times assured by the order creating the OIRA review regime. See Robbie Brown, 'US Requires Ships to Cut Speed in Waters Used by Right Whales', NY Times, 9 October 2008.

That the back-and-forth became public is due in substantial part to the increasing availability of information about governmental regulatory activities on the Internet. The EPA has been one of the leading agencies in developing public Internet databases associated with its rule-making activities. As a matter of the APA's text, the obligations to expose matters concerned with rule-making appear to be rather slight. Nonetheless, judicial decisions and the realities of the US Freedom of Information Act have resulted in thorough agency exposure of the scientific reports or data on which rule-making decisions may be based, as well as commentary received from outside the agency. The idea that this should happen is uncontroversial, and is strongly voiced in President Obama's recent executive order. To the extent such information is made available and searchable on the Internet, as increasingly it is, citizen monitoring is facilitated. And, responding in part to commitments made in the OIRA mandate, the computerised database for the ozone rule-making quickly included much material revealing the back-and-forth that had occurred. Perhaps a knowledgeable EPA official then suggested to the reporter that he have a look.

THE ROLE OF RULE-MAKING

Each of these examples could be thought to raise the question how the timeliness and internal integrity of government regulatory decision-making can best be promoted. Choices to prosecute (Connecticut), to allocate public funding (New Zealand), to approve an application (Australia) or to adopt a standard (EPA) can all be influenced by factors other than a reasoned judgement about 'best science'. Yet to recognise that this is so, in a democratic society, is not necessarily to condemn that outcome. In the New Zealand case, for example, one might well think that although a large corporation's profit motivations may have influenced the outcome, the spending choice between marginally beneficial breast cancer treatment regimes and other purposes was also a matter that had been contested in the citizenry and was proper for political determination. In this case that decision was openly made in a straightforwardly political way. In the other three cases, one could believe that timely public information about the objective realities underlying the decision could have produced different results. The issues are ones both of procedures employed, and of the place of politics in the determinations made.

The focus of inquiry in the paragraphs following will be on rule-making—the generation of regulations that if valid have the force and effect of statutes—rather than adjudication. Policy issues of broad interest more frequently arise in that context, and there are interesting parallels between the ostensible public procedures for rule-making, as they have developed in the United States, and the paradigmatic methods scientists use to inform their judgements. The 'paper hearing' of today's important rule-makings—marked by detailed notice including the availability of underlying data; a seriously taken opportunity for comment; an extensive explanation of agency reasoning in the face of that comment; followed by 'hard look' judicial review—seems remarkably like the scientific method for approaching truths.

The matrix for these paragraphs will be that suggested by President Obama's recent directive on restoring scientific integrity,[22] which focuses in turn on selection and retention of candidates; internal procedures including 'well-established scientific processes' such as peer review; and issues of arising out of central government control of rule-making, including transparency, protection for dissidents, and White House relations.

Selection and retention of candidates

The executive order directs that selection of candidates 'should be based on the candidate's knowledge, credentials, experience, and integrity.' Left off this list of desirable qualities are such typical criteria for political appointment as loyalty and a known predisposition to agree with the President/agency head's policy preferences. One might find room for these qualities in the interstices of 'credentials, experience, and integrity', the language President Obama used in his recent directive; and appraisals of President Obama's own appointments to scientific posts have not been lacking in suggestions that they have been used.[23] Nor can one imagine that persons possessing 'credentials, experience, and integrity' lack political commitments, or predispositions on issues in play in the scientific community respecting which final judgement has yet to be reached. In his short recent book, *The Honest Broker*, Roger Pielke, Jnr valuably distinguishes between the kinds of political issues that can be appropriately resolved by reliable inquiry into observable facts—is a tornado approaching? 'tornado politics'—and others that cannot, 'abortion politics'.[24] To the extent reliable inquiry cannot produce uncontested answers—very often the case in situations where politicians nonetheless feel required to act (say, respecting climate change)—the engaged scientist is faced with the choice between acting as 'stealth advocate', proceeding on the basis of his or her personal belief or preference, and acting as 'honest broker', stating clearly the alternatives and their associated uncertainties and implications while subduing as best he or she can his or her own priors.

[22] Text at n 15 above.
[23] eg, J Tierney, "Findings: Politics in the Guise of Pure Science," NY Times, 24 February 2009, at D1.
[24] Pielke, n 11 above, at 40.

Committing scientific data-gathering to the civil service?

In speaking to the 'selection of candidates', President Obama is of course addressing the appointees he and his political lieutenants choose and not the members of the permanent civil service. One mechanism that might be thought useful to encourage 'honest broker' behaviour is a definition of function to separate, so far as possible, the responsibility for appraising those issues for which scientific inquiry may be helpful, such as risk, from questions on what to do about such matters once identified. Such a separation could map onto the ostensible distinction in government employment between the permanent civil service, and political appointees who hold office at will and ordinarily change with administrations.

A distinction between risk managers and risk assessors is explicit, for example, in the standard setting activities of the Codex Alimentarius Commission under the aegis of the Food and Agriculture Organization (FAO) and the World Health Organization (WHO). This body undertakes setting international standards for food safety to ensure human health protection, in light of the best available scientific data.[25] Its documents conceive overall risk analysis as comprised of three functionally separated elements: risk assessment, risk management, and risk communication. The allocation is in the service of creating a zone in which 'scientific integrity' may be assured (risk assessment); another in which political judgements are made and from which guidance and standards emerge (risk management); and a third element of systematic, maximally sustainable transparency that may build public trust (risk communication). Risk assessors are encouraged to identify the data, assumptions and uncertainties bearing on their assessments, and the characteristics of the hazards they identify, and to report their conclusions in a manner permitting peer and public review. Risk managers, taking a range of economic and political factors into account, are to respect 'precaution' and public attitudes towards risk in deciding how best to respond to the assessments thus received; again, their processes and reports should be 'transparent, consistent and fully documented'. Both assessors and managers, while respecting 'legitimate concern to preserve confidentiality', are encouraged to communicate their activities and conclusions with the greatest accuracy and transparency possible, so as to strengthen working relationships and build public trust.

Distinguishing between risk assessors (scientists) and risk managers (the policy-setting overseers to whom they report) might be thought naturally to fit the presuppositions of a permanent civil service working within a framework of political management. That is, one might think, the data gatherers, the risk assessors, are unlikely to have political ambitions or roles; that is the whole point. If initially the impulse to creation of a civil service imagined a body of secretaries

[25] Its Working Principles for Risk Analysis for Food Safety for Application by Governments, CAC/GL 62–2007, is attached as Appendix B to this chapter.

and clerks, and was intended to control the financial and general competence risks of patronage, one may now see it as a means of assuring the best information for government managers—as an instrument for integrity in a different sense. Selection will be made on the basis of objective criteria. Of course some managers are also scientists, the ones whose appointment President Obama was addressing; the relationship between managers and responsible staff in general, ripe with potential for misuse, is addressed below.[26]

This intellectual separation is intuitively appealing, and certainly sends useful signals to those minded to heed them. It could be seen to reinforce the 'honest broker' vision of scientist function. But as appears amply in the literature, the uncertainties of outcomes and predispositions of analysts confound its reliability.[27] 'Stealth advocacy' can readily appear at the level of risk assessment, whether or not risk management is identified as a separate task. The scientist who has chosen a civil service career has often sacrificed financially more rewarding avenues, perhaps for competitive reasons suggesting his or her possession of a lesser skill set yet perhaps, instead, in order to serve normative preferences that make public service seem worth that sacrifice. One readily understands the political managers' fearing this influence, particularly politicians whose attitude toward the project of government is more sceptical than those who choose a lifetime career in it.[28] To them, at least, 'stealth advocacy' in the memos they receive will appear a significant threat.[29]

It is unlikely, moreover, that an agency's civil servants will themselves be able to amass and analyse the data required for risk assessment. Often they will be required to call upon outsiders more expert than themselves, perhaps as 'special government employees' or perhaps by requesting or contracting for relevant studies. Now their neutrality may not suffice to satisfy; the Lyme disease example from Connecticut underscores the importance of considering what controls exist over the potential conflicts of interest among outsiders relied on for help in assembling/assessing relevant data. If we are evoking 'science' as a rationale, moreover, that entails the values of transparency and openness to refutation. 'Whether a scientific finding is judged to be accurate is dependent on the quality and rigor of the methods used and whether that finding is replicable.'[30]

[26] See pp 133–37 below.

[27] eg, Jasanoff, *The Fifth Branch*, n 11 above.

[28] 'A bureaucrat is a Democrat who holds some office that a Republican wants.' (Alban Barkley, Harry Truman's Vice President, at the 1948 Democratic Convention, as reported in William Safire, *Safire's Political Dictionary* (Oxford, Oxford University Press, rev ed 2008) at 90; the quotation is sometimes attributed to President Truman himself, as at www.members.tripod.com/aldems/page20.html, visited 27 April 2009.

[29] See AF Wichelman, 'Administrative Agency Implementation of the National Environmental Policy Act of 1969: A Conceptual Framework for Explaining Differential Response' (1976) 16 *Natural Resources Journal* 263, on the motivation of government bureaucrats; also discussed in S Taylor, *Making Bureaucracies Think* (Stanford University Press, 1984) and M Painter, *Steering the Modern State* (Sydney, Sydney University Press, 1987).

[30] Note 1 above.

For reasons such as these, 'risk assessment' may be seen as an appropriately public procedure, one that ought to be as contestable and open as the debates over risk management that will follow it. Now the separation virtually disappears. 'Bending'—that is to say political rather than science-process reasons for decision—may have much to do with the arguments about procedure. Much of the (frequently industrial) pressure to formalise 'risk assessment' as an initial, distinct step preparatory to 'risk management' can be understood as an instrument of delay. The EPA should not be required to coordinate with the Department of Defense in assessing the 'toxicity of perchlorate, a component of rocket fuel detected nationally in drinking water, breast milk, and produce', one activist, consumerist science NGO has argued, as this 'could mean that the DOD and its contractors are liable for potentially billions of dollars in cleanup costs. The DOD has long sought to weaken any scientific standard that would mandate cleanup of perchlorate contamination.'[31]

Even at what may appear to be the apolitical, civil service level, as a recent fine analysis by Professor David Barron of Harvard points out, one of the significant threats to scientific integrity is the much enlarged penetration of 'political clearances' into agency bureaucracies. Like OIRA's regulatory review mechanisms, this trend became pronounced with the administration of Ronald Reagan. Barron reports that:

> the number of full-time political appointees serving in the federal government [in policy positions] jumped from 2150 in 1964 to 3687 in 1992. …These [positions, with 2300 others effectively open to political clearance] … dwarf, by orders of magnitude, the number of political appointees available to the executive leaders of most European nations. … The rise in the ranks of economists, engineers, scientists, and lawyers within the bureaucracy itself increases the opportunities for Presidents to remake the bureaucracy in ways that are likely to promote a particular view of regulatory policy.[32]

The increasing scope of political clearance for persons having policy responsibilities certainly renders American 'administration' more political than might be expected in the strong civil service regimes of many parliamentary democracies. Probably the move in this direction began during the presidency of Jimmy Carter, when a reform of the civil service laws created in the upper echelons of the civil service a Senior Executive Service, those persons responsible for policy direction and other matters involving substantial discretion. In the United States as in European democracies, important federal bureaus, elements perhaps of a cabinet department, might be under the direction of a senior civil servant, a

[31] 'Scientific Integrity', a submission of the Union of Concerned Scientists to the public comment files respecting revision of EO 12866, see note and accompanying text below, www.reginfo.gov/public/jsp/EO/fedRegReview/publicComments.jsp (visited 12 March 2009), citing Sass J 2004. US Department of Defense and White House working together to avoid cleanup and liability for perchlorate pollution in *International Journal of Occupational and Environmental Health* (abstract) 10:330–34.

[32] DJ Barron, 'From Takeover to Merger: Reforming Administrative Law in an Age of Agency Politicization' (2008) 76 *George Washington Law Review* 1095, 1123.

permanent government employee rather than a political appointee.[33] Perhaps, one would think, smaller numbers of politicians at the top, and a civil service enured to 'Yes, Minister' in parliamentary systems make for a rather different picture. It should not be hard to understand the stress such penetration can put on the interface between law and politics.

Scientific integrity at the management level

Turning to the context of risk management: the White House and the political heads of agencies do have significant control over agency management levels. At least three strata of management-level employee can be identified. At the highest level are heads of departments and others whose appointment requires Senate confirmation. Here one can find not only public processes for exploring the merits of appointment, but also the possibility of undertakings to others than the President—that is, to the Senators who confirm—that provide a kind of cover for independent judgement. Second come a much larger number of persons who are appointed by the President alone, or by the heads of departments, without need for Senate confirmation. Like those whose appointment do require that step, they generally[34] serve 'at will' but now without either the cover of undertakings to the Senate, or the same basis for belief that their summary dismissal might produce the kinds of political controversy that could make a President hesitate to act. Strikingly, 100 days into the Obama administration the Library of Congress was reporting 177 nominations submitted to Congress for civilian positions,[35] but as Professor Barron's analysis shows, thousands more politically cleared positions exist outside congressional control. Third and finally, there is the Senior Executive Service—lifetime civil servants in senior positions who, since President Carter's administration, have served in a regime considerably more exposed to reward and punishment for desired and undesired actions than the ordinary civil service. Bureau chiefs may in the past have had the independence of full civil service status and consequent effective room within which to manoeuvre;[36] their service today is much more subject to political controls.

Persons living in parliamentary systems built over permanent civil service bodies find the resulting level of politicality in American government astounding. Mutual understandings about the security of lifetime governmental employment are understood to be a major assurance of the integrity of technical assessments. While the creation of inspectors general (serving in this respect a function similar

[33] The classic study of their work, written at about the time of this change, is H Kaufman, *The Administrative Behaviour of Federal Bureau Chiefs* (Washington, The Brookings Institute, 1981).

[34] The reservation is made to recognise that Congress has occasionally limited dismissals of persons appointed with and without senatorial confirmation to 'good cause'. Thankfully, the Supreme Court has not yet had an occasion to address what might constitute 'cause' in a legal sense.

[35] www.thomas.loc.gov/home/nomis.html, visited 20 September 2009. The number had become 300 by mid-June, 477 by 20 September. By the last date, 328 of the nominations had been confirmed.

[36] Kaufman, n 33 above.

to ombudsmen in European administrations) and whistleblower protections such as President Obama recently re-emphasised provide some protection for scientific integrity, their cover is not complete. Thirty-two years ago, when the author was General Counsel of the US Nuclear Regulatory Commission, its Bureau 'executives' sometimes exercised rigorous control over what they would permit their staff members to tell the Commission about perceived nuclear power risks.[37] Nor were Commissioners wholly committed to transparency about possible risks; facing the chance that utilities or equipment manufacturers might bring similar pressures to bear on their personnel to suppress safety concerns they might wish to share with the Commission and aware that their statute affirmatively provided for whistleblower protection, they did not seem eager to encourage 'rat finks'. Such phenomena suggest what must be obvious, that personal integrity and a willingness to subdue personal preferences are irreducible elements of the 'bending' problem.

To the extent the White House controls the selection of agency personnel, the risk that judgements committed to the agency for decision will be made on bases other than those its constitutive statutes commit to it increases. Professor Barron has amply illustrated these risks in his recent article.[38] They are perhaps magnified by a quixotic Supreme Court decision taking the position that anyone holding an executive branch office with significant authority to act constitutionally, yet not senatorially confirmed, *must* be appointed by either the President or the head of a cabinet department, narrowly understood.[39] And the intensity of senatorial inquiry for those appointments that require confirmation may have at least two consequences promoting White House control. First, by encumbering that process—helping to explain the observable slowness of both nomination (as potential candidates are vetted to avoid embarrassments) and confirmation—it produces enduring *agency* vacancies in ostensible political positions,[40] inviting direct White House engagement in the interim. Second, the same costs rationally lead the President to prefer locating responsibility, to the extent he can, in persons he can place quickly in a position to act, and who are not required to answer Senate inquiry, perhaps creating a conflicting sense of political obligation. It is easy to understand the increasing use of White House 'czars' in this light.

While in parliamentary systems it may be natural for the prime minister to see himself as a persuader/conciliator open to constructive dialogue and shared

[37] Not without chastening consequence; one suppressed employee went to the CBS programme, 'Sixty Minutes' with his concerns, producing both public scandal and congressional hearings that consumed a great deal of the time the Commissioners might otherwise have had for regulatory matters.

[38] N 32 above.

[39] *Freytag v Commissioner*, 501 US 868 (1991).

[40] Seven months into the Obama Administration, just 43% of more than 500 positions requiring Senate confirmation had been filled. See P Baker, 'Obama Team Lacking Most of Top Players', NY Times, 24 August 2009, at A1.

responsibility, the 'unitary executive' idea, pursued to its theoretical limits, has other implications. In recent writings, Robert Post has pointed to the differences from the perspective of democracy between political conceptions that are centered on loyalty—you are with me or you are my enemy—and others that welcome disagreement, preferring a team of rivals from which judgements can emerge by a process of constructive conversation.[41] In the Bush administration, it often appeared that the first duties of civilian heads of departments, like generals of the Army, were thought to be loyalty and obedience—a perspective that may conduce to efficiency in executive governance but offers less promise to democracy. For President Harry S Truman, who regarded the President's office as one of conciliation and persuasion, 'Whenever you have an efficient government you have a dictatorship.'[42] In the first months of the Obama administration, some disposition to hear all sides—to enlist 'honest brokers'—might be suggested by the President's appointment of his principal political opponent to be his Secretary of State, and his reputation as a person committed to hearing all sides. His nomination of a former colleague, Professor Cass Sunstein, to head the office most directly concerned with domestic regulation, the Office of Information and Regulatory Analysis (OIRA) in the Office of Management and Budget (OMB), would put in that important post an academic whose recent writings have repeatedly stressed the importance of hearing all sides for sound decision.[43] Yet an 'Inside Account' of the President Bush's controversial decision on stem cell research persuasively portrays it, too, as the product of intense internal dialogue;[44] and President Obama's undertakings of increased transparency, unsurprisingly, have yet to result in significant public exposure of advice he has received from within the executive branch.[45] Truman again:

> The President cannot function without advisers or without advice, written or oral. But just as soon as he is required to show what kind of advice he has had, who said what to him, or what kind of records he has, the advice received will be worthless.[46]

[41] See, eg, R Post, 'Theorizing Disagreement: Re-Conceiving the Relationship between Law and Politics' *California Law Review* (forthcoming), *Yale Law School Public Law & Legal Theory Research Paper No. 195*, available at www.papers.ssrn.com/abstract #1434103.

[42] Harry S Truman, *Lecture at Columbia University, 28 April 1959*, www.quotationspage.com/quote/27058.html, visited 21 April 2009.

[43] See CR Sunstein, 'The Empiricist Strikes Back', *The New Republic*, 10 September 2008, at 9; T Kuran and CR Sunstein, 'Availability Cascades and Risk Regulation' (1999) 51 *Stanford Law Review* 683.

[44] J Lefkowitz, 'Stem Cells and the President—An Inside Account', Commentary (January 2008), www.commentarymagazine.com/viewarticle.cfm/stem-cells-and-the-president-br–an-inside-account-11024?page=all (visited 3 June 2009).

[45] Prominent among a number of public consultations begun by the Obama administration within its first 100 days in office was one in connection with its reexamination of Executive Order 12286, discussed further below. See text below accompanying n 78.

[46] H Truman, *Memoirs: Years of Trial and Hope* (New York, Garden City,1956).

Further discussion of the transparency side of these issues will be found below, as well as an examination of the White House control mechanisms.[47] But in concluding a discussion of the appointments issues, as such, some mention is warranted of the resistance of recent Presidents to congressional instructions about appointment qualifications; these Presidents have asserted an essentially constitutional right to propose whomever they wanted. President Clinton appended such a statement on signing a bill that, inter alia, sought to limit the pool of persons he might nominate for US Trade Representative to avoid arguable conflicts of interest. In the wake of the Katrina disaster and the deficiencies in Federal Emergency Management Administration (FEMA) management it revealed, Congress passed statutes requiring that the person appointed to head FEMA be a person experienced in the management of complex institutions and disaster management.[48] In a later statute, it directed that appointees to high office in the United States Postal Commission have similar experience-related backgrounds.[49] In signing the lengthy statutes including these provisions into law, President George W Bush identified these two provisions in particular, as against many he accepted, as unconstitutional infringements of his authority to nominate or appoint anyone he chose.[50] The obverse of congressional creation of appointments limits suggesting commitments to, for example, professional integrity is that openness to political direction in the face of those commitments can be highly valued.

One area of personnel control that has long been thought important, in science as in politics, is the subduing of personal financial advantage—not power, now, so much as greed. Both formal conflict of interest requirements and attention to the loyalties likely to persevere from prior activities and commitments operate here. The presuppositions of a civil service that invites transition between public and private life, as the American one does, at both leadership and staff levels, creates inevitable tensions. These are dealt with, but imperfectly, by financial controls and by restrictions on 'revolving door' service. One President appoints a construction executive to head the Occupational Safety and Health Administration; another, an industrial safety professional with union connections. Each on leaving office may return to a post similar to that from which he or she came; either may be preferable to appointing a skilled administrator who is inexperienced about issues of workplace safety; both may return to

[47] See pp 145ff.

[48] Department of Homeland Security Appropriations Act 2007 § 611(11), 6 USC § 313.

[49] Postal Accountability and Enhancement Act 2006 § 501, 39 USC § 202.

[50] Statement by President George W Bush Upon Signing HR 5441, 2006 USCCAN S49, S52 (4 October 2006) ('[the statute] purports to limit the qualifications of the pool of persons from whom the President may select the appointee in a manner that rules out a large portion of those persons best qualified by experience and knowledge to fill the office. The executive branch shall construe [section 611] in a manner consistent with the Appointments Clause of the Constitution.'); Statement by President George W Bush Upon Signing HR 6407, 2006 USCCAN S76 (20 December 2006) (making an almost identical statement).

private life with increased skills and understanding that in fact serve to aid their clients' attention to industrial safety realities. And for both, questions can be raised about the 'objectivity' of their attention to programmatic issues.

Conflict of interest regulation and revolving-door control have been recurrent issues in the United States. President Obama made strong commitments to avoiding appointments questionable on such grounds, yet some of his initial designees withdrew in embarrassment after compromising connections or lapses came to light. Others did not and, as with Secretary of the Treasury Geithner, it is not surprising that appointees bring with them prior commitments or experience that seem likely to influence their judgement. Attention to such issues is perhaps easier, and more readily regularised, at lower levels—as, for example, assurance of balance and lack of conflict in the advisory panels that work with the Food and Drug Administration or the EPA.[51] The literature is replete with examples of settings in which these efforts have not been successful and, indeed, it may be hard even in the academy to find a pharmacological expert who has not had financial dealings with the drug industry. The FAO-WHO Codex Alimentarius process already mentioned commits to having experts involved in risk assessment publicly known, transparently selected, and free of potentially disabling conflicts of interest. The FAO questionnaire on the subject explores in considerable detail, for individuals and also their families and business connections, a wide range of financial and other interests that could raise such questions—seeking explanations where potential conflicts arise, presuming consent to disclosure of the document, and suggesting that disqualification may occur if disclosure is refused.[52] But with disclosure, appointments are not disqualified.

Procedures

Incentives for integrity might also be found in objectivised, procedural controls over rule-making. We can briefly mention two—judicial review of the outcomes, and peer review of the relevant science. In doing so, however, one must bear in mind the caution suggested by the noted American scholar Jerry Mashaw, writing about procedural choices in the context of administrative adjudications affecting individual rights. Mashaw persuasively argued the point that there is no 'best' answer. He identified three perspectives from which this question could be approached: individual fairness, affording maximum attention to the process claims of the individuals whose rights are at stake; professional integrity, considering *both* the arguable contributions made to sound decisions by the professional commitments of the deciders *and* the possible interference with these

[51] See, eg, McGarity and Wagner, n 4 above, at 181–203.
[52] The questionnaire is attached as Appendix C to this chapter.

contributions that could be created by procedural details;[53] and bureaucratic rationality, which would value the confinement of likely error to cases 'on the borderline' and efficiency—low cost in relation to the issues to be determined.

> If these hypotheses are correct, then it may also follow that the best system of administrative adjudication may be the one most open to criticism. A compromise that seeks to preserve the values and to respond at once to the insights of all of these conceptions of justice will, from the perspective of each separate conception, appear incoherent and unjust. The best system of administrative adjudication that can be devised may fall tragically short of our inconsistent ideals.[54]

And, of course, procedural requirements may not only contribute to more accurate or efficient, or fair outcomes. They may also provide 'handles' that participants eager to add delay or expense to government determinations can use to achieve that. As long-time American Congressman John Dingell is reported once to have observed, 'If you let me write the *procedure*, and I let you write the substance, I'll screw you *every time*.'[55] Many believe that the notorious slowness and infrequency of rule-making on issues of occupational safety and health is the product of industrial success in securing cumbersome and expensive procedural requirements in a law whose purpose of improving worker safety they could not directly oppose. Claims to improving fairness and accuracy were a different matter.

So the same kinds of trade-offs as Mashaw remarked for the setting of adjudication may be implicit in providing procedures for standard-setting. Even if we start with the proposition that the standards to be set should reflect as is best possible the state of scientific knowledge, we can identify significant elements that will influence the timeliness, accuracy and acceptability of the outcomes. Rule-making in American law is a public procedure, with agencies statutorily required to solicit public comment on any proposal before acting on it, and to explain their reasoning in response to comments and other materials when they do act. American case law has largely established propositions central to the language in President Obama's recent executive order providing that:

> (1) … (c) When scientific or technological information is considered in policy decisions, the information should be subject to well-established scientific processes, including peer review where appropriate, and each agency should appropriately and accurately reflect that information in complying with and applying relevant statutory standards;

[53] Examples might be teachers or doctors, whose professional commitments have often been relied upon. In the welfare context, the proceduralisation of welfare administration in the wake of *Goldberg v Kelly*, 397 US 254 (1970), brought about a shift in hiring from social workers, professionally committed to the wellbeing of their clients, to caseworkers with an eye to the bottom line. See WH Simon, 'Legality, Bureaucracy, and Class in the Welfare System' (1983) 92 *Yale Law Journal* 1198.

[54] JL Mashaw, *Bureaucratic Justice: Managing Social Security Disability Claims* (New Haven, Yale University Press, 1983).

[55] M Foley and JE Owens, *Congress and the Presidency: Institutional Politics in a Separated System* (Manchester, Manchester University Press, 1996) (emphases added).

> (d) Except for information that is properly restricted from disclosure under procedures established in accordance with statute, regulation, Executive Order, or Presidential Memorandum, each agency should make available to the public the scientific or technological findings or conclusions considered or relied on in policy decisions.
>
> (e) Each agency should have in place procedures to identify and address instances in which the scientific process or the integrity of scientific and technological information may be compromised …

And as long as three decades ago, a thoughtful writer celebrated the proposition that judicial review of rule-makings, requiring what our courts have called a 'hard look' at matters in controversy, armed those within an agency who cared about reasoned decision-making (ie, acts of judgement) with a weapon with which to influence those who did not (ie, prefer acts of will).[56] The other side of this, however, has been the plaint recurrent in the American literature that the 'hard look' has produced ossification—by making it too costly for agencies to produce regulations, and providing the opponents of warranted regulation with too many tools by which to delay or obstruct it.[57]

Perhaps nowhere in American administrative law have ossification concerns been voiced more loudly than in connection with the issues of peer review and information quality—both issues on which the executive order appears to make commitments. Does peer review add another step to what is already a time-consuming, resource-expensive process? In the realm of 'pure science' (or review for publication in science journals), peer review might be characterised as merely the process that happens (assessments and efforts at replication that conduce to validity), and the passage of time is not so relevant as a factor. Add financial or power consequences to truth-seeking, and social consequences to delay, however, and matters become considerably more complex. If it is to be conducted outside government (that is, using scientists whose connection with public service is no more than as a special employee), can adequate assurances be attained that the reviewing peers will not be interested ones? The Bush administration's efforts to put peer review mechanisms in place were widely criticised for their perceived tendencies to produce delay and to arm regulatory opponents without notably improving regulatory outcomes. A so-called 'Information Quality Act' was inserted by stealth in an omnibus budget statute during the Bush administration, and seen by many to have similar tendencies. 'More study is required' is notoriously an obstacle to action—appropriate at times, but readily wielded in a wider range of circumstances.

One does not too readily find enforceably mandated procedures like the American ones for the adoption of regulatory measures in other political systems. The European Union engages in advanced public consultations about proposed

[56] WF Pedersen, Jr, *Formal Records and Informal Rulemaking* (1975) 85 *Yale LJ* 38, 59–60.

[57] A sceptical note has recently been sounded about these claims by S Shapiro, 'Explaining Ossification: An Examination of the Time to Finish Rulemakings' (11 August 2009). Available at SSRN: www.ssrn.com/abstract=1447337 (Visited 20 September 2009).

legislative actions; for subsidiary legislation corresponding to American rule-making, however, it deploys the somewhat obscure process of comitology, which lacks similar commitments.[58] In the development of Codex Alimentarius standards, FAO-WHO employs a process resembling American notice and comment rule-making, with some exposure of data, opportunities for comment by interested persons, and an ostensible commitment to objective, science-based judgement. Adoption, however, is political, by agreement of the Member States; the extent to which transparency is actually achieved, by documents or through the Internet, appears uncertain (perhaps especially at later stages); and it does not appear there is any objectivised test of the reasoning that may be employed. In parliamentary democracies the responsibility of ministers to the Parliament is often, if not invariably, accepted as a sufficient basis for their exercise of rule-making powers.

Recent, broadly grounded studies by members of the science community have emphasised the positive contributions of embracive participatory processes to the quality as well as the acceptability of judgements made in contexts like these.[59] Building on the dominant ethic of scientific inquiry—the full reporting of approaches, data, reasoning and results, with open acknowledgment of and attempts to frame uncertainties—these studies stress transparency and candour as root values of the iterative processes they imagine. Of course certain realities intrude when translating the conditions of scientific inquiry to the world of government action. Securing the cooperation of commercial participants, often essential, may depend on effective capacity to assure them that information they provide will not be revealed to competitors or in other respects imperil their interests. Government actors will not be disposed or able to await the definitive resolution of all issues in the face of needs for action, not merely knowledge. Not every participant in a process will be motivated simply by the pursuit of accurate understanding. Concerns for efficiency, and for protection against manipulative uses of opportunities afforded for participation, have consequent force.

A further complication is introduced by the fact, frequently remarked, that the public simply does not evaluate risks the same way experts do. New Zealand's experience with Herceptin might be taken as an exemplar of this problem: where administrators deemed the benefits of a full year of treatment too uncertain to justify diverting public funds, yet the public (whose funds they were) voted in favour of the diversion. In a democratic society, such electoral choices and the value judgements they reflect cannot be dismissed.

[58] See generally PL Strauss *et al*, *Administrative Law of the European Union: Rulemaking* (Chicago, American Bar Association, 2008).

[59] T Dietz and P Stern (eds), *Public Participation in Environmental Assessment and Decision Making* (Washington, National Research Council, 2008); J Chilvers, 'Deliberating Competence: Theoretical and Practitioner Perspectives on Effective Participatory Appraisal Practice' (2008) 33 *Science, Technology & Human Values* 421.

Central government controls and politics

Oversight or Control?

Recent years have seen both a significant expansion of agency control mechanisms in the White House itself and, as mentioned above,[60] much enlarged penetration of 'political clearances' into agency bureaucracies. While the controls centered in OIRA, discussed further below, have attracted the most scholarly and congressional attention, Lisa Bressman and Michael Vandenbergh's groundbreaking account of the EPA-White House interface from the perspective of EPA political appointees dramatically illustrates the number of White House voices (in both Republican and Democratic administrations) purporting to exercise 'presidential control'.[61] President Obama's appointments to White House positions—for example, a former EPA administrator, Carol Browner, to a new position as White House Coordinator of Energy and Climate Policy, 'climate czarina'—suggests that this reality may persevere. The prompt annulment of President Bush's Executive Order 13422, on the other hand, withdrew certain personnel requirements for responsibility *within* agencies that might have been seen as additional political controls.[62]

An entirely separate issue, and the one that initially catalysed this writing, concerns the place of political controls, and perhaps especially centralised executive political controls, over the outcomes of standard setting activities. American arrangements for the allocation of executive authority typically place responsibility for science-based decision-making in civil service-dominated agencies rather than the political White House. When the legislature has empowered a particular organ of government to create regulations—subsidiary norms—to carry forward a statutory scheme that imagines technical or scientific judgements being made, what is the appropriate reach of centralised executive oversight or control?

Consider the ozone regulation episode described above. The bureaucratic structures President Bush employed in interacting with EPA did not originate with him, but have been steadily developed by American presidents at least since the administration of Richard Nixon, most notably by Ronald Reagan and Bill Clinton.[63] Their current expression is in Executive Order 12,866, an order initially created by President Clinton and then somewhat modified by President Bush. The order, in basic outline, creates three stages for agency consultation with the White House during rule-making: first, consultation with the White House

[60] See text accompanying n 32 above.

[61] LS Bressman and MP Vandenbergh, *Inside the Administrative State: A Critical Look at the Practice of Presidential Control* (2006) 105 *Michigan Law Review* 47, 47–52.

[62] Exec Order No 13,422, 72 Fed Reg 2763 (23 January 2007), essentially required every agency to place control over its rule-making operations in the hands, not of the agency head, but of a staffer directly responsible to the White House.

[63] Such a regime was first given formal public shape by President Jimmy Carter (Exec Order 12,044); precursors can be found in the presidencies of Richard Nixon and Gerald Ford.

about their rule-making priorities (the 'regulatory plan', which is published annually in advance of any particular proposals); and then draft and final analyses of particular rules to be proposed and perhaps adopted in carrying out the plan. For the latter stages, the order directs agencies, to the extent consistent with law, to engage in structured analyses of the projected costs and benefits of rule-making proposals, assessing the projected costs and benefits of alternative approaches and choosing that policy which maximises benefits in relation to costs and in other respects conforms to presidential policy preferences. The intensity of this effort and of OIRA's supervision of it is to vary with the importance of the rule; the greatest effort is required for proposals likely to add $100 million or more annually to industrial costs or in other respects have a major economic impact.

Although not statutory, the existence and general shape of this regime have been accepted by Congress, which has passed several statutes assuming its existence and continuation, and by the academic community. Rule-making is understood to be too important to national well-being for there not to be a strong central voice and regime for coordination and settlement of interagency dispute. Through the Clinton administration at least, the disputes that have arisen about it could be characterised as marginal: the nature and extent of its transparency; the precise nature of the inquiry to be conducted; the balance OIRA should strike between supervision of agency processes in general and detailed attention to particular proposals; and the threshold beneath which only superficial OIRA engagement is appropriate.[64]

Probably the most important criticism has been that, as administered, Executive Order 12866 has too often proved not to be a neutral device, but rather a deregulatory device—a source of delay and diversion, a pressure point for reduction of burdens and not actions to protect the public. A narrow focus on monetised 'costs' and 'benefits', in relation only to regulatory actions agencies have in fact proposed (and not, then, to their priority choices), has largely been responsible for that. But beyond this is the possibility that presidential involvement has led to decision based on considerations other than those the agencies explain in their statutorily required 'statement of basis and purpose'.

In the American context, the controversy about the chief executive's engagement with rule-making has a number of elements, some of which are doubtless (and perhaps happily) unique to it and may be seen to illustrate ongoing disputes about the nature and extent of the American President's authority in relation to the decisions of domestic government. Our Constitution vests our President, our one elected executive official, with 'the Executive power', in a largely undefined way. Does that entitle him to *decide* every matter the Congress may delegate to

[64] OIRA will doubtless remain a small office, and one lacking the expertise to be found in the operating agencies. This makes it important that effort be focused on the most important rule-makings, and that it be prompt. No more than a few hundred rules annually, as such, should be in strong review.

cabinet Departments and other governmental agencies? Or is he merely to *oversee* their doing so, accepting that ultimate legal responsibility for action has been placed in them and that his authority is limited to persuasion, to replacing officers whose decisions displease him, and the like?

I have discussed this question at length elsewhere.[65] In a nutshell, my view is that control and influence are different matters. As our one elected executive official with a constitutionally defined active role, the President is certainly entitled to try to influence agencies; he would be shirking if he did not do so. He enjoys constitutional authority to demand the 'Opinion, in writing' from the leadership of executive departments on any matter Congress has assigned to them.[66] Certainly this supposes that, once informed of their opinion, he will have a chance at least to reason with them on any matter Congress has assigned to them (that is, their 'Duties', to which the same constitutional text also refers). For me, this must include the so-called independent regulatory commissions as well as the cabinet departments. And where responsibilities are shared among several agencies—to take an example I am a bit familiar with, radiation exposure protections, which concern the Nuclear Regulatory Commission, EPA, the Occupational Safety and Health Administration, the Department of Defense, the Department of Energy, the Department of Transportation (hazmats) and probably others—coordination must be part of what he has to do. He should have staff to help him with this, a matter of particular importance where multiple agencies are involved.

Control, in my judgement, is an entirely different matter. Congress has placed decisional responsibility in the EPA, say, not in the President. That placement, no less than the placing of the Forest Service in the Department of Agriculture and National Parks in the Department of the Interior, is a part of the law to whose faithful execution the President has undertaken to see. He is not assuring the faithful execution of the law if he purports to assign decisional responsibility to a place Congress has not put it, or takes on himself decisional responsibility for a matter Congress has delegated to someone else.

This is not to say that presidential supervision of rule-making is per se inappropriate. It seems at least possible that the new administration will pay more disciplined attention than its predecessors have to the first, priority-setting stage of the executive order process. Priority planning has been a part of the executive order at least since the second Reagan administration, but it has never been seriously used, so far as I have been able to tell. Strikingly, for example, a recent Government Accountability Office (GAO) Report,[67] while paying detailed

[65] PL Strauss, 'Overseer or "The Decider"? The President in Administrative Law' (2007) 75 *Geo Wash L Rev* 695.

[66] US Const art II, § 2, cl 1 (The President 'may require the Opinion, in writing, of the principal Officer in each of the executive Departments, upon any subject relating to *the Duties of their respective Offices*[.]') (emphasis added).

[67] See n 77 below.

attention to agency decision processes throughout the initiation and development of rule-makings, essentially ignores the formation of the regulatory plan. Conversation with agencies about their priorities—where the President believes it is important for them to put their effort—is in my judgement far more likely to be effective in improving government performance and administration than retrospectively checking sums on a series of particular rules. So also, engagement with agencies in how they structure their internal processes to promote sound and efficient analysis and decision, downplaying retrospective analysis of what is already well under way. Retrospective analysis threatens, and has been used to secure, considerable delay of initiatives already established as important priorities. And an emphasis on the regulatory plan element may also increase political responsibility *within* agencies. Chris DeMuth, the progenitor of the regulatory plan element, rationalised it as a way to give the political heads within agencies a mechanism for engaging with their staff at the outset of rule-makings, rather than also find themselves caught in retrospective exercises with effective *faits accomplis* perpetuated by staff.

Further, there are certain questions (foreign policy issues for example) as to which there is 'no law to apply', as the courts have said, and federal officials are merely the organs to express presidential will. Chief Justice Marshall famously addressed this setting in *Marbury v Madison*.[68] But where legality is central to our very tolerance of governmental authority, as it is for rule-making decisions like those of the EPA, then in my judgement our President's role under the laws, in a government of laws, requires him to respect Congress's placement of duties where Congress has placed them. When the EPA is authorised to adopt rules, it is the head of the EPA who has the responsibility to decide those matters. The President's place is one of oversight, not decision, making sure that he or she does that well. Which of course includes the agency head's acting only on the basis of those factors Congress has made relevant to his or her decision—precisely the issue President Bush's intervention on ozone appeared to compromise.[69] Of course consultation can often result in pressures, the substitution of judgement in fact. To turn from the presidency for the moment, the courts, too, know that they are responsible to review agency action (oversight) but are not to substitute their own judgements (decision); yet this does not keep them from doing things on occasion that to the observer seem like substitution. The important thing is the attitude—that agencies know what their responsibilities are, that courts are aware that they, like Presidents, are not supposed to substitute judgement, and that onlookers like myself can point to departures and cry 'Shame!'

[68] *Marbury v Madison* 5 US (1 Cranch) 137 (1803): an official obliged 'to conform precisely to the will of the President,' Marshall wrote, 'is the mere organ by whom that will is communicated. The acts of such an officer, as an officer, can never be examinable by the courts. ... The province of the court is, solely, to decide on the rights of individuals, not to enquire how the executive, or executive officers, perform duties in which they have a discretion. Questions, in their nature political, or which are, by the constitution and laws, submitted to the executive, can never be made in this court.'

[69] *Massachusetts v EPA* 549 US 497, 533 (2007).

My casebook colleague Todd Rakoff, reading an early draft of this chapter, remarked that it might be useful to note 'that our parties—or those that have a chance of coming to power—are based on very broad coalitions, such that each represents (albeit to differing degrees) most of the views to be found on public policy.' Over the years American political parties have enforced much less rigorous discipline, particularly in the Congress, than the parties of parliamentary democracies often deploy. Absent much party discipline or feeling that it ought to prevail, the result is to make even executive administration quite diverse. As President Harry Truman famously remarked when President Eisenhower, a former general, had been elected to succeed him, 'He'll sit here ... and he'll say, "Do this! Do that!" And nothing will happen. Poor Ike—it won't be a bit like the Army. He'll find it very frustrating.'[70] If presidential power is understood as the power to *persuade*—if those with whom he interacts understand that duties lie with them, that loyalty is not the *primum bonum* of holding executive office, and that the diversity of political view within their party creates wiggle room for them in performing their duties—then one might argue that the 2,500 or so presidential administrative appointments made without the benefit of Senate confirmation will still predictably represent, in some crude but real sense, the disparate views of a majority of the population. Introduce the emphasis on loyalty and effective party discipline that has characterised the Republican party in recent years, in Congress as well as in the White House, and this reassurance disappears.[71] The governing ethic of those taking the 'strong unitary executive' view is that the first duties of civilian heads of departments, like generals of the Army, are loyalty and obedience. Recall Truman's quip: 'Whenever you have an efficient government you have a dictatorship.'[72]

Transparency, Accountability, and the Honest Broker

Knowledge of what White House officials are doing is surely a prerequisite for presidential political responsibility, indeed for arming political response. Fortunately, there is at least some reason to believe the present executive order regime can facilitate the necessary watchdogging. The involvement of OIRA is perhaps the most regular and (although not completely) transparent means by which political officials may succeed in influencing decisions ostensibly committed to bureaucrats instructed to act on the basis of objective data and limited, stated considerations.[73] As noted previously, that OIRA's interventions in the ozone

[70] R Neustadt, *Presidential Power and the Modern President* (New York, Free Press, 1991).

[71] *cf* the decision of Senator Arlen Spector, a long-time moderate Republican from Pennsylvania, to switch parties, which appears at least in part to have been motivated by the prospect of strong opposition within his party in a coming election, given his moderate views.

[72] See n 145 above.

[73] Accounts of Vice President Dick Cheney's behaviour in office, eg, have included his repeated forceful and undisclosed interventions on a question concerning the amount of water (that might otherwise be used by farmers for irrigation) to be released from a single western dam in order to

rule-making became public owes something to precommitments it had made. These were made as part of the political price exacted by previous Congresses for accepting the role Presidents had established for it; the disclosures also had their source in bureaucratic initiative. And the ensuing proceedings, congressional and judicial, as well as the fact of a searchable Internet database, reflect possible controls on such interventions in the American context. President Obama's apparent taste for other central offices with oversight responsibilities[74] suggests a possible need to generalise these controls.

Indeed, new scholarship highlights a remarkable gap in the public record. In a piece appearing on SSRN,[75] Professor Nina Mendelson persuasively analyses the opaque disconnect between agency reasoning and White House influence.

> With a couple of notable exceptions, numerous searches of Federal Register statements issued since January 1981 have disclosed no proposed or final rules in which the agency referred to the content of OMB or OIRA review or presidential preferences, directives, or priorities.[76]

A recently published GAO study of rule development and OIRA reviews suggests that—as proved out in the Ozone case—presidential fingerprints are more readily to be found in rule-making dockets than statements of basis and purpose; the study also suggests considerable deficiencies in the transparency of the present process.[77]

Perhaps our President's promises of transparency will change all this—lift the veil of privilege, expose the influence of values on decision as Professor Mendelson urges. Or perhaps not. The public alarm over President Bush's apparent use of the EO 12,866 procedures to 'bend science' led President Obama, at the very outset of his administration, to announce a sweeping reconsideration of the practice. Without awaiting further public input, he revoked changes that President Bush had made in the order, that obscured the role of the Vice President, required the designation in each agency of political officers directly responsible to him to control rule-making, and expanded the reach and intensity of OIRA's review. This effectively restored it to the shape it had had during the Clinton administration—but in that administration as well the order did not lack critics

protect an endangered species of fish living in the river on which the dam was situated. Under the statute, wisely or not, the farmers' needs were not a relevant consideration; rather, the decision was to be based on a scientific assessment of the survival needs of the endangered species. J Becker and B Gellman, 'Leaving No Tracks', The Washington Post, 27 June 2007, at A1.

[74] See the text above, following n 61. Recent commentary on these offices, strongly suggesting their deficiencies in transparency alongside their legitimacy for securing coordination among the variety of agencies that may be charged with particular elements of a problem, appears in Czar Talk, www.ombwatch.org/node/10403, visited 21 September 2009.

[75] NA Mendelson, 'Including "Political" Reasons in Agency Decision Making', (2010) 108 *Michigan Law Review* 1127.

[76] ibid, at 1157.

[77] GAO, Report to the Chairman, Committee on Oversight and Government Reform, House of Representatives, 'Federal Rulemaking: Improvements Needed to Monitoring and Evaluation of Rules Development as Well as to the Transparency of OMB Regulatory Reviews', GAO-09–205, April 2009.

of its politicising and delay-promoting possibilities. Perhaps in consequence, President Obama has invited public as well as agency engagement with the question, how the order should be revised. As of 20 April, 183 public comments or meetings had been memorialised on the White House website,[78] reflecting the wide range of views held on the matter.

Strikingly, and perhaps an indicator of the sensitivity about exposing internal executive branch communications that will doubtless complicate President Obama's commitment to transparency, there is not a single comment from a public agency; two meetings are mentioned, but in each case only the names of agency attendees are given.

Indeed, one kind of issue about presidential control with proven implications for 'science-bending' concerns presidential control over executive branch communications with Congress, a sort of control likely to be much harder to achieve where ministers are members of parliament who must be prepared to respond, with their own re-electability on the line, in free flowing 'question time'. Transparency, and all the contributions to 'honest brokering' and effective democracy through the 'marketplace of ideas' that go with it, are impaired if the President takes the position that communications with Congress or the public must be pre-cleared politically. One notorious example during the Bush administration was the suppression of projections concerning the cost of certain health-care measures.

Some White House controls are of long-standing, however. During my tenure as General Counsel of the US Nuclear Regulatory Commission some three decades ago, the Office of Management and Budget was already 'coordinating' (ie, pre-clearing) communications and testimony to Congress about legislative proposals and budgetary matters. The Commission's nominal independence (it was of course an element of the executive branch, but its statutes provided explicitly for direct communication) softened these controls; but, as noted above,[79] within the Commission itself, Bureau 'executives' sometimes kept their staffers on a tight leash in terms of what the latter were permitted to tell the Commission about perceived nuclear energy risks. And similar pressures might be brought to bear on utility personnel to suppress safety concerns they might wish to share with the Commission. Such 'bending' did not conduce to public protection.

The legal basis for sweeping presidential control over communication by others in the executive branch, if not its political reality, can be questioned. To the extent the American Constitution speaks to the matter at all, it merely permits the President to recommend to the Congress such legislation as he regards as expedient. Citizens of parliamentary democracies, inured to the powers of their prime minister over legislative business, will easily grasp the weakness of this

[78] www.reginfo.gov/public/jsp/EO/fedRegReview/publicComments.jsp, visited 10 September 2009.

[79] See n 37 above and accompanying text.

provision, which addresses only presidential initiative and does not even suggest that a presidential suggestion must become legislative business. For that to happen, some member of Congress must introduce a bill, whose language the President cannot legally control. There is nothing here about keeping others from making any recommendations they might like. Nonetheless, as indicated, Presidents have long asserted the right to sit astride any such communications, at least outside the 'independent regulatory commission' context.

The strong Bush (and Reagan) administration theories of the 'unitary executive' can be found in a memorandum entitled 'Authority of Agency Officials to Prohibit Employees from Providing Information to Congress', explaining the withholding of projections of health programme costs from Congress, following a discussion properly reciting the Clinton, etc, invocation of executive privilege in more conventional contexts:

> The foregoing discussion does not mean that an agency's right to supervise its employees' disclosures to Congress is limited to privileged information. The discussion establishes only that the CRS interpretation that the 'right of disclosure' statutes prohibit Executive Branch supervision of employee disclosures unconstitutionally limits the ability of the President and his appointees to supervise and control the dissemination of privileged government information. However, the CRS position also unconstitutionally limits the President's ability to supervise and control the work of subordinate officers and employees of the Executive Branch more generally. See Constitutionality of Statute Requiring Executive Agency to Report Directly to Congress, 6 Op. O.L.C. 632, 633 (1982) (statutory 'requirement that subordinate officials within the Executive Branch submit reports directly to Congress, without any prior review by their superiors, would greatly impair the right of the President to exercise his constitutionally based right to control the Executive Branch'; provision would be unconstitutional if so construed); Authority of the Special Counsel of the Merit Systems Protection Board to Litigate and Submit Legislation to Congress, 8 Op. O.L.C. 30, 31 (1984) ('Congress may not grant [Special Counsel] the authority to submit legislative proposals directly to Congress without prior review and clearance by the President, or other appropriate authority, without raising serious separation of powers concerns').

This second, 'unitary Executive' position is based on the following rationale:

> The [judicial] decisions and the long practical history concerning the right of the President to protect his control over the Executive Branch are based on the fundamental principle that the President's relationship with his subordinates must be free from certain types of interference from the coordinate branches of government in order to permit the President effectively to carry out his constitutionally assigned responsibilities. The executive power resides in the President, and he is obligated to 'take care that the laws are faithfully executed'. In order to fulfill those responsibilities, the President must be able to rely upon the faithful service of subordinate officials. To the extent that Congress or the courts interfere with the President's right to control or receive effective service from his subordinates within the Executive Branch, those other branches limit the ability of the President to perform his constitutional function.

> 6 Op. O.L.C. at 638–39. Based on this rationale, we do not believe that the statutes relied upon by CRS could constitutionally be applied, as CRS would apply them, to the circumstance where a government official instructs a subordinate government employee not to provide an Administration's cost estimates to Congress, whether or not the estimates are viewed as privileged.[80]

On this issue, the Obama administration appears to be sending somewhat mixed signals. The recent executive order on scientific integrity is explicit that:

> (3) ... (b) Nothing in this memorandum shall be construed to impair or otherwise affect...:
>
> (ii) functions of the Director of the Office of Management and Budget relating to budgetary, administrative, or legislative proposals.

This seems to keep OMB's existing controls over direct agency communications firmly in place. On the other hand, the 'whistleblower' provisions of President Obama's directive on scientific integrity reflect one possible step toward openness—hopefully successful in [re]establishing an ethos, if not invariably successful in preventing suppression of data. And in a recent statement accompanying his signing of a piece of complex legislation, explaining his reservations about limited elements of the bill he was permitting to become law,[81] President Obama wrote:

> *Executive Authority to Control Communications with the Congress.* Sections 714(1) and 714(2) in Division D prohibit the use of appropriations to pay the salary of any Federal officer or employee who interferes with or prohibits certain communications between Federal employees and Members of Congress. I do not interpret this provision to detract from my authority to direct the heads of executive departments to supervise, control, and correct employees' communications with the Congress in cases where such communications would be unlawful or would reveal information that is properly privileged or otherwise confidential.[82]

Whether this is simply a reaffirmation that in some cases (nuclear weapons plans, for example) congressional demands for information must be denied in the interest of national security and the like, or rather a continuation of past practices of iron control over what information Congress sees remains to be seen. But note that in this statement President Obama, unlike his predecessors, limits

[80] www.usdoj.gov/olc/crsmemoresponsese.htm, visited 19 March 2009. Shortly before leaving office, President Bush's final Assistant Attorney-General in charge of the Office of Legal Counsel formally withdrew certain OLC opinions embracing 'unitary Executive' reasoning. In doing so, however, he mentioned only some that had become particularly controversial respecting presidential claims to emergency powers in the wake of September 11, 2001 attacks. NA Lewis, 'Memos Reveal Scope of Power Bush Sought in Fighting Terror', NY Times, 3 March 2009, at A1.

[81] On the controversy over 'signing statements', hardly necessary to explore here, see R Cass and PL Strauss, 'The Presidential Signing Statements Controversy' (2007) 16 *William & Mary Bill of Rights Journal* 11.

[82] Press Statement of 11 March 2009, www.whitehouse.gov/the_press_office/Statement-from-the-President-on-the-signing-of-HR-1105/, visited 13 March 2009.

his reservation to 'cases where such communications would be unlawful or would reveal information that is properly privileged or otherwise confidential.' This seems a more limited, and readily accepted, claim than appears in the Bush 'unitary President' explanation.

It is unreasonable to expect presidential-congressional struggles over executive privilege to cease.[83] As Congress itself recognised in including certain exemptions in the Freedom of Information Act, and as President Truman pungently remarked,[84] the President needs candid advice from his subordinates, and candour depends on confidentiality. Where the issue, however, is not advice, but data (viz, projections of the frequency with which orange-bellied parrots would be impinged on wind farm turbine blades at the projected Bald hills facility in Australia), the issues are quite different. The issue will be how widely and aggressively executive privilege is claimed.

One's impression is that the Obama administration understands these issues. But the proof will be in the pudding.

CONCLUSION

In concluding a paper presented to a conference on *global* administrative law, it may be appropriate to remind the reader that these are not simply American issues. One may be certain the issues of science-bending and the possible contributions to its control of transparency are present in *every* administrative law system—if not in connection with rule-making, then with contentious licensing issues.

The Internet and its ready searchability are global phenomena, so that questions about what information it should contain about governmental policy formation, made available to whom, and on what time schedule, are universal. Questions inviting scientific assessment frequently also involve uncertainties not completely resolvable by objective means, and/or kinds of risk to which the public is particularly sensitive. They may reflect matters of large public concern, on which the public, and politicians representing them, will understandably and acceptably wish to have a voice. The use of nuclear power, or of genetically modified organisms (GMOs) in the food chain, and the problems of global warming come readily to mind, and there are many like situations. One easily imagines situations like the more acceptable way of understanding the ozone controversy in the United States, in which generalist politicians are motivated by public interest considerations that may be missing from the particular law governing an agency's resolution of a matter. Understandable as it may be for them to inject these considerations into the decisional framework, that course

[83] See generally PM Shane, 'Negotiating for Knowledge: Administrative Responses to Congressional Demands for Information' (1992) 44 *Administrative Law Review* 197.

[84] See text accompanying n 46 above.

nonetheless presents troubling questions of legality. If the inadequacy of the existing legal framework is thus revealed, the proper response appears to be changing, not overriding, that framework. Beyond this lies the possibility that, less acceptably, individual politicians will act covertly in the interest of particular 'clients' to influence decision away from the point that an inquiry according to framework laws would determine.

To what extent is the data on which scientific assessments or political judgements may be based provided through the Internet, or in other ways exposed to public view? What are the contexts in which political interventions in an ostensibly objective (scientific) process may arise? To what extent are they transparent, so that the fact of them may be known? What if any controls are available to constrain their impact? These are questions of the broadest import. In the current day, given the high levels of concern about global warming, GMOs, and other matters, finding appropriate space both for the understandings science can bring and for the expression of democratic concerns that do not and need not regard all risks as commensurate, is challenging indeed.

Appendix A

THE WHITE HOUSE

Office of the Press Secretary

For Immediate Release March 9, 2009

March 9, 2009

MEMORANDUM FOR THE HEADS OF EXECUTIVE DEPARTMENTS AND AGENCIES

SUBJECT: Scientific Integrity

Science and the scientific process must inform and guide decisions of my Administration on a wide range of issues, including improvement of public health, protection of the environment, increased efficiency in the use of energy and other resources, mitigation of the threat of climate change, and protection of national security.

The public must be able to trust the science and scientific process informing public policy decisions. Political officials should not suppress or alter scientific or technological findings and conclusions. If scientific and technological information is developed and used by the Federal Government, it should ordinarily be made available to the public. To the extent permitted by law, there should be transparency in the preparation, identification, and use of scientific and technological information in policymaking. The selection of scientists and technology professionals for positions in the executive branch should be based on their scientific and technological knowledge, credentials, experience, and integrity.

By this memorandum, I assign to the Director of the Office of Science and Technology Policy (Director) the responsibility for ensuring the highest level of integrity in all aspects of the executive branch's involvement with scientific and technological processes. The Director shall confer, as appropriate, with the heads of executive departments and agencies, including the Office of Management and

Budget and offices and agencies within the Executive Office of the President (collectively, the 'agencies'), and recommend a plan to achieve that goal throughout the executive branch.

Specifically, I direct the following:

1. Within 120 days from the date of this memorandum, the Director shall develop recommendations for Presidential action designed to guarantee scientific integrity throughout the executive branch, based on the following principles:

(a) The selection and retention of candidates for science and technology positions in the executive branch should be based on the candidate's knowledge, credentials, experience, and integrity;

(b) Each agency should have appropriate rules and procedures to ensure the integrity of the scientific process within the agency;

(c) When scientific or technological information is considered in policy decisions, the information should be subject to well-established scientific processes, including peer review where appropriate, and each agency should appropriately and accurately reflect that information in complying with and applying relevant statutory standards;

(d) Except for information that is properly restricted from disclosure under procedures established in accordance with statute, regulation, Executive Order, or Presidential Memorandum, each agency should make available to the public the scientific or technological findings or conclusions considered or relied on in policy decisions;

(e) Each agency should have in place procedures to identify and address instances in which the scientific process or the integrity of scientific and technological information may be compromised; and

(f) Each agency should adopt such additional procedures, including any appropriate whistleblower protections, as are necessary to ensure the integrity of scientific and technological information and processes on which the agency relies in its decisionmaking or otherwise uses or prepares.

2. Each agency shall make available any and all information deemed by the Director to be necessary to inform the Director in making recommendations to the President as requested by this memorandum. Each agency shall coordinate with the Director in the development of any interim procedures deemed necessary to ensure the integrity of scientific decisionmaking pending the Director's recommendations called for by this memorandum.

3. (a) Executive departments and agencies shall carry out the provisions of this memorandum to the extent permitted by law and consistent with their statutory and regulatory authorities and their enforcement mechanisms.

(b) Nothing in this memorandum shall be construed to impair or otherwise affect:

(i) authority granted by law to an executive department, agency, or the head thereof; or

(ii) functions of the Director of the Office of Management and Budget relating to budgetary, administrative, or legislative proposals.

c) This memorandum is not intended to, and does not, create any right or benefit, substantive or procedural, enforceable at law or in equity, by any party against the United States, its departments, agencies, or entities, its officers, employees, or agents, or any other person.

4. The Director is hereby authorized and directed to publish this memorandum in the Federal Register.

BARACK OBAMA

Appendix B

WORKING PRINCIPLES FOR RISK ANALYSIS FOR FOOD SAFETY FOR APPLICATION BY GOVERNMENTS

CAC/GL 62–2007

1. SCOPE

1. The Working Principles for Risk Analysis for Food Safety for Application by Governments are intended to provide guidance to national governments for risk assessment, risk management and risk communication with regard to food related risks to human health.

2. GENERAL ASPECTS

2. The overall objective of risk analysis applied to food safety is to ensure human health protection.

3. These principles apply equally to issues of national food control and food trade situations and should be applied consistently and in a non discriminatory manner.

4. To the extent possible, the application of risk analysis should be established as an integral part of a national food safety system.[85]

5. Implementation of risk management decisions at the national level should be supported by an adequately functioning food control system/program.

6. Risk analysis should be:

- applied consistently;
- open, transparent and documented; and

[85] It is recognised that national governments will use different approaches and time frames in the application of these principles taking into account national capacities and resources.

- evaluated and reviewed as appropriate in the light of newly generated scientific data.

7. The risk analysis should follow a structured approach comprising the three distinct but closely linked components of risk analysis (risk assessment, risk management and risk communication) as defined by the Codex Alimentarius Commission,[86] each component being integral to the overall risk analysis.

8. The three components of risk analysis should be documented fully and systematically in a transparent manner. While respecting legitimate concerns to preserve confidentiality, documentation should be accessible to all interested parties.[87]

9. Effective communication and consultation with all interested parties should be ensured throughout the risk analysis.

10. The three components of risk analysis should be applied within an overarching framework for management of food related risks to human health.

11. There should be a functional separation of risk assessment and risk management to the degree practicable, in order to ensure the scientific integrity of the risk assessment, to avoid confusion over the functions to be performed by risk assessors and risk managers and to reduce any conflict of interest. However, it is recognized that risk analysis is an iterative process, and interaction between risk managers and risk assessors is essential for practical application.

12. Precaution is an inherent element of risk analysis. Many sources of uncertainty exist in the process of risk assessment and risk management of food related hazards to human health. The degree of uncertainty and variability in the available scientific information should be explicitly considered in the risk analysis. The assumptions used for the risk assessment and the risk management options selected should reflect the degree of uncertainty and the characteristics of the hazard.

13. National governments should take into account relevant guidance and information obtained from risk analysis activities pertaining to human health protection conducted by Codex, FAO, WHO and other relevant international intergovernmental organizations, including OIE and IPPC.

[86] See Definitions of Risk Analysis Terms Related to Food Safety, Procedural Manual.

[87] For the purpose of the present document, the term 'interested parties' refers to 'risk assessors, risk managers, consumers, industry, the academic community and, as appropriate, other relevant parties and their representative organizations' (see definition of 'Risk Communication').

14. With the support of international organizations where appropriate, national governments should design and/or apply appropriate training, information and capacity building programs that are aimed to achieve the effective application of risk analysis principles and techniques in their food control systems.

15. National governments should share information and experiences on risk analysis with relevant international organisations, other national governments (e.g. at the regional level through FAO/WHO Regional Coordinating Committees) to promote and facilitate a broader and, where appropriate, more consistent, application of risk analysis.

3. RISK ASSESSMENT POLICY

16. Determination of risk assessment policy should be included as a specific component of risk management.

17. Risk assessment policy should be established by risk managers in advance of risk assessment, in consultation with risk assessors and all other interested parties. This procedure aims at ensuring that the risk assessment is systematic, complete, unbiased and transparent.

18. The mandate given by risk managers to risk assessors should be as clear as possible.

19. Where necessary, risk managers should ask risk assessors to evaluate the potential changes in risk resulting from different risk management options.

4. RISK ASSESSMENT

20. Each risk assessment should be fit for its intended purpose.

21. The scope and purpose of the risk assessment being carried out should be clearly stated and in accordance with risk assessment policy. The output form and possible alternative outputs of the risk assessment should be defined.

22. Experts, involved in risk assessment including government officials and experts from outside government should be objective in their scientific work and not be subject to any conflict of interest that may compromise the integrity of the assessment. Information on the identities of these experts, their individual expertise and their professional experience should be publicly available, subject to national considerations. These experts should be selected in a transparent manner on the basis of their expertise and their independence with regard to the interests involved, including disclosure of conflicts of interest in connection with risk assessment.

23. Risk assessment should incorporate the four steps of risk assessment, i.e., hazard identification, hazard characterization, exposure assessment and risk characterization.

24. Risk assessment should be based on scientific data most relevant to the national context. It should use available quantitative information to the greatest extent possible. Risk assessment may also take into account qualitative information.

25. Risk assessment should take into account relevant production, storage and handling practices used throughout the food chain including traditional practices, methods of analysis, sampling and inspection and the prevalence of specific adverse health effects.

26. Constraints, uncertainties and assumptions having an impact on the risk assessment should be explicitly considered at each step in the risk assessment and documented in a transparent manner. Expression of uncertainty or variability in risk estimates may be qualitative or quantitative, but should be quantified to the extent that is scientifically achievable.

27. Risk assessments should be based on realistic exposure scenarios, with consideration of different situations being defined by risk assessment policy. They should include consideration of susceptible and high-risk population groups. Acute, chronic (including long-term), cumulative and/or combined adverse health effects should be taken into account in carrying out risk assessment, where relevant.

28. The report of the risk assessment should indicate any constraints, uncertainties, assumptions and their impact on the risk assessment. Minority opinions should also be recorded. The responsibility for resolving the impact of uncertainty on the risk management decision lies with the risk manager, not the risk assessors.

29. The conclusion of the risk assessment including a risk estimate, if available, should be presented in a readily understandable and useful form to risk managers and made available to other risk assessors and interested parties so that they can review the assessment.

5. RISK MANAGEMENT

30. National government decisions on risk management, including sanitary measures taken, should have as their primary objective the protection of the health of consumers. Unjustified differences in the measures selected to address similar risks in different situations should be avoided.

31 Risk management should follow a structured approach including preliminary risk management activities,[88] evaluation of risk management options, implementation, monitoring and review of the decision taken.

32. The decisions should be based on risk assessment, and should be proportionate to the assessed risk, taking into account, where appropriate, other legitimate factors relevant for the health protection of consumers and for the promotion of fair practices in food trade, in accordance with the Criteria for the Consideration of the Other Factors Referred to in the Second Statement of Principles[89] as they relate to decisions at the national level. National Governments should base their sanitary measures on Codex standards and related texts, where available.

33. In achieving agreed outcomes, risk management should take into account relevant production, storage and handling practices used throughout the food chain including traditional practices, methods of analysis, sampling and inspection, feasibility of enforcement and compliance, and the prevalence of specific adverse health effects.

34. Risk management should take into account the economic consequences and the feasibility of risk management options.

35. The risk management process should be transparent, consistent and fully documented. Decisions on risk management should be documented so as to facilitate a wider understanding of the risk management process by all interested parties.

36. The outcome of the preliminary risk management activities and the risk assessment should be combined with the evaluation of available risk management options in order to reach a decision on management of the risk.

37. Risk management options should be assessed in terms of the scope and purpose of risk analysis and the level of consumer health protection they achieve. The option of not taking any action should also be considered.

38. Risk management should ensure transparency and consistency in the decision-making process in all cases. Examination of the full range of risk management options should, as far as possible, take into account an assessment

[88] For the purpose of these Principles, preliminary risk management activities are taken to include: identification of a food safety problem; establishment of a risk profile; ranking of the hazard for risk assessment and risk management priority; establishment of risk assessment policy for the conduct of the risk assessment; commissioning of the risk assessment; and consideration of the result of the risk assessment.

[89] See *Statements of Principle Concerning the Role of Science in the Codex Decision Making Process and the Extent to which other Factors are Taken in to Account*, Procedural Manual.

of their potential advantages and disadvantages. When making a choice among different risk management options, which are equally effective in protecting the health of the consumer, national governments should seek and take into consideration the potential impact of such measures on trade and select measures that are no more trade-restrictive than necessary.

39. Risk management should be a continuing process that takes into account all newly generated data in the evaluation and review of risk management decisions. The relevance, effectiveness, and impacts of risk management decisions and their implementation should be regularly monitored and the decisions and/or their implementation reviewed as necessary.

6. RISK COMMUNICATION

40. Risk communication should:

i) promote awareness and understanding of the specific issues under consideration during the risk analysis;

ii) promote consistency and transparency in formulating risk management options/recommendations;

iii) provide a sound basis for understanding the risk management decisions proposed;

iv) improve the overall effectiveness and efficiency of the risk analysis;

v) strengthen the working relationships among participants;

vi) foster public understanding of the process, so as to enhance trust and confidence in the safety of the food supply;

vii) promote the appropriate involvement of all interested parties;

viii) exchange information in relation to the concerns of interested parties about the risks associated with food; and

ix) respect the legitimate concern to preserve confidentiality where applicable.

41. Risk analysis should include clear, interactive and documented communication, amongst risk assessors and risk managers and reciprocal communication with all interested parties in all aspects of the process.

42. Risk communication should be more than the dissemination of information. Its major function should be to ensure that all information and opinion required for effective risk management is incorporated into the decision making process.

43. Risk communication involving interested parties should include a transparent explanation of the risk assessment policy and of the assessment of risk, including the uncertainty. The decisions taken and the procedures followed to reach them, including how the uncertainty was dealt with, should also be clearly explained. It should indicate any constraints, uncertainties, assumptions and their impact on the risk analysis, and minority opinions that had been expressed in the course of the risk assessment (see para. 28).

Appendix C

DECLARATION OF INTERESTS FOR FAO EXPERTS

The assistance of distinguished authorities knowledgeable in a variety of scientific professions is essential to the work of the Food and Agriculture Organization of the United Nations (FAO). **It is expected that persons qualified to serve as an expert for FAO may have private interests related to the subject of their expertise. At the same time, it is imperative that situations be avoided in which such interests may unduly affect, or may be perceived to affect, an expert's impartiality or the outcome of work in which he/she was involved.**

To assure the highest integrity, and hence public confidence, in the activities of the Organization, FAO's regulations and policies require that all experts serving in an advisory role disclose any circumstances which could give rise to a potential conflict of interest (i.e., any interest which may affect, or may reasonably be perceived to affect, the expert's objectivity and independence). Accordingly, in this Declaration of Interest (DOI) form, you are requested to disclose any financial, professional or other interest relevant to the subject of the work or meeting in which you will be involved and any interest that could be significantly affected by the outcome of the meeting or work. You are also asked to declare relevant interests of others who may, or may be perceived to, unduly influence your judgment, such as immediate family members, employers, close professional associates or any others with whom you have a substantial common personal, financial or professional interest. If you do not provide, where requested, the amount or value of the interest, it will be assumed to be significant.

Kindly complete this form and submit it to FAO Secretariat, well in advance of the meeting or work. You are also asked to inform the Secretariat of any change in this information that occurs before or during the course of the meeting or work. If FAO considers that a potential conflict of interest exists, one of several outcomes can occur, depending on the circumstances involved: (i) you may be invited to continue to participate in the meeting or work, provided that your interest would be publicly disclosed; (ii) you may be asked not to take part in the portion of the meeting, discussion or work related to your interest, or not participate in related decisions; or (iii) you may be asked not to take part in the meeting or work altogether. Non-completion of the DOI form would preclude further consideration of an expert's participation.

Experts are requested to agree that any relevant conflicts may be **publicly disclosed** to other meeting participants and in the resulting report or other work product. The Secretariat will assume that you consent to such a disclosure, unless you check 'no' in the space provided on the last page of this form. In addition, the information disclosed by you **may later be made available** to persons outside of FAO if the objectivity of the work or meeting in which you are involved is questioned and the Director-General considers disclosure to be in the best interests of the Organization, although only after discussion with you.

Date and title of meeting or work, including description of subject-matter to be considered (if a number of substances or processes are to be evaluated, a list should be attached):

____

____

Please answer each of the questions below. If the answer to any of the questions is 'yes', briefly describe the circumstances on the last page of the form.

The term 'you' refers to yourself, your employer and your immediate family members (i.e., spouse (or partner with whom you have a similar close personal relationship) and your minor children). The term 'commercial entity' includes—aside from any commercial venture—an industry association, research institution or other organization whose funding is significantly derived from commercial concerns having an interest related to the subject of the meeting or work. The term 'meeting' also includes a series or cycle of meetings.

EMPLOYMENT AND CONSULTING

Within the past 3 years, have you worked for a commercial entity or other organization with an interest related to the subject of the meeting or work? Please also report any application or negotiation for future work.

1a Employment — Yes □ No □

1b Consulting, including service as a technical or other advisor — Yes □ No □

RESEARCH SUPPORT

Within the past 3 years, have you or your department or research unit received support or funding from a commercial entity or other organization with an interest related to the subject of the meeting or work? Please also report any application or award for future research support.

2a Research support, including grants, collaborations, sponsorships, and other funding — Yes□ No □

2b	Non-monetary support valued at more than US$1000 overall (include equipment, facilities, research assistants, paid travel to meetings, etc.)	Yes □ No □
	INVESTMENT INTERESTS Do you have current investments (valued at more than US$10 000 overall) in a commercial entity with an interest related to the subject of the meeting or work? Please also include indirect investments such as a trust or holding company. You may exclude mutual funds, pension funds or similar investments that are broadly diversified.	
3a	Stocks, bonds, stock options, other securities (e.g., short sales)	Yes□ No □
3b	Commercial business interests (e.g., proprietorships, partnerships, joint ventures)	Yes □ No □
	INTELLECTUAL PROPERTY Do you have any current intellectual property rights that might be enhanced or diminished by the outcome of the meeting or work?	
4a	Patents, trademarks, or copyrights (also include pending applications)	Yes □ No □
4b	Know-how in a substance, technology or process	Yes □ No □
	PUBLIC STATEMENTS AND POSITIONS (during the past 3 years) (questions relate to balanced composition of committee or group)	
5a	As part of a regulatory, legislative, judicial, or other governmental process, have you provided an expert opinion or testimony, related to the subject of the meeting or work, for a commercial entity or other organization?	Yes □ No □
5b	Through your articles, editorials or speeches, could you be perceived as having taken a prominent or well-known position related to the subject of the meeting or work?	Yes □ No □
5c	Do you hold an office or other position, paid or unpaid, where you may be expected to represent interests or defend a position related to the subject of the meeting or work?	Yes □ No □
5d	Have you served as a principal investigator, as lead expert in an expert committee or scientific or advisory group, and/or a member of a steering committee, an advisory board or equivalent body in relation to the same product or subject matter?	Yes □ No □

ADDITIONAL INFORMATION

6a If not already disclosed above, have you worked for the competitor of a product which is the subject of the meeting or work, or will your participation in the meeting or work enable you to obtain access to a competitor's confidential proprietary information, or create for you a financial or commercial competitive advantage? Yes☐ No ☐

6b To your knowledge, would the outcome of the meeting or work benefit or adversely affect interests of others with whom you have substantial common personal, financial or professional interests (such as your adult children or siblings, close professional colleagues, administrative unit or department)? Yes☐ No ☐

6c Is there any other aspect of your background or present circumstances not addressed above that might be perceived as affecting your objectivity or independence? Yes ☐ No ☐

EXPLANATION OF 'YES' RESPONSES: If the answer to any of the above questions is 'yes', check above and briefly describe the circumstances on this page. If you do not provide, where requested, the amount or value of the interest, it will be assumed to be significant.

Nos. 1–4 Type of interest, question number and category (e.g., Intellectual Property 4.a copyrights) and basic descriptive details.	**Name of company, organiza-tion, or institution**	**Belongs to you, a family member, employer, research unit or other?**	**Amount of income or value of interest (if not disclosed, assumed significant)**	**Current interest (or year ceased)**
Nos. 5–6: Describe the specific circumstances, parties involved, time frame and other relevant details				

CONSENT TO DISCLOSURE. The Secretariat will assume that you consent to the disclosure of any relevant conflicts to the other meeting participants and in the resulting report or work product, unless you check 'no' in the space provided here. If you check 'no', the Secretariat will not disclose the information without your prior approval, although this may result in your not being able to participate in the meeting or conference. **No:** ☐

DECLARATION. I hereby declare that the disclosed information is true and complete to the best of my knowledge. I undertake to inform the responsible staff of FAO of any change in this information or any new information that needs to be reported, which occurs before or during the meeting or work itself and through the period up to the publication of the final results.

Date: _________Signature___________________________________

Name

Institution

Address

Fax

Email

Telephone

7

Accountability as a Value in Global Governance and for Global Administrative Law

CAROL HARLOW*

INTRODUCTION

IN THIS CHAPTER I consider whether the term 'accountability' is a purely mechanistic concept, in the sense of a process for limiting and legitimating government, or whether it possesses a normative sense. In the first section, I argue that the concept has, in the English-speaking world, climbed rapidly to the top of the political ladder, to emerge as a constitutional principle approximating in value to the foundational liberal principle of the rule of law. In the second, moving to transnational level, I consider reception of the accountability concept in the most developed multi-level governance regime, the European Union (EU). Here I conclude that the most salient concepts in constitutional debates concerning the EU governance system remain those of legitimacy and democratic deficit. Accountability has made some progress as a standard to evaluate the conduct of public administration but has not yet acquired the status of a normative or 'constitutional' principle. In the third section, I turn to the international level, where accountability is promoted by international organisations as a 'good governance standard' for the evaluation of national governance systems. It is, however, seen as part of a package of values closely linked to economic liberalism and American hegemony, raising questions about legitimacy, and how real its acceptance is by national governments and peoples we can only guess. Its growing use inside international organisations and transnational systems of governance also raises questions about both legitimacy and effectiveness. The final question, as yet unanswered is whether accountability can ever become a reality outside the framework of a liberal democratic State?

* London School of Economics. My thanks are due to the editors and Richard Rawlings, who read a draft of this chapter.

Carol Harlow

ACCOUNTABILITY IN THE ENGLISH-SPEAKING WORLD

Shifting understandings

Mulgan suggests that the term 'accountability' 'leapt to prominence' in the last two decades of the twentieth century to become 'one of the core values of democratic governance in the English-speaking world'.[1] The term has certainly made rapid headway since the millennium, when Mulgan described it as 'a commonplace of the public administration literature', observing that:

> A word which a few decades ago was used only rarely and with relatively restricted meaning (and which, interestingly, has no obvious equivalent in other European languages) now crops up everywhere performing all manner of analytical and rhetorical tasks and carrying most of the burdens of democratic 'governance'.[2]

Since those words were written, the concept has climbed still higher. In the English-speaking world, where the term is generally understood to have originated, it has become a political slogan with totemic resonance in every area of public life, capable of bringing down governments. Academic analysis has been more considered and the literature has mounted up. Accountability found a significant place, for example, in the CONNEX research agenda funded by the European Commission under the sixth framework programme.[3]

Some of the indeterminacy noted by Mulgan has dissipated as interdisciplinary study has enabled more precise definitions to be agreed. The term still retains, however, a multiplicity of usages: at political level, an iconic use to express public dissatisfaction with the incumbents of office; a tool for analysis in the political science literature; a normative concept of good governance; and much more besides. Its 'complex and chameleon-like' characteristics[4] suggest a portmanteau word with multiple, overlapping meanings. Closely linked to the notion of democratic legitimacy, the primary reference is to a principal/agent relationship between political actors and their electorate. This is, however, a minimal interpretation of accountability, easily satisfied by the largely empty ritual of election, requiring reinforcement from the machinery of democratic government.

The classical notion of responsibility then comes into play, in which accountability is rooted; Beaud, a French constitutional lawyer, is indeed content to equate the two notions.[5] Bovens on the other hand, in the set of studies that he has contributed to the growing body of accountability literature, sees the two

[1] R Mulgan, *Holding Power to Account, Accountability in Modern Democracies* (London, Macmillan, 2003) at ix.

[2] R Mulgan, '"Accountability": an Ever-Expanding Concept?' (2000) 78 *Public Administration* 555.

[3] See D Curtin and A Wille (eds), *Meaning and Practice of Accountability in the EU Multi-Level Context* (CONNEX Report Series No 07).

[4] Mulgan, n 2 above.

[5] O Beaud, 'La responsabilité politique face à la concurrence d'autres formes de responsabilité des gouvernants' in Special Issue, 'La Responsabilité des Gouvernants' (2000) 92 *Pouvoirs* at 18.

concepts as distinguishable.[6] He singles out an element of subjectivity in the term 'responsibility', which signals both a causative component, ie, that a given actor is answerable for events directly attributable to him, and also an ethical dimension, namely that the actor is morally responsible for events that he has caused. Responsibility, to rephrase this argument, comprises a moral or subjective dimension. In just this sense, the Committee of Independent Experts, set up by the European Parliament to investigate allegations of corruption in the Commission, famously spoke of 'a growing reluctance among the members of the hierarchy to acknowledge their responsibility. It is becoming difficult to find anyone who has even the slightest sense of responsibility.'[7] Here the normative content of the term emerges clearly.

Accountability may, on the other hand, be read objectively as referring to narration: it is simply the obligation to 'give an account' of events. Here the narrator may not be the principal actor and no direct causal connection may exist between him and the train of events. This diminished content has allowed British politicians to turn to the word 'accountability' in an effort to dilute the classical constitutional doctrine of ministerial responsibility, which, in its classical format, requires a minister 'to accept full responsibility for any mistakes and inefficiency of his officials', a process culminating if necessary in resignation. Where, however, action has been taken by a public servant of which the political representative had no prior knowledge and would not endorse, the doctrine requires the latter to 'render an account of his stewardship' to Parliament. This well-approved formulation[8] suggests more than merely giving an account in the sense of narrating. It is significant that a House of Commons committee firmly refuted this attempt to dilute the stricter doctrine of personal responsibility. Instead, the committee twinned the notions of responsibility and accountability, upgrading the latter with the assertion that ministerial resignations, although rare, were 'in effect, the final stage in a process of accountability'.[9]

Should we then conclude that accountability is a *political* concept in which representative government and political responsibility, key elements of democratic legitimacy, are combined? That would be to overlook more obvious semantic links between accountability and the vocabulary of counting, accounting and accountancy. Hood is not alone in tracing the modern idea to public

[6] M Bovens, 'Analysing and Assessing Public Accountability. A Conceptual Framework', European Governance Papers, No C-06-01 (2006).

[7] Committee of Independent Experts, *First Report on Allegations of Fraud, Mismanagement and Nepotism in the European Commission* (15 March 1999) at [9.4.25]. A Second Report, *Reform of the Commission—analysis of current practice and proposals for tackling mismanagement, irregularities and fraud*, was published on 10 September 1999.

[8] Taken from ministerial resignation speeches in the British House of Commons: see HC Deb, vol 530 (20 July 1954) at cols 1186 and 1285–87. And see G Marshall, *Constitutional Conventions, The Rules and Forms of Accountability* (Oxford, Clarendon Press, 1984) ch 4; S Finer, 'The Individual Responsibility of Ministers' (1956) 34 *Public Administration* 377.

[9] House of Commons Public Service Committee, *Ministerial Accountability and Responsibility*, HC 313 (1995–96) at [33].

audit and the mediaeval office of Comptroller and Auditor-General. Financial accountability and public audit are, Hood argues, 'deeply embedded in the European tradition of constitutional (limited) government and formal public accountability in financial affairs'.[10] This is a point of some importance. In recent years, audit has played a central part in the rewriting of public administration as a system of 'public management'[11] in which people 'are constantly checking up on each other, constantly monitoring the ongoing stream of communicative exchanges and accounts that make up daily life'.[12] This shift in ideology has installed audit as a centrepiece of the machinery by which accountability is established, an evolution clearly visible in the mandate of the Committee of Experts (above) to 'examine the way in which the Commission detects and deals with fraud, mismanagement and nepotism, including a fundamental review of Commission practices in the awarding of all financial contracts'. Equally it is implicit in the brief of the British Nolan Committee set up to examine allegations of corrupt behaviour by members of the British House of Commons (below). This is to stress the mechanical aspect of audit but audit does at the same time represent a value-system or cluster of values, including independent validation, efficiency, rationality, visibility and transparency. Power highlights these values as symbolic of the reinvention of government 'almost irrespective of the mechanics of the practice'.[13] This suggests that, by linking accountability to audit and public management, the term is made (at least seemingly) more objective, while at the same time its field of operation is extended from the realm of politics into financial affairs and public administration.

A definition adopted by Mark Bovens is capable of encompassing these ideas. For Bovens accountability entails three main elements:[14]

(i) giving an account, in the attenuated sense of narration;
(ii) questioning or debating the issues;
(iii) evaluation, or passing judgement.

In this definition, accountability is essentially retrospective; indeed, from such a standpoint, even elections take on a retrospective character as an occasion to pass judgement on the activities of the existing government ('throw the rascals out') rather than to legitimate a package of policy measures for an incoming government. This is to exclude from the definition the popular participation in

[10] C Hood, 'The hidden public sector: the "quangocratization" of the world' in F Kaufmann, G Majone and V Ostrom (eds), *Guidance, Control and Evaluation in the Public Sector* (Berlin, de Gruyter, 1986) at 7.

[11] See for explication C Hood, 'A Public Management for All Seasons' (1991) 69 *Public Administration* 3 and 'Emerging Issues in Public Administration' (1995) 73 *Public Administration* 165.

[12] M Power, *The Audit Society, Rituals of Verification* (Oxford, Oxford University Press, 1997) at 1.

[13] M Power, *The Audit Explosion* (London, Demos, 1994) at 17.

[14] M Bovens, 'Public accountability' in E Ferlie, L Lynne and C Pollitt (eds), *The Oxford Handbook of Public Management* (Oxford, Oxford University Press, 2005). And see M Bovens, *The Quest for Responsibility, Accountability and Citizenship in Complex Organisations* (Cambridge, Cambridge University Press, 1998).

policy-making seen by proponents of direct democracy as an essential element in accountability to the people. Here, I shall suggest later, is an important point of difference with usage in the EU.

A prospective approach to accountability is necessary too if parliamentary input into legislation is to be included in the machinery for accountability. Auel argues, for example, that in the case of national parliaments in the EU, both parliamentary input into legislation and parliamentary scrutiny and monitoring are necessarily ex ante forms of accountability; ex post or retrospective accountability, after policy is adopted and becomes law, 'is possible but, for legal reasons, virtually useless'.[15] Bovens too admits that 'the line between retrospective and proactive policy making can be thin in practice' but believes that, for analytical purposes, policy making and accountability should be kept distinct.[16]

As Bovens also admits, his is a 'thin' definition of accountability. As understood by the modern media and in popular parlance, accountability invariably contains a fourth element of sanction: 'heads must roll' for accountability to be sufficiently 'thick'.[17] This is one reason why France, according to Beaud, has in recent years suffered popular pressure for a move to legal, and more particularly criminal, liability, with a view to avoiding the many opportunities to shuffle off responsibility provided by the political system and modern systems of governance.[18] More restrained is Oliver's requirement, if not of sanction, then at least apology and redress. She sets accountability in place as the keystone of the modern liberal-democratic constitution, seeing it as:

> a framework for the exercise of state power … within which public bodies are forced to seek to promote the public interest and compelled to justify their actions in those terms or in other constitutionally acceptable terms (justice, humanity, equity); to modify policies if they should turn out to have been ill conceived; and to make amends if mistakes and errors of judgement have been made.[19]

Bovens himself is less concerned with sanction, seeing it as likely to exclude from the list of accountability forums some of the most effective forms of redress: those, such as ombudsmen, who 'do not have the authority to sanction formally, but who can nevertheless be very effective in securing redress or reparation'.[20] Instead, he treats accountability in terms of social relationships, where the 'actor may face consequences', which may on occasion 'only be implicit or informal,

[15] K Auel, 'Democratic Accountability and National Parliaments: Redefining the Impact of Parliamentary Scrutiny in EU Affairs' (2007) 13 *European Law Journal* 487.

[16] M Bovens, 'Analysing and Assessing Accountability: A Conceptual Framework' (2007) 13 *European Law Journal* 447, 453.

[17] A Schedler, 'Conceptualizing Accountability' in A Schedler, L Diamond and MF Platner (eds), *The Self-Restraining State: Power and Accountability in New Democracies* (New York, Lynne Rienner, 1999).

[18] Beaud n 5 above, at 23.

[19] D Oliver, *Government in the United Kingdom: The Search for Accountability, Effectiveness and Citizenship* (Milton Keynes, Open University Press, 1991) at 28.

[20] Bovens, n 16 above, at 452.

such as the very fact of having to render account in front of television cameras, or…. the disintegration of public image and career as a result of the negative publicity generated by the process'.[21]

The best way to think of accountability then is as a portmanteau word into which is packed a bundle of notions pertinent to modern systems of government. The concepts of democratic legitimacy, political responsibility, financial probity and audit are all contained within it. This is enough to make accountability a contested concept, which can never be wholly objective. As Mulgan has observed, 'no analysis of accountability can pretend to be wholly without ulterior purpose',[22] while for Fisher, arguments for more or less accountability are always arguments 'about wanting to align governance regimes to a particular normative regime'. Arguments about accountability are arguments about *standards* and 'the process of holding a decision-maker to account is a process of debating what those standards should be'.[23] Accountability, to put this differently, is more than mere machinery; it is a value-loaded concept and if it is contestable this is less because we do not understand its meaning than because we disagree as to what the constituent elements should be.

A principle of normative value

Bovens suggests that, within the strong accountability traditions of the English-speaking world, a different emphasis is placed on accountability. In American academic and political discourse:

> Accountability is used predominantly as a normative concept, as a set of standards for the evaluation of the behaviour of public actors. Accountability or, more precisely, 'being accountable', is seen as a *virtue*, as a positive quality of organizations or officials. It is evaluative not analytical—close to responsiveness and a sense of responsibility contested and contestable.[24]

American governance, Bovens is suggesting, contains a built-in expectation that government will be accountable. This belief plays an important part in underpinning the legitimacy of the governmental system. In British, Australian and European scholarly debates, on the other hand, the term is 'used in a much more narrow, descriptive sense. Accountability is seen as a social *mechanism*, as an institutional relation or arrangement in which an actor can be held to account by a forum.'[25] The emphasis, in other words, falls on *machinery* for accountability.

[21] ibid.
[22] Mulgan, n 2 above, at 556.
[23] E Fisher, 'The European Union in the Age of Accountability' (2004) 24 *Oxford Journal of Legal Studies* 495, 513.
[24] Bovens, 'New Forms of Accountability' at 106.
[25] ibid.

Bovens is drawing on Dubnick, who treats accountability as a value, linking it to ethics and standards of responsible behaviour and professional integrity in public administration.[26] Dubnick sees the concept as deeply rooted in American constitutional history and 'linked to the principles implicit in the Magna Carta as well as our system of checks and balances'. He goes on, however, to stress the mechanistic dimension of the concept, which has 'traditionally been regarded as the means used to control and direct administrative behaviour by requiring "answerability" to some external authority'.[27] He focuses the so-called Friedrich/Finer debate as 'one of the core debates that set the intellectual agenda for American public administration during the Cold War era'.[28] The debate concerned machinery for accountability within the public service. Friedrich on the one hand argued for *subjective* accountability through reliance on 'the judgment of administrators whose sense of professional responsibility and loyalty could be trusted when they carried out public policy in the national interest'. Finer on the other hand asserted the *objective* view that, 'despite the greater sense of professional responsibility among today's administrators, democracy still requires enhanced public control and direction of administrative agents':[29]

> Fundamental to that view is the assumption that the commitment of modern administrators to conduct themselves responsibly (i.e., ethically, in accord with 'democratic morality') was not sufficient to insure that the will of the people would be carried out. Accountability, in the form of external (i.e., democratic) constraints and controls, was necessary as well. Accountability mechanisms were required to render the decisions and behaviour of public officials responsible, not merely in the legal, political or bureaucratic senses of that term, but morally as well ... Ethical behaviour, in short, required the presence of external accountability mechanisms in all their various forms.

The march of accountability structures in modern governance is encapsulated in this debate. Friedrich's discretionary 'soft law' model of administrative accountability was sufficient until the late 1980s but would be widely regarded as insufficient in an era when a hard law framework coupled to an external accountability forum is a standard requirement. This must be a crucial point in any discussion of accountability in transnational governance systems or international bodies.

It is true that the British debate tends to focus on the pragmatic; British dislike of theory is well known. The common law tradition is factual and pragmatic, an approach enhanced in constitutional matters by the absence of a written constitution. This does not mean, however, that accountability has no normative

[26] M Dubnick, 'Accountability and Ethics: Reconsidering the Relationships' (2003) 6 *International Journal of Organization Theory and Behaviour* 405.

[27] ibid, at 406.

[28] ibid.

[29] ibid. Dubnick is referring to H Finer, 'Administrative responsibility in democratic government' (1941) 1 *Public Administration Review* 335 and CJ Friedrich, 'Public policy and the nature of administrative responsibility' in CJ Friedrich and ES Mason (eds), *Public policy: A yearbook of the graduate school of public administration* (Cambridge MA, Harvard University Press, 1940) 3.

aspects or that these have never been debated. The Nolan Committee, for example, set up to deal with one of many crises of confidence following a corruption scandal in the House of Commons, highlighted seven standards as essential principles for public service, of which accountability was one:[30]

> Holders of public office are accountable for their decisions and actions to the public and must submit themselves to whatever scrutiny is appropriate to their office.

A leading contemporary constitutional law textbook takes the same line, listing accountability alongside democracy, parliamentary sovereignty, the rule of law and separation of powers as one of a set of ideas central to the British constitution. The authors stress the dual link with democracy and the rule of law:[31]

> A link with democracy in that people are given power not for their own ends but for the public good; and a link with the rule of law, which demands that those to whom power is granted should not exceed the limits of their authority. Accountability for the use of power is supportive of both democracy and the rule of law and we may claim it as a leading principle of our constitution even if it is only imperfectly realised in practice.

Not only is the normative character of accountability taken for granted in this passage but its status as a principle of constitutional law is tacitly assumed.

If Bovens is correct in seeing the English debate to be about machinery, this may be because the normative quality of accountability is assumed. The idea has, after all, a long historical pedigree and common origins in Anglo-American constitutional theory. Philosopher and historian Quentin Skinner traces the ideal of limited government at least to the seventeenth century,[32] encouraging Tomkins to ground modern ideals of accountability in a 'normative theory of constitutionalism', which he calls republicanism. This he believes can provide 'a normative foundation for our practices of responsibility and political accountability (and, as we shall see when we come to examine our history, this is a normative foundation that already inheres within the British constitutional order).' The republican vision of political accountability, derived as it is from familiar historical models, is both normative and mechanistic: it provides 'a standard to which we can aspire and, just as importantly, against which we may judge current

[30] Lord Nolan, *First Report of the Committee on Standards in Public Life*, Cm 2850 (1995) at 14 and, for comment, D Oliver, 'Standards in public life—what standards?' [1995] *Public Law* 497. The seven principles are: selflessness, integrity, objectivity, accountability, openness, honesty and leadership.

[31] C Turpin and A Tomkins, *British Government and the Constitution*, 6th edn (Cambridge, Cambridge University Press, 2007) at 132.

[32] Q Skinner, *Liberty before Liberalism* (Cambridge University Press, 1998), on which A Tomkins, *Our Republican Constitution* (Hart Publishing, Oxford, 2005) draws heavily.

practices'.[33] The machinery of accountability and the forums in which accountability is claimed are closely linked; without these, Tomkins argues, the ideal is valueless. The historical model differs, however, from the modern quest for accountability in that the former is premised on representative institutions while the latter seeks:

> systematic possibilities for ordinary people to contest the doings of government. This points us towards the ideal of a democracy based, not on the alleged consent of the people, but rather on the contestability by the people of everything that government does.[34]

The ideal has in other words shifted from government *for* to government *by* the people.

ACCOUNTABILITY AND THE EUROPEAN UNION

European Correspondences

In the context of the EU, it is important to establish the origins of the accountability concept, since the EU is a polity in which political ideas must be blended. It has by and large to accommodate the traditions of its members and to proceed so far as possible—to borrow the language of the Treaties—in accordance with the general principles common to the laws of the Member States. Yet scholars have argued that other languages (French, Portuguese, Spanish, German, Dutch) 'have no exact equivalent and do not (yet) distinguish semantically between "responsibility" and "accountability"'. If there is growing familiarity with the term and its use as an organising principle of public administration, then this is 'due to experience with the Anglo-Saxon tradition'.[35] Tomkins adds that 'it is not just the word that is difficult to translate: British political practices of political accountability have few parallels elsewhere in Europe', though he exempts from his strictures Ireland, the Netherlands and Denmark.[36] The suggestion is then that accountability is an Anglo-American *arriviste* on the political scene without resonance in other European systems.

We should not, I think, be quick to adopt these assumptions. None of those to whom the remarks are attributed are linguists; the best that can be said is that

[33] Tomkins, n 32 above, at 51–52. There is no space here to explore these ideas further but see also R Bellamy, *Political Constitutionalism* (Cambridge University Press, 2007). On the authoritarian strand in the British constitution see M Loughlin, 'Tinkering with the Constitution' (1988) 51 *Modern Law Review* 531.

[34] P Pettit, *Republicanism: A Theory of Freedom and Government* (Oxford, Clarendon Press, 1997) ch 6, discussing the concept of contestation in a democracy, cited by Tomkins, above.

[35] M Bovens, 'New Forms of Accountability and EU-Governance' at 105, citing Mulgan; an unpublished paper by M Dubnick; and C Harlow, *Accountability in the European Union* (Oxford, Oxford University Press, 2002) at 14–15.

[36] A Tomkins n 32 above, at 5.

each has access to one or more of the languages mentioned by Bovens. Moreover, words do not usually possess a single, incontrovertible meaning. Accountability is a portmanteau word into which differing concepts have been packed. The terminology is both shifting and complex, made up of bundles of overlapping meanings (some contestable and contested). When borrowed or transplanted, these may acquire new and unexpected meanings.[37] Thus Avril sees the term 'accountability' as borrowed by the French to encapsulate a cluster of ideas contained within the notion of 'responsabilité devant le peuple'; this would lend the term the dual meaning of 'accounting for' one's actions (rendre compte) and of 'taking into account' (tenir compte de) or responsiveness to the people's views.[38] Though possible, this last sense is not normal English usage. Again, the French word 'responsabilité' combines political accountability with legal liability, lending a further dimension to the term. This may reflect the French constitutional tradition of reliance on a strong and well-established system of public law to provide the main machinery of accountability in a political system which, at least until the Second World War, lacked a strong parliamentary tradition. Political vocabulary ideas and values must always in short be interpreted in the context of cultural and institutional framework.[39]

The EU: legitimacy and accountability

In the discourse surrounding the EU system of governance, legitimacy rather than accountability has taken centre stage. Initially, the basis of legitimacy was, if not the Treaties, then delegation theory,[40] in which accountability plays a part that may in practice be minimal. Scharpf's important theory of EU legitimacy contrasted 'input' and 'output' legitimacy. Democratic self-determination, Scharpf argued, relied on the metaphor of a chain of accountability linking the governors to the governed: elections, parliaments and other devices associated with democratic government. This was 'input legitimacy'. But the success of any democratic system of government must equally be measured against its 'output legitimacy' or effectiveness in meeting the wishes and expectations of the governed, assumed to be the achievement of economic and social policy goals. The legitimacy of the EU governance system should be judged on success in this sphere rather than on the democratic notions of accountability discussed

[37] See G Teubner, 'Legal Irritants: Good Faith in British Law or how Unifying Law Ends Up in New Divergences' (1998) 61 *Modern Law Review* 11.

[38] P Avril, 'Les Fabriques des politiques', in JL Quermonne et N Wahl (eds), *La France presidentielle* (Paris, Presses de la FNSP, 1995) at 65.

[39] C Harlow, 'Voices of Difference in a Plural Community' (2002) 50 *American Journal of Comparative Law* 339.

[40] See A Stone Sweet and M Thatcher (eds), *Theory and Practice of Delegation to Non-majoritarian Institutions* (2002) 25 *West European Politics* (Special Issue); B Rittberger, 'The Creation and Empowerment of the European Parliament' (2003) 41 *Journal of Common Market Studies* 203.

above.[41] This approach allows issues of democratic deficit to be circumvented—perhaps just as well, the elitist governance structures established by the EC Treaties were not designed for accountability. This was neither government *for* nor government *by* the people but 'government by organisations for organisations'.[42]

In alternative accounts of the EU as a 'post-parliamentary democracy'—or system of divided democracy, where 'the people back home are represented by their heads of states with cadres of advisors'[43]—accountability does not feature significantly. Instead, legitimacy is secured through the traditional relationship between national governments and their electorate, free at least in theory to withdraw support for the European project at any point. Moravcsik feels it necessary to defend the EU from charges of 'unaccountable technocracy', arguing that 'robust mechanisms' of direct accountability are in place at Union level, where 'the mode of EU delegation to its constitutional court, central bank and other semi-autonomous authorities, is consistent with the late twentieth-century practice of most advanced industrial democracies'.[44] Even if this were correct, it takes no account of the impact on popular opinion of the upward drift of power from States to Union as a factor fuelling the phenomenon of de-legitimation.[45] It overlooks also the 'growing democracy assertiveness' and 'mounting demand for accountability' that is rapidly undercutting the 'late twentieth-century practice of advanced industrial democracies'.[46] Tomkins, for example, deduces that 'it would have been greatly to the benefit of the EU's citizens had its constitution more enthusiastically embraced British ideas and practices of political accountability'.[47]

The widespread perception of democratic deficit at European level fuelled interest in alternative notions of deliberative democracy,[48] where decision-making is legitimated by a process of 'justifying the results to the people who are affected by them'. This would make 'thin' accountability an important element in

[41] F Scharpf, *Governing in Europe: Effective and Democratic?* (Oxford, Oxford University Press, 1999); A Menon and S Weatherill, 'Legitimacy, Accountability and Delegation in the European Union' in A Arnull and D Wincott, *Accountability and Legitimacy in the European Union* (Oxford, Oxford University Press, 2002).

[42] S Andersen and T Burns, 'The European Union and the Erosion of Parliamentary Democracy: A Study of Post-parliamentary Governance', in S Andersen and KA Eliassen (eds), *The European Union: How Democratic Is It?* (London, Sage, 1996) at 229.

[43] ibid.

[44] A Moravcsik, 'Reassessing Legitimacy in the EU' (2002) 40 *Journal of Common Market Studies* 603, 611.

[45] J Weiler, U Haltern, F Mayer, 'European Democracy and its Critique' in *The crisis of representation in Europe* (1995) 18 *West European Politics* 4, 6 (Special Issue).

[46] Mulgan, n 1 above, at 4.

[47] Tomkins, n 32 above, at 5–6. See also A Tomkins, 'Responsibility and Resignation in the European Commission' (1999) 62 *Modern Law Review* 744.

[48] See, eg, J Cohen and C Sabel, 'Directly Deliberative Polyarchy' (1997) 3 *European Law Journal* 313; O Gerstenberg and C Sabel, 'Directly-Deliberative Polyarchy: An Institutional Ideal for Europe?' in C Joerges and R Dehousse (eds), *Good Governance in Europe's Integrated Market* (Oxford, Oxford University Press, 2002); C Joerges, 'Deliberative Supranationalism: Two Defences' (2002) 8 *European Law Journal* 135.

a legitimation process.[49] The term does indeed make a fleeting appearance in the *White Paper on European Governance*, an attempt by the Commission to 'get more people and groups involved in shaping and delivering EU policy', which can be read as an effort to introduce at least a elementary form of participatory and deliberative democracy. Each of the five fundamental principles on which the *White Paper* was premised—openness, participation, accountability, effectiveness and coherence—is said to be important for underpinning democracy and the rule of law at every level of the EU system of governance. Accountability receives, however, a strangely attenuated meaning bearing little resemblance to definitions discussed in the previous section:[50]

> Roles in the legislative and executive processes need to be clearer. Each of the EU Institutions must explain and take responsibility for what it does in Europe. But there is also a need for greater clarity and responsibility from Member States and all those involved in developing and implementing European Union policy at whatever level.

This is little more than a weak institutional requirement to keep the public informed.

It is instead in the Report of the Experts (mentioned earlier) that we find the first use of the term 'accountability' in the sense discussed in Section 1. Making reference to the Nolan standards,[51] the Experts state unequivocally that Commissioners and officials must all behave:

> with *integrity* and *discretion* and—the Committee would like to add—in accordance with the principles of *accountability* and *openness* to the public, which implies that, when decisions are taken, the reasons for them are made known, the processes by which they were taken are transparent and any personal conflicting interests are honestly and publicly acknowledged.[52]

The Interim Conclusions put the finishing touches to this definition, highlighting accountability as 'the ultimate manifestation of democracy':[53]

> The principles of openness, transparency and accountability ... are at the heart of democracy and are the very instruments allowing it to function properly. Openness and transparency imply that the decision-making process, at all levels, is as accessible and accountable as possible to the general public. It means that the reasons for decisions taken are known and that those taking decisions assume responsibility for them and are ready to accept the personal consequences when such decisions are subsequently shown to be wrong.

[49] E Erikssen and J Fossum, 'Europe in Search of Legitimacy: Strategies of Legitimation Assessed' (2004) 25 *International Political Science Review* 435.

[50] European Commission, *White Paper on European Governance* (COM(2001) 428 final) [2001] OJ C287 p 1 at 10.

[51] Above n 16.

[52] *First Report*, at [1.5.4] in the English-language version. The French version uses *responsabilité*, the Italian *responsabilità*, the Dutch *rekenschap* and the German *Rechenschaftspflich*.

[53] *First Report* at [9.3.3] and [9.4.25].

Here prospective and retrospective accountability in the objective sense that explanations must be made if things go wrong are combined with subjective accountability in the sense of personal acceptance of responsibility. Finally, the element of sanction is added. Apparently for the first time in EU public administration the term 'accountability' is used in its true Anglo-American and presented as a standard by which administrators are to be judged.

The two Reports from the Experts mark a significant stage in the evolution of accountability machinery in the first transnational regime. Perhaps surprisingly, it succeeded in establishing accountability as a standard of conduct in public life, forcing recognition on a Commission later shown by its *White Paper* (above) to be reluctant. An internal programme of reform was inaugurated within the Commission, which for the first time introduced the standard accountability machinery of public management techniques to the European public service.[54] Most significant, the two Reports, produced for the European Parliament, established and enhanced the role of that institution as a key engine of accountability in EU space. At least from this time on, the European Parliament would undertake its role as the Community's main accountability forum with increasing seriousness, taking every opportunity to strengthen its scrutiny powers[55] and using its influence to bring within the Community institutional structure areas of 'soft' EU governance that did not conform to its standards.[56] In a second stage, this concern for greater accountability would spread to national parliaments, whose role as scrutinizer was acknowledged and enhanced by the Amsterdam and Lisbon Treaties, both of which contain protocols on the role of national parliaments in the EU. The seeds of political accountability had been sown and were sprouting in the first developed transnational system of governance.

ACCOUNTABILITY IN THE GLOBAL SPHERE

The appearance of the term accountability in the discourse of European public administration must also reflect its growing influence at global level, where it was beginning to establish itself as a 'good governance' principle. Just as the Committee of Experts was reporting, the Organisation for Economic Co-operation and Development (OECD), an organisation of States committed to democratic

[54] See European Commission, *Reforming the Commission*, COM 200 (2000) and Code of Conduct for Commissioners SEC(2004) 1487/2 and for comment, L Cram, 'Governance to Go' (2001) 39 *Journal of Common Market Studies* 595.

[55] See R Corbett, F Jacobs and M Shackleton, 'The European Parliament at Fifty: A View from the Inside' (2003) 41 *Journal of Common Market Studies* 353; V Mamadouh and T Raunio, 'The Committee System: Powers, Appointments and Institutional Roles' (2003) 41 *Journal of Common Market Studies* 333; K Bradley, 'Comitology and the Courts: Tales of the Unexpected' in H Hofmann and A Turk, *EU Administrative Governance* (Cheltenham, Edward Elgar, 2006).

[56] See further J Scott and D Trubek, 'Mind the Gap: Law and New Approaches to Governance in the European Union' (2002) 8 *European Law Journal* 1; G de Búrca, 'The Constitutional Challenge of New Governance in the European Union' (2003) 28 *European Law Review* 814.

governance, was finalising a paper on European principles for public administration in the context of its substantial Sigma programme, jointly underwritten by the EU. The paper envisioned a 'European Administrative Space', composed of 'a set of common standards for action within public administration which are defined by law and enforced in practice through procedures and accountability mechanisms'.[57] For our purposes, the interest of this paper is first, that it provides advice on governance to 'countries in transition' or candidate States for admission to the EU, in this way linking European standards to the wider global scene; and secondly, that the term is given a purely mechanistic characterisation (comprising explanation, justification and scrutiny), its purpose being to act as a buttress for other more important principles. These comprise the administrative values of efficiency, effectiveness, reliability and predictability and, at a higher level, the rule of law, openness, transparency, impartiality, and equality before the law.[58] The most significant aspect of the paper is, however, that its standards, including accountability, are said to form part of administrative law and to be enforceable through it:

> These administrative principles are not simply ideas based on goodwill; they are embedded in institutions and administrative procedures at all levels. Actors in the public sphere are legally obliged to comply with these legal principles, which must be upheld by independent control bodies, systems of justice and judicial enforcement, parliamentary scrutiny, and by ensuring opportunities for hearing and redress to individuals and legal persons.[59]

This passage, which has a German ring, is an important pointer, I suggest, to a shift from political to legal accountability in international regimes, which lack strong political institutions. It is replicated in the present growth of interest in a global administrative law.

The OECD is by no means the only international organisation to concern itself with good governance and accountability. The World Bank has also played a leading part in establishing accountability as a 'good governance' principle, adopting the concept as one of its six standard indicators for evaluating the quality of governments.[60] It views the accountable administration of public funds and an independent auditor responsible to a representative legislature as essential components of good governance.[61] How is this rise of interest in accountability to be explained?

[57] *European principles for public administration*, Sigma Paper No 27, CNM/SIGMA/PUMA(99)44/REV1, available on-line at www.oecd.org/ at 6.

[58] *European principles for public administration* at 12.

[59] ibid at 8.

[60] D Kaufman, A Kray, P Zoido-Lobaton, 'Aggregating Governance Indicators', World Bank Research Working Paper 2195 (1999).

[61] World Bank, *Sub-Saharan Africa: From Crisis to Sustainable Growth* (1989); OECD Council, 'Improving Ethical Conduct in the Public Service' (23 April, 1998).

The most hopeful explanation, if accountability is to be grounded at the global level, would be that there is (as Mulgan suggests) a 'mounting demand for' and 'worldwide movement in favour of increased accountability'. As a sign of 'growing democracy assertiveness',[62] accountability would then take its place alongside the movement for elections—which can truly be accounted a worldwide movement—as a serious step in progression towards democratic government. This is, however, unlikely or perhaps merely too ambitious for the present times.

A more probable explanation lies in American hegemony. The United States (US) has influence in both the international institutions discussed above and in other aid institutions, including the International Monetary Fund (IMF) and the World Trade Organization (WTO), both converts to accountability as a good governance tool. For Leftwich, the 'new orthodoxy' that today dominates official Western aid policy and development thinking is an aspect of neo-liberalism, associated with a 'functional theory of politics', which 'links its concern with markets and economic growth to its concern with democracy'. At its core is 'the confident assertion that "good governance" and democracy are not simply desirable but essential conditions for development in all societies'. Both are, however, handmaidens to a thriving free market economy, for which democratic politics is a *sine qua non*:

> It follows that neo-liberal political theory holds that democratisation in the context of a free economy would compel governments to be more accountable, less corrupt and hence more efficient developmentally, for they would be judged on their performance and thrown out if they did not deliver public goods effectively.[63]

If, as Leftwich argues, accountability is a concession to the interests of aid donors, trading partners and other economic actors, then it has to be conceived as a principle, like the rule of law, of universal application. Petersmann couples the two principles and links them to *legal* accountability when he says:

> Recourse to domestic court proceedings offers the most effective and most democratic means for the decentralized enforcement of precise unconditional WTO rules by, and for the benefit of, citizens interested in defending individual freedom and rule of law against protectionist abuses of government powers.[64]

If, on the other hand, accountability is a truly democratic value, then it is owed to the constituents of the polity. The One World Trust, a non-governmental or civil society organisation, which aims 'to generate wider commitment to the *principles and values* of accountability; increase the accountability of global organizations

[62] Mulgan, n 1 above, at 4.

[63] A Leftwich, 'Government, Democracy and Development in the Third World' (1993) 14 *Third World Quarterly* 605 and 609. For the counter-argument that law can further the interests of those on the receiving end of policies, see D Hunter, 'Using the World Bank Inspection Panels to Defend the Interests of Project-Affected People' (2003) 4 *Chicago Journal of International Law* 201.

[64] E-U Petersmann, 'Dispute Prevention and Dispute Settlement in the Transatlantic Partnership between the European Union and the USA' in G de Búrca and J Scott, *The EU and the WTO, Legal and Constitutional Issues* (Oxford, Hart Publishing, 2001).

to those they affect; and strengthen the capacity of civil society to better engage in decision-making processes', is quite clear about this. The Trust defines accountability as 'the processes through which an organization makes a commitment to respond to and balance the needs of *stakeholders in its decision-making processes and activities*' and the Trust seeks 'practical ways to make global organizations more responsive to the people they affect, and on how the rule of law can be applied equally to all'.[65]

This duality of purpose, identified in the previous section as a core feature of the accountability debate in the EU, has been theorised by Grant and Keohane to provide a framework for analysis of accountability in global environments.[66] In their 'model of democratic participation', accountability lies to those affected by the use of power; in their 'delegation or trustee model', the emphasis is on legal authority and office. The American authors do not question the need for 'a public standard of legitimacy to which public actors are held', although they do note that international organisations and regimes are increasingly judged on their conformity with the model of democratic participation if they are to be seen as legitimate. They conclude, however, that by focusing too narrowly on democratic models of accountability, much of the existing machinery for accountability in the global environment may go unnoticed or be undervalued. There must be maximum flexibility as to machinery, since it is more helpful to seek a 'working set of accountability systems' than to wring one's hands over a shortfall in democratic ideals.

The authors move on to examine machinery, identifying seven 'structures of accountability'—hierarchical, fiscal, legal and market accountability, peer and reputational accountability in the sense of prestige and esteem amongst colleagues and public—which fit different transnational regimes. Notably all the structures, with the possible exception of public reputational accountability, fall within the delegation model. Of these structures, the most objective, hence possibly the most widely acceptable, forms of accountability are fiscal and legal accountability. Here the European Court of Justice (ECJ) serves as a precedent. The control of legality by the ECJ led to the court-dominated construction of general principles of administrative law, based on 'general principles common to

[65] Citations from M Blagescu, L de Las Casas and R Lloyd *Pathways to Accountability: The GAP Framework* (One World Trust, 2005) at 3 (emphasis mine). See for an overview of the Trust's work, R Lloyd, 'Promoting Global Accountability: The Experiences of the Global Accountability Project' (2008) 14 *Global Governance* 273.

[66] R Grant and R Keohane, 'Accountability and Abuses of Power in World Politics' (2005) 99 *American Political Science Review* 29. The authors distinguish the delegation model, a principal/agent model where 'power-wielders act as faithful agents of principals who empower them', from the trustee model, based on the professional ethics of office, as envisaged by Friedrich, n 28 above. See also G Majone, 'Two logics of delegation: agency and fiduciary relations in EU governance' (2001) 2 *European Union Politics* 103.

the member states'.[67] These in turn allowed the Court to claim its position as the most influential accountability forum in the EU.

There is a possible analogy here with a movement (as yet in its infancy) to distil from the normative standards and procedures applied by bodies such as the dispute resolution panels of the WTO the germs of a globalised system of administrative law.[68] This movement crystallised around the celebrated '*Shrimps/Turtles* decision'[69] from the appellate panel of the WTO, concerning the application of 'due process procedures' to a partly transnational rule-making process. Cassese sees this as the starting point for a globalised administrative law, which could in time provide both standards and procedures for accountability. Perhaps because of his European background, Cassese passes easily over questions of legitimacy, satisfied that 'we have come to expect and accept international organizations that set *substantive* standards..., so it is easy to argue that national administrations ought to respect global substantive goals, standards and criteria'.[70] Here we have the paradigm of the elite, delegate model of accountability. Chesterman hives this off as wholly 'distinct from demands that globalization be made more *democratic*', the justifiable aim of the delegate model being only 'to make it more *reasoned*'. The normative response to questions of value would not be 'uniform' but 'the concept of a global administrative law can help frame these questions of accountability and sketch out some appropriate responses'.[71] According to Chesterman, the standards being imported into this 'entirely new area of law that may provide a set of rules for accountability in globalization' draw 'upon existing administrative law principles common in many jurisdictions, such as transparency, participation, and review'.[72]

The slight sense of unease over legitimacy that colours this passage finds expression also in Stewart's case for modelling global administrative law on American administrative law. Stewart's first concern is legalistic: the absence at global level of any parallel to the strong judicial monitoring that exists in the US (or, as argued earlier, in the EU). To translate American procedures and processes outside the legitimating constitutional framework that gave them birth 'will not provide strong assurances of legality accountability, and indeed might even

[67] Wording from Art 288 of the EC Treaty. And see J Schwarze, 'Developing Principles of European Administrative Law' [1993] *Public Law* 229; J Schwarze (ed), *The Birth of a European Constitutional Order* (Baden-Baden, Nomos, 2000); and on the substance, T Tridimas, *The General Principles of EC Law*, 2nd edn (Oxford, Oxford University Press, 2006).

[68] B Kingsbury, N Krisch and R Stewart, 'The Emergence of Global Administrative Law' (2005) 68 *Law and Contemporary Problems* 15.

[69] *United States—Import Prohibition of Certain Shrimp and Shrimp Products*, WTO Appellate Body WT/DS58/AB/R Document No 98–3899 (12 October 1998).

[70] S Cassese, 'Global Standards for National Administrative Procedure' (2005) 68 *Law and Contemporary Problems* 109, 110–11.

[71] ibid at 39–40.

[72] S Chesterman, 'Globalization Rules: Accountability, Power, and the Prospects for Global Administrative Law' (2008) 14 *Global Governance* 39, citing Kingsbury, Krisch and Stewart, (n 68 above) at 15–18.

undermine legality'.[73] But Stewart, a long-time opponent of 'interest-representation politics' and advocate for participatory administrative law procedures,[74] also expresses concern over 'the potential linkage, if any, between global administrative law and democracy'. Stewart hopes for a 'bottom up' solution; global administrative law should:

> work to strengthen representative democracy at the national level by making global regulatory decisions and institutions more visible and subject effective scrutiny and review within domestic political systems, and thereby promote the accountability of international regulatory decisionmakers through those systems.[75]

Globalised accountability machinery should, in other words, so far as possible operate within and work to strengthen the 'model of democratic participation'.

Slaughter's pioneering study attempts to come more directly to grips with the phenomenon of 'network governance', which she sees as the distinguishing feature of a coming 'new world order', which she hopes will prove just as well as effective. She too sees the answer as lying partly in US domestic procedural guarantees. These should apply to all trans-governmental activity in which the US participates, including all attempts to 'replace the variety of product standards and other regulatory policies adopted by nations in favour of uniform global standards'.[76] But Slaughter sees a second answer lying in government networks and 'their capacity for self-regulation and for socialization and support of their members'.[77] This idea, which bears some resemblance to 'soft governance' networks developing in the EU,[78] is, however, an imperfect solution to problems of accountability, as the 'informal order of global networks operates largely without norms, or, at least, without specific norms'.[79]

Scott, working within the delegate or trustee model, delineates two rather different accountability models within governance networks. In Scott's 'interdependence model', the network actors are reliant on each other:

[73] R Stewart, 'US Administrative Law: A Model for Global Administrative Law' (2005) 68 *Law and Contemporary Problems* 63, 105.

[74] R Stewart, 'The Reformation of American Administrative Law' (1975) 88 *Harvard Law Review* 1667; 'Madison's Nightmare' (1990) 57 *University of Chicago Law Review* 335; 'Administrative Law in the 21st Century' (2003) 78 *New York University Law Review* 437. And see J Mashaw, 'Structuring a "Dense Complexity": Accountability and the Project of Administrative Law' in Berkeley Electronic Press, *Issues in Legal Scholarship*, 'Symposium: The Reformation of American Administrative Law' (2005), available on-line.

[75] R Stewart, 'US Administrative Law' n 73 above, at 108. See similarly A Aman, *The Democracy Deficit* (New York, New York University Press, 2004).

[76] A-M Slaughter, *A New World Order* (Princeton, New Jersey, Princeton University Press, 2004) at 223.

[77] ibid, at 195–215.

[78] See n 58 above.

[79] Slaughter, n 76 above, at 215.

> because of the dispersal of key resources of authority (formal and informal), information, expertise, and capacity to bestow legitimacy such that each of the principal actors has constantly to account for at least some of its actions to others within the space, as a precondition for action.[80]

This elite model, which lacks the externality required by both Bovens and Mulgan,[81] does not resolve the normative problems; values are impliedly generated internally by the network. It may even add to accountability problems by failing to provide for accountability of the network as a whole. Certainly this cannot satisfy demands for democratic accountability. In Scott's 'redundancy' or 'belt-and-braces' model, 'overlapping (and ostensibly superfluous) accountability mechanisms' are said to replicate and 'reduce the centrality of any one of them'.[82] This is open to criticism in that it ignores the potential for gaps to be left at crucial points in the multi-level decision-making processes by both national and supranational accountability machinery—precisely the experience with parliamentary accountability in the EU.[83]

With a view to strengthening accountability in systems of multi-level governance, Harlow and Rawlings have suggested that 'networks of accountability' be constructed to offset governance networks. These would be built up from traditional accountability machinery and forums of national systems (courts, auditors, ombudsmen and parliaments)—a 'bottom up' approach.[84] Some legitimacy for the internally generated norms would here be borrowed from national accountability systems to which network members would remain ultimately accountable. Based on the EU, a system of multi-level governance with relatively strong accountability networks, it is however doubtful that such a model could function effectively in the global environment.

CONCLUSION

This chapter has traced the onward march of accountability as a good governance value and legitimating principle of contemporary governance systems. With origins in Anglo-American constitutional systems, in which the concept is today securely anchored, accountability is only beginning to scrape a toe-hold elsewhere. In the EU, to date the most sophisticated system of multi-level governance, its advance has been stalled by competition from the concept of legitimacy, which, more prominent in European legal orders, has consequently

[80] C Scott, 'Accountability in the Regulatory State' (2000) 27 *Journal of Law and Society* 38, 50. See also C Scott, 'Spontaneous Accountability' in MW Dowdle (ed), *Rethinking Public Accountability* (Cambridge, Cambridge University Press, 2006).

[81] See Mulgan, n 1 above and Bovens, n 6 above.

[82] C Scott, n 80 above, at 52.

[83] See, eg, J Lodge, 'The European Parliament' in Andersen and Eliassen (eds) n 42 above.

[84] C Harlow and R Rawlings, 'Promoting Accountability in Multi-Level Governance: A Network Approach' (2007) 13 *European Law Journal* 542.

attracted more attention in the literature. At global level, there must be doubts over accountability as a universal democratic principle or even as a good governance value. Such recognition as has been achieved is in great part owed to American dominance in international affairs and organisations and to creditable concern on the part of American scholars that key democratic values should be maintained and extended. As Cerny warns, 'the kind of world which is crystallizing through globalization is not only inherently less permeable to democratically-grounded values and conceptions of the public interest or collective good, but also less capable of generating the public policy outcomes that people want. Democratic governance must therefore possess a significant element of collective accountability and authoritative (but not just repressive) policy capacity if it is to be democratic'.[85] If governments have been able to resort to globalised governance with a view to avoiding democratic and political accountability, this option may in the future no longer be available—nor should it be.

[85] P Cerny, 'Globalization and the End of Democracy' (1999) 36 *European Journal of Political Research* 1, 6.

8

Would International Courts be Able to Fill the Accountability Gap at the Global Level?

TOM ZWART*

INTRODUCTION

ONE OF THE most interesting aspects of the discussion on globalisation is the lack of accountability at the global level. Global organs take numerous far-reaching decisions which affect the daily lives of billions of people, either directly or indirectly. However, the mechanisms put in place to hold them accountable tend to be rather weak.[1]

Several important suggestions have been made on how to tackle this accountability deficit. This contribution deals with a possible solution which has generated only limited attention, ie, the suggestion to leave it to the courts to hold the global organs accountable.[2] In order to determine whether courts will be able to play such a role at the global level, the practices of one such court, the Appellate Body of the World Trade Organization (WTO) will be analysed.

The notion that courts may step in if the ordinary checks and balances are not working properly, is not new. Such action has been described and defended by Lord Woolf when he was serving as the Master of the Rolls of England and Wales. His approach will be discussed in section 2. There are signs that courts at the national level have tried to counterbalance the fact that national parliaments have lost their grip on administrative agencies. Those developments will be described in section 3. Because courts are intended to adjudicate disputes between parties, rather than act as a countervailing power to administrative agencies, such role

* Professor of Law, Utrecht School of Law, and Director of the Netherlands School of Human Rights Research; the author is indebted to Amy Day for her invaluable assistance during the drafting process.

[1] N Krisch and B Kingsbury, 'Introduction: Global Governance and Global Administrative Law in the International Legal Order' (2006) 17 *European Journal of International Law* 1–13.

[2] See, on the role of courts in the global legal order, S Cassese, *Lo Spazio Giuidico Globale* (Bari, Laterza, 2003)

changes assume strategic behaviour on the part of the courts. These strategic models of judicial behaviour will be discussed in section 4. Section 5 will be devoted to an analysis of the case law of the Appellate Body. Section 6 contains some concluding observations.

LORD WOOLF'S THEORY

During the 1990s, a Conservative government, led first by Prime Minister Margaret Thatcher and then her successor John Major, enjoyed a very comfortable majority in the British House of Commons. The Labour opposition was not only small in number, but was also ineffective at holding ministers accountable. At the same time the relationship between the government and the courts was very tense. The most senior judges, who were also members of the House of Lords, frequently voiced their criticism towards government proposals. On the other side, ministers felt that judges were scrutinising their decisions too strictly and quashing too many of them for the wrong reasons. Consequently, Conservative politicians and parts of the media felt that the judges, many of whom they suspected were Labour sympathisers, were making life difficult for the government as a substitute for the ineffective opposition in the Commons.[3]

In 1997, Lord Woolf, one of the most senior members of the English judiciary,[4] felt that the time had come to intervene, in order to prevent irreparable damage to the relations between the government and the judiciary. Invited to give the annual Neill lecture in Oxford, he used this opportunity to put things into perspective.[5] He admitted that the courts were indeed highly critical of government decisions, but he denied that this attitude was politically motivated, as some Conservatives had argued. In Lord Woolf's view, the judiciary scrutinised the government's actions for constitutional reasons.

According to Lord Woolf, checks and balances define the British constitutional system. These checks and balances were not working properly at the time in Britain, because the government effectively controlled its majority in Parliament. Consequently, Parliament failed to exercise meaningful oversight of executive action, which is the backbone of any parliamentary system. In addition, the local government was under the pressure of increasing centralisation, which also meant that there was no meaningful vertical division of powers. Finally, the government had taken a number of measures which had negative implications for the justice system and vulnerable groups, such as prisoners and asylum

[3] J Rozenberg, *Trial of Strength, The Battle Between Ministers and Judges over Who Makes the Law* (London, Richard Cohen, 1997) at 79–115.

[4] At the time Lord Woolf of Barnes was the Master of the Rolls, the leading judge dealing with administrative law cases. He went on to become the Lord Chief Justice of England and Wales, the head of the judiciary in England and Wales. He later served as a member of the House of Lords.

[5] H Woolf, 'Judicial Review—The Tensions between the Executive and the Judiciary' (1998) 114 *Law Quarterly Review* 579–80.

seekers, who rely on the courts for their protection. To restore the balance within the British constitutional system, Lord Woolf asserted that the only remaining branch, the judiciary, had started to compensate for the shortcomings of Parliament. This resulted in a more rigorous examination of executive action by the courts.

The view that there are circumstances under which courts should no longer feel restrained by the boundaries of their constitutional territory has an impressive pedigree. A similar sentiment has been expressed before, by US Supreme Court Chief Justice Stone in a footnote 4 in the *Carolene Products* case, although it related to the review of legislation rather than executive acts.[6]

THE INSTITUTIONAL MODEL AT THE NATIONAL LEVEL

Some general comments

Although Lord Woolf's thesis related to the British system, it lends itself well for an application to any other system based on checks and balances or the separation of powers.[7] There are certainly strong indications that such developments are taking place in other jurisdictions as well. Increasingly courts are demonstrating a willingness to subject the acts of administrative authorities to a more probing review in the absence of effective legislative oversight. In doing so, these courts have been developing a new conception of judicial review, which replaces what might be termed the 'private rights model' of the judicial role by an 'institutional model' of review.

Traditionally, courts have restricted their review to the legality of administrative acts in suits initiated by private individuals. The gravamen of these claims is usually that administrative action has violated their rights or interests. In order to be successful, the plaintiffs must convince the court that the allegedly illegal act had caused damage to their body, property, or reputation. This approach can be referred to as the 'private rights model'. Within the framework of this type of review, courts focus on whether the agency had committed an unlawful act. Therefore, one could argue that even in the private rights model, courts were holding the administration accountable for their actions. However, this supervision was an incidental outcome of addressing the claim of the affected individual, rather than part of a more systematic and structural assessment of the conduct or the agency.

Alongside this private rights model, a new 'institutional model' has developed, which accords a new role to the courts. Underlying this model is the idea that courts have an institutional obligation, mandated by the separation of powers, to

[6] *US v Carolene Products Co* 304 US 144 (1938).

[7] For a critical assessment of this kind of approach see WH Rehnquist, 'The Notion of a Living Constitution' (1975–76) 54 *Texas Law Review* 693, 695, 700 and 706.

see to it that the other branches remain within their constitutionally designated spheres. In order to ensure effective supervision, the institutional model requires the courts to closely monitor the performance of the agencies and to provide them with guidance for future cases. In other words, no potentially unlawful act should go unchallenged.

From the institutional model's perspective, courts need to be able to take on more cases rather than less. Cases are the fuel that keeps the engine of supervision running. Requiring the plaintiff to show a violation of a private interest could keep cases from reaching the court, cases which judges need as vehicles to exercise supervision. The institutional model, therefore, essentially relies on a lowering of the standing barrier and a reduction of the ambit of the non-justiciability doctrine. This new model reflects a growing fervour of judicial review of administrative actions.

Standing

In the area of standing, courts in many jurisdictions have replaced the private rights approach with the institutional model. For example, the Indian Supreme Court in their 1981 decision in *SP Gupta v President of India* substantially lowered the standing barrier to allow public interest litigation.[8] The government of India, led by Prime Minister Indira Ghandi, decided to start rotating judges between the different High Courts to prevent the courts from becoming hotbeds of opposition. This measure was challenged, not by the judges themselves, but by several practicing lawyers who often appeared before them. The government in turn challenged their standing.

Under the traditional standing rules, judicial redress was available only to a person who had suffered a legal injury by reason of violation of their legal right or legal protected interest by the impugned action of the public authority. The traditional basis of entitlement to judicial redress was personal injury to property, body, mind or reputation arising from actual or threatened violation of the legal right or legally protected interest of the person seeking such redress. However, in the case at hand, the petitioners' claim was not that of private injuries, but rather of public injuries. Therefore, the question before the Court was, whether the petitioners had the necessary standing to maintain an action for redress of this public wrong. The Court felt that standing was present, because of the separation of powers.

The Court based its reasoning that the petitioners had standing primarily on the separation of powers. The Court emphasised that it is an essential element of the rule of law that every organ of the State must act within the limits of its power. Moreover, it is the function of the judiciary to confine the legislative and executive organs within their powers. To fulfil that function, courts must be able

[8] AIR 1982 SC 149.

to review acts performed by the legislative and executive branches that are beyond the scope of their powers. If an act is unlawful and causes injury to the public interest rather than to private individuals, there must be a mechanism of redress.

On the other hand, if courts were limited to claims seeking redress for private wrongs, this would be disastrous for the rule of law. Courts would not be able to intervene, and consequently it would be open to the organs of the State to act with impunity beyond the scope of their powers. In the words of Justice Bhagwati: 'the observance of the law is left to the sweet will of the authority bound by it'.[9] According to his Honour, in order to prevent such a lacuna from arising, courts must allow any member of the public acting in good faith to maintain an action for redress of public wrongs or injuries.

The non-justiciability doctrine

Another potential obstacle of judicial review on the institutional model is the 'non-justiciability' concept or political question doctrine, which allows courts to avoid deciding sensitive cases. Some issues belong so clearly to the core activities of the executive that the courts feel that it would not be appropriate for them to look into them, and therefore the courts will declare them to be non-justiciable. These issues are mainly in the area of foreign relations, financial and economic policy, and national security. The courts feel that these issues are sensitive because they involve making policy choices and require expertise, which the courts themselves may lack. Over the past few decades the sphere of non-justiciability has diminished considerably. Issues which many judges deemed too sensitive for judicial consideration 20 years ago,[10] like granting mercy or decisions involving national security, have by now become a normal part of judicial business.[11]

The reduction in the number of non-justiciable issues, however, is not the only recent development of relevance in this regard. Judges have also developed a way to at least partially review matters of high policy. This development began in France, where judges have traditionally refused to look into matters relating to foreign affairs and relations between the government and Parliament. A 1993 case, concerning a UK request to the French government to extradite a person accused of certain financial offences, reflected the clear change in judicial attitude.[12] When France refused to hand the person over, the United Kingdom contested the denied extradition request before the French Council of State. The French government argued that the refusal was immune from judicial review

[9] ibid, at 185.

[10] See the so-called 'negative list' presented by Lord Roskill in *Council of Civil Service Unions v Minister for the Civil Service* [1985] AC 374.

[11] As *R v Home Secretary ex p Bentley* [1994] QB 349, and *A and others v. Secretary of State for the Home Department* [2005] 2 AC 68, the so-called *Belmarsh* case, demonstrate.

[12] *Royaume-Uni de Grande Bretagne et d'Irlande du Nord* CE 15 October 1993.

because it related to French foreign relations. The *Commissaire de Gouvernment*, who is the judicial advisor to the Council of State analogous to the Advocate General at the European Court of Justice (ECJ), argued that the decision not to extradite a person was circumscribed in detail by Treaty and was therefore justiciable. The Council of State agreed, and held that a decision rejecting a request for extradition was 'detachable' from the conduct of diplomatic activity between the two States concerned. The Council made it clear that it is prepared to consider elements of a decision, when those elements are detachable from the policy aspects, ie, can be reviewed independently thereof.

Scope of review

Since World War II, courts have also been introducing more rigorous standards to review administrative action. The deferential tests applied by the courts to review the lawfulness of discretionary acts, exemplified by the *Wednesbury* unreasonableness standard,[13] have gradually been replaced by grounds which subject administrative acts to a more probing review, such as proportionality.

This has happened first and foremost in human rights cases.[14] The German *Multiple Choice Exam* decision is a case in point.[15] A medical student, who had failed a multiple-choice exam, challenged some of the questions before the administrative courts. These courts pointed out that, on the basis of existing case law, they were supposed to accord great deference to the experts that had composed the exam. The courts would only intervene if a question was manifestly wrong or had no foundation in science. Since neither could be said of the contested questions, review was denied.

The student subsequently filed a constitutional complaint with the Federal Constitutional Court, challenging the limited review exercised by the administrative courts. She claimed that her right laid down in Article 19, Section 4 of the German constitution had been infringed. Under this provision any person whose rights have been violated ought to have recourse to a court. The Constitutional Court felt that the applicant's complaint was well founded. Since the administrative courts had been unwilling to look into her objections to the contested exam, they had denied her right to an effective remedy. According to the Court, Article 19(4) does not only confer a right of access to a court, but it also implies that one is entitled to an effective review by that court. Therefore, courts should undertake a thorough examination of both of the law and the facts concerning the challenged decisions, and not simply rely upon the determinations made by the administrative authorities.

[13] *Associated Provincial Picture Houses Ltd v Wednesbury Corporation* [1948] 1 KB 223.

[14] As exemplified by Lord Bridge's speech in *R v Secretary of State for the Home Department, ex p Brind* [1991] 1 AC 696.

[15] BVerfGE 84, 59 (1991).

Consequently, according to the Court, the margin of discretion to be accorded to the authorities with regard to exams should be very limited, since otherwise it would be impossible to guarantee an effective review by the courts. The courts are expected to review whether the exam authorities have adhered to the prescribed standards. As far as medical exams were concerned, the courts should ascertain whether the questions were understandable, clear and not open to debate. A question which does not meet these standards is unlawful. It is the task of administrative courts to exercise this kind of review, with the help of experts if necessary.[16]

THE STRATEGIC BEHAVIOUR OF COURTS

It is clear that by moving from the private rights to the institutional model courts are performing a role which has not been scripted for them in constitutional and statutory law. Courts are meant to settle disputes between opposing parties, one of which may be a government agency. Their job is to adjudicate rather than to monitor agency action. In other words, to a certain extent there is a difference between what courts are supposed to do in theory, and what they actually do in practice. The fact that courts are turning themselves into the supervisors of agency decision-making is the result of strategic behaviour. The research conducted by Epstein and Knight in particular, offers support to this thesis.[17]

In the literature on courts, three models of judicial behaviour are usually distinguished. The first is called the legal approach, which regards the role of judges as being apolitical. Judges are seen as 'mechanical' decision-makers who interpret the law and apply it to the case. Judges are motivated by their desire to honour the doctrine of stare decisis rather than to follow their personal policy views.[18] The second approach, which is the political scientists' answer to the legal ideal type, is called the attitudinal model. The proponents of this school, who are also called behavioralists, assume that judges act directly on their own ideological preferences.

The third model, which was put on the map in particular by Epstein and Knight, perceives judges and courts as strategic operators. Like the attitudinal model, the strategic approach assumes that pursuing their own policy preferences is one of the main goals of judges, albeit not the only one. There are also other goals, including the desire to reach 'principled' decisions based on impartial

[16] The German administrative courts are not altogether happy with this approach, because they feel caught between a rock and a hard place. While the Constitutional Court pushes for exacting review, administrative authorities complain about government by the judiciary, see N Niehues, 'Die Bindungswirkung und Umsetzung Verfassungsgerichtlicher Entscheidungen' (1997) *Neue Juristiche Wochenschrift* 557.

[17] L Epstein and J Knight, *The Choices Justices Make* (Washington DC, CQ Press, 1998).

[18] ibid, at 23.

doctrines, which underlies the legal approach;[19] strengthening institutional legitimacy of the court;[20] and using their career on the court as a stepping stone for political office.[21]

In addition, the strategic model assumes that judges carefully calculate the consequences of their choices.[22] It postulates that judges are strategic actors who realise that their ability to achieve their goals depends on a consideration of the preferences of others, such as their colleagues on the bench, the political branches and the public at large, and of the choices they expect others to make. They will also have regard to the institutional context in which they act, like the concept of stare decisis, which can constrain them from acting on their individual policy preferences.[23]

The main difference between the legal and attitudinal model on the one hand and the strategic account of judicial decision-making on the other, is the assumption that judges pursue multiple goals rather than one, and that they act strategically rather than mechanically. The strategic approach comprises three main ideas, ie, that judges' actions are directed towards the attainment of goals; that judges act strategically; and that institutions structure judges' interactions.[24] The choices judges make therefore flow from strategic considerations rather than from their personal ideology or an apolitical jurisprudence.[25]

In *The Choices Justices Make* Epstein and Knight focus on the micro-level, ie, the way in which individual judges within a court, more particularly the Justices within the US Supreme Court, behave strategically towards each other. They acknowledge, however, that this model also applies to courts behaving strategically towards the political branches.[26] They have further elaborated the macro-approach in an article in the *Emory Law Journal*.[27]

THE OVERSIGHT EXERCISED BY THE APPELLATE BODY

Some general comments

The main rationale for transforming the General Agreement on Tariffs and Trade (GATT) into the WTO was the desire to replace the political settlement of trade

[19] ibid, at 40 and 44.
[20] ibid, at 11–12.
[21] ibid, at 36 and 39.
[22] ibid, at xiii.
[23] ibid, at 10, 12, and 17.
[24] ibid, at 11.
[25] ibid, at xiii.
[26] ibid, at 13, 14–15, and 47–48.
[27] L Epstein, J Knight and A Martin, 'The Supreme Court as a Strategic National Policy Maker' (2001) 50 *Emory Law Journal* 583.

disputes by adjudication.[28] Not surprisingly, therefore, the judicial dimension of the WTO has been much better developed than the oversight role of the political bodies. Thus, unlike other international organisations, the WTO lacks an executive body consisting of the most important Members.[29] In addition, the decision-making for all matters other than dispute settlement is by consensus, which makes it slow and cumbersome. Consequently, there is a stark contrast between the fast and effective operation of the judicial dispute settlement bodies and the inefficiency and weakness of the political structure.[30]

The lack of effective political checks and balances may tempt the Appellate Body, the supreme judicial body within the WTO, to exercise some of these checks instead, in a manner which is comparable to the behaviour of its national counterparts. The question therefore is, whether there are indications that the Appellate Body is developing an institutional model similar to the one that is being put in place by national courts and judges?

The Appellate Body has been acting as the constitutional engine of the WTO by shaping and filling in its constitution,[31] by forging constitutional relations at the central level.[32] The case law of the Appellate Body in the areas of standing, scope of review and non-justiciability, which will be discussed below, does indeed show signs of the development of an institutional model. In addition, the Appellate Body has accorded a role to non-governmental organisations (NGOs) by allowing them to act as amicus curiae in the proceedings before it, which can also be regarded as a mechanism to hold the Members accountable more effectively. This development will also be discussed below.

This evidence is of a circumstantial nature, and there may be other plausible explanations for the behaviour of the Appellate Body. It makes life for court watchers difficult by keeping its cards close to its chest and by applying a literalist or textualist approach to WTO law. In their lectures and publications, the present and former members of the Appellate Body tend not to stray far from the material which is already in the public domain. The only exception is the article written by Ehlermann on his six-year term on the Appellate Body.[33] In this publication he seems to suggest that the weakness of the political structure within the WTO may have had an impact on the approach adopted by the dispute settlement bodies.

[28] P van den Bossche, *The Law and Policy of the World Trade Organization, Text, Cases and Materials*, 2nd edn (Cambridge, Cambridge University Press, 2008) at 170–71.

[29] ibid, at 128.

[30] C-D Ehlermann, 'Six Years on the Bench of the "World Trade Court", Some Personal Experiences as Member of the Appellate Body of the World Trade Organization' (2002) 36 *Journal of World Trade* 632–36.

[31] DZ Cass, 'The Constitutionalization' of International Trade Law: Judicial Norm-Generation as the Engine of Constitutional Development in International Law' (2001) 12 *European Journal of International Law* 39, 51 and 42.

[32] ibid, at 42, 44, and 56.

[33] Ehlermann, n 30 above, at 632–36.

Standing

Standing is usually not much of an issue in WTO cases, because the complaints are brought by Members that clearly have a stake in the outcome. However, there has been one case in which one of the complainants seemed to lack such a direct interest. In *EC-Bananas III*,[34] which was decided in 1997, a complaint had been brought against the European Communities (EC) by Ecuador, Guatemala, Honduras, Mexico and the United States (US). The complaining parties argued that the EC regime for the importation, sale and distribution of bananas was inconsistent with its obligations under the GATT 1994 Agreement (GATT 1994).

Before the Appellate Body the EC contested the standing of the US to bring a case under the GATT 1994. It argued that the US had no actual or potential trade interest justifying its claim, since its banana production is minimal, and it has never exported bananas, which is unlikely to change due to climatic and economic conditions, while production alone is insufficient basis for bringing a claim.

The EC asserted that, as a general principle, in any system of law, including international law, a claimant must typically have a legal right or interest in the claim it is pursuing. It relied on judgments of the Permanent Court of International Justice (PCIJ) and the International Court of Justice (ICJ) to demonstrate that international law does not allow an *actio popularis*. Therefore an *actio popularis* like the one brought by the US would be acceptable only if the WTO Agreement would expressly set aside the requirement of a legal interest. The absence of such an explicit rule indicated that the US lacked the necessary standing. In addition, the EC argued that Article 10.2 of the Dispute Settlement Understanding (DSU) allows only those WTO Members to participate as third parties that have 'a substantial interest in the matter before the panel'. According to the EC this means a fortiori that a party to a dispute must show a legal interest.

The Appellate Body found that the judgments of the PCIJ and the ICJ on which the EC relied did not establish a general rule that in all international litigation a complaining party must have a legal interest in order to bring a case. Furthermore, these judgments did not deny the need to resort to the applicable multilateral treaty, in this case the WTO dispute settlement provisions, in order to determine the question of standing. The Appellate Body pointed out that the text of Article XXIII:1 of the GATT 1994 allows a complaint to be brought 'if any Member should consider that any benefit accruing to it directly or indirectly under this Agreement is being nullified or impaired'. In addition, Article 3.7 DSU states that 'before bringing a case, a Member shall exercise its judgement as to whether action under these procedures would be fruitful'. According to the

[34] *European Communities—Regime for the Importation, Sale and Distribution of Bananas*, DS27, 9 September 1997; see WJ Davey, 'Has the WTO Dispute Settlement System Exceeded its Authority? A Consideration of Deference Shown by the System to Member Government Decisions and its Use of Issue-Avoidance Techniques' (2001) 79 *Journal of International Economic Law* 97–99.

Appellate Body, the language of both provisions suggests that a Member is expected to be largely self-regulating in deciding whether any such action would be fruitful. It therefore believed that a Member enjoys broad discretion in deciding whether to bring a case against another Member under the DSU.

Accordingly, the Appellate Body was satisfied that the US was justified in bringing its claims under the GATT 1994 in this case. The US is a producer of bananas, and a potential export could not be excluded. The internal market of bananas for the US could be affected by the EC banana regime, in particular, by the effects of that regime on world supplies and world prices for bananas. The Appellate Body referred with approval to the statement made by the Panel in this case that with the increased interdependence of the global economy, Members have a greater stake in enforcing WTO rules than in the past, since any deviation from the negotiated balance of rights and obligations is more likely than ever to affect them, either directly or indirectly.

Although the Appellate Body has made it clear that its ruling on standing may not have precedential value, in this case it has laid down a very low standing barrier, which basically allows Members to decide for themselves whether or not to bring a case. This liberal attitude of the Appellate Body in the area of standing is comparable to the leniency displayed by the Indian Supreme Court in *Gupta*.

Scope of review

There are clear indications that over time the Appellate Body has become more probing in its review of decisions taken by the Members, both in fact and in law.[35] Its review of the facts is rather intrusive and on the spectrum of standards of review it is much closer to *de novo* review than total deference.[36] In law the Appellate Body has moved away from the rather deferential 'objective assessment test',[37] while there are indications that the standard of review of law is turning into a proportionality test.[38] Both Cass and Zleptnig have related these developments to a shift in the institutional balance within the WTO.[39]

The most visible development has taken place in relation to the standard laid down in Article 17.6 of the Anti-Dumping Agreement. It may be true that in

[35] M Oesch, *Standards of Review in WTO Dispute Resolution* (Oxford, Oxford University Press, 2003) at 105–230.

[36] M Oesch, *Standards of Review in WTO Dispute Resolution* (2003) 6 *Journal of International Economic Law* 649 and 651.

[37] Oesch, n 36 above, at 656–57, 658; R Becroft, 'The Standard of Review Strikes Back: The *US—Korea Drams* Appeal' (2006) 9 *JIEL* 211; H Spamann, 'Standard of Review for World Trade Organization Panels in Trade Remedy Cases: A Critical Analysis' (2004) 38 *Journal of World Trade* 540.

[38] P Van den Bossche, 'Looking for Proportionality in WTO Law' (2008) 35 *Legal Issues of Economic Integration* 293–94.

[39] Cass, n 31 above, at 58; S Zleptnig, 'The Standard of Review in WTO Law, An Analysis of Law, Legitimacy and the Distribution of Legal and Political Authority' (2002) *European Business Law Review* 434 and 444.

theory this standard is an exception to the rule,[40] but it is undoubtedly the most commercially significant.[41] The negotiators have laid down a special standard of review for national anti-dumping measures. A manufacturer engages in dumping when he charges a lower price for a good in a foreign market than the one he charges for the same good in the domestic market. National authorities often impose anti-dumping duties on goods imported from the dumper's country. Article 17.6 of the Anti-Dumping Agreement contains the standard for reviewing such anti-dumping measures. According to this provision, WTO panels shall interpret the relevant provisions of the Agreement in accordance with customary rules of public international law. If the Panel finds that a provision of the Agreement admits more than one permissible interpretation, the Panel shall find the measure taken by the national authority to be in conformity with the Agreement, so long as it rests upon one of those permissible interpretations.

This standard closely resembles the one adopted by the US Supreme Court in the *Chevron* case.[42] This case concerned rules issued by the Environmental Protection Agency (EPA) under the Clean Air Act. The Carter EPA had promulgated very strict regulations that were environmentally friendly, but were not received very well by the business community. When the Reagan Administration came into office, the EPA replaced the existing rules by regulations that gave companies more leeway. Not surprisingly, these rules were then challenged by the National Resources Defense Council, an environmental organisation. Since these different sets of rules were rooted in an interpretation of the same statutory language, the question before the Supreme Court was how courts should treat agency interpretations of Acts of Congress. Should judges rely upon their own construction of the statute or should they respect the agency's interpretation?

The Supreme Court applied a two-step analysis which became known as the '*Chevron* two-step'. The first question is whether Congress has directly addressed the precise question. If the intent of Congress is clear, the agency and the court have to defer to the position of Congress, and thus cannot amend its views. If the court determines that Congress has not directly addressed the precise question, by being silent or ambiguous, the answer of the agency will be decisive. In such a case, a court may not substitute its own construction of a statutory provision for a reasonable interpretation made by the agency. As a result of the Court's holding in *Chevron*, courts should ordinarily yield to the agencies' interpretations of the statutes they administer, unless their construction was unreasonable. Not surprisingly, *Chevron* has signalled a substantial increase in agency discretion to make policy through statutory interpretation.[43]

[40] Ehlermann, n 30 above, at 619.

[41] JP Durling, 'Deference, But Only When Due: WTO Review of Anti-Dumping Measures' (2003) 6 *JIEL* 125.

[42] *Chevron v Natural Resources Defense Council* 467 US 837 (1984).

[43] CR Sunstein, '*Chevron* Step Zero' (2006) 92 *Virginia Law Review* 187, 190.

This parallel with *Chevron* is no coincidence. The text of Article 17.6 was the result of an initiative taken by the US government, which felt that some of the decisions reached by GATT panels in the anti-dumping area had been too intrusive.[44] By putting forward this lenient standard, the US tried to insulate its anti-dumping decisions from the review to be exercised by the WTO Panels, which would not only be binding, but also highly legalised.[45]

The bottom line was that an interpretation of a provision of the Anti-Dumping Agreement by a national authority should stand even if the Panel would have reached a different conclusion. However, research conducted by Daniel Tarullo has demonstrated that in anti-dumping cases the WTO Panels and the Appellate Body apply the Article 17.6 standard in a way which does not at all resemble the *Chevron* type of review intended by the US.[46] The Appellate Body effectively turned Article 17.6 into a dead letter in *US-Hot-Rolled Steel*.[47] In this case, the Article 17.6 standard was collapsed into the general standard of review laid down in Article 11 of the DSU, which calls for a more probing review.

The Appellate Body noted that Article 17.6 is identified in Article 1.2 and Appendix 2 of the DSU as one of the special or additional rules and procedures which prevail over the DSU to the extent that there is a difference between those provisions and the provisions of the DSU. The Appellate Body pointed out that in *Guatemala-Cement I*[48] it had decided that the special or additional rules of a covered agreement will prevail when they are in conflict with the provisions of the DSU, but not if they can be read as complementing those provisions.[49] It then set out to interpret the text of Article 17.6 in such a way that it had little to add to the text of Article 11 of the DSU and therefore lost its status as a special, more lenient standard of review.

The Appellate Body reiterated that under Article 17.6 Panels are obliged to determine whether a measure rests upon an interpretation of the Anti-Dumping Agreement which is in accordance with customary rules of public international law. Therefore, according to the Appellate Body, the interpretation has to be permissible under the rules of treaty interpretation laid down in Articles 31 and 32 of the Vienna Convention on the Law of Treaties. Consequently, if the rules of

[44] SP Croley and JH Jackson, 'WTO Dispute Procedures, Standards of Review, and Deference to National Governments (1996) 90 *American Journal of International Law* 195–96; RP Alford, 'Reflections on *US—Zeroing*: A Study in Judicial Overreaching by the WTO Appellate Body' (2006–07) 45 *Columbia Journal of Transnational Law* 201, in particular fn 19.

[45] DK Tarullo, 'The Hidden Costs of International Dispute Settlement: WTO Review of Domestic Ant-Dumping Decisions' (2002–03) 34 *Law & Policy in International Business* 112; the wording of Art 17.6 is slightly different from the original proposal submitted by the US, see Tarullo at 117, in particular fn 21.

[46] Tarullo, n 45 above, at 118–47.

[47] *United States—Anti-Dumping Measures on Certain Hot-Rolled Steel Products from Japan*, DS184, 24 July 2001.

[48] *Guatemala—Anti-Dumping Investigation Regarding Portland Cement from Mexico*, DS60, 2 November 1998.

[49] *United States—Anti-Dumping Measures on Certain Hot-Rolled Steel Products from Japan*, DS184, 24 July 2001 at § 51.

treaty interpretation as articulated in Articles 31 and 32 of the Vienna convention could give rise to at least two interpretations of a provision of the Anti-Dumping Agreement, a measure will be deemed to be in conformity with the Agreement if it rests upon one of those permissible interpretations.[50] Although the Appellate Body stopped short of determining in general whether there are provisions of the Anti-Dumping Agreement which admit more than one permissible interpretation under those conditions, it is, of course, highly unlikely that the rules of treaty interpretation will result in different interpretative scenarios.

The Appellate Body noted that Article 11 of the DSU require Panels to make an 'objective assessment of the matter' as a whole. Thus, under the DSU, when examining claims, Panels must make an 'objective assessment' of the legal provisions at issue, their 'applicability' to the dispute, and the 'conformity' of the measures at issue with the covered agreements. According to the Appellate Body, nothing in Article 17.6 of the Anti-Dumping Agreement suggests that Panels examining claims under that Agreement should not conduct an 'objective assessment' of the legal provisions of the Agreement, their applicability to the dispute, and the conformity of the measures at issue with the Agreement.

Therefore, to this extent, Article 11 of the DSU and Article 17.6 of the Anti-Dumping Agreement are in conformity rather than in conflict with each other. It is true that Article 17.6 adds that a Panel shall find a measure to be in conformity with the Anti-Dumping Agreement if it rests upon one permissible interpretation of that Agreement. After having considerably reduced the significance of this standard by tying it to Articles 31 and 32 of the Vienna convention, the Appellate Body emphasised that insofar as Article 17.6 imposes obligations on Panels that are not found in the DSU, it supplements rather than replaces Article 11 DSU.

Non-justiciability

The GATT Panels have introduced a distinction between two types of rules, ie, mandatory and discretionary legislation. Mandatory legislation prescribes one single course of action, which leaves no room whatsoever to the administrative agency to deviate from. Discretionary legislation, on the other hand, enables the agency to choose from different options.[51] Members were permitted to challenge legislation that mandated an alleged violation of GATT obligations as such. However, discretionary legislation could only be challenged if the national agency had opted for a course that was contrary to its GATT obligations, as exemplified by a concrete act. In other words, mandatory laws could be subjected to abstract review, while discretionary laws would only be reviewed as applied. In *US-1916*

[50] ibid, at § 59–60.

[51] Y Naiki, 'The Mandatory/Discretionary Doctrine in WTO Law, The *US—Section 301* Case and its Aftermath' (2004) *JIEL* 23 and 24.

Act (EC)[52] the Appellate Body noted that under Article XVI:1 of the WTO Agreement both it and the Panels would be bound by the mandatory/discretionary doctrine, since it formed part of the GATT *acquis.*

In *US-Oil Country Tubular Goods Sunset Reviews*,[53] the Appellate Body explained why 'as such' review is far-reaching. It noted that 'as such' claims challenge laws, regulations, or other instruments of a Member that have general and prospective application, and therefore seek to prevent Members ex ante from engaging in certain conduct. By limiting the possibility of 'as such' challenges to mandatory legislation, the GATT Panels, and therefore also the Appellate Body, have declared such challenges concerning discretionary legislation to be non-justiciable. This approach is similar to the concept of ripeness as developed by US courts.[54]

Over the years the Appellate Body has been gradually reducing the scope of this non-justiciability doctrine. The first step on this road was taken in *US-1916 Act (EC)*, the case in which the Appellate Body seemed to embrace the mandatory/discretionary doctrine. The US, the appellant in this case, had argued that the Panels and the Appellate Body were not allowed to review the challenged legislation, the United States Revenue Act of 1916, as such, because it constituted discretionary legislation within the meaning of the mandatory/discretionary doctrine. The US pointed out that, with respect to both criminal and civil proceedings, US courts have in the past interpreted the 1916 Act in a manner consistent with the WTO obligations of the US, and could do so again in the future. Furthermore, the US Department of Justice has discretion to decide whether or not to initiate criminal proceedings under the 1916 Act.

The Appellate Body referred to a statement made by the Panel in *United States Tobacco*[55] that legislation which merely gave the discretion to the executive of a contracting party to act inconsistently with the General Agreement could not be challenged as such. The Appellate Body interpreted this statement to mean that legislation can only be discretionary for purposes of the mandatory/discretionary doctrine if it vests discretion in the executive branch of government.[56] The Appellate Body then noted that there is no relevant discretion accorded to the executive branch of the United States' government in the 1916 Act. A judge faced with proceedings under the 1916 Act must simply apply it,[57] and the discretion enjoyed by the US Department of Justice is not of such nature or of such breadth

[52] *United States—Anti-Dumping Act of 1916*, DS136, 28 August 2000, § 61.

[53] *United States—Sunset Reviews of Anti-Dumping Measures on Oil Country Tubular Goods from Argentina*, DS268, 29 November 2004, § 172.

[54] Naiki, n 51 above, at 26; Alford, n 44 above, at 217 explains the rationale of the doctrine as respect for the legislative autonomy of the Members to allow them to delegate decision-making authority to the executive branch and the rejection of the assumption that a national organ will act in a way which is inconsistent with the Member's WTO obligations.

[55] *United States—Measures Affecting the Importation, Internal Sale and Use of Tobacco*, Panel Report, adopted 4 October 1994, BISD 41S/131.

[56] *United States—Anti-Dumping Act of 1916*, DS136, 28 August 2000, § 89.

[57] ibid, at § 90.

as to transform the 1916 Act into discretionary legislation, as this term has been understood for purposes of distinguishing between mandatory and discretionary legislation.[58]

The second step on the road to broaden the ambit of the 'as such' concept was taken in *US—Corrosion-Resistant Steel Sunset Review*.[59] In this case the Appellate Body, although conceding that in the practice under the GATT most measures which were subject to 'as such' challenges were of a legislative nature, pointed out that in *Guatemala-Cement I* it had observed that a broad range of measures could be subjected to such review.[60] It is submitted, however, that the paragraph and the footnote in the report to which the Appellate Body referred was not related to the mandatory/discretionary doctrine.

It also found support for the view that non-legislative measures may be challenged as such in Article 17.3 of the Anti-Dumping Agreement, which establishes the principle that a Member can complain if it considers that its benefits are being nullified or impaired by another Member or Members. According to the Appellate Body, this language underlines that any measure attributable to a Member may be submitted to dispute settlement and that Article 17.3 does not contain a threshold requirement that the measure in question be of a certain type.[61] It also relied on Article 18.4 of the Anti-Dumping Agreement, which contains an explicit obligation for Members to take all necessary steps, of a general or particular character, to ensure that their laws, regulations and administrative procedures are in conformity with the Anti-Dumping Agreement. According to the Appellate Body, the phrase 'laws, regulations and administrative procedures', taken as a whole, encompasses the entire body of generally applicable rules, norms and standards adopted by Members in connection with the conduct of anti-dumping proceedings. The Appellate Body expressed the view that if some of these types of measures could not, as such, be subject to dispute settlement under the Anti-Dumping Agreement, it would frustrate the obligation of conformity set forth in Article 18.4.

The Appellate Body therefore came to the conclusion that there is no basis, either in the practice of the GATT and the WTO generally, or in the provisions of the Anti-Dumping Agreement, for finding that review 'as such' is only restricted to certain types of measures. In the case at hand it decided that the Sunset Policy Bulletin, which was a policy document, could be subjected to an 'as such' challenge.

[58] ibid, at § 91.

[59] *United States—Sunset Review of Anti-Dumping Duties on Corrosion-Resistant Carbon Steel Flat Products from Japan*, DS244, 15 December 2003.

[60] *Guatemala—Anti-Dumping Investigation Regarding Portland Cement from Mexico*, DS60, 2 November 1998, § 69, n 47.

[61] *United States—Sunset Review of Anti-Dumping Duties on Corrosion-Resistant Carbon Steel Flat Products from Japan*, DS244, 15 December 2003, § 86.

In *US—Zeroing (EC)*,[62] the Appellate Body further limited the ambit of the non-justiciability doctrine by determining that measures that are not expressed in a written form may also be subjected to 'as such' challenges. Again it relied on the text of the Articles 17.3 and 18.4 of the Anti-Dumping Agreement. It pointed out that the determination of the scope of 'laws, regulations and administrative procedures', which are mentioned in Article 18.4, must be based on the content and substance of the alleged measure, and not merely on its form.[63] Accordingly, the mere fact that a rule or norm is not expressed in the form of a written statement does not separate it from review 'as such'.[64]

Amicus briefs

The number of checks and balances has been increased as a result of the acceptance by the Appellate Body of amicus curiae briefs, which are filed by third parties unrelated to the dispute. In the *Shrimp-Turtle* case,[65] which was brought by India, Malaysia, Pakistan, and Thailand against the US, the US government had attached three amicus briefs, filed by NGOs, to its appellate submission. The US made it clear that it acted as a channel for these NGOs and that the arguments made in the brief could only be attributed to it to the extent to which those arguments concurred with the arguments set out it its main submission.[66]

The Apellees objected to the submission of these briefs and requested the Appellate Body not to consider them. They pointed out that the submission of documents which present the views of NGOs is not contemplated in or authorised by the DSU or the Working Procedures for Appellate Review. Nevertheless, in a preliminary ruling the Appellate Body decided to accept the briefs for consideration. It noted that the attaching of a brief or other material to the submission of either Appellant or Appellee, no matter how or where such material may have originated, renders that material at least prima facie an integral part of that participant's submission. On the one hand, it is for the participant in an appeal to determine for itself what to include in its submission. On the other hand, a participant filing a submission is properly regarded as assuming responsibility for the contents of that submission, including any annexes or other attachments.[67]

[62] *United States—Laws, Regulations and Methodology for Calculating Dumping Margins (Zeroing)*, DS294, 18 April 2006.
[63] The Appellate Body referred to *United States—Sunset Review of Anti-Dumping Duties on Corrosion-Resistant Carbon Steel Flat Products from Japan*, DS244, 15 December 2003, § 87.
[64] *United States—Laws, Regulations and Methodology for Calculating Dumping Margins (Zeroing)*, DS294, 18 April 2006, §§ 192–93.
[65] *United States—Import Prohibition of Certain Shrimp and Shrimp Products*, DS58, 12 October 1998.
[66] ibid, at § 86.
[67] ibid, at § 89.

By closely linking the amicus briefs to the appellant submission filed by the US, the Appellate Body clearly limited the impact of the legal arguments made in them. Since the US had itself accepted the briefs in a tentative and qualified manner only, the Appellate Body decided to focus on the legal argument made in the main US submission.[68] The moral dimension, however, was clearly significant. The briefs had been submitted by a number of reputable environmental organisations and it did the US no harm that its position based on trade considerations was perceived as being in the interest of the environment as well.

Since the Panel in this case had also received a few amicus briefs directly from NGOs, the Appellate Body decided to come back to this issue in the main body of its Report. It pointed out that under the DSU, only Members who are parties to a dispute, or who are involved as third parties, have a legal right to make submissions to and have them considered by a Panel.[69] However, Article 13 of the DSU authorises Panels to seek information and advice as they deem appropriate in a particular case from any individual, body or relevant source. The Appellate Body considered that a Panel also has the authority to accept or reject any information or advice which it may have sought and received, or to make some other appropriate disposition thereof. In sum, the Panel has the discretionary authority to determine the need for information and advice in a specific case, to ascertain the acceptability and relevancy of information or advice received, and to decide what weight to ascribe to that information or advice.[70] The Appellate Body also pointed to Article 12.1 of the DSU which authorises Panels to depart from, or to add to, the Working Procedures set forth in Appendix 3 of the DSU, and in fact to develop their own Working Procedures, after consultation of the parties to the dispute.[71]

According to the Appellate Body, the thrust of Articles 12 and 13, when taken together, is that the DSU accords to a Panel ample and extensive authority to undertake and to control the process by which it informs itself both of the relevant facts of the dispute and of the legal norms and principles applicable to such facts. That authority is indispensably necessary to enable a Panel to discharge it duty imposed by Article 11 of the DSU to make an objective assessment of the facts of the case and the applicability of and conformity with the relevant covered agreements.[72] Considering the context of broad authority vested in Panels by the DSU, and given the object and purpose of the Panel's mandate as revealed in Article 11, the Appellate Body felt that the word 'seek' in

[68] ibid, at § 91.
[69] ibid, at § 101.
[70] ibid, at § 104.
[71] ibid, at § 105.
[72] ibid, at § 106.

Article 13 should not be read in too literal a manner. A Panel has the discretionary authority to either accept and consider, or to reject information and advice submitted to it, whether requested by a Panel or not.[73]

In the *Carbon-Steel* case[74] the Appellate Body revisited the amicus issue. It had directly received amicus briefs from two organisations which represented the interests of steel manufacturers.[75] While the amici in *Shrimp-Turtle* were NGOs representing the public interest, the amici in this case represented an industry which had a stake in the outcome of the proceedings. The Appellee in this case, the EC, objected to the briefs being taken into consideration. It pointed out that in *Shrimp-Turtle* the Appellate Body had relied on Article 13 as the basis for allowing amicus briefs in Panel proceedings. According to the EC, Article 13 does not apply to the Appellate Body and, in any case, that provision is limited to factual information and technical advice, and would not include legal arguments or legal interpretations received from non-Members. Furthermore, the EC argued that neither the DSU nor the Working Procedures allow amicus briefs to be admitted in Appellate Body proceedings, given that Article 17.4 of the DSU and Rules 21, 22 and 28.1 of the Working Procedures confine participation in an appeal to participants and third participants, and that Article 17.10 of the DSU provides for the confidentiality of Appellate Body proceedings.[76]

The Appellate Body observed that nothing in the DSU or the Working Procedures specifically authorises nor prohibits it to accept and consider submissions or briefs from sources other than the participants and the third participants. It emphasised, however, that under Article 17.9 the Appellate Body has broad authority to adopt procedural rules. Accordingly, the Appellate Body was of the view that as long as it acts consistently with the provisions of the DSU and the covered agreements, it has the legal authority to decide whether or not to accept and consider any information that it believes is pertinent and useful in an appeal.[77]

The Appellate Body also reiterated that in *Shrimp-Turtle* it had made clear that under the DSU only parties and third parties to a dispute have a legal right to participate in Panel or Appellate Body proceedings, and that individuals and organisations which are not Members of the WTO lack such a legal right.[78] The Appellate Body came to the conclusion that it has the legal authority under the DSU to accept and consider amicus briefs in any appeal in which it finds it

[73] ibid, at § 107.

[74] *United States—Imposition of Countervailing Duties on Certain Hot-Rolled Lead and Bismuth Carbon Steel Products Originating in the United Kingdom*, DS138, 10 May 2000.

[75] This point has been made persuasively by A Kupfer Schneider, 'Unfriendly Actions: The Amicus Brief Battle at the WTO' (2001) 7 *Widener Law Symposium Journal* 98 and 100.

[76] *United States—Imposition of Countervailing Duties on Certain Hot-Rolled Lead and Bismuth Carbon Steel Products Originating in the United Kingdom*, n 74 above, at § 36.

[77] ibid, at § 39.

[78] ibid, at § 40–41.

pertinent and useful to do so. Interestingly, in the case at hand it did not find it necessary to take the two amicus briefs that had been filed into account.[79]

The third step on this road was taken in the *EC—Asbestos* case,[80] in which the Appellate Body again received a number of amicus briefs. It decided to adopt an Additional Procedure, pursuant to Rule 16(1) of the Working Procedures, do deal with such briefs, for the purposes of the *EC—Asbestos* appeal only.[81] The core of these new procedural requirements was that any natural or legal person, who wished to file an amicus brief, was obliged to apply for leave to file such a brief from the Appellate Body before a certain date.[82]

After the adoption of the Additional Procedure, the Appellate Body returned the amicus briefs which had been submitted to their senders, along with a letter informing them of the new procedural requirements. Thereafter the Appellate Body received 17 applications for leave to file an amicus brief. It denied such leave in six cases, because those applications had been received after the deadline specified in the Additional Procedure. In the 11 remaining cases the Appellate Body denied leave on other grounds.[83]

This brought the Appellate Body into hot water. Some Member States are steadfast objectors to the filing of amicus briefs and they were disappointed by the fact that the Appellate Body was willing to entertain them at all. The amici who had been denied access were irritated by the fact that their brief had been rejected out of hand, apparently because they had ignored some simple procedural rules.[84]

Although the Appellate Body has not yet pronounced itself on the rationale of this practice, it has been widely perceived as being meant to fill the democratic deficit.[85] Allowing such briefs to be filed generates input from civil society and at the same time may assist the WTO in alleviating itself of its reputation as an organisation which is out of touch with the mainstream of society. For the Appellants and the Appellees it may be important to show that they enjoy the support of groups in society that have an interest in the issue.

[79] ibid, at § 42.

[80] *European Communities—Measures Affecting Asbestos and Products Containing Asbestos*, DS135, 12 March 2001.

[81] ibid, at § 50.

[82] ibid, at § 52; the idea to introduce a 'leave to file' procedure has probably been taken from national law.

[83] ibid, at §§ 53–56; the rounds were not specified, which allowed the Appellate Body to retain its discretion.

[84] R Howse, 'Membership and its Privileges: the WTO, Civil Society, and the *Amicus* Brief Controversy' (2003) 9 *European Law Journal* 505.

[85] Howse, n 84 above, at 509; M Laidhold, 'Private Party Access to the WTO: Do Recent Developments in International Trade Dispute Resolution Really Give Private Organizations a Voice in the WTO?' (1999) 12 *Transnational Law* 432; J Keller, 'The Future of Amicus Participation at the WTO: Implications of the Sardines Decision and Suggestions for Further Developments' (2005) 33 *International Journal of Legal Information* 457 and 460; P van den Bossche, 'NGO Involvement in the WTO: A Comparative Perspective' (2008) 11 *JIEL* 720.

CONCLUSION

This contribution has focused on the extent of the ability of courts to hold global organs accountable. In order to illustrate whether courts are able to perform this role at the global level, a discussion of the thesis of Lord Woolf was first briefly considered. There are signals that national courts have attempted to compensate for the lack of parliamentary hold on administrative agencies by introducing an 'institutional model'. By lowering the standing barrier, by restricting the ambit of the non-justiciabilty doctrine and by subjecting administrative decisions to a more probing review, courts have been able to turn themselves into monitoring bodies, which oversee the behaviour of administrative agencies in general. This transformation from adjudicator to overseer fits into the strategic model of judging as developed by Epstein and Knight.

Finally, the case law of the Appellate Body of the WTO was examined in order to evaluate if international courts are able to hold global organs to account. The Appellate Body has also developed an 'institutional model', which does not only cover standing, non-justiciability and standards of review, but also extends to the acceptance of amicus briefs. It is likely that through developing this 'institutional model' the Appellate Body is trying to compensate for the democratic deficit which is inherent to the WTO system. The fact that the Appellate Body performs this role, implies that generally, international courts are able to fill the accountability gap at the global level. A complication is that not every global organ is subject to the jurisdiction of an international court. This could be remedied by the establishment of a Global Administrative Court to which global organs which are not yet covered can subscribe.

9

The Place of Public Interest

JOHN MORISON AND GORDON ANTHONY*

INTRODUCTION

THE THEME OF this chapter is 'public interest' and global administrative law. Public interest, for these purposes, is the (ill-defined) term that has traditionally occupied a range of abstract and more practical places in administrative law and which can be invoked by legislative, executive and judicial actors, as well as those drawn from civil society.[1] The central point in the chapter is that public interest may have an important role to play in global administrative law but that this requires a pluralist approach to the challenge of post-State governance.[2] The contrasting approach links global administrative law more immediately to the realm of the 'global administrative space' and suggests that accountability mechanisms there can ensure some degree of control over extra-State decision-makers.[3] However, while the merit in that approach is that it seeks to identify a means partly to legitimate global governance,[4] it can be criticised for distancing global administrative law from wider debates about constitutionalism and anterior values such as democracy.[5] Although we will not claim, in this chapter, to have the answers to the problematic of post-State democracy, we will suggest that a concept such as public interest—which is central to much administrative law theorising—can enjoy meaning in the global setting only insofar as it maps onto identifiable publics and institutional processes. We will thus suggest

* The authors wish to acknowledge support from the Economic and Social Research Council through the award of a grant (RES-062-23-1996) to explore wider concepts of public interest. We are also grateful to Leanne Cochrane who provided research assistance.

[1] See generally R Brownsword (ed), *Law and the Public Interest* (Stuttgart, Franz Steiner Verlag 1993).

[2] On which see C Harlow, 'Global Administrative Law: The Quest for Principles and Values' (2006) 17 *European Journal of International Law* 187; N Krisch, 'The Pluralism of Global Administrative Law' (2006) 17 *EJIL* 247; and Ch 1 this volume.

[3] See B Kingsbury, N Krisch, and R Stewart, 'The Emergence of Global Administrative Law' (2005) 68 *Law and Contemporary Problems* 15.

[4] See generally N Krisch, 'Global Administrative Law and the Constitutional Ambition', *LSE Legal Studies Working Paper No 10/2009*, available through www.lse.ac.uk/collections/law/wps/.

[5] See pp 6–10, this volume.

that pluralism's emphasis on a multiplicity of legal orders is important precisely because it regards global governance as conditioned by cross-cutting norms and preferences that have constitutional origins in a range of sites found above, below, and at the level of the State itself.[6]

The corresponding objectives of the chapter are twofold. First, it seeks to explain how conceptions of public interest have moved from a position of State-centricity towards one of increased interdependence and interaction within the post-Westphalian order. The focus, here, will be very much on the idea of overlapping national, international and supranational norms and the fact that legal systems increasingly regulate one another through a range of direct and indirect linkages associated with Europeanisation and globalisation.[7] Although the idea of linkages is by no means new[8] the intensification of regional and global processes in recent decades has removed real and imagined boundaries to the transfer of norms and entailed that legal orders are ever-more permeable, even if they do not wish be so.[9] In practical terms, this means that domestic governmental preferences can be influenced by external national actors who work within policy networks[10] as well as by international and supranational organisations that impose significant obligations upon their Member States. Of those organisations the most commented upon perhaps remain the Council of Europe and the European Union (EU), which have facilitated not only a part fusion of legal traditions in Europe[11] but also positioned themselves as new public spheres and constitutional orders.[12]

The second objective is to consider the meaning that should be ascribed to 'publicness' in debates about global administrative law. Here, the starting point for lawyers and political scientists is often the idea of 'political community' that sustains shared political institutions and which justifies legal and political decisions taken for reasons of the 'public interest'. Of course, such discourses have historically included an element of artificiality as political communities have been constructed within State boundaries, given order by a State's internal constitutional norms, and enfranchised (at least in democratic systems) by voting rights that offer a gateway to political participation. However, with the fusion of

6 On which see N Walker, 'The Idea of Constitutional Pluralism' (2002) 65 *Modern Law Review* 317.

7 J-B Auby, *La globalisation, le droit et l'État* (Paris, Montchrestien, 2003); and Battini, ch 3 in this volume.

8 DB Goldman, *Globalisation and the Western Legal Tradition: Recurring Patterns of Law and Authority* (Cambridge, Cambridge University Press, 2007).

9 M Hunt, *Using Human Rights Law in English Courts* (Oxford, Hart Publishing, 1997) chs 1–3.

10 A-M Slaughter, *A New World Order* (Princeton, Princeton University Press, 2004).

11 See, generally, J-B Auby and J Dutheil de la Rochère (eds), *Droit Administratif Européen* (Brussels, Bruylant, 2007) and J Schwarze, *European Administrative Law*, 2nd edn (London, Sweet & Maxwell, 2006).

12 See, in respect of the ECHR, *Loizidou v Turkey* (1996) 23 ERR 99; and on the EU see Joined Cases C 402/05P and C-415/05P, *Kadi & Al Barakaat International Foundation v Council and Commission* [2008] 3 CMLR 41.

State boundaries and a proliferation of extra-State institutions, that artificiality has assumed a much more troubling dimension and the gap between decision-maker and governed has become a chasm.[13] With that in mind, much of the literature on global administrative law suggests an incremental approach to the attainment of legitimacy in global governance rather than a more ambitious search for a constitutional settlement centred upon a model of democracy for the globe.[14] We would agree with that caution in respect of a foundational constitution but, as we have outlined in the introduction to this collection,[15] we consider that the pursuit of a 'one size fits all' constitution is in any event misguided. There are many reasons for this, but the one that is most germane here is the underlying assumption that there can be a singular global public that defines a global legal space and lends legitimacy to decisions taken in the global public interest. We will suggest that any such construction of a global public has the potential to reduce to an exercise in safeguarding elite interests in global governance rather than those that truly belong to a range of publics. To put the point differently—and to return to the above comment about pluralism—we will contend that legitimacy lies more in the equal recognition of many publics rather than in the construction of one.

The chapter begins with a section that considers some of the literature on public interest and national administrative law and how those traditional models are now subject to external influences associated with globalisation. The second section develops the point about the nature of publicness in the global legal space; and the conclusion ties the various themes together with reference to pluralism.

PUBLIC INTEREST AND ADMINISTRATIVE LAW: OLD AND NEW PARAMETERS

Debates about 'public interest' find many of their origins in literature on political philosophy and sovereign Statehood.[16] In one of the most famous attempts at definition Walter Lippmann wrote that 'the public interest may be presumed to be what [people] would choose if they saw clearly, thought rationally, acted disinterestedly and benevolently'.[17] Of course, this is to attribute to individuals altruistic qualities that, in early social contract theory, had led to the State being

[13] P Cerny, 'Globalization and the End of Democracy' (1999) 36 *European Journal of Political Research* 1. But compare A Moravcsik, 'Is there a "Democratic Deficit" in World Politics? A Framework for Analysis' (2004) *Government & Opposition* 336.

[14] Krisch, n 4 above.

[15] At pp 8–10.

[16] For discussion of the term see B Bozeman, *Public Values and Public Interest: Counterbalancing Economic Individualism* (Washington, Georgetown University Press, 2007) esp chs 1 and 5; RC Box, 'Redescribing the Public Interest' (2007) 44 *Social Science Journal* 585; and M Feintuck, *The 'Public Interest' In Regulation* (Oxford, Oxford University Press, 2004) ch 1.

[17] W Lippmann, *The Public Philosophy* (London, Hamish Hamilton, 1955) at 44.

entrusted with the power to take decisions for reasons of the 'common good'.[18] For some, the State thus became 'the formal expression and visible symbol of the "public interest"'[19] and the pursuit of the greater good 'the ultimate ethical goal of political relationships'.[20] However, such reasoning also begged questions about how to gauge the public interest within polities that inevitably had a variety of cross-cutting individual and sectional interests, as well as those that may have appeared irreconcilable. Here, the answers were sometimes said to lie in 'preponderance', 'unitary', and 'common interest' theories that situated individual interests within that of a broader collective.[21] While each theory was criticised for reasons of artificiality—they rested upon assumptions about, among other things, aggregated individual interests and the arbitrary rejection of other subjectively legitimate preferences[22]—they all presupposed an inherent normative appeal to the idea of public interest. The theories were in that sense communitarian in outlook, at least within State-based, democratic meanings of that term.[23]

Other literature was more critical of the normative vision of public interest precisely because of the artificiality that underwrites it. At their height, such criticisms held that the term should simply be removed from public discourse given its 'fundamentally undemocratic' assumptions about shared individual interests.[24] However, a more moderate argument noted the flaw in the normative vision while accepting that public interest could retain procedural meaning. The point here was that the virtue of government lay not in its assumed ability to represent shared values but rather in 'the multiplicity of points of access it affords for the manifold conflicting interests which necessarily arise' in society.[25] National government, on this approach, was therefore about reconciling interests through deliberation and debate and about having procedures that could yield agreed—or certainly acceptable—policies and outcomes. Indeed, while an emphasis on procedure raised doubts about majoritarianism[26] and about how to ensure coherent reasoning in respect of substantive choices,[27] the procedural

[18] J-J Rosseau, *The Social Contract* (London, Penguin, 1968; first published 1762).

[19] W Friedmann, 'The Changing Content of Public Interest: Some Comments On Harold D Lasswell' in CJ Friedrich (ed), *Nomos V: The Public Interest* (New York, Atherton Press, 1967) at 84.

[20] CW Cassinelli, 'Reflections on the Concept of the Public Interest' (1958) 69 *Ethics* 48.

[21] V Held, *The Public Interest and Individual Interests* (New York, Basic Books, 1970).

[22] ibid. See too H Campbell and R Marshall, 'Utilitarianism's Bad Breath? A Re-evaluation of the Public Interest Justification for Planning' (2002) 1 *Planning Theory* 163.

[23] For the point that the term can equally be used by totalitarian regimes see WD Zarecor, 'The Public Interest and Political Theory' (1959) 69 *Ethics* 277. And for its worth in a democracy see A Downs, 'The Public Interest: Its meaning in a Democracy' (1962) 29 *Social Research* 1.

[24] The term is HR Smith's: see *Democracy and the Public Interest* (Athens, University of Georgia Press, 1960) at 27. For the abolitionist approach see further CE Cochran, 'Political Science and "The Public Interest"' (1974) 36 *Journal of Politics* 327.

[25] GA Schubert, *The Public Interest: A Critique of the Theory of a Political Concept* (Illinois, Glencoe Free Press, 1960) at 136.

[26] A Lijphart, *Thinking About Democracy: Power Sharing and Majority Rule in Theory and Practice* (Routledge, 2007) esp chs 7 and 8.

[27] See J Bell, 'Public Interest: Policy or Principle' in R Brownsword (ed), n 1 above, at 30.

approach recognised that individuals necessarily interact with one another within the framework of broader society. Bozeman described this as the compromise position of those who could not 'accept a normative view of public interest but (were) not ready to altogether abandon the concept'.[28]

Aspects of the normative and procedural approaches can then be found, at least analogically, in models of national administrative law. The normative vision of 'State', for instance, has a clear parallel in French administrative law where it is used to justify 'the public service [as] a legal structure by which a need of *public interest* is satisfied'.[29] In German administrative law, too, emphasis is placed on the idea of public bodies acting in the 'public interest'[30] and, while UK law historically had no public/private divide,[31] UK courts now frequently refer to the 'public interest' or 'public policy' when resolving administrative law disputes in favour of public bodies.[32] The procedural dimension can in turn be seen in fair hearing and consultation requirements which are familiar throughout administrative law traditions that span Europe, North America, Latin America, and elsewhere.[33] Although fair hearing and consultation guarantees may be subject to limitation for reasons of, most obviously, national security, they speak to ideas of 'input' legitimacy in systems with diverse individual and group interests.[34] And while it is, of course, true that participation in administrative and political processes can be inhibited by economic capacity and by the lobbying of others,[35] liberal standing rules can allow for residual participation through 'public interest litigation'.[36] This has certainly been the (occasionally controversial) experience of

[28] Bozeman, n 16 above, at 93.

[29] Conclusions Corneille in CE 7 April 1916, *Astruc*, RDP 1916.364, quoted in J Bell, S Boyron, and S Whittaker, *Principles of French Law*, 2nd edn (Oxford, Oxford University Press, 2008) at 169. Emphasis added.

[30] M Nierhaus, 'Administrative Law' in J Zekoll and M Reimann (eds), *Introduction to German Law*, 2nd edn (The Hague, Kluwer Law International, 2005) at 87.

[31] JWF Allison, *A Continental Distinction in the Common Law: A Historical and Comparative Perspective on English Public Law* (Oxford, Oxford University Press, 2000).

[32] See, eg, *Tomlinson v Birmingham City Council* [2010] UKSC 8, para 5, Lord Hope ('not in the public interest that an excessive proportion of the funds available for schemes for the regulation of social welfare should be consumed in administration and legal disputes'); and *Hill v Chief Constable of West Yorkshire* [1989] AC 53, as read with *Van Colle v Chief Constable of Hertfordshire; Smith v Chief Constable of Sussex* [2008] UKHL 50; [2009] 1 AC 225 (public policy arguments entail that the courts should be reluctant to impose common law duties of the care on the police when they are investigating and suppressing crime).

[33] See Sérvulo Correia, ch 14 in this volume. See too, e.g., L Ortega Alvarez and Carmen Plaza Martin, 'Administrative Procedure' in L Ortega, L Arroyo and Carmen Plaza (eds), *Spanish Administrative Law Under European Influence* (Groningen, Europa Law Publishing, 2010), ch 2.

[34] On input legitimacy see A Moravcsik and A Sangiovanni, 'On Democracy and "Public Interest" in the European Union' in Wolfgang Streeck and Renate Mainz (eds), *Die Reformierbarkeit der Demokratie. Innovationen und Blockaden* (Frankfurt, Campus Verlag, 2002) at 122.

[35] L Graziano, *Lobbying, Pluralism, and Democracy* (London, Palgrave Macmillan, 2001).

[36] C Harlow and R Rawlings, *Pressure Through Law* (London, Routledge, 1992).

many common law systems that have heard challenges brought by pressure groups, representative organisations, and statutory bodies.[37]

Public interest is also important at the interface between administrative law and human rights law, where it may be used to justify interferences with individual freedoms.[38] To take as an example the European Convention on Human Rights (ECHR) that was moulded with first reference to the experience of national legal orders,[39] some Articles refer expressly to the 'public interest'[40] while others base limitations upon the related language of 'national security' (as above), 'public safety', 'the economic well-being of the country', 'the prevention of disorder or crime', and 'the protection of health or morals'.[41] In each instance, human rights law finds itself drawing upon the abstract notions of 'public' and 'community' that have divided political philosophers, and some commentators have argued that the uncertainty in such notions means that courts have yet to achieve a coherent jurisprudence on individual interests and those of the broader public.[42] On the other hand, it is axiomatic that human rights standards are intended to offset the arbitrary rejection of individual interests and this should lessen concerns about the place that 'preponderance' and other theories may assume in the human rights sphere. Although judicial approaches to the protection of individual rights are often problematised by judicial restraint,[43] European standards (to take that example once more) require that public interest justifications are linked to minimum requirements of transparency, proportionality, and

[37] See B Dickson (eds), *Judicial Activism in Common Law Supreme Courts* (Oxford, Oxford University Press, 2007); M Rao, *Public Interest Litigation in India: A Renaissance in Social Justice*, 2nd edn (Delhi, Eastern Book Co, 2004); C Harlow, 'Public Law and Popular Justice' (2002) 65 *MLR* 1; G Whyte, *Social Inclusion and the Legal System: Public Interest Law in Ireland* (IPA, Dublin, 2002); and D Feldman, 'Public Interest Litigation and Constitutional Theory in Comparative Perspective' (1992) 55 *MLR* 44.

[38] A McHarg, 'Reconciling Human Rights and the Public Interest: Conceptual Problems and Doctrinal Uncertainty in the Jurisprudence of the European Court of Human Rights' (1999) 62 *Modern Law Review* 671.

[39] A Lester, 'Fundamental Rights: The UK Isolated?' (1984) *Public Law* 46.

[40] eg, Art 1, Prot 1: 'Every natural or legal person is entitled to the peaceful enjoyment of his possessions. No one shall be deprived of his possessions except in the public interest and subject to the conditions provided for by law and by the general principles of international law. The preceding provisions shall not, however, in any way impair the right of a State to enforce such laws as it deems necessary to control the use of property in accordance with the general interest or to secure the payment of taxes or other contributions or penalties.'

[41] See, illustratively, Arts 8–11 ECHR.

[42] McHarg, n 38 above.

[43] On the manner in which restraint takes form see, eg, RA Edwards, 'Judicial Deference Under the Human Rights Act' (2002) 65 *MLR* 859 and H Yourrow, *The Margin of Appreciation Doctrine in the Dynamics of European Human Rights Jurisprudence* (The Hague, Kluwer, 1996).

rationality.[44] This is so even where the legal instrument that 'authorises' interference has been adopted by a sovereign, democratic legislature.[45]

Of course, the real story about the ECHR is how it has evolved to occupy its own public—or constitutional—space, and this returns us to the dynamics of Europeanisation and globalisation and, indeed, to the idea of pluralism. In a range of important pronouncements the European Court of Human Rights (ECtHR) has emphasised that the ECHR is, among other things, a 'living instrument' that is unlike other international Treaties,[46] 'autonomous' in terms of its meaning and content,[47] founded upon the principles of democracy and respect for the rule of law,[48] and a 'constitutional instrument of European public order'.[49] Such statements have marked out the ECHR as an essentially self-legitimating public space that draws inspiration from national legal traditions[50] as well as the parallel experiences of the EU[51] and international treaties.[52] While we will query, below, just how far it is feasible to speak of shared public space at the international level, the point to note here is that the 'public' to which the ECtHR lays claim is one that is found at the intersection of legal traditions and norms. By positioning the ECHR in that way, the ECtHR has thus consciously adopted a 'cosmopolitan' jurisprudence that speaks to a plurality of legal systems and norms that are more complementary in nature than conflicting.[53] The out-workings of that jurisprudence are at their most apparent in relation to the 'margin of appreciation' doctrine whereby the ECtHR exercises restraint in the face of 'public interest' choices taken by its contracting parties.[54]

Even more striking has been the construction of ideas of public and constitutional space in the context of the EU.[55] In an historical sense this centred upon the contested supremacy doctrine and the limitation of national economic and social preferences in accordance with the terms of the EU's founding Treaties and

[44] J Jowell and J Cooper (eds), *Understanding Human Rights Principles* (Oxford, Hart Publishing, 2001).

[45] *Gillan & Quniton v UK*, ECtHR judgment, 12 January 2010 (police powers of stop and search under the Terrorism Act 2000, ss 44–47, were too wide, potentially open to abuse, and violated Art 8 ECHR).

[46] *Cossey v UK* (1991) 13 EHRR 622, 639, para 35.

[47] See, eg, *Engel v Netherlands* (1976) 1 EHRR 647.

[48] See, eg, *Refah Partisi (the Welfare Party) v Turkey* (2003) 37 EHRR 1.

[49] *Loizidou v Turkey* (1996) 20 EHRR 99, 134.

[50] DA Leonardi, 'The Strasbourg System of Human Rights Protection: Europeanisation of the Law Through the Confluence of Western Legal Traditions' (1996) 8 *European Review of Public Law* 1139.

[51] See, eg, *Goodwin v UK* (2002) 35 EHRR 447, 480, para 100, referring to Art 9 of the then non-binding Charter of Fundamental Rights of the EU in a dispute about the interpretation of Art 12 ECHR.

[52] See, eg, *A v United Kingdom* (2009) 49 EHRR 29, para 109, considering the notion of a 'public emergency' under Art 4 of the International Covenant on Civil and Political Rights.

[53] HP Glenn, 'Cosmopolitan Legal Orders' in A Halpin and V Roeben (eds), *Theorising the Global Legal Order* (Oxford, Hart Publishing, 2009) at 25.

[54] ibid, at 35; and on the margin of appreciation see Yourrow, n 43 above.

[55] J Weiler, *The Constitution of* Europe (Cambridge, Cambridge University Press, 1999).

general principles of law.[56] However, the European Court of Justice's (ECJ) project in constitution building has since gone far beyond internal matters of the relationship between the EU and its Member States to include questions of the EU's place and space in global law and politics. The leading authority is now the seminal *Kadi*[57] judgment, where the ECJ used EU law's fundamental rights standards to review the legality of EC Regulations that implemented UN Security Council Resolutions in the field of international terrorism.[58] In doing so, the ECJ made clear that EU law now occupies its own sphere of influence at the extra-State level and that public interest/safety arguments formulated by other global actors would not automatically trump procedural and property guarantees recognised by EU law. While this, in effect, challenged the international law 'rule' whereby UN measures enjoy primacy over other treaty obligations,[59] it brought to its fullest stage of maturation the ECJ's belief that the EU supranational order is *sui generis* and that it stands in a relationship of equality with other constitutional orders (whether national or otherwise). *Kadi* was, in that sense, a further manifestation of constitutional pluralism albeit that international law orthodoxy would regard it as an exercise in unilateralism and 'fragmentation'.[60]

One further point that *Kadi* opens up concerns the indirect interaction of norms and what this reveals about inter-order linkages in the global setting. In short, the judgment is widely understood to have influenced decision-making in the UN insofar as the expected outcome in the case led the Security Council to revise aspects of its anti-terrorism procedures.[61] Any influence for EU law in this regard was, in strict legal terms, entirely incidental as the ECJ does not (of course) have any jurisdiction over the legality of UN Resolutions. However, by adopting a robust approach to the legality of EC Regulations the ECJ was more

[56] See M Jarvis, *The Application of EC Law by National Courts: the Free Movement of Goods* (Oxford, Oxford University Press, 1998). On the still contested nature of supremacy, at least in judicial reasoning, see D Doukas, 'The Verdict of the German Federal Constitutional Court on the Lisbon Treaty: Not Guilty but Don't Do it Again!' (2009) 34 *European Law Review* 866.

[57] Joined Cases C 402/05P and C-415/05P, *Kadi & Al Barakaat International Foundation v Council and Commission* [2008] 3 CMLR 41.

[58] Principally Council Regulation (EC) 881/2002, OJ L 139/9. For commentary see G Anthony, 'EU Law's Fundamental Rights Regime and Post-national Constitutionalism: *Kadi's* Global Setting' in P Birkinshaw and M Varney (eds), *The European Union Legal Order After Lisbon* (The Hague, Kluwer, 2010) at 179.

[59] Art 103 of the UN Charter; and compare the approach of the ECtHR in *Behrami v France; and Saramati v France, Germany and Norway* (2007) 45 EHRR 10.

[60] See G de Búrca, 'The EU, the European Court of Justice, and the International Legal Order' (2009) 51 *Harvard International Law Journal* 1; and K Ziegler, 'Strengthening the Rule of Law, but Fragmenting International Law: The *Kadi* Decision of the ECJ from the Perspective of Human Rights' (2009) 2 *Human Rights Law Review* 288.

[61] *Kadi* in this way fed into an ongoing debate about the need for change to procedures. For aspects of that debate see, B Fassbender, *Targeted Sanctions and Due Process: The responsibility of the UN Security Council to ensure that fair and clear procedures are made available to individuals and entities targeted with sanctions under Chapter VII of the UN Charter*, Study Commissioned by the UN Office of Legal Affairs 2006, available at www.un.org/law/counsel/Fassbender_study.pdf.; and UNSC Resolution 1822 (2008)

generally able to limit the reach of the UN norms and the ruling thereby had a wider—and positive—effect simply on account of overlap in a globalising world. That said, the vindication of individual freedoms in *Kadi* is not the inevitable endpoint in all instances of overlap, and other cases have shown how legal and political linkages can undermine important democratic values. A particularly strong example is *R (Corner House Research) v Director of the Serious Fraud Office*,[62] where the claimant challenged the Director's decision to end an investigation into allegations of bribery in the context of arms contracts between British Aerospace and the Kingdom of Saudi Arabia. The decision, which was said to have been taken for reasons of 'public interest', was made against a backdrop of Saudi threats to the effect that close intelligence and diplomatic contacts between Saudi Arabia and the United Kingdom would cease in the event that the Serious Fraud Office's investigation continued. Holding that the Director had acted lawfully, the House of Lords considered that the central question for the Director had been whether the public interest in pursuing an important investigation into alleged bribery was outweighed by the public interest in protecting the lives of British citizens. This clearly pointed to competing public interests within the national system that were generated by external pressures and, while the House of Lords emphasised the importance of upholding the rule of law, it accepted that that imperative could not trump all other considerations.[63] In this latter context, pluralism and overlap thus had less happy connotations.

A GLOBAL PUBLIC SPHERE: DEMOCRACY, PUBLICNESS AND PUBLIC INTEREST WITHOUT CONSTITUTIONAL FOUNDATIONS?

So what then of public interest and more current debates about global administrative law? Certainly, global administrative law may remain a problematic idea in many senses but as the whole project of this volume attests there is now little doubt that there is at least a reasonably well accepted idea of a global legal space. States, international bodies and sub-State organisations have combined and coalesced around various regulatory themes to create what Cassese describes as a 'saprophyte legal order'[64] that opens up national systems and creates a public legal space at a global level. The nature of this public legal space is itself complex, and it is perhaps even more problematic to consider if actions within this public legal space could be said to be for the 'public interest'. As we have shown this concept does have some conceptual grip at the national level, and it appears to have an intuitive resonance for a wider world. But in the absence of the constitutional foundations, and a real connection to mechanisms of democratic decision making, how does this idea of public interest—as mobilised by lawyers,

[62] [2008] UKHL 60; [2009] 1 AC 756.

[63] For criticism see J Jowell, 'Caving in: threats and the rule of law' [2008] 13 *Judicial Review* 273.

[64] S Cassese, 'Administrative law without the State: The Challenge of global Regulations' (2006) 37 *International Law and Politics* 680.

judges and academics—root itself and begin to operate as a normative standard with any real meaning? If we remain committed to at least some version of the traditional democratic understandings that, as we noted earlier, informed ideas of public interest historically in the national context and which depend on understandings of the general interest filtered through fair and inclusive argumentation, open to everyone potentially affected, can we find any foundation for a global public interest?

In this section we explore some of the arguments suggesting that a global public space is capable of yielding up a sensible notion of a global public interest, as well as those that are more hostile to the whole project of extending any offshoot of democracy beyond the context of a constitutional framework and an idea of common citizenship. This is territory explored in a number of ways within various literatures including a wide range of democratic theorists and those interested in developing constitutional foundations for the EU project. Within the burgeoning literature on transnational democracy it is possible to distinguish perhaps four distinctive types of theory.[65] First there is democratic intergovernmentalism which sees the project as one of constructing an international order of cooperation and voluntary pluralism among states within conditions of maximum transparency.[66] Secondly radical republican democracy concentrates on building 'good communities' based upon normative principles of equality and active citizenship within a bottom-up account which can challenge international structures.[67] Next there is cosmopolitan democracy which requires the construction of a new global settlement in which democratic principles are firmly entrenched across all areas within the public realm between and across states.[68] Finally there is deliberative or discursive democracy which seeks to establish deliberative democratic control over the terms of political discourse within the international system as well as elsewhere and so establish a genuine transnational sphere of public deliberation.[69] One of the most interesting recent areas of inquiry approaching this same issue comes from those who are wondering if new advances in information and communication technology which have produced a global communication revolution have resulted in new social

[65] See the useful review provided by T McGrew, 'Transnational Democracy: Theories and Prospects' Center for Globalisation, Europeanisation and Democracy Discussion Paper Series, No 1, (2004) available at www.ihis.aau.dk/ged/Mcgrew.pdf.

[66] See, eg, M Doyle, 'A Liberal View: Preserving and Expanding the liberal Pacific Union', in J Hall and T Paul (eds), *International Order and the Future of World Politics* (Cambridge, Cambridge University Press, 1999); R Faulk, 'Liberalism at the Global Level: The Last of the Independent Commissions?" (1995) 24 *Millenium* 563–78; R Keohane, 'International Institutions: Can Interdependence Work?' (1998) *Foreign Policy* 82–96.

[67] See, eg, J Bernheim, *Is Democracy Possible?* (Cambridge, Cambridge University Press, 1985) and K Hutchings, *International Political Theory* (London, Sage, 1999).

[68] See D Held, *Democracy and Global Order* (Cambridge, Cambridge University Press 1995) or U Beck, *Power in the Global Age* (Cambridge, Polity Press, 2005).

[69] See J Dryzek, *Discursive Democracy* (Cambridge, Cambridge University Press, 1990); *Deliberative Democracy and Beyond* (Oxford, Oxford University Press, 2000); and P Pettit, *Republicanism: A Theory of Freedom and Government* (Oxford, Oxford University Press, 1997).

domains of cultural hybridity and deterritorialised cyberspace where a new demos emerges.[70] In this section we skirt unsystematically through some of these debates in order to consider our more specific inquiry about the fundamental possibility of a global public interest. In particular we will focus on larger questions about how a postnational polity can be constituted in order to form a communicative space supporting democratic deliberation and decision-making.

No demos, no democracy, no public interest?

Although ideas of publicness have not been inevitably coterminous with the nation State since at least enlightenment notions of an international republic of letters, and transnational movements such as abolitionism and socialism, and of course religious and imperial forces have always spilled over national boundaries, there remains a stubborn attachment to State-centred ideas of publicness. Indeed there is an argument, familiar from the EU context and taken up again in the global administrative law world, that without a State there can be no common cause, no democracy, no public interest. For example, Daniel Esty refers to the modern democratic tradition which connects the right to exercise power to the expression of majority will—'making legitimacy a function of electoral success', and argues that to 'the extent that this is true, global governance is doomed to illegitimacy'.[71] This approach suggests that despite the way globalisation binds the fate of communities together the reality is, as Kymlicka puts it, 'the only forum within which genuine democracy occurs is within national boundaries'.[72] This emphatic conclusion seems to indicate that although public opinion is undoubtedly circulating across wider global forums and involving more people, this does not mean that there is really a global public interest, or at least one that can be connected to democratic understandings. While we may have a global public sphere it has been created by the operation of global institutions which may purport to operate in the public interest but cannot in fact be doing so insofar as they are unanchored from the State and the legitimacy that this brings.

This apparently simple insistence on a State is in fact more complex than it first appears and covers a variety of perspectives. There is the view that democracy, at least in its representative form where it is capable of yielding up a coherent public interest, cannot work properly beyond a certain size and scale, and that the global sphere is simply too large to have the necessary democratic machinery.[73] This argument of scale is separate from, yet connected to, the idea

[70] See M Castells, *The Rise of the Network Society* (Malden, MA, Blackwell, 1996); *The Power of Identity* (Malden, MA, Blackwell, 1997) and *End of Millennium* (Malden, MA, Blackwell, 1998).

[71] 'Good Governance at the Supranational Scale: Globalising Administrative Justice' (2006) 115 *Yale Law Journal* 1490.

[72] W Kymlicka, 'Citizenship in an era of globalisation' in I Shapiro and C Hacker-Gordon (eds), *Democracy's Edges* (Cambridge, Cambridge University Press, 1999).

[73] R Dahl, 'Can international organizations be democratic?' in I Shapiro and C Hacker-Gordon (eds), n 72 above, at 19–36.

that a common or truly public interest cannot reside or flourish outside a sufficiently defined political community or demos where there can be said to be a collective interest in, and shared responsibility for, the decisions and norms enacted by that community.[74] In other words, if there is no community there can be no public interest. Ideas of public interest are connected to ideas of democracy and they, indeed like all the various goods of liberalism such as justice, rights and perhaps accountability, require a State, and all elements of commonality that this brings, as a necessary pre-condition. As Thomas Nagel puts it simply, there is 'no justice outside the state'.[75]

We need to look a bit more closely at why and how exactly the absence of State removes the possibility of discerning or developing a collective public interest. Issues of scale and diversity are no doubt daunting, but is there something about the absence of a common constitutional framework and a shared collective purpose that means there can be no global public interest beyond the individual national interests (as coloured by their international context)?

Clearly it is possible to develop ideas of constitutionalism for changing circumstances at many levels: for example we can see attempts to infer new understandings of constitutionalism at the national level,[76] in international law,[77] in Europe[78] and even in a world context.[79] However there is perhaps a more serious objection to the idea of a global public interest and it comes from a fuller parsing out of the requirements of democracy. This involves asking the question if a globalised public sphere could ever conceivably provide the basic minimum

[74] This sort of argument takes us perilously close to the idea that, as Carl Schmitt famously said, 'democracy requires . . . homogeneity" (*The Crisis of Parliamentary Democracy* ((trans E Kennedy) Cambridge, MA, MIT Press, 1926) at 185). See also JHH Weiler, 'Does Europe need a Constitution? Demos, Telos and the German Maastricht Decision' (1995) 1 *European Law Journal* 219.

[75] T Nagel, 'The Problem of Global Justice' (2005) 33 *Philosophy and Public Affairs* 113. Nagel indeed maintains that the only situation that actually triggers supra-humanitarian norms of justice (beyond the very basic level that operates in any combination of people) is one in which a group of people are all subject to a common sovereign, who imposes coercive rule on the member of the group—ie only a group of people who live together as both subjects in law's empire and citizens in law's republic. In the evident absence of a Hobbesian sovereignty on a world scale, neither the increase in global interdependence nor global administrative effort to coordinate responses to the effects of this globalisation are justice-generative.

[76] See, eg, J Murkens, 'The Quest for Constitutionalism in UK Public Law Discourse' (2009) 29 *Oxford Journal of Legal Studies* 427–55.

[77] eg, B Fassender, 'Sovereignty and Constitutionalism in International Law' in N Walker (ed), *Sovereignty in Transition* (Oxford, Hart Publishing, 2003).

[78] See, eg, P Eleftheriadis, 'The Idea of a European Constitution' (2007) 27 *Oxford Journal of Legal* Studies 1; J Weiler, n 55 above; P Craig, 'Constitutions, Constitutionalism and the European Union' (2001) 7 *European Law Journal* 125; J Weiler and M Wind (eds), *European Constitutionalism beyond the state* (Cambridge, Cambridge University Press, 2003).

[79] See, eg, B Akerman, 'The Rise of World Constitutionalism' (1997) 83 *Virginia Law Review* 771; A Peters, 'Global Constitutionalism Revisited' (2005) 11 *International Legal Theory*, 40; R Macdonald and DM Johstone (eds), *Towards World Constitutionalism: Issues in the Legal Ordering of the World Community* (Leiden, Martinus Nijhoff 2005); N Walker, 'Taking Constitutionalism beyond the State' (2008) 56 *Political Studies* 519; D Held, *Global Covenant* (Cambridge, Polity 2004); and A Kuper, *Democracy Beyond Borders: Justice and Representation in Global Institutions* (Oxford, Oxford University Press, 2004).

framework for the operation of a plausible form of democracy, and so the foundation for developing a tenable notion of public interest. If we turn to Habermas and his classic analysis of the public sphere, *Structural transformation of the Public Sphere*[80] we can see a deliberative model where the public sphere is concerned with generating legitimate public opinion in the sense of considered understandings of the general interest filtered through fair and inclusive argumentation, open to everyone potentially affected. Public opinion is legitimate only if all who are potentially affected are able to participate as peers in deliberations concerning the organisation of their common affairs. *Inclusiveness* and *participatory parity* are thus central. For some critics this would seem to tie the Habermasian account to a State-centric view.[81] In the latest stage of her ongoing critique of Habermas, Nancy Fraser directly takes issue with the implicit Westphalian presuppositions of Habermas's public sphere theory (as well as the Westphalian assumptions in her own critique of the masculinist, bourgeois nature of the standard liberal view of what counts as a significant in the public sphere).[82] In considering whether a genuinely critical and democratising role for a transnational public sphere could ever come about, Fraser (helpfully for our purposes here) unpacks the two features that are important to see if public opinion has any value in the process whereby communicative power generated in civil society is effectively translated into a legislative and administrative power in government. These relate to the *normative legitimacy* and the *political efficacy* of public opinion. In order for communicative action to be viable in any constellation of power it must pass tests of legitimacy as to what passes for public opinion (so that the excluded and marginalised are not left out as not truly full members of the national political public), and it must pass tests as to the efficacy of public opinion (so that there are not obstacles of political muscle, private economic influence and entrenched bureaucratic interest that deprive discursively generated public opinion of its power).

Developing each of these in turn we can see first that in any public sphere public opinion is legitimate only if it is inclusive and passes the test whereby all potentially affected are able to participate. Within the context of a State centred

[80] Trans T Burger (Cambridge, MA, MIT Press, 1989).

[81] Of course Habermas and others have been anxious to extend the idea of a public sphere into (at least) a European public space where communication can take place among all those who are politically affected. See J Habermas, *Between Facts and Norms: Contributions to a Discourse Theory of Law and Democracy* (Cambridge MA, MIT 1996) where he argues that 'the pan-European political public sphere is the solution to the problem of insufficient social integration in the processes of Europeanization' (at 65). See also J Habermas and J Derrida, 'February 15, or What Binds Europeans Together: A Plea for a Common Foreign Policy, Beginning in the Heart of Europe' (2003) 10 *Constellations* 291 and J Habermas, 'The Kantian Project of the Constitutionalization of International Law: Does it still have a Chance?' in O Shabani (ed), *Multiculturalism and Law: A Critical Debate* (Cardiff, University of Wales Press, 2007). See also the useful, if ultimately sceptical, review of research in C de Vreese, 'The EU as a public sphere' 2 *Living Reviews in European Governance* (2007) at www.livingreviews.org/Ireg2007–3.

[82] N Fraser, 'Transnationalising the Global Sphere: On the legitimacy and efficacy of the public opinion in a post-Westphalian world' (2007) 24 *Theory, Culture and Society* 7.

view, this requirement of inclusive participation can be passed over (albeit inadequately according to the critique) by reference to ideas of common citizenship within a bounded community. However this is even less plausible in a globalised post-Westphalian space where increasingly it appears that it is only transnational elites who possess the material and symbolic prerequisites for global networking and thus are equipped to participate fully. In a globalised world where political membership and even language is not coextensive with the putative public sphere, this idea that shared citizenship as a proxy for inclusive participation is no longer sustainable. Of course even if we cannot have a citizenship argument to cover the requirement of inclusiveness needed to bring normative legitimacy this still leaves the 'all-affected' principle—all those affected by political decisions should be able to participate on a basis of equality in the informal processes of opinion formation to which decision takers should be held accountable—and this may be achieved in different ways. It may be possible to find other means whereby all potentially affected can participate as peers regardless of political citizenship. Indeed, while Fraser remains sceptical, she does suggest that the most promising way of reconstructing a valid and critical conception of inclusive public opinion in a globalised context is to abandon attempts to create a shared citizenship among diverse peoples and concentrate instead on 'their co-imbrication in a common set of structures and/or institutions that affect their lives'.[83] This is a large project which as we shall see later remains largely unfulfilled.

Turning next to the *efficacy* feature of public opinion as an essential element of a successful notion of any claim of publicness in this context, there are again problems as we move from the national context to a global one. The issue here is how any democratically generated political will can be mobilised into action in a way that is in line with and remains accountable to the considered will of civil society. This has two distinct aspects. First there is the *translation* condition requiring that communicative power generated in civil society can be translated first into binding laws and then into administrative power. Then there is the *capacity* condition which concerns the ability of the administrative power to realise the designs of public opinion and at the same time rein in private powers and ensure effective implementation of the democratic consensus. As Fraser argues, in the past this was understood within the Westphalian frame of the sovereign territorial State where the State was seen as the appropriate vehicle for fulfilling both the translation and the capacity conditions of public sphere efficacy. The State had control of its own destiny and the main focus within this sovereign, territorial perspective was how well does it manage the translation of power between civil society and the State. Now, however, when global institutions have overtaken territorially based national bodies, and when the turn towards

[83] ibid, at 22. This of course is a 'those affected' approach that resonates strongly with cosmopolitian approaches. See further, eg, D Held, 'Restructuring Global Governance: Cosmopolitanism, Democracy and the Global Order' (2009) 37 *Millennium* 533.

transnational politics overwhelms much of domestic administrative capacity, we need to ask the more basic question as to how well the capacity condition is addressed. There is reduced efficacy in depending on the national State to deliver any democratically determined will. To whom then should public opinion be addressed as it pertains to transnational issues? And also, no less importantly, in order to complete the circuit of flow in communicative power, to whom is any new administrative power accountable? As Fraser puts it, the challenge now is 'twofold: on the one hand, to create new, transnational public powers; on the other, to make them accountable to new, transnational public spheres'.[84] Again this is a huge challenge and one that we are far from responding to effectively as yet.

Politics and Publicness

This excursion into the some of the problems of public sphere theory in the transnational context has indicated some of the serious difficulties in developing an idea of publicness in a global context in any way that connects meaningfully with ideas of democracy as understood from a Habermasean perspective. As we search for a foundation for public interest in a global context it appears increasingly difficult to maintain a link with what are essentially political ideas about agency coming from the public opinion of civil society. This is not simply a problem about fitting older ideas about the State as the proper forum for democracy into a new global context. It is rather about finding a way in which the politics that comes from people actively and equally deciding things can maintain a leading role. Indeed, instead of some sort of more or less imperfect means whereby an idea of a public interest can be generated within the political institutions of a nation State, the impact of globalisation leaves us with a wider sphere of public action where it is more likely to be international capital markets, multinational business networks or their transnational regulatory bodies that determine essentially political issues. Teubner complains that the legal order that emerges from such a fragmented process where private actors negotiate their own interests, and '"invisible colleges", "invisible markets and branches", "invisible professional communities" [and] "invisible social networks"' set the boundaries of global law, is one where politics is no longer central.[85]

Indeed we may go even further and suggest that the replacement of the public in some (albeit imperfect) format of the State and its political institutions by transnational agencies of control has more to do with reversing the democratic project of politics. Instead of using politics to tame markets it is more likely that markets will be seen as the overwhelming determinants of social and political life. The whole idea of a global public order (and any associated notion of a global

[84] N 82 above, at 23.

[85] G Teubner, '"Global Bukowina": Legal Pluralism in the World Society' in G Teubner (ed), *Global Law without a State* (Sudbury MA, Dartmouth, 1996) at 8.

public interest) may even be seen as a construction that could operate as a disciplinary tool, or at least an instrument of governance, by causing us to 're-imagine' politics and the public, and re-assemble the nation State and the limits of political action in line with ideas and concepts that have all the eloquence that comes from being bigger than national interests, and newer and seemingly more sophisticated than simple domestic understandings. In contrast to the nineteenth century world, where economies were organised largely within borders and the social was located within the nation, the influence of globalisation seems to be requiring us to think differently about some of the fundamental building blocks. The essential elements of this are well known. There is the dispersal of economic power to a global field where even elementary aspects of the national economy are seen as conditioned by wider international and supranational networks of finance, insurance, trade and investment. There is the growth of global institutions such as the World Bank, the World Trade Organzation (WTO), and the International Monetary Fund (IMF) as well the global reach of the banking crisis which revealed the interdependent nature of the securitised global economy.[86] Even in relation to law itself, once regarded as the very expression of sovereignty and nationhood, there is the huge growth in numbers of international regulating bodies and regimes as well as the increased reach of such bodies so that it now seems to appear that, as Cassese puts it, 'the centrality of the state to the notion of public powers has become an optical illusion'.[87] At the same time the social realm too is seen to have moved beyond the State and ideas of community have become de-coupled from territory.[88] All of these factors bear down on the perceived capacity of nations to act politically in shaping the effects of a world market. It seems to require a re-thinking of the way in which government operates; how its role and resources are conceptualised and its consequences calculated.[89] Such an understanding of the new space of government, and the apparently limited resources of the State to deliver effectively upon a common political agenda, are taken up in various new forms of politics. These are now focused on facilitating what is seen as a new global reality. Within this revised image of the governable space, and its relation to the global economic

[86] There is a growing literature trying to expose and explain how the economies of the developed world failed both separately and together. See, eg, L Elliot and D Atkinson, *The Gods that Failed* (London, Bodley Head, 2008); V Cable, *The Storm: The World Economic Crisis and What it Means* (London, Atlantic, 2010).

[87] See S Cassese, n 64 above, at 673. It is here also that Cassese notes the growth in international regulatory bodies from 245 organisations in 1988 to 7,306 in less than 10 years (while pointing out that there are only 191 States in the UN).

[88] See, eg, ideas of the 'Muslim community' or the 'Asian community' in Britain which encompass not only British nationals but also a range of people who are from Pakistan, India, Yemen or Turkey.

[89] This even goes to the spatialising gaze of government, or how it models its space and role. As Rose explains, 'governmental thought territorializes itself in different ways ... central to modern governmental thought has been a territorializaton of national spaces: states, countries, populations, societies'. Now the project of government has changed both its object and its scope. See N Rose, *Powers of Freedom: Reframing Political Thought* (Cambridge, Cambridge University Press, 1999) at 34.

context, the whole project of government is seen differently. As Rose points out, it is not so much a politics of economic abstentionism in the face of apparently unmanageable global currents but rather a politics which seeks to intervene actively to create the conditions—an open economy, a flexible regulatory regime, a skilled but de-regulated labour market etc—to support this view of the globalised economy. Both neo-liberal and neo-social politics are re-calibrated within this more limited view of the national political project.[90]

Meanwhile, as ideas of the public become unrooted from the State, the idea of public interest becomes more ambivalent. As with an idea such as multiculturalism, which is promoted as a way of accommodating difference and producing new ways of thinking about the nation in the context of changing demographics, so the creation of a global public interest is attractive, especially if linked to a recognition of a range of stakeholders beyond the major nations and most powerful interest groups. It seems to acknowledge the complexity of (particularly) economic and financial relations, and the interconnectedness of markets, economies and peoples. Also it seems to offer the possibility that it might provide a way of simultaneously framing and serving all those whose needs must be recognised. However, as with multiculturalism, it is subject to critiques (from the left and feminism in particular) about how it both acknowledges and flattens difference.[91] As we have noted already, a notion of a global public interest may easily come to be seen simply in terms of bolstering up one particular view of what this should be, and so require the integration of wider subaltern interests within a newly defined greater interest that silences more diversely democratic interests.

But is this thinning of publicness within the global constellation an inevitable result of losing the connection to Stateness? (Or perhaps more accurately we should ask if the changed nature of state within the dynamic of globalisation—whereby States stand to lose their role within a democratic, public culture and risk becoming merely agents in a wider process[92]—inevitably results in the displacement of a democratic publicness?)

Democracy through process?

There is of course a series of approaches that seek to move beyond the simple no demos, no democracy, no global public interest argument to find a way in which internal procedures of decision-making can provide the basis for a legitimate

[90] See Rose, n 89 above, at 144 ff.

[91] See, eg, W Brown, *Regulating Aversion: Tolerance in the Age of Identity* (Princeton, Princeton University Press, 2006).

[92] See, eg, the discussion of the 'market state' as the successor to the post-war nation State in P Bobbitt, *The Shield of Achilles: War and Peace and the Course of History* (London, Penguin, 2003) or B Jessop's account of the 'Schumpererian workfare post-nationalist regime' in *The Future of the Capitalist State* (Cambridge, Polity, 2002).

form of global governance without recourse to any idea of publicness as found in the State or uncovered in any global polity. This reproduces many of the issues that we saw in the context of procedural approaches in national administrative law and, for us, suffers many similar failings in addition to a few extra ones.

In a useful review De Búrca collects together some of these attempts to move understandings of democracy beyond the State context.[93] These approaches vary in how exactly they claim to overcome the absence of State but all maintain, more or less, that the way in which a decision is taken, its internal procedural integrity, can prevail over the absence of direct connection to the more traditional democratic environment associated with a State. Thus for some, the independence, expertise and authority of the decision-maker can compensate for absence of democratic participation.[94] It may seem extraordinary, particularly in wake of the international financial crisis, to argue that "experts" such as financiers and bankers have particular legitimacy as a result of their skills. However, the argument does extend to a more functional claim that while this may not amount to an idea of public interest as such, it is a reflection of a particular policy community or network who are most directly affected and so are best placed to take the decision. In this way such an account seeks to make a connection to ideas of corporatism or at least governance by networks in its search for legitimacy.[95] At another level there are approaches that suggest that the quality of the outputs of decisions taken—in terms of quality, efficiency or acceptability—might itself be sufficient justification to overcome any democratic insufficiency.[96]

Of course such an argument about outputs only is not one about democracy at all. It is simply a claim that good ends are more important than valid democratic means. A more interesting variation on this involves the claim, familiar from the EU context, that the nature and character of the decision-making process may be such that it somehow delivers democracy as a side-project. If there is transparency and, more ambitiously accountability,[97] in the governance process, and it is

[93] See G De Búrca, 'Developing Democracy beyond the State' (2008) 46 *Columbia Journal of Transnational Law* 101.

[94] See S Smismans, *Law, Legitimacy and European Governance: Functional Participation in Social Regulation* (New York, Oxford University Press, 2004).

[95] See the overview provided by AM Slaughter and D Zaring, 'Networking goes international: An update' (2006) 22 *Annual Review of Law and Social* Science 211; and P Craig, ch 4 in this volume.

[96] See, eg, F Scharpf, *Governing in Europe: Effective and Democratic?* (Oxford, Oxford University Press, 1999).

[97] Perhaps this argument has some attraction because the idea of accountability is being used in a slightly different way in this context. Unlike in traditional democracy, it is not political accountability to the public that is involved but accountability to a selected group of actors. This introduces an interesting dimension. Kirsch maintains that many global regulatory institutions are highly accountable up to the point where they enjoy little freedom of independent action and are tied to their constituents. The problem is that they are accountable in the wrong way or to the wrong constituencies. Thus, eg, the World Bank is accountable to the developed countries that fund it and not to the people who are affected by its decisions; and the UN Security Council should be accountable to those who are the subject of sanctions not just member governments. See N Kirsch, 'The Pluralism of Global Administrative Law' (2006) 17 *European Journal of International Law* 247.

genuinely open and fully scrutinised with reasons for decisions given to peers, states, markets or individuals, then its acceptability is considerable enhanced.[98] Of course unlike in traditional democracy, it is not political accountability to the public but to a selected group of actors. This is not yet the same as being democratic, but, its adherents point out, if we add regard for human rights standards and emphasise protection of minority rights, then this can (in some rather unspecific way), overcome the missing participatory-representative dimension of democracy and public-oriented character of such governance. Also, it is argued, if the quality of deliberation at global level is such that it is, if not inclusive, then at least on the basis of well-informed debate and with an openness to change, it may be said to provide some guarantee as to the substantive merit and quality of the decision-making which could compensate for its non-democratic nature.

De Búrca distances herself from these approaches involving various sources of compensatory legitimacy but remains optimistic that what she terms 'a democratic striving approach' can be developed to translate the principle of political equality into a requirement of the fullest possible participation in effective processes of decision-making by those concerned.[99] In doing this De Búrca refers to ideas of 'democratic experimentalism' as developed by Cohen and Sabel who ask could it not be that interdependence and organised cooperation in the absence of a State might in fact trigger normative demands that although short of a full idea of domestic distributive justice, might be regarded nevertheless as greater than a base level, simple humanitarianism?[100] Elaborating the sort of argument about the expertise of the decision-maker mentioned above, Cohen and Sabel develop an idea of deliberative polyarchy whereby decision-making works through mutual reason-giving, and is deliberative in the sense that the stronger argument will prevail in a context of mutual reason-giving when making decisions.[101] Accountability, it is argued, is not always about constraining the actions of a decision-maker but rather can be brought about when agents are required to explain and justify their actions to those who have the necessary knowledge to understand and evaluate those actions. This is supposedly more than a technocratic argument about who is best placed to make a decision. It is claimed that it is instead about the procedural quality of the process where a decision-maker has to show how his or her decision has taken into account the impact on others, and be able to explain the decision perhaps even where it may be liable to peer review or judicial challenge. The argument is that this brings a

[98] See also P Nicolaides et al, *Improving Policy Implementation in an Enlarged European Union: The Case of National Regulatory Authorities* (Maastricht, EIPA, 2003) who argue that accountability is strengthened when 'the agent is required to explain and justify his actions to those who have the necessary knowledge to understand and evaluate those actions' (at 46).

[99] N 93 above, at 133.

[100] J Cohen and C Sabel, 'Global Democracy?' (2005) 37 *International Law and Politics* 763.

[101] See further J Cohen and C Sabel, 'Directly-Deliberative Polyarchy' (1997) 3 *European Law Journal* 313.

form of accountability that does not require a central, delegating authority or State. Neither does it necessarily require even a global civil society to act as a counterweight or control.[102]

This idea of deliberative polyarchy is so termed because it is deliberative (with its commitment to mutual reason-giving) and polyarchic (because of the use of situated deliberation within decision-making units and deliberative comparisons across those units). In the global administrative space, Cohen and Sabel argue, interactions of a deliberatively polyarchic nature, developing rules and vindicating rights, may in time produce a form of global governance without recourse to the classic nation State. The process of decision-making may add further to the already existing standards, goals, metrics and mores of all the various actors who together are developing and refining new versions of global democracy beyond States.[103] The very action of decision-making in the correct manner in a whole range of supranational institutions is, they seem to argue, endogenously producing standards that not only now pertain globally but bind in the subaltern national units too.[104] As Cohen and Sabel express it, 'in joining these regimes [EU and WTO], member states are agreeing to remake their rules, in domain after domain, in light of the efforts of all the others to reconcile their distinctive regulations with general standards in whose determination they participate and that are assumed to be attentive to the interests of others elsewhere.'[105] Indeed, they claim people more generally might in this way come to share a new identity as common members of an organised global populace. They believe that this would be so especially if 'such rule making is increasingly accountable, preceded by hearings, shaped by participation of affected parties, subject to review, and defended by reference to what are commonly cognised as reasons in an emerging public reason of global political society'.[106]

This attempt to produce global democracy without a global State or nation but through process alone may seem extraordinarily naive. A single group of actors

[102] On this idea see, eg, J Keane, *Global Civil Society?* (Cambridge, Cambridge University Press, 2003) or M Kaldor, *Global Civil Society: An Answer to War* (Cambridge, Polity Press, 2003).

[103] In the EU context, eg, Cohen and Sabel argue that there are broadly defined goals—full employment, social inclusion, unified energy grid—and measures for gauging their achievement are established by joint action of the Member States and EU institutions. Goals, metrics and procedures are periodically revised by the same actors, fora, networked agencies, councils of regulators and through open methods of coordination and other processes. As this works across a number of EU areas such as health care, anti-discrimination and pension reform, EU administrative law requires decision-making at key points to be transparent, accessible to relevant parties and deliberative in the sense of providing reasons for decisions. See n 100 above, at 763 ff.

[104] Kingsbury, Krisch and Stewart endorse this idea of a relatively autonomous space of global administration operating beyond the State and acknowledge indeed that domestic administrations are increasingly constrained by substantive and procedural norms developed at global level. As they see it, global rule-making is not simply the product of State power, and domestic rule-makers are constrained in their procedures, policy deliberations and decisions by that global rule-making. See 'The Emergence of Global Administrative Law' (2005) 68 *Law and Contemporary Problems* 26.

[105] Cohen and Sabel, n 100 above, at 786.

[106] N 100 above, at 795.

who are themselves involved in the decision are supposed to produce, if not a democratic legitimacy per se, then a legitimacy that can equal it or substitute for it.[107] This is to be achieved simply by making the decisions with the correct procedure and with a good heart. The whole history of the exercise of power seems to scream at the unlikeliness of such an idea. How can the practices of decision-makers generate their own legitimacy simply through the way in which such decisions are taken and how can this compensate for an absence of democratic nexus? While we may well be in favour of deliberation, and even believe in a sort of enlarged mentality',[108] or transformative personal experience,[109] that this is supposed to bring, we are all too aware of the problems of this even in the context of the nation State. Their calls for a genuinely participatory democratic approach challenge the conflation of the State apparatus with the public sphere of discourse and association. There is a considerable body of critique arguing for the inadequacy of ideas that State arenas, as provided by representative democracy, parliament, legally guaranteed free speech and the rest, could ever be the sole, exclusive or adequate spheres of public, civic interaction. This is in addition to the range of feminist critiques arguing that existing State institutions are inherently exclusionary because of their masculinised nature.[110] All of these problems are of course written even larger in the global context and there are additional ones besides.

After challenging what he describes as the inherent difficulties of the deliberative vision, Shapiro picks up on the theme that we have urged relating to the de-politicising character of global structures. Shapiro suggests that the record of EU policy-making history, where supposedly the Council engages in national interest aggregation while the committees of experts are deliberative in seeking the best economic and technical outcomes, amply illustrates how 'the whole paraphernalia of deliberation is employed as a cover for technocratic

[107] Extraordinarily Cohen and Sabel even go as far as to assert that establishing new forms of accountability at the global level will, because of the way that global administration connects with national rule-making, help reshape national politics and reinvigorate democracy there. They describe this as 'the democracy destabilizing hunch': n 100 above, at 766 ff.

[108] See H Arendt, *Between Past and Future* (London, Penguin Books, 1977) at 220 and 241. See also M Canovan, *Hannah Arendt: A Reinterpretation of her Political Thought* (Cambridge, Cambridge University Press, 1992)at 229 ff.

[109] For S Wolin 'democracy is not about where the political is located but how it is experienced' with the constitutional arrangements of liberal democratic States being the ultimate 'domestication' of a more real and personally transformative politics: see 'Fugitive Democracy' (1994) 1 *Constellations* 11.

[110] See, eg, IM Young, *Inclusion and Democracy* (Oxford, Oxford University Press 2000); K Ferguson, *The Feminist Case Against Bureaucracy* (Philadelphia, Temple University Press, 1984); K McKinnon, *Towards a Feminist Theory of the State* (Cambridge, MA, Harvard University Press, 1989) and W Brown, *States of Injury: Power and Freedom in Late Modernity* (Princeton, Princeton University Press, 1995).

government'.[111] Similarly, Shapiro argues, the experience of supposedly independent agencies in the United States such as the Environmental Protection Agency (or indeed the Federal Reserve in the context of the credit crisis) illustrates 'the substitution of technocratic legitimacy for a supposedly deficient democratic legitimacy'.[112]

If we return to Teubner's critique mentioned earlier[113] we can see clearly some of the inadequacies in the idea of global decision-making that is supposedly democratic as a result of its procedures. The participants are members of a club generally unknown to those affected: the 'invisible colleges', 'invisible professional communities' and 'invisible social networks'. (Even the most ambitious advocate of virtual networks and cyber worlds could not say that the global communication revolution has yet overcome issues of language and access to power.)[114] The soft law that these invisible groups generate is without the characteristics of transparency, predictability and uniformity of application traditionally associated with the rule of law. Instead it is a law that grows and changes according to the exigencies of global economic transactions and organisations. As Teubner points out, it is thus 'extremely vulnerable to interest and power pressures from economic processes, because it is "indeterminate" and can change in its application from case to case'.[115]

Even an enthusiast for the general idea of a public legal space at a general level such as Cassese, who accepts that pressures towards greater openness, participation and transparency in processes can go some way to make up for the democratic deficit caused by the absence of a constitutional foundation, and more generally seems to believe that the absence of top-down legitimacy in the global legal order could be, at least partially, compensated by means of reinforced guarantees for civil society, remains sceptical.[116] He acknowledges the very spread of principles of these nascent general principles as they are being consolidated in global arena actually 'highlights their meagreness compared to the richer panoply of rights recognised by national legal systems'.[117] We would see ourselves siding with those who are perhaps even more sceptical. Harlow points out how 'sceptics of legal globalisation are in the main more concerned with structures than with principles. In the modern nation-state, power is "billeted" and powers are "bounded"; in global space, power is diffused to networks of private and public actors, escaping the painfully established controls of democratic government and

[111] M Shapiro, '"Deliberative", "Independent" Techocracy v Democratic Politics: Will the Globe Echo the EU' (2005) 68 *Law and Contemporary Problems* 341 at 351.

[112] ibid, at 353.

[113] N 85 above.

[114] L Cederman and P Kraus, 'Transnational Communication and the European Demos' in R Lathan and S Sassen (eds), *Digital Formations: IT and New Architectures in the Global Realm* (Princeton, Princeton University Press, 2005).

[115] Teubner n 85, above at 21.

[116] N 64 above, at 688.

[117] ibid, at 692.

public law.'[118] These structures, like the very idea of a demos that they are intended to reflect however imperfectly, along with the controls that have been established, seem an irreducible element.

CONCLUSION: PUBLIC INTEREST AS PLURALISM

The argument of this chapter is one that is essentially sceptical of the project of finding or creating a workable notion of public interest within the emerging global administrative space. It is accepted that conceptions of public interest have moved on from more wholly State-centric understandings. As the *Corner House* and *Kadi* cases illustrate so well, public interest in a national or even European context is increasingly conditioned by wider forces beyond the individual State and there is a complex pattern of linkages between overlapping and often interdependent national, regional and supranational bodies and systems. As we look for workable notions of publicness and public interest within this new constellation of power existing in the emerging global administrative sphere it is apparent that ideas from an earlier, Westphalian world, where concepts of the State, citizenship and democracy can be deployed, have limited conceptual grip. The no demos, no democracy argument that is familiar from a European context is difficult to get around in this context too. Process arguments seeking to find a way in which internal procedures of decision-making can somehow provide a democratic basis without recourse to any idea of publicness found in the State or in a global polity remain unsatisfactory. Indeed, as this element of democratic publicness is downplayed it looks increasingly as if it is a thinner, more elitist version of politics that has come to dominate. Despite being significantly larger in scope this new global sphere is more contracted in terms of how it is ordered. In place of an admittedly imperfect democratic model based on the State there is a larger but narrower, mostly invisible network which sets the boundaries of global law without the same input from ordinary politics.

Of course one way around this problem is simply to accept it. We may say that the classical methods of legitimating rules have little application in this context: we cannot reproduce domestic, State level mechanisms here and efforts to find procedural techniques to compensate will remain incomplete at best. But this does not mean we should accept some sort of free for all. Rather (as we have argued in the introductory chapter) we must settle for the sort of pluralist approach advocated by Krisch where he talks in terms of 'mutual challenges between different regimes and different levels in global regulatory governance' within an overall order which is 'heterarchical, not hierarchical', and where stability comes not from final decisions based on authority but on 'processes of negotiation and compromise as well as challenge and concession between the

[118] See C Harlow, 'Global Administrative law: The Quest for Principles and Values' (2006) 17 *European Journal of International Law* 187, 212.

different constituencies involved'.[119] This sort of model will not be ideal in terms of democracy. It will challenge civil society to ensure that it is involved and it will require authority to be open to such involvement. It will be messy and incomplete and the political struggle that will be possible there will be unequal and unfair. However it does acknowledge both the reality of the new global order and that within some form of political contestation is the appropriate place of public interest.

[119] N 97 above, at 278.

10

Public Goods and Global Administrative Law

JEAN-BERNARD AUBY

INTRODUCTION

THE QUESTION ADDRESSED by this chapter is at the crossroads of three contemporary sources of thought about public action, public affairs, and relevant legal mechanisms in post-modernity: economic analysis of law, the globalisation theory, and one of its particular branches, which is global administrative law.

The first one gave birth to the concept of public goods, which is a way of approaching some of the duties with which States and other public entities are charged. The second one elevated the concept of public goods up to the international level in order to circumscribe the common tasks which international institutions must accomplish because they are common concerns of the global community. The third one is a recent development in the globalisation theory, which aims at improving the way the numerous international bodies which are of an administrative nature conduct public affairs, and deliver the tasks with which they are entrusted.

The overall purpose of this book is, in tribute to two scholars who have shown their constant dedication to administrative law, internationalisation of the law and the protection of public values, to reflect on the 'values' dimension in the global administrative law theory. This chapter would like to contribute by putting together some reflections on how the consideration of serving general interest purposes is and could be better taken into account in the global administrative law theory.

Three questions will be considered in turn: public goods and law (section 2), public goods and legal globalisation (section 3), public goods and global administrative law (section 4).

Jean-Bernard Auby

PUBLIC GOODS AND LAW

It is not within the scope of this chapter to provide a long discussion about the concept of public goods and its use in economic analysis of law, but some basics elements must be recalled before we consider its application in the ambit of legal globalisation.

The concept of public goods[1] derives from the economic theory of welfare. It designates various types of economic goods whose common characteristic is that they are non-excludable—it is impossible to deprive somebody from benefiting from them, and/or non-rival—when somebody is using them, it does not lower the quantity which is available for other possible consumers. Goods which are both non-excludable and non-rival are called pure collective goods: such as national security, or a national health care system. Those which are non-excludable but rival are called common goods: a school of fish, for example—everyone can go fishing in it, but what is caught by one person is no longer available for others. Those which are excludable but non-rival are club goods: this is the case of a TV programme, for example—the access can be limited by a code or the like, but what a particular consumer watches does not reduce what is available for other consumers.

Public goods are an archetypal case of market failure. Because of their particular characteristics, their provision and their consumption tends to be different from what would be the economic optimum.[2] That is true in particular for pure collective goods: because it is difficult to make people pay for them—it is easy to use them freely—their provision, if it is purely left to the market, will automatically be under-optimal.

For that reason, it will generally be desirable that the State intervenes in order to make sure that they are produced in sufficient quantity. This does not mean necessarily that the State will directly take charge of their production, but that it will see to it that they are sufficiently produced.

The transposition of this economic concept into legal concepts is not quite straightforward, but it can be approximately operated through the following considerations.

Public goods are not necessarily goods in the ordinary legal sense of physical assets: sometimes they are services. At least when it comes to pure collective goods, they correspond well enough to the idea of general interest services, including the fact that they can be provided either by public entities, or by private ones, but within a framework of public supervision and incentives, possibly under contracting out schemes.

[1] See eg, S Shavell, *Foundations of Economic Analysis of Law* (The Belknap Press of Harvard University Press, 2004) at 110 ff; and R Geuss, *Public goods, private goods* (Princeton University Press, 2001).

[2] G Napolitano, *Les biens publics et les tragédies de l'intérêt commun* (2007) *Droit Administratif* 5.

In fact, there are both similarities and differences between the economic concept of public goods and the way the law usually comprehends general interest services. There are similarities in the sense that these notions try to identify analogous realities—public intervention vs market and the autonomous functioning of the society—but also commonly meet a normative perspective, since they try to answer the question: what is the (acceptable or desirable) scope of State intervention, on matters which could, in theory, be governed by the market or by ordinary social interplay?

The main differences between the economic concept and its legal equivalents are twofold. First, while the starting point of the public goods concept is the market—then the theory moves on to its failures, and what the State can do, and its own failures—when the law refers to public interest duties, it is not necessarily as a limit to the market and other spontaneous social mechanisms which would be considered as 'normal': in many traditions, there is the vision of a certain 'normality' of the State, which is considered as entrusted with some duties by essence, and not just where these duties are not properly accomplished by the market or spontaneous social life. Secondly, like the whole 'neo-classic' theory it belongs to, the concept of 'public goods' is built upon a methodological individualism stance which is not a kind of basic theoretical position on which all public law theories are based, by far.

Notwithstanding these differences, lawyers can use the concept of public goods without being too greatly disoriented, and they are well aware what kinds of problems are posed by legal equivalents. Limiting our reflection to domestic laws for the moment, we will summarise the related basic questions, and the main contemporary evolutions.

The basic questions are about how public goods are identified, defined, and how they are provided. Who, in the legal system, decides what tasks will be assumed by public authorities: is it stated in the Constitution—which would provide, for example, that the State must secure a certain level of education, or public health—is it left to the legislator, is it in some proportion, left to judges, who would, for example, be in a position to arbitrate on the 'general interest' character of a service that would justify its being taking charge of by public authorities? What are the criteria under which it will be decided that one social need or another has the nature of a public good? In French administrative law, for example, there is abundant case law on the issue of determining whether an economic activity is of a sufficient 'local public interest' to justify its service by a local government.[3]

Each legal system possesses its own solutions as to how public goods are provided. The way they are performed depends on how, in one particular system, the distribution of functions between public institutions and private entities

[3] eg, Conseil d'Etat, 30 May 1930, Chambre syndicale de commerce en detail de Nevers, Rec at 583.

taking part in the management of public duties is legally arranged: this is about the delineation of those public duties which must be directly performed by public institutions, and those which may be partly assumed by private entities; about the type of contracts through which part of public tasks can be entrusted to private entities; about the recognition of something like a 'third sector', acting between public authorities and the market, and so on.[4] What can also vary is the means by which the performance of public goods is monitored, assessed, and whether there are legal remedies available to those dissatisfied with the quality of provision.

Two principal changes currently affect the way public goods are provided. The first one is the large tendency to privatisation, deregulation and outsourcing which has influenced more or less all countries since the 1970s. It has transformed the management of public goods by transferring a large part of their provision to private entities, either in a pure, although regulated, market context—in telecommunications, for example—or by reliance on non-profit 'third sector' institutions, or in contracting out frameworks, where public authorities remain ultimately responsible for the service, but delegate it for a certain period of time under their supervision.

The second change derives from the fact that, more and more often, public goods become bigger than the States themselves, which are no longer the proper level for handling them. Public affairs and their management are now undergoing the process of globalisation, to which we must turn now.

PUBLIC GOODS AND LEGAL GLOBALISATION

Based upon the concept of public goods as it has just been briefly described, some authors and institutions[5] have evolved the notion of 'global' public goods,[6] in order to discern the general interest duties which must be taken charge of by the international community because States do not have the individual capacity to cope with them. These 'common concerns of mankind'[7] include the action against climate change, or the fight against corruption, but also some more

[4] It is not possible, within the limits of this chapter, to provide a more detailed look at this 'third sector'.. For some of the issues see SP Osborne (ed), *The Third Sector in Europe: Prospects and Challenges* (New York, Routledge, 2008).

[5] Such as the United Nations, which has fully adopted the idea: see the 'Global Public Goods' website, on one of the United Nations Development Programmes (http://www.undp.org/globalpublicgoods/), and: Inge Kaul, Isabelle Grundberg and Marc Stern (eds), *Global Public Goods: International Cooperation in the 21st century* (Oxford, Oxford University Press, 1999).

[6] I Kaul and P Conceicao (eds), *Providing Global Public Goods : Managing Globalization* (Oxford, Oxford University Press, 2003); F Constantin, *Le bien commun comme réponse politique à la mondialisation* (Paris, L'Harmattan, 2003); O Delas et C Deblock (eds), *Le bien commun comme réponse politique à la globalisation* (Brussels, Bruylant, 2003); M-C Smouts, *Forêt tropicale, jungle internationale* (Paris, Presses de Sciences Po, 2001).

[7] P Birnie, A Boyle and C Redgwell, *International Law & the Environment* (Oxford, Oxford University Press, 2009) at 339.

traditional ones such as peace, growth of developing countries, and so on. They exist as global public goods because they address 'public evils', such as financial crises, transnational pollution, money-laundering, and so on, which are impossible to combat at the national level.

Critics will argue that, extended in this manner to the international level, the concept loses its scientific purity, because it only has the meaning afforded by neo-classic economics where it applies to a particular territory, to a particular jurisdiction—only then can the 'free-riding' problem and the response to it be clearly identified.[8] The problems which are identified by the 'global public goods' theory correspond more, in, economic terms, to the concept of externalities than to the one of public goods: this applies typically, for example, to solutions to transnational pollutions.[9] Moreover, it can also be objected that what the idea of 'global public goods' highlights is more about the limits of States' powers—State failures in a sense—than about market failures, which are the origin of the public goods concept.

However, one cannot deny the fact that, in the international community as it is now, there is a large consensus on the existence of some 'common concerns', which are similar to the general interest duties States care about in the domestic ambit, but which have to be dealt with at the international level. The struggle against climate change and the financial crisis are certainly the ones which come to our mind most immediately in current times.

The question, for us, is to determine what content law is able to give to this idea. The question is, in fact, considering the complexity and fragmented character of global law, whether it is possible to discern in it some systemic—ie not attached only to one particular regime—pattern of what could be global public interests. And the answer to that question is yes, in two different ways.

The most obvious is in the fact that a large array of public needs and common concerns, is formally put forward in a range of international legal instruments, concerning environmental protection, free trade, protection of public health as well as food safety or the rule of law. One of the strongest characteristics of contemporary international law is that, while its predecessor essentially sought to ensure coexistence between States—in that sense, it had a function akin to the one assumed by private law in domestic ambits—it is concerned more and more with issues related to the international community as a whole, and conveys more and more corresponding public values.[10]

[8] F Lévêque, *Economie de la réglementation* (La Découverte, 2004) at 78.

[9] See eg, M Faure, *L'analyse économique du droit de l'environnement* (Brussels, Bruylant, 2007) at 12.

[10] GZ Capaldo, *The Pillars of Global Law* (Aldershot, Ashgate, 2008); J d'Aspremont, 'Contemporary International Rulemaking and the Public Character of International Law', IILJ Working Paper, New York University, 2006/12.

The second way is less direct, but not less strategic. It is the fact that the definition of global public interests derives indirectly from the various public order exceptions States have carved out in various international legal instruments in order to protect their sovereignty.

Most of the main legal instruments in globalisation, the ones concerning economic globalisation as well as the ones related to human rights at least, consent to the fact that, when public powers, public order, public health, and so on, are at stake, then 'ordinary' rules may be adapted, and in fact leave the way to specific ones, more adapted.

That is true in World Trade Association (WTO) law as well as in EU law. Both admit their 'ordinary' principles related to free trade and freedom of circulation, to be subject to some alleviations when concerns related to the public order, public health, and so on, are faced. EU competition law both is deemed non applicable where a matter of public authority is at stake, and applies in a specific and alleviated manner to services of general economic interest.[11]

This is also the case with global law on human rights. All the major international instruments in that field allow exceptions to the principles they lay down where proportionate public order, public security and public health needs are present.

Then, even if the States remain in principle competent for deciding what the public interest, the public order, the public health, and so on requirements are in their territory, the international institutions in charge of the various mentioned regimes—as well as national judges if they are in the position of applying the international regimes in question—will be entitled to check whether their claims in that respect do correspond to what the treaties provide for, and that the departures from 'normal' rules the States ask for are proportionate to the public interest, public order, public health, and so on concerns they invoke. Therefore, what is normally meant to protect the States'autonomy becomes a way of internationalising the definition of public goods.

Given these two factors, it is possible to admit that the concept of global public goods can have a meaning in legal terms.

Then, it must also be accepted that both properly identifying public goods, and arranging for their efficient provision, two issues which domestic systems already struggle to cope with, become even more difficult in global law.

The first obstacle to successfully identifying international public goods comes from the fact that the different legal traditions which compose the international community do not apprehend in the same way the problem of how to justify public intervention on economic and social issues. Some will tend to prefer to

[11] See eg, M Karayigit, 'The Notion of Services of General Economic Interest Revisited' (2009) 15 *European Public Law* 575.

base this justification on economic arguments,[12] whereas others will rather rely on pure political justifications, on a vision of common welfare without too many economic considerations.

This 'horizontal' obstacle stems from the existence of a variety of national legal cultures. One must also consider the 'vertical' aspect of complexity which results from the fact that, in globalisation, and in legal globalisation, the conduct of public affairs, and the legal arrangement of it, are fundamentally 'multi-level' businesses. Public affairs are assumed by various layers of public governance, from the State—and even infraState—level up to the worldwide one, with intermediate ones—regional, in particular—bearing in mind that, at most of these levels, there is also a division of work between several specialised institutions, and between specialised institutions and more generalist ones.

This tends to create a fragmented approach to general interest concerns, thus to public goods. Not that it would frequently give way to huge differences in the 'decalogue' of public goods: all international public actors, whether States or international organisations roughly agree on the same list, and none of them would publicly claim that reducing climate change, corruption, diseases, and so on, are not suitable objectives. But what changes from one level to another is the importance accorded to the various public goods. A good example of that is how, respectively, WTO law and EU law accommodate the combination between the free trade objectives and the environmental protection: the latter finds its way in WTO law with difficulty, while it is a prominent policy in the EU.

Moving from the national level to the global one also makes various questions concerning the provision of public goods more difficult.[13] The breadth of actors involved in the conduct of public affairs in globalisation is wide, and what has already sometimes become quite a complex scene at the domestic level, tends to be, at the global level, a jigsaw puzzle of contributors of many types, from States and traditional international organisations, to an array of private actors among which some clearly take part in public functions: some of them have a role in regulations,[14] others are more associated with implementing tasks. At the domestic level, it is already difficult to make sure that the more disparate set of actors who are associated with public tasks through privatisation and contracting out processes remain sufficiently accountable, and respectful of the basic public law values: this is obviously even more problematic at the global level.[15]

These difficulties concerning the identification and provision of public goods at the international level are one source of the wide debate which is evolving in

[12] eg, the traditional common law jurisprudence on common carriers.

[13] S Barrett, *Why Cooperate? The Incentive to Supply Global Public Goods* (Oxford, Oxford University Press, 2010).

[14] A Peters, L Koechlin, T Förster and G Fenner Zinkernagel, *Non-State Actors as Standard Setters* (Cambridge, Cambridge University Press) 2009.

[15] L Dickinson, 'Public Law Values in a Privatized World' (2006) 31 *Yale Journal of International Law* 383; J-B Auby, 'Contracting Out and Public Values' in S Rose-Ackerman and P Lindseth (eds), *Comparative Administrative Law* (Cheltenham, Edward Elgar, 2010).

current legal literature about how to make global governance more adjusted to the common interest of the world community, more accountable to it, and more efficiently submissive to the common values which are ordinarily imposed upon public bodies in the national traditions.

Within this set of reflections, the global administrative law theory, to which we now turn, already holds a recognised position.

PUBLIC GOODS AND GLOBAL ADMINISTRATIVE LAW

The global administrative law theory is a broad research and teaching project initiated at New York University by Richard Stewart and Benedict Kingsbury, and elaborated in Europe by Italian lawyers, headed by Sabino Cassese.

The theory[16] is based upon two observations. The first one is that, in the current globalising organisation of the world, there are many international bodies, embedded in international organisations or not, public or private, or public-private, which have all the features of administrative bodies: they deal with typical administrative issues—fisheries, drugs, environmental issues and so on—and they are made up of experts rather than diplomats or politicians.

Global administrative law theorists[17] have discerned five types of these global administrative bodies: apart from 'administration by formal organisations', they belong to 'administration based on collective action by transnational networks of cooperative arrangements between national regulatory officials', or to 'distributed administration conducted by national regulators under treaty, network or other cooperative regimes', or to 'administration by hybrid intergovernmental-private arrangements', or, finally, to 'administration by private institutions with regulatory functions'.

The second observation is that these various global administrative bodies are often insufficiently accountable, for three reasons. The first one is that, in general, they stay clear from national legal disciplines normally imposed upon public bodies: either they are international law entities, or they are domestic law ones, but then, they belong to networks whose legal functioning cannot be mastered by national law.

The second reason is that international law does not contain the same rules as the ones which constitute the ordinary legal disciplines imposed upon national public bodies, in terms of accountability, rationality, fair process, transparency, non-discrimination, and the like.

[16] Of which basic elements can be found in: B Kingsbury, N Krisch, R Stewart and J Wiener (special eds), 'The Emergence of Global Administrative Law' (2005) 68 *Law and Contemporary Problems*. See also S Cassese, *La crisi dello Stato* (Bari, Editori Laterza, 2002); *Lo spazio giuridico globale* (Bari, Editori Laterza, 2003).

[17] See Kingsbury et al, n 16 above.

The third one is that some global administrative bodies are private or semi-public, and therefore avoid both national and international disciplines concerning public bodies.

Considering this twofold observation, the global administrative law theory articulates its programme on the following ideas. The question asked is: who has the best 'know-how' in terms of making public bodies accountable? The answer given is: administrative law, whose function is to impose upon public bodies the respect of legality, transparency, due process.

Upon these bases, the global administrative law theory opens on a middle term project, consisting in: identifying all global administrative bodies, discerning if they are properly based on principles such as fair hearing, transparency, and so on, and if their decisions can be appealed in one way or another, and, when necessary, issuing proposals about ways of making them more accountable.

What is, then, the possible contribution of the global administrative law theory to the apprehension of global public goods and the search for the best ways of having them best produced?

The answer can be summed up in the idea that global administrative law's realm is more on the side of processes than on the one of substances. The entire purpose of global administrative law is to better submit global bodies to sound procedures, reviewing mechanisms, accountability devices; it is not a theory about what these bodies ought to do, what aims they should follow, or what tasks they are supposed to serve.

Accordingly, the global administrative law theory's possible input as to the identification of global public goods is limited to the improvement of rulemaking procedures through which it is determined how the objectives of global administrative bodies are supposed to be pursued. In general, the choice of these objectives is not made within the body itself. Rather, it will usually be made through traditional diplomatic ways and provided for in the treaty creating the body—or any other kind of act defining its statute. In any case, there is an aspect of the global public goods qualification on which global administrative law does not seem to be able to shed any light: it is the criteria upon which something can be considered as constituting a public good, and a global one.

On the other hand, the global administrative law work is of significant use when it comes to the performance of global public goods. Indeed, under the banner of accountability, the main effort of the theory is dedicated to the determination of the best procedural solutions through which it is ensured that the tasks devolved to the body are performed in the most effective and accountable manner, including in cases where part of them is contracted out. Thus, in its proper realm, the global administrative law theory can make an important contribution to the improvement of global public goods' performance.

Whilst the global administrative law theory can indeed make a significant contribution, it is not yet equal to the challenges of the global public goods issue, because it lacks two dimensions.[18]

The first one is about the 'multilevel' character of public action in globalisation.[19] The conduct of public affairs in the international ambit is managed more and more by complex arrangements of two or more levels of governance, and the distribution of roles between the different levels of public action is, for that reason, blurring.

One of the consequences of this is that the identification and the provision of public goods in the global ambit is never the duty of one institution solely, but always involves several institutional levels in an intricate manner. This means that one cannot impose much rationality in that identification and provision by simply adjusting the procedures which are followed at one institutional level – which makes the theory ingenious.

The second one is about the democratic and constitutional background of the identification of public goods, and the determination of their ways of implementation. There, the global administrative law theory must necessarily be complemented by reflections concerning international and European citizenship and democracy,[20] and others concerning the constitutionalisation of international bodies,[21] and of European institutions.[22]

It has now been fully demonstrated that international and European institutions[23] need to be equipped with constitutional bases. One reason why this is much needed is that such a constitutionalisation is the only way by which the public goods of which global bodies are in charge of, and the main modalities of their provision, would clearly be determined on the face of the record.

This line of thought should, then, be added to the global administrative law theory. And it is quite feasible, in fact. In domestic ambits, we know how strong

[18] J-B Auby, 'The EU and Global Administrative Law' in P Birkinshaw and M Varney (eds), *The European Union Legal Order after Lisbon* (Dordrecht, Kluwer Law International, 2010) at 57.

[19] N Bamforth and P Leyland (eds), *Public Law in a Multi-Layered Constitution* (Oxford, Hart Publishing, 2003); I Bache and M Flinders, *Multilevel Governance in Practice* (Oxford, Oxford University Press, 2004); P Taylor, *International Organization in the Age of Globalization* (London, Continuum, 2003); C Joerges and E-U Petersmann, *Constitutionalism, Multilevel Trade Governance and Social Regulation* (Oxford, Hart Publishing, 2006).

[20] R Burchill (ed), *Democracy and International Law* (Aldershot, Ashgate, 2006); J-A Scholte, 'Global civil society' in N Woods (ed), *The political economy of globalization* (London, Macmillan, 2000); P Fitzpatrick and P Tuitt (eds), *Critical beings. Law, Nation, and the Global Subject* (Cambridge, Cambridge University Press, 2004).

[21] A Peters, J Klabbers and G Ufstein, *The Constitutionalization of International Law* (Oxford, Oxford University Press, 2009); D Schneiderman (ed), *Constitutionalizing Economic Globalization* (Cambridge, Cambridge University Press, 2008); Joerges and Petersmann (eds), n 19 above; D Feldman, 'Modalities of internationalization in Constitutional Law' (2006) 18 *European Review of Public Law* 131.

[22] J Weiler and M Wind (eds), *European Constitutionalism Beyond the State* (Cambridge, Cambridge University Press, 2003).

[23] Perhaps including private entities taking part to the management of public affairs: Gavin Anderson, *Constitutional Rights after Globalization* (Oxford, Hart Publishing, 2005).

the links between administrative law and constitutional law are, due especially to the wide development of constitutional review nowadays. There is no reason for thinking that, at one time or another, a similar junction will not occur at the global level. The weak degree of constitutionalisation of international bodies is certainly an obstacle, but this kind of obstacle also existed in domestic systems, and most of today's national public laws are made on a basis which strongly combines constitutional law and administrative law. The same could, and probably will, be the case in legal globalisation.

11

Global Citizenship and Global Legitimacy

LUIS ORTEGA

INTRODUCTION

IF WE FOLLOW the approach of Santi Romano[1] concerning the elements of any legal concept (such as community, organisation or rule) global administrative law is concerned primarily with how administrative rules are implemented—both in a procedural and a substantial way. This chapter attempts to open up a new focus within global administrative law centring on the legal status of the community, and more precisely, on the status of the individuals and groups within such a community. The argument centres on building a multi-level order of law defining the legal status of any individual or group who is subject to the legal consequences of global administrative law, and on ensuring that the legal status thus established is binding within the global legal order. This involves creating a notion of citizenship based on principles of democracy, welfare protection and the rule of law, which gives an individual a status based on membership of that community. These principles are common across the world and are drawn from well known sources such as the Treaty of Lisbon, on the Political and Civil Rights Charter of the UN of 1966, and many national constitutions worldwide.

While the reality of this new legal status can only be shown as it is employed to successfully guaranteeing fundamental rights in legal actions, this chapter is concerned to sharpen the concept of global citizenship and develop it as a more complex idea moving beyond the global protection of fundamental rights to encompass political action, citizens' organisations, and public opinion. Additionally the chapter seeks to make the point that if global rules do not include recognition of this idea of citizenship as special status they will lack a very important source of legitimacy.

[1] S Romano, *L'ordinamento giuridi: Studi sul concetto, le fonti e i caratteri del diritto*, (Pisa, Spoerri, 1918).

GLOBAL CITIZENSHIP AS A LEGITIMATING ELEMENT OF GLOBAL LAW

This understanding of legal legitimacy has been raised also by Gerard Timsit who argues that in the global context neither rules originating simply from the bureaucracy of the individual State nor the operation of the free market have the necessary elements to legitimise restrictions upon citizens. Timsit proposes the use of a negotiated and dialogued legal order as the best way to guarantee the rights and needs of the political community of any legal order.[2] Indeed, it can be said that if there is one single element in the development of administrative law as a legal science in the second half of the twentieth century it has been without doubt this methodological approach of explaining administrative law as having a constitutional basis.[3]

This approach has two main consequences: first, the important place that respect for fundamental rights and human rights has in legitimising public authorities acting in their different roles in regulating, adjudicating and controlling; and, second, the fact that administrative law principles have to be challenged with other constitutional principles closely related to our discipline, such as the democratic and the welfare state principles. In this situation, global citizenship is implicated in both these consequences: citizenship as the subject of fundamental and human rights, and citizenship as a reference of the principles of democracy and welfare state. Indeed, as already stressed, when global citizenship is mentioned here in relation to global administrative law it should be taken to mean more than simply respect for fundamental rights and human rights, and should encompass this more dynamic approach relating to the role of the individual as a political actor and, indeed, the main component in any democratic system. Viewed from this perspective, we must be concerned not only with considering the existence of decision-making processes in global organisations but also with questions about how, and the extent to which, those mechanisms influence the democratic functioning of the State.

GLOBAL CITIZENSHIP, GLOBAL LAW AND DEMOCRACY

The fact that global administrative law has expanded in parallel with the expansion of a global economy has produced some conceptual limits of constitutional relevance. These include most notably an affirmation of the autonomy of economic decisions in the global market from the rules of democracy. This is an unacceptable situation. In public law we have seen how, through a long period of legal evolution, some very important concepts have appeared such as abuse of

[2] G Timsit, 'La reinvention de l'État', 6th Braibant Lecture delivered at the International Institute of Administrative Sciences 2007 and published as 'Braibant Lecture 2007: Reinventing the State—to be continued' (2008) 74 *International Review of Administrative Sciences* 165–75.

[3] See S Cassese (ed), *Le basi costituzionali. Trattato di Diritto Ammnistrativo Parte Generale*, Tomo I. 2 (Milano, Giuffrè, 2003) at 173–250.

power, social function of property and the submission of wealth to an idea of public interest as declared by parliaments. Inherent in all of these concepts is the philosophy that the economy is merely instrumental in achieving political objectives as defined by a democratic process.

The global economy has developed largely in the absence of a political environment stressing global democracy. The recent economic and financial global crisis shows how global decisions affect national States but without allowing them any capacity to react and to give rational answers to citizens. The United Nations has not been a useful instrument in setting new rules for a global economy, and the same can be said of the role played by the different 'Gs': G-7, G-8 or G-20. In fact, to have a world authority with the power successfully to rule a global economy requires national States to renounce a very important part of their sovereignty over economic affairs. Such a relinquishment of power remains impossible. Against this background where the establishment of supranational democratic institutions with a global scope remains so difficult, there is still the possibility of requiring democratic rule from any agent who wishes to participate in the global economy. Furthermore there is also the possibility of requiring a further conformity with global public law principles in order to be allowed to participate as an actor on the global scene. Among those principles should be respect for a minimum status of citizenship.

We know that according to theories of deliberative democracy which require an extended procedure of active, rational argumentation over values and interests, there is requirement for a rational and comprehensible relationship between global and national realities.[4] The construction of any multi-level structure of power requires clear and consistent connections between the different levels of such structures. The way in which a decision is taken at a global level, even if taken by majority rule, cannot be separated from the consequences of such decision at any other level of the multi-level system. In many cases, global rules are made under a philosophy of aggregated democracy where the various interests are mediated in private, with only the result of these transactions being made known to the public. In contrast, the multi-level system, in which global law functions, requires that those rules have to be set under the principles of reciprocity, transparency and accountability. There cannot be a properly conceived multi-level structure with two or more separated levels of democracy. In fact the whole of a multi-level structure should be evaluated in terms of all of its elements, so that at least the main rules of democracy are respected,[5] especially

[4] J Besssette, 'Deliberative Democracy: The Majority Principle in Republican Government' in R Goldwin and W Schambra (eds), *How Democratic is the Constitution?* (Washington DC, American Enterprise Institute, 1980) at 102–16; A Gutmann and D Thompson, *Why deliberative democracy?* (New Jersey, Princeton University Press, 2004); J Rawls, 'The idea of public reason revisited' in S Freemann (ed), *Collected Papers*, (Cambridge, MA, Harvard University Press, 1999) at 573–615.

[5] A McGrew, 'Democracy beyond borders? Globalization and the reconstruction of democratic theory and politics' in A McGrew (ed), *The transformation of democracy? Golobalization and territorial democracy* (London, Polity Press, 1999).

the rule that guarantees that consent given by citizens to the multi-level structure is followed by a mechanism of accountability.[6] At the global level the absence of a higher and hierarchical authority, cannot be allowed to mean that there is governance without government or that the principles of democracy and of rule of law play a different role.[7]

The concept of higher authority is also relevant and valid in the context of a global legal order, because it also operates in relation to the sources of law in a system. The way in which a legal order is in a higher position is not only given by the elements of organisation, but also by the relationship between norms. In this case, the non-democratic authority (the global organisation) imposes a rule that modifies the rule approved by a democratic assembly. This means that it cannot be denied that the hierarchy among norms places a hierarchical relation between the organisations that control these norms. The limits imposed on domestic rule by global rule is a fact of authority insofar as it comes from a higher and effective power. If, at the end of the day, there is a situation of governance without government, the structure should be reviewed in order to avoid the situation where any multi-level structure that has a global presence within it simply ends up submitting to the requirements of the global economy, without regard to the fact that States, even where they are acting in a global context, represent a plurality of public interests.

The ongoing processes of deregulation, and the choice that has been made for a minimal system of public control, has created a kind of regulatory deficit, especially at the global level. This has been denounced by important legal scholars, as a potential danger to the ideas of the public interest of citizens who are at the lower end of the multi-level scale.[8] Indeed, the global economy has shown itself not to be responsible to such citizens as the consequences of the recent financial failures needed resolution by national governments using the fiscal resources, taxes and revenues of citizens.

This reality of the role played by national States in ultimately solving the global financial and economic crisis of September 2008 has to be analysed at least from two perspectives. First of all, considering the capacity of the national States to play such a role, Habermas has pointed out three elements relating to the constitutional function of the national State: the decline of the capacity of the State to exercise powers of control; the deficit in the legitimacy of its decision-making process; and the impossibility of acting in favour of certain political options that may be voted by citizens, such as economic planning or an expansive financing of social rights.[9] This situation emphasises the important question

[6] R Cox, *Approaches to World Order* (Cambridge, Cambridge University Press, 1996).

[7] S Cassesse, *Il diritto globale*, (Torino, Einaudi, 2009) at 166.

[8] L Ferrajoli, 'Por una esfera pública del mundo' in R Soriano and J Mora (eds), *El nuevo orden americano. La muerte del Derecho?* (Cordoba, Almuzara, 2005).

[9] J Habermas, 'El valle de lágrimas de la globalización' (2001) 10 *Claves de la razón prectica* 109.

relating to the real capacity of national States to react and to solve problems affecting national citizens that originate from a crisis developed at the global level. The potential inability of national States to manage properly the solution to a global crisis generates a rejection by citizens of the democratic model of the State as it does not seem to be providing adequate answers to citizens' needs. It is in this sense that the absence of democracy at the global level has negative consequences on the operation of democracy at the national level. At the same time it not possible to design global structures, rules or organisations that exist separately from the national level since it is at the global level that solutions to national problems must be found.

The implications of this are that it becomes of primary importance to ensure that ideas of global democracy (weak as they are) do not operate to assist the deterioration of democracy within national States. It may be useful here to draw lessons from history. After the Great Depression of 1929, the United States had the capacity and the resources to propose the 'New Deal', but Europe was sunk into a very deep democratic crisis. We have to remember that the ideal of a perfect political regime is as ancient as the work of Hippodamus of Miletus,[10] and even if democracy is commonly accepted as the best political system in the world, there are many problems and questions still unresolved. However if we concentrate on the question of legitimacy at the global level, there is a lack of a fundamental democratic basis. Global rule wishes to have not only the same legal structure and effect as rules approved under a democratic system but the same legitimacy.[11] While we may have to accept global law and global institutions as necessary in light of the global nature of the economy and the reality of a global world, it is important to remember too that this global dimension has to exist in relation to the national and indeed local level. National systems of judicial review use national legal standards to protect citizens, even from global law. As we shall see later, global law itself, including global judicial review, will need to set its standards based on values of global citizenship because if it does not, national systems of judicial review will be employed, with the consequences that large elements of diversity will be introduced into the global context.

By way of example to illustrate what global citizenship might mean in this context, the global legal order should require that every regulatory authority and every institution that is subject to legal review should be aware of the full range of interests that are inherent in the idea of citizenship, and how they apply to anyone who complains before a global organisation or institution, irrespective of whether they relate directly to the area of competence of the global body. The rationale for this is to ensure the same rights where a global decision is being challenged as the citizen may have if he or she were in a domestic court where his or her full constitutional status would be respected.

[10] Aristotles, *Política*, vol II.8 b (Madrid, CEC,1267) at 22.

[11] D Held, *La democracia y el Orden Global* (Barcelona, Paidós, 1997).

The upshot of all this is, to quote Bobbio's brilliant observation, that the problem today in relation to human rights is not the need to justify them but to guarantee their protection.[12]

GLOBAL CITIZENSHIP: UNIVERSALITY AND DOMESTIC PECULIARITIES

It follows from all this that there must be a complementary process whereby we simultaneously demand the universality of institutions and principles of public law to represent the paradigm of global civilisation, and require respect for national differences within an understanding of legal pluralism.

In some ways, the experience of European public law, since the French Revolution, has been a continuous process of finding mechanisms to facilitate the universality of political, philosophical, social or moral ideas in different legal orders. In this way the idea of justice with a moral background was transformed into constitutional values and into general principles. Understandings of family relations were modified as sexual roles changed and racial prejudices were reduced in relation to ideas of equality. Secularisation diminished the deference of national law to religious dogma. When these principles were enshrined in constitutional law they were heralded as coming from universal ideals of free citizenship. In a similar process we can see the potential for global public law as an instrument to unify legal orders.

However, in the same experience of European public law, we can also find elements of pluralism and decentralisation as with the principles of subsidiary and proportionality. These in particular indicate a degree of recognition of the necessity to provide adequate space for the peculiarities of social groups and different levels of political communities. This seems to combine the republican ideal of citizenship within the French Republic, where all are equal before the law of the State irrespective of the place of residence, with an ideal of democracy coming from the United States, where the individual is equal in relation to the specific community to which he or she belongs, although various communities may have a different a political status. This thought sets us the task of formulating an equilibrium between the idea of universal, homogeneous legal status and the recognition of some amount of diversity where principles of public law are interpreted according to specific cultures, social behaviours or national legal orders.

In any event at this point we need to follow three separate steps: first, to note if the law is expressed in the same way; secondly, to observe how different public authorities implement the law; and thirdly, to assess if there is the same level of protection given by the courts.

The Charter of Fundamental Rights of the European Union provides an example of unification though public law of legal cultures as different as, for

[12] N Bobbio, *El tiempo de los derechos* (Madrid, Editorial Sistema, 1991) at 61.

example, Finland and Spain. Here, although both countries have the same fundamental rights proclaimed in their Constitutions, the interpretation of the limits that each fundamental right places on another fundamental right can be different. This can be seen, for example, in relation to freedom of speech versus privacy, or the extent of the concept of dignity, fairness or proportionality.

It is also true that there may be variation in this way in which the legal understanding of a fundamental right may evolve. This is demonstrated in the experience of the European Court of Human Rights where there are many examples demonstrating evolution in the interpretation of the extent of a single right, as with the recent ruling in which bad odour or loud noise has been interpreted as an infringement of privacy. However, for the sake of the Charter of Fundamental Rights on the European Union and the jurisprudence of the European Court of Justice, there will be the same interpretation in Finland and in Spain. The effect of this is that some appropriate sources of law can provide a unifying tendency for several legal orders that would otherwise demonstrate a tendency historically to develop individual peculiarities.

However this tendency to develop peculiarities is something that may have structural roots. When law is implemented, especially in the European Law area through the mechanism of European directives, it is national rules that control the implementation of the directive. In this mechanism the directive unifies the scope of the European legal command but leaves to Member States certain flexibility in the application of the directive. Also one should remember the tendency in the bureaucratic practice of all public administrations to adapt law to the specific case. Finally, there are different degrees of judicial review before various courts. There is the European Convention of Human Rights in which certain rights can be modulated by some factors such as national security, public order or cultural heritage. Also, if we look carefully at the content of many rights in the Charter of Fundamental Rights of the European Union, they are conditioned by the specific way they are protected by the law of each Member State.

So we may conclude that there is a tendency to create universal rules with a minimum of dogmatic content, even though in the interpretation and in the application of law, and even in the degree of judicial review, there can be some differences concerning the subjects, the object and the circumstances as applied to the single case. If we move now to a comparative legal context, we can see very often that the focus of conceptual effort is on finding by which measure public law in a variety of countries copes with the traditional principles of the rule of law and democracy as a universal form of political organisation. It remains true that these principles are taken as a goal for most legal orders, and even exist as the paradigm in China, Vietnam or Iran. Of course in some circumstances there are historical, cultural and socio-economic conditions that make it difficult to achieve these traditional principles. In some cases there are problems of transition of traditional societies to modern patterns of civilisation and legal orders; in others there is a lack of capacity of public law to develop new political systems, or the appearance of new negotiation procedures that allow the participation of private agents in giving solutions to public problems. But at the same time we must also take into account that the mere presence of one of the formal elements of a democracy, even the presence of the typical institutions of a democracy, does not mean that there is a truly democratic political system. In some non-democratic countries there can be developments around legal reforms that are misleading, such as those that have been introduced because of the presence of these countries in international or global organisations. This is the case especially in relation to the principle of legal certainty in commercial law which may be recognised in order that such countries can take part in the global economy. Also, there are examples of countries with two different levels of legality: the formal legality, which may cope with the standards of the Universal Declaration of Human Rights, and the real one where social, family or cultural factors interfere with the effective exercise of individual rights.

All these possibilities make it increasingly important that individual legal systems contain the most appropriate and widespread legal remedies to guarantee individual and collective rights. It also requires vigilance so that coherence can be maintained within the global legal system with regard to dealing with inadequacies in those universal rules and principles. Indeed it is especially important because, as has been pointed out already, some elements of public law need to be interpreted through a pluralistic approach and the paradox remains whereby there are calls about the need to universalise democratic values at a national level while the same values are forgotten when global or international action is in question.

Public law has been an effective instrument in the national context in organising issues such as formal democracy, political and economic sovereignty, effective legal remedies, redistribution of wealth and public interventions to cope with the social needs through instruments that replace market options. Public law also has been able to create guarantees for citizens as to the adequate means for the formulation of responsibility, liability and accountability of any public or private body. However, when we move to the global and international level, those achievements of public law are less clear-cut. There it is global and international law which must take on not only the global and international dimension of individual States but also the global and international dimension of citizenship.

GLOBAL LAW IN THE NATIONAL AND LOCAL CONTEXTS AND NATIONAL LAW IN THE GLOBAL CONTEXT

Sabino Cassese gives us some indications about how global problems are controlled by local decisions in three different cases.[13] The first one deals with a legal action placed by the State of California before the District Court of Northern

[13] S Cassese, 'Nel laberinto delle globalización' (2007) 4 *Rivista Trimentrale di diritto pubblico* 57, 923 ff.

California against the six biggest car manufacturers. It was argued that automobile pollution increases global temperature and this global problem is directly related to issues about sea level, pollution of big cities, the risk of fires, and the reduction of quality of drinking water. In this instance we have a global phenomenon that is controlled by the local criteria. The second case relates to the American Supreme Court case of *Massachusetts v Environmental Protection Agency*[14] in which the Court states that the Environmental Protection Agency (EPA) must take global warming into account when regulating environmental issues, or at least give reasons as to whether or not the green house effect is responsible for global climate change. In this case, the global phenomenon required a local reasoning. The third case deals with the anti-sweatshop laws. Here a law approved by the City of New York in 2002 requires that textile products sold in New York City should come from a 'responsible manufacturer'. This is defined as one who pays salaries that allow a family of three members to live above the poverty line. In this case it is the local rule that limits the effectiveness of a global market, requiring that such global markets meet local standards in order to become a legitimate activity.

There is also the very well known European Union Court case of *Kadi and Al Barakaat v Council of European Union and Commission of the European Communities.*[15] This deals with an issue where global law is controlled under the criteria of a regional legal order—here the European Community's human rights standards. In this case there is a judgment that the global rule breaches the right to a hearing, the right to judicial protection and the right to property. The importance of this case comes from the doctrine that Community courts must guarantee and control the legality of all community acts and decisions (from the point of view of the fundamental rights that integrate the general principles of Community Law) in principle exhaustively and even when applying global law. In the case of *Katrin Krabbe v IAAF,*[16] the District Court of Munich (LG Munich) reviewed the decision taken by the Council of the International Association of Athletic Federations suspending an athlete from competition. The Court held the suspension to be unconstitutional on the basis of competence, a denial of the constitutional right to fair hearing and a disproportionate interference with the constitutional right to freedom of occupation. Here, besides the control of fundamental rights, we can see the how the case illustrates the full nature of the citizen: several values are covered by the case as the review is not limited to the sporting aspects of the issue but also relates to issues about freedom of occupation.

[14] 549 US 497 (2007).

[15] Joined Cases C 402/05P and C-415/05P, *Kadi & Al Barakaat International Foundation v Council and Commission* [2008] 3 CMLR 41.

[16] LG Munich, available at SpuRt 1995, 161. See also the paper presented to the 4th Global Administrative Law Seminar, in Viterbo in June 2008 by A Lang, *Global Administrative Law in Domestic Courts: Holding Global Administrative Bodies Accountable.*

Another example that should be mentioned is one that relates to the principles that rule the spatial implementation of criminal law such as the principle of universal jurisdiction as this involves the Spanish criminal law applying to certain crimes committed by any person in any country in respect of a threat posed to humanity. This principle of universal jurisdiction establishes an important exception to the basic principle of territoriality in criminal law, in accordance with which States are competent to try crimes committed within their frontiers. This can be seen as the expression of the unquestionable link between criminal law and the exercise of sovereignty, a concept which is also linked to the State's territory. The principle of universal jurisdiction is a step forward in order to prevent impunity and is, by definition, additional to the jurisdiction of the country where the crimes have been committed. This is why it applies especially when that country refuses to prosecute those crimes. It is not only a way to allow international laws to apply when the principle of territoriality does not, but it is also clearly inferred, *contrario sensu*, from the tenor of Article 23.4 LOPJ.[17] Here it is required that the culprit should have not been 'acquitted, convicted or pardoned' in the past, and so the Spanish extraterritorial jurisdiction only stops applying when the jurisdiction has been previously exercised.

The resolution of the Spanish court of the 'Audiencia Nacional' of 5 March 1998, which confirms the Spanish jurisdiction, interprets the principle of universal jurisdiction as an expression of a commitment to the prosecution of international crimes, with special reference to genocide. It is regulated in Article 23.4 LOPJ (written according to the Organic Law 13/2007, of 19 November, for the extraterritorial prosecution of the illegal trafficking or immigration):

> The Spanish jurisdiction will be equally competent to try those crimes committed by Spaniards or foreigners outside the national territory which can be considered, according to the Spanish criminal law, as one of the following:
>
> Genocide
>
> Terrorism
>
> Piracy and unlawful seizure of aircrafts
>
> Forgery of foreign currencies
>
> Crimes relating to prostitution and those of corruption of minors or incapables
>
> Illegal trafficking of psychotropic, toxic and stupefacient drugs
>
> Illegal trafficking or immigration of humans, whether they be workers or not
>
> Crimes relating to female genital mutilation, provided that those responsible are in Spain

[17] Organic Law 6/1985, of 1 November, on the Judiciary.

And any other crime which, according to international treaties or agreements, should be prosecuted in Spain

By virtue of the principle of universal jurisdiction, the State keeps its competence to prosecute crimes committed by Spaniards or foreigners outside the national territory whenever they damage certain legally protected interests recognised by the entire international community. The principle focuses on this protection. From this point of view, the recognition of the principle by States not only involves an assumption of competence, but also the commitment to prosecute those crimes which damage international interests, and which are often committed by forms of international criminality. Therefore, it is an instrument whose adoption by any State allows the prosecution of any crime committed outside its frontiers, but in whose punishment the State is interested as a member of the international community.

CONCLUSIONS

It is important to make the point that essentially the general and universal principles of public law concerning the status of the citizen also need to be applied to global law as a mean of legitimising its operation. At the same time, global rules must pass through the test of compliance with those rules and principles as they are applied at a local/national level, because in those rules can be found the core of the status of citizenship.

The approach of seeing global law as autonomous and on a separate level from domestic or national legal orders needs to be modified since ultimately it is national systems which must solve problems created at that global level which impact directly into the economic, social or cultural status of the citizen.

In a recent conference held under the auspices of a Global Administrative Law Seminar,[18] Armin von Bogdandy concluded that 'the normative vantage point of an international judiciary in the postnational constellation should be the idea of global citizenship'. This is a view with which I would concur.

[18] Conference held in Viterbo, at La Tuscia University (12–13 June 2009). See www.iilj.org/GAL/ViterboV.asp.

12

Affirmative Action: A New Challenge for Equality

GEORGE GERAPETRITIS

INTRODUCTION

THE TRADITIONAL CONCEPT of formal equality, stemming from the essence of the great revolutions of the eighteenth century, has been proven somewhat unsatisfactory and this has led to conceptual and institutional reconsideration of its basics. This is so because formal equality not only presupposes that all people are inherently equal but also that they have the same starting point in their social, professional and political lives—a premise that is patently false. Furthermore, society itself has been subject to great modifications: the nation State ideal of the nineteenth century has collapsed and the rational limits of society's self correction mechanisms have been diminished, as reflected in the recently developed and widely elaborated doctrine of 'clash of civilisations'.

Affirmative action has been the most striking response to the shortfalls of formal equality. In fact, it constitutes a doctrinal subversion of its rudiments because it tends to award privileges to certain groups that have historically suffered discrimination or have been underrepresented in specific social sectors by using criteria of differentiation that are in principle unacceptable. The underlying rationale is that one cannot place at the same starting point people who have been treated differently in the past because in this way one merely perpetuates a state of difference and, in turn, social gaps are exaggerated and social cohesion is endangered.

Although affirmative action has a long tradition at the national and international levels, there is not a universally accepted terminology. Usually there is a two-word term used: 'positive' or 'affirmative' in order to imply that State activity is required to materialise these plans, and 'action' or 'discretion'. The latter distinction is of major significance: in the United States (US) the widely accepted notion is that of action *(affirmative 'action')*; whereas in Europe some legal doctrines use the idea of action (thus in Greece *positive 'action'*) and some others the notion of discretion (thus to a large extent in France '*discrimination*' *positive*, in the United Kingdom (UK) *positive 'discrimination'* and in Germany *positive 'Diskriminierung' or zulässige 'Diskriminierung')*. In yet other cases mixed definitions apply.[1]

This chapter will use all terms, following the terminology applied by the legal system under consideration at any time. Literally, however, the most expedient linguistic approach would suggest that when the measure is of direct effect, such as the imposition of rigid quotas, there is essentially a case to use the terminology of positive discrimination, whereas if the measure is of an indirect effect, thus encouraging participation of underrepresented groups without establishing quotas, the language of positive/affirmative action is more appropriate.

SOCIAL TASKS AND LEGAL JUSTIFICATION

Identifying the task of an affirmative action plan is not merely a doctrinal experiment; it also connotes significant legal implications. This is so because in order to assess the constitutionality of a particular positive measure there is a conceptual precondition that the measure pursues a legitimate aim. If this is so, the judiciary must first evaluate the particular side effects of the measure in question (mostly adverse consequences for the human rights involved) against the scope and quality of the goal pursued. This legal approach may take place either in a more pragmatic way, through the application of the reasonableness/rational basis test, or through a more doctrinal approach, broadly speaking the application of proportionality test. Thus, the relative value of the goals pursued by each legal system when introducing an affirmative action plan not only provides the substantive legitimacy of this State intervention but also constitutes the legal foundation for the technical/legal evaluation of the measure.

There are basically two ratios justifying the enactment of affirmative action measures: a remedial purpose, ie compensation for past discriminations; and a cultural purpose, ie diversity. The former has been the initiating force for the introduction of such measures, whereas the latter tends to become the most up to date expression for seeking substantive equality.

The remedial purpose: compensation for past discrimination

The most easily conceivable social task of affirmative action policy is to compensate groups that have suffered discrimination in the past. It sounds reasonable, fair and morally acceptable that society should bridge the gap of opportunities that has occurred due to the unequal distribution of social benefits and the historically disadvantageous position of societal actors. Thus, women, racial

[1] 'Corrective inequality' (*'inégalités correctrices'*) according to the Belgian Cour d'arbitrage, Judgments 53/93 of 1 July 1993 and 9/94 of 27 January 1994 or 'standarisation' in Sri Lanka.

minorities, religious groups, etc ought to gain some advantage in the fields of education, economy and political participation.

The first relevant question is under what conditions remedial action can be justified. According to the 'societal' version of remedy, affirmative action can be introduced when there is evidence of past discrimination in society as a whole; according to the 'segmental' version, a remedy must be provided when it is exactly the same authority or institution initiating the affirmative action plan that committed discriminatory activities in the past. The former version seems to be the prevailing one when remedial purposes are recognised as legitimate, although the latter version has on occasions been invoked by the courts.[2]

Probing beneath the equity façade of remedial purposes, this type of affirmative action becomes rather vulnerable. A first level of objections lies with the technical issue of the delineation of the beneficiaries. The basic generic question raised is why there should be a group remedy in the first place. Compensation is not, and could not be, a value per se, but functions only as a means to liberate the human value that has been suffocated due to past discrimination. In that case, group compensation is merely an out-of-date break even process between competing social groups. This process, however, does not necessarily result in fair awards precisely because of its non-individualistic methodology. In other words, this balancing process may statistically provide satisfaction to members of subordinate groups but, technically, not to all members of these groups and most probably not all those individuals who have suffered discrimination in the past.

A group remedy presupposes, first, that all members of a group carry the same idiosyncrasy and, second, that the members of the group have suffered discrimination in the past. However, neither of these hypotheses is true. Members of groups do differ significantly; and discrimination is suffered not by groups per se but rather by some members of a group (most probably the majority in the case of subordinate groups). Only in very exceptional cases where there has been institutional differentiation, such as in general terms under the apartheid or segregation regimes or the deprivation of political rights of women, could group discrimination be claimed altogether. One could counter argue against affirmative action policy on the basis that, by definition, it lacks a distinctive approach upon the issue of societal damage and merely constitutes a confession of State failure to identify those in true need.

Failure to identify the persons who have suffered past discrimination may lead to unsatisfactory results in relation to the determination of the groups that should be treated preferably. There are two stages in the process of delineating the affirmative action beneficiaries. First, the policy criteria should be set out, eg race, sex, religion; and, second, there must be a process of inclusion of groups into the

[2] In *Hopwood v Texas*, 78 F 3d 932, 944–45 (5th Cir 1996), the Court of Appeals held that Texas Law School could not act to alleviate the effect on its applicant pool of past discrimination in elementary, secondary and undergraduate education, since the effects of such discrimination were too difficult to measure and the Law School was not responsible for those effects in any event.

settled criteria. The former decision is mostly a political one based on historical assumptions about past discrimination. This choice, however, is not free of objections. In a sense, given the wide differences between the members of a group, one might convincingly argue that instead of using a more or less authoritarian criterion, a more objective and secure yardstick, such as class or financial capacity, should apply. In this way, institutional encouragement could be given to the individuals in true need in a more Marxist approach to State intervention in social relations. Otherwise, any generic affirmative action plan constitutes an over-simplistic approach to a rather complicated social phenomenon.

On the other hand the group inclusion process is even more delicate. In fact, there is no automatic, or even easy, answer, as to which groups should fall within the benevolent umbrella of affirmative action. The inherent subjectivity of this process is an obvious hindrance in introducing a fair and rational awarding system. What races should be considered as having suffered discrimination; how much blood is required in such a case; and what is the priority amongst the various group that might benefit from measures?—these are only a few of the questions indicating the inclusion problem.[3] Moreover, a secondary doctrinal problem is that any inclusion suffers as a matter of fact from over-inclusiveness (thus benefiting individuals not in true need) and under-inclusiveness (thus not benefiting individuals in true need). Over-inclusiveness can occur because some beneficiaries have suffered no past discrimination and do not need any benevolent treatment, but will nevertheless benefit undeservedly: for instance, *most* blacks and women have suffered discrimination in the US and in Europe respectively, but not *all* blacks or women and, in any case, not all of the beneficiaries would need favourable treatment.[4] Under-inclusiveness can occur when members of the historically dominant groups carry the burden of an affirmative action plan without having been engaged in any discriminatory activity in the past but instead having themselves been the victims of social inequalities. A female from a politically strong family will qualify for the reserved seats in a parliament due to an affirmative action plan and will do this over a male who has no social, political or financial means and who should, himself, ideally be the beneficiary of a plan. At the end of the day, the price to be paid for

[3] 'How much "blood" of a given race is enough to justify one's claim that she is of one race? Is "one drop" enough? If the absurd "one drop" rule were applied to "Caucasians", we might agree that since the drops of white blood are very widely spread, we are all whites', Carl Cohen in C Cohen and JP Sterba, *Affirmative action and racial preference. A debate* (Oxford and New York, Oxford University Press, 2003) at 172.

[4] In a random survey in the US it emerged that two thirds of non-white entrepreneurs who benefited from affirmative action plans and were awarded a public contract had net incomes over $1 million each: see T Sowell, *Affirmative action around the world. An empirical study* (New Haven and London, Yale University Press, 2004) at 120.

affirmative action is not left to dominating groups but rather particular members of such groups. A group remedy necessarily suffers from a certain degree of improper classification.

The last statement leads us to the core of the political issue relating to this topic. Affirmative action is, at source, a policy that is intended to redistribute power or wealth. Independently of whether such measures apply in labour, academia or political representation, they converge on one major target: they incline to subvert historical divergences by (institutionally) redrafting the balance amongst normally competing social groups. If this is the essence of affirmative action, it is merely one form of State social policy. What makes the difference between a typical social policy plan and affirmative action is that that the former aims *directly* at redistributing social resources whereas the latter does the same thing but only *indirectly*. From this standpoint, the implementation of social policy entails cost for the State budget, essentially drawn from taxation, whereas affirmative action plans in principle bear no cost since it is not necessary for the State to launch funds to initiate them. However, these plans do have cost, albeit not necessarily in a monetary form. An affirmative action approach to entry to university entails that a *specific* non-benefiting person fails despite his or her better record. The cost for the latter individual is indeed significant: apart from the immediate, mostly psychological, damage there is a potential future loss in professional life. This cost is not borne by the State, not even by a class of people. It burdens a single individual. And, normally, the harmed individual is not amongst the privileged persons of his or her class who would ordinarily have the resources to access academia since they might have had the chance to have better high school education, better access to out-of-school knowledge, and better opportunities to gain additional qualifications. What follows is that affirmative action is in fact a form of social policy, which, unlike other social policies, burdens only individuals. Crudely speaking one might speak of an outsourcing of State obligations with respect to the social State.

The second level of objection against the remedial character of affirmative action is based on psychology. The supporters of affirmative action argue often invoke that the implementation of the policy contributes to the elimination of social stereotypes by softening a de facto relationship of social submission and by strengthening the self-esteem of underrepresented groups. This statement, however, seems to contradict the very essence of the policy which, strictly speaking, presupposes or at least intimates the historical bias that led to inequality. In fact, an affirmative action plan may improve representation statistics but might result in secondary discrimination due to the fact that in the same environment there are individuals who entered through different standards. Consequently, it is not only the stereotypical stigma that might survive for those who have entered under affirmative action, but a correlating bias might also emerge suggesting that the privilege awarded is due to the (inherent) inability of the beneficiaries to be successful in a State of free social competition. Given that the criteria of the beneficiaries of any affirmative action plan, such as the race or the sex, are in principle inherent and immutable, there is a danger of perpetuation of the stigma involved. If a group carries the same idiosyncrasy, which is an implicit presupposition of affirmative action, any stereotype will apply not only to the actual beneficiaries but will be diffused to the totality of group membership. The result is: a) those benefiting from affirmative action continue to suffer from (or start feeling) an institutionally originated inferiority syndrome and b) those not falling in the affirmative action categories continue to have (or start having) a strong bias against those benefiting.

The extent of the psychological stigma may vary depending on the nature of the measure in question. The imposition of rigid quotas might conceivably be very harmful, not only because they constitute a direct, if not oppresive, intervention in social competition, but also because they lack a fundamental characteristic that any remedial action must comprise, namely the impact upon the origins of the pathology. Indeed, quotas do not aspire directly to cure causal roots of discrimination, in which case they might have had an increased level of substantive legitimacy, but their end objective is mainly to redress the balance of participants in social or political arenas. Even if one takes into account that law also performs a pedagogic role in society, still in that view the use of criteria of discrimination, which is otherwise impermissible, produces the opposite effects.

Although not strictly justiciable, the issue of the psychological effect of affirmative action has sometimes been part of judicial reasoning, especially in the case law of the US Supreme Court. In *Brown v Board of Education*, Chief Justice Warren made a very strong statement to the effect that 'to separate them [children in grade and high schools] from others of similar age and qualifications solely because of their race generates a feeling of inferiority as to their status in the community that may affect their hearts and minds in a way unlikely ever to be undone'.[5] By the same token, it was stated in *Richmond v Croson*, that 'classifications based on race carry a danger of stigmatic harm' and 'unless they are strictly reserved for remedial settings, they may in fact promote notions of racial inferiority and lead to a politics of racial hostility'.[6] The greatest case law contribution in relation to the psychological effects of affirmative action came with the landmark decision *Regents of the University of California v Bakke*. The problem set out in this case was whether affirmative action requirements for university entries had any adverse effect upon the new students. The most powerful judicial opinion on the case[7] suggested that the contested plan did not simply advance less qualified applicants but rather compensated applicants who

[5] *Brown v Board of Education*, 347 US 483, 494 (1954).

[6] *Richmond v Croson*, 488 US 469, 493 (1989). The language of 'perpetuation of traditional biases between men and women' has been used by the Spanish Constitutional Court in Tribunal Constitucional no 103/1983, Judgment of 22 November 1983.

[7] *Regents of the University of California v Bakke*, 438 US 265, 357–358 (1978), opinion (in part concurring, in part dissenting) of Justices Brennan, White, Marshall and Blackmun.

were fully qualified to study for educational disadvantages which it was reasonable to conclude were a product of State-fostered discrimination. The fact that, once admitted, these students should satisfy the same degree requirements as regularly admitted students and their performance was evaluated by the same standards by which regularly admitted students were judged, led the justices to conclude that, irrespective of their mode of entry, the performance and degrees of all students should be regarded equally. Thus, there was no reasonable basis for the Court to conclude that affirmative action students would be stigmatised as inferior and it abstained from exercising strict scrutiny, like any other racial differentiation, which could reasonably have resulted in annulment of the plan. In this way *Bakke* introduced the distinction, rather blurred of course in practice, between 'benign' and 'invidious' racial preferences. This jurisprudence was essentially confirmed in the *Michigan Cases* where the majority of the Court took the view that academic diversity serves to mitigate stereotypes because a mixed environment reasonably leads to better understanding amongst the students.[8]

The cultural purpose: diversity

In the US, 'diversity' in the context of affirmative action theory constitutes a technical term implying the legitimate interest in ensuring that, in every segment of human interaction, whether social, political or academic, a critical mass of group representation should exist so that the societal body can become richer and more representative. In this way, members of the underrepresented groups should not be afraid that, when expressing their opinions, they might become victims of a stereotypical treatment and left isolated, as that would certainly jeopardise their future uninterrupted social interaction.

Although diversity in general is closely linked to the formal concept of multiculturalism in its specific legal perception it also embraces the active expression of differentiation through participation.[9] In this view, diversity produces directly or indirectly benevolent results for all participants in the social struggle. Thus, members of the benefiting groups draw direct earnings from their participation in the schemes; members of the non-benefiting groups have indirect positive results because of their exposure to various non-familiar incentives that raise their social awareness and enriches their cultural background; and, finally, society as a whole benefits collectively from the creation of a productive environment of human variety, within which every different group contributes according to their own experience and knowledge.

It is particularly interesting to see the different historical backgrounds to the demand for diversity. In the US, diversity reflects the anxiety to develop a

[8] *Gratz v Bollinger*, 539 US 244 (2003) and *Grutter v Bollinger*, 539 US 306 (2003).

[9] In this meaning diversity is also traceable in constitutions such as the 1996 Constitution of the Republic of South Africa, which declares in its Preamble that 'South Africa belongs to all who live in it, united in our diversity'.

homogenous society through the establishment of actual equality. The fact that diversity is mostly related to race relations is easily explicable given the discrimination institutionally imposed upon minorities. Race in the US has been the axis around which an effort to establish national identity revolves. On the other hand, although in Europe race has not traditionally been a point of acute dispute, due to the rise and dominance of the idea of national State, the co-existence of various nations in the Union renders diversity a *sine qua non* condition to maintain a level of national identity. It is not, therefore, a surprise that, by way of contrast to the US where diversity is a notion shaped by case law, in the European Union (EU) the Treaties make direct reference to this notion stipulating that 'the Community shall contribute to the flowering of the cultures of the Member States while respecting their national and regional diversity and at the same time bringing the common cultural heritage to the fore'.[10] Thus, diversity in Europe reflects the antithesis inherent in a free market transnational union: while each nation struggles to maintain national idiosyncrasy (not an easy task in a very powerful international community that naturally tends to expand the fields of its competence), at the same time societies must become more tolerant towards outside intrusions as free movement of persons within the community otherwise becomes impossible. Unlike in the US where diversity is a cohesion mechanism aimed at melting identities in a single national pot, in Europe it serves the conflicting ideals of national distinction and tolerance.

The diversity doctrine is founded upon two premises: one anthropological, and one sociological. The anthropological premise entails that all members of a group, mostly of an underrepresented one, carry the same idiosyncratic features that will undoubtedly contribute to the body. However, the statement that cultural difference follows race or sex is a notion that is rather vulnerable, if not dangerous.[11] Although long term suppression may indeed bring people of a group together, it does not necessarily imply that the group is homogenous in its constituent elements. The sociological premise presumes, in turn, that the mere participation of all different groups within a body will by itself make it diverse. However, in this way diversity is mostly conceived of as a means formally to bring together various bodies and not as a substantive principle requiring true expression of the various social groups. By assimilating the goal with the means, the doctrine becomes rather circular in its argumentation: instead of the goal legitimising the means, it becomes vice versa. In order for there to be genuine diversity, it is necessary that the members of groups participating in a body, irrespective of how proportionate this representation is, *do* contribute their own experience and social understanding. In other words, the essence of diversity is not accomplished if affirmative action beneficiaries do not themselves carry the

[10] Art 151 para 1 of the Treaties.

[11] According to D Ingram, *Group rights: reconciling equality and difference* (Lawrence, University Press of Kansas, 2000), esp at 42–43, affirmative action presupposes common characteristics or values of a group, which is nevertheless the core of racism.

typical characteristics of their respective groups. It is very often the case, however, that those individuals are either unrepresentative of their group or after their accession to the body they change so as to assimilate with the majority in order to avoid the easy accusation that their success is not to be attributed to their own qualities.[12] From this viewpoint, the goal of essential diversity would be better served if a member of the dominant group, supporting minority rights, was selected instead of a member of the minority group who would nevertheless be biased against his or her own race or sex. This point clearly illustrates the inherent deficiencies of all institutional means that purport to establish substantive equality: they are all formal, for they presuppose the segmentation of society and, within this segmentation, certain generic criteria of distinction are selected which do not actually secure the expression of differentiation.

THE POLICY WORLDWIDE

International law

After World War II, the first international law texts intended to safeguard human rights at a global or regional level, mostly written at the United Nations (UN), imposed an unconditional obligation on States to guarantee equality without any reference to its substantive form.[13]

The first reference to 'special', essentially positive, measures was made in the context of the International Labour Organisation and the Discrimination (Employment and Occupation) Convention, adopted in 1958 and according to which the States, after consultation with representative employers' and workers' organisations, may take special measures designed to meet the particular requirements of persons who, for reasons such as sex, age, disability, family responsibilities or social or cultural status, are generally recognised to require special protection or assistance.[14]

An essential move towards more substantive equality was made by the International Convention on the Elimination of All Forms of Racial Discrimination of the UN, which was signed in 1965 and entered into force four years later. This provides that the States may introduce special measures for the sole purpose of

[12] Beyond any doubt, Justice Clarence Thomas of the US Supreme Court (the second black judge to be appointed in the history of the Court after Justice Thurgood Marshall) provides the most vivid illustration. After having graduated from Yale Law School as an affirmative action entry, he was appointed to the Court by President Bush and became the most pro-active opponent of this policy. It was exactly his views on the matter (as well as matters of ethics attributed to him) that led to a fierce split of the Congress when called to give its consent for his appointment.

[13] See, eg, Recital 4 of the Preamble to, and Art 2 of, the 1948 Universal Declaration of Human Rights. See also international instruments aiming at securing equality of men and women, ie the 1952 Convention on the Political Rights of Women (Art 3), the 1966 International Covenant on Economic, Social and Cultural Rigts (Art 3) and the 1993 Vienna Declaration and Programme of Action (ch I, para 18).

[14] Art 5 para 2 of the convention.

securing adequate advancement of certain racial or ethnic groups or individuals requiring such protection as may be necessary in order to ensure equal enjoyment or exercise of human rights and fundamental freedoms, provided that such measures do not lead to the maintenance of separate rights for different racial groups and that they shall not be continued after the objectives for which they were taken have been achieved.[15]

Furthermore, the International Covenant on Civil and Political Rights, which was signed in 1966 and entered into force 10 years later, provides that the States shall take the necessary steps to adopt such laws or other measures as may be necessary to give effect to the rights recognised in the Covenant, which include equality before the law and non-discrimination of any kind whether on grounds of race, colour, sex, language, religion, political or other opinion, national or social origin, property, birth or other status.[16]

The Convention on the Elimination of All Forms of Discrimination Against Women, signed in 1979 and entered into force in 1981, provides an explicit and detailed reference to the UN Member States' obligation to take positive measures in favour of women. According to it, adoption of temporary special measures aimed at accelerating de facto equality between men and women are not considered discrimination, albeit that shall in no way entail as a consequence the maintenance of unequal or separate standards and shall be discontinued when the objectives of equality of opportunity and treatment have been achieved.[17] In fact, the convention not only elevates positive action to the level of international law, but essentially requires the States to use it in all fields, in particular in the political, social, economic and cultural fields.[18]

In relation to the equality of sexes, the Committee of Ministers of the Council of Europe adopted on 5 February 1985, a Recommendation on Legal Protection against Sex Discrimination, which includes a special section entitled '*special temporary measures (positive action)*'. This provides that, in order to promote equality of sexes, European States should adopt suitable machinery, such as draft legislation and advice for public authorities, guidelines and codes of conduct, encouragement for collective bargaining that promotes equality, action to eliminate and avoid sex discrimination in commercial advertisements, conciliation between parties to a dispute, imposition of sanctions and initiation of legal proceedings where appropriate.[19]

[15] Art 1 para 4 of the convention.

[16] Art 2 para 2 in conjunction with Arts 26 and 2 para 1 of the covenant. Special protection for the equality of men and women is awarded by the covenant in Art 3 stipulating that the parties undertake to ensure the equal right of men and women to the enjoyment of all civil and political rights set forth in the covenant.

[17] Art 4 para 1 of the convention. Para 2 of the same Art provides for the adoption of special state measures aimed at protecting maternity.

[18] Art 3 of the convention.

[19] Recommendation No R (85) 2, Art III.

In this respect, the Framework Convention for the Protection of National Minorities, signed under the auspices of the Council of Europe in Strasbourg in 1995, is worth mentioning. Through this convention, the parties undertake to adopt, where necessary, adequate measures in order to promote, in all areas of economic, social, political and cultural life, full and effective equality between persons belonging to a national minority and those belonging to the majority by taking due account of the specific conditions of the persons belonging to national minorities.[20]

An international law evaluation of positive action would be incomplete if reference was not made to the European Convention on Human Rights signed in Rome on 4 November 1950. In the same way as other regional human rights Treaties, it makes no explicit or implicit reference to positive action as part of the equality principle.[21] Although formal equality is expressly acknowledged in Article 14, according to the European Court on Human Rights the clause can only be invoked in an auxiliary way, namely only in cases where another right recognised by the Treaty has allegedly been violated.[22] Only obiter has the Court implied that when a deviation from formal equality occurs through action of a positive measure, there must be a legitimate aim and the principle of proportionality ought to be respected.[23] On 26 June 2000, the twelfth protocol of the convention was signed by the Committee of Ministers of the Council of Europe representing 25 European States. The specific aim of this protocol was to address the inadequate protection offered by the principle of equality by upgrading it to the status of a right protected per se. The protocol entered into force only five years later, after ratification from 10 contracting States of the Council of Europe, thereby being enforced as of 1 April 2005. Until the end of 2009, the protocol has been ratified by 14 States, whereas 21 States have signed but not ratified it. The protocol makes reference to positive measures in its Preamble according to which the contracting States 'reaffirm' that 'the principle of non-discrimination does not prevent States Parties from taking measures in order to promote full and effective equality, provided that there is an objective and reasonable justification for these measures'. It is noteworthy that there is an issue concerning the language of 'reaffirmation'. In fact, it is not self-evident that the statement refers to any prior statutory or jurisprudential rule. Given that positive measures were treated in the same way as any other deviation from the principle of formal equality, reaffirmation can only imply that they are still to be considered as an exception to

[20] Art 2 para 2 and 3 of the convention.

[21] A formal version of equality is also found in the African Charter on Human and Peoples' Rights, widely known as the *Banjul Charter*, which was adopted on 27 June 1981 and which entered into force on 21 October 1986, despite multiple references to equality in Arts 2, 3, para 2, 13, para 2 and 3, 15, 19, 22, para 1.

[22] See for this issue the principal ECHR Judgment of 23 July 1968, *Belgian Linguistic Case (*No *2),* 1 (1979) EHRR 252.

[23] ECHR Judgment of 24 September 2002, *Posti and Rahko v Finland,* 37 (2003) EHRR 6:158 and Commission Decision on Application no 11089/84, *DG and DW Lindsay v UK* (1986) 49 DR 181.

the non-discrimination clause. This interpretation becomes more convincing if one takes into account the prerequisites of a legitimate positive measure. 'Objective and reasonable justification' constitutes (along with the principle of proportionality, if conceived of as conceptually different from objective and reasonable justification the criterion of any deviation from the principle of equality.[24] In that sense, the Preamble to the protocol really reaffirmed that positive action is *en bloc* tantamount to an exception from the general principle of equality.[25] In any event, the fourteenth protocol does not mandate the contracting States to take positive measures to curtail factual discriminations.[26] Positive action in the domain of equality thus remains at the stage of political declaration and not a clear-cut enforceable right.

Domestic legal orders

Of course, in addition to international law measures, affirmative action has today acquired a worldwide significance. Broadly speaking, this policy has become very widely acknowledged in three types of State: States with a strong tradition on social policies; those that are multicultural; and those that are federal.

Long standing social States tend to employ affirmative action in their broader political agenda of social justice and democracy.[27] On the contrary, States where the social State has traditionally been weak and where market economics and politics predominate are normally suspicious, if not hostile, towards these policies. The latter tendency is rather evident in the UK both on the level of regulation,[28] as well as on the level of case law,[29] where the adherence to formal equality excludes the use of any differentiation criteria. The divergence between 'social' and 'liberal' States in Europe is reflected in the proceeding before the European Court of Justice (ECJ) in the *Marschall* case, in which the question was whether a positive labour measure introduced by a German Länder in favour of

[24] See indicatively ECHR Judgment of 26 February 2002, *Fretté v France*, 38 (2004) EHRR 21: 438, para 34.

[25] See the Explanatory Report on the 12th Protocol drafted by the Steering Committee for Human Rights and adopted by the Committee of Ministers on 26 June 2000 (para 16).

[26] ibid, para 16.

[27] See, eg, in Sweden, Ch 2, Art 16 of the 1974 Constitution. It is noteworthy that States with a long tradition on social rights have not upgraded positive measures to a constitutional level because this would presumably be unnecessary. This is so because the reading of equality in the light of social State arguably provides a more fertile ground for the implementation of positive measures because unlike this latter policy, temporary by nature, the social State is a standing and permanent pursuit.

[28] Although legislation does not typically allow quotas, both the Sex Discrimination Act 1975 and the Race Relations Act 1976 provide for the introduction under certain conditions of indirect positive measures, such as special education, or encouragement to national groups when there is underrepresentation of these groups for more than 12 months, or special measures of social security, see especially ss 49 and 71(1)(b) respectively.

[29] Although not directly referring to positive measures, the most relevant decision of the UK courts is the House of Lords judgment, *James v Eastleigh Borough Council* (1990) 2 AC 751, where the House strictly adhered by the formal version of equality.

women was compatible with the Union law.[30] Finland, Sweden and Norway intervened in favour of upholding the measure, arguing that positive action helps women to gain access to high responsibility posts, previously outside their reach. On the other hand, the governments of France and the UK intervened against the measure on ground that it resulted in unacceptable discrimination.[31]

Furthermore, historically multicultural States, mainly those composed of a great number of different races in Asia and Oceania, less so in Europe, have introduced affirmative action plans in order to minimise or even eliminate the possibility of the dominant race suppressing minorities.[32] This was particularly evident in the case of States, such as the US or South Africa, where racism had an institutional status. Accordingly, these States tried to launch measures that would go beyond tolerance.[33]

A similar situation also occurs in the case of States religiously fragmented, where each community enjoys a higher level of self-administration. This is certainly the case of Northern Ireland, within which the hard task of establishing peace between the religious communities focused on relevant quotas for governmental posts. In fact, Council Directive 2000/78 establishing a general framework for equal treatment in employment and occupation[34] provides a special geographically located clause for the acknowledgment of positive measures in order to safeguard peace and conciliation among the main local communities.[35] Accordingly, positive measures are expressly provided in relation to the police service and in education in order to maintain a religious balance of teachers.[36] These stipulations were largely used in order to secure representative quotas in the region.[37]

[30] ECJ Judgment of 11 November 1997, Case C-409/95, *Hellmut Marschall v Land Nordhein–Westfalen*, Rec 1997, I-6363.

[31] ibid, esp paras 16, 20.

[32] eg in Malaysia and in the Netherlands. In the latter country, the statute for the encouragement of minorities to access labour market ('Wet stimulering arbeidsdeelname minderheden', widely known as Wet Samen), in its original version obliged the employers to introduce work quotas in favour on minority employees through a special archive (later abolished to protect personal data), in which the employees noted the birthplace of their parents and of themselves, see F Goudappel, 'Race equality: The Netherlands' 11/2 (1999) *European Review of Public Law* 881, 894–95.

[33] According to Art 9 para 2 of the 1996 Constitution of the Republic of South Africa: 'Equality includes the full and equal enjoyment of all rights and freedoms. To promote the achievement of equality, legislative and other measures designed to protect or advance persons or categories of persons, disadvantaged by unfair discrimination may be taken.' The case of South Africa is in terms of affirmative action a rather unique case study in the sense that these measures purport to compensate for past discriminations not against the minority but against the majority race.

[34] OJ L 303 of 2 December 2000, at 16.

[35] This teleology stems from Recital 34 of the Preamble of Directive 2000/78.

[36] Art 15 para 1 and 2 respectively of Directive 2000/78.

[37] The basic peace text is that of the Good Friday Agreement signed in Belfast on 10 April 1998 by the British and Irish governments, endorsed by most Northern Ireland political parties and by the voters of the region in a referendum on 23 May 1998. Particular legislative measures provide for quotas for the religious communities, eg, the Police (Northern Ireland) Act 2000, s 46, providing that entries to the body will include 50% Catholics and 50% non-Catholics, and arts 55 and 56 of the Fair

Federal States are very often composed of diverse communities in terms of their national origin, language or religion.[38] A vivid illustration is that of Nigeria, a State created rather artificially at the end of the British colonial era and composed of a very extensive, and potentially explosive, mixture of religions, classes, races, languages and traditions. Not surprisingly, the newly emerged State was composed as a federal State and a wide range of affirmative action plans was introduced to serve the task of social simulation and, in turn, of synthetic national identity.[39] India was essentially built on the same premise. A country with the largest number of races in the world, and with more than 100 spoken languages, came out of British colonisation and become a sovereign State in 1947. Even before that landmark year, positive measures applied to the representation of various races, especially the 'untouchables'. In fact, the implementation of such measures went far beyond their original ratio of race participation and also embraces, today, political participation of women since, according to the national constitution, one third of the elected posts in the local government councils are occupied by women of certain origins, ie rigid quotas.[40] It has been historically indicated that coming out of a colonial domination is a fertile ground in order to apply positive measures, because normally the new States lack social cohesion and suffer from political segregation and the apathy of certain social groups due to the long abstention from the active exercise of political rights. In such a case the goal of affirmative action plans is to raise public awareness in relation to a large scale political participation.

Amongst the federal States in Europe, the 1994 Belgian Constitution also provides for positive measures for a balanced representation of the ethnic communities clearly facilitated by the federal structure of the State. Thus, according to a constitutional prescription that the Cabinet (composed of a maximum of 15 members) should include an equal number of French and Dutch speaking ministers, except—reasonably—for the Prime Minister, there must be wide representation of the Communities at the Senate.[41] The addition of a new constitutional prescription institutionally facilitates the access of Belgian citizens to public posts. This clause not only requires the legislature to enact measures to reach this goal but constitutes a direct set of positive measures. Thus, both sexes

Employment and Treatment [Northern Ireland] Order 1998 using the term rather uncommon in the EU, 'affirmative action' to entail reasonable and appropriate measures to secure fair participation in employment.

[38] See, eg, in Canada (Art 15(2) of the 1982 Charter of Rights and Freedoms). The most analytical approach to affirmative action, both conceptually and technically, is made in the Quebec Charter of Human Rights and Freedoms.

[39] The same is also true for the 1999 Constitution of the Federal Republic of Nigeria (Art 14 para 3) The constitutional encouragement, however, did not produce spectacular results given the huge national divisions. An analogous, albeit based on different historical incidents, situation in Europe is that of the creation of post-war Yugoslavia, where, however, positive measures were unknown due to the imposition of an authoritarian regime.

[40] Arts 243D and 243T.

[41] Arts 99 and 67 respectively.

ought to be represented in the Cabinet and the governments of the three State communities and the districts, as well as in principle in the permanent delegations of the regional councils, the mayoral colleges, the committees and the standing social welfare offices and the administrations of other intra-community organs.[42]

Apart from multicultural and federal States that normally introduce racial positive measures, a great number of legal orders, especially in Europe, have in the last two decades placed emphasis on this policy in favour of women and have occasionally upgraded their status to a constitutional level. In France, after the 1999 constitutional amendment, there is a clear mandate to the legislature to encourage equal access of men and women to political functions.[43] Accordingly, a statute provides that parties' candidate lists should include women, otherwise State subsidy is curtailed in proportion to the extent of the violation.[44]

In Germany, the original wording of Article 3, paragraph 2 of the Constitution, according to which men and women had equal rights, was amended in 1994 and a new clause was added according to which 'the state shall promote the actual implementation of equal rights for men and women and take steps to eliminate disadvantages that now exist'. Although the new provision does not embrace positive measures *eo nomine*, it entails that there is an interpretation of the clause to that effect. Unlike federal legislation that has not, as yet, extensively use this tool, the Länder have largely introduced positive measures in their respective labour legislation.

The constitutional acknowledgment of affirmative action policy also follows as a matter of interpretation from the constitutions of Italy,[45] Spain[46] and Portugal,[47] which all use similar language in this domain. Accordingly, the States have

[42] Art 11b of the Belgian Constitution.

[43] Arts 3 and 4 of the 1958 French Constitution respectively.

[44] The statute demands separate women candidate lists for the election for the European Parliament and for some of the seats of the Senate determined on the basis of proportionate representation, equal participation of men and women (in sections of every six candidates) for the municipal elections and marginal deviation up to 2% for the lists for the national elections.

[45] Art 51 para 1 of the Constitution was revised by Constitutional Law 1/2003 and a new clause was added: 'Citizens of one or the other sex are eligible for public office and for elective positions under equal conditions, according to the rules established by law. To this end, the republic adopts specific measures ("appositi provvedimenti") in order to promote equal chances for men and women'. Furthermore, Art 117 para 2 provides that 'regional laws have to remove all obstacles which prevent the full equality of men and women in social, cultural, and economic life, and promote equal access of men and women to elective offices'.

[46] According to Art 9 para 2 of the 1978 Spanish Constitution, 'it is the responsibility of the public authorities to promote conditions ensuring that freedom and equality of individuals and of the groups to which they belong are real and effective, to remove the obstacles preventing or hindering their full enjoyment, and to facilitate the participation of all citizens in political, economic, cultural and social life'. On this legal ground the Spanish Constitutional Court upheld the constitutionality of positive measures in favour of women with small children (Tribunal Constitucional no 128/1987, Judgment of 16 July 1987).

[47] The Portuguese Constitution makes no explicit reference to positive measures although it is the most detailed among the European constitutions and has been revised seven times since its introduction in 1976. The general equality clause reads 'no one is privileged, favored, injured,

the obligation to remove all obstacles in order to achieve equality and facilitate the participation of everyone in all aspects of human activities.[48] The friendliest attitude towards positive measures on a constitutional level is traced in the new clause of Article 116, paragraph 2 of the 1975 Greek Constitution, after its revision in 2001. The new stipulation introduces both a principle of interpretation, according to which adoption of positive measures for promoting equality between men and women does not constitute discrimination on the basis of sex, and a constitutional mandate to the legislature according to which the State shall attend to the elimination of inequalities actually existing, especially to the detriment of women. Following the new constitutional clause, two statutes enforcing the participation of women in the electoral process were introduced requiring that at least one third of all parties' candidate lists should be composed of members of each sex both for local government authorities (for each candidate list) and national parliament elections (for the total number of candidates of each party).[49] After the 2002 elections for municipal and prefect authorities, the Council of State upheld the constitutionality of the legislative quota.[50]

There is one last comment that should be made about the dialogue that has been developed between the constitutional legislator and the judiciary in each legal order. While in Germany,[51] Italy[52] and Greece[53] the constitutional upgrade of positive measures merely confirmed the position on substantive equality that had pre-existed in the case law, the constitutional amendment was necessary in

deprived of any right, or exempt from any duty because of his ancestry, sex, race, language, territory of origin, religion, political or ideological convictions, education, economic situation, social condition or sexual orientation' (Art 13 para 2).

[48] See, too, the 1999 Swiss Constitution, which effectively acknowledges positive measures by stipulating in Art 8 para 3 that: 'Men and women have equal rights. Legislation shall ensure equality in law and *in fact,* particularly in family, education and work…' (emphasis added).

[49] Art 75 para 1 of Law 2910/2001 (later confirmed by Art 34 para 3 of Law 3463/2006) and Art 3 of Law No 3636/2008 respectively.

[50] Judgments of the Council of State (3rd Section) 2831–3/2003, 3027–8/2003, IN 3185–9/2003, 192/2004, 2388/2004 and 3353/2004.

[51] In the principal decision, *BVerfGE* 74, 163 (1987), the Constitutional Court held that the different treatment of men and women in social security was in conformity with the Basic Law on grounds of the social State and legitimately aimed at balancing biological variations and compensating for past discrimination. In the context of the law prohibiting women's night work the Court used for the first time the language of positive measures.

[52] Even before the constitutional upgrade of positive measures, the Constitutional Court had already demonstrated a favourable attitude towards this policy when interpreting Art 3 para 2 of the Constitution ('it is the duty of the republic to remove all economic and social obstacles that, by limiting the freedom and equality of citizens, prevent full individual development and the participation of all workers in the political, economic, and social organisation of the country') first in its judgment of 3rd June 1987 215/1987 and eventually in judgment 109/1993 of 24 March 1993 when it ruled that 'positive action constitutes the main tool of the legislator to perform the duty prescribed in Art 3 para 2'.

[53] Judgment 1933/1998 of the plenary of the Council of State.

France to overcome the obstacles raised by the Constitutional Council which had ruled that such measures were, in the absence of an explicit constitutional clause to that effect, unconstitutional.[54]

The case of the US

There is a major difference in the cultural background of the French Revolution and the American war of independence. In the former case, the revolution was doctrinally strengthened by the spiritual current of the enlightenment suggesting formal equality as a means to trespass the ancient regime and curb the unlimited powers of the monarchy. In the latter case, the war only targeted the nation's independence without any regard to the issue of equality of people; as a matter of fact, at that time, the most brutal violation of equality and human dignity existed in the form of recognised slavery. The new State had to wait for about a century, until the end of the civil war, in order constitutionally to embrace equality through the enactment in 1868 of the Fourteenth Amendment and the Equal Protection Clause. In spite of the explicit recognition of the principle and the formal abolition of slavery, in reality the constitutional declaration was merely a façade. Until the mid-1950s racial discrimination was imposed through segregation meaning that certain places of human interaction were isolated from racial mixing. Accordingly, in most southern and central states, there were either distinct installations of public services (eg schools, hospitals) or distinct areas within the same installations (eg sanity places, restaurants, leisure places and mass transportation means). In both cases the treatment of racial minorities was degrading; schools for whites were of much higher quality in relation to infrastructure and the personnel employed, while in the buses the front seats were reserved only for whites. Blacks were not allowed to use these seats even if they were on occasions vacant.

In this context, the Supreme Court, in 1883, found the Civil Rights Act 1875, permitting access for blacks to hotels, restaurants, trains, theatres and other premises unconstitutional on the ground that the delegation of the Fourteenth Amendment to the Congress did not allow for positive State intervention to combat existing discriminations. This decision unequivocally established racial segregation.[55]

[54] Conseil Constitutionnel décision no 82–146 du 18 novembre 1982, *Quotas par sexe,* Rec 66, (1983) AJDA 128, RJC, I-134, Journal officiel du 19 novembre 1982, 3475. The Council held that the mandatory quota of 25% participation for both sexes for the municipal election was incompatible with the constitutional right of equality as set out in Art 3 of the Constitution and Art 6 of the Declaration of Rights of Man and Citizen.

[55] *Civil Rights Cases,* 109 US 3 (1883). A basic argument used by Justice Bradley to declare the incompatibility of the legislation to the Constitution was that entrepreneurs could not be deprived of their right to select their own clients on the ground of non-discrimination since this clause was not applicable in the sphere of private relations.

By the same token, the Supreme Court with a large 8–1 majority launched in 1896 with *Plessy v Ferguson*[56] the doctrine of 'separate but equal', which haunted social cohesion in the US for more than half a century. According to this doctrine, equality did not necessarily suggest that all racial groups were the same but their differences might be reflected in all aspects of social activities so that it would be permissible to isolate them by maintaining separate places. Thus, the Court held that a Louisiana statute providing for distinct train wagons for blacks and whites was in conformity with the Federal Constitution.

During World War II, privileged treatment for whites acquired a new perspective mainly towards Americans with Asian, especially Japanese, origin. The well-known *Korematsu case*,[57] legitimised the institutional isolation of these individuals but left an indication for future change in judicial attitude by establishing the rule that any restriction towards the principle of racial equality was automatically considered as a suspect classification, which essentially introduced a much higher judicial threshold in these cases, namely the strict scrutiny test; indeed, *Korematsu* remains to this day one of the very few cases where this standard has been successfully met by the government.

Explicit recognition of racial equality came in 1954 with the Supreme Court decision of *Brown v Board of Education*.[58] In this case the Court ruled that racial segregation was contrary to the Fourteenth Amendment to the extent that it was 'inherently unequal' for the minorities. The almost metaphysical declaration of 'self evident' equality, which was supported by arguments of the mentality of the US people and culture, did not have an immediate effect. Restoration of full racial equality should according to the judgment occur 'with all deliberate speed'. Through this obiter statement, the Court tried to absorb the estimated social and state reaction, which indeed followed.[59] At any rate, this landmark decision, in conjunction with the human rights movement at the time, strengthened the demand for the elimination of all forms of racial discrimination.

A symbolic heyday of the human rights movement came with the march to the capital city and the historical speech of Martin Luther King Jr, on 28 August 1963, pleading for work and freedom in his seminal 'I have a dream' speech. Of course, the social pressure for wide human rights recognition found a fertile ground in economic growth and the prevailing political ideology of that era. Essentially, the policy of incorporating racial minorities into industry in a broader sense—education, labour market, entrepreneurial activities—was part of a larger scale

[56] 163 US 537 (1896).

[57] *Korematsu v United States*, 323 US 214 (1944).

[58] 347 US 483 (1954).

[59] States supporting segregation suffered from wide riots known as 'massive resistance'. In traditionally segregated Arkansaw, the Governor, wishing to express his opposition to the Supreme Court ruling, came into conflict with the federal police when he tried to prohibit black pupils from entering schools reserved for whites.

scheme to improve an already thriving economy. This is why social tensions that were bound to happen with the introduction of measures in favour of the black community were partially absorbed.

Although some aspects of positive State intervention in favour of under-represented races were intimated in an Executive Order during World War II, through which President Roosevelt allowed African Americans to access the labour market in the field of defence and mandated that public contractors abstain from any discriminatory practice,[60] the actual implementation of the policy began in the 1960s. Indeed, two months after his inauguration in 1961, President Kennedy issued an Executive Order to introduce the Committee on Equal Employment Opportunity.[61] It is exactly this Order that used for the first time the language of *affirmative action* as a means to prevent racial discrimination on the ground of race, beliefs, colour or national origins. A more solid policy was, however, introduced through Executive Orders of President Johnson that obliged public contractors to take affirmative action measures in hiring blacks and women.[62] A further boost was given when President Nixon introduced the 'Philadelphia Plan', a financial project aimed at producing a fairer racial balance in the construction market in the long run.[63]

The judicial reaction to the Civil Rights Act 1964 and the Executive Orders in favour of affirmative action was positive. The Supreme Court not only consolidated the *Brown* case law by upholding the legitimate aim to achieve substantive equality,[64] but on occasions did not hesitate to demand the State introduction of such measures.[65] The new judicial authority on affirmative action came in 1978 with the leading decision of *Bakke*. The majority of the members of the Supreme Court held that the admission policy of the University of California reserving places for minority candidates was against the principle of equality because it did not entail assessment of non-minority candidates for all university entries.

After 30 years of case law fluctuation and ambivalence, the Supreme Court revisited its doctrine on affirmative action in cases concerning the entry of new students to the University of Michigan. On 23 June 2003, the Supreme Court rendered two much belated decisions on the issue, known as the *Michigan Cases*. Although the cases had different outcomes, their composite reading is necessary to trace what is acceptable according to the jurisprudence and what is not. In fact, two different affirmative action plans introduced by the University of Michigan at different times in order to facilitate admission to the university for minority candidates were challenged. In *Gratz v Bollinger*, a 'strict' admission policy was

[60] Executive Order 8802 of 25 June 1941. The same Order launched the significant Fair Employment Practices Committee.

[61] Executive Order 10925 of 6 March 1961.

[62] Executive Order 11246 of 24 September 1965 and amending Executive Order 11375 of 13 October 1967 respectively.

[63] Office of Federal Office Compliance (OFCC) Revised Order No 4.

[64] *Loving v Virginia*, 388 US 1 (1967).

[65] *Green v County School Board of New Kent County*, 391 US 430 (1968).

challenged according to which a number of variables had to be be taken into account for deciding admission (these included high school grades, entry test results, quality of graduating high school, curriculum vitae, the geography of the origins of applications, the relations of candidates with university alumni, leading capacities and race). For candidates falling within these criteria, the university added a bonus of 20 points out of a total possible maximum of 150 points. This practice essentially meant that all average candidates of the benefiting categories would be admitted since 100 points would normally suffice in order for a candidate to be admitted. The 'flexible' university admission policy, which was challenged in *Grutter v Bollinger*, suggested that candidates should be admitted on the basis of an evaluation of their academic qualifications in conjunction with a flexible judgement of their talents, experience and potential, as revealed through their dossier (especially their statement as to why they wished to pursue particular areas of study), their recommendation letters, a statement on what they perceived their contribution to academic life would be, their high school grades, their entry test results, as well as a series of 'soft variables' such as the enthusiasm of those providing recommendations, the quality of their high school and the difficulty of graduating from the particular high school. Throughout the period that the two admission policies applied, the university considered African-Americans, Hispanics and Native Americans as 'underrepresented' races.

The legal proceedings were initiated in 1997 when two white males filed an application with the Michigan federal courts against the rejection of their applications to the university. The university did not admit the candidates although admittedly one of them was deemed 'well qualified' and the other 'within the qualified range'. On the grounds of the Fourteenth Amendment and the legislation implementing this clause, the applicants claimed compensation for damages, recognition that their rights to non-discrimination had been violated, and the issuance of injunctions requiring the university to abstain from future discriminatory practices and to offer the applicants a university place that would allow them to be transferred from other universities in which they had already enrolled.

The Court discussed the cases on 1 April 2003. In *Gratz v Bollinger* the Court found in favour of the applicant and struck down the strict admission policy. The six judges' majority opinion, written by Chief Justice Rehnquist himself, applied the strict scrutiny test and accepted that securing diversity within an academic environment constituted a compelling public interest and therefore 'some' measures could be taken in favour of this goal. However, the Court held that the particular policy was not 'narrowly tailored' to achieve the legitimate aim of diversity. Building upon the *Bakke* case law, the Court held that although it is permissible for a university to adopt an admission policy that takes into account the national or racial origin of a candidate as a '"plus" factor', this policy should not prevent an individualised assessment of the candidates qualifications, ie their capacity to contribute to the academic environment. Accordingly, while the Court accepted that assessment of each candidate might entail administrative difficulties (an argument invoked by the university during the judicial proceedings), it rejected the system of automatic addition of points for minority candidates. Thus, the Court essentially declared that race might be one of the considerations of the admission policy but could not go as far as to set up a 'racial point-system' that would clearly violate the Constitution and the law. On the contrary, the Court upheld the constitutionality of the flexible admission policy with a narrow 5–4 majority in *Grutter v Bollinger* by placing emphasis on the fact that the policy in question did not award direct benefits to candidates but merely set out the criteria of assessment, thus allowing for an overall evaluation of all candidates. The Court found that the flexible admission policy was not drafted in generic terms but was narrowly tailored to serve the compelling public interest of diversity in the academia.

The *Michigan University* decisions received a very enthusiastic welcome both from the supporters and the opponents of affirmative action. This paradox clearly reflected the Solomon approach of the Supreme Court towards the policy. Thus, it declared that racial affirmative action narrowly tailored to serve the compelling public interest of diversity was constitutional as a means of encouraging minority participation but rejected measures entailing quotas or reserved seats or automatic preferences or measures of equivalent effect ('indirect' quotas). However, the precise nature of this distinction remains unclear. This is because, on the one hand, there is still a range of unacceptable measures which, nevertheless, do not entail rigid or effectively rigid quotas and, on the other hand, because there can be no clear-cut definition of what constitutes a (direct or indirect) quota. In a sense the Court specified only what measures are considered clearly unconstitutional and left the issue of the constitutionality of the remaining measures to be decided on an ad hoc basis.

Even after *Grutter* and *Gratz*, the case law still remains unstable. Justice Scalia in his dissenting opinion predicted that these decisions would not put an end to social anxiety and judicial dispute due to the adverse reading of the equality clause and the fluid criteria employed. Only three years later, on 7 November 2006, the majority of the people of Michigan approved with a 58 per cent majority a ballot initiative (the 'Michigan Civil Rights Initiative') introducing an amendment to the State Constitution to the effect that any affirmative action awarding privileges to groups or individuals on the grounds of race, sex, colour, national origin in the fields of labour, education or public procurement should be prohibited. This prohibition entered into force on 22 December 2006. The constitutional amendment was challenged before the federal courts by a great number of non-governmental organisations (NGOs) and individuals. The Court of Appeal decided on 29 December 2006, that there was no violation of the Federal Constitution and rejected the application.[66] The plaintiffs then appealed

[66] *Coalition to Defend Affirmative Action et als v Jennifer Granholm, Governor of Michigan*, App no 06–2640 (6th Cir 2006).

to the Supreme Court for interim relief that was rejected on 19 January 2007 on the opinion of Justice Stevens.[67] On 21 March 2008 Judge David M Lawson of the District Court for the Eastern District of Michigan finally dismissed the case.[68]

On 28 June 2007, the Supreme Court decided the case *Parents Involved in Community Schools v Seattle School District No 1 et al.*[69] Here, the respondent school districts had voluntarily adopted student assignment plans that relied on race (white or non-white) to determine which schools certain children may attend (the petitioners contended that allocating children to different public schools based solely on their race violated the Fourteenth Amendment). All state courts found that that the school district had asserted a compelling interest in maintaining racially diverse schools, and that its plan was, in all relevant respects, narrowly tailored to serve that interest. However, the Supreme Court reversed the lower courts in a 5–4 decision, holding that the School Boards did not present any 'compelling state interest' that would justify the assignment of school seats on the basis of race.

The latest Supreme Court decision of affirmative action interest is *Ricci v DeStefano* decided on 29 June 2009.[70] The applicant city firefighters alleged race discrimination due to the state of New Haven's decision to disregard written promotion tests because of a disparate impact on minorities caused by the fact that none of the black candidates had managed to score high enough to be considered for the positions and that there was therefore a risk of law suits by the rejected minority candidates. The Court held with a 5–4 majority that New Haven's decision to ignore the test results violated Title VII of the Civil Rights Act 1964. The decision is of major importance for racial discrimination in general in that it raises again the issue of strict scrutiny and suspect classification that is almost unbearable for the administration to support. On the facts of the case, the state failed to produce evidence to uphold the constitutionality of the measure.

Generally speaking, it seems that there is a tendency to overestimate the position of affirmative action within the American legal system. The truth is, however, that neither the State organs nor society more generally have been unanimously in favour of these measures. Most of the relevant federal or State laws either set out the general principle of equality, in which case a formal reading would result in the negation of affirmative action, or apply in very particular segments of social interaction and cannot have spill-over effect. By the same token, the judiciary has not been altogether in favour of the constitutionality of the policy. The more or less explicit judicial premise is that the prevailing notion of equality is that of equality of chances, not of end results; accordingly, measures introducing inflexible quotas are not acceptable by the Court. In all

[67] App no 06A678.
[68] Case no 06–15024.
[69] 551 US 701 (2007).
[70] No 07–1428.

other cases, although affirmative action has in principle been declared constitutional, each particular plan, especially those using race as a criterion of differentiation, is subject to a thorough ad hoc judicial review of a rather pragmatic nature, which implies a test as to whether the measure in question is drafted in a way that serves a compelling public interest.

The case of EU law

The non-discrimination principle has a significant status within EU law as a rudimentary condition for the smooth operation of the economic transnational union whose main goal historically has been the creation of an internal market. In fact, although equality may present a social perspective in the sense that it broadly determines the model of social interaction, its concrete aspects, such as equality of market access, equality of labour conditions and equality of pay, also have economic implications and, therefore, clearly fall within the ambit of EU law. From an institutional point of view, the recognition of positive action as part of the boarder non-discrimination principle followed a different path in relation to the hierarchy of norms of EU law. It was first acknowledged at the level of secondary law, then became part of the revised Treaties and was, eventually, incorporated in the draft Constitutional Treaty.

In relation to non-discrimination on grounds of sex, the first measure of secondary Community law was Council Directive 76/207 of 9 February 1976 on the implementation of the principle of equal treatment for men and women regarding access to employment, vocational training and promotion, and working conditions, applying both to public and private labour relations. According to Article 2, paragraph 4 of the directive, its implementation 'shall be without prejudice to measures to promote equal opportunity for men and women, in particular by removing existing inequalities which affect women's opportunities'. Directive 76/07 was later amended by Directive 2002/73 of the European Parliament and of the Council of 23 September 2002, which in relation to the application of affirmative action makes reference to Treaty of Amsterdam, which had been entered into force in the meantime.[71] The most explicit reference to positive measures was made in Council Recommendation 84/635 of 13 December 1984. Thus, the Council recommends that Member States adopt a positive action policy designed to eliminate existing inequalities affecting women in working life and to promote a better balance between the sexes in employment, comprising appropriate general and specific measures, within the framework of national policies and practices. The purposes of those measures should be to eliminate or counteract the prejudicial effects on women in employment or seeking employment which arise from existing attitudes, behaviour and structures based on the idea of a traditional division of roles in society between men

[71] OJ L 269 of 5 October 2002, 15, Recital 15 of the Preamble.

and women and to encourage the participation of women in various occupations in those sectors of working life where they are at present underrepresented, particularly in new employment sectors of the future, and at higher levels of responsibility in order to achieve better use of all human resources.

In relation to non-discrimination on other grounds apart from sex, positive measure clauses are also included in Council Directive 2000/43 of 29 June 2000 implementing the principle of equal treatment between persons irrespective of racial or ethnic origin,[72] in Council Directive 2000/78 of 27 November 2000 preventing discrimination on grounds of religion or belief, disability, age or sexual orientation,[73] in Council Recommendation 86/379 of 24 July 1986 on the employment of disabled people[74] and in Council Resolution of 17 June 1999 on equal employment opportunities for people with disabilities.[75]

At the level of the Community Treaties, positive action was acknowledged through the Agreement on Social Policy annexed to the Protocol on Social Policy of the Treaty on European Union through Protocol 14, which confirmed that the equal pay principle does not prevent Member States from introducing measures awarding benefits to women to prevent or compensate disadvantages in their professional careers.[76] The Treaty of Amsterdam upgraded positive action policy through the introduction of a new paragraph 4 in Article 141 (former 119) according to which Member States may maintain or adopt measures providing for specific advantages in order to make it easier for the underrepresented sex to pursue a vocational activity or to prevent or compensate for disadvantages in professional careers.[77]

Two particular aspects of the new provision are worth noting. First, there is no mention of the beneficiaries of the positive measures but merely a reference to the 'underrepresented sex'. Accordingly, even men could be the subjects of positive action provided that they are underrepresented within a particular labour environment; it seems that no other criterion apart from sex, such as race or religion, can be an acceptable ground for the application of the clause. Second, the goals for the introduction of positive measures are clearly set out and delineated, namely help to pursue a vocational activity, prevention of disadvantages and compensation for disadvantages in professional careers. Strictly speaking, however, only help to pursue a profession or compensation for past discrimination is causally linked to the implementation of a positive action plan. Due to the inherent fluidity of the criterion 'prevention' cannot be a strictly legal

[72] EE L 180 of 19 July 2000, 22, Arts 5 and 14.

[73] EE L 303 of 2 December 2000, 16, Art 7.

[74] EE L 225 of 12 *August* 1986, 43. The Recommendation envisages in Art 2(b) a series of positive measures that the Member States should introduce in their respective legal orders.

[75] EE C 186 of 2 July 1999, 3.

[76] EE C 191 of 29 July 1992, 91. Art 6 para 3 of the Agreement.

[77] Official Journal C 321 E of 29 December 2006, 110. The Treaty of Amsterdam generally adopted the concept of substantive equality by providing in its general principles that the Community shall have as its task equality between men and women and prevention of discrimination (Art 2).

ratio that might justify the introduction of a measure in favour of substantive equality, quite apart from the fact that it does not come within the terms of the general remedial purpose of positive action as recognised by the ECJ.

Finally, at the level of 'constitutional' EU law, equality constituted a special seven-article chapter (III) of the Charter of Fundamental Rights. According to Article 43 of the Charter, the principle of equality shall not prevent the maintenance or adoption of measures providing for specific advantages in favour of the underrepresented sex. The Treaty establishing a Constitution for Europe enhanced the Charter and further made reference to positive action in the section concerning the policies and functioning of the Union by providing that a European law or a framework law shall establish measures to ensure the application of the principle of equal opportunities and equal treatment of women and men in matters of employment and occupation, including the principle of equal pay for equal work or work of equal value.[78] The Treaty also reaffirmed the EU's adherence to positive action with a view to ensuring full equality in practice between women and men in working life in the same line with the Treaty of Amsterdam.[79] Eventually, on 1 December 2009, the Treaty of Lisbon entered into force, upgrading the Charter of Fundamental Rights on the level of European primary law through an amendment of Article 6, paragraph 1 of the Treaty on European Union.[80]

As regards the community jurisprudence on the issue, even before the explicit recognition of positive action, there were judicial voices arguing in favour of this policy as part of the overall structure of equality.[81] In *Commission v France*, the ECJ placed emphasis upon the goal of equality of chances as the prevailing notion of equality.[82] In the cases of *Kalanke, Marschall and Badeck*, the Court held that a measure aiming at facilitating women's path to work in labour areas that are male dominated is in principle compatible with EU law provided that the law does not establish a direct and unreserved priority to women.[83] In *Abrahamsson and Anderson*, the ECJ held that a selection procedure can include some

[78] Art III-214 para 3 of the Treaty.

[79] Art III-214 para 4 of the Treaty.

[80] According to the protocol on the Application of the Charter to Poland and to the UK, national and EU courts do not have the ability to find that national provisions of the two countries are inconsistent with the rights and freedoms of the Charter, whereas these rights and freedoms only apply to these countries insofar as they are recognised by domestic law.

[81] Advocate General Darmon in ECJ Judgment of 12 July 1984, Case 184/83, *Ulrich Hofmann v Barmer Ersatzkasse*, Rec 1984, 3047, para 9.

[82] ECJ Judgment of 25 October 1988, Case C-312/86, *Commission v France*, Rec 1988, 6315.

[83] ECJ Judgment of 17 October 1995, Case C-450/93, *Eckhard Kalanke v Freie Hansestadt Bremen*, Rec 1995, I-3051; *Hellmut Marschall*, n 30 above, I-6363; ECJ Judgment of 28 March 2000, Case C-158/97, *Georg Badeck et als*, Rec 2000, I-1875.

priority clauses in favour of women as long as their implementation is transparent and any arbitrary assessment is prohibited.[84] By the same token, the European Free Trade Area Court in decision *Surveillance Authority v Norway*, rejected a measure according to which permanent or temporary academic posts were reserved for women on the ground that there was no flexibility in the system which automatically excluded men from these very posts.[85] On the same ground, the ECJ held in *Griesmar* that the stipulation of the French civil and military pension's retirement scheme excluding men from a service credit for children, even in a case where a man could prove that he was responsible for the care of his children, was contrary to EU law.[86] In the same way, it was decided in *Briheche* that provisions reserving for widows who had not remarried the benefit of the exemption from the age-limit for obtaining access to public sector employment was contrary to EU law because it treated differently men who were in the same factual situation with women of the same status.[87] In *Lommers* the Court upheld a Dutch measure according to which there were places in nurseries reserved only for children of female officials, save in cases of emergency to be decided by the employer, on the ground that there were no labour places reservations but merely the establishment of better working conditions for working mothers. The measure was deemed suitable to advance equality of opportunity in the sense that it prevented women from resignation due to a potential inability to accommodate both professional and family tasks.[88] Finally, in the recent judgment of *Commission v Greece*, the ECJ held that different pension ages based on gender and length of service violated the principle of equal treatment, since they were not of a nature to offset the actual disadvantages of women's careers in work.[89]

In the above cases the ECJ intimated that EU law merely acknowledged the prevalence of the doctrine of equality of opportunity and not of equality of end-results. This resulted in upholding the exceptional nature of positive measures that in turn meant that there should be a narrow interpretation of the clauses enabling the introduction of such plans.[90] Thus, in *Kalanke*, the scheme

[84] ECJ Judgment of 6 July 2000, Case C-407/98, *Katarina Abrahamsson and Leif Anderson v Elisabet Fogelqvist*, Rec 2000, I-5539.

[85] EFTA Court Decision of 24 January 2003, Case E-1/02, *EFTA Surveillance Authority v* Νορβηγίας, EFTA Court Report 2003, 1.

[86] ECJ Judgment of 29 November 2001, Case C-366/99, *Joseph Griesmar v Ministre de l'Economie, des Finances et de l'Industrie et al*, Rec 2001, I-9383.

[87] ECJ Judgment of 30 September 2004, Case C-319/03, *Serge Briheche v Ministre de l'Intérieur, Ministre de l'Éducation nationale and Ministre de la Justice* [2004] ECR I-8807.

[88] ECJ Judgment of 19 March 2002, Case C-476/99, *Lommers v Minister van Landbouw, Natuurbeheer en Visserij* [2002] ECR I-2891

[89] ECJ Judgment of 26 March 2009, Case C-559/07, *Commission v Greece*, www.curia. europa.eu/ jurisp/cgi-bin/form.pl?lang=EN&Submit=rechercher&numaff=C-559/07 (last accessed on 30 December 2009).

[90] See ECJ Judgment of 15 May 1986, Case C-222/84, *Johnston v Chief Constable of the Royal Ulster Constabulary*, Rec 1986, 1651, para 36; ECJ Judgment of 26 October 1999, Case C-273/97, *Angela Maria Sirdar v The Army Board and Secretary of State for Defence*, Rec 1999, I-7403, para 23.

providing an unreserved priority of women against men of the same qualifications for access to public service was considered as violating EU law. This judgment attracted much criticism mainly on the ground that it failed to tackle the contemporary call for more substantive equality. This reaction came to the attention of the European Commission which issued a Communication addressed to the Council and the Parliament essentially delineating the ratio decidenti of the Court by 'clarifying its interpretation of the judgment'.[91] According to the Communication, the only form of positive action condemned by the Court is the rigid quota system; there are still, however, many forms of positive action which are not affected by the judgment in question and Member States and employers may avail themselves of a wide range of positive measures such as State subsidies granted to employers, positive training-oriented action, vocational guidance, child care and flexible quotas. A few months later, the Commission 'in the light of the case-law ... Kalanke' issued a proposal for a Council Directive, amending Directive 76/207, to the effect that measures to promote equal opportunity for men and women, in particular by removing existing inequalities which affect the opportunities of the underrepresented sex, such as giving preferential access to employment or promotion, are tolerated, provided that they do not preclude the assessment of the particular circumstances of an individual case.[92] The European Parliament rejected the proposal as inadequate in the course of the consultation procedure and asked the Commission to submit a new proposal.[93]

Two years after *Kalanke*, the ECJ had the oppportunity to revisit its positive action doctrine in *Marschall*.[94] The pressure on this case was immense not only because of the delicate issue involved but also because of the participation of a significant number of Member States and of the Commission itself, which intervened in favour of upholding the compatibility of the positive measure in question. The facts of the case were identical to *Kalanke* save for the point that the crucial statute provided a saving clause from the priority of women over men with the same qualification. Accordingly, the Law on Civil Servants of the German Land Nordrhein-Westfalen provided that where, in the sector of the authority responsible for promotion, there were fewer women than men in the particular higher grade post in the career bracket, women were to be given priority for promotion in the event of equal suitability, competence and professional performance, 'unless reasons specific to an individual [male] candidate tilt the balance in his favour'. This saving clause constituted the ground for upholding the statute. According to the judgment, 'unlike the rules at issue in *Kalanke*, a national rule which ... contains a saving clause does not exceed those limits if, in

[91] COM 96/88 of 27 March 1996. The Communication cited an indicative list of measures that might be accepted and suggested an amendment to Directive 76/207 in order for the *Kalanke* ruling to be overcome.

[92] COM 96/93, EE C 179 of 22 June 1996, 8.

[93] COM 96/93, EE C 175 of 21 June 1999, 67. The validity of the suggested amendment expired on 9 January 2004.

[94] *Hellmut Marschall*, n 30 above, I-6363.

each individual case, it provides for male candidates who are equally as qualified as the female candidates a guarantee that the candidatures will be the subject of an objective assessment which will take account of all criteria specific to the individual candidates. … In this respect, however, it should be remembered that those criteria must not be such as to discriminate against female candidates.'[95]

The composite reading of the ECJ case law provides the following principles of interpretation. First, equality of opportunity is the prevailing version of equality, whereas quotas and other measures of direct effect are not acceptable. All other positive measures are compatible with EU law provided that they ensure an objective and individualised judgement and respect the principle of proportionality. The Court strictly adheres to a more liberal approach to equality and is reluctant to adopt a more social reading of the principle, even after the upgrade of positive action through the Treaty of Amsterdam. Thus, the ECJ still insists upon fundamental community rights and the prevailing notion of the free market with certain, albeit not extensive, concessions to the need for social cohesion.

CONSTITUTIONAL INTERPRETATION

Affirmative action vis-a-vis equality

A basic preliminary question is if, after the constitutional recognition of affirmative action, the principle of equality has been subject to change. If the answer is positive, equality has arguably obtained a more social character and affirmative action is an intrinsic aspect of equality. If the answer is negative, equality is still conceived of in a more liberal manner and affirmative action is, therefore, deemed to be a permissible exception from the principle.

With only minor exceptions, most legal systems, certainly those of the US and the EU, seem to treat affirmative action not as a *novum* or a post expression of equality. In these orders formal equality still remains the prevailing dogma with only minor concessions concerning measures of a temporary character to restore substantive equality. However, these concessions do not go so far as to establish equality of end-results but merely purport to apply equality of chances. The major doctrinal development set out by affirmative action is that the two key factors for determining the implementation of the legal principle of equality, namely resemblance and differentiation, are subject to alteration so as under-representation or past discrimination become relevant issues that distinguish social groups thus providing the necessary foundation for the awarding of privileges. Accordingly, inherently equal individuals are treated temporarily as different and the State selectively awards benefits. Treating positive measures as

[95] ibid, paras 24, 33.

exceptions from formal equality means that they must be justified on grounds of a permissible goal and are proportionate to the aim pursued, just like any other deviation from equality.

The case law of the US Supreme Court, by adhering today to the version of equal opportunities as a dominant version of the principle of equality treats affirmative action plans as any other exception to the principle of equality. Accordingly, affirmative action measures, especially in favour of minorities, are considered to be suspect classifications, controlled through the methodological tool of strict scrutiny. Given the intensity of this judicial vehicle, these positive measures are particularly vulnerable to constitutional review and only rarely manage to trespass the judicial threshold. In contrast, affirmative actions in favour of women, which are very rare in practice, are more easily upheld by the Court due to the application of a less penetrating judicial control, namely the intermediate control that allows the legislator a much wider margin of appreciation in determining its policy. This different approach is justified by the fact that affirmative action was originally set out in the US with reference to racial discrimination, mainly against African Americans and less so against Hispanic and native Americans. On the other hand, in Europe, even though positive measures have only recently been widely applied, it seems that they have gained a higher level of social and judicial acceptance, especially when they purport to benefit women in relation to their access to politics and the labour market—positive measures in favour of minorities are rather marginal in Europe.

At any rate, on both sides of the Atlantic, there are three elements that lower the significance of affirmative action vis-a-vis equality. First, affirmative action does not entail equal distribution of benefits but only equal opportunities to achieve the level of substantive equality. Secondly, unlike equality which is a standing and consolidated feature of the liberal State, affirmative action is by definition temporary and transitionary until actual equality is established. Thirdly, although affirmative action has received a constitutional status by law or jurisprudence, the States are not legally bound to take such measures and underrepresented groups do not have a legally enforceable right to that effect and, therefore, the introduction of positive measures remains primarily at the level of politics.

Constitutional ratio

The starting point here is the question of which goal a particular measure pursues. In most systems, the identification of the ratio of affirmative action fluctuates in relation to the beneficiaries and the area of application of the measure. Positive measures in favour of racial or religious groups are particularly akin to the goal of diversity in the form of multiculturalism, whereas measures in favour of women mostly tend to compensate for past discriminations. On the other hand, in the field of education or broadcasting, diversity plays a dominant role because obviously an enriching academic environment can have particularly benevolent side effects in the same way that broadcasting diversity secures the expression of a wide range of voices,[96] whereas in the fields of labour or public procurement the remedial character of affirmative action is more apparent since there is not an equal need to address the cultural issue.

Europe and the US employ a fundamentally different approach when it comes to the interest served by affirmative action. In Europe, particularly in the EU legal order, the basic ratio of positive action lies in the idea of compensation for past discrimination with a view to restoring full equality, conceived of primarily as equality of opportunity.[97] Thus, merely remedial purposes are considered as legitimate, whereas the argument of diversity has been disregarded. Despite the fact that in this way the emphasis is put on redressing the statistical imbalance, what lies beneath is the constitutional choice to address the unfair results of past discrimination against women. By way of contrast, in the US, after much fluctuation in the case law between the goals of diversity and compensation,[98] the former seems today to have become the prevailing compelling public interest in the context of affirmative action. In fact, the Supreme Court in *Bakke* rejected the argument of compensation on the grounds that collective damage cannot be established and that concrete damage can only be asserted if based on judicial, legislative or administrative findings of constitutional violations.[99] The *Bakke* case law was reaffirmed in the Michigan Cases, especially in *Grutter v Bollinger* where the Court emphasised that a 'critical mass' of minority students was necessary for their uninhibited progress in the academia through the creation of a 'diverse student body'. The Court did not set out a fixed number of minority students that would satisfy the critical mass requirement but merely demanded that some minority students be admitted so as they did not feel isolated. This particularly fluid criterion essentially conveys the diversity requirement form the level of objective ratios in group representation to the level of psychological

[96] See *Metro Broadcasting Inc v Federal Communications Commission*, 497 US 547 (1990) where the Court with a 5–4 majority upheld the Federal Communications Commission's policy to award an enhancement for minority ownership in comparative proceedings for new licences and to permit a limited category of existing radio and television broadcast stations to be transferred only to minority-controlled firms.

[97] See the extremely illustrative Opinion of Advocate General Tesauro in *Kalanke*, paras 18–19.

[98] See *United Steelworkers of America v Weber* 443 US 193 (1979), where the Supreme Court invoked the history of the enactment of the Civil Rights Act 1964 and equity as well as the 'broad remedial purposes' of the measure and upheld the constitutionality of voluntary labour affirmative action in favour of minorities without any reference to diversity. Also see *Richmond*, n 6 above, 493, where a six-Justice majority ruled that affirmative action measures were reserved strictly 'for remedial settings', and the Court of Appeal cases *Contractors Association of Eastern Pennsylvania v Secretary of Labor*, 442 F 2d 159 (3rd Cir 1971) and *Podberesky v Kirwan*, 956 F.2d 52, 57 (4th Cir 1992).

[99] According to Justice Powell only the legislature and the executive and not other institutions, such as the universities, can identify such findings in order to justify the introduction of affirmative action plans.

security.[100] At any rate, the Court left a wide margin of appreciation to the university to define what the critical mass really stands for in numbers, a discretion which is nevertheless judicially controllable. *Grutter* not only enhanced diversity as a compelling public interest but categorically rejected remedial purposes of affirmative action, essentially prompting the university to withdraw from the argument that its admission policy aimed at compensating for past discrimination and to retreat from certain extracts of its regulations to that effect. The argument of diversity was not, however, unanimously embraced by the members of the Court. Justice Thomas used a very technical line of argument in order methodologically to combat diversity and, in turn, affirmative action in general. In his view, in order for a goal to be assessed as being of public interest and most importantly as 'compelling' it must be acknowledged as such unanimously from the federal State and States: although it is not suffice *ipso facto* that certain states adopt this policy, if some states reject it then it cannot by definition be a compelling public interest. In consequence, given that certain US states institutionally overrule the policy, it cannot qualify as public interest.[101] The dominance of diversity over compensation was in any case reaffirmed in *Parents Involved*, where Justice Roberts classified the two legitimate compelling interests for the use of race and further exemplified diversity by requiring a compact plan to achieve this measure and not merely incremental measures.

Occasionally, other public interests, more or less relative to the idea of diversity, have been invoked by judges of the Supreme Court to justify affirmative action, such as social cohesion and inclusion, mainly the prevention of stigma and social bias against minority groups,[102] the improvement in service provision given the tendency of minority members to professionally address members of the same group,[103] the need to have members of minorities in significant posts to operate as role models for their fellows[104] and the need to treat cases of social emergency.[105] It seems that after the *Michigan* cases, diversity remains as the sole ground for justification of affirmative action in the US. However, a serious doubt is expressed according to which the adoption of diversity is merely an opportunist approach, in the sense that it transfers the focus of discussion of the intensely heated issue of past discrimination (for which a sense of social guilt is not to be excluded) to the objective and neutral issue of racial balance.

[100] According to the dissenting opinion of Justice Scalia, the critical mass is so 'mystical' that it 'challenges even the most gullible mind'.
[101] *Grutter*, n 8 above, 357–58.
[102] *Brown*, n 5 above, 494 (1954).
[103] *DeFunis v Odegaard* 416 US 312 (1974).
[104] *Wygant v Jackson Board of Education* 476 US 267 (1986).
[105] Justice Scalia in the cases *Hirabayashi v United States*, 320 US 81 (1943) and *Korematsu*, n 57, above.

Areas of application

In the US, affirmative action is nowadays quite widespread not only in the public sector but also in private industry, where several programmes in favour of underrepresented groups have been voluntarily introduced. From a statistical point of view, affirmative action measures in the US apply mostly in education and public contracting and less so in the field of access to the labour market and to political representation. The Supreme Court seems to be very cautious when assessing the constitutionality of political positive measures on the ground that in such a case there is an intrusion beyond the traditional scope of civil rights to political rights and representative democracy. Indeed, the foundation of political equality is not to be traced primarily on the conventional liberal right to equality but mostly on the very essence of popular sovereignty and representative democracy. This variation in relation to the very quality of the constitutional derivative of political equality calls for a different, presumably stricter, constitutional review.

This does not seem to be the case in Europe. In most European countries positive measures purport to facilitate and encourage access of women to elected political posts as a means to treat the phenomenon of under-representation which, in this view, undermines the substantive legitimacy of any elected body. Alongside with political representation, access to labour is the other privileged area of application of positive measures in Europe, especially in the EU. By way of contrast positive measures in relation to university admissions or public contracting are almost unknown in Europe.

Vehicles of constitutional review

In the US, as well as in Europe, neither the legislature nor the executive have the constitutional obligation to introduce positive measures. On the other hand, the judiciary has refused to provide altogether *ipso jure* constitutional cover to such measures but has upheld them only ad hoc and provided that certain conditions have been met. The US Supreme Court explicitly, albeit not always strictly, requires that the measure impugned serves a compelling public interest and that it is narrowly tailored to serve the legitimate interest involved. In Europe, certainly in the EU, the main tool of judicial control is the principle of proportionality and the tools of suitability and of necessity, ie the test of the least restrictive alternative. The most typical such example is provided in 2009 judgment, *Commission v Greece*,[106] where the ECJ examined the provision of the Greek Civil and Military Pensions Code according to which women had a lower retirement age and a minimum length of service in order to address the disadvantages faced by them as a result of their social roles and the fact that they

[106] *Commission v Greece*, n 89 above.

have generally fewer years of paid employment. The ECJ, after having ruled that the pension scheme in question was based on an employment record and was not a social security scheme, considered the benefits attributed to women as pay and, accordingly, that no discrimination could be tolerable. Although the ECJ explicitly acknowledged that Member States can introduce positive action measures to ease labour disadvantages, different retirement ages could not by their nature serve legitimate remedial purposes since the multiple roles of women in society, especially that related to motherhood, were not by any means alienated if women workers retired earlier. What would have satisfied the proportionality test was the timely establishment of motivation for mothers of young children, such as flexible working conditions, full child care services, modes of distant working etc, so as to enable women in fact to conduct their professional lives on an equal footing with men. While there are these alternatives, which are milder from the point of view of those affected by the measures, namely male workers who are obliged unequally to support the social security system for the early retirees, the measure was patently disproportionate.

This typical proportionality test, very well known in European legal systems unlike the Anglo-Saxon tradition focusing mainly on a more pragmatic approach to the evaluation of the reasonableness of a measure, presents some similarities with the American demand for a narrowly tailored measure, only in a more methodologically finely tuned form. The results of judicial control are in any case very similar. Inflexible quotas are not tolerable because, according to the American jurisprudence, they cannot conceivably be narrowly tailored since they could apply generically in any case of statistical inequality. From this viewpoint they are not combating the roots of discrimination that have caused this social pathology and, at any rate, there can be milder means to achieve this purpose, ie measures that do not penetrate so intensely to the rights of non benefiting individuals. So, if the early retirement scheme for female workers was challenged before the US Supreme Court, the outcome would most probably be annulment on the ground that it was not narrowly tailored to serve the compelling interest of supporting motherhood. The scenario remains the same even in legal systems where domestic constitutions have explicitly recognised and upgraded affirmative action. Thus, the judiciary is bound to apply the standards of constitutional review on each particular measure and asses the compatibility of the measure with the fundamental equality principle. In this way, it seems that in terms of constitutional review, it makes no real difference if affirmative action has been constitutionally acknowledged, such as in many EU Member States and the EU itself, or stems as a matter of interpretation from the constitutional principle of equality. Constitutional recognition is not—and cannot be—open ended.

EPILOGUE

Affirmative action reflects the contemporary call for substantive equality as a quasi fourth generation right. The basic philosophy of the liberal State, entailing the abstention of State from a sphere of unobstructed human activity, has become out-of-date due to the complexity of State power as well as the growth of multicultural States. Accordingly, traditional liberal rights seem to be on the road to transformation in order to gain an intense social dimension. Affirmative action thus constitutes a means of redistributing State benefits through the award of special rights to those who are in a less competitive position, mainly because of past discrimination against them. At the same time, affirmative action is seemingly violating a fundamental principle upon which the human rights dogma has been founded, namely that the individual is the subject of each right. Insofar as positive measures are addressed to a certain social sub-category, the group seems to be worked out through the person. This conversion obviously causes a series of doctrinal and practical problems that need to be treated, such as the question of (self-) determination of one's identity or issues of social inclusion. In this context, the traditional tools of interpretation used by the judiciary as a means of delineating constitutional rights seem out of date, if not methodologically inadequate. The conventional liberal approach of rights vested merely to individuals concedes as rights attributed to groups seem to receive more and more constitutional accommodation. History, which is rather marginal when it comes to constitutional interpretation, becomes a necessary component when reading the requirement for positive measures or assessing their compatibility with the Constitution. Therefore, a Constitution transcends time and at the same time history becomes a contemporary actor that brings a large portion of past factual situations into legal reasoning. In Benedetto Groce's words 'history refers to present needs and present situations within which [past] events vibrate'.

13

Fundamental Rights in the Global and European Law Order

JACQUELINE DUTHEIL DE LA ROCHÈRE

INTRODUCTION

IS THERE A European approach of fundamental rights/human rights in a global world? The question may seem surprising as we are accustomed to associate human rights and universalism, by reference either to the French Declaration of the man and citizen of 1789 ('Men are born and remain free and equal in rights') or to Article I of the Universal Declaration of Human Rights of 10 December 1948 ('All human beings are born free and equal in dignity and rights'). On the other hand it appears that legal systems have different conceptions of human rights: cultural, political, ideological differences as to what should be regarded as fundamental and how rights should be protected.

Human rights are not purely declaratory; they are more and more used by individuals and their advocates to defend cases, at least in those parts of the world where the level of education and political consciousness has grown. During the last 50 years or so, the European subcontinent engendered the most sophisticated system of supranational protection of human rights combining definition of rights and control of their implementation through the mechanism of the European Convention on Human Rights (ECHR) and the European Court of Human Rights. The European Union (EU) followed the same trend borrowing extensively from the ECHR system, while the national systems of protection of human rights developed alongside the international norms of human rights at global level. One may wonder whether or not developments at the global level benefit the regional and local levels. We will examine the conditions of adjustment between the European level and the others as regards, first, the definition of human rights and, secondly, their implementation.

Jacqueline Dutheil de la Rochère

DEFINITION OF HUMAN RIGHTS:
UNIVERSAL *JUS COMMUNE* V EUROPEAN *JUS COMMUNE*

A universal conception of human rights was born in Europe or at least in the western world at the age of the enlightenment. But the development of European institutions as from the middle of the twentieth century coincided with the progressive identification of a proper European corpus of human rights.

Europe and the development of a universal concept of human rights[1]

No one would contest that the philosophy of human rights was born in Europe or more generally in the western world. Having its roots in the greco-latin tradition and the judeo-christian civilisation, the philosophy of the enlightenment inspired the famous declarations of the American independence and of the French revolution, anticipated by the English revolution of 1689. The subsequent intellectual evolution of Europe remains indebted to Locke, Rousseau and Kant. What is proclaimed is that human beings have indefeasible rights. The individual is considered at the heart of society as having a supreme value; the role of the liberal and democratic State is to serve the interests of the citizen. As from the end of the eighteenth century these conceptions passed from a theoretical approach to a practical one in documents such as the Declaration of Rights of Virginia (1776) or the Declaration of the Rights of Man and Citizen of 1789; it implies a total revolution concerning the role assigned to public authorities in the western world. The fact that in modern history the consciousness of the universality of human rights took place in Europe or the western world makes it difficult at first to distinguish a European approach of human rights from a universal approach.

When trying to identify what is specific to the European approach of human rights, it is important to recall that the philosophy of human rights, presented as universal when it was born at the end of the eighteenth century, took a long time to instil positive law in European countries. The doctrine of human rights and *jus naturalis* incurred criticism during the nineteenth century up until the middle of the twentieth century. In France criticism came from conservative thought and combined with certain contradictions in the heritage of the French revolution. The most significant cause of contradiction is linked to the affirmation of the value of statute law: in a democratic system of government, the law voted by Parliament is the expression of the general will; it can do no wrong. As a consequence, under the Third Republic in France there prevailed a sort of tyranny of the legislator. Civil liberties were defined and protected by the law voted by Parliament and no one could usefully argue in court that a statute law did not comply with the principles of the Declaration of 1789. The Declaration

[1] See Charles Leben, 'Y a-t-il une approche européenne des droits de l'homme?' in P Alston (ed), L'Union européenne et les Droits de l'Homme (Bruxelles, Bruylant, 2001) at 78–98.

remained prestigious but it was deprived of any proper judicial value, except perhaps as a source of inspiration of the development of general principles in the case law of administrative courts, namely the Conseil d'Etat.

For different reasons, England has experienced a similar restriction to the practical effects of the universal philosophy of human rights. The dominant trend of utilitarianism promoted by Jeremy Bentham and John Stuart Mill condemned the idea of natural rights: in a democratic government, the rights of the individuals are engendered by a system of positive law where the law voted by Parliament plays a prominent role. Later on, Marxist philosophy inspired a radical criticism of the heritage of the enlightenment, with human rights as conceived in traditional democracies being qualified of bourgeois liberties. As a consequence the reference to human rights, solemnly proclaimed in declarations of the eighteenth century, was occulted in Europe during most of the nineteenth century, up to the middle of the twentieth century. A similar phenomenon is to be observed in the United States although the declarations of independence and the 10 first amendments to the constitution adopted in 1791 were rich with potential concerning human rights.[2]

The main difference between Europe and the United States lies in the fact that the Supreme Court as from the famous case of *Marbury v Madison*,[3] has allowed any judge in the country to evaluate the compatibility with the federal constitution of any statute or regulation, including law voted by Congress. As a consequence, human rights as defined in the amendments to the constitution were recognised as part of positive law of the country and their violation could be sanctioned by any judge and in the last resort by the Supreme Court. However, as it is well known, the history of American democracy was deeply affected by the question of slavery; it cost the country a civil war which did not immediately bring a solution to the question of civil rights. The Supreme Court in *Plessy v Fergusson*,[4] accepted the compatibility with the constitution of legislation in southern states maintaining segregation. It was only in 1954 in the case *Brown v Board of Education of Topeka*[5] that the Supreme Court introduced a systematic policy of defence of civil rights.

So in both Europe and America, and for different reasons, it was only after the middle of the twentieth century that the potentialities of the doctrine of human rights, proclaimed 150 years earlier, really inspired positive law. The horrors of Nazi Germany and the experience of fascism in parts of Europe obviously played a role. A drastic evolution occurred after 1945. Not only was the Rome Convention (ECHR) adopted, but most countries introduced in their own constitutions a bill of rights and a system of control of constitutionality of the laws voted by

[2] As examples, the first amendment protects freedom of speech and religion, and the fourth, fifth and sixth are related to criminal procedure protection.

[3] 5 US 137 (1803).

[4] 163 US 539 (1896).

[5] 347 US 483 (1954).

Parliament. This evolution took place in countries like Germany just after the war; for others, it was when fascist regimes came to an end, and for central European countries, it was when the Berlin wall fell down (1989). Without going into the specifics of each national constitution of the various European States, it is interesting to try underlining the characteristics of a common European approach of human rights.

European jus commune v jus commune universalis

Identification of a European approach to human rights

The first common European approach to human rights appeared in the Rome convention of 1950, adopted in the framework of the Council of Europe, conceived as an instrument of harmonisation of the substance of human rights and of the means of their protection. The European convention, including the various protocols progressively added, played a decisive role in the protection of the rights of individuals against public authorities, namely with the development of the possibility of individual recourse to the Strasbourg Court. This role was subsequently increased with the adhesion to the ECHR of most central and east European countries, even if their arrival en masse could at first be felt as a threat to the homogeneity of the system. It must be underlined that even if the substance of the European convention has remained oriented towards the protection of civil and political rights, to the exclusion of social rights, the system of control with the intervention of an independent court able to provide adequate compensation to the aggrieved person[6] has no equivalent in any other supranational system, either regional or global. This is the first characteristic of the European approach to the protection of human rights: not only does it formulate a list of human rights which have to be respected, but it provides individuals with a system of effective judicial remedy in case of violation of their rights by the public authorities of their own country.

In the EU the protection of fundamental rights followed a different track but progressively converged with that provided by the system of the ECHR. The founding Treaties of the Communities did not make any express reference to fundamental rights; such a reference did not seem to be necessary as the competence conferred to the Communities by the Treaties pertained essentially to the economic area and it was not apparent at the time that they could in any way affect the rights of the individuals. At the end of the 1960s, the ECJ had to decide cases in the area of common agricultural policy or competition which incidentally raised questions of protection of fundamental individual rights. It occurred that the question of respect of fundamental rights was tightly linked to that of the primacy of EC law upon the national law of Member States. In a

[6] Art 50 ECHR.

landmark case decided in 1970,[7] where the question centred around the level of protection of individual rights guaranteed by EC law in comparison to the level of guarantee provided by the German Fundamental Law, the Court forcefully denied that the validity of a Community measure could be judged against principles of national constitutional law. It held that fundamental rights formed an integral part of the general principles of Community law protected by the ECJ; on the other hand, the ECJ emphasised that, when formulating fundamental rights, it would draw inspiration from the constitutional tradition common to the Member States. The Court found a common formulation of protected individual rights in international Treaties, to which Member States are parties, namely the ECHR.[8] After the mid-seventies, there were frequent references to the ECHR and to its annexed protocols in the case law of the ECJ.[9] The Court not only imposed the respect of fundamental rights in the acts adopted by EC institutions, but confirmed that those rights were binding on Member States when they act within the sphere of Community law, either when implementing EC law[10] or when deciding whether a derogation to EC law is lawful.[11]

The Treaty of European Union signed in Maastricht (1992) explicitly introduced in primary law the concept of fundamental rights, reproducing in Article F.2 TEU—at the time not justiciable—the exact formulation used by the ECJ: 'The Union shall respect fundamental rights, as guaranteed by the European Convention of Human Rights and as they result from the constitutional traditions common to the member States, as general principles of Community law'. Respect for human rights and fundamental freedoms was also mentioned among the objectives of the common foreign and security policy (second pillar, Article J.1 §2) and of the policy of cooperation with developing countries (Article 177 §2 EC). A commitment to respect the ECHR and the Geneva convention of 1951 relating to the status of refugees is expressed as regards justice and home affairs (third pillar, Article K.2 §1).

The Treaty of Amsterdam (signed in 1997) strengthened the reference to fundamental rights. The amended provision of Article 6(1) TEU states that 'the Union is founded on the principles of liberty, democracy, respect for human rights and fundamental freedoms, and the rule of law, principles which are common to the Member States'. Article 6(2) which stipulates that the Union should respect fundamental rights as guaranteed by the ECHR and as they result from the constitutional traditions common to the Member States as general

[7] Case 11/70, *Internationale Handelsgesellschaft*, 17 December 1970, R, 1125.

[8] All six initial members of the communities were members of the Council of Europe and party to the ECHR, even if they had not all accepted yet the individual recourse to the European Court of Human Rights; France did so in 1974.

[9] A first reference to the ECHR appeared in *Rutili*, Case 36/75, 28 October 1975, R, 1219, concerning the limit to the powers of national States as to the control of foreigners when the respect of Arts 8, 9, 10 and 11 ECHR were in question.

[10] Case 5/88, *Wachauf*, 13 July 1989, R, 2609.

[11] C-260/89, *ERT*, 18 June 1991, R I-2925.

principles of Community law, is made justiciable to the ECJ under Article 46(d) TEU. The ECJ is given jurisdiction with regard to respect of fundamental rights by the European institutions, but only insofar as the Court has substantial jurisdiction under the EC and EU Treaties. Clearly the jurisdiction of the Court remains quite limited as regards the third pillar and non-existent as regards the second one. Article 7 TEU as modified enables the Council to suspend certain Member State rights under the TEU and the TEC (Article 309) where the Member State has committed 'serious and persistent breach' of principles mentioned in Article 6(1) TEU. The respect for these principles has also been made a condition of application for membership to the EU (Article 49 TEU). Finally, the Amsterdam revision has added a new basis of legislative competence concerning discrimination. Article 13 EC provides that the Community institutions may, within the limits of the conferred competences, take 'appropriate action to combat discrimination based on sex, racial or ethnic origin, religion or belief, disability, age or sexual orientation'. This enables the Community to adopt measures to combat such discrimination within the scope of the various policies and powers granted to it otherwise in the Treaty. For example, Article 13 was used as a legal basis for the creation of a European Monitoring Centre on Racism and Xenophobia by a Council Regulation of 2 June 1997 (Regulation No 1035/97, OJ No L 151, 10 June 1997) and established in Vienna, subsequently replaced by the Fundamental Rights Agency created by Council Regulation No 168/2007 of 15 February 2007.

Thus appear three concentric circles in the EU system of protection of fundamental rights. A first circle concerns the respect of human rights by European institutions and by Member States when they implement EC/EU law or derogate from it. A second type of obligation imposed on potential or actual Member States is to respect liberty, democracy and human rights in the common course of their activities, any persistent breach being liable of sanction under Article 7 TEU. A third circle concerns the international projection of the EC/EU; they expect that their partners respect fundamental rights. A good example is that of the successive Lomé agreements which, as from 1989 (Lomé IV), included a provision imposing on ACP countries[12] a clause of respect of fundamental rights and democratic principles. The same sort of formula was included in the Treaties of Association with eastern and central European countries as from 1991/1992, the so-called 'European agreements' prior to admission of these countries to the EU. The various initiatives taken by the EU towards third countries are reported annually,[13] presented by theme (capital punishment, torture, rights of the child, trafficking in human beings, etc) and by geographical areas (dialogue on human rights with China, Iran, central Asia, Africa, Federation of Russia, etc).

[12] Africa, Caribbean and Pacific Group of States.

[13] See Annual report of the EU on human rights 2008 14146/2/08 REV 2 COHOM 105.

In parallel with the modifications brought to the EC/EU Treaty, a Charter of Fundamental Rights of the Union was negotiated in 1999/2000 among representatives of EU institutions and national parliaments in the framework of a convention, and solemnly proclaimed by the presidents of the Parliament, the Council and the Commission at the occasion of the Nice intergovernmental conference (December 2000). This Charter, which did not immediately become part of EU primary law, has been welcomed quite unanimously by Advocates General as a full realisation of the general principles of Community law/Union law.By comparison with the ECHR, the Charter of Fundamental Rights, in its six chapters (entitled Dignity, Freedoms, Equality, Solidarity, Citizens' Rights and Justice), reveals a conception of human rights which has identical philosophical roots: the dignity of the human being is at the heart of both documents. But the Charter, appearing 50 years after the ECHR, not only introduces new conceptions of certain rights (see right to a family life) and of threats to individual freedoms (see biology or personal data protection), but also gives space to socio-economic rights which are not present in the ECHR. These rights are significant for the EU, which is primarily an economic common venture although it has now acquired a comprehensive political dimension covering most aspects of social life. The structure adopted for the 50 Articles of substance of the Charter has the merit of breaking with the traditional opposition between, on one side, civil and political rights, enforceable in court, and on the other side social and economic rights of a more declaratory type; it underlines the essential unity of fundamental rights.

The Charter would have been the part II of the unborn Constitutional Treaty. According to the Lisbon Treaty, the Charter, which is not included in the treaty, should 'have the same legal value as the treaties' (Article 6(1) TEU). Initially the Charter was only an interinstitutional agreement, reproclaimed in Strasbourg in December 2007. However, considering its format, substance and the way it was drafted—borrowing a lot from existing sources such as widely agreed international or regional conventions, common constitutional traditions of the Member States or case law of the ECJ—the Charter, through its underlying concepts and principles, proved capable of influential effect. It is noticeable that it has become a document of reference for the Union, either in decision-making or through case law. However the Charter in no way designed to become the exclusive reference of human rights in the Union. On the contrary, the Lisbon Treaty reproduces the various other elements of the constitutional Treaty concerning the question of fundamental rights. The consolidation and support of democracy, the rule of law and human rights should remain among the objectives of the Union's external action (Article 21(2)(b) TEU). Potential and actual Member States must comply with this triptych (Articles 2, 7 and 49 TEU). A legal basis for the accession of the Union to the ECHR is precisely provided and the Court should continue to discover in the ECHR and the constitutional traditions common to the Member States the substance of the general principles of EU law (Article 6(2) and (3) TEU).

European approach to human rights compared with other possible approaches

The present situation of the EU reveals an approach to the question of human rights in line with that of the ECHR, with some elements of differentiation both in the substance of the rights and the techniques of implementation. Limiting our observations to the substance we could easily pinpoint certain differences between national conceptions of human rights by European States, with the consequence that a common perception cannot emerge at regional European level for lack of consensus. An obvious example is the question of respect of the life of the unborn child. The Irish object fiercely to any recognition of a right to abortion; for that reason such a right is not mentioned in the Charter of Fundamental Rights of the EU. Freedom of religion is treated very differently in a country like the UK where the head of State is also the head of the established religion, and in France where religious neutrality of public authorities, the so-called *laïcité,* is considered as a dogma. Nevertheless the principle of religious freedom appears in the Charter in terms very similar to that used in the ECHR, but France strongly objected to any reference to the 'christian origins of the Europe' in the preamble of the Charter, a proposition which on the contrary was welcome by most other Member States, with the notorious exception of Portugal.

More significant in our reflection on the position of Europe in a global world is to wonder what, in the European approach of human rights, is properly kept to the regional level and what can pretend to universality. At each level of a possible legal approach of human rights, national, European or global, there is a part which belongs exclusively to that level and another part which reflects common values likely to be protected also or more efficiently at the next level. As mentioned earlier, the triptych democracy/rule of law/ protection of human rights is presented by the EU primary law as an obligation for its Member States and an objective of its external action. This ambitious programme did not appear in the Universal Declaration of Human Rights of 1948, nor in the United Nations (UN) covenants. But following the breaking down of the Sovietworld, which defended another conception of democracy, the European/western conception of democracy is in the course of universalisation. Various international documents of the UN, International Monetary Fund (IMF) and other organisations, refer to the triptych which becomes a common reference. On the other hand, other values expressed in Community primary law and secondary legislation and reproduced in the EU Charter of Fundamental rights, such as social rights and principles of solidarity, appear as proper European principles which at the moment are not located in the global world. The same could be said of cultural pluralism which is not considered positively outside Europe.

Quite instructive also would be a comparison between the European and the North American approach to the protection of human rights. Although these parts of the world have both contributed to the birth of the modern approach of the defence of rights of the individuals, there are today significant differences. America remains influenced by a deep diffidence as regards public intervention while the European social-democracies, specially France and Germany, consider that the public authorities have a role to play in order to make the rights of the second generation become effective (social rights, health, education, protection of the environment). At the beginning of the twenty-first century, the need to face one of the most dramatic financial and economic crises ever met by the capitalist world may induce the United States (US) to initiate certain changes. Another example of differences between both sides of the Atlantic could be the right to free speech. It is considered as vital for democracy in the US, while European countries—having experienced the deviations of fascism—tend to accept that there are limits to the free expression of individual opinions in the interests of security and public order. But the development of actions against terrorism may here again induce the US to adapt their traditional attitude in a way which would be more balanced and more similar to the European approach.

There is a matter in which Europe remains definitively different from the US: it is the question of capital punishment. Such punishment is excluded by Article 2 of the EU Charter of fundamental rights and by protocol 6 to the ECHR. It has been abolished by all the Member States of the EU, while the evolution in North America remains slow despite sustained efforts of the EU on the international scene. At the 62nd General Assembly of the United Nations, 104 countries voted a moratorium on capital punishment in the expectation of its legal abolition everywhere.[14]

To sum up one may consider that there is a common European approach to human rights which has played a pioneering role and continues to lead the way with a justifiable pretension to a certain degree of universalism. This common approach was made possible by the significant degree of cultural, economical and political homogeneity of European countries assembled in the Council of Europe and the EU. One of the challenges presently facing these institutions is the question of their ability to cope with the consequences of enlargement due to the change of political configuration of Europe. More numerous and less homogeneous, will European States be able to let the European institutions continue to inspire the global evolution in the domain of the defence of human rights? There is no clear answer. At least the European institutions provide an interesting framework for the control of the effective implementation of human rights in that part of the world.

REGIONAL EUROPEAN LEVEL: THE MOST ELABORATE SYSTEM OF ACCOMMODATING POTENTIAL CONTRADICTIONS

We will limit our observations to the question of cohabitation between various but not contradictory systems of protection of fundamental rights. In the European area, outstanding efforts to overcome contradictions have developed

[14] See EU Annual report on human rights 2008, at 4.

quite successfully over the last 50 years. Recurrent questions remain on the relation between European level and other levels of protection of fundamental rights, national constitutions, on one side, international law order on the other.

A policy of mutual respect

The adoption of the ECHR by the Member States of the Council of Europe is anterior to the development of a Community law concern for fundamental rights. It provides not only a comprehensive list of rights but also a sophisticated system of judicial review—at the initiative of either other Member States or individuals, once national remedies have been exhausted—in order to guarantee the full practical respect of human rights by States in relation to those under their jurisdiction. When the Luxembourg Court started producing its case law on fundamental rights as general principles of Community law, a policy of mutual respect between both systems developed. The case law of the ECJ is well known; it regards the ECHR as a very important source of inspiration of its own decisions in the field of fundamental rights and always tends to adopt in specific cases an interpretation which is compatible with that retained by the Strasbourg Court. In certain circumstances, the ECJ has been willing to revise some previous judgments in order to bring them in line with subsequent case law of the Strasbourg Court.[15] As to the European Court of Human Rights, it has not hesitated in *Matthews*[16] to review an act of an EU Member State held to be in violation of the ECHR where the cause of the breach was an act of the EU and where the EU system did not provide an adequate remedy for breach of a rule of primary law. In fact, EU primary law excluded the citizens of Gibraltar from voting to elect representatives of the European Parliament; the European Court held the UK responsible for this breach of the right to vote.

The *Bosphorus* case is paradigmatic of the relationship between fundamental rights protection afforded by the EU and by the ECHR. In a case concerning the seizure in Ireland of an aircraft of Yugoslav airlines, Ireland having taken the aircraft pursuant to an EC regulation enacted in furtherance of UN sanctions, the Strasbourg Court found that in principle the protection afforded to fundamental rights by the EU was equivalent to that for which the ECHR provides, and that in this particular case, the protection afforded was not manifestly deficient. The general approach of the Strasbourg Court is based on equivalence leading to a presumption of compliance with the convention, presumption which could only be rebutted by showing manifest deficiency in a particular case.

[15] In C-94/00, *Roquette Frère SA*[2002] ECR I-9011, para 28, the ECJ tacitly acknowledged that it had erred in its interpretation of Art 8 ECHR in its earlier decision in *Hoechst AG v Commission*, Joined Cases 46/87 and 227/88 [1989] ECR 2859.

[16] *Matthews v United Kingdom*, App No 24833/94, judgment of 18 February 1999 (1999) 28 EHRR 361.

The adoption of the EU Charter of Fundamental Rights and its acquisition of 'the same legal value as (that of) the treaties', under the Lisbon Treaty should not significantly modify the present situation. The question of the relationship between the Charter and the ECHR was fiercely and lengthily discussed during Convention talks which had the task of drafting the Charter. Some governments such as Italy, Spain and, to a lesser degree, France pleaded for the autonomy of the Charter with respect to the ECHR, while other countries such as the UK, anxious that a maximum of legal certainty be maintained, would rather have a Charter as similar as possible to the ECHR and that a reference be made in the Charter to the necessary compliance with the case law of the European Court of Human Rights. It was at the time that the UK had just adopted the Human Rights Act 1998 which incorporated the ECHR in UK law. On the basis of an amendment proposed by the government of the Netherlands, Article 52(3) of the Charter provides: 'In so far as this Charter contains rights which correspond to rights guaranteed by the Convention for the Protection of Human Rights and Fundamental Freedoms, the meaning and scope of those rights shall be the same as those laid down by the said convention. The provision shall not prevent Union law providing more extensive protection'. In order to help identifying those Charter rights which 'correspond' to rights guaranteed by the ECHR, the explanatory memorandum provides some help. The memorandum contains a first list of Articles which have the same meaning and scope as the corresponding Articles of the ECHR.[17] A second list enumerates Articles of the Charter which have the same meaning as corresponding Articles of the ECHR, but whose scope is wider.[18] In fact, in a number of situations the relationship between Charter rights and the ECHR is more complex. For instance, Article 5 dealing with slavery and forced labour is partly based on the ECHR but goes beyond by expressly prohibiting trafficking in human beings. Article 8 dealing with personal data is based on an ECHR right, but also on an EC Treaty Article and a directive. Article 9 of the Charter, on the right to marry and to found a family, modifies Article 12 of the ECHR as it provides for the possibility of marriage by those of the same sex, where this is permitted by the relevant national law. The drafters of these lists have cautiously indicated that they were established without precluding development in case law, legislation and the Treaties.

The injunction of Article 52(3) that the meaning and scope of Charter rights and ECHR rights be the same makes an implicit reference to the case law of the Strasbourg Court. The explanations under Article 52(3) say clearly that the meaning and scope of the guaranteed rights are determined not only by the text but also by the case law of the European Court of Human Rights and by the ECJ.

The current conventional wisdom is that the problem of potential divergence between EU law and the law of the convention would be resolved if the EU

[17] Arts 2, 4, 5 (1) and (2), 6, 7, 10 (1), 11, 17, 19 (1) and (2), 48, 49(1) of the Charter.
[18] Arts 9, 12(1), 14(1) and (3), 47(2) and (3), 50 of the Charter.

became a party to the European Convention on Human Rights, which is far from simple.[19] A proposal in that direction led the Court to express the opinion[20] that accession to the ECHR would be impossible without Treaty amendment because of lack of sufficient legal basis. Article 6(2) TEU of the Lisbon Treaty provides such legal basis stating that 'the union shall accede to the European Convention'. On the Council of Europe side, Article 17 of protocol 14 to the ECHR[21] adds a new paragraph to Article 59 of the Convention saying that the EU may accede to the convention. The organisation of such accession would imply the finding of solutions to some difficult questions such as demarcation between actions of Member States acting independently or implementing EU law, or the relationship between the courts and representation of the EU in the Strasbourg Court. The idea has been put forward of introducing a new procedure permitting either of the Luxembourg Courts to request an interpretation of the European convention from the Strasbourg Court. The main purpose would be to avoid divergences in the case law. On the whole, accession would permit the development of a system of supervision of actions of the EU at a time where it develops a new set of constitutional principles in an enlarged space.

Recurrent questions

At regional level, the cohabitation between the European convention and the EU system of protection of fundamental rights has developed quite smoothly over the years, following the policy pattern of mutual respect. The situation appears more questionable when it concerns the relationship between different levels of protection of fundamental rights: national level on one side, the general international law level on the other. Is a policy of mutual respect equally practicable?

European protection of fundamental rights and national constitutions

The question is not new. It was raised at the end of the 1960s when it appeared through the case law of the ECJ that Community law in its area of implementation pretended to primacy over the law of the Member States, including constitutional law. The answer of some national constitutional courts, namely those of Germany and Italy, relied on the assumption that national constitutional protection of human rights continued to be generally applicable, but that national courts might choose not to exercise their jurisdiction if satisfied that the

[19] See R White, 'The Strasbourg perspective and its effect on the Court of Justice: is mutual respect enough?' in A Arnull, P Eeckhout and T Tridimas (eds), *Continuity and change in EU law, Essays in the honour of Sir Francis Jacobs* (Oxford, Oxford University Press, 2008) at 139–56.

[20] Opinion 2/94 on accession by the Community to the European Convention on Human Rights [1996] ECR I-1759.

[21] Protocol 14 was signed on 13 May 2004.

protection of rights within the Community legal order was sufficient.[22] Subsequently, the approach of the *Bundes fassungsgericht* has softened; it has accepted that the level of protection provided by the ECJ could differ from that of the German courts in individual cases. It is only if the overall level of protection falls below an acceptable level that the German courts would revive their control. On the other hand, constitutional courts of other Member States have accepted the primacy of EC law to the extent that a guarantee of fundamental right equivalent to that of national constitutional law is granted.[23]

On the EC/EU law side, the ECJ has always maintained its commitment to apply fundamental rights as they result from the constitutional traditions common to the Member States as general principles of Community/Union law. This formula, introduced in Article F.2 TEU of the Maastricht Treaty, has been maintained all along the various Treaty amendments of the last decades. Therefore it is not surprising that Working Group II of the Convention on the future of Europe recommended the adjunction to Article 52 of the Charter of a new provision stating: 'Insofar as this Charter recognises fundamental rights as they result from the constitutional traditions common to the Member States, those rights shall be interpreted in harmony with those traditions'. This provision now appears in Article 52(4) of the Charter re-proclaimed at Strasbourg in December 2007. The duty of harmonious interpretation is less strict than the duty of identity of result imposed in relation to Charter rights corresponding to ECHR rights. As the ECJ has already built a body of case law which takes into account the constitutional traditions common to the Member States, this obligation of harmonious interpretation should not be insuperable.

Article 53 on the 'level of protection' guaranteed by the Charter contains another obligation of substance in relation with national constitutions: 'Nothing in this Charter shall be interpreted as restricting or adversely affecting human rights and fundamental freedoms as recognised, in their respective fields of application ... by the Member States' constitutions'. What is meant by 'in their respective fields of application' is certainly questionable. As mentioned above, from the point of view of national constitutional courts, the assumption is that national constitutional protection is generally applicable but that national courts may choose not to exercise their jurisdiction if satisfied that the protection of rights within the EU order offers sufficient guarantees. However, the new formulation introduced in the Charter takes into account this attitude of national constitutional courts. Therefore although the concept of respective fields of application is not easy to conceive in the area of fundamental rights, this express reference to mutual consideration between national constitutional courts and the ECJ, which corresponds to a long standing practice, is to be welcomed. It may

[22] *Re Wunsche Handelgesellschaft*, Dec of 22 October 1986 [1987] 3 CMLR 225; *SpA Granital v Administrazione delle Finanze*, Dec 170, 8 June 1984; *SpA Fragd v Administrazione delle Finanze*, Dec 232, 21 April 1989.

[23] See for instance the French Conseil Constitutionnel, Dec 2004–496 of 10 June 2004.

help new Member States to find their own way of living with the EU system of guarantee of human rights and its proclaimed primacy.

European protection of human rights and international law standards

As regards the general objectives of protection of human rights there is no contradiction between regional European level and the global level. The ECJ has always marked its openness to general international law and international treaties and covenants have been sources of inspiration for various European initiatives, in the area of human rights—for instance the Geneva convention on refugees, or social rights—for instance ILO conventions. As an illustration, a number of international agreements or declarations have been used as sources of inspiration for the drafting of the EU Charter of Fundamental Rights, as indicated in the explanatory memorandum.[24] However it is not until recently that a direct confrontation between the international level of guarantee of human rights and the regional European level took place, on the occasion of the fight against terrorism engaged in by the western world.

The *Kadi* case underlined the difficulties of that relationship. What was in question was the respect of fundamental rights in relation to sanctions adopted by the Committee of Sanctions of the United Nations concerning those suspected of terrorism. The applicant challenged a Community regulation which, pursuant to Security Council Resolutions, included the names of people subject to freezing orders. As regards the inscription on the list of the applicant's proper name, he pleaded violation of the right of property, the right to be heard and the right of access to court. The CFI[25] (now known as the General Court) declined to exercise generalised review of the contested EC regulation for compliance with fundamental rights as protected by the Community legal order, since this would entail indirect review of the Security Council Resolutions for compliance with those rights. On the other hand, the CFI held that it could review the Security Council Resolutions for compliance with *jus cogens* since this was a body of international law rules, binding on all including the UN. The CFI concluded that in this instance there had been no violation of any rule of *jus cogens,* neither the right to property, nor the right to be heard, nor the right to judicial review. According to *jus cogens* as interpreted by the CFI, the right of access to court was not absolute and the limitation on that right in the instance case was justified by the nature of the decision taken by the Security Council and the legitimate objective pursued.

On appeal, the ECJ[26] partly following the opinion of its Advocate General Poiares Maduro who had insisted on the autonomy of EC legal order, decided to review the contested regulation and examine its compliance not with *jus cogens* but with fundamental rights as protected by the Community legal order. It

[24] See for instance Art 1 (human dignity), Art 24 (the rights of the child).
[25] Case T-315/01, [2005] ECR II-3533.
[26] C-403/06 P, 3 September 2008.

observed that the control by the Court of the compatibility of any Community law act with fundamental rights appeared as a constitutional guarantee in a system such as that of the EC/EU where the rule of law prevailed. The mechanism of control of sanctions granted by the UN institutions which is an important derogation to the judicial protection of fundamental rights provided by the EC Treaty manifestly does not provides sufficient guarantees (point 322). The ECJ concluded that the CFI had erred in law in deciding that the EC regulations implementing UN resolutions were immune to any control of compatibility with EC law principles and could only be evaluated with reference to the principles of *jus cogens* (point 327). Finally the Court proceeded to the appreciation of the validity of the regulations with reference to the general principles of Community law. It concluded that, in this instance, there had been a violation of the right of property, the right to be heard and the right of access to court.

The case highlights the dangerous absence of proper guarantees of fundamental rights at the global level and the need to find substitutes at other levels as long as common initiatives do not provide serious mechanisms of effective guarantee.

CONCLUSION

This brief outline of protection of human rights in a multi-level system of law and institutions leads to some general observations. Whatever the pioneering role played by Europe in the development of formulation and protection of human rights, it cannot any longer pretend to universality. At each level of legal approach to human rights—national, European or global—there is a part which belongs exclusively to that level and another part which reflects common values likely to be protected also or more efficiently at the next level, either closer to individuals or with a wider dimension. This is an illustration of the concept of subsidiarity. As to the policy of mutual respect initiated by European institutions but not denied by a number of national constitutional courts, this is probably the best path to explore, as illustrated by recent case law.

14

Administrative Due or Fair Process: Different Paths in the Evolutionary Formation of a Global Principle and of a Global Right

SÉRVULO CORREIA

INTRODUCTION

Purpose

ADMINISTRATIVE PROCESS TODAY plays an irreplaceable role as an element or concept of administrative law *qua* normative legal system. In contemporary legal thought, administrative process is well established as a structure for managing relationships and dealings between public administration and individuals. In general, participation by interested parties and the rational and efficient conduct of administrative affairs are the two supreme goals, or the raison d'être, of administrative process.[1]

For its part, administrative law has from the outset played a prominent role in the web of rules, institutions and decision-making proceedings which give a shape to global law. The distinctive traits of administrative law can easily be recognised in many of the legal frameworks for transnational situations: organisations endowed with powers of authority, which prepare and take decisions of an administrative nature addressed to other subjects, which decisions tend in turn to be subject to procedures for judicial or proto-judicial review.[2] In contrast with the national administrative models, the global administrative activities are carried on without dependency on a (non-existent) overarching political and

[1] The Portuguese Constitution says as much in Art 267, s 1.
[2] S Cassesse, *Oltre lo Stato* (Roma, Editori Laterza, 2007) at 42.

legal unity and are largely founded on functional cooperation between institutions which remain organisationally separate.[3] But this difference does not affect the role of the administrative process as a constituent element of global administrative law.

In today's world, as a rule there is no such thing as non-proceduralised administrative action. Of course, the universe of global administration presents a density of regulation far lower than that of national law systems or of international organisations. This leaves more room for decision-making processes to be shaped freely on a case-by-case basis. However, even so, the imperative of rational decision-making, combined with the need to determine who takes part, and how and when, will in practice require a choice of the type of proceedings and the respective sequencing. So bit by bit, administrative procedures specific to global administrative action have taken shape. These procedures have emerged in different types depending on the nature and characteristics of the administrative tasks in hand.[4]

We should add that the relative importance of administrative process in global law is more than proportional to the already large position occupied in this sphere by administrative law. The large number and diversity of global regulatory bodies and the fluid organisation of many[5] makes it difficult to determine the common traits of an organisational framework for global administration. And 'legislative weaknesses'[6] mean, amongst other things, that, in many global regulatory systems, 'law disciplines are weak or absent'. 'The overall result is a spontaneously evolving, untidy regulatory mass without centre or hierarchy.'[7] In such an environment, we should not expect in most cases to find bodies of material administrative law rules organised under the leading idea of accommodating the pursuit of public interests with respect for individual rights.

All the same, it is easy to detect in every global administrative instance the consistent presence of principles, rules and practices of administrative process. First, at least some of these principles are nowadays anchored in a broad segment of our universal consciousness. Moreover, in their core aspects, the requirement of fairness in the process of adjudication (or of rule-making or of proto-judicial or judicial review) is posited on the same basic terms irrespective of the economic or social sector in which global administrative activity is being

[3] *cf* A von Bogdandy and P Dann, 'International Composite Administration: Conceptualizing Multi-Level and Network Aspects in the Exercise of International Public Authority' (2008) 9(11) *German Law Journal* 2015 and 2016.

[4] On the tendency for different types of administrative procedures to take shape in line with distinct administrative tasks, see W Hoffmann-Riem, E Schmidt-Aßmann and A Voßkuhle, *Grundlagen des Verwaltungsrechts, II* (München, Beck, 2008) at 614 ff.

[5] S Cassesse, 'Administrative Law Without The State? The Challenge Of Global Regulation' (2005) *Journal Of International Law And Politics* 663, 670 ff.

[6] M Delmas-Marty, *Global Law—A Triple Challenge* (New York, Transnational Publishers, 2003) at 122.

[7] R Stewart, 'The Global Regulatory Challenge to U.S. Administrative Law' (2005) *Journal of International Law And Politics* 695, 702–03.

conducted. And procedural requirements such as notice, the right to be heard, guarantees against bias or giving reasons, in addition to their intrinsic value, serve to offset a certain deficit in the democratic legitimacy of the decision-making structures[8] and the vagueness of the substantive rules.

A broader acceptance of the procedural requirements corresponding to principles and policies centred on the values of transparency and participation[9] does not, however, signify that we can today look to a mature body of global law of administrative process. As, for instance, Sabino Cassese has shown on the basis of concrete examples, 'participation in the global administrative arena is not precisely defined; it is loosely structured and not always enforceable by a court'.[10] Law will only stop evolving when we reach the mythical 'end of history'. However, with regard to the present state of global administrative process, we cannot even claim that it has attained a degree of relative stability, from where it could slowly accrue changes in detail to underpin a necessarily distant qualitative leap.

The still incipient definition of the value standards and structural framework of global administration means that we should try to identify the axiological and dogmatic matrix towards which it is evolving. But, before projecting the likely outline of its future shape, we need to understand the route that global administrative process has travelled in order to reach its present state. We should not therefore overlook this field of analysis, which can to some extent offset the limitations raised by the elementary stage of development of 'global proceduralism'. It is a fact that many of its elements are still rudimentary in structure. Due to the shortage of specific jurisprudence, it is difficult to set up autonomous explanatory legal doctrines and to outline an integrated system of values and functions. Nonetheless, global administrative process has not come out of the blue in the rarefied atmosphere of a transnational legal system which is not properly (or merely) national or international. Notwithstanding its particular features and the embryonic and sketchy nature of its emblematic concepts, we may, to a significant degree, regard and understand the global administrative process as a projection of the same functional type as is today framed by the so called 'Euro-Atlantic constitutional arch or circle'.[11] With the globalisation of the

[8] S Marks, 'Naming Global Administrative Law' (2005) *Journal Of International Law And Politics* 995, 998 ff.

[9] J-B Auby, 'Globalisation et Droit Public' (2002) 14 *Revue Européenne de Droit Public* 1219, 1237.

[10] N 2 above, at 172.

[11] We are here alluding to the 'circle of constitutional states' (Kreis der Verfassungsstaaten) or the 'joint Euro-Atlantic interactive connection of constitutions' (Gemeineuropäisch-atlantischen Wirkungszusammenhang der Verfassungen) of Häberle. The formation of a 'common legal thought' (Gemeinrechtsdenken) has played a special role in the phenomenon of the 'Europeisation of Europe', this based on the shared respect for human rights and other fundamental principles. But it would be wrong to circumscribe this 'shaping of a new common law' to the European arena. The legal-cultural heritage on which this is based is in fact transatlantic. In the constitutional State, the European heritage intersects first with that of the US and then also with other important countries on the other side of the Atlantic, including Brazil. There is therefore a 'Euro-Atlantic arch or circle' cemented by

administrative process, we have in fact witnessed the continuation (or a fresh phase) of a dynamic which, over more than half a century, has left its mark on a considerable number of domestic systems of administrative law. It is therefore important to understand how these have come together around an idea of intrinsic justice in the design of administrative procedure. This movement has amounted above all to harmonisation and not unification of national systems. Common guiding principles lay down the general thrust without specifying the details of implementation. Compatibility derives from sufficient proximity without completely eliminating differences[12].

In short, the principle of *due or fair administrative process* is not exclusive to the transnational or international experience. Instead, it has a bearing on all dealings between those exercising administrative authority and those on the receiving end, irrespective of setting. The different ways in which the principle is fleshed out in domestic systems therefore offer an important platform for reflection on how developments in the field of administrative process might unfold, internationally and transnationally, in the years to come. But before predicting evolution on the lines of a possible synthesis of national experiences, or else envisaging a wholly novel tendency at the global level, we need first to understand the common, and uncommon, ground between the various antecedents in the formulation and application of due or fair administrative process. It would not appear utopian to point to *due or fair administrative process* as the value cementing the globalisation of administrative process, provided it is based on a sufficient definition of the patterns of fairness. But in adopting this point of departure, we presuppose that the differences we may find between the evolutionary dynamics within the 'Euro-Atlantic constitutional arch or circle' have not undermined the essential shared position on the scope and the requirements of due or fair administrative process and on its nature as both an objective legal principle and a legal right.

The central purpose of the present study is therefore to decide whether the different routes travelled in the affirmation of *due process* as the principle of administrative adjudication and rule-making processes in Anglo-Saxon legal systems (in particular, that of the United States (US)) and of *fair* or '*equitable*' or '*equitativo*' *process* as the correlative principle in Romano-Germanic systems have created shared axiological benchmarks, or whether they have generated an array of sub-principles and modes of application which would be difficult to reconcile. Needless to say, in the latter event, the consolidation of a form of global administrative process around a single set of legal values and the functional structures for implementation would prove more problematic.

adoption of the dignity of the human being as an anthropological cultural premise of the constitutional State. *cf* Häberle, 'Gemeineuropäisches Verfassungsrecht' (1991) 18 *EnGRZ-Europäische Grundrechte Zeitschrift* 261, 261, 262, 267, 269 and 274.

[12] Delmas-Marty, n 6 above, at 87.

The Notion of 'Due or Fair Administrative Process'

Before proceeding with this analysis, two points should be clarified by way of demarcating more precisely the scope of our study. The first concerns the meaning of 'administrative process'; and the second concerns our use of the expression 'due or fair process' instead of the term 'due process' that is more usual in legal writings in the US or those systems that have been closely influenced by US legal culture.

For the purposes this study, 'administrative process' means the sequential structure, established by legal rules, of conduct on the part of the administrative authorities and the private parties with which they have dealings, with a view to the preparation, adoption and execution of administrative decisions through the gathering and processing of relevant information. The term 'decisions' is used here with a broad meaning: initially conceived of and legislated for with regard to administrative adjudication (that is, individualised determinations), administrative process has since seen its field of action expanded. To a greater or lesser extent, depending on the domestic legal systems and without prejudice to the differentiation of legal disciplines, administrative process has been extended to the formation of contracts (legal procurement procedures, *marchés publics*), to the drafting and issuing of legal rules by the administration and even to the preparation and follow-through of the material operations of the administrative authorities as provided for in law.

The interrelations between administrative process and judicial review of administrative action are clear and are tending to increase due to the growing powers of judges over the administrative authorities in most of the domestic systems of the 'Euro-Atlantic constitutional arch or circle'.[13] But although both these forms fit within a very broad concept of *process* (where there is also room for other realities, such as the legislative process and the electoral process), they are not to be confused, not least because they correspond to the exercise of different State powers in constitutional systems characterised by the separation of powers.

[13] The expansion of judges' powers of review of administrative action—particularly with regard to interim measures, to the final remedial orders available in new types of urgent procedure (for instance, enforcement measures provided by the EC Remedies Directives in the context of EC procurement law), to injunctions requiring public authorities to take decisions unlawfully omitted or refused (eg in Verpflichtungsklagen in Germany, or in acções de condenação à prática de acto administrativo devido in Portugal) or to the powers of substitution of the administration by the judge for the purpose of enforcement of judicial review decisions—has resulted in a greater number of situations where the judicial review process and administrative process overlap chronologically. It is no longer possible to point, as a rule, to a linear sequence in which judicial review follows on from administrative process, the latter being first concluded.

In national legal systems, such as those of Germany, Italy, Portugal or Spain, the distinction has given rise to semantic tags, with the expressions Verwaltungsverfahren,[14] procedimento amministrativo,[15] procedimento administrativo[16] or procedimiento administrativo[17] corresponding to the sequential ordering of administrative conduct, whilst Verwaltungsprozess, processo amministrativo or processo administrativo are used to designate the sequential plan whereby the courts take cognisance of, and decide upon, disputes arising from situations governed by administrative law and which normally have the administrative authorities as at least one of the parties.

In contrast with these national examples, in contemporary French law, the administrative courts remain a jurisdictionalised arm of the administrative authorities, forming a part of the country's administrative structure. For this reason, procedure in the courts and the procedure of 'active administration' (as opposed to 'litigious administration') are qualitatively indistinguishable, as they do not represent the exercise of constitutionally separate powers. However, the term 'procédure', commonly used to designate the two forms, is qualified as 'contentieuse' (litigious or judicial) or 'non contentieuse',in order to distinguish the organisational setting.[18]

In the US and English legal systems, the terms 'process', 'procedure' and 'proceedings' are used indiscriminately to refer to procedural forms of administrative action and to judicial proceedings for direct review of administrative action, as well as to process rights before an agency or before the courts.[19] But the expression 'administrative process' is used to designate the procedures that agencies are required to use in order to reach decisions, in other words regulatory process and procedural rights in interaction with an administrative decision-making process. And whilst there is the idea that the courts conduct different types of process depending on the subject matter (eg civil process, criminal

[14] On the distinction between Verwaltungsverfahren and Verwaltungsprozess in German law, see, by way of example, E Schmidt-Aßmann, 'Einleitung' in F Schoch, E Schmidt-Aßmann, and R Pietzner (eds), *Verwaltungsgerichtsordnung*, I (München, Beck, 2008) paras 196 ff.

[15] On the distinction between procedimento amministrativo and processo amministrativo in Italian law, see, by way of example, L Mazzorolli et al, *Diritto Amministrativo*, I (Bologna, Monduzzi, 2005) at 536 and 567 ff.

[16] On the distinction between procedimento administrativo and processo administrativo in Portuguese law, see, by way of example, M Rebelo de Sousa and A Salgado de Matos, *Direito Administrativo Geral*, III, (Lisboa, Dom Quixote, 2006) at 56 ff.

[17] On the distinction between procedimiento administrativo and processo administrativo in Spanish law, see, by way of example, E García de Enterría and TR Fernández, *Curso de Derecho Administrativo*, II, 11th edn (Madrid, Civitas, 2002) at 442 ff.

[18] M Fromont, *La Procédure Administrative Non Contentieuse En Droit Français* (London, Esperia, 2000).

[19] See, by way of example, P Strauss, *Administrative Justice In The United States*, 2nd edn (Durham, Carolina Academic Press, 2002) at 187 and 297; P Craig, *Administrative Law*, 5th edn (London, Thomson, 2003) at 10, 11, 408 and 409.

process), judicial process as relates to administrative law uses the legal language of 'judicial review' and its attendant references to procedures and remedies.[20]

The 'administrative process' considered in this chapter as the general framework of analysis is precisely the collection of procedural forms of administrative action as shaped by procedural requirements and safeguards.

Let us also clarify why, in the title of this chapter, we qualify administrative process as 'due or fair'. If, in this context, the two adjectives go together, why not use just one of them, opting perhaps for 'due process', which is the oldest expression?

The fact is, however, that even in a comparison of US and English law, the two notions are not without specific connotations. *Due process* is expressed as a fundamental right in both the Fifth and the Fourteenth Amendments of the Constitution of the United States. It assures that no person may be deprived of 'life, liberty or property without due process of law'. Historically, this clause reflects the early common law rules of natural justice relating to hearing and bias. So the literal meaning of due process is *fair procedure*. 'Due process guarantees that the state will treat individuals with fundamental fairness.'[21] But, in contemporary English administrative law, not everybody agrees that 'the distinction between the terms *natural justice* and *fairness* is linguistic rather than substantive'. One interpretation sees the emergence of *fairness* as having a broader implication leading to different sets of procedural norms for distinct forms of decision-making.[22] And, today, the US due process doctrines 'differ in a number of respects from British doctrines of natural justice and procedural fairness'.[23]

But, for the purposes of this chapter, we will use the expression 'due or fair process' not only to accommodate the differing particularities of contemporary US and English law. Our intention—which is to encompass a broader reality—would be more readily intelligible if, instead of in English, this study were to be published in a latin language. An example is provided by the various versions of Article 41.1 of the Charter of Fundamental Rights of the European Union. This provision, which will in future serve to underpin the movement towards asserting a right to fair administrative process in the Union's space, is rendered in English as 'the right to have his or her affairs handled … fairly', whilst in French, 'fairly' appears as 'équitablement', and also in the Portuguese version as 'equitativamente'. Now, these terms may allude, in the light of other domestic legal traditions, to normative values not necessarily restricted to the English doctrines of fair process and even less confined to the scope and safeguards of the US due process.

[20] H Woolf, J Jowell, and A Le Sueur, *DeSmith's Judicial Review*, 6th edn (London, Sweet & Maxwell, 2007) at 779.

[21] B Schwartz, *Administrative Law*, 3rd edn (Boston, Toronto and London, Little Brown, 1991) at 224 and 225.

[22] Craig, n 19 above, at 415–17.

[23] D Galligan, *Due Process and Fair Procedures* (Oxford, Clarendon Press, 1996) at 73.

With Article 41, the Charter establishes an obvious parallel between the right to fair administrative process and the right to fair judicial process, in turn enunciated in Article 47. This Article 47 of the Charter corresponds in its core concepts to the central guarantee contained in Article 6.1 of the European Convention on Human Rights (ECHR), which for European legal systems is the closest provision to the due process clause in the US Constitution. In the latin languages versions of Article 6 of the ECHR, we also find 'équitablement' or 'equitativamente' in the place of the English 'fairly'.[24]

The parallel between the appeal in the Charter of Fundamental Rights of the European Union (the Charter) to basic values of judicial process and administrative process represents a move towards the present dualism of the concept of due administrative process in US law. Except in the case of English law, the gradual elaboration of the requirements of fair administrative process has not taken place as a rule in the different European domestic systems through an extended application of a fundamental principle of judicial process, but rather through the ground-breaking affirmation (and not through application by analogy) of principles able to shape the dealings of the administrative authorities with individuals in accordance with the legal value of the 'rule of law' (Rechtsstaat, État de Droit, Stato di Diritto).

However, whilst the Charter expresses a rapprochement between the two shores of the 'Euro-Atlantic constitutional arch or circle' as to the dual direction of due administrative process in the system of public law, this does not signify that doctrines and domestic forms of application have been unified. Accordingly, when we seek to view the principle in the wider setting of global administrative law, we feel it is appropriate to use the composite expression 'administrative due or fair process'. This evokes the melting pot of concepts and implications which recognition of this legal value involves and the need to take into account in this regard the contributions from different national and regional cultures.[25] [26]

[24] But the letter of this article is addressed in principle to process taking place before a court. As happened with the efforts of the US Supreme Court, it is up to the European Court of Human Rights to assess the possibility of extending to administrative process a number of inferences from the idea of fundamental fairness in the way in which the State will exercise decision-making powers in dealing with individuals.

[25] Art 5, s LIV of the Brazilian Constitution enshrines the principle of due process of law ('devido processo legal'), without which 'no person shall be deprived of his or her freedom or property'. Whilst accepting in general that this extends to administrative process, the case law and legal scholarship appear not to have reached uniform understandings as to the reach of this principle.

Argument has raged around a 'property-focused' vision, centred on administrative process leading to immediate limitations to property, such as the case of fiscal process, or on a restricted concept of administrative process, circumscribed to types of adversarial process which involve a dispute between an individual and the public authorities (such as disciplinary process and other punitive processes). By way of example, see on this matter, H Lopes Meirelles, *Direito Administrativo Brasileiro,* 30th edn (São Paulo, Malheiros, 2005) at 664–72; S Ferraz and A Dallari, *Processo Administrativo* (São Paulo, Malheiros, 2003) at 22–25. Doubtless in order to underline the applicability of its principles to all administrative processes handled by the federal authorities irrespective of the type of interests regulated by these processes, Federal Law no 9784, of 29 January.1999 does not

The Dualistic Rationale for Administrative Process

Before turning our attention solely to administrative due or fair process, we should stress that, although fundamental, this is not the only normative concept involved in administrative process.

Due or fair process is a legal value, legal right or (and) legal principle which functions as a guarantee. The ancient components of *audi alteram partem* and *nemo iudex in causa sua*, initially conceived as the necessary requirements for a fair trial, also apply today, brought up to date in the guise of participation and impartiality, to the protection of individuals confronted with the exercise of decision-making powers of the administrative authorities. Although, in the national legal systems of continental Europe, this did not come about as a pure and simple extension to administrative action of the same principle as initially conceived in relation to the exercise of the jurisdiction of the courts, the fact is that the essence of due or fair process is maintained, on the premise that it is fundamental for respect for human dignity that an individual should take part in decisions relating to him or her and should in principle be able to rely on the objectivity of the decision-maker.

But just like administrative law in general, administrative process has not come into being and been structured only to protect the individual from public power. Administrative law, and administrative process as one of its basic institutions, is also designed to realise the public interest through the efficiency of administrative conduct. This means that administrative process should also be organised so as to contribute to the effective application of the law irrespective of whether the recipient of the decision has benefited, and also to assure that administrative discretion is exercised in accordance with a rational judgement as to the best policies.[27]

It follows from this that not all the principles and rules of administrative process may be explained as standards of due or fair process. An example of this

invoke the principle of the due process of law, instead enunciating a set of general principles of administrative process, some of them designed to serve as guarantees (Arts 2 and 3).

[26] It is curious to note that, despite its usual facility for encapsulating legal concepts, the German language is less successful in expressing the legal value known in English as 'due or fair' when applied to process. In the ECHR, the phrase (in Art 6.1) 'everyone is entitled to a fair … hearing' or 'Toute personne a droit à ce que sa cause soit entendue équitablement' is rendered in the German language version as 'Jedermann hat Anspruch darauf, dass seine Sache in billiger Weise … gehört wird'. 'Billigkeit' does actually mean 'equity'. But the use of this term for the present purpose does not appear to offer much comfort, and legal scholars often prefer to have direct recourse to the English expressions 'fair' or 'fair trial'. See, for instance, JA Frowein and AV Peukert, *EMRK—Kommentar*, 2nd edn (Kehl, Strassburg and Arlington, NP Engel, 1996) at 213. Mixed words like 'Verfahrensfairness' reveal the same difficulty. F Huffen, *Verwaltungsprozessrecht*, 2nd edn (München, Beck, 1996) at 593.

The German language version of the Charter of Fundamental Rights of the European Union once again reflects the difficulty in finding a sufficiently accurate term. The concept to which the English version refers, in both Arts 41 and 47, by use of the terms 'fairly' and 'fair' is expressed by two distinct words in the German version: 'gerecht' (just) and 'fairen'.

[27] P Moor, *Droit Administratif* II, 2nd edn (Berne, Staempfli, 2002) at 227.

is offered by the principle—in Article 56 of the Portuguese Code of Administrative Process of 1991 (PCAP)—whereby agencies enjoy powers to enquire on their own initiative into the facts relevant to the decision, even if these facts are not alleged by the interested parties, and to decide on terms broader than or different from those set out in an individual's petition when the public interest so requires. In some countries' legal systems, this capacity amounts to a principle of administrative process, albeit not (at least directly) one of due or fair administrative process, because its main purpose is not to guarantee individual interests.[28]

However, most of the principles of administrative process are directly designed to protect the individual in his or her procedural relations with the administrative authority. This is the case, for instance, of the guarantees of an unbiased authority, of notice of the bringing of proceedings, of being represented by counsel, of having access to the record, of presenting evidence, of being given notice of proposed action and of presenting reasons why it should not be taken, of receiving notice of the final decision and of its reasons and, in due course, of appealing to another administrative authority.[29]

It should however be recalled that most of these principles present a measure of ambivalence seeing that, in addition to their function as guarantees, they also play a role in realising the public interest. For example, participation by the interested parties in the finding of facts in administrative process may also make a functional contribution to the objective of reconstituting the factual situation on which the public administration is called to pronounce. Contact, and even confrontation, between the individual and the agency may bring to the process facts and legal arguments which contribute to a correct administrative decision.[30]

As a further example, we may cite the multiple functions served by the duty on agencies to give reasons for adjudicative decisions. Some domestic legislation establishes a general duty for the public authorities to state grounds for these decisions.[31] In other countries, instead of a general clause, a detailed list is laid

[28] § 26 of the German Law of Administrative Process of 1976 (Verwaltungsverfahrensgesetz—VwVfG) lays down that agencies shall use the means of proof which they deem, at their discretion, to be most appropriate for establishing the matter of fact. The discretion enjoyed by agencies offers them a number of alternatives as they set about the finding of facts, which results in an investigatory strategy based on a balancing act. For the purpose of choosing the means of procuring evidence, a judgment is sought, in the light of the specific circumstances, on the means of investigation which best satisfy the public interest of the administrative decision being reached on the basis of full and accurate knowledge of the relevant factual situation. See D Duarte, *A Norma de Legalidade Procedimental Administrativa* (Coimbra, Almedina, 2006) at 531 s, 565 s and 621 ff.

[29] The right to an effective judicial review remedy is not a matter of administrative process in the strict sense, because it relates to court procedures.

[30] Sérvulo Correia, 'O direito à informação e os direitos de participação dos particulares no procedimento e, em especial, na formação da decisão administrativa' (1994) 9/10 *Legislação* 133, 149–51; J Loureiro, *O Procedimento Administrativo Entre A Eficiência E A Garantia Dos Particulares* (Coimbra, Coimbra Editora, 1995) at 91–93; P Machete, *A Audiência Dos Interessados No Procedimento Administrativo* (Lisboa, Universidade Católica, 1995) at 273 ff.

[31] Art 3, s 1 of the Italian Law of 7 August 1990, no 241 on administrative process and the right of access to documents.

down of the decisions for which grounds must be stated in view of the particular nature of their effects.[32] Now, where the law establishes a general duty to give reasons, the function of this will not be to protect private legal positions whenever—as frequently happens in the 'social State'—the decision has no negative impact on the party concerned or on any other private parties. However, a favourable decision may be unlawful and its illegality may be more easily detected if the reasons for it are known. On the other hand, in the case of lists of decisions for which reasons must be given, whilst these lists include types of decision where the requirement of giving grounds serves the purpose of protection of the individual (for instance, in the Portuguese and Spanish laws, decisions extinguishing or otherwise undermining rights or other legally protected interests), in relation to other types of administrative decisions, the duty of giving reasons corresponds to direct realisation of the public interest, such as preservation of administrative legality and transparency. This is the case, for instance, when the same laws require that reasons be given for decisions where the exercise of discretion results in a deviation from normal practice or from the recommendations of advisory bodies. In any case, it appears undeniable that, even in cases where the duty to state grounds exists primarily for the purpose of individual protection, the objective goals of respect for legality, transparency and for the utmost care in the decision-making process are also served by compliance with this obligation.[33]

The dualistic rationale works usually as a methodological tool concerning the assessment of the sufficiency of the proceedings for the enforcement of the procedural principles.[34]

We should add that, alongside procedural principles, there are also procedural rules and that many of these impose on the public authorities duties of procedural conduct geared only to objective aims of rationality and efficiency. And some of these rules establish duties or impose obligations on individuals as parties to the administrative process. All these normative elements of administrative process fall outside the scope of the requirement of due or fair administrative process and relate instead to the imperative of efficient administrative process.

The consequences of the dualistic rationale vary significantly between different domestic legal systems. In systems such as Germany, where a subjectivist vision predominates, what matters most is the reinstatement of the individual rights breached rather than the reconstitution of the unity of an objective system of legal commands which has been undermined by the exercise of public power at

[32] Art 124, s 1 of the PCAP; Art 54, s 1 of the Spanish Law 30/1992 of 26 November, on general administrative process.

[33] JC Vieira de Andrade, *O Dever Da Fundamentação Expressa De Actos Administrativos* (Coimbra, Almedina, 1990) at 65 ff.

[34] As an example of the recognition of the dualistic common rationale for administrative process, we may cite Art 267 s 5 of the Portuguese Constitution. This states that, 'Administrative procedure shall be the subject of a special law which shall ensure the rationalisation of the instruments used by agencies and the participation by citizens in the formation of decisions which affect them'.

variance with the relevant rules. Accordingly, non-compliance with procedural rules will only result in the invalidity of the adjudication when, as a consequence of a rule's purpose of individual protection, we might consider that breach of that rule represented violation of an individual right to a certain procedure (Schutznormlehre).[35]

In other national systems, judicial review remedies may serve simultaneously to reconstitute the offended individual right and to remove the unlawful administrative decision (this approach is highly developed in Portuguese law and also exists to a lesser extent in, for instance, French law). In these circumstances, standing does not depend on allegation of an offended individual right and it is sufficient for the private party to demonstrate that he or she will enjoy a personal benefit from annulment of the contested decision. The advantage of this approach lies in the less rigorous requirements for the interest needed in order for the individual to have standing to bring personal proceedings to the benefit of preserving the integrity of the pyramid of legal commands.

Within the framework of these systems, the distinction between rules of administrative process with or without a direct purpose of individual protection ceases to be of practical relevance, given that breach of either type of rule may form grounds for an application for judicial review.

However, in the legal framework for the invalidity of administrative adjudication (or rule-making, or contracting) due to breach of the rules of administrative process by the agencies, another variable comes into play, which adds to the complexity. This new factor relates to the degree to which the procedural norms are instrumental to the substantive outcomes. This is a question of philosophy and legal methodology which falls outside our present scope. We may nonetheless say that the central issue here is whether the role of procedural principles and rules is always the reduction of administrative costs resulting from incorrect decisions or whether they (or some of them) serve inherent values irrespective of particular outcomes.[36]

The inherent value of certain procedural principles transcends all questions of instrumentality, with regard either to the pursuit of the public interest, or else to the protection of individual's interest in a certain outcome, or even of both. The value of procedural rules, when viewed from the perspective of instrumentality, is always relative. When a procedural rule is observed, the outcome may nonetheless be legally incorrect because of a material error of law. But similarly a procedural rule may be disregarded and the outcome still be correct in the light of the applicable substantive norms.

[35] *cf* F Kopp and WR Schenke, *VwGO—Verwaltungsgerichtsordnung*, 12th edn (München, Beck, 2000) at 282–84. Under the terms of s 2 of §42 of VwGO (the German Law on the administrative courts), in principle, application for judicial review is only admissible when the claimant pretends that an administrative decision (or the refusal or abstention from adjudication) offended an individual right in his or her legal sphere.

[36] M Bayles, *Procedural Justice: Allocating to Individuals* (Dordrecht, Boston and London, Kluwer, 1990) at 127–39.

This is so because the procedural rule does not regulate the conflict between the final outcomes sought: the process does not exist only in and for itself, but rather with a view to enforcing the effects of substantive rights whose immediate parameters are not procedural.

There are at least two ways in which a procedural illegality can be discounted or disregarded.

The first occurs when the procedural rule is not observed but, due to fortuitous or other circumstances, the individual or public interest that it is designed to safeguard is assured. It may be, for instance, that the interested party was not notified of the bringing of proceedings, but that he or she learned of them by some other means and intervened in due time. If the interest to which the procedural requirement is directed is assured, it would be obdurate to insist on complying with a formality just because it failed to play the role which justifies it being required by law. In such an event, even if the rule has an inherent value, this value is assured albeit by aleatory means.[37]

There is however a second and more radical means of discounting a procedural illegality relating to the *principle of the upholding or conservation of substantively correct administrative decisions*, asserted by the legal scholars and case law of several countries. It is generally understood that, despite any procedural defects, a final decision will be deemed valid when its content could not have been different in the light of the applicable legal rules and the factual circumstances of the specific case. It makes no sense for the courts to overturn an administrative decision, even if adopted without observance of the legal requirements as regards procedure, when the agency is obliged by law to decide the case again and to adopt a decision identical in all respects to the previous decision.[38] It

[37] By way of example, see M Caetano, *Manual de Direito Administrativo* I, 10th edn (Lisboa, Coimbra Editora, 1973) at 471–72; R Chapus, *Droit administratif général* I, 15th edn (Paris, Montchrestien, 2001) at 1035.

[38] In some cases, the solution expounded follows directly from the law. For instance, under the terms of §46 of the German VwVfG, the administrative decision will not be quashed on the basis of procedural defects when it is apparent that the procedural impropriety had no influence on the decision. This wording is designed to encompass even certain situations where discretion is exercised, and replaced, in the 1996 review, a different wording under which the decision could not be quashed when, by law, no other decision could have been reached. See F Kopp and U Ramsauer, *VwVfG-Verwaltungsverfahrensgesetz*, 7th edn (München, Beck, 2000) at 954 and, in more general terms, C Starck, *La Constitution Cadre et Mesure du Droit* (Paris, Economia, 1994) at 138.

The solution, in which a procedural illegality is only regarded as of no essential importance when the content of the decision could not have been different from that actually adopted, is today followed or provided for in other European countries. See, by way of example, F Caringella, *Corso di Diritto Amministrativo* II, 3rd edn (Milano, Giuffrè, 2004) at 1382; García de Enterría and Fernández, n 17 above, vol I, at 646. The Portuguese Supreme Administrative Court has taken the same line. For instance, in one decision of the Plenary of the First Section of 25 May 2006, it was affirmed that the principle of the upholding of conservation of the administrative decision makes it possible to disregard the failure to comply with the duty of hearing the interested party on the draft administrative decision when the decision is pronounced by an agency under the objective incidence of injunctive rules that impose an adjudication to that effect and countenance no other in the light of the specific circumstances.

is in this sense that frequent claims can be heard today that there is an increasing tendency for procedural illegalities to be disregarded for the sake of preserving the right outcomes. It is hazardous to make generalisations in this regard, given that the shift of the emphasis from formal procedures to substantive outcomes stumbles upon the particular emphasis on procedures in certain domestic legal systems.[39]

In any case, we presume that the question is posed in similar terms in relation to the English remedy of *mandamus*, the German Verpflichtungsklage or of the Portuguese acção de condenação à prática de acto administrativo devido, whereby the applicant asks the court to order an agency to carry out a public duty owed to him or her and consisting of a certain administrative decision. In these cases, a prior administrative process will have taken place in the course of which the agency rejected a request or kept silent, failing to exercise its power. This administrative process may have contained procedural flaws but as the application is not for the quashing of a decision but rather for an order for a certain decision to be taken, the previous failure to observe procedural requirements has no role as grounds for the award of the judicial remedy. The only possible grounds are the applicant's right to an administrative decision with a particular legal content.

In short, the scope for alleging procedural defects as grounds for a judicial remedy tends to be circumscribed by the exercise of discretion and by situations which combine both procedural and substantial illegalities.

In the latter event, the procedural illegality will nonetheless be sidelined, given that the judicial decision will centre above all on the legal flaws in the substantial outcome. The grounds for the decision will reveal, with greater or lesser accuracy, the material parameters for an alternative administrative decision. In such an event, the parallel judicial review for process irregularity would not be needed for founding a quashing order. Reasons of procedural economy would make it dispensable were it not for the advantage of preventing the repetition of the same improprieties in the fresh administrative process (or as from the reopening of the previous administrative process) in the case of resumption of the exercise of the agency's jurisdiction for adjudication in respect of the same concrete situation.

On the other hand, the observance of procedural requirements retains its full importance wherever the exercise of discretion is involved. The fact that there is no legally binding solution adds to the value of the proceduralist approach as a basis for the gathering of the relevant facts, the identification of public and private interests deserving consideration, and the relative assessment or balancing of these interests in keeping with criteria of proportionality.

If the content of the decision is to be reached not through compliance with fixed legal patterns for administrative adjudication but by taking into account in

[39] Galligan, n 23 above, at 167–68.

a rationally balanced way the public and private interests meriting legal protection as they present themselves in the circumstances of a specific case, then the agency cannot claim to have taken proper account of the particular case if the legal way to act was ignored. In the exercise of discretion, procedural requirements, together with a number of methodological standards (proportionality, equality, impartiality, good faith), provide the only means of avoid arbitrariness. Without them, no outcome can be considered correct and, therefore, their being disregarded will inevitably have an invalidating effect.

But when, in the situations and on the terms described above, the procedural defects are irrelevant with regard to the validity of the administrative decision, the difficult question is raised of the nature of due or fair administrative process and of the procedural principles which should be regarded as essential elements of such process, such as the hearing (participation) and guarantees of impartiality. This question leads us to ask whether the depletion of legal worth resulting from failure to observe these principles comes down solely to the possibility of generating wrong outcomes or whether the procedural rationality embodied in these fundamental principles is not also rooted in an inherent autonomous legal value.

With the extension of due process (in a modified form) to administrative processes, the US Supreme Court acknowledged the constitutional value of the individual's right to due process of law when he or she is subjected to the exercise of executive powers. But, under this constitutional mantle, the 'participatory approach' (one of the main ingredients of due process) is linked with the 'dignitary approach'.

Participation is 'fair' in the sense of providing equal opportunities to affected parties to influence the ultimate administrative decision. It responds to deep strains of individualism and political egalitarianism in the US character.[40] The dignitary approach invokes process-oriented arguments to counter mere outcome-oriented motives. 'We do distinguish between losing and being treated unfairly.' And 'process efforts [can be described] as somehow related to disrespect for our individuality, to our not being taken seriously as persons'.[41]

In the jurisprudence of countries of the 'Euro-Atlantic arch or circle', or even expressly affirmed in the wording of their constitutions, human dignity is the supreme value imbued in every fundamental right. Consequently, fundamental rights are distinguished from other legal norms and rights precisely because they are directly instrumental and essential to safeguarding and protecting the value of the human dignity from which they derive their unity of meaning.[42]

[40] J Mashaw, excerpt in P Schuck, *Foundations of Administrative Law*, 2nd edn (New York, Foundation Press, 2004) at 132.

[41] J Mashaw, *Due Process in the Administrative State* (New Haven and London, Yale University Press, 1985) at 162–63.

[42] See the following passages in constitutional texts: Germany, Art 1, 1; Brazil, Art 1, 3; Greece, Art 2, 1; Portugal, Art 1; Spain, Art 10, 1.

Also the Preamble to the Universal Declaration of Human Rights 1948 invokes in the first place

Accordingly, the gradual incorporation in constitutional texts of due or fair administrative process, or of some of its most commonly held principles (such as those of 'hearing', 'representation' or 'reasons'), can only be understood as signifying recognition of the essential role of these norms and rights in the preservation and promotion of human dignity.

This process of incorporation in constitutions is currently underway. In the US, it is simply a further development of the extension to certain forms of administrative conduct of a constitutional principle already in force in relation to judicial adjudication. The same is true in English law having in view that the common law principle of natural justice constitutes judge-made constitutional law.[43] The extension of the requirement of fairness to other forms of administrative decision making other than adjudication (such as mediation, arbitration, contract and managerial decision) does not appear to involve a shift in this constitutional basis of procedural intervention.[44]

In domestic legal systems belonging to the Romano-Germanic family, certain principles of administrative process have in turn been gradually finding their way into constitutional texts. Despite in most cases referring to the legislator the task of detailed regulation, several constitutions enunciate the rights of private parties with interests in administrative proceedings. The constitutions of Spain (Article 105, c)), Greece (Article 20, 2) and Portugal (Article 267, 5) assert the right of individuals to a hearing in administrative proceedings which may lead to a decision affecting their interests. The constitutions of Spain (Article 105, b)), Greece (Article 10, 3) and Portugal (Article 268, 1) proclaim the right to information from the administrative authorities. The Portuguese Constitution specifically states that individuals are entitled to this information regarding administrative processes in which they may have an interest, but the right

'recognition of the inherent dignity … of all members of the human family'. The same is true of the Preambles to the International Covenants on Civil and Political Rights 1966 and on Economic, Social and Cultural Rights 1966.

On the same issue, see the following legal texts, amongst others: R Claytyon and H Tomlinson, *The Law of Human Rights* I (Oxford, Oxford University Press, 2000) at 23; LM Díez-Picazo, *Sistema de Derechos Fundamentales*, 2nd edn (Navarra, Thomson/ Civitas, 2005) at 68s; G Lebreton, *Libertés publiques et droits de l'Homme*, 7th edn (Paris, Armand Colin, 2005) at 158; J Melo Alexandrino, *A Estruturação Do Sistema De Direitos, Liberdades E Garantias Na Constituição Portuguesa* II, (Coimbra, Almedina, 2006) at 294–95, 368–69; J Miranda, *Manual De Direito Constitucional* IV, 3rd edn (Coimbra, Coimbra Editora, 2000) at 180s; M Perry, *The Idea of Human Rights—Four Inquiries* (New York and Oxford, Oxford University Press, 1998) at 13; B Pieroth and B Schlink, *Grundrechte—Staatsrecht* II, 16th edn (Heidelberg, CF Müller, 2000) at 79–84; P Saladin, *Grundrechte Im Wandel*, 3rd edn (Berne, Staempfli, 1982) at 283–84 and 427s; I W Sarlet, *Dignidade da Pessoa Humana e Direitos Fundamentais*, 3rd edn (Porto Alegre, Livraria do Advogado, 2004) at 84s; K Stern, 'Sinn und Form der Grundrechte' in J Isensee and P Kirchhof (eds), *Handbuch des Staatsrechts*, V, *Allgemeine Grundrechtslehren* (Heidelberg, CF Müller, 1992) at 6–7; JC Vieira de Andrade, *Os Direitos Fundamentais na Constituição Portuguesa de 1976*, 3rd edn (Coimbra, Almedina, 2004) at 82s.

[43] S De Smith and R Brazier, *Constitutional and Administrative Law*, 7th edn (London, Penguin Books, 1994) at 24 and 602 ff.

[44] G Anthony, *Judicial Review in Northern Ireland* (Oxford, Hart Publishing, 2008) at 104–05; Craig, n 19 above, at 415–18; Galligan, n 23 above, at 185–86.

recognised in other constitutional texts also encompasses this entitlement. In addition, the constitutions of the Netherlands (Article 18, 1) and Portugal (Article 20, 2) recognise the right to legal counsel in administrative process. The Portuguese Constitution (Article 268, para. 3) lays down that the interested parties shall be notified of 'administrative acts' (decisions rendered through administrative adjudication) and that, when such acts affect rights or other legally protected interests, the authorities must expressly state their reasons in an accessible formulation.

Contrary to what is now the case with Article 41.1 of the Charter of Fundamental Rights of the European Union, national constitutions do not yet proclaim an essential right to due or fair process, but instead, as we have seen, incorporate some of the respective sub-principles or requirements.

This is, however, no obstacle, at least in some of these countries, to the courts considering that the 'super-principle' of due or fair administrative process is rooted in the constitution. In Germany, for instance, grounds are drawn from two constitutional sources: the principle of Staatsrecht and the radiant strength of 'classical' or 'first generation' human rights whose defence necessarily involves certain prerequisites of administrative process.[45] The same understanding has been defended in Portugal.[46]

The classification as fundamental rights (and not mere non-constitutional rights) of due or fair administrative process (as a super-principle or Oberbegriff) and of some of its sub-principles or dimensions (such as the dimension of participation—hearing, the dimension of transparency—notice of the proceedings and access to the record, and the dimension of information—notice of the decision and giving of reasons) nonetheless generates difficulties in terms of systemic consistency. If they are fundamental rights, this means that the constitution regards them as a requirement and a direct means for assuring respect for human dignity. But if this is the case, how can we justify the systematic subordination of due or fair administrative process to the principle of legality, albeit only in those cases where the law imposes a particular substantive outcome as the only valid one?

As principles, human rights must be balanced against other fundamental rights or objective values with which they clash in specific cases. But this balancing means more or less rigorous solutions for enforcing standards of fair treatment and not the total irrelevance of the absence of procedural fairness in preference to the substantive legality of the outcome. If fairness corresponds to respect for the dignity of human beings when confronted with the exercise of public authority, how might such respect be completely dispensed with?

[45] P Kunig, *Das Rechtsstaatsprinzip* (Tübingen, Mohr, 1986) at 373–78; R Pitschas, *Verwaltungsverantwortung und Verwaltungsverfahren* (München, Beck, 1990) at 521–25; P Stelkens, *Verwaltungsverfahren* (München, Beck, 1991) at 56–57.

[46] J Loureiro, *O Procedimento Administrativo entre a Eficiência e a Garantia dos Particulares* (Coimbra, Coimbra Editora, 1995) at 255–58.

As it makes no sense to invalidate an administrative decision which would only have to be reiterated, on precisely the same terms, other tools will be needed to maintain the axiological consistency of the system.

In terms of global administrative law, we would set out three suggestions.

In the first place, each global sub-system should avoid over-formalisation and over-regulation of procedural principles, leaving it to jurisdictional and para-jurisdictional bodies to adjust the flexible standards to the scale of the interests at stake in different types of concrete situations. This would help to limit the number of problematic situations and to prevent procedural guarantees from serving too frequently as an impediment to the smooth attainment of the correct outcomes.

A second measure for reducing the weight of contradictions between substantive and procedural legality would consist of promoting urgent judicial or para-judicial review proceedings able to overcome the infringement of essential procedural requirements before the conclusion of the administrative process. The European 'Remedies Directives' relating to the application of review procedures to the award of public contracts might serve as source of inspiration.[47]

Thirdly, it would make sense to develop means of determining public liability for moral damages in more serious cases where, although the legally imposed outcomes are substantively correct, failure to comply with procedural requirements has clearly caused loss, albeit a non-pecuniary loss. Several domestic legal systems, such as the English, French and Portuguese systems, today accept public liability for non-pecuniary loss.[48]

DIFFERENT PATHS IN THE FORMATION OF DUE OR FAIR ADMINISTRATIVE PROCESS IN THE FRAMEWORK OF THE 'EURO-ATLANTIC CONSTITUTIONAL ARCH OR CIRCLE'

The Dual Itineraries

As regards its legal nature, its material threshold and its procedural blueprint, due or fair administrative process, as known today on both sides of the Atlantic, has evolved along two itineraries.

In the US and England, this took place fundamentally by transposing one of the core principles of judicial process into the scope of administrative action. It was therefore necessary to define gradually the fields encompassed by the new

[47] Consolidated text of the EC public sector remedies Directive 89/665/EEC including the amendments introduced by the Directive 2007/66/EC.

[48] Craig, n 19 above, at 885–88; C Harlow, *State Liability: Tort Law and Beyond* (Oxford, University Press, 2004) at 109–16; M Deguergue, *Jurisprudence Et Doctrine Dans L'Élaboration Du Droit De La Responsabilité Administrative* (Paris, LGDJ, 1994) at 424; C Cadilha, *Regime da Responsabilidade Civil Extracontratual do Estado e Demais Entidades Públicas* (Coimbra, Coimbra Editora, 2008) at 77–78.

version of the principle, both in terms of the different types of administrative activity (adjudication, rule-making, contracting, planning, inspection or investigation) and in terms of the types of interests affected by these activities (whether all or only some, and, in the latter case, which). And at the same time adjustments had to be made to the judicial model for the exercise of executive powers, modifying the old procedural requirements and satisfying the need for new requirements.

In short, this was a *deductive itinerary*, which consisted of extracting multiple elements of a material and functional legal framework from an overarching principle of great axiological importance, albeit vague in content.

In contrast, in continental Europe, the route followed over the last two centuries can be best described as an *inductive itinerary*, moving from the particular to the general. This happened over several stages. During the first stage, which we may locate in the nineteenth century and the early decades of the twentieth, the courts laid down isolated procedural safeguards and requirements for the rational preparation of administrative decisions. Gradually, and especially in the final quarter of the twentieth century, these isolated topics were organised into laws or codes of administrative process on the basis of a composite rationale founded on a dualistic dignitary and utilitarian approach. A general tendency towards constitutional incorporation of the foundations of administrative law was also reflected on the procedural plane, with the enunciation of the fundamental rights of participants and of functional requirements. Finally, although there was not yet any express provision to this effect in constitutional texts, legal scholars and the courts started to infer from various constitutional passages an implicit unitary foundation consisting of an overarching principle of fair administrative process. The recent Charter of Fundamental Rights of the European Union has explicitly enshrined just such a principle.

The processes summarised above were not linear. Suffice it to recall the importance of the Administrative Procedure Act 1946 in US law and the influence of the judicial procedural model on the first European law on administrative process: the Austrian law of 1925. But the principle did not take shape in continental Europe from a unitary idea and was not conceived with the purpose of extending one of the principles of judicial process to administrative action and to the legal relations between agencies and the subjects of regulation. Moreover, the legislative definition of procedural safeguards and functional requirements in the US cannot be considered as a part of a unitary movement to set detailed rules for due administrative process, given that this remains confined to the plane of constitutional law.[49]

In the following section, we shall not attempt an in-depth analysis of due or fair administrative process in different domestic legal systems, but instead

[49] 'There is a common tendency to confuse nonconstitutional procedural rights with due process procedural rights… The cases laying down the basic principle that an agency must follow its own procedural rules enunciate principles of a federal administrative law rather than of constitutional law

endeavour only to outline how it has been gradually implemented or asserted. This evolutionary course is of interest to this study as it reveals a dynamic process which will continue to unfold in global administrative law.

The Legal Systems of the United States and England: The Deductive Itinerary

On its procedural side,[50] the doctrine of due process refers to certain procedures regarded as necessary for the fairness of a trial and which were later extended in modified form to administrative processes.

Due process is required by the Fifth and Fourteenth Amendments to the Constitution of the United States: 'No person shall ... be deprived of life, liberty or property, without due process of law', nor shall any State do it. This is an open textured clause, 'wonderfully vague' for the purpose of affirming a values frame to the procedures required by increasingly interventionist government.[51] Centred on a participatory ideology (notwithstanding its wider reverberations), the clause has proven particularly well able to adapt either to shifts in the paradigmatic legal techniques of social control or to different ideals or models of constitutionalism.[52]

The definition of the doctrine of due administrative process provided by the US Supreme Court has focused on two fundamental aspects: delimitation of the interests protected (*scope*) and definition of the procedural safeguards required (*proceedings*). Due process offers a highly indeterminate notion of a legal value. And its application to administrative process has exacerbated the climate of uncertainty surrounding it due to the uselessness of part of the traditional thinking concerning the judicial process. The courts have therefore found themselves impelled to specify how this is to be applied in order to demarcate the scope of application of the constitutional imperative and to stipulate the actual procedural safeguards involved.

As an unavoidable result of the piecemeal way in which the courts define the law—as and when issues arise—construction of the architecture of due process has not been a wholly consistent and linear process.[53] This has negative and

binding up on the States. This issue is one of practical as well as semantic significance. To elevate a procedural right to the due process plane would make it binding on the states under the Fourteenth Amendment. See Schwarz, n 21 above, at 226.

[50] Galligan, n 23 above, at 172. The doctrine of due process as a constitutional standard has also had a substantive side meaning which is that administrative action is subject to the law and to certain general constitutional principles. This chapter does not deal with 'substantive due process', a rather confusing notion for a continental European legal mind.

[51] Mashaw, n 41 above, at 7. State and local activity only became subject to due process review under the federal Constitution after the ratification of the Civil War amendments.

[52] Mashaw, n 41 above, at 3, 7, 30 and 31.

[53] R Pierce, S Shapiro, and P Verkuil, *Administrative Law and Process*, 3rd edn (New York, Foundation Press, 1999) at 248. In particular with regard to the nature of the interests in liberty or

positive consequences. The negative consequences lie in uncertainty and insecurity as to the future determinations of the courts. On the other hand, that 'uncertainty' corresponds with a flexibility that allows the courts to fashion different approaches to disputes depending on socio-economic circumstances and dominant conceptions of what is needed.

In any case, there are some identifiable trends that permit a fuller understanding of the role of due process in relation to administrative action. In the first place, this is a constitutional imperative, making it a yardstick for assessing the validity of legislative rules. And secondly, it is a fundamental right. Its purpose is therefore merely to protect individuals. The efficiency of administrative action in pursuing the public interest is an autonomous value, which can guide the legislator in setting procedural administrative rules, but it is not part of the idea of due process. The courts have inferred from this postulate that due process requires procedural safeguards only in the case of adjudication with disadvantageous effects for individuals. There are, however, broad swathes of proceduralised administrative activity which fall outside the due process clause. This is the case of rule-making by administrative authorities.[54]

As regards the scope of due process, in other words, the interests which it protects from administrative action, the courts (and in particular, the Supreme Court) are faced with the need to decide on how to understand the constitutional clause. One possible understanding would be an updated construction of the formula 'life, liberty and property', seeing in this the expression of all individual interests deserving of the protection of law and potentially vulnerable to adverse impact from a government decision.[55] But, instead of reading 'life, liberty and property' together in such a way that would encompass any important interest of an individual, the Court has preferred to analyse whether each concrete interest fits comfortably in one of the three categories, considered as specific and limited areas not embracing all the elements of the individual legal sphere.

'Life' has not been qualified by the courts for the purpose of administrative process because no agency has the power to deprive an individual of his or her life. In relation to agency actions, we need only determine which situations are regarded by the courts as corresponding to 'liberty' and 'property'.

In deciding whether the interest affected is 'liberty', the Supreme Court has not attempted to offer a precise definition but instead considers that it denotes not merely freedom from bodily restraint but also the right of the individual to contract, to engage in any of the common occupations of life, to acquire useful knowledge, to marry, establish a home and bring up children, all of them

property protected by due process, '[the Supreme] Court's decisions are not linked by a consistent set of principles or by a consistent analytical approach'.

54 Galligan, n 23 above, at 189; Pierce et al, n 53 above, at 254.

55 This is the alternative interpretation advanced by scholars such as Davis and Van Alstyne. See Pierce et al, n 53 above, at 228.

'essential to the orderly pursuit of happiness by free men'.[56] However, despite specifications of this type, the Court has experienced difficulties in determining the scope of liberty interests for the purposes of due process. According to respected authors, the Court has been retreating from its previous broad interpretation, limiting the scope of protection accorded to interests that previously qualified as liberty and its treatment of this subject deserves to be termed as inconsistent.[57]

The Supreme Court has also had difficult delimiting the content of property. Here, the Supreme Court was initially reluctant to develop an approach that would take 'property' beyond narrow meanings of the right to ownership towards one that would include entitlement to welfare provision as a necessary correlate of life in a modern urban and industrialised society. For a period, the Court considered that such entitlements (for instance to the continuation of welfare payments or even government employment) were 'privileges' and not 'rights' and consequently not included within the scope of due process under the umbrella of 'property'.

This distinction, which severely limited the benefits of due process clause protection in the light of modern living conditions, was set aside in 1970 in the leading case of *Goldberg v Kelly*. For the first time, the Court held that a welfare payment should be considered as a property interest within the scope of the due process clause.[58]

At that time, however, the Court had yet to develop criteria for adjusting the range of procedural requirements to the interests actually combined in the specific case in hand. Without the completed roadmap for adapting to administrative process an instrument first developed for judicial process, the Court assumed that the interest was included within the scope of the clause that a judicial-type hearing would be required prior to terminating the welfare benefit. Although positive insofar as it broadened the scope of the due procedure clause, the *Goldberg* decision pointed to a procedural solution almost impossible to apply to the millions of agency decisions concerning eligibility for every form of government benefit.[59] This is why, in the years that followed, the Court sought to limit the possible reach of the *Goldberg* decision, circumscribing the number of interests classifiable as 'property' for the purposes of the scope of the due process clause. The threshold condition was again used to narrow rather than to widen the scope of constitutional procedural protection through 'disparate attitudes' which are difficult if not impossible to reconstitute through systemic logic.[60]

[56] *Meyer v Nebraska*, 262 US 390, 399 (1923), quoted by Pierce et al, n 53 above, at 243–44.

[57] Pierce et al, n 53 above, at 243–47.

[58] Mashaw, n 41 above, at 99–101; Pierce et al, n 43 above, at 231–32; Strauss, n 19 above, at 53–56.

[59] Pierce et al, n 53 above, at 232.

[60] Galligan, n 23 above, at 190; Pierce et al, n 53 above, at 232–36.

Viewed in retrospect, the *Goldberg v Kelly* case permits a clearer understanding of the dilemma posed by extending to administrative process a due process clause still wrapped in the 'placenta' formed in the womb of judicial process. In modern democracies, growing importance has been attached to the requirement that administrative decision-making should present attributes such as participation by the interested parties, transparency and the absence of bias. But if the aim were to satisfy these requirements through the judicial trial form instead of through other more flexible and less costly procedural instruments, many administrative decisions would necessarily have to be excluded from the scope of the clause.

As soon as this risk of an impasse loomed more clearly in legal thought, the Supreme Court could no longer excuse itself from cutting the Gordion knot (or, at least, trying to do so). This is what happened with the decision in another leading case for the doctrine of due administrative process: *Mathews v Eldridge* decision.[61] The issue was once again the role of the Constitution in procedures for terminating welfare benefits. But this time the decision was to have repercussions for 'the largest and most vexing welfare program in existence: the Social Security disability program'.[62] Between the Scylla of denying protection from the due process clause in complete negation of the *Goldberg* decision and the Caribdis of requiring in all instances a trial-type pre-hearing which would be functionally inappropriate and incompatible in terms of the human and financial resources it would absorb, the Court found a middle course in the methodology of *interest balancing*.

In order to characterise due process, the Court conducted an analysis leading to its classification as a *principle*:

> Due process, unlike some legal rules, is not a technical conception with a fixed content unrelated to time, place and circumstances.

And it went on to elucidate:

> identification of the specific dictates of due process generally requires consideration of three distinct factors: First, the private interest that will be affected by the official action; second, the risk of an erroneous deprivation of such interest through the procedures used, and the probable value, if any, of additional or substitute procedural safeguards, and finally, the Government's interest, including the function involved and the fiscal and administrative burdens that the additional or substitute procedural requirement would entail.[63]

This balancing test enables the Court to choose, between a range of procedural safeguards, the one able, in the light of the specific circumstances, to ensure a practical concordance between the public and private interests in the use of

[61] 424 US 319 (1976).

[62] C Farina, 'Due Process At Rashomon Gate: The Stories of *Mathews v. Eldridge*' in P Strauss (ed), *Administrative Law Stories* (New York, Foundation Press, 2006) at 230.

[63] Quoted from Pierce et al, n 53 above, at 259.

procedures. The prognosis of a malfunction due to the insufficiency of procedural requirements acts as a criterion for weighing up the sacrifices required from conflicting interests: preventing the risk of a legally incorrect outcome and making a judicious employment of bureaucratic and fiscal resources.

But the Court has not subsequently been consistent in following the *Mathews* approach. Whilst in some cases this appears to be due to the judges hesitating as to the legislator's margin of autonomy in deciding on the appropriateness of the procedural solutions,[64] in others this may reflect criticisms of the cost-benefit analysis in *Mathews*, accused of being founded on unpredictable judicial valuations[65] or else, in adopting an utilitarian perspective, of losing sight of the dignitary approach.

One of the main bases of the US administrative law system is the distinction between non-constitutional procedural rights and due process procedural rights.[66] In this context, the role of the US Constitution in the administrative process is more one of limiting legislative discretion than one of a central core from which the entire legislative construction of the system will irradiate.

For each agency, the two main legislative sources of administrative process are the Administrative Procedure Act 1946 (APA) and the organisational law governing the particular agency.[67] In principle, the APA provisions must be read with those of the agency's organisational law in order to determine the nature of the procedures to be followed.[68] The APA lays down four types of procedures: formal adjudication, informal adjudication, formal rule-making and informal rule-making. The requirements for both types of informal proceedings are less rigorous than for the corresponding formal proceedings and the procedural requirements for informal adjudication are less rigorous than those for informal rule-making. It is therefore of interest to know whether a given administrative action qualifies as *adjudication* or as *rule-making*, but this is not always easy to determine. The definitions contained in the APA are not much help and the courts tend to distinguish between them depending on whether an action is focused on resolution of actual disputes concerning a specific party or on policy issues underlying a general rule or standard.

The due process clause does not apply to rule-making, which adds to the importance of distinguishing rule-making from adjudication and also provides justification for tighter legal requirements for rule-making: judges have no power to require the agency to use rule-making procedures more rigorous than those resulting from its founding charter, and no constitutional provision can be invoked to this end.

[64] See the reference to decisions geared to a 'legislative judgement approach' in Pierce et al, n 53 above, at 261–62.

[65] Pierce et al, n 53 above, at 262–70.

[66] Schwarz, n 21 above, at 226.

[67] Pierce et al, n 53 above, at 275.

[68] ibid, at 307.

On the other hand, the APA cannot be read as a codification of the minimum procedural safeguards required for adjudication within the scope of protection of the due process clause. The purpose of the APA is not to elaborate on the constitutional clause. Under the APA, informal adjudication requires merely prompt notice of the rejection of any written application, petition or other request, accompanied by a brief statement of the grounds for denial. The thinness of these procedural requirements leaves the judge with the responsibility of extracting any other requirements from the due process clause, depending on the balancing of interests present in each case.[69]

Informal rule-making is also subjected by the APA to a modest set of procedural requirements (although, in this regard, US legislation goes further than most European legislation): public notice of the proposed rule, opportunity for affected members of the public to comment on the proposal, and publication of the final rule accompanied by a statement of its bases and purpose.[70]

The APA does not enunciate the preconditions for application of formal or informal procedures, referring this task to the founding instruments of agencies or other special legislation. In most cases, it is the informal arrangements which are adopted (for instance, in approximately 75 per cent of government actions classifiable as 'adjudication'). It is easy to conclude that the procedural arrangements are extremely varied, as the founding instruments and statutes establish specific rules for the different agencies. The APA does not therefore play a standardising role similar to that of the codes or general laws of administrative process in Western Europe and Latin American countries such as Brazil.

Procedural fairness in the English common law shares its historical origins with those of the US doctrine of procedural due process. The starting point for both is *natural justice*, a common law principle since medieval times. But as a consequence of the judicial application in the US of a written constitution and of the commanding and pervasive effect of the principle of separation of powers in US Constitutional law, distinct models have taken shape over time in the two main Anglo-Saxon legal systems. In contrast to the situation in England, the US soon developed an awareness of the difference between the functions of the executive and the judiciary, even when the first involve adjudication and even after the rise of independent agencies in the administrative State. As Tribe has noted, 'the indeterminacy of labels like "executive" or "judicial" does not mean that "anything goes" with respect to the distribution of governmental power'.[71]

In contrast, in England, separation was not easily achieved between what is meant by *judging* and what consists of *administering*. Only by the end of the nineteenth century, had the justices been largely replaced by elected authorities in

[69] ibid, at 278; Strauss, n 19 above, at 211.

[70] Pierce et al, n 3 above, at 315.

[71] L Tribe, *American Constitutional Law*, 3rd edn (New York, Foundation Press, 2000) at 122, 124, 131, 138 and 140.

the exercise of the main administrative responsibilities.[72] The combination of judicial and administrative functions in the same authorities made it difficult to classify their decisions as judicial or administrative, especially when they affected a person's rights. From a certain point onwards, the courts began to draw a distinction between judicial and quasi-judicial decisions. The latter could be distinguished from other administrative decisions insofar as they required the application of a right to a hearing.

However, as the concept of 'quasi-judicial' was gradually set aside to the benefit of the simple dichotomy of judicial/administrative decisions, the courts were first inclined to consider that, when the authority acted administratively, natural justice would not apply. And as it was considered that the scope of judicial review was natural justice, this reasoning was carried to its logical extreme: the conclusion that administrative decisions enjoyed immunity from judicial review. This finally put an end to the assumption that any adjudication (in other words, any imperative application of law to individual cases) constituted jurisdictional activity. The essential role of the organisational element in identifying a court in the face of other authorities endowed with determinative power was therefore reinstated. But this step in the right direction was accompanied by another in a wrong one: considering that judicial review would only make sense in connection with the relationship between lower and higher courts and not with the relationship between public administration and the courts.[73]

However, soon 'judges grew more sensitive to natural justice' and it became clear that its principles applied to the procedural part of statutory procedures 'even though the final decision was one of policy'.[74] The turning point was reached in the ruling rendered on *Ridge v Baldwin* ([1964] AC 40). In it, the House of Lords decided that a chief constable, who could only be dismissed with due cause, was entitled to notice of the charge and an opportunity to be heard. The idea prevailed that the judicial element (for the purpose of the duty to act in conformity with natural justice) should be inferred from the nature of the power exercised and its effects on the individual, not from the technicalities of the different writs or by identifying interests as rights or privileges.[75]

[72] P Leyland and G Anthony, *Textbook on Administrative Law*, 6th edn (Oxford, Oxford University Press, 2008) at 11–12.

[73] On the periods of *judicial quietism*, in the twentieth century 'when the judiciary generally retreated from applying the *ultra vires* doctrine, save on narrowly defined grounds' in part because of hesitation on the scope of natural justice, see Leyland and Anthony, n 72 above, at 14; W Wade and CF Forsyth, *Administrative Law*, 9th edn (Oxford, Oxford University Press, 2004) at 473 and 487, in particular with regard to the decisions of *Franklin v Minister of Town and Country Planning* [1948] (*Stevenage*), *Nakkuda Ali v Jayaratne* [1951] and *R v Metropolitan Police Commissioner ex p Parker* [1953].

[74] Wade and Forsyth, n 73 above, at 473.

[75] In 1973, we criticised the position taken by the English courts in requiring the existence of a 'duty to act judicially'—unsuited to the need to distinguish between judicial activity and administrative action—in order to impose participation and guarantees of unbiased decision-making in connection with administrative process. In the same work from 1973, we praised the then recent *Ridge v Baldwin* decision, for confirming that administrative action is subject to judicial review and for the

This important decision opened the way for application of the natural justice principle to all administrative action capable of generating harmful effects on individuals. Even so in the post-*Ridge* period, the courts continued to be faced with numerous cases concerning the material criterion for the applicability of natural justice.[76]

In English administrative law, the general principle of procedural fairness gradually delineated by the courts may still be called *natural justice*. But to the extent to which it has become clear that it applies not only to judicial decision-makers but also to administrative bodies when they decide over rights, interests and legitimate expectations, the expressions *fairness* and *duty to act fairly* have increasingly come into favour, as if to remind us that there has been a qualitative broadening of the concept's meaning.[77]

As happened with the construction of administrative *due process* in the US, the development of *fairness* may be analysed from two main perspectives: that of applicability and that of the panoply of procedural safeguards necessary to ensure fair treatment. But these concepts have been fleshed out differently on both sides of the Atlantic. With regard to the scope of the duty to act fairly, there is no need in England to classify situations in terms of concepts such as *liberty* and *property*, given that no constitutional rule limits the fundamental requirements of procedural protection to these aspects of human existence. Moreover, the minimal procedural blueprint is not rooted in norms of a formal constitutional nature, conferring on them a clearly supra-legislative value. Rather than the yardstick of the validity of legal rules on administrative process, 'the rules of natural justice/fairness are a set of uncodified common law rules offering procedural safeguards that have been developed over time by the judiciary themselves to ensure that decision makers act according to basic standards of fairness'.[78] These rules continue to develop and, in that regard, the common law is nowadays influenced in particular by Article 6 ECHR, guaranteeing the right to a fair trial.[79]

The fact that, in English law, there is no need to waste time on highly abstract discussions of what should be understood as *property* or *liberty* for the purpose of the applicability of the rules of fairness does not mean that there are no questions as to the scope of applicability of the duty to act fairly.

For as long as the only rationale for natural justice was an idea of protection against the exercise of the powers of the courts, the problem centred on the scope of the duty to act judicially. But the new awareness that the imperative of fairness also applied to the exercise of powers by administrative bodies without this

possibilities it opened up of releasing the issue of administrative fairness from the constraints deriving from inappropriate application of the rules of judicial process. See Sérvulo Correia, 'O Controlo Jurisdicional Da Administração No Direito Inglês' in *Estudos de Direito Público em Honra do Professor Marcello Caetano* (Lisboa, Ática, 1973) at 130–34.

[76] Craig, n 19 above, at 411–12.

[77] ibid, at 415 and 416; Leyland and Anthony, n 72 above, at 342–43.

[78] Leyland and Anthony, n 72 above, at 342.

[79] ibid, at 343.

meaning that their decisions (or rather, some of their decisions) would have to be assimilated into those of the courts rendered this limitation obsolete. In its place, an awareness grew up that what really mattered as a baseline was the effect of a decision, irrespective of the legal nature of the decision maker and the decision-making process. The main reason for procedural protection is now that the decision may potentially affect an individual's rights or interests.[80]

Acceptance of this broad base for applicability of the 'acting fairly' doctrine also led to the setting aside for this purpose of the classical distinction between *rights* and *privileges*. In reality, the interest of the claimant, and not the discretionary power of the decision-maker, underlies the right to a fair hearing and to other procedural protections.[81]

The nature of administrative action is not irrelevant to the applicability of the common law duty to act fairly. Albeit with some exceptions, administrative rule-making is not subject to natural justice. But whilst the traditional point of view is that fairness fits simply into an adjudicative framework, it is today considered likely that, in future, fairness may be applied in other forms of decision-making, such as mediation, arbitration, contract or managerial direction. As Paul Craig has noted, 'a general concept of procedural fairness could … lead the courts into developing procedural forms other than classical adjudication. If this transpires then fairness will have a substantial effect on the procedural due process.'[82]

Application of the principle of fairness causes certain procedural safeguards to be required. These correspond not only to more or less meticulous application of *audi alteram partem*, today converted into the *right to a hearing*. The old rules of *audi alteram partem* and *nemo judex in causa sua* are now seen as specific applications of the deeper principle of *procedural fairness*, 'the idea being that in other contexts the requirements of procedural fairness may be different'.[83]

One possible set of safeguards deriving from the principle includes notice, oral hearing, representation, discovery, cross-examination and reasoned decisions.[84] This list presents a double spectrum, given that, on the one hand, not all these procedural safeguards are required in each case and, sometimes, others are mentioned, such as consultation, appeals and rehearing and time limits for the making of decisions. In addition, in relation to all of these, but especially to some of them such as a *hearing*, there are different types which vary depending on the nature of the interests being asserted, the different areas or the stage of the proceedings.

[80] Craig, n 19 above, at 416; Leyland and Anthony, n 72 above, at 352; Wade and Forsyth, n 73 above, at 494.
[81] Craig, n 19 above, at 414–15; Woolf et al, n 20 above, at 365–68.
[82] Craig, n 19 above, at 417–18.
[83] Galligan, n 23 above, at 186.
[84] Craig, n 19 above, at 417.

It was particularly in regard to the *hearing* that the growing awareness that fairness was a principle that could be applied to administrative actions without any judicial character that led to the acceptance of non-adversarial hearings as best suited to administrative processes, emphasising a cooperative approach rather than a confrontational approach. In these cases, certain standard features of judicial practice, such as cross-examination, do not make sense.[85]

With the exception perhaps of the *hearing* (although in many cases this may be non-adversarial, conducted in writing or even waived in certain circumstances), no general common law duty requires the employment of any particular procedural safeguards. But in some cases, such as the giving of reasons, the common law seems to be moving in that direction. In others, such as with representation, administrative tribunals enjoy, according to the courts, discretion as to whether to allow it and the way this discretion is exercised is subject to judicial review.[86]

Insofar as procedural fairness is 'a general principle which applies across the spectrum of administrative processes … its precise content [is] to be determined in each context'.[87] Although it is also acknowledged, with regard to judicial process, that the requirements of natural justice vary according to the facts, the courts have gradually developed classes or types or situations which each correspond to a different variant of the requirements of natural justice. Apparently, when fairness is applied to administrative action, the aim has been to achieve greater flexibility, frowning on categorisation of cases and making the requirements more closely dependent on evaluation of the facts in the actual circumstances.[88]

Today, it is often statute and EU law which establish the procedural requirements for certain kinds of administrative action. But when there is recourse to the common law, the adjustment by the courts of the types of requirements and their degree of severity to the circumstances of each case inevitably involves the methodology known as balancing.

The factors that determine the content of procedural rights in any given case will include the nature of the individual's interest at issue, the benefits to be derived from added procedural safeguards and the costs to the administration of complying with the procedural constraints.[89] The negative effect on the individual of non-compliance with certain procedural requirements encompassed by the common law concept of fairness is not necessarily, or only, economic. The risk of moral harm corresponds to the understanding of the rationale for fair procedure in keeping also with the dignitary approach and not merely in the light

85 ibid, at 433–34; Leyland and Anthony, n 72 above, at 361–62.
86 Craig, n 19 above, at 435–37; Leyland and Anthony, n 72 above, at 338 and 368.
87 Galligan, n 23 above, at 186.
88 P Cane, *Administrative Law*, 4th end (Oxford, Oxford University Press, 2004) at 160.
89 Craig, n 19 above, at 425.

of a utilitarian approach.[90] For this reason, it makes sense to set stricter requirements when the individual interest served by the procedural safeguard has in turn the nature of a fundamental right.[91]

In recent years, the English courts have assigned particular importance to the role of Article 6 ECHR as a yardstick of procedural fairness for the decisions of administrative bodies. In our view, there are two reasons for this rule to be more actively applied to administrative process than in the Romano-Germanic legal systems of the continent.

The first is the role of *administrative tribunals* in the British system. These are not courts, but rather administrative bodies. And yet they exist to provide justice as like ordinary courts, albeit as a simpler, speedier, cheaper and more accessible form of justice. And their decisions bring them close to judicial model in the sense that the tribunal has to find the facts and then apply legal rules to them impartially, without regard to executive policy.[92] We should add that the English language version of Article 6 ECHR uses the term 'tribunals' and not 'courts'. This was a deliberate choice, given that what matters as reference are the organisational characteristics of section 1 of Article 6 and not whether the activities carried on by these structures are best classified functionally as judicial, administrative or disciplinary.[93] The large number of administrative tribunals and the volume of decisions generated each year directly submits a significant portion of administrative adjudication to the procedural requirements of Article 6 ECHR, given that many of these tribunals fall with the provisions of section 1 of Article 6.

As a second reason, we point out the frequency of the situations where judicial review does not involve assessment of errors of fact and where the court cannot substitute its decision for that of the administrative body. When this happens, the principle developed by the European Court of Human Rights and known as *composite compliance* with Article 6 applies. This means that the administrative and the judicial process as a whole must meet the requirements of Article 6 ECHR. If some parts of the original decisions cannot be reviewed and/or substituted by a court, then the procedures that govern the original decision must be compliant with Article 6 ECHR.[94]

We should finally point to the continuing role of the second level of natural justice, today seen from the broader perspective of the need to dispel the appearance of bias as well as actual bias. The rule against bias applies strictly to courts of law, adjudicating members of tribunals and even to ministers. If an

[90] Craig, n 19 above, at 431.
[91] Leyland and Anthony, n 72 above, at 352.
[92] Wade and Forsyth, n 73 above, at 906 and 909.
[93] *cf* Frowein and Peukert, n 26 above, at 248–49.
[94] Leyland and Anthony, n 72 above, at 358–87.

adjudicator who is likely to show bias has not been disqualified from acting and has participated in the decision-making process, the process will be invalidated.[95]

The Roman-Germanic Legal Systems: The Inductive Itinerary

It is our belief that in the countries of continental Europe and Latin America, where administrative law was shaped and initially evolved under the influence of the post-revolutionary French model, the principle of fair (or due) administrative process constitutes not the starting point but the point of arrival in a process of evolution which occurred over approximately two centuries. Rather than serving as the engine for deductive elaboration of legal rules, the principle was eventually asserted as the outcome of an inductive process. The original baseline was a loose collection of statutory rules or procedural good behaviour standards for administration defined by the courts as and when the need arose. This piecemeal affirmation of administrative process requirements from legislative or judicial sources was followed by their affirmation in codes or general laws of administrative process. The inclusion of procedural impositions, and in particular of those serving as guarantees, in a systematic legislative vision of administrative process did not however mean moving beyond the piecemeal way in which it was affirmed. This was maintained, given that the legislative rules on hearings, disclosure, notice or giving reasons, amongst other things, emerged not as manifestations of a central principle, but as autonomous values. At the most, we can point to a common raison d'être for these separate rules: the dual need to enhance the quality of administrative decisions and, in the light of the extremely broad principle of Rechtsstaat (État de droit, Statto di Diritto, Estado de Direito), to defend the individual sphere against the arbitrary exercise of power.

For the same reason, the incorporation into constitutional law of administrative procedural requirements, which has occurred in some domestic legal systems, has not yet ousted the piecemeal vision of minimum procedures.

These forms of piecemeal affirmation were only replaced by a more unified form of affirmation thanks to the Europeanisation of the doctrine of administrative fairness. It was, in effect, in section 1 of Article 41 of the Charter of Fundamental Rights of the European Union, that, under the legally not very precise heading of 'Right to good administration', the 'right to have his or her affairs handled *impartially*, *fairly* and within a reasonable time by the institutions, bodies, offices and agencies of the Union' was enunciated. As clearly shown by the examples given by section 2 of Article 41, including the individual's right to be heard and to have access to his or her file and the duty of the administrative authorities to give reasons for their decisions, the right to a fair process is seen as a core or basic entitlement which can be developed into various procedural requirements.

[95] Galligan, n 23 above, at 220; Leyland and Anthony, n 72 above, at 378–79.

Insofar as the Charter 'reaffirms ... the rights as they result, in particular, from the traditions and internal obligations common to the Member States',[96] it is legitimate to conclude that the scattered administrative procedural impositions contained in domestic systems are now seen as manifestations of an implicit general principle which confers on them all a common raison d'être.

The fact that, in domestic Romano-Germanic systems, the recognition of an overarching principle is a point of arrival, after a process of inductive evolution moving gradually from the particular to the general, does not mean that the question of procedural fairness is now posed in these countries in the same way as in common law countries. It is clear that both systems now recognise a legal requirement that citizens and corporate entities with an interest in an administrative decision be treated fairly in the process in which it is prepared and issued. And, in both legal families, the dynamic irradiating from the core principle, consisting of its objective capacity to set directives and impulses for the legislator (or the common law judge), is leading to the development of a web of rules on application. However, due to the inductive course whereby it has taken form in Romano-Germanic systems, the general principle of fairness already presents a much more highly developed system of application. We might say that, in these systems, the waters in which we navigate have been charted in much greater detail.

In addition, in the Romano-Germanic systems, the codes or general laws of administrative process—in contrast to the situation of the APA in relation to the US Constitution—display a relationship of axiological derivation vis-a-vis the constitutional texts. Insofar as the constitutional texts contain, in more or less explicit form, the enunciation of requirements such as notice, participation, representation or giving reasons, further elaborations on these in statutory law can be traced to a constitutional source. So, as the impositions for the administrative process start to be seen themselves as reflecting the overarching principle of fair administrative process, the statutory rules which embody them should be regarded not only in the light of a requirement not to diverge from the constitution, but as instruments for developing constitutional directives which here also play a role as an interpretative framework.

The central role played until very recently by the concept of the 'administrative act' (acte administratif, Verwaltungsakt, provvedimento amministrativo, acto administrativo) in the development of the general doctrine of administrative law in domestic legal systems influenced by the model emerging from the French Revolution explains, on at least two counts, why, in these systems, the principle of fair administrative process was not affirmed through an extension and adaptation of a fundamental value in criminal and civil process.

On the one hand, the 'administrative act' took a lead role in assuring the constitutional objective of separation between the exercise of the judicial and

[96] Preamble to the Charter.

administrative functions of the State. What happened was the creation or 'discovery' of a new legal category and not the recasting of judicial decisions as already characterised by the legal system. As an imperative declaration by the administrative authorities of what, in the specific case, has the value of law for the individual, 'administrative acts' represented a different route from that taken by judicial adjudication. The rules on judicial decisions were in no way applicable to them.[97]

Moreover, the 'administrative act' was for many decades regarded by legal doctrine as an isolated reality which congregated, for the purposes of judicial review, all the criticisms of legality which could be made of the conduct of the administrative authorities. The 'administrative act', as a typical form of exercise of State power in relation to individuals, provided the focus, through the detailed elaboration of its own legal discipline, of efforts to establish the Rechtsstaat (État de Droit) through the submission of administrative decisions in specific cases to the force of law. As noted by Otto Mayer (the true founder of the general German theory of administrative law), the Rechtsstaat was realised through self-subjection of inherent State power to development along the forms and with the content established in law.[98]

From this perspective, centred on the typical form and the situation in the instant of the administrative adjudication, the preceding moments—which today present themselves clearly as the phases of the administrative process given over to preparation of the decision—are not clearly separated from the 'administrative act' and appear merely as 'formalities' relating to the decision. Also absent at this stage—which encompassed the early decades of the twentieth century—was an interrelated and omnipresent set of these 'formalities' designed to protect the dignity of the individual as the person subject to administrative power *in fieri*. The omission, or the incorrect or irregular observance of 'formalities' required by law, is not seen as breaching subjective guarantees, but rather guarantees 'offered to the interested parties, the public and the administrative authorities themselves against hurried and ill-conceived decisions'.[99] These formalities consisted above all of requests for recommendations from other administrative agencies, inquiries or expert reports. In the words of Laferrière, the first great theorist of administrative law emerging from the Napoleonic reforms and strongly influenced by the case law of the Conseil d'État, 'forms are imposed on administrative

[97] O Mayer, *Deutsches Verwaltungsrecht* I, 3rd edn (München and Leipzig Duncher & Humblot, 1924) at 59, 62 and 93; F Fleiner, *Institutionen des deutschen Verwaltungsrechts* (Tübingen, Mohr, 1928; Reprint of 1963, Scientia Verlag Aalen) at 183–85; L Meucci, *Instituzioni di Diritto Amministrativo* (Torino, Fratelli Boca, 1892) at 143; M Hauriou, *Précis de Droit Administratif et de Droit Public*, 7th edn (Paris, Sirey, 1911) at 422; R Schmidt-de Caluwe, *Der Verwaltungsakt in der Lehre Otto Mayers* (Tübingen, Mohr Siebeck, 1999) at 20 and 50.

[98] Mayer, n 97 above, at 55. On the ordering power of legal forms see E Schmidt-Aßmann, *Das Allgemeine Verwaltungsrecht als Ordnungsidee* (Berlin,Springer, 2006) at 252–53.

[99] E Laferrière, *Traité de la Juridiction Administrative et des Recours Contentieux* II (Paris, Berger-Levrault, 1888; Reprint of Paris, LGDJ, 1989) at 492.

acts not in the distinct interest of one or other party, but in the interest of the administrative act itself, its correctness, its maturity, in short, with the aim of good administration'.[100]

So, in the last quarter of the nineteenth century, it was difficult to conceive of the exercise of administrative power of adjudication as a process. Moreover, it was difficult to regard it as a process that took form through administrative duties to keep the interested individual informed and to allow his or her participation. The intense activity of legal scholars and the courts in considering the act in which administrative adjudication took form and assumed its content, overshadowed the importance of the whole preliminary and preparatory process and the space which this offered for a legal relationship between the individual and the administration.

From time to time, some of the elements later to be regarded as typical features of just such a procedural relationship are to be observed in the early years of the twentieth century, but only as an exception, in specific situations where they were instituted as express legal requirements. This was the case of hearings[101] or of giving reasons.[102] Gradually, however, the courts began to consider some of these isolated legislative provisions as manifestations of unwritten general principles, to which they assigned normative power inferior to that of statute but superior to that of administrative rules.[103] Moreover, there was an ever-growing number of legislative exceptions to the principle that this or that procedural requirement was unnecessary.[104]

The next stage of evolution in the legal systems belonging to the Romano-Germanic family consisted of the appearance of statutes (some of them called codes) establishing a general set of rules for administrative process. Initially at least, the procedural requirements or safeguards still appear in these texts in a disparate manner. We mean by this that there was no clear awareness of their common allegiance as utterances to a higher-level principle of fair administrative process. The purpose of these laws was not, moreover, merely to provide individual guarantees, but above all to assure a standardised sequencing of administrative action with a view to rational use of scarce resources and to assure the quality and general acceptance of decisions.

To an extent, the shift away from a situation of scattered rules towards one with laws on general administrative process was achieved thanks to the bridge provided by the earliest laws on some special administrative processes. The most important of these were the rules on disciplinary proceedings for civil servants.

[100] ibid, at 495.

[101] Fleiner, n 97 above, at 228–29.

[102] ibid, at 191; Hauriou, n 97 above, at 420.

[103] eg, although, in Portugal, until 1976, no general rule was considered to require reasons to be given for unfavorable 'administrative acts', the courts ruled that a principle of consistency required the administrative authorities to give reasons whenever the adjudication was contrary to proposals or opinions from departments and contained in the record: Caetano, n 37 above, at 478.

[104] Fromont, n 18 above, at 88.

In continental European countries, the administrative law of the nineteenth century was to a large extent the law governing organisational aspects of public administration, including the civil service rules. Disciplinary proceedings have something in common with criminal proceedings: both involve the investigation of alleged reprehensible conduct, the imputation of this conduct to the perpetrator, classification of the conduct as an offence belonging to a certain type and the setting of the corresponding penalty. The punitive nature of the decision alerted the legal conscience of the period to the necessity of no punishment being accorded without the party concerned first being informed of the accusation and given a reasonable period in which to present his or her defence, including the production of evidence, with the option of assistance by legal counsel. It is surely no coincidence that, in these situations, the term 'procedure' quickly came into use.[105] According to Guimarães Pedrosa—a professor of law at Coimbra University, writing in 1908—the right of civil servants to a defence is a general principle parallel to the principle of the punitive power belonging to the hierarchical superior. And 'the first right of the civil servant, as a means of defence, is that of being heard'.[106]

During the interwar years, legal scholars in a number of countries, amongst whom it is fair to point to the special contribution by the Italian universities, and a number of legislators, including those of Austria, played an essential role in shaping a 'procedural awareness' in administrative law.

Since the nineteenth century, students of administrative law in France, Germany, Italy, Spain and Portugal (amongst other countries) had concerned themselves with administrative process, but not in the sense with which we use the term here (that of procédure non contentieuse, Verfahren, procedimento)—in other words, that of the process which gives legal form to administration action—but rather in the sense of judicial review procedure (procédure contentieuse, Prozess, processo).

Despite the absence of a unitary and systematic body of legislation and the scarcity of normative data, Italian legal scholars set out to construct a theoretical framework for administrative process. They avoided (in contrast to what happened in Austria) considering this kind of process as a phenomenon analogous to the judicial process and delineated it in the light of concepts drawn from the general theory of administrative law: the legal purpose of administrative conduct, the legal administrative relationship, administrative acts and instrumental or

[105] *cf* Laferrière, n 99 above, at 497; Mayer, n 97 above, at 200.

[106] *Curso de Ciência da Administração e Direito Administrativo* I, 2nd edn (Coimbra, Imprensa da Universidade, 1908) at 301. On the insufficiency of subjecting the public administration to the law when there are no 'forms and processes to bind it' and on the guarantee of the use of a process by operation of the principle of État de Droit in the case of disciplinary penalties applied by the administrative authorities, see M Stassinopoulos, *Le Droit de la Défense devant les Autorités Administratives* (Paris, LGDJ, 1976) at 54s and 81s.

accessory acts, functional connections between the conduct of administrative bodies or agents cooperating in the regulation of aspects of social life, and so on.[107]

A different approach was taken in Austria, resulting from the combination of a jurisprudential current with the doctrinal innovations introduced by the 'Viennese School' headed by Hans Kelsen. A Law of 1875 determined that the courts should annul administrative decisions adopted in breach of the essential rules of administrative process. In the absence of any law specifying these rules, the Supreme Administrative Court formulated a body of principles drawn from the higher principle of the Rechtstaat, including those of hearing and the giving of reasons. Legal practitioners called for these guidelines to be codified. At the same time, the Viennese School rejected the vision developed by the great German public law scholars of the nineteenth century—such as Laband and Otto Mayer—of the law as a limit on a State power which precedes legal rules and lies outside them. For Kelsen and his disciples, chief amongst whom was Merkl, a professor of administrative law, the State only existed in law and through law and the law was a dynamic phenomenon creating increasingly detailed layers of rules framed by other norms of higher legal force. According to this vision, process is a legal method, governed by its own rules, for pursuing State functions through the creation of rules (including individualised acts which give rise to legal bonds). Process is therefore a single legal category, in which judicial process and administrative process are mere sub-forms. Justice and administration are the two arms of the enforcement of the law (Gesetzesvollzug). Given that judicial process is more highly developed, it may justifiably serve as the model and basis for analogical application for administrative process. And, as administrative action is administrative process, it makes sense to think of administrative action in a form close to that of judicial adjudication (Justizförmigkeit der Verwaltung).[108]

Under the influence of these ideas, the Austrian General Administrative Procedure Law of 1925, revised in 1959, acknowledges subjective rights in legal proceedings, including the right of access to the record, the right to a hearing, the right to the orderly delivery of a decision, the right to know the reasons for such decision, and the right to have it enforced.[109]

An important difference from judicial process may however be noted in the powers of the administrative authorities to assess *ex officio* all the facts they consider may be relevant to reaching a correct decision.[110] This constitutes

[107] A Sandulli, *Il Procedimento Amministrativo* (Milano, Giuffrè, 1940; Reprint of 1964) at 17 ff.

[108] A Merkl, *Allgemeines Verwaltungsrecht* (Wien,Verlag Österreich, 1827; Reprint of 1999) at 213–17; B Sordi, *Tra Weimar e Vienna—Amministrazione Pubblica E Teoria Giuridica Nel Primo Dopoguerra* (Milano,Giuffrè, 1987) at 186–209; C Wiener, *Vers Une Codification De La Procédure Administrative—Étude de Science Administrative Comparée* (Paris, PUF, 1975) at 77–81.

[109] H Schäffer, *Administrative Procedure in Austria—80 Years of Codified Procedure Law* (2005) 17 *European Review of Public Law* 871, 876–81.

[110] ibid, at 877.

obvious acknowledgement that, through administrative process, the administration enforces the public interest and not only the alleged rights of the individuals.

Despite the obvious differences, centred on the procedural safeguards recognised in the Austrian model of 1925 and all but absent from the theoretical model brilliantly erected by Sandulli in 1940, the two constructions are not diametrically opposed. In fact, they shared the positivist and formalist vision of law, dominant at that time in continental Europe, resulting from the demotion of the 'État de Droit' (Rechtsstaat) to mere 'État legal' and an understanding of the legal order as a logical order not structured by any fundamental values.[111]

The milestones in the transition to the next stage were the adoption of new democratic constitutions based on value systems. Constitutions are no longer imaginable without the function of protecting fundamental rights. Legality is no longer a neutral quality: no longer the mere servant of positive law, it serves law as an idea of value endowed with its own materiality. Administration is no longer merely an activity consisting of enforcing legal rules, but rather a subject of law in a legal relationship with the parties affected by the exercise of its powers. Administrative law ceases to be an isolated entity and instead becomes constitutional law put into practice.

This opened the way to new laws or codes of administrative process based on the relational or participative idea of process. The legal rules for process started to feature requirements or safeguards able to assure effective participation by those possibly affected by the decision and respect for their dignity.

The paradigm is perhaps provided by the German Law of Administrative Process of 1976, which is a code in all but name.[112] Despite the visible differences in structure and many of the rules adopted, the German Law may be said to have influenced the Portuguese Code of Administrative Process (1991/1996).[113] The same is true of the Spanish Law on the Legal Framework for Public Authorities and Administrative Procedure (1992/1999).[114]

Important general laws governing administrative process have also been published on the other side of the Atlantic, such as Brazilian Federal Law Number 9784, of 29 January 1999, which enshrines the rights of citizens to whom a decision prepared through process relates: those to be treated with respect, to have access to the record, to set out their position before a decision is taken, to be assisted by legal counsel, to request the replacement of the officer with decision-making powers when he is known to be a close friend or an enemy of any other

[111] J Chevallier, *L'État de droit* (Paris, Montchrestien, 1992) at 47–49; M-J Redor, *De L'État Legal à l'État de Droit* (Paris, Economica, 1992) at 302–04; Sordi, n 108 above, at 157–209.

[112] Kopp and Ramsauer, n 38 above, at 3.

[113] M Esteves de Oliveira, P Costa Gonçalves, and J Pacheco de Amorim *Código do Procedimento Administrativo Comentado* I and II (Coimbra, Almedina, 1993, 1995).

[114] JM Alvarez-Cienfuegos, B Huesca, R Sala, R Xiol, *Comentarios a la Reforma de la Ley del Régimen Jurídico de las Administrationes Públicas y del Procedimiento Administrativo Común* (Elcano, Aranzadi, 1999).

interested parties, to the reaching of a decision within a legal time limit, to notice of the decision and to be given the reasons for any unfavourable decision.[115]

Other countries also published laws which, although falling short of general laws on administrative process, enunciate a range of common requirements or safeguards for administrative processes. This was the case, in France, of the Law of 11 July 1979, on the giving of reasons for administrative decisions, and of the Decree of 28 November 1983, on the right to a hearing prior to the issue of different categories of 'actes administratifs'.[116] This also happened in the Italian Law of 7 August 1990, Number 241, on administrative process and the right of disclosure concerning the documents in the record. This Law regulates the duty of the administrative authorities to decide by express act, with the giving of reasons, notification, participation and disclosure.[117]

One development which has not yet been widely taken up is the inclusion in constitutional texts of provisions expressly enunciating certain safeguards or requirements concerning administrative process. More commonplace, so far, have been the efforts of legal scholars and the courts to deduce these safeguards and requirements from other principles (such as the Rechtsstaat) or guarantees (considering, for instance, that the guarantee of the effectiveness of judicial review presupposes the giving of reasons for administrative decisions). However, we can find such provisions in some constitutional texts. A good example is that of the Hellenic Republic (1975), which safeguards in administrative process the right to disclosure with regard to information on the process (Article 10, 3), the right to be heard before an administrative decision is taken and before it might affect rights or interests (Article 20, 2) and the right to be given the reasons for it (Article 10, 1). Probably, in Western Europe, the constitution with the most precepts on the subject of safeguards and requirements for the administrative process is that of Portugal (1976): the right to appoint a lawyer (Article 20, 2); the right to a decision in a reasonable period (Article 52, 1); the right (on the terms established by law) to participate in an administrative process where decisions may affect the individual (Article 267, 5); the right to be informed of the proceedings and to notification of the decision (Article 268, 1 and 3); and the duty of giving reasons for decisions that affect rights or legally protected interests (Article 268, 3). The Constitution of Brazil also safeguards the right of petition to any authorities (Article 5, XXXIV, (a)); the right to be heard in processes where administrative penalties may be applied (Article 5, LU); the right of the parties to obtain official transcriptions of the record (Article 5, XXXIV, (b)); and the principle of publicity (Article 37).

[115] MS Di Pietro, *Direito Administrativo*, 13th edn (São Paulo, Atlas, 2001) at 493–510; J Santos Carvalho Filho, *Processo Administrativo Federal* (Rio de Janeiro, Lumen Júris, 2001).

[116] Fromont, n 18 above, at 11.

[117] V Itália and M Bassani, *Procedimento Amministrativo e Diritto di Acesso ai Documenti* (Milano, Giuffrè, 1991).

We should stress that even the constitutions most attentive to the administrative process limit themselves to enunciating a series of separate safeguards and requirements, without organising them in an intentional or systematic manner around fair process as the central and common denominator principle.

Lines of convergence and subsisting differences

In addition to the difference pointed out above with regard to the relationship between statutory laws on the administrative process and constitutional law (considered, from a material point of view, to encompass also the natural justice principle of the common law), the main point where Anglo-Saxon systems (and especially the US system) and the Romano-Germanic system differ has to do with the scope of the principle of due (administrative) process. Indeed, the codes and laws on general administrative process tend to encompass all administrative action irrespective of the material interests at stake. The preparation of any administrative adjudication is subject to them. And, increasingly, the codes or laws on general process regulate not only administrative adjudication but also the formation of administrative contracts[118] and administrative rule-making.

In the field of procedural requirements and safeguards, the differences are tending to fade even though the use of trial-type proceedings as the form for the hearing requisite is more widespread in the administrative process of common law systems. We should nonetheless note a common trend in both types of system towards recognition that, in many processes, participation by the interested parties need not be adversarial in character, with the emphasis placed squarely on cooperation by these parties in reaching a decision appropriate to the situation of fact and compliant with the law.

The main safeguards or requirements may taken a multiplicity of forms, making greater or lesser demands on the administrative authorities in terms of human and financial resources. In the Anglo-Saxon systems, the decision on the mix of safeguards to be used and the respective degree of severity is left to the judge, who will determine the appropriate formula for practical concordance by weighing up the interests at stake. In Romano-Germanic systems, this assessment is entrusted in the first instance to law-makers who have two methodologies at their disposal. When dealing with interests which justify distinct procedural treatment, the law-maker may establish special administrative processes. This is the case of disciplinary and of public procurement administrative processes. In these instances, the legal rules of general administrative process do not apply or apply merely on a subsidiary basis. Besides, in the actual codes or laws on general

[118] On the instigation of EU law and the case law of the ECJ, laws have today been developed (and even codes, as in Portugal) on public procurement. This amounts to legislation on important special administrative processes.

administrative process, law-makers frequently employ open-textured rules, or accept situations where application of the general rules is waived.[119]

We may point very briefly to just some of the common traits of the different types of systems. These include reserving a role for the *ex officio* initiative of the administrative body, in opposition to the passivity of the judge. Another example is the structuring of the administrative process to accommodate the dual aims of providing guarantees and functional effectiveness. Lastly, we may cite the dual position occupied by administrative process in respect of fundamental rights: in some cases as a subject matter of procedural fundamental rights, and in other cases as an instrument for the realisation of substantive fundamental rights.

DUE OR FAIR ADMINISTRATIVE PROCESS: ITS PRESENT AND ITS FUTURE IN GLOBAL ADMINISTRATIVE LAW

The globalisation of the principle

The scope and coordinates of global administrative law will certainly continue to be discussed but its existence leaves no room for doubt. And whatever place is properly assigned to this legal phenomenon, it also seems certain that what distinguishes it from other fields of global law is something it has in common with domestic systems of administrative law and those of international organisations.

In this shared essence, the principles of administrative law play a leading role. They mean goals and synthesised values, concerning administrative activities and situations. The flexibility of this kind of legal norms facilitates their adoption as markers of the many fields of the disparate administrative activity at global level. On the one hand, principles combine the purpose of optimisation in the attainment of ideal targets with recognition of the need for mutual adjustment, using formulas for practical concordance between their competing contents. The same central ideas may therefore give rise to distinct solutions without undermining their common axiology. On the other hand, the ease of adopting a more or less common set of administrative law principles for very different institutional settings derives from the fact that these principles tend today to serve two main goals: the definition of individual rights and the protection of collective interests.[120]

[119] An example of this is Art 103, 1 of the Portuguese Code of Administrative Process (Código de Procedimento Administrativo) which lays down that no pre-termination hearing of the interested parties is needed when the decision is urgent, or when it may be reasonably foreseen that such a hearing might compromise the enforcement or usefulness of the decision, or else, when the number of interested parties to be heard is so great that a hearing is not appropriate, when a public consultation process should instead be conducted.

[120] R Alexy, *A Theory of Constitutional Rights* (Oxford, Oxford University Press, 2002) at 80 and 396.

It is no surprise that scholars of global administrative law have so far focused mostly on 'equivalents or potential equivalents to procedural administrative law'.[121] In the field of transnational regulatory systems, the subject matters are extremely diverse, and the organisation tends to be fluid. The field where the convergence of basic criteria is easiest is therefore that of techniques for action or decision-making processes in the light of the shared imperatives of good governance.[122]

In global administrative law (as in domestic administrative law), due process is merely a smaller concentric circle within a wider circle of principles of administrative process. This is the case because the due process values interconnect with the wider methodology of administrative adjudication, rule-making and making and performing contracts. A very significant portion of the rules governing these activities and some of their principles are geared solely or primarily to the interests of society and government and not to the protection of individual interests.

However, the universal acceptance of basic administrative process requirements has moved fastest in the field of protection of the individual from governmental power. Centred on due or fair process with the essence of an administrative procedural structure affording guarantees for individuals, we are today witnessing the gradual formation of a *jus commune*. This is the result of the convergence of domestic and regional legal systems throughout the 'Euro-Atlantic constitutional arch or circle'. But the phenomenon may also be observed in other important areas of the world (Japan, India and Australia, in particular) and manifests itself, albeit to differing degrees, in the working of international organisations and transnational decision-making structures. At the supra-, trans- and international levels, the driving forces in this movement have been, in increasing order of importance, the norm-emitting bodies, the courts, tribunals or similar bodies and legal doctrine. At the supra-national level, we still find ourselves in general at a pre-codification stage, where, as Schmidt-Aßmann has observed (referring to the administrative *Jus Europaeum Commune*), scholarly reflection is (still) preferable to normative codification.[123] Faced with highly disparate situations, and above all those lacking structured systems of sources of law, the law has in part evaded the dominance of the State to return—as at the time when the *jus commune* or *common law* took shape—to contemplation of 'what ought to be' (*dever-ser*) determined through reflexive, theoretical and value-oriented recognition achieved through jurisprudential debate between lawyers committed to discovering the logic of what is reasonable.[124]

[121] D Dyzenhaus, *Accountability and the Concept of (Global) Administrative Law*, IILJ Working Paper 2008/7 (Global Administrative Law Series), (www.iilj.org) at 2.

[122] Cassese, n 2 above, at 51 ff.

[123] 'Europäisches Verwaltungsrecht als Gemeinsame Aufgabe' (2000) 12 *European Review of Public Law* 11, 12.

[124] R de Albuquerque, 'Direito de Juristas—Direito de Estado' in *Revista da Faculdade de Direito da Universidade de Lisboa* (2001) XLII 751, 752 ff.

In short, the nascent doctrine of global administrative law, as well as the doctrines of domestic systems and of international administrative law, through research in the field and the respective methodological treatment, have conveyed the material on which judicial decisions and normative texts are founded. It is no simple coincidence that due or fair administrative process has been simultaneously asserting itself at national, international and global levels and increasingly presents common features. It is not due to chance that, at the start of the twenty-first century, we have seen the emergence of written norms of constitutional or equivalent value such as Article 41 of the Charter of Fundamental Rights of the European Union, seminal judicial decisions such as the judgment of the ECJ in the *Kadi* case,[125] or scattered procedural rules, adopted in the form of transnational regulatory structures, which recognise that interested parties in administrative adjudication have the right to a pre-decision hearing and also impose on adjudicators the duty to state reasons. These are all consequences of the circulation, within the community of legal scholars and practising lawyers' of methods and ways of shaping the legal universe. Despite continuing debate on essences and meanings, sources of reference have been adopted which are regarded as inalienable. This provides the basis for what Häberle has called 'common legal thought' (Gemeinrechtsdenken).[126]

The value of legal reasoning lies in its intellectual and persuasive qualities and easily traverses the historical boundaries of the 'principal legal systems of the world'[127] when it combines methodological modernity with values deserving of greater acceptance by those open to the manifestations of free debate and rational discourse.

The enshrinement of due or fair administrative process in global administrative law therefore reflects, to a large extent, the ability of contemporary jurists to overcome the 'strong introversion'[128] in their domestic legal cultures and to see in the public law doctrine a field for the free movement of methodologies, concepts and values drawn from other environments but which merit analysis and use on a much broader scale.

The actual nature of many of the entities which today take part in the exercise of transnational administrative activity offers a particularly favourable setting for broad accession to the value of due or fair administrative process. A widespread democratic deficit within organisations and broad margins of appreciation with regard to standard clauses are to a certain extent offset by the role of participatory

[125] Joined Cases C-402/05 P and C-415/05 P, *Yassin Abdullah Kadi and other v Council and Commission* [2008] 3 *Common Market Law Reports* 41.

[126] N 11 above, at 261.

[127] Expression used in Art 9 of the Statute of the ICJ.

[128] Schmidt-Aßmann, n 123 above, at 24.

and transparent proceedings in the adjudication or rule-making models. Participation and transparency here present themselves as constitutional principles capable of enhancing accountability and legitimacy.[129]

The peculiar correspondence between due or fair administrative process and the needs inherent to administrative process allows the principle to keep a clearer distance from natural justice, historically conceived to protect the individual from the power of a court. This makes it easier to avoid the problems posed in domestic legal systems such as that of the US by the principle's remaining judicialist elements with regard to demarcation of the scope and to requirements such as that of a trial-type hearing (in cases other than those where administrative penalties are applied).

Whilst, in Anglo-Saxon legal systems, the principle of due administrative process evolved along predominantly deductive lines and, in legal systems belonging to the Romano-Germanic family, the principle of fair administrative process was asserted by following a primarily inductive route, in global administrative law we can today see these two lines of development overlapping.

The *deductive route* appears to be the weakest, given the difficulty of finding in 'global governance' systems any foundation sufficiently firm to confer legal force on the value of due or fair administrative process as a whole. Indeed, this is also the case of the actual sub-principles forming the requirements for due or fair administrative process.[130] But, in global administrative litigation, litigants resort increasingly to the principle of due or fair administrative process, or (even more diffuse) to that of 'good administration' as a sort of 'multifunctional weapon' in order to obtain a degree of procedural protection.[131] And the entities conducting judicial review are gradually leading the way to a situation where these principles are generally applicable.

In the ECJ decision in the *Kadi* case, the Court took a concept of Community law as its basis—the 'fundamental rights which are an integral part of the general principles of Community law'—which is not automatically extendable to all aspects of global administration. But the fact is that, on the grounds that obligations imposed by an international agreement cannot have the effect of breaching the principle whereby all Community acts should respect fundamental rights (section 285) and that also Community acts implementing resolutions adopted by the Security Council under chapter VII of the Charter of the United Nations should be monitored in the light of the same fundamental rights, the

[129] Marks, n 8 above, at 998–1001; H-P Nehl, *Principles of Administrative Procedure in EC Law* (Oxford, Hart Publishing, 1999) at 168.

[130] According to Cassese, despite the existence of a 'universal legal heritage, which strengthens the legal unity of the world' (albeit counterbalanced by the 'extreme variety of local legal systems'), the right to take part in decision-making processes, the right to be heard and the procedures for notification and comment have not yet been fully asserted in the legal system of 'global governance', meaning that they should only be deemed assured when prescribed by a specific rule: n 2 above at 102, 103, and 174–76.

[131] Nehl, n 129 above, at 35.

Court reasserted the duty of giving reasons for unfavourable decisions and the right to be heard in relation to such decisions (sections 336, 337, 338, 348 and 352). The ECJ implicitly (but unmistakably) let it be understood that the Security Council should also respect the procedural human rights at issue. This corresponds in our view to the assertion of unwritten,[132] jurisprudential standards with a global nature (sections 322 and 325). The Court expressly accepts the need for adjusted, ie *deductive*, application of these principles in the light of the need to accommodate them with conflicting public interests which justify the respective limitation. In the case, the conflicting interest at issue consisted in the just requirements of public security.

The *Kadi* judgment is also a good example of *articulated deduction* of various sub-principles from due or fair administrative process: the statement of reasons is a requirements for the effectiveness of the right of defence (section 348) and also for the right to an effective remedy before a court. And failure to observe these requirements in an administrative process leading to limitations to property has the consequence of violation of the fundamental right to property (sections 370 and 371).

The dominant dynamic is, however, *inductive*. Starting out from scattered rules, principles have gradually been constructed to provide them with a rationale and value system. And alongside this bottom-up reasoning, we may also point to other, horizontal, arguments, which extend the restricted scope of application of isolated rules to other fields of administrative decision-making.

The deductive and inductive dynamics are connected within an all-embracing dialectic: the principles created or reinforced through an inductive line of argument can then serve fresh deductive dynamics for which the main vehicles are decisions of a jurisdictional nature.

Scope

The scope of procedural rights is determined by the criteria for its applicability. This is therefore a question not to be confused with that of the contents of these rights.

One of the criteria for determining the scope—the importance of which derives above all from the history of due process in the law of the US—is that of the material nature of the interests affected. Its adoption has historically had the consequence of restricting the principle's application to matters such as freedom and property, which are seen as fields of administrative activity.

But 'global governance' is exercised nowadays over an extremely diverse range of economic, social, cultural and environmental matters. And the positions thereon are often not ascribable to individuals, but rather to institutions and

[132] Given the still ambiguous status of the Charter of Fundamental Rights of the European Union at the time of writing. But see now Art 6(1) TEU.

corporations, or even to social groups, of the most varied complexions. This therefore justifies the alternative approach of including within the scope of due or fair administrative process any decision that may have a significant adverse impact on any legal subject or social groups provided these have institutionalized representation.[133] The solution consisting of looking at the adverse effect, instead of at a tight circle of legal positions, is moreover followed today not only in legal systems belonging to the Romano-Germanic family, but even in the English system.[134]

Regarding the scope of due or fair administrative process, it is necessary to avoid the risk of getting trapped in concepts unconnected to the material reality of the interests. An example of a distinction where the conceptual arguments distract from the constitutional system of values is that drawn between 'rights' and 'privileges'. We believe this distinction serves no useful purpose in global administrative law.

There is also no reason why—on a global scale—due or fair administrative process should not extend its protection to all the typical forms of administrative conduct capable of damaging interests worthy of legal protection. This should encompass not only adjudication, but also rule-making and even public procurement and the performing of contracts.

The distinction between general rules and the regulation of individual companies or institutions tends, as a matter of fact, to blur when only a small number of entities are involved.

A third criterion for demarcating scope has to do with the relative unimportance of procedural requirements in cases where the content of the adjudication could not have been different in the light of the facts and the applicable substantive norms. It might be said that, when the outcome corresponds to the only legally possible model, the situations in which this occurs fall at least *a posteriori* outside the scope of due process. But these cases should be subject to careful examination, requiring more than a fallible conviction that the procedural wrong exerted no influence over the decision. And in extreme cases, although the decision may be upheld as the only legally possible outcome, the dignitary approach and the duty of institutional accountability may determine recourse to other remedies other than annulment: compensation for moral damages or a disciplinary reaction against the procedural wrongdoing.[135]

[133] On this proposal for the US legal system see Pierce et al, n 53 above at 248 and 249.
[134] Craig, n 19 above, at 418 ff.
[135] On this subject see M Fromont, *Droit Administratif des États Européens* (Paris, Thémis, 2006) at 230–33.

The requirements

It would be fruitless to seek to establish a detailed catalogue of common requirements for due or fair administrative process applicable to all fields of 'global governance'. Even in domestic legal systems, these lists vary considerably between general laws of administrative process and laws on special administrative processes. In other cases, the requirements vary depending on court decisions, adjusting different sets of safeguards for different types of administrative situations.

In certain institutions involved in global administration, established practice will allow administrative process to be codified around the leading principles of participation, transparency and impartiality. But, even then it should be acknowledged that basic procedural principles have a normative force which goes beyond the rules which specify some of their aspects. The fact that a 'radiant core' is not exhausted through statute will permit a dense web of case law to take shape. The formulas whereby standards are applied in practice will also have to vary depending on the type of situations over which regulatory power is exercised and the type of individuals and other parties subject to this power. For instance, the same form of participation will not be used in procedures leading to adjudication, rule-making or procurement. And participation by the representatives of institutions will be subject to requirements for standing different from those applying to individuals directly affected.

It will also be necessary to guard against the risks of procedural over-protectionism. Inordinate participation will increase the risks of capture of the decision-maker or inefficiency.[136] Trial-type hearings are not the only means for effective participation and—because they are costly and time consuming—should in principle be reserved for situations where penalties are at issue, these being the only instances where guarantees similar to those of criminal procedure are required.

In many cases where the type of procedural solution desirable will not be yielded by a simple 'yes or no' answer to a precise rule, the methodology should consist of balancing the conflicting fundamental rights between themselves and with the public interests worthy of legal protection, such as the containment of expenditure and administrative efficiency.

Procedures used for similar ends should not vary within the same 'global agency'. And special procedures should be reserved for the regulation of fields whose substantive peculiarity requires different procedural treatment in the light of the protection of the dignity of the persons affected or of the adequacy of the administrative action to the policies required.

[136] L Netto, *Participação Administrativa Procedimental—Natureza Jurídica, garantias, riscos e disciplina adequada* (Belo Horizonte, Fórum, 2009) at 119 ff.

Legal nature

In areas where the exercise of a power of an administrative nature[137] is still only rudimentarily constrained (or not at all) by texts with a constitutional value or function, legal principles offer themselves as a possible alternative for the purpose of taming it.[138] This is, par excellence, the role of administrative procedural principles in global administrative law. But this raises a series of questions. We need only outline these issues here as topics for study in the field of global administrative law, and in effect to briefly assess the extent to which this new setting poses fresh questions or requires distinctive answers.

On the question of the legal nature of due or fair administrative process in the context of global administrative law, we would point to the following as the main methodological questions:

a) Whether the expression corresponds to a legal principle or a mere heuristic tool for a clearer understanding of procedural principles, such as those of transparency, participation and impartiality;
b) The extent to which due or fair administrative process and (or) the principles which can be isolated from this central idea simultaneously possess the nature of rights;
c) The extent to which administrative procedural rights whose existence can be determined deserve to be classified as fundamental rights of global administrative law.

We can only offer extremely brief answers to these three questions, on the basis of our considerations in this chapter. A less constricted response to these issues would have to be based on a comprehensive analysis of rules and practices in a sufficiently representative range of fields of global administrative law.

In our opinion, due or fair administrative process merits consideration as a legal principle in the context of global administrative law.

It is clear that, historically, its role as a radiant norm, progressively elaborated into sub-principles and rules by evolving case law and legislation (in turn based on, or interconnected with, the construction of legal doctrine), was developed above all in Anglo-Saxon systems. But, at least within the broad legal territory of the EU, a long inductive process is about to culminate in the unitary assertion of a principle of good administration whose content draws on the procedural values of impartiality and fairness manifested in a minimum platform comprising the rights of the individual to a hearing and of access to his or her file and the administration's duty to the giving of reasons.

[137] An investigation using the methodology of legal science to determine which situations and actions shall be regarded as 'administrative' in present times for the delineation of the right scope of administrative law would offer the subject matter for another (difficult) legal essay.

[138] A von Bogdandy, 'General Principles of International Public Authority: Sketching a Research Field' (2008) 9 (11) *German Law Journal* 1909, 1913.

Given that global administrative law is not an integrated legal system, these incipient movements produce no binding legal effect on many transnational or international situations. But the examples of the US and Europe also serve as an irrefutable demonstration that, in the contemporary world, it is not possible to conceive of administrative activity being carried on without procedural parameters assuring a degree of compatibility between the aims of individual protection and of efficient satisfaction of the public interest. When the logic of the system transforms the means for assuring personal protection into essential factors for satisfactory achievement of the public interest, then due administrative process cannot but be regarded as a legal imperative, albeit, perhaps, on a minimalist scale.

Some of the legal values into which the idea of due or fair administrative process divides undoubtedly take on the nature of rights because this follows from the normative texts or from judicial precedent. But even when these values are not expressly classified as such, the right naturally asserts itself when interpretation of the legal norm leads to the conclusion that it serves a primary and immediate purpose of protecting individual subjects of law.[139] This is the case of the normative texts or judicial precedents which require the public authorities to grant a hearing to the individual, impose a requirement of notice and comment, or require disclosure of the record in relation to the parties with an interest in the decision being prepared.

Opinions are divided on the giving of reasons, considering that the grounds for decision are of direct interest to the decision-maker as a methodology for organising and weighing up the relevant reasons and as a foundation for granting an egalitarian treatment. Even so, we believe that, as pointed out in the ECJ's ruling in the *Kadi* case, the duty to give reasons is primarily intended to permit the person affected by the decision to make a judgement as to whether it would be useful for him or her to contest it, and to defend his or her rights to the best possible effect (section 337). Protection is therefore an immediate purpose, and is not merely a reflexive effect. And not being subordinate to realisation of a public interest, it is therefore primary. This means that to the duty of the administration corresponds a right of the addressee.

The context offered by global administrative law has added new perspectives on the general theory of fundamental rights.

The first new perspective is the observation that a position such as the claim for due or fair administrative process is either a fundamental right or else it is not a right. Its nature as a general clause does not allow for immediate enforceability. The role of the concept is therefore that of a 'right as a whole' (Recht als Ganze), a right consisting of a bundle of rights positions.[140] The irradiation of rights

[139] J Wolff, O Bachof, and R Stober, *Verwaltungsrecht*, 11th edn (München, CH Beck, 1999) at 646–47.

[140] Alexy, n 120 above, at 159. We prefer 'right as a whole' for 'Recht als Ganze' to 'complete constitutional right' as in the English translation by Julian Rivers.

from a 'mother right', in which only the rights generated from the original core are sufficiently precise in content to be enforceable, is a typical feature of fundamental rights. Only these rights present simultaneously the nature of an objective rule as a principle and of a subjective position as a right.[141]

In addition, because they are also principles, fundamental rights are 'prima facie rights', and therefore not immutable entitlements, because they can be displaced, at least in part, by competing principles through balancing in the light of the specific circumstances of the case.

In many sectors of global administrative law, it may prove problematic to classify certain propositions as 'fundamental' due to the absence of a structure of sources headed by a charter endowed with formal constitutional force. Might the inclusion, in these global legal layers lacking in any openly constitutional cornerstone, of 'as a whole' and prima facie principles such as due or fair administrative process point to the hierarchically superior role of norms of this nature, albeit without any constitutional character?

Probably, a rather different explanation should be preferred: that the absence of any formal constitution in certain global administrative systems does not preclude the existence of a material constitution, if only at the level of unwritten general basic principles.

[141] *cf* IW Sarlet, *A Eficácia dos Direitos Fundamentais—Uma Teoria Geral dos Direitos Fundamentais na Perspectiva Constitucional*, 10th edn (Porto Alegre, Livraria do Advogado, 2009) at 141 ff.

15

Access to Justice, Legal Certainty and Economic Rationality

AGUSTIN GORDILLO

INTRODUCTION

MY AIM IN this chapter is to say some words about 'access to justice' as a global value, and to consider its relationship with related ideas of 'legal certainty' and 'economic rationality'.[1] I have chosen 'access to justice' as the focal point for the chapter as it is perhaps the sole value that can at least be argued to have a global reach.[2] Although the value is at its most advanced in developed and democratic States, it also exists in a procedural sense in failed and rogue States, in frontier economies, in developing and underdeveloped States, as well as in primitive societies and indigenous tribes. This means that access to justice is a procedural value with a global relevance—even if its workings may vary significantly from context to context.

The chapter's main point is, that in order for access to justice to be a meaningful value in global administrative law,[3] it must correspond with wider

[1] Or convenience. There are many possible variations, which we will mention later.

[2] Although we shall see—both in this subject and others—that values are so much entrenched in each language's choice of words, that translation sometimes becomes an issue by itself, thus making it difficult to deal with global values in a meaningful way. Yet mankind has always been making that effort, and it certainly is worth it. Language and its implied values, not so clear to foreigners, is just another difficulty to surmount.

[3] Formerly, the more modest 'international administrative law' was preferred, for it merely suggested something which went over national boundaries; 'global' suggests universality, completeness, no country excluded. If this is the case, one must explain whether *failed* or *rogue* States are included in global administrative law, as well as States that may fall somewhere between different categories. I would argue that global administrative law, in order to have meaning, must restrict itself to States that have the minimum qualities of *Rechtsstaat, État de Droit, Estado de Derecho*, or *rule of law*, and that have enough *control over their territory* to impose the order for that rule of law to prevail. That may exclude a hundred or more independent or sovereign countries, at any given moment. See, however, S Flogaitis, 'The General Principles of Law in the Jurisprudence of the United Nations Administrative Tribunal', forthcoming, § III: 'The United Nations Administrative Tribunal ... has proven from its early days ... that there is a Global Administrative Law, that there is a common ground in all legal systems of the world and this is because at the end of the day there is only one legal

notions of substantive justice and fairness.[4] As we will see, substantive justice can be achieved only where there is a respect for the 'rule of law' and a corresponding certainty in decision-making in public law.[5] Without that, access to justice will remain as an essentially procedural construct that does not give full weight to related rights such as the protection of property.

science, the one created by the Romans as it was understood and further developed through adaptations by the various nations around the Globe, especially through general principles of law, that specific way of understanding the man and the world.'

In any event, we may of course have a debate about the list of such countries, but the exercise is unnecessary if we admit the limits of the word 'global'. When, in 1962, I undertook the task of defining administrative law, traditional and even contemporary notions always included the characterisation of its being exclusively 'internal', 'domestic', 'national', municipal, local, etc, as opposed to international. I decided at that time to omit such characterisation: see A Gordillo, *Introducción al derecho administrativo* (Buenos Aires, Perrot, 1962). However, it was obvious, even then, that there were international elements of administrative law and I developed the idea in the second edition of the work (Buenos Aires, Abeledo-Perrot, 1966). See, too, the various editions of A Gordillo, *Tratado de derecho administrativo*, 1st and 10th edns, (Buenos Aires, Macchi, 1974; Buenos Aires, FDA, 2009). In the second volume, recent editions currently include such chapters as 'International Administrative Justice': see *La defensa del usuario y del administrado*, 9th edn (Buenos Aires, FDA, 2009) ch XVII.

[4] There are different variations such as natural justice, fairness, substantial due process of law, reasonableness, proportionality, according to each one's country or language. In Argentina, we use the words reasonableness, interdiction of arbitrariness, and also due process of law in both procedure and substance. Occasionally we use the word *fairness* in its original language. The French and Portuguese translation of fairness as equitableness is slowly gaining ground in Latin American Spanish too. See further Sérvulo Correia, ch 14 of this volume.

[5] The non native English speaker is mystified by the fact that the words which are commonly used in other languages to convey the meaning of *Rechtssicherheit, sécurité jurídique*, etc., do not translate well into English into the more direct 'safety' or 'security'. In English both 'safety' and 'security' have usually been associated with physical protection from criminal acts of a predominantly private nature (burglary, theft, more recently national security), and those wishing to translate *Rechtssicherheit, sécurité juridique*, etc, into English have first toyed with the idea of *legal certainty*, of which mostly the antonym *uncertainty* seems satisfactory to this foreigner, and later *legal predictability*, of which yet again *unpredictability* looks more satisfactory to the foreign ear. When we foreigners worry about *Rechtssicherheit, sécurité juridique*, etc, we worry about the legal system and the State itself: we worry about physical criminal acts of private individuals, of course, but we worry more about decisions by the State and the legal system. The native English speaking people have managed not to have to worry about that choice of words, by creating and keeping a system and a State that are meant precisely to provide a modicum of certainty, predictability, and confidence in the legal system. That is why also *rule of law* is so hard to translate into other languages, where *Rechtsstaat* and *Estado de Derecho* are more apt than, say, *Imperio de la ley, gobierno de la ley* or the unskillful sounding '*Regla del derecho*' which someone has unfortunately tried.

Perhaps the lack of meaning of the direct nominal translation of *Rechtssicherheit, sécurité juridique*, etc, as 'legal security' and 'legal safety', probably an abomination to the contemporary English native speaker, is indicative that for the English speaking people the notion is so obvious (if forced to, then: legal predictability, legal certainty) as not to have merited the ruminations of other languages. That says a lot about both kinds of systems.

ACCESS TO JUSTICE[6]

So, it may be said with only a limited degree of certainty that one of the few fundamental values that has a global reach nowadays is the basic human right of access to justice, or procedural due process of law. For instance, at the time of the making of the first Draft Constitution for the European Union an agreement was reached between countries with a prevailing judicial system and those with independent administrative tribunals:[7] there would be a difference in wording but not in essence, and that is why the French version is a different translation of the same ideas.

The 2003 English version of Article II-47, which was made Article II-107 in 2004, and which now has effect under the terms of the Treaty of Lisbon,[8] states:

> [The] right to an effective remedy and to a fair trial: Everyone whose rights and freedoms guaranteed by the law of the Union are violated has the right to an effective remedy before a tribunal in compliance with the conditions laid down in this Article. Everyone is entitled to a fair and public[9] hearing within a reasonable time by an independent and impartial tribunal previously established by law. Everyone shall have the possibility of being advised, defended and represented.[10] Legal aid[11] shall be made available to those who lack sufficient resources insofar as such aid is necessary to ensure effective access to justice.[12]

[6] When we mention access to justice we assume that the rule of law does also exist. Otherwise it is simply not possible to comment on other values such as the economic rationality we are going to explain. See for instance Pia Heikkila, 'Afghans swap poppies for wheat as food costs soar' in *The Guardian*, 13 May 2008 at 5.

[7] See European Group of Public Law, 'Proposal on the Debate on the European Constitution' in (2002) 14 *Revue Européenne de Droit Public/ European Review of Public Law* 1451–99; and A Gordillo, 'The Draft EU Constitution and the World Order' in *The Constitution of the European Union/La Constitution de l'Union Européenne* (London, Esperia Publications Ltd, 2003) at 281–94. See, too, A Gordillo, 'El control jurisdiccional en el mundo contemporáneo' at www.tcadf.gob.mx/congreso/internacional/control_jurisdiccional.html; E Garcia de Enterria and TR Fernandez, *Curso de Derecho Administrativo* (Buenos Aires, Thomson/Civitas-La Ley, 2006) at 618-A and 618-B, paras XXIV.1 and XXIV 2.

[8] Art 6 TEU. The corresponding version that now has binding force of law is Art 47 of the Charter of Fundamental Rights of the European Union.

[9] Obviously, the universal value is here that the aggrieved individual has a right to access all parts of the proceedings, in order to avoid any 'Kafkaesque' process: it cannot be secret for the parties, it must be public. But, even if the words 'public hearing' are used here (which cannot be translated as *enquête publique* or *audiencia pública*, in this case), it is not meant that the process itself should always be free to the public in general. Whether or not, or to what extent, it is depends on the nature of the process and national legislation and general principles of law, which vary considerably from one country to another. The tribunal's deliberation, on the contrary, is almost always not public in either sense, although there are countries with a tendency to make some court deliberations public (eg, the Swiss Federal Court).

[10] In international administrative organisations and tribunals, advice and representation is also undertaken by colleagues within staff associations, without cost to the staff member.

[11] Legal aid is the second phase after formal access to justice is established. Since Roman times access to justice does not favour the needy. The tendency nowadays is to try to make justice really accessible both to the well-to-do and the needy.

[12] www.european-convention.eu.int/DraftTreaty.asp?lang=EN.

The French version states:

> 'Droit à un recours effectif et à accéder à un tribunal impartial': 'Toute personne dont les droits et libertés garantis par le droit de l'Union ont été violés a droit à un recours effectif devant un tribunal dans le respect des conditions prévues au présent article. Toute personne a droit à ce que sa cause soit entendue équitablement, publiquement et dans un délai raisonnable par un tribunal indépendant et impartial, établi préalablement par la loi. Toute personne a la possibilité de se faire conseiller, défendre et représenter. Une aide juridictionnelle est accordée à ceux qui ne disposent pas de ressources suffisantes, dans la mesure où cette aide serait nécessaire pour assurer l'effectivité de l'accès à la justice.'[13]

At the risk of being obvious, direct translations were made of 'independent and impartial tribunal', viz 'un tribunal indépendant et impartial'; and 'access to justice', viz 'l'accès à la justice'. On the other hand, the following words have not been meant to be a direct translation, although they are roughly comparable: 'effective remedy', ie 'recours effectif'; 'to a fair trial' ie 'à accéder à un tribunal impartial'; and a 'fair hearing', ie 'équitablement'.

Both versions agree that an independent and impartial tribunal should provide, within a reasonable time, fair or equitable[14] public access to justice for all,[15] by either an 'effective remedy' or a 'recours effectif'. The French word *recours*, as with its direct Spanish direct translation *recurso*, may have an implicit distinction in Latin America, evoking the absolute monarchy of the *Ancien Régime* which some countries not in Latin America still consider their way of government (Saudi Arabia): a limited access to judicial or jurisdictional review. Any such ambiguous distinction is, however, tentatively being prevented by the emphasis put on 'effective'.

Anyway, in some countries judicial review may also be limited; or at least have some judicial deference to administrative adjudication by administrative tribunals (Canada);[16] while in some other countries it has evolved to allow for more intensive review and full access to justice (Spain).

So we might say that in practice both versions tend to be equivalent, even if they are not meant to be direct translations of each other. Obviously, a very careful evaluation has been made of the different versions, which further explains the added emphasis in the phrase 'in compliance with the conditions laid down in this Article'. This is meant to assure an homogeneous, yet nationally adaptable, interpretation of the different texts.

[13] www.constitution-europeenne.info/special/part_2_fr.pdf.

[14] That is to say, due process of law in substantive sense (fairness, etc).

[15] Viz, due process of law in a procedural sense (access to an impartial and independent tribunal). So, the relevant provision of the Charter of Fundamental Rights of the European Union intends to assure both procedural and substantial process of law. For the purpose of analysing its global reach, we are distinguishing between the two senses.

[16] It should be noted that this applies to judicial review of adjudication made by impartial and independent administrative tribunals, of which there are about 5,000 in Canada.

International organisations, some as large as the United Nations (UN) (with almost 40,000 employees worldwide), all have independent and impartial administrative tribunals available to their staff and even former staff members.[17] However, third parties have to suffer their otherwise general immunity from either international or national jurisdictions, which the organisations' legal departments always defend before local courts. These third parties usually have access to conventional arbitration proceedings, not to national or international courts or tribunals.[18] If that is applied to companies, it would seem to be above the threshold of access for all; however, it is quite frequently also applied to individual contracts for personal employees, who may not be as well-protected as an organisation with the recourse to arbitration.

JUSTICE[19] OR SUBSTANTIVE DUE PROCESS OF LAW, ETC, LEGAL CERTAINTY[20] ECONOMIC RATIONALITY OR CONVENIENCE[21]

A citation from Radbruch may be a starting point to develop another line of reasoning. Radbruch stated that there are legal values above the normative system: 'human rights that surpass all written laws'. His now accepted perception of law was that there are both 'statutory lawlessness and supra-statutory law', as translated from his masterfully titled, *Gesetzliches Unrecht und übergeseztliches*

[17] See S Flogaitis, 'The General Principles of Law in the Jurisprudence of the United Nations Administrative Tribunal', n 3 above, at § I. 'There is a terrain which is by definition Global and Universal: the legal system of the United Nations, the place where all civilizations come together; [rules] 'which have been decided upon by representatives of the nations of the world, and therefore is universal by definition.' See also A Gordillo, 'Tribunales administrativos internacionales' in Universidad Austral *Cuestiones de procedimiento administrativo* (Buenos Aires, Rap, 2006) at803–06. Also, 'La justicia administrativa internacional' in A Gordillo, *Tratado de derecho administrativo*, vol 2, *La defensa del usuario y del administrado*, 9th edn (Buenos Aires, FDA, 2009) ch XVI.

[18] National courts sometimes try to assert local jurisdiction over these bodies when there is no other venue that can provide access to justice against them (Germany, France, USA, etc).

[19] The word justice does not present translation problems, albeit that it has a very deep and different resonance in one's mind and culture. It can be traced to the notion of substantive due process of law and natural justice, and that is what prompted Justice Jackson of the US Supreme Court to say at the height of the Cold War, in 1952, that if he had to choose between American laws without due process of law, or Soviet laws with due process of law, he would undoubtedly choose the second.

[20] *Legal certainty* is the usual English translation of the original *Rechtssichercheit*, which can also be translated as *sécurité juridique, seguridad jurídica*, etc. To those of us who are non-native English speakers, the English *legal certainty* does not seem to be wholly satisfactory, even if we feel more at ease with the antonym *uncertainty*. But this is a problem that we have to tolerate: it is not, after all, our own language.

[21] Gérard Timsit has kindly reminded me that many people would adopt a rather extensive interpretation of the words 'economic rationality', namely absolute free market self-regulation and the absence of the principle of solidarity that pervades the Welfare State. Thanks to this kind suggestion, my use of the word is therefore firmly linked to the Welfare State and solidarity, but also within the context of the rule of law, *Rechtstaat, État de Droit*, etc. Social and economic equality have to be pursued, but this does not mean that all and any regulation is conducive to that end. That depends on the efficiency of regulation, on its lack of corruption and its reasonableness, or it may have unintended consequences. The same is true for national security, the public interest, and so on.

Recht.[22] He dealt mainly with three values: purposiveness, justice, and legal certainty. Without going into Radbruch's view on purposiveness for now, I suggest that the other two values, legal certainty and justice or fairness,[23] have to be considered as values in contemporary global administrative law, even if many issues will forever be contentious[24] in some cases.

There is also a factor which Adam Smith called 'tolerable security of property' and 'tolerable administration of justice'. In his view, capital provided with those protections would lead to economic growth and the 'wealth of nations', which we all know is not necessarily true in every case. But there is still more to that. J Bradford Delong explains '*Reverse the process, however, and you get the poverty of nations.*' (Emphasis added.) That is why a 'large net flow of capital from rich to poorer nations simply never materialized.[25] In fact, the principal outcome was *an enormous flow of capital from the periphery to the rich core.*' (Emphasis added.) 'The reason is ... that the core ... offers a form of protection for capital against unanticipated political disturbances.' It can be argued, then, that at least partly it is these 'institutions ... that have made the core so wealthy.'[26]

Flight capital from poor to rich nations, by foreigners and nationals who are better off in developing nations, is born out of the fact that they feel developed countries can provide them with a 'tolerable security of property', even if the

[22] Radbruch, 'Statutory lawlessness and supra-statutory law' (2006) 26 *Oxford Journal of Legal-Studies* 1 (translation by B Litschewski Paulson and Stanley L Paulson). See also Rabdruch, 'Five minutes of Legal Philosophy' (2006) 26 *OJLS* 1 (translation by B Litschewski Paulson and Stanley L Paulson). Radbruch's work represents the first major step in the current formulation of the idea, although it has also roots in the common law world, in Ihering, and even in the old Roman law, where Cicero referred to as universal law, as opposed to the dominant explanation of the legal system provided by scholars and jurists, not practitioners, lawyers, praetors. See App A, 'Cicero the Outsider' in A Watson, *The Spirit of Roman Law* (Athens and London, University of Georgia Press, 1995) at 195–200, specially 197–99. The prevailing exposition of the old Roman system is further explained at 71, 73, 79, 83, 89, 93, and ch 8, 'Jurists and Reality' at 88–100. Flogaitis also says, in this tradition of legal thinking and its evolution, that 'Modern administrative law has evolved from a very positivistic branch of law into the branch of law par excellence which is the law of general principles, those ideas and rules which derive from a certain conception of the man and the world.' See 'The General Principles of Law in the Jurisprudence of the United Nations Administrative Tribunal',n 3 above, at § I.

[23] That is to say, substantial due process of law, reasonableness, etc.

[24] For instance, the question whether social improvement should be led by normative or judicial bodies, as in the case of the diverse forms of discrimination. See A Gordillo, 'The administrative Law of International Organisations: Checks and Balances in Law Making—The Case of Discrimination' in *Internationalisation of Public Law/ L'Internationalisation du Droit Public* (London, Esperia Publications, 2006) at 289–312. This has also some relationship to the subject matter I deal with in 'Statutory Limitations of International Administrative Tribunals' in *XXth Anniversary*, Inter American Development Bank, Administrative Tribunal, Washington DC, 2003; 'Restricciones normativas de los tribunales administrativos internacionales' in D Ahe (ed), *El derecho administrativo de la emergencia, II*, (Buenos Aires, FDA, 2002) at 285–98.

[25] Or, when it did, it did not always contribute to the overall wealth of the recipient nation. Old memories still relive the initial times of colonialism, as retold by Barack Obama in *Dreams from My Father, A Story of Race and Inheritance* (New York, Three Rivers Press, 2004) at 400–01, 409–12, 414. Examples, of course, abound and differ widely.

[26] 'Gambler's ruin', *Buenos Aires Herald*, 3 June 2008 at 6.

rules may change:[27] yet they are not expected to change as unpredictably and to such an extent as they may do in frontier economies, underdeveloped or most developing countries. They may adhere to the Welfare State or not, foreign or national capital does not care; what it does care about is a certain measure of legal predictability.[28] When that is highly endangered or even disappears, capital flees from those places to more secure shores.

That is why Adam Smith's qualification of 'tolerable' highlights well the zone of uncertainty around words in any language. In any case, the rule of law, due process of law, access to justice, etc, are not merely good legal values; they can also make good long-term economic sense even in the Welfare State.

It is thus economically irrational, or at least economically highly inconvenient in the short or long term, not to have those legal values, because capital goes where it feels there is a tolerable security, and flees those countries where that sense of security falls below what they think is admissible.[29]

Some countries such as Argentina have occasionally had the idea that one can make a fundamental legal distinction between long-term investment and temporary investment, trying to help the former and hinder the other. Sunken investments cannot of course summarily flee a country; but a country that does not comply with the minimal requirements of due process of law cannot reasonably expect more sunken investment to be made in them. Even then, sunken investment can be sold at a loss to locals friendly to the government,[30] if the owner does not trust the legal system, and so he or she flees the country anyway.

In Russia, '[o]ver $30 billion of foreign capital fled since the August war in Georgia and the ruble's decline against the dollar spooked investors.'[31] Its own previous weak rule of law and then its intervention in Georgia meant to its own

[27] According to current international banking regulations on prevention and detection of money laundering, banks have the duty to 'know' their clients. This leads to certain documents being asked of prospective foreign non-resident aspiring account holders, and sometimes also of lengthy interviews where one of the questions is: 'Why do you want to bring your capital here?' If the customer is at a loss to provide an answer, a helpful 'capital protection' will be provided: that, and no other, is the reason for capital flow from developing countries to central ones or even developing ones which provide such 'tolerable security' (Uruguay). That goes to show the need to establish legal protection of property, predictability, etc, to be universally required as fundamental values above any legal system, at least as a matter of principle.

[28] For that reason, even socialist countries that provide some predictability, such as China, receive foreign investments even though they do not have developed concepts of the rule of law or the administration of justice.

[29] Nor is it enough to invoke the public interest, which is a notoriously imprecise 'concept'. It can have very bad consequences if it is not tempered with the rule of law and procedural and substantial due process of law. On public interest see further Anthony and Morison, ch 9 in this volume.

[30] Or 'oligarchs', to use the contemporary terminology adopted in Russia in 1990s. Opposition leaders in Latin American countries have now also started to use the Spanish equivalent of the term to describe the same phenomenon, albeit as exists on a smaller scale. See, for instance Elisa Carrió, interview in *La Nación. Enfoques*, 11 January 2009 at 1, 2 and 5.

[31] GL White, 'Russian economic recovery tested', *The Wall Street Journal*, 20 October 2008 at 10, See also L Harding, 'Moscow's old communists rejoice as oligarchs look to a future of *nyet* profit', *The Guardian*, 21 October 2008 at 13: 'Spooked foreign investors have fled, because of the global credit crisis but also because of the war in Georgia and the Kremlin's interventions in the market.'

nationals and foreigners alike that recent axioms did not apply anymore. The tolerable security of property, the tolerable administration of justice, seemed not applicable for the time being. Whatever the reasons for the country's actions, it included—after the fact—lack of economic rationality; as things turned out, it was economically inconvenient not just in the long term, but in the very short term too.

Or, to express Radbruch's thought in today's words, that which is not just, fair and predictable is not good either for the public interest, national security or convenience of the national economy.[32] In a similar vein, Flogaitis stresses that in the case law of the UN administrative tribunal, 'Fairness, rationality, good administration, *non venire contra factum proprium* are principles which the Tribunal *has established as interconnected*.'[33] (Emphasis added.) As the tribunal stated in Judgment 951, *Al-Khatib* (2000), 'It would not be in the interest of the Agency to make decisions that are patently unjust or irrational and to act thereon.'[34]

Of course, not only does reality change and so does its perception and public policy by regulatory agencies of every kind and level, but so too, in turn, do the rules and regulations, both local and global, that guide any given economic activity: we are now suggesting a focus on economic activities. The chance for both groups and individuals to effectively challenge regulatory decisions is part of normal democratic behavior, as much in economic activities as in civil liberties.

However, predictability or legal certainty is not enough if it is also fundamentally unfair, for there is an 'immemorial law that denies validity to the criminal dictates of inhuman tyrants.' In such cases justice should prevail over legal certainty. The criminal dictates of inhuman tyrants have not disappeared, but they do not seem to be accepted as something which the law would encompass.

Some minimal principles of economic rationality in normal circumstances include currency stability or inflation control, fiscal surplus, open economies[35] and the rule of law. They began to appear as rather universal indications of long-term economic rationality or convenience for the public good. Yet in a moment of financial panic, an intervention[36] by the United States and an *ad hoc*

[32] The case has been made recently that the same applies to the national public interest in any of its forms, for instance national security considerations, not just economic convenience. See notice of an OECD 2008 report about an arms deal with Saudi Arabia, in the *International Herald Tribune*, 18–19 October 2008 at 3.

[33] Flogaitis, n 3 above, at 4.

[34] The case has been highlighted by Flogaitis, n 3 above, at § III, 4 and is also applicable, necessarily, in nation States; not that all countries can be counted to rely on such interconnectedness in the practicality of each one's system: but those countries that do not adhere to this line of reasoning necessarily pay the price in their own economic downturn.

[35] There is a wide range of opinions as to the proper balance between tolerable freedom of the market and tolerable State intervention. See G Timsit, 'La réinvention de l'État—Suite' (2008) 74 *Revue internationale des Sciences administratives* 179.

[36] Some developing countries at times express satisfaction that their own intervention is deeper than in developed countries. But regulation is only as good or bad as the regulators are able and

informal or virtual network[37] of European countries and organisations has been made. That seems to prove that no easy solution really exists to satisfy everyone.

Standards and values (such as access to justice, fairness and natural justice,[38] the rule of law, and so on), do not automatically solve cases but they can provide guidelines. I suggest including economic rationality or convenience for the country's economy among them, in the sense that no long-term economically sound idea or lasting solution is born out of the realm of due process of law.[39] I fully understand, of course, that current policy issues perhaps make that, at least momentarily, a somewhat unrealistic suggestion.[40]

Be it the old ideas about stability and open markets or the current ideas, not necessarily opposed, of State intervention[41] in acute crisis, economic rationality or convenience has to be factored in as a guiding value in global administrative law. The tolerable security of property that Adam Smith suggested for the wealth of nations, if absent, translates into flight of capital and poverty for the national economy and a substantial part of its population. The long-term well-being of a country, or the wealth of nations, depends to a large degree in its compliance with universal values of administrative law.[42] It is just one reason why long-term

honest, or inefficient and corrupt. Intervention in developed countries mostly fulfils the requisites of efficiency and honesty; intervention in some underdeveloped countries does not.

[37] While I do not pretend to represent their thoughts, I am indebted to Paul Craig and Thumen Koopman for their comments on this point. The theory of networks registers such informal use: see for instance A-L Barabasi, *Linked* (New York, Penguin, 2003); and DJ Watts, *Six Degrees. The Science of a Connected Age* (New York, Norton, 2003). And on networks see Craig, ch 4 in this volume.

[38] As Paul Craig has pointed out to me, if due process of law in both procedural and substantive sense is accepted, then that is a huge body of law indeed. That is why one always needs to bear in mind Justice Jackson's words at n 22 above.

[39] In the same sense, the OECD made an International Anti-Bribery Convention, ratified by individual countries, Art 5 of which prohibits considerations of national economic interest, whether short term or long term, when prosecuting foreign bribery. Of late, the need has been observed also to include in such prohibition considerations of 'national security' or 'national public interest': no pro-bribery decision can really be considered to be in the national public interest or national security; no more than convenience for the national economy. See notice of the 37 nations OECD 2008 special report, referring to Serious Fraud Office investigation of an arms deal with Saudi Arabia, in the *International Herald Tribune*, 18–19 October 2008 at 3. And for judicial consideration see the decision of the UK House of Lords in *R (Corner House) v Director of the Serious Fraud Office* [2009] 1 AC 756.

[40] That is obvious when my own idea corresponds up to a point with Adam Smith's ideas, which were later overshadowed by Keynes, who was then superseded by others, only to be given partial credence again later on, and so on. The story has not ended yet.

[41] Again, a crucial factor is what kind of intervention? If it is inept and corrupt, as in countries whose administrations share those characteristics, it will almost always be deleterious. In a similar vein, the first 2008 government proposal for US intervention was rejected by Congress, who considered it to be an attempt to introduce absolute discretionary powers, thereby adding a constitutional issue to the economic one. Checks and balances provided the answer: intervention without discretionary powers.

[42] A majority of writers and all international tribunals adhere to such values, as well as developed countries, and they are explained in, for instance, Flogaitis, n 3 above. But the question remains whether they are real or not in all countries of the world, as I explained at the beginning of this chapter.

economic rationality or long-term convenience for the country's economy, with the above explained caveats,[43] has to be included in the search for values in global administrative law.

[43] As a rule of thumb, developed societies tend to have smaller numbers of people under the level of poverty or in indigence, compared to developing or underdeveloped ones. When developing countries want to reduce inequality and foster growth without regard to the rule of law and other legal values, they usually do not achieve those ideals. They just promote more poverty and more inequality.

16

Processes of Transnationalisation of Administrative Values: Administrative Regulation and Transparency in the EU

FLORA GOUDAPPEL AND TON VAN DEN BRINK

INTRODUCTION

THE EUROPEAN UNION (EU) is often used as some form of example for the globalisation of administrative law or at least of principles of administrative law.[1] Yet, although it is clearly a prime example, it can be argued that the European influence in this respect cannot solely be described as such. As it has been noted concerning the internationalisation of public law,[2] the influence of principles of administrative law on other legal systems works in several ways. Not only does globalisation of principles of administrative law involve mostly soft law instead of black letter law, it is usually not a top-down influence but rather a bottom-up or transnational influence. This is certainly true for principles of administrative law in the EU system. Not many principles, if any, were originally laid down in any of the Treaties; they stem from national systems which have first influenced other Member States, and they sometimes have even been used as a yardstick for other States.

A good example of a principle for which this mechanism has worked is the principle of democracy. Article 6, paragraph 1 TEU states:

[1] See for instance, E Petersmann, 'European and International Constitutional Law: Time for Promoting "Cosmopolitan Democracy" in the WTO' in G de Búrca and J Scott (eds), *The EU and WTO: Legal and Constitutional Issues* (Oxford, Hart Publishing, 2001) at 81–110; or M Shapiro, 'The Institutionalization of European Administrative Space' in A Stone Sweet, W Sandholtz and N Fligstein (eds), *The Institutionalization of Europe* (Oxford, Oxford University Press, 2001) at 94.

[2] F Goudappel, 'Making Sense of Internationalization—General Conclusions' (2006) 18 *Revue Européenne de Droit Public* 641–56.

> The Union is founded on the principles of liberty, democracy, respect for human rights and fundamental freedoms, and the rule of law, principles which are common to the Member States.

This provision indicates that democracy is considered a principle common to the Member States, and the EU is therefore founded on it as well. A legal definition of what a democracy entails is not included but implied.[3] The notion of democracy has later become part of the so-called Copenhagen criteria, necessary for prospective Member States to be fulfilled before accession, thus giving it effect above and beyond the EU:

> Stability of institutions guaranteeing democracy, the rule of law, human rights and respect for and protection of minorities.[4]

The purpose of this contribution is to explore the influence of the EU on the development of transnational administrative values. The focus—and umbrella—is therefore on how the EU triggers the emergence and development of transnational administrative values at a regional level. The 'top-down' influence of the EU on national legal orders (facilitated by the specific, binding nature of EU law) would be an obvious perspective from which to view these processes. Indeed, supremacy of European law[5] is meant to influence State behaviour and seek Member State compliance. As mentioned above, the EU not only enforces transnational administrative values, but it also facilitates bottom-up processes to influence the development of such values.

It needs to be noted that part of these transnationalisation processes either stem from the fact that the European Community especially is a supranational system, or such processes are influenced by it. Although transnational influence as such cannot be directly influenced by supranational processes, principles which have developed in this way in several Member States may be forced upon other Member States through the European legislative process which often describes a qualified majority voting. This may ease the spreading of such principles, giving them a larger or quicker impact than they would otherwise have had. The EU must therefore be seen as a platform on which upstream, downstream and horizontal processes take place that enable cross fertilisation of legal orders to the benefit of the transnationalisation of administrative values. A bottom-up approach, for instance is very common in creating the EU as such

[3] The Charter of Fundamental Rights of the European Union contains a similar reference to democracy as a founding principle in its Preamble.

[4] As formulated on the website of the EU, www.europa.eu/scadplus/glossary/accesion-criteria-copenhague-en.htm, accession criteria (Copenhagen criteria) (last visited on 26 September 2008).

[5] J Steiner, L Woods and C Twigg-Flesner, *EU Law*, 9th edn (Oxford, Oxford University Press, 2006) at 69–88; or K Alter, *Establishing the Supremacy of European Law* (Oxford, Oxford University Press, 2001).

because the Member States use their own national experiences 'as a means to shape the developing polity according to their interests and objectives'.[6]

Two principles that are relevant for European administration will be analysed in this chapter. The first is the management of the regulatory role of the administration. On the basis of the principle of separation of powers, the regulatory role of the administration is subordinate to that of the legislature. Although this is a common value in western States, the way it is applied differs substantially. The EU introduces a complete new dimension. Not only does the distinction between statutory and administrative legislation emerge at the European level, but EU membership also changes the way the distinction is applied domestically. Moreover, the issue is also relevant in the vertical relationship between the EU and its Member States. Thus, various ways of influence (top-down, bottom-up, horizontal) may be distinguished.

The second principle to be analysed is the principle of transparency of administration. Based in the Nordic legal and administrative tradition, openness used to be quite alien to the EU. Indeed, effective and efficient decision-making in an international organisation such as the EU may benefit from a certain level of secrecy. Since the 1990s, however, the principle of transparency has been developing rapidly into a general principle of EU law. As such, it provides the second example of transnationalisation of an administrative value on the EU 'platform'. In the end, the question can be posed whether or not this relatively random (yet well founded) choice of examples shows that a degree of supranationalism is necessary for a process of globalisation of principles in administrative law.

MANAGING THE BORDER BETWEEN LEGISLATION AND REGULATION

> There is no more characteristic administrative activity than legislation.[7]

One might easily be under the impression that administrative powers in political systems influenced by Montesquieu are merely concerned with taking concrete decisions for individual cases. The quotation above helps us to understand that this is an illusion: administrative authorities adopt general applicable rules and norms as well. This has to with efficiency arguments: legislatures are far from able to regulate each and every aspect of modern life, but there is also a normative argument involved. It is the argument that legislatures should not be bothered with highly detailed and technical rules.

Thus, in modern western political systems both the legislature and administrative authorities adopt legally binding rules. Given the idea that the legislature possesses the ultimate legislative authority, how should administrative legislation

[6] W Song and V Della Sala, 'Eurosceptics and Europhiles in accord: the creation of the European Ombudsman as an institutional isomorphism' (2008) 36 *Policy and Politics* 481.

[7] W Wade and CF Forsyth, *Administrative Law*, 8th edn (Oxford, Oxford University Press, 2000) at 839.

be distinguished from statutory legislation? What substantive and procedural requirements should be applied? States have developed different ideas and norms in this respect.

In this contribution, three Member States will be analysed in terms of how they manage the border between statutory and administrative legislation. Apart from two contrasting states: Germany (a country in which the constitution takes a central place) and the United Kingdom (in which the principle of parliamentary sovereignty prevails), the relevant provisions from the Greek constitution (home to Professor Flogaitis) will also be analysed.

In the EU, the distinction between statutory and administrative legislation is relevant as well. Three perspectives are chosen in this regard:

- Statutory and administrative legislation at the level of the EU;
- Influences on the organisation of the legislative powers of the Member States; and
- Influences of national legislatures and the organisation thereof. In this respect, we will specifically focus on the Treaty of Lisbon which carries clear examples of Member States' influences.

ADMINISTRATIVE LEGISLATION IN THREE EU MEMBER STATES

United Kingdom

In most EU Member States, the organisation of the legislative function, or at least the important elements thereof, are laid down in a codified constitution. Provisions of such constitutions usually prevail over ordinary statute law and are adopted on the basis of special constitutional procedures. In the absence of a codified constitution in the United Kingdom, no clear distinction may be drawn between constitutional law and statutory law as both may be altered or repealed by a simple majority in Parliament. Thus, the ordinary legislature is not bound to higher ranking constitutional norms. This opens the way for the leading principle governing the organisation of the legislative function in the United Kingdom, *sovereignty of Parliament*. As early as 1689, it was described as follows:

> The Parliament is that supreme and absolute power, which gives live and motion to the English Government.[8]

> The principle of Parliamentary sovereignty means neither more nor less than this, namely, that Parliament [defined as the Queen, the House of Lords, and the House of Commons, acting together] has, under the English constitution, the right to make or

[8] Earl of Shaftesbury, *Some Observations concerning the Regulation of Elections for Parliament*, cited in A Bradley, 'The Sovereignty of Parliament—Form or Substance?' in J Jowell and D Oliver (eds), *The Changing Constitution*, 6th edn (Oxford, Oxford University Press, 2007) at 28.

unmake any law whatever; and further, that no person or body is recognised by the law as having the right to override or set aside the legislation of Parliament.[9]

Consequences of parliamentary sovereignty

The first consequence of the principle of parliamentary sovereignty is that Acts of Parliament are not subject to judicial review. In academic writing this consequence has been extensively analysed, but since it concerns primarily the relation between the legislature and the judiciary rather than the executive, we will consider it here no further.

Another consequence that does relate to the relation between legislature and executive is the rule that the Queen in Parliament cannot bind its successors.[10] Conversely, existing Parliaments may undo legislation of their predecessors by a simple Act of Parliament. This even applies to matters that would be subject to a special constitutional procedure in other Member States. Bradley refers, by way of example, to decisions to hold referenda.[11]

It seems a paradox that in a system in which parliamentary sovereignty prevails, administrative legislation would occupy such a prominent place. In some cases, however, the Crown enjoys what is called the 'royal prerogative' which allows for independent governmental legislation, ie, legislation for which no statutory basis is required. Most powers under the royal prerogative, however, are nowadays limited to 'pure', non-legislative powers.[12] Most subordinate legislation is therefore delegated legislation.

The principle of parliamentary sovereignty as such is hardly affected by the phenomenon of delegated legislation. Indeed, part of the power associated with the principle is that the Queen in Parliament is not obliged to regulate all aspects itself but rather that it may be decided to leave certain aspects to the Crown. This is not to say, however, that delegated legislation is an unproblematic phenomenon in the United Kingdom. Wade and Forsyth point in particular at the scale on which delegated legislation is produced.[13] Delegated legislation outweighs statutory legislation by far.[14] Moreover, delegated legislation is certainly not always restricted to the details of a matter. Parliament sometimes delegates quite general and extensive legislative power. Critics of such practices are not only to be found in academic circles but in Parliament itself as well. Thus, in 1998 the House of Lords established the Delegated Powers Scrutiny Committee with the

[9] V Dicey, *Law of the Constitution*, 10th edn (London, MacMillan, ECS Wade (ed), 1959) at 39–40.
[10] Bradley n 8 above, at 37.
[11] ibid.
[12] Wade and Forsyth, n 7 above, at 221.
[13] ibid, at 840.
[14] In 1998 by four times: Wade and Forsyth, n 7 above, at 841.

explicit task of controlling provisions on delegation. Externally, the Better Regulation Task Force scrutinizes proposed delegated legislation (as well as statutory legislation) as well and advises the legislature on the issue.

Particularly troublesome are so-called 'Henry VIII-clauses'. These provisions empower the executive to amend statutory legislation. As these provisions need to be explicitly laid down in an Act of Parliament, they are considered by some to comply with the principle of parliamentary sovereignty. As Wade and Forsyth state: 'It is quite possible for Parliament to delegate a power to amend its own Acts.' They accept Henry VIII-clauses moreover on the argument of the necessary flexibility. Others are much more critical: The Committee on Ministers' Powers considered such clauses as 'inconsistent with the principle of parliamentary sovereignty'.[15]

Effects of European Union membership

An obvious link between Henry VIII-clauses and the effect of EU membership is the European Communities Act 1972. Article 2 section 2 reads as follows:

> (2) Subject to Schedule 2 to this Act, at any time after its passing Her Majesty may by Order in Council, and any designated Minister or department may by regulations, make provision—
>
> (a) for the purpose of implementing any Community obligation of the United Kingdom, or enabling any such obligation to be implemented, or of enabling any rights enjoyed or to be enjoyed by the United Kingdom under or by virtue of the Treaties to be exercised; or
>
> (b) for the purpose of dealing with matters arising out of or related to any such obligation or rights or the coming into force, or the operation from time to time, of subsection (1) above;
>
> and in the exercise of any statutory power or duty, including any power to give directions or to legislate by means of orders, rules, regulations or other subordinate instrument, the person entrusted with the power or duty may have regard to the objects of the Communities and to any such obligation or rights as aforesaid.

On the basis of this provision, the UK government as well as individual Cabinet ministers are empowered to adopt any EU implementing measure. Obviously, the centre of gravity in legislating shifts from the legislature to the executive, even though the legislature may decide to implement EU legislation itself. The legislature may go for this option when the issue concerned is considered of substantial political importance, or when EU law implicates a major domestic policy change. An example is the Data Protection Act 1998 by which the EC Data Protection Directive was implemented. These examples must, however, be considered exceptions.

[15] *Report of the Committee on Ministers' powers*, Cmnd 4060 [1932].

Germany

The organisation of the legislative power in Germany contrasts with that in the United Kingdom. The most remarkable difference is the constitutional embedding in Germany: the legislative power is in all respects subject to the German constitution.[16] The legislative power is thus curtailed in procedural terms (who may initiate legislation, involvement and roles of federal institutions etc), but also in terms of substance.

The catalogue of competences attributes federal and State powers on the basis of substance, and the constitution also limits legislative power in the field of fundamental rights protection. The constitutionality of legislation and the legislative process is carefully reviewed by the constitutional court, a prominent and vital element of the German constitutional system.

The key legislative institution is the *Bundestag*, but the *Bundesrat*, the Federal Government and the Federal President are also involved in the legislative process.

The German constitution acknowledges the existence of administrative legislation, but restricts its use and formulates certain conditions with which administrative legislation must comply. Article 80 of the Basic law reads as follows.

> Article 80
>
> [Issuance of statutory instruments]
>
> (1) The Federal Government, a Federal Minister or the Land governments may be authorised by a law to issue statutory instruments. The content, purpose and scope of the authority conferred shall be specified in the law. Each statutory instrument shall contain a statement of its legal basis. If the law provides that such authority may be further delegated, such subdelegation shall be effected by statutory instrument.
>
> (2) Unless a federal law otherwise provides, the consent of the Bundesrat shall be required for statutory instruments issued by the Federal Government or a Federal Minister regarding fees or basic principles for the use of postal and telecommunication facilities, basic principles for levying of charges for the use of facilities of federal railways, or the construction and operation of railways, as well as for statutory instruments issued pursuant to federal laws that require the consent of the Bundesrat or that are executed by the Länder on federal commission or in their own right.
>
> (3) The Bundesrat may submit to the Federal Government drafts of statutory instruments that require its consent.
>
> (4) Insofar as Land governments are authorised by or pursuant to federal laws to issue statutory instruments, the Länder shall also be entitled to regulate the matter by a law.

In the German legal doctrine, administrative legislation is still seen by some to conflict with rule of law and democratic principles and as such, they argue, it

[16] Art 20 s 3 *Grundgesetz* (Basic law).

should be restricted as much as possible.[17] Nevertheless, the Basic law establishes the right of existence for administrative legislation, and at the same time carefully curtails its use. Unlike in the United Kingdom, the German legislature is thus unable to unilaterally decide the scope and content of the power of the executive to adopt regulations. It is also possible to view Article 80 of the Basic law as a manifestation of the underlying constitutional idea, ie that the German parliament lacks the comprehensive supremacy of the UK parliament but that a systems of checks and balances applies according to which various institutions have been attributed specific tasks and powers.

Despite the different constitutional outlook on administrative legislation, in Germany too the phenomenon has become a substantial empirical reality.[18]

Greece

The Greek constitution explicitly applies the concept of separation of powers to the organisation of the Greek state functions. Article 26 reads as follows:

> Article 26
>
> 1. The legislative powers shall be exercised by the Parliament and the Presidents of the Republic.
>
> 2. The executive powers shall be exercised by the President of the Republic and the Government.
>
> 3. The judicial powers shall be exercised by courts of law, the decisions of which shall be executed in the name of the Greek People.

In other sections of the constitution, more detailed provisions are to be found, most notably on the regulatory powers of the executive. In the light of the explicit foundation of the constitution on the principle of separation of powers, it may hardly come as a surprise that delegation of regulatory powers to the executive is subject to specific provisions, most notably Article 43.

> Article 43
>
> 1. The President of the Republic shall issue the decrees necessary for the execution of statutes; he may never suspend the application of laws nor exempt anyone from their execution.
>
> 2. The issuance of general regulatory decrees, by virtue of special delegation granted by statute and within the limits of such delegation, shall be permitted on the proposal of

[17] R Wahl, 'Verwaltungsvorschriften. Die ungesichterte dritte Kategorie des Rechts' in E Scmidt-Aßmann, D Sellner and G Hirsch, *Festgabe 50 Jahre Bundesverwaltungsgericht*, (Cologne, Carl Heymanns Verlag, 2003) at 594.

[18] In his PhD thesis Schröder analyses a number of policy areas in which administrative regulation is often used: R Schröder, *Verwaltungsrechtsdogmatik im Wandel* (Dresden, Mohr Siebeck Verlag, 2007).

the competent Minister. Delegation for the purpose of issuing regulatory acts by other administrative organs shall be permitted in cases concerning the regulation of more specific matters or matters of local interest or of a technical and detailed nature.

* 3. [Paragraph 3 repealed by the 1986 Amendment].

4. By virtue of statutes passed by the Plenum of the Parliament, delegation may be given for the issuance of general regulatory decrees for the regulation of matters specified by such statutes in a broad framework. These statutes shall set out the general principles and directives of the regulation to be followed and shall set time-limits within which the delegation must be used.

5. Matters which, as specified in article 72 paragraph 1, belong to the competence of the plenary session of the Parliament, cannot be the object of delegation as specified in the preceding paragraph.

Thus, the Greek constitution not only prohibits Henry VIII-provisions as well as delegation of certain substantive matters, but it also prescribes that statute law must contain specific elements in relation to the delegation of regulatory power.

Administrative regulation in three member states: An overview

In the three Member States that were analysed, administrative regulation is a common phenomenon, as well as the realisation that setting abstract norms is first and foremost a responsibility for the legislature rather than the executive. In this sense, although the mere existence of executive regulation is not considered to be contrary to the principle of separation of powers, the notion that the border between statutory and executive legislation must in some way or another be 'managed', may be considered a common value of the States that were analysed. In Greece and Germany, this 'management' takes a constitutional form as their respective constitutions contain provisions on the issue. Nevertheless, EU Member States make different choices. The constitutional management of the border between the executive and the legislature in Germany and Greece means that the legislature itself is restricted by rules. In the United Kingdom, on the other hand, managing the border is essentially up to the Queen in Parliament. Outcomes differ less.

LEGISLATION AND REGULATION IN THE EUROPEAN UNION BEFORE AND AFTER LISBON

Statutory and executive legislation might not easily be distinguished at the EU level. The previous Treaty texts simply lacked a legislative vocabulary. In various EU policy areas legal instruments are adopted by the Council alone. In such areas the European Parliament only enjoys the right to advise the Council. Hence, statutory legislation, in the sense of rules which are the product of a directly elected institution, is an a priori impossibility in such areas. Conversely, legal instruments which were the result of the co-decision procedure might by considered statutory legislation, but they were not formally distinguished from delegated regulation, ie, Commission or Council regulations and directives.

The Treaty of Lisbon, more specifically the Treaty on the Functioning of the European Union (TFEU), includes new provisions on 'legal instruments of the Union'. The most striking new feature of these provisions is the formal distinction between 'legislative acts' and 'non-legislative acts'. This distinction, which is common in the Member States, will now achieve a European dimension as well. Moreover, the way in which legislative acts are distinguished from non-legislative acts resembles that of the Member States as well.

The distinguishing factor is the procedure according to which an act has been adopted (Article 289 TFEU). Unlike the Member States, in which usually just one legislative procedure may be followed—apart from procedures to amend constitutional texts—the TFEU opens the possibility for the EU legislature to adopt legislation on the basis of different legislative procedures. This oddity is, however, mitigated by the explicit determination of the co-decision procedure as the regular legislative procedure of the EU.[19] Nevertheless, in the 'special' legislative procedures it is precisely the democratic involvement of the European Parliament that is affected; whereas at the national level democratic legitimacy is the defining factor for distinguishing statutory legislation from executive regulation.

Yet, substantive elements are also relevant for the distinction between legislative and non-legislative acts. Similar to the German and Greek constitutions, Article 290 TFEU provides that: 'the essential elements of an area shall be reserved for the legislative act and accordingly shall not be the subject of a delegation of power'. Legislative acts delegating regulatory powers must, furthermore, specify the objectives, content, scope and duration of the delegation of power. These may be considered the minimum requirements of legislative acts, although the criterion 'essential elements' is obviously open for interpretation. The existing framework of comitology, which is based on the same distinction between essential and non-essential elements of a regulation, provides for a rather clear framework of reference.[20]

Highly interesting is the second type of executive EU legislation, implementing measures (Article 291 TFEU). These measures are truly of an executive nature as they serve to contribute to the proper functioning of legally binding EU acts. As such, it may concern measures of general application but also measures designed for individual cases. The latter fall outside the scope of this contribution. Implementing acts are, however, ambiguous in another sense as well. Although implementing acts will normally be adopted by the Member States (see above),

[19] Art 289 § 1 TFEU.
[20] Art 2 of the Comitology decision 2006.

should uniform conditions be necessary, the Commission or (in exceptional cases) the Council may adopt implementing measures as well.

What is interesting is that the Member States are endowed with the primary responsibility for adopting implementing measures. The most obvious example here are measures to implement EU directives. The observation that the distinction between statutory and executive legislation extends beyond the mere EU level and is indeed of a multi-level kind, adds to the complexity. Whereas the Member States may adopt implementing measures in the form of statutory legislation, these will indeed be considered to be non-legislative acts according to the terminology of the TFEU.

The TFEU contains a parallel with the British legislative system. As was discussed above, Henry VIII-provisions are a relatively common phenomenon in British legislative practice. The TFEU allows for non-legislative acts amending legislative acts as Article 290 TFEU provides that delegated measures may 'supplement or amend' non-essential aspects of legislative acts.

How may the explicit introduction of the distinction between legislative and non-legislative acts be assessed? The first conclusion that may be drawn is that the organisation of the European legislative power is converging with those of the Member States. The distinction between statutory and administrative legislation will become increasingly meaningful at the European level. The underlying democratic idea of a directly elected institution being responsible for legislation has been formally acknowledged, although it is not fully implemented at the moment.

A development of convergence is taking place at the substantive level as well. The substantive delineation of legislation and administrative legislation as laid down in the Treaty of Lisbon shows strong similarities with the Greek and German constitutions. These constitutions contain similar provisions which are, obviously, moreover, older than the Treaty of Lisbon (although they consolidate the existing comitology practice). The EU, thus, not only exercises top-down influence on the Member States, but is in its turn influenced by the way the Member States organise their respective legislative structures.

Apart from top-down and bottom-up influences, transnational (in other words: vertical) relations also become increasingly important. It is interesting to observe that such relations are increasingly embedded in an EU framework. Parliaments meet in the framework of COSAC (Conference of Community and European Affairs Committees of Parliament of the EU), for instance. Recently, the Council adopted a resolution to establish a legislative network, involving the Member States' ministries for justice.[21] The objective of this network is to exchange information on legislation, case law and major legislative reform projects. Obviously, no obligation will emerge to take over ideas or legislation in

[21] Council Resolution 2008/C 326/01 on the establishment of a Network for legislative cooperation between the Ministries of Justice of the European Union.

the other Member States. But the 'soft power' which emerges from learning from practices in other Member States will surely have its effects in terms of 'cross fertilisation'.

The general position on administrative legislation

Administrative legislation is a common feature in the EU Member States. This practice is subject to the idea that administrative legislation should be clearly distinguished from and subordinate to statutory legislation, and, furthermore, that its use and content should be restricted. This does not make for a clear cut administrative principle as its implementation in practice differs greatly throughout the Member States. It would be fair, though, to label it as an administrative value of an international kind. It is international as various political systems share it and derive it from elementary democratic and rule of law principles.

It is truly remarkable that a value which is so deeply rooted in constitutional requirements should lead to such different outcomes in different Member States. In particular, the contrast between the continental systems of Germany and Greece on the one hand, and the United Kingdom on the other, is striking. It may be explained by the differences in the respective constitutional systems at large. Whereas in Greece and Germany not only the administrative but also the legislative powers are subject to the constitution, in the United Kingdom it is largely the legislative power which restricts and controls the administrative power.

The EU has created its own distinction between administrative and legislative power. Whereas in the Member States the principle of democracy and separation of powers determine the issue, at the European level the principle of legitimacy through the Member States is added. This has meant for the organisation of the legislative power that the Council (Member States' legitimacy) needed to prevail over the European Parliament. This often rendered the legislative procedures more complex or left the European Parliament with less power.

But it also affected the administrative power of the EU. Administrative legislation is in fact an ambiguous phenomenon in the EU. Implementing EU law (especially directives) is normally a task of the individual Member States. It may be, however, that—for the sake of uniformity—the EU itself adopts administrative regulations. At the substantive level, the distinction between statutory and administrative regulation is determined by the Member States' perspective as well. They are not inclined to delegate legislative power to the Commission in sensitive policy areas. Another peculiarity at the EU level is the system of comitology which smoothens the sharp edges of the distinction between statutory and administrative legislation.

The effect of EU membership on the Member States is twofold. First of all, the EU takes away parts of the legislative power of the Member States: in areas in which the EU has adopted legislation, the Member States need to refrain from legislative action. This top-down effect of the EU is parallelled by a development of a more voluntary nature. EU membership leads to a shift in the relation between administrative and statutory legislation as many Member States prefer to implement EU law by way of administrative rather than statutory legislation. The constraints of the transposition deadlines, as well as the fact that the most important policy choices have been made at the European level are the most important arguments for this shift, which is explicitly laid down in the UK European Communities Act.

But the Member States have an effect on the organisation of the legislative power of the EU as well. This 'bottom-up' effect may be discerned rather clearly by the Treaty of Lisbon in which various elements have been laid down of the administrative value discussed in this contribution. Elements that are peculiar to the EU will remain, however, as Member States' legitimacy will continue to be crucial. The last interesting development is the emergence—next to top-down and bottom-up developments—of transnational 'cross fertilisation', which will be increasingly facilitated by the EU framework.

TRANSPARENCY

One of the ways in which democratic control can be exercised in the EU system is by means of transparency. As the Commission itself indicates: 'The Union must be open to public scrutiny and accountable for its work. This requires a high level of openness and transparency.'[22] The importance of transparency at the EU level is significant. Not only is it considered to be one of the basic rights on which the EU was founded,[23] it is also deemed important for an understanding by the public in general of what is happening at the European level. Some state that the Irish rejection of the Treaty of Lisbon in 2008 was partially based on a lack of transparency.[24]

What is meant by the notion of 'transparency' turns out to be manifold. It would be useful, therefore, to look at a selection of interpretations of this notion by the ABA working group on Transparency:

> Specifically, we deal here with (1) the citizen's ability to obtain information about the structure and foundation of the principal Community institutions of government and to have access to and participate in their processes; (2) the important subset of obtaining information that consists of access to documents produced and accumulated by government; and (3) the increasingly siginificant and complex issue of data

[22] *Strategic objectives 2005–2009; Europe 2010: A Partnership for European Renewal; Prosperity, Solidarity and Security. Communication from the President in agreement with Vice-President Wallström*, COM((2005) 12, at 5.

[23] Art 42 of the Charter of Fundamental Rights of the European Union.

[24] S Peers, 'Statewatch analysis. Proposals for greater openness, transparency and democracy in the EU, October 2008' at 1, www.statewatch.org/analyses/proposals-for-greater-openness-peers-08.pdf (last visited on 27 October 2008).

protection and privacy, which has dimensions in the EU absent in the U.S. and which often conflicts with attaining transparency.[25]

This selection comprises the most important elements which are more than relevant for the process of transnationalisation as well. It needs to be noted that the word 'transparency' itself is already the result of the globalisation of administrative values. While is was apparently meant to be the French equivalent of 'openness', it is an old, wrong translation of the French 'transparence' at a time when English was not an official language of the then European Communities.[26]

The approach to transparency of EU decisions and actions manifests itself in two ways: in the stages leading to legislation by means of consultation, and in access to documents afterwards. In order to give these approaches form and substance, legislation has been adopted and internal EU documents have been created. In order to obtain a full overview of the width of transparency in the EU, four manifestations will be discussed in detail. First, the process and procedures of consultation rounds by—most notably—the Commission will be described, along with an evaluation of the transparency of the process. Access to documents used by any of the institutions will then be discussed, both from a legislative point of view and from case law. A third method of transparency goes via the European Ombudsman, whose main task is the following:

> The Ombudsman shall help to uncover maladministration in the activities of The Community institutions and bodies, with the exception of the Court of Justice and the Court of First Instance acting in their judicial role.[27]

Finally, the voting in the Council has to be taken into consideration, especially the public voting in the co-decision procedure.

The following expectations can be deduced from the European experience as far as transparency is concerned:

- to enhance democratic accountability;
- to assist political decisions about legislation, policies, and programmes;
- to promote closer understanding between stakeholders; and
- to support the implementation and management of existing programmes.[28]

[25] ABA working group on Transparency, 3/10/08 version, 7296073_1.doc, at 1.

[26] P Nikiforos Diamandouros, 'FOI: A European Perspective', Speech by the European Ombudsman, Professor P Nikiforos Diamandouros, at the 4th International Conference of Information Commissioners, Manchester, 23 March 2006, to be found at www.ombudsman.europa.eu/speeches/en/2006–05–23.htm (last visited on 2 December 2008).

[27] Art 2 para 1 of the Decision of the European Parliament on the regulations and general conditions governing the performance of the Ombudsman's duties, adopted by Parliament on 9 March 1994 (OJ L 113, 4.5.1994, at 15) and amended by its decisions of 14 March 2002 (OJ L 92, 9.4.2002, at 13) and 18 June 2008 (OJ L 189, 17.7.2008, at 25).

[28] Taken from H Summa (rapporteur) and H Schmitt von Sydow (pilot), *Report of the Working Group 'Evaluation and Transparency'* (Group 2b), White Paper on European Governance, Work Area no 2, Handing the Process of Producing and Implementing Community Rules, July 2001, at 20–21.

The idea of transparency or openness in the European context developed from national systems which had a need to evaluate government and governmental actions over the last 30 years, especially in the United Kingdom and Sweden.[29] In the 1990s, a similar system was adopted for achievements and cost-effectiveness by the EU, based on experiences in the Member States.[30] The need for evaluation is thus seen as part of the claim for sovereignty, accountability, legitimacy and effective implementation.[31] However, the terms 'transparency' and 'openness' can be used interchangeably.[32] In European terms, an important part of transparency is formed by the need for 'traceability' of Community legislation.[33] This is of course not just a European issue, the European transparency demands can increasingly be seen at the national level in the Member States and even in national case law.[34] Moreover, in the EU Charter of Fundamental Rights, the elements are laid down in Article 41 (right to good administration), Article 42 (right of access to documents) and Article 43 (European Ombudsman). Not only will this Charter be part of the system of the Treaty of Lisbon through the Declaration to the Treaty, several of these rights are laid down in the Treaty itself. In this way, the principle of transparency will become an even stronger right in the European system.

The European Ombudsman

The institution of the European Ombudsman was meant to help limit the democratic deficit through the European Parliament as a 'complementary instrument of political accountability over other Community institutions and bodies'.[35] This institution was proposed by Spain and Denmark on the basis of their own national experiences with national ombudsmen.[36] Eight of the 12 Member States at the time had Ombudsman-type institutions in their national system. The remaining Member States, therefore had a top-down influence from the European level because of this new institution.[37] It needs to be noted here that, because the concept of the European Ombudsman was adopted in the text of the EC Treaty in Article 195 EC, all (new) Member States had to accept this notion, even if they did not recognise it in their national constitutional structure since the procedure for amending the EC Treaty has always required unanimity of the Member States. For Member States which acceded later, the institution of the

[29] ibid, at 4.
[30] ibid, at 6.
[31] ibid, at 4.
[32] P Nikiforos Diamandouros, n 26 above.
[33] H Summa and H Schmitt von Sydow, n 28 above, at 16.
[34] S Prechal, "De emancipatie van 'het algemene transparantiebeginsel'"(2008) 9 *Sociaal-Economische Wetgeving* 316.
[35] Song and Della Sala, n 6 above, at 482.
[36] ibid, at 493.
[37] ibid.

European Ombudsman was part of the whole package and might therefore have entered their legal system without prior express consent.

Yet, before the ombudsman concept became part of the European system, the development of this concept was subject to transnational influence, developing from a Nordic invention in the early twentieth century to a more general Western European concept in the second half of the twentieth century.[38] Of the two models for an ombudsman which have developed in this period (control or redress),[39] the European Ombudsman has proven to be more of a redress type of ombudsman.[40] This means that only part of the bottom-up development has taken place, the remaining part of model development is more horizontal cross fertilisation.

Access to Documents

Access to documents is a traditional part of transparency in view of democratic control of decisions taken by institutions. In the European system, the first steps towards this were taken in 1992 in an Annex to the Treaty of Maastricht:

> The Conference considers that transparency of the decision-making process strengthens the democratic nature of the institutions and the public's confidence in the administration. The Conference accordingly recommends that the Commission submit to the Council no later than 1993 a report on measures designed to improve public access to the information available to the institutions.[41]

The most notable results of the process of providing access to documents were subsequent decisions in which this was ensured for the respective institutions.[42] In 2001, these separate decisions were replaced by one comprehensive regulation on the issue.[43] In the Treaty of Amsterdam, the right to access to documents for the EU citizens was laid down in Article 255 EC, on the basis of which specific legislation was adopted in order to ensure this access to document.[44] Access to documents will re-obtain a direct legal basis in the Treaty of Lisbon in Article

[38] ibid, at 490.

[39] K Heede, *Control and Redress at Union level: the European Ombudsman* (Alphen aan den Rijn, Kluwer Law International, 2000) at 112.

[40] ibid, at 27–271.

[41] Declaration 17 to the Treaty of Maastricht.

[42] Council Decision 93/731/EC on public access to Council documents, OJ L 340 31 December 1993; Decision 94/90/ECSC, EC, Euratom on public access to Commission documents, LJ L 46, 18 February 1994; 97/632/EC, ECSC, Euratom Decision of the European Parliament of 10 July 1997 on public access to document of the European Parliament OJ L 263 25 September 1997.

[43] Regulation (EC) 1049/2001 of the European Parliament and of the Council of 30 May 2001 regarding public access to European Parliament, Council and Commission documents.

[44] ibid.

16A of the Treaty on the Functioning of the European Union (TFUE), if ratified. The system is being reviewed on a regular basis, the latest review process started in 2007.[45]

Apart from the bottom-up influence that the access to documents holds because all Member States had of course some tradition in this subject, new influences can be detected. As case law of the European Court of Justice (ECJ) shows,[46] Member States may be forced to give access to documents following from European law even when their national legislation does not provide for this option.[47] This top-down process goes even further because the EU also experiences top-down influence on this issue from international obligations, which may then influence the national level. As the implementation of the Arhus Convention shows,[48] environmental issues are a matter for everybody, which means that access to information needs to be ensured at all levels. In several of the European anti-terrorism cases, on the other hand, the ECJ has decided that this European principle even applies to European obligations which follow directly from international obligations.[49]

Voting in the Council

Several practical measures have been taken at the European level in order to promote openness in the decision-making process as a result of Article 1 TEU, in which it was stated:

> This Treaty marks a new stage in the process of creating an ever closer union among the peoples of Europe, in which decisions are taken as openly as possible and as closely as possible to the citizen.

This can also be seen as a method to implement the constitutional traditions common to the Member States as Article 6 paragraph 2 states. The most important decision in this striving for openness was taken in 2006, when the Council adopted new Rules of Procedure.[50] Part of these new Rules is the public voting of the Council in co-decision procedures under Article 251 EC. As stated in the preamble to the Council decision, the reason behind the public voting is

[45] *Public Access to Documents held by the institutions of the European Community; A Review*, Commission Green Paper, 18 April 2007, COM(2007) 185 final.

[46] A prime example is case *C-64/05 Sweden v Commission*, of 18 December 2007.

[47] S Prechal and M E de Leeuw, 'Transparency: A General Principle of EU Law?' in U Bernitz, J Nergelius and C Cardner (eds), *General Principles of EC Law in a Process of Development* (The Hague, Kluwer International, 2008) at 212–14.

[48] See *Public Access to Documents held by the institutions of the European Community; A Review*, Commission Green Paper, 18 April 2007, COM(2007) 185 final, for a review of this influence. See also Prechal and de Leeuw, n 47 above, at 214–15.

[49] For instance Joined Cases C 402/05P and C-415/05P, *Kadi & Al Barakaat International Foundation v Council and Commission* [2008] 3 CMLR 41.

[50] Council decision of 15 September 2006 adopting the Council's Rules of Procedure (2006/683/EC, Euratom).

openness and transparency because a Member State can be outvoted in this procedure. Because the Council is composed of members of governments of the Member States, the actions of these members can only be checked by national parliaments according to national rules. As a consequence, the voting in the Council needs to be public so that a control system can be maintained. It goes without saying that such a public vote is not necessary in cases in which unanimity is prescribed[51] because it is clear that each member has voted in favour of adoption of the legislation.

It is important to note that this way of voting in the Council goes further than is usual at Member State level. However, it is at the same time a method to open possibilities for the national parliaments for transparency. In this way, the openness in the voting in the Council does not represent a traditional top-down approach but one which functions as a trigger to develop new systems of democratic control at the national level.

Opposite effect: Right to Privacy and Data Protection

The right to privacy and data protection may often lead to conflicting results compared to the principle of transparency. Yet, the European Parliament in particular fights to retain the importance of transparency within the European context. This element is therefore laid down in Article 286 EC. In the Treaty of Lisbon, the protection of personal data has also been given a legal base, together with access to documents.[52] Different directives have been adopted in order to achieve a broad protection of personal data.[53] Apart from a general framework directive,[54] there are specific directives on the protection of personal data in the electronic communications sector[55] and a specific regulation on personal data in the possession of EU institutions.[56]

The fact that the general framework directive 95/46 has been given extraterritorial application[57] indicates that the globalisation process continues in this respect. For instance, the United States, which has a less broad application of the

[51] See, for examples, voting in the second and most of the third pillar, and voting in an advisory procedure when it is different from the draft legislation of the Commission under Art 250 EC.

[52] Art 16B TFEU.

[53] ABA working group on Transparency, 3/10/08 version, 7296073_1.doc, at 5.

[54] Directive 95/46/EC of the European Parliament and of the Council of 24 October 1995 on the protection of individuals with regard to the processing of personal data and on the free movement of such data.

[55] Directive 2002/58/EC of the European Parliament and of the Council of 12 July 2002 concerning the processing of personal data and the protection of privacy in the electronic communications sector (Directive on privacy and electronic communications).

[56] Regulation (EC) 45/2001 of the European Parliament and of the Council of 18 December 2000 on the protection of individuals with regard to the processing of personal data by the Community institutions and bodies and on the free movement of such data.

[57] ABA working group on Transparency, 3/10/08 version, 7296073_1.doc, at 5.

protection of data[58] has to (partially) follow the EU standards when dealing with the EU.[59] In fact, in many cases professional secrecy has to be upheld (for instance in competition law) against transparency.[60] The protection of the interests of third parties is important in this respect. Notable in this regard is that the right to privacy is an example of a national legal concept transposed to the European system, but having a wider scope as a fundamental right.[61]

In conclusion, the concept of transparency shows a broad process of transnationalisation: most elements discussed from the EU point of view are the result of cross fertilisation and bottom-up influence from the Member States. In its own unique form, it has materialised at the European level, from which it influences the Member States again.

CONCLUSION

In this chapter the contribution of the EU to the development of regional administrative values was analysed. Does the EU take administrative values out of their purely domestic context and what mechanisms are used in this regard?

Both the 'border management' between administrative and statutory legislation and transparency have been domestic administrative values which have increasingly influenced the EU legal system. In case of regulation, it was concluded that the Member States have an effect on the organisation of the legislative power of the EU. This 'bottom-up' effect may be discerned clearly by the Treaty of Lisbon in which various elements have been laid down of the administrative values discussed in this contribution. For transparency this was possibly even more clear, as some Member States actively advocate transparency.

The more 'traditional' element of European integration, top-down influence as a result of the supranational nature of the EU may be discerned in the development of administrative values as well. The Transparency regulation contains, for example, provisions that may require a higher level of transparency than prescribed domestically. Nevertheless, not all top-down influences of the EU may be explained by the binding nature of its provisions. The European Communities Act in the United Kingdom indicates that Member States may choose to come to other conclusions on how they want to manage the border between administrative and statutory legislation. Although the EU in no way prescribes such choices, they are obviously the result of EU membership.

[58] ibid.

[59] Joined Cases C-317/04 and C-318/04, *European Parliament v Council of the European Union and Commission of the European Communities*, judgment of 30 May 2006.

[60] Public Access to Documents held by the institutions of the European Community; A Review, Commission Green Paper, 18 April 2007, COM(2007) 185 final, pp 8–9.

[61] Regulation (EC) No 45/2001 of the European Parliament and of the Council of 18 December 2000 on the protection of individuals with regard to the processing of personal data by the Community institutions and bodies and on the free movement of such data, preamble.

The last interesting development is the emergence—next to top-down and bottom-up developments—of transnational 'cross fertilisation'. In this regard, it is not a vertical relationship between the EU and the Member States, but the horizontal relationship among the Member States which is key. Obviously, such processes of transnational 'cross fertilisation' may flourish without an explicit role for the EU. Nevertheless, some interesting examples indicate that the EU is increasingly used to stimulate and coordinate such processes.

These three developments that lead to the convergence of administrative values do not stand alone. Indeed, in some cases they function as a combination of instruments that is applied jointly. This works best in areas of mutual interest, ie, when the EU wants to implement changes in the Member States, when the Member States advocate changes beyond the sphere of their respective territory and when they have the desire to learn from other legal systems.

What do these conclusion mean for the supranational nature of the EU? Has this—in the light of all concurrent developments—become irrelevant, or even outdated? Supranationalism remains a powerful force which has made the implementation of administrative values in the Member States possible. This is still true today. Taking over elements of administrative values from the Member States in the EU's political system allows for a greater convergence of national systems and the European system. In doing so, the alternative mechanisms of convergence are not to be considered as competing with the supranational method but rather as strengthening it.*

* This chapter was completed before the Treaty of Lisbon entered into force.

17

Globalisation of Administrative Law—the European Experience

TIM KOOPMANS

THE BACKGROUND

THE TWENTY-first century may very well become the age of globalisation. Many indications point in this direction: some political developments tend to show that important problems are increasingly considered as problems which are common to the international community and cannot be left to the care of one or two nations; and economic and technical developments imply that obstacles to communication and to trade resulting from national boundaries are rapidly losing their importance, sometimes to the point of vanishing completely. At the same time, increasing mobility of capital, persons and goods is accompanied by the establishment of virtual spaces not linked to territory. The famous aphorism that we are living in a 'global village', where the dividing walls have been levelled out and people interact worldwide as if they were living in one single village community, looks more and more like a true description of common reality.[1] As far as we can see now, the process has the appearance of being continuous and irreversible.

For lawyers, the ensuing question is whether these new situations are compatible with the main paradigm of modern legal thinking, namely that legal systems are primarily national systems of law. This proposition is certainly prevailing in the area of administrative law. In traditional thinking, the very concept of administrative law is linked to the administration of a country; and the birth of administrative law as a separate legal discipline is mainly due to the activities of national judicial and legislative bodies, such as the French Conseil d'Etat, or the common law courts in England and Wales.[2] The least one can say is that there seems to be some kind of antagonism between the evolution of globalisation in

[1] The expression 'global village' seems to reach back to HM McLuhan, *The Gutenberg Galaxy: The Making of Typographic Man* (Toronto, University of Toronto Press, 1962).

[2] See also J Bell, 'Comparative Administrative Law' in *Oxford Handbook of Comparative Law* (Oxford, Oxford University Press, 2006) ch 39.

the field of politics and economics on the one hand, the traditional roots of administrative law in national systems of law on the other.

It is certainly possible to study this problem on an abstract and conjectural basis: by analysing the direction taken by the developments usually considered as elements of the globalisation process, we could try to reflect on the legal consequences and to construct new ways of defining sources of administrative law. However, it is also possible to opt for a more empirical approach by examining legal developments in international organisations whose aim is to reduce the influence of national boundaries on the exchange of goods and services. The European Union (EU) can nowadays be considered as the most conspicuous example of such an international organisation. That has not been obvious from the start: one of the specific characteristics of the European economic integration process is that there was never any common consent with regard to its final aim. Particularly in the early days of the European Economic Community, many observers believed that it might develop into a European federation, to be fashioned after the American model. In 1955, an 'action committee for the United States of Europe' was established by some influential politicians; it tried to mobilise support for far-reaching forms of European integration, which, ultimately, did not materialise.[3] Nevertheless, an evolution of the European Community into a complete federal system could not be entirely excluded at the time. However, with the entry of Great Britain, Ireland and Denmark to the Community in 1973, this possibility began slowly to recede.[4] In the twenty-first century, in an EU of 27 Member States with diverging views on the future of Europe, and after the failure to establish a 'European Constitution', the urge towards new constitutional forms seems to have disappeared below the horizon. The EU remains true to one of its initial missions, that of making up a strong international organisation, albeit with some particular characteristics, such as the common market, the monetary union, the decision-making system, with independent Union institutions consisting of political, administrative and judicial bodies, the direct effect of rules issued by the legislative machinery of the Union, and the close collaboration of the Member States, even in matters not, or not yet, covered by the European treaties. The EU could therefore provide a scene exhibiting the evolution of public law in the process of internationalisation of commerce.

DEFINITION OF THE PROBLEM

If the EU does not, or not any more, foreshadow a State-like entity, the problems it met over the years might very well show a prefiguration of difficulties to be

[3] See J Monnet, *Mémoires* (Paris, Fayard, 1976) ch 19.

[4] See H Young, *This blessed plot—Britain and Europe from Churchill to Blair* (London, Macmillan, 1998), in particular ch 7.

overcome at the global level in the future. In international trade, the World Trade Organization (WTO) is already facing some of the same problems the European Community had to cope with in the early years of its existence. These problems concern, for example, public health as a justification for protectionist measures, or tax systems which charge imported goods more heavily than nationally manufactured products, or the use of intellectual property, such as rights of patent or trade marks, as a means of screening off national markets, etc.[5] There is no intrinsic reason why similar developments will not occur in the field of administrative law.

In matters of administrative law, the EU experience centres round three lines of development:

(a) sometimes, the European treaties[6] explicitly lay down rules of administrative law; it is up to the courts to apply and to interpret those rules;
(b) sometimes, well known problems of administrative law turn up in practice, for which the treaties fail to provide a solution; courts will then have to find their way;
(c) a third category is developed by the courts on the basis of rule of law requirements, written or unwritten, which must necessarily apply to the administrative behaviour of the Union institutions as they apply to public authorities elsewhere.

I shall try to give examples of the growth of a European body of administrative law, taken from each of these three categories.

I shall then examine the influences on these developments one can discern, in particular the possible influences of certain national systems of administrative law, such as French or German systems.

Finally, I shall come back to my central theme, namely, the possible occurrence of similar problems, and of similar solutions, at the global level. In doing so, I also hope to show, quite incidentally, that the traditional view concerning the link of administrative law with the operation of a national administration may need some revision. The working of the 'European laboratory' does indeed convincingly show that the evolution of administrative law is not necessarily linked to national legal or administrative systems.[7]

[5] An interesting example is Case 40/82, *Commission v United Kingdom* ('Newcastle disease') [1982] ECR 2793.

[6] The Treaties establishing the European Communities, the Treaty on European Union, and the Conventions and Protocols revising or complementing these Treaties. Now also the Treaty on the functioning of the European Union (TfEU).

[7] I borrow the metaphor of the 'laboratory' from M Delmas-Marty, 'Comparative Law and International Law: Methods for ordering pluralism' (2006) 3 *University of Tokyo Journal of Law and Politics* 44.

WRITTEN RULES

The written rule is generally considered as being the true instrument for producing legal certainty. Lawyers are aware, of course, that this is only a half-truth. Even if the written rule is clear and precise, the odds are that many unexpected questions will arise for which no solution is provided: life usually shows more variation than even the shrewdest law-giver could possibly imagine.

My first example concerns a simple kind of procedural problem, which provides a clear illustration of this statement. If a Member State fails to comply with one of its obligations under the EC Treaty, the EC Commission can bring an action for infringement before the European Court of Justice (ECJ), asking for a declaration that the Member State in question failed to fulfil its obligations. The Treaty provides that the Commission, before applying to the Court, will deliver a 'reasoned opinion' on the matter, after having given the government of the Member State the opportunity to submit its observations.[8] The Treaty rules are, therefore, based on a process in three stages: after some initial correspondence, the Commission will first issue a formal notice of default, inviting the Member State to give its comments; next, when these comments are not considered as convincing, the Commission will issue its reasoned opinion, ordering the Member State to take the necessary measures within a certain period of time. When the Member State does not act in conformity with the reasoned opinion, the Commission brings its action before the Court. First problem to occur in practice: is it necessary that the petition is identical to the reasoned opinion? The Court answered in the affirmative: the Treaty provision assumes that the subject matter of the lawsuit, and the arguments in favour of the Commission's point of view, are fixed in the reasoned opinion. Second question: should the reasoned opinion be identical to the notice of default? Here, the Court said no: it is the purpose of that notice to elicit the observations of the Member State and, consequently, to enable the Commission to take these observations into account when formulating its reasoned opinion.[9] Thus, the Court specified the Treaty rules by laying down some simple procedural standards.

My second example concerns sanctions. The common agricultural policy of the EC is chiefly laid down in a great number of regulations of the EC Council, which organise different regimes for different basic agricultural products and their derivatives (wheat, milk, sugar, rice, pork etc). Export subsidies, and restitution of amounts paid as a security, used to constitute important elements of these regimes. The regulations defined the sanctions to be imposed on operators who failed to comply with the administrative formalities, such as time limits for the application for subsidies, or for the production of evidence, for example evidence that the exported product did actually arrive in the country of destination (so that the security can be restored). The normal sanction the

[8] Initially Art 169 EEC treaty. Now Art 258 TfEU.

[9] For one example among many see Case C-279/94, *Commission v Italy* [1997] ECR I-4743.

regulations provided was forfeiture of the subsidy or of the restitution. However, the ECJ held that the sanction to be imposed can never go beyond the limits of necessity and appropriateness;[10] there should be some proportionality between the negligence committed and the sanction to be imposed. Exceeding a time limit by one day cannot justify, said the Court, the complete forfeiture of a subsidy or a restitution of, maybe, millions. The result was that the sanction regime did not entirely correspond to the written rules of the regulations, although these rules were clear enough. By interpreting the rules in the light of rule of law requirements, the Court limited indeed the effect the rules on sanctions might have.

LACK OF WRITTEN RULES

In an early staff case, the ECJ had to examine the question whether a Community institution is entitled to repeal an earlier decision that turns out to have been illegal, even if that decision grants rights to individual persons. The Court said that this is a well known problem of administrative law but that it is not governed by any Treaty provision (at the time: provision of the ECSC Treaty). Under these conditions, the Court held that, unless it decided to deny justice, it was 'obliged' to solve the problem by reference to the rules recognised by legislation, literature and case law of the Member States.[11] A comparative study of this legal problem revealed, said the Court, that an administrative decision conferring individual rights on the person concerned cannot be withdrawn if it was a lawful decision; but that, on the other hand, revocation is possible under the law of all the Member States (six, at the time) if the administrative decision is illegal.

In later cases, the Court was less explicit. When the EEC Treaty came into force, in 1957, it embodied a provision which, for a somewhat technical problem (extra-contractual liability), refers to 'the general principles common to the laws of the Member States'.[12] This rule seems to have been conceived by the Court as a general encouragement to look for such common principles if the Treaties themselves are silent or ambiguous on the matter. Thus, the right to hearing, though not mentioned by the Treaty or by the applicable regulation, was explicitly recognised in a 1974 competition case, on the basis of common principles of administrative law.[13]

The most famous instance of the lack of written rules concerns protection of human rights and fundamental freedoms. Initially, the European Treaties were completely silent on this point. However, the proposition that human rights protection would not extend to activities of Community institutions could hardly be sustained. The legal question was how to justify judicial intervention for that

[10] eg, Case C-118/89, *Lingenfelsen* [1990] ECR I-2637.
[11] Joined Cases 7/56 and 3–7/57, *Algera and others* [1957] ECR 39 (English language edition).
[12] Initially Art 215 EEC treaty. Now Art 340 TfEU.
[13] See Case 17/74, *Transocean Marine Paint* [1974] ECR 1063, and the opinion of Adv-Gen Warner.

purpose: even in the absence of any directly applicable written rule, the courts could not leave the problem unsolved. The application of national constitutional law could not be envisaged, as it was settled case law of the ECJ that rules of national law, national constitutions included, can never detract from the full force of provisions of Community law. In this, somewhat uneasy, situation, the Court decided, first rather hesitantly but more and more firmly as time went by, that human rights protection is a 'general principle of law', to be applied even in the absence of any written rule; this protection is therefore part of the law, the observance of which the Court is to ensure. In safeguarding these rights, as the Court repeatedly said in a series of judgments, judges are bound to draw inspiration from the constitutional traditions common to the Member States as well as from the provisions of the European Convention on Human Rights.[14] In the course of the further evolution of its case law, the Court gradually began to take the position that it is to review measures of Community institutions for their compatibility with fundamental rights as protected by the European Convention. That view was later embodied in the Treaties.[15] It may be true that this is a matter of constitutional law rather than administrative law; but the development of German administrative law and the case law of the European Court of Human Rights have both abundantly shown how much of the recent evolution of administrative law is due to the developing case law on human rights protection. In particular, the very nature of administrative law has gradually changed under the influence of the growing importance of individual rights, such as, for example, the general right to submit conflicts with the administration to the judgment of independent and impartial judicial bodies.[16]

VALUES

It is the task of the ECJ, as an institution of the EU, to ensure that in the application of the European Treaties, 'the law is observed'.[17] 'Law', in this sense of the word, includes not only rules but also certain legal values. The rule of law implies indeed a certain value orientation: observing 'the law' is more than just respecting written provisions. The judicial method for imposing these legal values is the recourse to what is called 'general principles of law'. In recognising and elaborating these general principles, the ECJ did not break any new ground. Already in 1945, the French Conseil d'Etat had ruled that respecting legality does not only mean that statutory rules are to be observed by the administration, but that it also implies the obligation not to violate the general principles of law ('les principes généraux du droit'). French commentators agreed, at the time, that this

[14] See J Weiler, *The Constitution of Europe* (Cambridge, Cambridge University Press, 1999) ch 2.

[15] See Art. 6 s.3 Treaty on European Union.

[16] Eg, ECtHR 27 October 1987, *Pudas*, Series A vol 125; ECtHR 19 April 1994, Van de Hurk, Series A vol 288.

[17] See Art. 19 Treaty on European Union.

1945 judgment merely gave a name to methods which had already been used by the administrative courts for a long time ('the concept preceded the terminology', as one observer put it).[18]

As far as the substance of the general principles of law is concerned, the case law of the ECJ stays close to the findings of the Conseil d'Etat. Apart from the particular position of human rights protection in the Community, which I mentioned earlier, the general principles developed by the ECJ belong chiefly, if not exclusively, to two large categories: first, procedural requirements to be met by the administrative authorities, whether mentioned in the applicable rules or not (the right to a hearing and, more generally, the rights of the defence, constitute important examples); and secondly, traditional legal values which can be traced back to the legal evolution over the centuries (such as legal certainty, equal protection, proportionality). In France, some of the principles of the second category find support in written texts, in particular the preamble to the French 1958 Constitution; the ECJ, for its part, relies entirely on traditions common to the laws of the Member States. Nevertheless, the definition and elaboration of the general principles of law served the same ends in both systems of law, French and European: namely, that governing, managing and administering matters by public authorities is not merely a question of administrative discretion enclosed in responsibility towards political institutions, but that it is also submitted to legal restraints, whether expressly laid down in the applicable texts or not. The gradual construction of these restraints represents the slow growth of administrative law into a true system of law.[19]

The history of the Conseil d'Etat confirms this view. In its early days, the French administrative court considered its task as exclusively checking the jurisdiction of the administrative body in question (its 'compétence'), while leaving matters of substance to the administration and its political masters. By relying on new concepts it developed itself, such as misuse of power ('détournement de pouvoir') and general principles of law, the Conseil d'Etat then began to penetrate into matters of substance. One of the general principles, the principle of proportionality, is a good example. It means, in a colourful Dutch expression, that one should not use a cannon to shoot a midge, no matter how irksome the animal happens to be. In administrative law, this precept implies that the purpose to be attained by the decision should be determined and that the different ways of arriving at that purpose should be defined. It is only thus that one can find out whether less burdensome ways of reaching the same end had been possible. In other terms: under the principle of proportionality, the courts

[18] See T Koopmans, *Courts and political institutions, a comparative view* (Cambridge, Cambridge University Press, 2003) ch 6.2. The 1945 judgment was *Aramu*, Rec 213.

[19] See R Widdershoven, 'European administrative law' in RJGH Seerden (ed), *Administrative law in the European Union, its Member States and the United States, a Comparative Analysis*, 2nd edn (Antwerp and Oxford, Intersentia, 2007) at 289–350.

must examine very closely the substance of the administrative decision.[20] However, in doing so they trace the limits of administrative discretion; that helps to instil a certain frame of mind among the administrative bodies. It happened in France and also in some other countries such as Germany; it is now happening at the level of the EU.[21]

INFLUENCES

In matters of administrative law, the influence of the French legal system on the evolution of the European Communities has been pervasive. The European Treaties borrowed much of their terminology from French administrative law. The first Treaty, the one establishing the European Coal and Steel Community, referred to some of the key concepts of the case law of the French Conseil d'Etat, such as 'détournement de pouvoir' (in a not quite adequate translation: misuse of power). Already in the nineteenth century, the Conseil d'Etat had ruled that the requirement of legality not only implies that statutory provisions must be respected by the administrative body in question, but also that a power conferred on that body cannot be used for a purpose different from that for which it has been granted. The ECJ held that the concept should be interpreted against that background.[22] Later developments, such as the recourse to general principles of law I mentioned earlier, owe much to the French administrative law tradition as well.

However, other national systems of law have also helped to promote the gradual realisation of a European system of administrative law. I am thinking, in particular, of German influences. Germany has, as France, a long tradition of administrative law, but the case law of the German courts is different from that of their French counterparts on two important points. First, the influence of constitutional thinking on legal evolution is clearly noticeable. The decisions of the federal constitutional court ('Bundesverfassungsgericht') have been giving guidance to different important developments in administrative law and in procedural law. And secondly, German courts put the emphasis somewhat differently: they are not primarily concerned with enforcing the legality ('la légalité') of the action of the administration, but rather with finding a 'just' solution to the case at hand. In this view, the facts of the case are not just fixed data to which courts are to apply the legal norm; their true meaning 'colours' the norm to be applied. Thus, there is a subtle interplay between the facts and the law. Slowly, this more relaxed approach to problems of administrative law found

[20] See J Jans, R De Lange, S Prechal and R Widdershoven, *Europeanisation of Public Law* (Groningen, Europa Law Publishing, 2007) ch V-4.

[21] For a general view, see J Schwarze, *European Administrative Law*, 2nd edn (Andover, Thomson Sweet, 2006); P Craig, *EU Administrative Law* (Oxford, Oxford University Press, 2006).

[22] See, in particular, opinion of Adv-Gen Lagrange in Case 3/54, *Assider* [1954–56] ECR 63 (English language edn).

its way to the case law of the ECJ. The Court considers, for example, that certain provisions of the European Treaties have 'constitutional value' and will thus require an added protection.[23] Besides, the Court's judgments are nowadays less abstract than they used to be in the early years, and more closely related to the facts of the case.

It is undeniable that the common law tradition also began to make its influence felt after the accession of Great Britain and Ireland to the European Communities in 1973. In a general way, one could say that common law courts put more emphasis on the rights of the parties than, for example, the French Conseil d'Etat, with its different role perception as guardian of the legality. The significance of the rights of the parties and of procedural requirements has slowly developed into an important element of the case law of the ECJ. I referred already to the recognition of the right to a hearing. Since the 1980s, the Court is also inclined to re-open oral argument when it feels tempted to decide a case on the basis of legal grounds not yet discussed by the parties: it will first ask them to give their views.[24]

This rapid overview of a long and slow evolution shows one very interesting characteristic of European administrative law: it integrated some strong points of national legal traditions into the new body of European administrative law. Thus, it gradually accepted the concepts of 'légalité' and of general principles of law; it began to embody elements of constitutional and rule of law thinking; and it insisted on procedural guarantees in administrative practice. Nevertheless, the administrative law of the EU is not a juxtaposition of national systems: it is a separate system, still in an early phase of its development, but having its own particular role to play in the institutional framework of the Union.[25]

LOOKING BACKWARDS

In retrospect, the evolution of a new and independent body of European administrative law was mainly due to four quite different factors.

The first determining influence was the construction of the institutional system of the Communities, with independent bodies which had to establish their relationships with each other, with their staff, with the institutions of the Member States and with the subjects of their rules and decisions such as European citizens, and business corporations operating on the European common market. This complex of relationships was partially governed by the rules laid down in the European Treaties themselves, partially by practices adhered to because they seemed obvious, and occasionally by no rule or well-established practice at all. The ECJ was to interpret and develop this body of rules and

[23] eg, Case 294/83, *Les Verts* [1986] ECR 1339.
[24] eg, Case 99/79, *Lancôme* [1980] ECR 2511.
[25] See also W van Gerven, *The European Union, a Polity of States and Peoples* (Oxford, Hart Publishing, 2005) ch 3.

customs. The development of a complex administration preceded, therefore, the birth and growth of a system of administrative law. Consequently, the link with an administration seems a necessary condition for the evolution of a system of administrative law; but European experience shows that this administration is not necessarily a national administration. To this extent, the traditional paradigm I mentioned earlier, on the national character of administrative law, cannot be upheld any longer.

The second factor was the necessity to submit administrative bodies of the EC to the rule of law. If, for example, correspondence between a solicitor or an 'avocat' or 'Rechtsanwalt' with his or her client is protected from searches and seizures by public authorities under national laws, it would be difficult to comprehend why a similar protection would be absent from European Community law, for example in the enforcement of competition law.[26] The sheer necessity of finding guarantees against arbitrary actions of Community agents stimulated further developments of European administrative law. The Treaty makers in the EU recognised as much in 1990, when they amended the European Treaties in the sense that the Union is based on the principles of freedom, democracy, respect for human rights and fundamental freedoms, and the rule of law.[27]

The third important element was the coexistence of European Community law with national systems of administrative law. These national systems had sometimes been established by judicial bodies, such as the French Conseil d'Etat, sometimes primarily by legislative action, for example in the Netherlands. In both instances, however, the national systems played the same double role: on the one hand, they were a source of inspiration for the evolution of a body of administrative law of the EU and its predecessors; on the other hand, they were also the competitors of European administrative law, in particular in the sense that national courts were tempted to revert to applying their own national system if European law did not provide comparable guarantees (such an attitude would, of course, provoke the risk of discomposing the European common market). As a result, a kind of dialectical relation between European and national systems of administrative law has slowly been developing, sometimes leading to an uneasy kind of companionship. The same difficult relation has also strongly influenced the European debate on human rights protection.[28] I call these relations 'dialectical', because they are not based on a classical dichotomy ('national' v 'European') but on polar distinctions in which both 'poles' are continually influencing each other.

[26] See Case 155/79, *AM&S* [1982] ECR 1575.

[27] Now Art. 2 Treaty on European Union..

[28] See H Ragnemalm, 'Leading by example or leaning on supremacy? Some reflections on the Union, the individual and the protection of fundamental rights' in U Bernitz and J Nergelius (eds), *General Principles of European Community Law* (The Hague, Kluwer Law International, 2000) ch 2.1.

Fourthly, of course, from the very start of the EC, there were judicial bodies as part of the institutional system, with the power to have a final say in conflicts between institutions, or between the institutions and Member States, individual citizens and business corporations.

LOOKING FORWARD

It is unlikely that the European experience can be quite simply repeated at the global level. The European Communities started their life in the post-war years in a particular situation: the material and moral destruction caused by the war were still clearly perceptible; the relationship between the French Republic and the new Federal Republic of Germany continued to raise political problems; Central and Eastern Europe were subjected to Soviet domination; there was a general feeling in Western countries that the difficulties afflicting Europe could only be overcome if European States did things together. The American diplomacy, then still considered as a leading force in the Western world, exercised pressure in the same direction. These conditions are absent on a world scale: nowadays, the necessity of a more intense collaboration is not felt by the political elites in the most important world powers such as the United States, Russia and China. In recent years, the US administration has believed it can rely entirely on the American economic and military might; and the US Supreme Court is traditionally averse from accepting the influence of internationally accepted rules and practices.[29] Things may change, but that will happen very slowly.

Nevertheless, certain international developments seem to arise in spite of the resistance of the great powers, or some of them. The creation of the International Criminal Court took place in spite of strong, and sometimes heavy-handed, American opposition; and when the so-called Doha-round, in the framework of the WTO, will finally be concluded, it will probably have a result which was not wanted in that form by most of the participating countries but accepted because there was no clear alternative. Occasionally, events have a stronger influence than opinions. More particularly, a process of economic integration, once started, can only be stopped by the States if governments are prepared to accept heavy losses. In other words: some events are just bound to occur. It is not excluded, therefore, that the near future will show that the globalisation process requires some guidance to economic, cultural and legal developments, with the gradual creation of international institutions as a result. The growth of international trade and communication may require somewhat firmer structures than a negotiating machinery like the WTO. The same may happen with regard to other pressing international problems: for example those resulting from the likelihood that many inhabitants of Central and Western Africa (perhaps millions) will continue to flock to Europe, considered as safe and wealthy by most of them; no single

[29] eg, *United States v Alvarez-Machain* 504 US 655 (1992).

State is able to face the resulting difficulties alone, and collaboration in some institutionalised form may very well be the final consequence. A certain parallelism with the European experience would then become possible.

Experience has also taught us that standards for administrative behaviour of international institutions can only develop if some form of judicial or semi-judicial supervision is available. Without courts, or comparable bodies, a system of administrative law can hardly come to maturity. Nearly a century of history of international courts has convincingly shown how hard it is for many States to comply with the judgments of international judicial institutions. The concept of sovereignty of States is still a mighty obstacle to efforts directed at enforcing rules and principles of international law.[30] However, some examples of judicialisation at the global level have already found a modest beginning. Thus, WTO Member States are no longer allowed to respond to protectionist measures of other States by imposing countervailing duties unilaterally: they are now obliged to lay the matter first before a WTO arbitration panel and, eventually, before its Appellate Body.[31] So far, this important norm has been respected by the main parties to trade disputes such as the United States, the EU, Japan and India. Sometimes, the evolution of international law accelerates in ways which are not always foreseeable. The rapid development of international criminal law, and international criminal courts, in the last 25 years bears witness to this peculiarity. One of the main reasons behind the growth of an international judiciary may be the growing insight that many of the world's modern problems cannot be solved any more by national political and administrative measures alone, or by decisions of national courts.[32] If that is true, it may have its consequences for the process of economic globalisation.

The next question is whether courts or arbitration panels will be able to develop and elaborate sets of standards for administrative behaviour when there are no or few applicable rules and no internationally recognised rule-making institutions. Before judicial or semi-judicial bodies can try to enforce rule of law requirements without any support in written texts, they must already have acquired a strong position in the system in which they are operating. The EU experience shows indeed that a system of administrative law could develop although written rules were absent or incomplete, because the ECJ was already an important actor in the evolution of European law and had established a close relationship with the national judicial systems. It will be difficult to achieve such a situation at the global level.

Quite unexpectedly, however, the European experience may give another indication of future developments. For nearly two centuries, lawyers have been

[30] See the elegant but somewhat simplified description of P Allot, *Eunomia* (Oxford, Oxford University Press, 1990, paperback edn 2004) ch 15(3).

[31] See P Vanden Bossche, *The constitution and policy of the World Trade Organisation*, 2nd edn (Cambridge, Cambridge University Press, 2008) ch 1.

[32] See also A Cassese, *International Criminal Law* (Oxford, Oxford University Press, 2003) ch 1.

generally preoccupied with one legal system, their own national system; but an important change in that situation began to occur when transnational competition problems had to be discussed. As a result, a specialised multinational bar began to develop in cities like Brussels and Luxemburg, where negotiations with the EC Commission and litigation before the ECJ took place. Similarly, networks of business corporations began to have their own lobbyists in Brussels, who tend to develop their own codes of behaviour—European rather than national standards.[33] Some kind of transnational practice is slowly developing. That has led to a somewhat different view on the very nature of business morals, administrative behaviour and legal relationships. Mentalities change as situations change, and that may very well happen at the global level as well.

QUO VADIMUS?

The main charm of the future is that we know so little about it. International relations, which seemed to stabilize in the 1990s, have been thrown into disarray since the beginning of the twenty-first century. The United Nations and its specialised agencies have survived this turmoil so far. Important specialised organisations such as the Food and Agriculture Organization (FAO), International Labour Organization (ILO) and United Nations Educational, Scientific and Cultural Organization (Unesco) might play a role in the future, if globalisation of trade, commerce and communication continues and gathers strength. An evolution in that sense could, in its turn, lead to a further institutionalisation and, concomitantly, to a gradual creation of worldwide standards of administrative law.[34] For the moment, however, it is not clear whether, and when, the main players in the game of international relations will actually accept such an evolution. And when they finally do, the true difficulties only begin to occur: what kind of judicial and semi-judicial protection will be available as part of a new accountability regime, and in what way the unity of the resulting judge-made law can be achieved? New forms of international governance may be framed, which could also require new forms of political responsibility and of judicial protection.[35] It is all in the lap of the gods.

It is my own conviction that the movement towards international integration will have its ups and downs, but that it will ultimately prevail. The world's statesmen will finally find out that the planet can only be saved from destruction by drastic limitations of national sovereignty through formalised methods of international collaboration and through mechanisms of integration. In that

[33] See K Middlemas, *Orchestrating Europe—the informal politics of European Union 1973–1995* (London, Fontana Press, 1995) part III.

[34] See P Allot, n 30 above, preface to paperback edition (*New world*).

[35] See also D Curtin, 'European legal integration: paradise lost?' in D Curtin, J Smit, A Klip and J McCahery, *European Integration and Law* (Antwerp and Oxford, Intersentia, 2006) at 1–54.

perspective also, the European experience constitutes a useful precedent.[36] Things may go slowly, albeit perhaps with accelerations, but I have no doubt about the direction developments will take.

Nevertheless, the uncertain course of history remains its chief characteristic. However, the uncertainties cannot be the exclusive guides to our action and to our reflection. When globalisation will begin to lead to institutionalisation, and to the slow germination of new forms of administrative law, the lawyers should be ready to face the challenges.

However that may be, Martin Shapiro's question 'will the globe echo the EU?' has not yet been answered;[37] the option is still open.

[36] See already P Pescatore, *The Law of Integration* (Leiden, Sijthoff, 1974).
[37] M Shapiro, '"Deliberative", "independent" technocracy v. democratic politics: will the globe echo the EU?' (2005) 68 *Law and Contemporary Problems* 341.

Index

Introductory Note

References such as '178–9' indicate (not necessarily continuous) discussion of a topic across a range of pages. Wherever possible in the case of topics with many references, these have either been divided into sub-topics or only the most significant discussions of the topic are listed. Because the entire work is about the 'global administrative law' and 'values', the use of these terms (and certain others which occur constantly throughout the book) as entry points has been minimised. Information will be found under the corresponding detailed topics.

www.ingramcontent.com/pod-product-compliance
Ingram Content Group UK Ltd.
Pitfield, Milton Keynes, MK11 3LW, UK
UKHW021904150926
475560UK00007B/372/J

9 781849 460095